Wolfgang Gaul · Martin Schader (Eds.)

Data, Expert Knowledge and Decisions

An Interdisciplinary Approach with Emphasis on Marketing Applications

With 117 Figures

Springer-Verlag
Berlin Heidelberg New York
London Paris Tokyo

Professor Dr. Wolfgang Gaul
Institut für Entscheidungstheorie und Unternehmensforschung
Universität Karlsruhe (TH)
Kollegiengebäude am Schloß, Bau III
7500 Karlsruhe 1, FRG

Professor Dr. Martin Schader
Institut für Informatik
Universität der Bundeswehr
Holstenhofweg 85
2000 Hamburg 70, FRG

ISBN-13:978-3-642-73491-5 e-ISBN-13:978-3-642-73489-2
DOI: 10.1007/978-3-642-73489-2

Softcover reprint of the hardcover 1st edition 1988

2142/7130-543210

Preface

The discussion of how computer-assisted decision making can be supported, e.g. by sophisticated data analysis techniques and by recent developments of so-called knowledge-based systems, is attracting increasing attention. The multitude of information and the variety of kinds of data together with the different possibilities of how knowledge can be processed and stored is requiring cross-disciplinary research efforts.

Against this background activities to combine various research areas have been undertaken in order to stimulate and strengthen the exchange of information, ideas and first results. In this context an international conference was incited, which—due to the research interests of colleagues with related intentions—should deal with interdisciplinary aspects of fields such as data analysis, decision support, expert knowledge representation, and marketing and related areas of research.

A meeting of the above mentioned kind was organized together with

Phipps Arabie, Champaign, USA,
J. Douglas Carroll, Murray Hill, USA, and
Paul E. Green, Philadelphia, USA.

We all, gratefully, take the opportunity to acknowledge support by

Deutsche Forschungsgemeinschaft,
Karlsruher Hochschulvereinigung,
Universität Karlsruhe (TH),
IBM Deutschland,
Kölnische Rückversicherung,
UNISYS Deutschland,

which made it possible to hold such a workshop on

Data Analysis, Decision Support and Expert Knowledge Representation
in Marketing and Related Areas of Research

at the University of Karlsruhe (TH) from June 21 to 23, 1987, with local organization by the Institut für Entscheidungstheorie und Unternehmensforschung. It provided the possibility to present recent research in the mentioned areas and was the starting-point for most of the papers in this volume.

The volume consists of five parts. The first part contains two introductory papers which discuss the foci of research interests sketched above in more detail. The arrangement in the four following parts resulted from the keywords assigned to each paper by the referees.

We thank all authors for their contributions and the referees for their comments. Furthermore, we would like to thank Werner A. Müller from Springer Publishing Company for excellent cooperation.

W. Gaul and M. Schader Karlsruhe and Hamburg, December 1987

Contents

Part 1

Introduction

Characterization of Research Papers by Data Analysis Techniques

W. Gaul † and M. Schader ‡

† Institut für Entscheidungstheorie und Unternehmensforschung, Universität Karlsruhe

‡ Institut für Informatik, Universität der Bundeswehr Hamburg

Summary

When editing a volume of papers on interdisciplinary research efforts, editors' tasks comprise a classification of the papers submitted and an assignment of subsets of papers to important topics of research covered. On the basis of key words attached to the different papers by the referees of the papers and with the help of well-known data analysis techniques a characterization of the papers is given which serves as a starting-point for structuring the underlying volume.

1 Motivation

Contributions to research about how computer-aided processing of knowledge and reasoning should be performed, how it could be combined with other research directions such as data analysis and decision support, and how it could be used in interesting application areas, are attaining increasing attention in today's scientific discussion. In this context, it is argued that abilities to evaluate certain types of data (preferably, of course, arbitrary information) in order to support decision making, to assess consequences of different choice alternatives in a decision situation, to examine the quality of—either considered or already performed—actions, etc., should belong to the features of any system for decision support.

To cope with these objectives, knowledge from different areas is needed, e.g. about

- the underlying problem (e.g. about debt management, media planning or new product introduction—to give just a few examples of applications dealt with in this volume),
- the specific scientific background (e.g. about known models and methods and their relationships covering such areas as data analysis/statistics and operations research/optimization), and
- possibilities how problem solutions can be achieved (e.g. about the availability of and experience with existing software tools and computer languages).

Of course, such a listing of areas from which knowledge is needed could serve as a starting-point for attempts to structure (or combine) interdisciplinary research and, indeed, the label which was used in the correspondence with those interested to stimulate and strengthen research efforts of the kind mentioned stood as a symbol for such cross-disciplinary intentions (see Fig. 1).

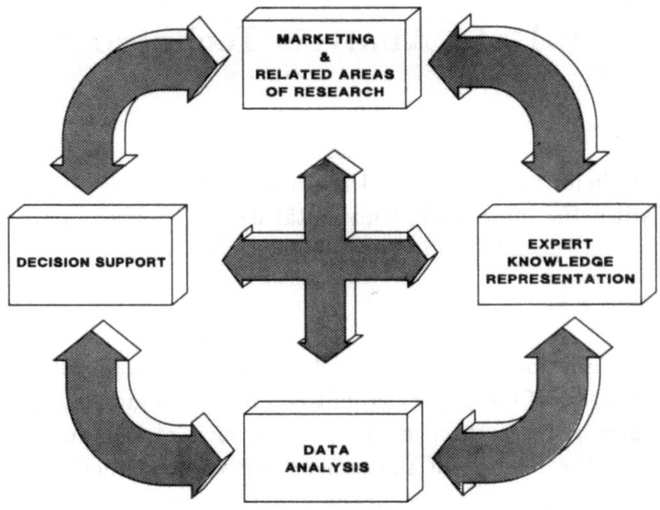

Figure 1: Cross-disciplinary Research Intentions

Among the many possible application areas special emphasis was laid on marketing because, here, the interface between data analysis, market research and marketing has a certain tradition to which some of the authors of this volume have contributed considerably. Additionally, the interface between decision support and marketing has gained increasing interest already in the past, see e.g. Little (1970) for an introduction into the well-known decision calculus discussion and Little (1979) for comments on decision support systems for marketing.

On the contrary, research concerning problems of expert knowledge handling is rather new to all application areas. Thus, papers which cover the interface between application areas and expert knowledge handling—no matter which application areas they are tackling—are of interest here.

In this introductory paper no attempt to survey literature concerning the research topics mentioned (and their interconnections) will be made. This is left to Arabie and Daws (1987) who in the following introductory paper give their view of the nature of the linkages among the foci of research interests described above.

Instead, on the basis of key words attached to the different papers by the referees of the papers and with the help of well-known data analysis techniques a characterization of the papers is given which serves as a starting-point for structuring the underlying volume.

2 Key Words for Research Papers

As the area of data analysis belongs to one of the joint research interests of nearly all authors of this volume, we thought that it would be a good idea to try to use data analysis techniques to achieve a first arrangement of the papers submitted and an assignment of subsets of papers to important research topics. For this purpose, we asked the referees of the papers submitted to provide key words for every paper. The result is given in the list of key words of Tab. 1.

Analysis of Residuals	Financial Modeling	Personnel Disposition
Annealing	Forced Classification	Pick k(any)/n Data
ANOVA	FORTRAN	Planning
Assertions	Frames	POPLOG
Assignment Problem	Fuzzy Pattern Matching	Portfolio Management
Asymmetric Associations	Geographical Data	Positioning & Segmentation
Asymmetric Cross Elasticities	Hierarchical Clustering	Possibility Theory
Asymmetric Dominance Data	Hybrid System	Prediction
Biplots	Hypersphere Representation	Predictive Validation
Bond Energy Algorithm	Ideal Point Model/Unfolding	Preference Data
Brand Switching Data	Inexact Reasoning	Principal Clusters
BTX	Interfaces	Principal Component Analysis
Budgeting	Interpretation of Representations	Probabilistic Multidim. Scaling
Carry-over Effect	KEE	PROLOG
Categorical Data	Knowledge Based System	Prototype Development
Combinatorial Data Analysis	Knowledge Representation	Qualitative Data
Combining Rules	Likert-Type Data	Redundancy Analysis
Competitive Maps	LISP	Regression Analysis
Conjoint Analysis	Local Optima	Relaunch of Product
Consumer Behavior Data	Longitudinal Data	Second Order Regression
Consumer Choice Data	Long-term Effects of Advertising	Sensitivity Analysis
Correlation Analysis	Machine Learning	Sequencing/Seriation
Correspondence Analysis	Marketing Application	Simulation
Credit Checking	Market Segmentation	Statistical Models
Crew Rostering	Market Share Models	Supplement. Elements Algorithm
Data Analysis	Maximum Likelihood Estimation	Symmetric Associations
Debt Management	Media Planning	Symmetric Proximities
Decision Support System	Mixed Data	Telecommunications Pricing
Distances	Monte Carlo Methods	Tests
Dominated Options	Multidimensional Scaling	Three Mode Factor Analysis
Dual Scaling	New Product Introduction	Time-Dependent Data
Error-perturbed Data	Number of Clusters	Transfer Algorithm
Estimation Methods	Option Valuation	Two-Mode Data
Events	Pareto-optimal Options	Unidimensional Scaling
Factor Analysis	Partitioning	Urban Mass Transit
Factorial Axes	PC Implementation	Vehicle Scheduling

Table 1: List of Key Words

On the one side, such a collection of key words allows a quick overview and a first impression of what special topics have been tackled in the papers of this volume. On the other side, the set of key words together with the information which key words have been attached to which papers can serve as fundamentals for the application of data analysis techniques. There are 108 key words and 29 papers. However, we omit the corresponding 29×108 incidence matrix for the sake of brevity.

When trying to arrange the given key words we found that some kind of hierarchy between the key words had to be considered, see Fig. 2 which depicts part of the key words hierarchy and shows that some key words can be considered as generic terms of subsets of certain key words.

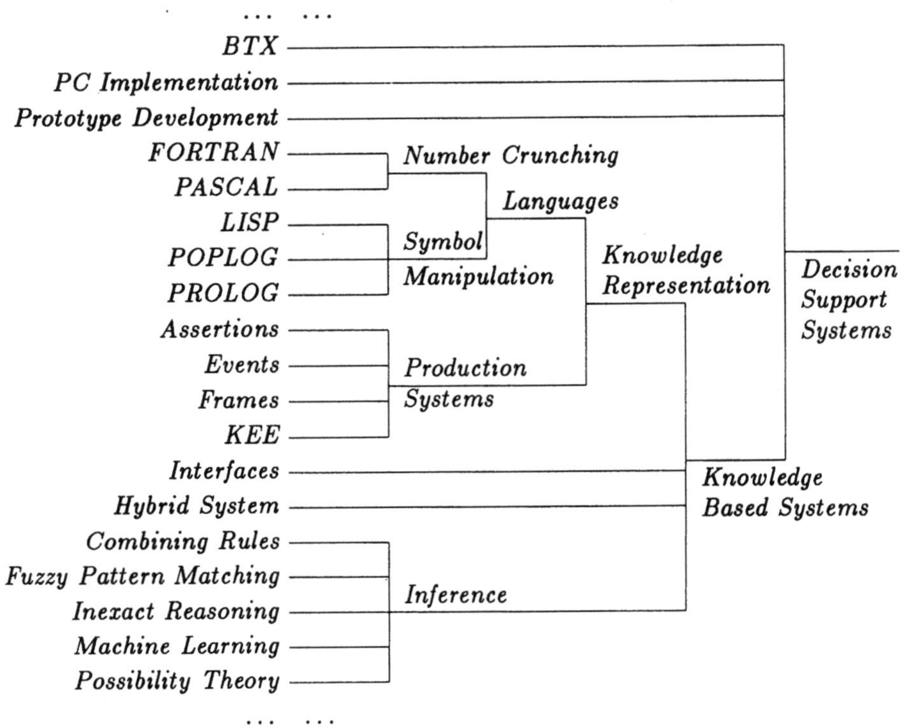

Figure 2: Part of Key Words Hierarchy

Although there exist methods to determine (dis)similarities between papers from such a hierarchy of key words, see e.g. contributions in Opitz (1978) in relation with marketing applications, we restricted ourselves to techniques easily available in standard software packages because this contribution is not to demonstrate own new or otherwise highly sophisticated methodological developments.

3 Clustering and Positioning of Research Papers

Research papers are—for abbreviation—marked by the first two letters of the corresponding author(s), e.g. *GeRaDi* denotes the paper by Gettler-Summa, Ralambondrainy and Diday. Fig. 3 shows the dendrogram of research papers obtained by weighted average-linkage clustering. Already a first glance reveals that there exist two large clusters.

The first cluster is, again, divided into two sub-clusters where we can clearly distinguish between the classes of papers which describe knowledge-based decision support for marketing applications (*BöBoGa, GaSch, GeTaWa, Mi*), of KEE-LISP applications (*BüSch, DeIr, DeSchTü, Tü*) and of two papers which combine decision support (knowledge-based in one case) with other applications (*Da, Tr*). Also the remaining two classes of the first cluster ((*Es, FrGr*) and (*GeRaDi, Gr*)) are well interpretable and their fusion with the other classes appears to be very reasonable.

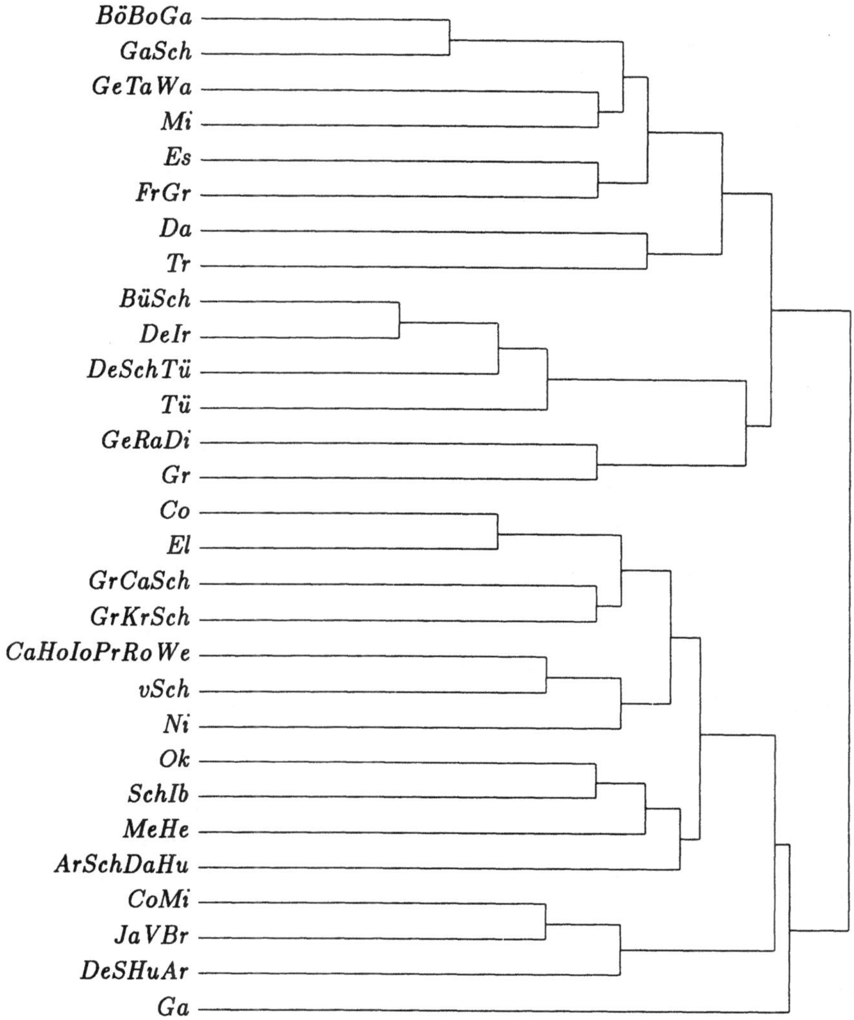

Figure 3: Weighted Average-Linkage Clustering of Research Papers

Altogether, the first cluster contains papers which rather deal with the topics of decision support and expert knowledge representation/expert systems.

On the contrary, the second cluster rather contains papers which deal with data analysis aspects where a class of marketing applications (*Co, El, GrCaSch, GrKrSch,*

CaHoIoPrRoWe, vSch, Ni) can immediately be recognized. The remaining papers (*Ok, SchIb, MeHe, ArSchDaHu, CoMi, JaVBr, DeSHuAr, Ga*) seem to emphasize data analysis aspects to a larger extent.

Similar structural relationships are shown in Fig. 4 which depicts a two-dimensional ALSCAL-representation of the research papers.

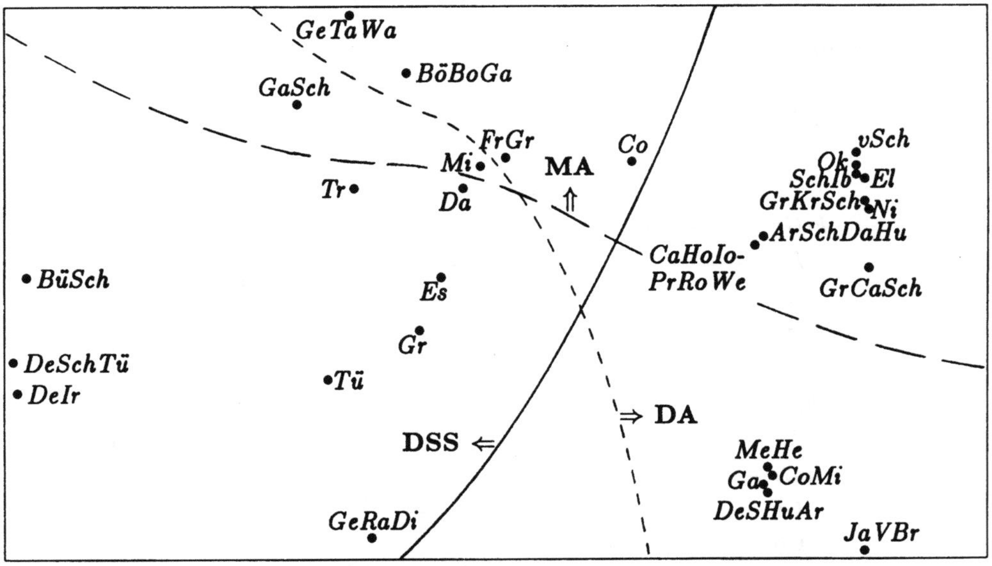

Figure 4: ALSCAL Representation of Research Papers

Here, papers on the right side of Fig. 4 rather deal with data analysis aspects while papers in the upper part, additionally, include marketing applications. Papers on the left side of Fig. 4 rather tackle decision support aspects and include first attempts of expert knowledge handling. These general remarks are illustrated by the border lines drawn in Fig. 4.

To sum up, the expert knowledge of the referees, who provided the key words for the papers, together with the solutions of the data analysis techniques applied have resulted in decision support for the editors' task to structure a volume of papers on the interdisciplinary research areas mentioned above.

4 Conclusions

The just described results confirmed us to arrange the volume into the chapters

- Decision Support for Marketing Problems,
- Decision Support, Knowledge Representation, Applications other than Marketing,
- Data Analysis and Marketing,
- Data Analysis.

In each chapter contributions are ordered alphabetically according to authors' names. We hope that this straightforward demonstration of how data analysis, expert knowledge and decision support can be combined may serve as another stimulating example to further development of interdisciplinary research in the areas discussed for which this volume is just a starting-point.

References

Arabie P, Daws J (1987) The Interface Among Data Analysis, Marketing, and Representation of Knowledge. This Volume

Little JDC (1970) Models and Managers: The Concept of a Decision Calculus. Management Science 16:466–485

Little JDC (1979) Decision Support Systems for Marketing Managers. Journal of Marketing 43, 3:9–26

Opitz O (Hrsg.) (1978) Numerische Taxonomie in der Marktforschung. Vahlen, München

Papers of All Other Authors of this Volume

The Interface Among Data Analysis, Marketing, and Representation of Knowledge[1]

P. Arabie and J. Daws
Department of Psychology, University of Illinois at Champaign
603 E. Daniels St., Champaign IL 61820

Summary

We selectively review the linkages among the foci of this conference, emphasizing areas of current and intense interest, and we predict some directions for future developments.

1 Introduction

In convoking a conference of such ambitious scope, it seems reasonable to ask: (I) which areas of research are heavily represented, (II) what is the nature of the linkages—which justify having the conference—among these areas, and (III) what ongoing and future benefits should result from interactions among the areas?

Concerning Question I, our subjective organization of the papers to be presented at this conference emphasizes three categories. "Statistical Methodology and Data Analysis" are exemplified by papers on the topics of regression, continuous spatial models and/or representation of preference, and discrete representations and optimization. "Representation of Knowledge" is characterized by papers covering decision support systems, expert systems, and knowledge-based representations. Finally, "Marketing, Consumer Behavior, and Advertising" are depicted by papers on prediction of market share, software for conjoint analysis, and managerial decision-making.

2 Linkages that Constitute the Interface

Since the emphasis of this conference is to examine and further the development of the interface among these three areas of research, we propose to sketch our personal view of the ways these three areas of activity interact with and strengthen each other (Question II), and to speculate on the promise of recent and future developments (Question III). In pursuing the latter objective, we will not be emphasizing results being presented at this conference, since they will speak for themselves through both the presentations and the ensuing conference volume.

In Figure 1, the six directional links constituting the interface between the three foci of this conference have been labeled. Under the corresponding headings in Table 1, we have offered a brief description of our view of the nature of these linkages.

[1]This work was supported by AT & T Information Systems through the Industrial Affiliates Program of the University of Illinois and a Fulbright Award to the first author. We are indepted to Francesca Lundström and Carolyn Simmons for comments on an earlier version and to Mary Kay Burns for bibliographic assistance.

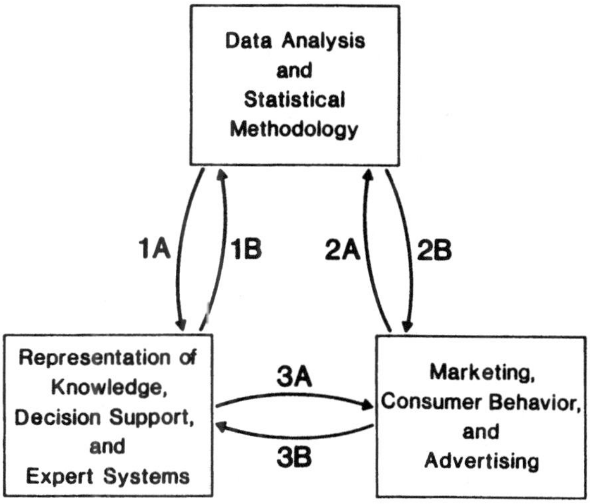

Figure 1: The three foci of this conference, with the six linkages labeled according to usage in Table 1.

Table 1: The Nature of the Six Linkages in Figure 1

Link 1A	Link 1B
Data Analysis and Statistical Methodology provides new algorithms and models for Representation of Knowledge. For example, there is Mirkin's (1979) scheme for evaluating the panelists rendering expert judgments.	Representation of Knowledge contributes new paradigms for collecting data (Hirtle (1982, 1987)) and new models (Doignon and Falmagne (1985); Degreef, Doignon, Ducamp, and Falmagne (1986)) for representing structure of knowledge to Data Analysis.
Link 2A	Link 2B
Marketing provides substantive motivation for the development of more refined models for Data Analysis. Belk and Srivastava and their respective collaborators have emphasized usage-situational influences of perceptions in marketing, thus providing impetus for three- and higher-way models of scaling and clustering.	Data Analysis provides concrete and (sometimes) testable models embodying substantive propositions originating in Marketing (e.g., the introduction of conjoint analysis; also, work on consumer choice behavior, by Rao and Sabavala (1981), and DeSarbo and De Soete (1984))
Link 3A	Link 3B
Representation of Knowledge provides formal models for the quantity and type of information utilized by consumers (e.g., Srull's (1986) model of consumer memory and judgment).	Marketing provides feedback on and evaluation of suitability and utility of representations of knowledge (e.g., Michaelsen and Michie (1983); Lutz (1985); Srull (1986))

Link 1A

Links 1A and 2B are perhaps the ones most familiar to participants at this conference. The former is the contribution of new algorithms and models for the representation of knowledge. Mirkin (1979, Ch. 4) provided a particularly interesting example: after independently reinventing correspondence analysis (see Nishisato (1980), and his chapter in this volume), Mirkin proposed to use the technique for evaluating the congruity between each of a group of "expert" panelists and the corresponding consensus judgment. Given the current emphasis on "Expert Systems" (e.g., Assad and Golden (1986)), it seems highly appropriate to examine the structure of concordance (or lack thereof) among such "experts."

Link 1B

This reciprocal link from Representation of Knowledge to Data Analysis, is nicely illustrated by Hirtle's (1982, 1987) research, providing a logically rigorous framework for earlier work by Reitman and Rueter (1980). Hirtle has demonstrated that it is possible to reconstruct a dendrogram with seriated nodes (i.e., a tree diagram with the nodes in a mathematically preferred order), using replicated orderings of the set of objects/nodes as input (viz., subjects' various orders of recall for the remembered items corresponding to the nodes). Concretely, data from multi-trial free-recall experiments will suffice to produce such a tree, so that the data analyst is potentially spared the traditional and more cumbersome requirement of having a (pairwise) proximity matrix. Similarly, Doignon and Falmagne (1985); Degreef, Doignon, Ducamp, and Falmagne (1986) have provided a new logical framework for representing an individual's knowledge of a given field. One goal of this impressive research is to predict which questions within the field can be answered by the individual. In addition to the elegant models already proposed by those authors, the work will no doubt lead to further models and algorithms for analyzing relevant data.

Link 2A

Shepard and Arabie (1979, p. 89) noted that the first three- way approach to multidimensional scaling, the INDSCAL approach of Carroll and Chang (1970), "began as a psychological model around which a computer program was then developed" and not the other way around. Nonetheless, the explosive growth of three-way approaches since then (reviewed in Arabie, Carroll, and DeSarbo (1987)) has occasionally met with the skeptical reaction that models have been devised in vacuo with neither current substantive need nor interesting data available. Those of us who feel obligated to answer this criticism owe considerable gratitude to Belk and to Srivastava and their respective collaborators for contributions to link 2A.

In an impressive and enduring program of research, Belk and his colleagues (Belk (1974a, 1974b, 1975a, 1975b, 1979); Belk, Mayer, and Bahn (1982)) have emphasized the substantive and methodological importance of situational effects and individual differences in buyers' behavior. Belk (1975a, p. 430) explicitly called for three-way analyses (e.g., situation by buyer by product) utilizing Tucker's (1964) techniques, to replace traditional two-way analyses that use data aggregated over either individuals or usage situations. Similarly, Srivastava and his colleagues (Srivastava (1980, 1981); Srivastava, Shocker, and Day, (1978); Day, Shocker, and Srivastava (1979); Srivastava, Leone, and Shocker (1981); Srivastava and Alpert (1982); Srivastava, Alpert, and Shocker (1984)) have emphasized usage-situational influences on perceptions of product markets. Srivastava et al. (1984) provided an elegant demonstration of the usefulness of a product specific usage-situational taxonomy. The success of Srivastava's programmatic research has provided justification for such methodological developments as three-way multivariate conjoint analysis (DeSarbo, Carroll, Lehmann, and O'Shaughnessey (1982)).

Link 2B

This link is characterized by the formal, concrete, and (sometimes) falsifiable models Data Analysis provides for gauging substantive propositions from Marketing. Of course, the classic example here is the introduction of conjoint analysis (Green and Wind (1973, 1975); Green and Srinivasan (1978)) in marketing research. The successful adoption of this technique throughout marketing is demonstrated by the abundance of software now available. More recent examples illustrating link 2B have included the translation of theoretical statements of consumers' hierarchical choice processes into schemes for data analysis (Kalwani and Morrison (1977); Rao and Sabavala (1981); DeSarbo and De Soete (1984)).

Link 3A

Srull's (1986) model of consumer memory and judgment is a good example of a link 3A contribution from the Representation of Knowledge to Marketing and Consumer Behavior. This model seeks to account for the protean and elusive link between memory for information presented in advertisements and the evaluation of the product being advertised.

> *"The model postulates that when a consumer acquires ad information with the (implicit or explicit) objective of making an evaluative judgment of the product, the global evaluation will be made at the time of information acquisition and stored in memory separately and independently from the specific episodic facts that are learned.... There are occasions in which an alternative process will apply. Specifically, when a person acquires ad information with no specific objective [such as purchasing] in mind, ... a global evaluation of the product will not ... be incorporated into the resulting mental representation. If later asked to make a specific judgment, the consumer will be forced to retrieve the previously acquired information ... and use it as a basis for his/her evaluative judgment of the product ... computed on the spot"* (Srull (1986, p. 644)).

Thus, the relationship between effectiveness of advertisements (as gauged by recall) and a consumer's evaluation of a product for potential purchase is a function of more variables than had previously been realized.

Link 3B

The implications of Srull's model call in turn for the very kinds of methods for higher-way analyses mentioned earlier in the discussion of link 2A. Moreover, since Srull (1986, p. 646) notes that "the exact format of knowledge representation has been left unspecified" in the current version of his model, there is thus the motivation arising in Marketing for contributions from Representation of Knowledge (link 3B). Similarly, the renewal of interest in the nature and effects of consumers' affective responses to advertising has led to more concern for how brand information may be stored and updated in memory (see review by Lutz (1985)). More routine activity along this link includes evaluation of the usefulness of efforts to provide software for representing knowledge relevant to management (e.g., Michaelsen and Michie (1983)).

References

Arabie P, Carroll JD, DeSarbo WS (1987) Three-Way Scaling and Clustering. Sage, Newbury Park, CA

Assad AA, Golden BL (1986) Expert Systems, Microcomputers, and Operations Research. Computers and Operations Research 13: 301–321

Belk RW (1974a) Application and Analysis of the Behavioral Differential Inventory for Assessing Situational Effects in Buyer Behavior, in: Ward S, Wright P (eds.) Advances in Consumer Research, Vol 1. Association for Consumer Research, Urbana, IL, pp 370–380

Belk RW (1974b) An Exploratory Assessment of Situational Effects by Buyer Behavior. Journal of Marketing Research 11: 156–163

Belk RW (1975a) The Objective Situation as a Determinant of Consumer Behavior, in: Schlinger MJ (ed.) Advances in Consumer Research, Vol 2. Association for Consumer Research, Ann Arbor, MI, pp 427–437

Belk RW (1975b) Situational Variables and Consumer Behavior. Journal of Consumer Research 2: 157–164

Belk RW (1979) A Free Response Approach to Developing Product-Specific Consumption Situation Taxonomies, in: Shocker AD (ed.) Analytic Approaches to Product and Marketing Planning. Marketing Science Institute, Cambridge, MA, pp 177–196

Belk RW, Mayer R, Bahn K (1982) The Eye of the Beholder: Individual Differences in Perceptions of Consumption Symbolism, in: Mitchell A (ed.) Advances in Consumer Research, Vol 9. Association for Consumer Research, Ann Arbor, MI, pp 523–530

Carroll JD, Chang JJ (1970) Analysis of Individual Differences in Multidimensional Scaling Via an N-Way Generalization of "Eckart-Young" Decomposition. Psychometrika 35: 283–319

Day GS, Shocker AD, Srivastava RK (1979) Customer-Oriented Approaches to Identifying Product-Markets. Journal of Marketing 43: 8–19

Degreef E, Doignon J-P, Ducamp A, Falmagne J-C (1986) Languages for the Assessment of Knowledge. Journal of Mathematical Psychology 30: 243–256

DeSarbo WS, Carroll JD, Lehmann D, O'Shaughnessey J (1982) Three-Way Multivariate Conjoint Analysis. Marketing Science 1: 323–350

DeSarbo WS, De Soete G (1984) On the Use of Hierarchical Clustering for the Analysis of Nonsymmetric Proximities. Journal of Consumer Research 11: 601–610

Doignon J-P, Falmagne J-C (1985) Spaces for the Assessment of Knowledge. International Journal of Man-Machine Studies 23: 175–196

Green PE, Srinivasan V (1978) Conjoint Analysis in Consumer Research: Issues and Outlook. Journal of Consumer Research 5: 103–123

Green PE, Wind Y (1973) Multiattribute Decisions in Marketing: A Measurement Approach. Dryden, Hinsdale, IL

Green PE, Wind Y (1975) New Way to Measure Consumers' Judgments. Harvard Business Review 53: 107–117

Hirtle SC (1982) Lattice-Based Similarity Measures Between Ordered Trees. Journal of Mathematical Psychology 25: 206–225

Hirtle SC (1987) On the Classification of Recall Strings Using Lattice-Theoretic Measures. Journal of Classification 4, in press

Kalwani MU, Morrison D G (1977) A Parsimonious Description of the Hendry System. Management Science 23: 467–477

Lutz RJ (1985) Affective and Cognitive Antecedents of Attitude Toward the Ad: A Conceptual Framework, in: Alwitt LF, Mitchell AA (eds.) Psychological Processes and Advertising Effects. Erlbaum, Hillsdale, NJ, pp 45–63

Michaelsen R, Michie D (1983) Expert Systems in Business. Datamation 29 (11): 240–246

Mirkin BG (1979) Group Choice. VH Winston, Washington, DC (Original work published 1974)

Nishisato S (1980) Analysis of Categorical Data: Dual Scaling and its Applications. University of Toronto Press, Toronto

Rao VR, Sabavala DJ (1981) Inference of Hierarchical Choice Processes From Panel Data. Journal of Consumer Research 8: 85–96

Reitman JS, Rueter HR (1980) Organization Revealed by Recall Orders and Confirmed by Pauses. Cognitive Psychology 12: 554–581

Shepard RN, Arabie P (1979) Additive Clustering: Representation of Similarities as Combinations of Discrete Overlapping Properties. Psycholcgical Review 86: 87–123

Srivastava RK (1980) Usage-Situational Influences on Perceptions of Product Markets: Response Homogeneity and its Implications for Consumer Research, in: Olson JC (ed.), Advances in Consumer Research Vol 7. Association for Consumer Research Ann Arbor, MI, pp 644–649

Srivastava RK (1981) Usage-Situational Influences on Perceptions of Product-Markets: Theoretical and Empirical Issues, in: Monroe KB (ed.) Advances in Consumer Research, Vol 8. Association for Consumer Research, Ann Arbor, MI, pp 106–111

Srivastava RK, Alpert MI (1982) A Customer-Oriented Approach for Determining Market Structures, in: Srivastava RK, Shocker AD (eds.) Proceedings of the Second Conference on Analytic Approaches to Product and Marketing Planning. Marketing Science Institute, Cambridge, MA, pp 26–57

Srivastava RK, Alpert MI, Shocker AD (1984) A Customer-Oriented Approach for Determining Market Structures. Journal of Marketing 48: 32–45

Srivastava RK, Leone RP, Shocker AD (1981) Market Structure Analysis: Hierarchical Clustering of Products Based on Substitution-in-Use. Journal of Marketing 45: 38–48

Srivastava RK, Shocker AD, Day GS (1978) An Exploratory Study of the Influences of Usage Situation on Perceptions of Product-Markets, in: Keith HH (ed.) Advances in Consumer Research Vol 5. Association for Consumer Research, Ann Arbor, MI, pp 32–38

Srull TK (1986) A Model of Consumer Memory and Judgment, in: Lutz RJ (ed.), Advances in Consumer Research, Vol 13. Association for Consumer Research, Provo, UT, pp 643–647

Tucker LR (1964) The Extension of Factor Analysis to Three-Dimensional Matrices, in: Frederiksen N, Gulliksen H (eds.) Contributions to Mathematical Psychology. Holt, Rinehart, and Winston, New York, pp 109–127

Part 2

Decision Support for Marketing Problems

PROLOG-Based Decision Support for Data Analysis in Marketing*

I. Böckenholt, M. Both and W. Gaul
Institute of Decision Theory and Operations Research,
Faculty of Economics, University of Karlsruhe
F. R. G.

Summary

Against the background of numerous developments of models and methods for solving marketing planning and decision problems, there is empirical evidence that some of the potential users refrain from applying existing tools. Decision support systems, combined with expert knowledge components, can increase acceptance and provide additional knowledge concerning e.g. the possibilities and preconditions of proper usage of certain models and methods in this field.

In this paper, a prototype implementation is presented which aims at supporting data analysis situations which frequently occur in market research.

In its present version, the prototype comprises e.g. the demonstration of a user specific consultation trace, the explanation why a specific solution was not chosen, a what-if component, offers help functions, revises specifications made by the user, and performs consistency checks during the identification process of a data structure.

The prototype has been implemented by means of PROLOG and runs on PC. A marketing example is used to show how and what support can be made available by the prototype.

1 Introduction

The discussion about expert knowledge research and representation has reached the marketing area. Of course, the interest in such problems is not that new. In order to support decision makers in marketing, approaches having become known under labels such as "marketing information systems", "marketing decision support systems", and, just recently, "knowledge-based systems for marketing problems" or "marketing expert systems" have been discussed and (in some cases claimed to have been) developed. But the question of what marketing people would accept as supporting tools (with or without emphasizing the expert knowledge representation viewpoint) within the area of marketing decision making is referring to a problem too complex to allow both a quick/easy and complete/straightforward answer.

Additionally, there are, at least, two ways of exploiting the potential of knowledge-based systems for marketing purposes.

*Research has been supported by the Deutsche Forschungsgemeinschaft

On the one hand, closely adhering to the intention originally pursued by knowledge-based systems, it would be of interest to tackle problems characterized by qualitative relationships and, thus, requiring the processing of symbols.

On the other hand, quantitative models and methods, incorporating mainly algorithmic expertise, could be enriched by qualitative knowledge concerning e.g. handling of these techniques, preconditions of their usage, and clues for an adequate interpretation of the results obtained. This coupling of quantitative and qualitative knowledge would stimulate the application of sophisticated and powerful techniques to problems in practice, and could, simultaneously, prevent misuse.

However, this paper is not aimed at giving a review concerning basic principles with respect to the different kinds of systems mentioned, their common features and differences and their potential benefits, and assessing whether and how well existing systems have coped with theoretical requirements (see e.g. Little (1970) for an introduction into the well-known decision calculus discussion, Little (1979) for comments on decision support systems for marketing and Hayes-Roth, Waterman and Lenat (1982), Harmon and King (1985) and Waterman (1985) for an introduction into the field of expert systems).

A further question in this context would have to deal with what part(s) of the marketing area would be appropriate and/or worthwhile to be tackled by knowledge-based decision support. Of course, there exists a broad spectrum of tools to support the marketing decision maker, ranging from simple data handling facilities to complex, sophisticated methods and models (to be more concrete, at least, the two fields ",marketing data analysis" with connections to statistics (see e.g. Ferber (ed.) (1974) for an early collection of corresponding methodology, or Green and Tull (1982) for a more recent introduction into this field) and "marketing planning" with connections to operations research (see e.g. Lilien and Kotler (1983) for an overview) should be mentioned).

This paper will concentrate on decision support aspects with respect to marketing data analysis. Although also in this field—as in others—quite a number of models/methods and corresponding software tools are available, there is empirical evidence that some of the potential users refrain from applying existing marketing data analysis methodology to an extent desirable. A survey conducted among German market research agencies (Gaul, Förster and Schiller (1986a,b), Gaul (1987) and Gaul and Homburg (1987)) has revealed that within the spectrum of data analysis methods certain new and sophisticated techniques would need support in order to increase their usage. Although, compared with results obtained by Greenberg, Goldstucker and Bellenger (1977), the willingness to apply advanced data analysis techniques in practice has increased, there is still lack of usage for some of them.

Thus, efforts to extend the capabilities of conventional software in this field and to bridge the gap between the requirements of advanced methods and the skills of potential users are needed.

First attempts of providing intelligent assistance for data analytic and statistical tasks are mentioned in Nelder (1977). In his opinion, the amount of uncritical usage of standard procedures is enormous, since it is left to the potential user to check the preconditions of their proper employment. Chambers (1981) made similar observations concerning uninformed, unguided, and incorrect data analysis enhanced by the increasing availability of statistical software. Against this background, he proposed that expert system techniques would be useful for building more intelligent statistical software and should play an active role in the process of data analysis.

In response to these directive papers, subsequently some attempts were made to encode knowledge within programs designed for supporting inexperienced users. In this context, at least two major lines of developments have to be mentioned.

On the one hand, there are user interfaces to complex statistical software systems, so-called front-ends (see e.g. the front-end to MULTIVARIANCE by Smith, Lee and Hand (1983) or the front-end to GLIM by Wolstenholme and Nelder (1986)). On the other hand, there are prototypes which advise the user in performing analyses and, to a certain degree, carry out the analyses automatically (see e.g. the regression expert prototype REX by Gale and Pregibon (1982)).

Simultaneously with these application-oriented developments, contributions concerning design aspects (see e.g. Hand (1984) and Hahn (1985)), necessary attributes (see e.g. Hand (1985)) and ways of implementation and study of statistical strategies (see e.g. Oldford and Peters (1986)) with respect to knowledge-based decision support for data analysis were made.

In the next section, the question of how to implement a data analysis strategy is discussed while the third section describes an own decision support prototype for data analysis applications within the context of specific marketing problems. In the fourth section, parts of a prototype consultation are described to give an impression about the support available from the current version of the prototoype. In the final section, some conclusions concerning the evaluation of the prototype will be given and directions of future research will be outlined.

2 How to Implement a Data Analysis Strategy

Before describing the current version of a prototype of a decision support system for data analysis in marketing, some remarks concerning what has been named a "data analysis strategy" or "statistical strategy" in the literature will be given.

In this regard, Pearl (1984, p. 19) states that " a strategy is not simply a sequence of actions but a prescription for choosing an action in response to any possible external event such as an outcome of a test,..., or the output of a complicated computational procedure". Hand (1986, p. 356) defines a statistical strategy "as a formal description of the choices, actions, and decisions to be made while using statistical methods in the course of a study", and, furthermore, cites a number of reasons indicating their importance. Similary, Oldford and Peters (1986, p. 337) use this term "to label the reasoning used by the experienced statistician in the course of the analysis of some aspects of a substantive statistical problem".

When trying to implement parts of such a strategy in a knowledge-based system, one is faced with two complementary requirements regarding the software representation (see Oldford and Peters (1986)). On the one side, the representation should be well targeted, in order to exhibit a performance comparable to that of an expert working on the same problem. On the other side, the representation should be as complete as possible, i.e. it should be applicable not only to a single, specific problem but also to other problems in the domain to be studied. Human expertise for performing data analysis tasks, however, is so diverse and complex (see e.g. Thisted (1986)) that for many of the strategies complete representations cannot be achieved for the time being.

In order to determine which kind of strategy exhibits the largest potential for complete software representations, it is useful to consider the following two components. First, the level at which the strategy operates within the overall analysis indicates the complexity of the operations to be performed. At a low level, the operations can be specified in general more precisely than at a higher level. Second, the importance of the input from the surrounding subject-matter context to the performance of the strategy plays an important part with respect to the efficiency of the representation. Typically, the importance of the subject matter context, i.e. problem-specific or more general knowledge, is the greater the higher the operational level is. Oldford and Peters (1986, p. 336) express the opinion "that a reasonably accurate software representation will be possible only for certain kinds of statistical strategies, namely those which do not require computer determination of the relevant properties of the substantive subject-matter context". To sum up the previous discussion, low-level, low-context strategies can be more easily represented and should, therefore, be the starting point for the development of knowledge-based systems intended to support data analysis tasks.

3 A Decision Support Prototype for Data Analysis in Marketing

In the following, a decision-support prototype development of our own, which takes into account design aspects mentioned previously and which is intended to meet the demand for intelligent support in the process of data analysis, will be illustrated. This prototype aims at supporting some aspects of analyzing data structures frequently encountered in marketing research. In this context, frequently, consumer preferences, perceived similarities or dissimilarities in one-mode or higher-mode settings have to be evaluated. For performing such evaluations, a lot of data analysis techniques have been developed either being part of standard software packages or being available as individual programs (see e.g. Böckenholt and Gaul (1986) (advanced scaling methods) and Both and Gaul (1987) (advanced clustering techniques)—to mention just a few own contributions—and the references cited there).

As argued previously, knowledge about the suitability of different methods with respect to the user's objectives, and knowledge about the properties the data structures to be analyzed have to exhibit, is required in order to ensure proper application. Obviously, different levels of knowledge appertaining to the typical stages of the data analysis process can be distinguished. At the present implementation stage, knowledge about the preconditions for the usage of a spectrum of multidimensional scaling and cluster analysis methods is represented. By means of this knowledge, important characteristics of the data structures can be related to the requirements of specific analysis procedures, and proper procedures can be identified and executed.

As far as the data analysis procedures themselves are concerned, it cannot be the objective of the prototype to compete with large statistical software systems such as SAS or SPSS which require various skills from the user. Rather, focus is laid on advanced

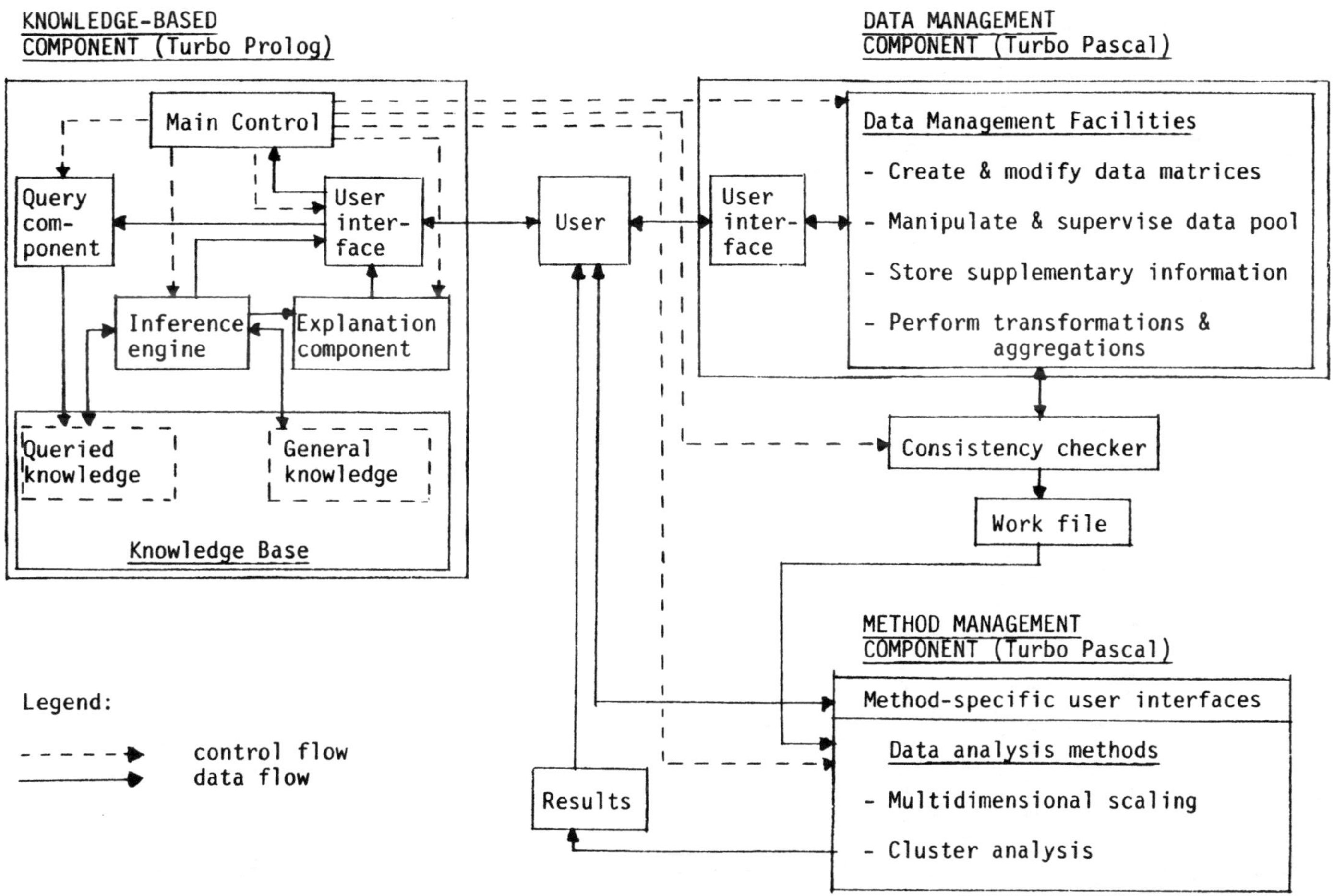

Fig. 1: Architecture of the prototype

data analysis techniques which have not been integrated in standard software systems in a desirable extent. Additionally, the quantitative procedures can be made more easily accessible and their misuse can be prevented by employment of knowledge-based approaches as described later on. In conjunction with the precondition of providing a microcomputer implementation, the above objectives entail that only a limited number of data analysis procedures can be reasonably incorporated. Therefore, references to sources of procedures not implemented in the prototype, e.g. because of excessive runtime, will be provided in an extended version.

The architecture of the current version of the prototype, depicted in Fig. 1, is characterized by a division into three components.

The *knowledge-based component* consists of an expert-system shell implemented by means of TURBO-PROLOG[1] and of a knowledge base structured as a production system. Some of the main functions of this knowledge-based component tailored with respect to the requirements of the specific consultation task will be illustrated in the following.

At the beginning of a prototype consultation session, the knowledge-based component is operating, and the user is asked to specify—among other things—the data structures to be analyzed. To that end, important characteristics, appertaining to the data, are asked by a *query component*, and are, subsequently, stored in the temporary part of the knowledge base. In Fig. 2, an example screen, illustrating the underlying mechanism, is depicted.

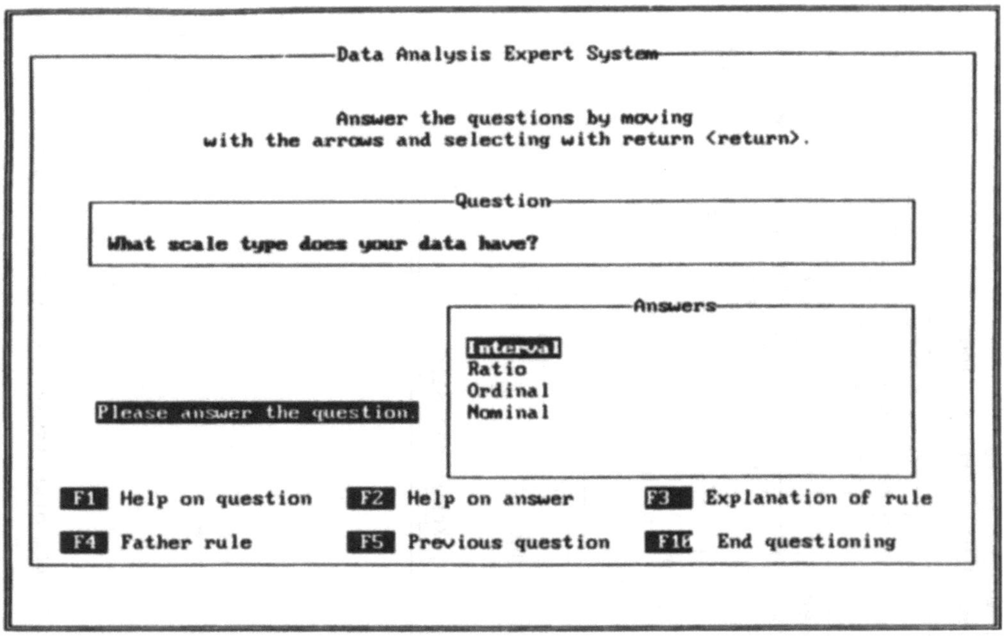

Figure 2: Example screen of the query component

[1]A preceding version of the knowledge-based component was written in ARITY-PROLOG together with H. Kleine Büning and coworkers from the Institut für Angewandte Informatik und Formale Beschreibungsverfahren, Fakultät für Wirtschaftswissenschaften, Universität Karlsruhe (TH).

In an upper window of a screen—like that of Fig. 2 where the scale type of the underlying data is asked for—questions concerning the characterization of the data structures are formulated while respective answer categories are depicted beneath. The answer categories are constrained according to the specifications previously made by the user as a result of internal consistency checks. On the bottom of such a screen, some help functions are listed which can be activated by means of function keys. F1 provides an explanation of terms used in the questions whereas F2 gives explanations with respect to the answer categories depending on the actual cursor position. While these help functions are of a static nature, F3 and F4 help to understand the dynamic behaviour of the system. F3 elucidates why a certain question is asked by giving an explanation of the rule which caused this question to be formulated, F4 indicates the father rule which may be of interest in multistage rule bases, while F5 allows the user to return to the previous question and to alter specifications made there.

Dependent on the kind of specifications, some questions need not be addressed to the user explicitly by the query component but may be answered implicitly. This abbreviation of the specification process helps to avoid lengthy and boring parts at the beginning of the prototype consultation session.

When the characterization of the data structure has been completed, the information provided by the user and the general knowledge being represented in the knowledge base can be processed by the *inference engine.* This component draws on the resolution mechanisms provided by PROLOG and works in a goal-driven manner to search for appropriate data analysis techniques in the frame of the momentary description of the data analysis problem.

Additionally, the user can consult the *explanation component* where he/she is offered a screen with a menu as depicted in Fig. 3 from which the prototype consultation can be traced back.

One can select a list of all questions and answers where, as argued previously, a distinction is made between specifications explictly given by the user and answers which can be derived implicitly.

Moreover, the user can get a list of all successful rules. For that purpose, all of the rules which led to the proposal of a specific data analysis technique are presented in a verbalized way. Analogously, the complementary set of rules, namely the falsified ones, may be indicated. Additionally, a "why not" mechanism may be invoked, which gives reasons, why a certain data analysis technique, the user had in mind, is not proposed by the system. Finally, this part of the explanation component is complemented by a list of all solutions possible with respect to the specifications regarding the data structures to be analyzed.

Besides getting explanations with respect to proposed solutions and with respect to the way the conclusions were arrived at, the user can also modify specifications given in previous parts of the consultation session. Fig. 4 shows how the screen looks like if one wants to alter the description of mode, scale type or type of matrix of the underlying data.

In the upper window, specifications previously made by the user are summarized. When the user indicates which answer is to be altered, the respective answer categories are presented in a window built up in the lower part of the screen, and the alteration

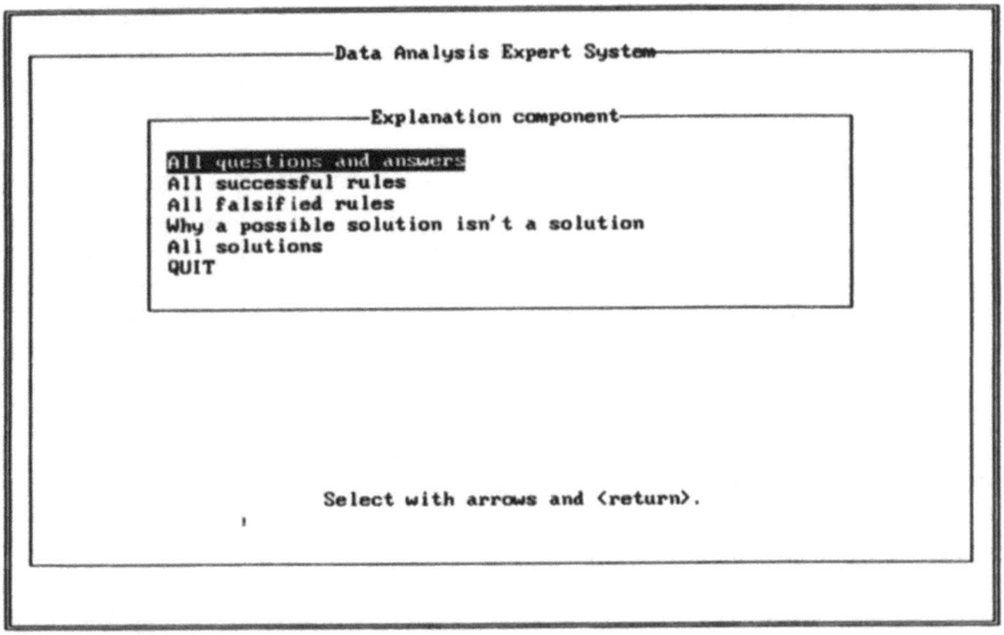

Figure 3: Example screen with explanations of user specific consultation trace

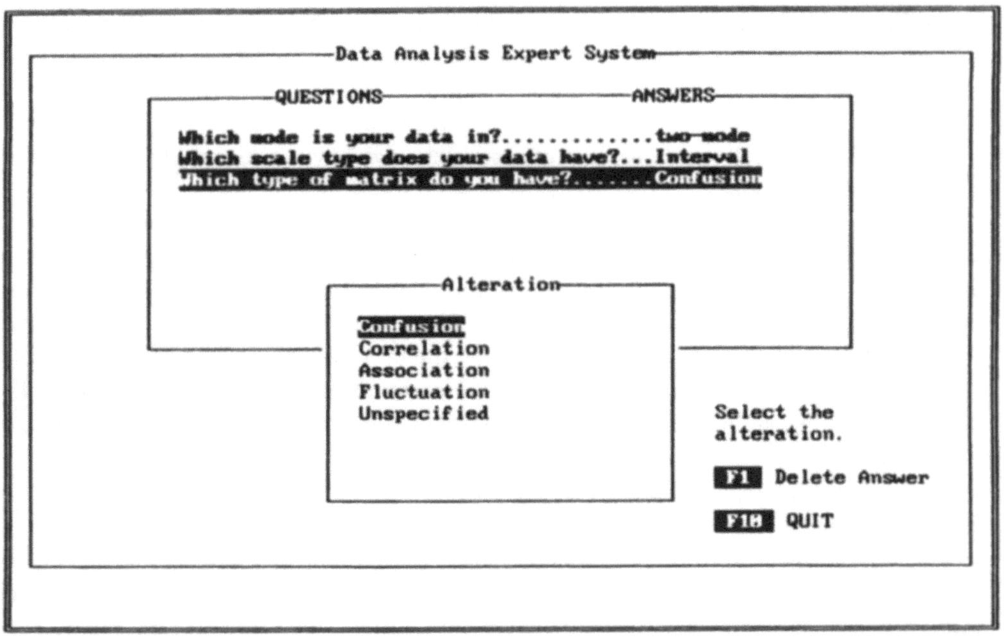

Figure 4: Example screen of alteration possibilities

can be carried out by selecting the proper item. The specifications changed in this alteration component are processed by rules by which consistency is checked and which allow to detect incorrect combinations and prompt the user to make proper corrections.

The other parts of the prototype—a data management component and a method management component—are both implemented by means of TURBO-PASCAL.

The *data management component* provides facilities which are oriented by the kind of data structures to be processed, including e.g. comfortable editing functions, transformations and aggregations of the data to be analyzed. When transformations or aggregations have to be performed, e.g. similarities may have to be transformed into dissimilarities or vice versa, data structures change and another part of the consultation session can be initiated on the basis of such a modification. The data management component can be invoked independently from the knowledge-based component in order to allow the user to handle the data structures. Nonetheless, several checks concerning consistency and plausibility are performed automatically, e.g. when data matrices are being edited or when transformations/aggregations are being carried out.

The *method management component* can be invoked by the user on the basis of the recommendations given by the knowledge-based component. After one of the data analysis procedures proposed has been selected, the data actually to be analyzed is checked automatically. If all of the requirements are met, the data are stored in a workfile and can subsequently be processed by the specific data analysis procedure. To that end, control is being transferred to a corresponding subroutine which is in charge of the user interface and of the numerical computations. After having displayed the results of a specific data analysis method graphically or in tabular form, control is taken over again by the knowledge-based component, and the user can decide on the next analysis steps. The user, however, is not allowed to invoke the method management component at random, since otherwise, it would not be possible to ensure the consistency between the requirements of the data analysis techniques used and the characteristics of the underlying data structures.

4 Demonstration of Prototype Consultation Session

In this section, the usage of the just described prototype will be illustrated by evaluating a data set collected in the course of an advertising research experiment (Experimental design and execution of the advertising research study is described in Gaul and Böckenholt (1987). Here, emphasis is laid on evaluation possibilities of a special data set from the advertising research experiment within the prototype consultation demonstration.).

In order to show how the data looks like, part of the data matrix to be analyzed is visualized in Fig. 5 within the matrix editing environment.

The data matrix to be analyzed during the prototype consultation session is an aggregated two-mode matrix reflecting associations between print ads and appropriate features or properties (two print ads for five cognac brands, labelled brand name 1 and brand name 2, respectively, and constituting the rows of this matrix, and seven properties, making up the matrix columns). Each of the print ads had to be characterized with respect to the mentioned properties on a seven point rating scale.

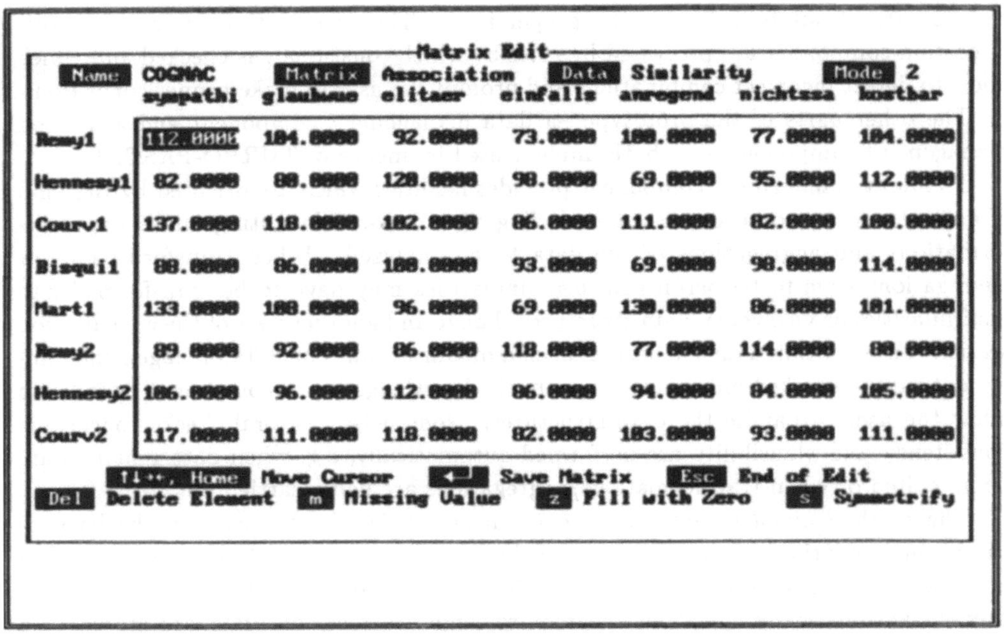

Figure 5: Part of a two-mode association matrix reflecting relationships between cognac brands (row objects) and associated features (column objects)

For the purpose of editing data matrices, some useful features have been implemented such as symmetrifying a matrix on the basis of the upper triangle or filling up an incomplete matrix with zeros or indicating missing values. These commands are listed on the bottom of the screen. On the top, entries concerning matrix type, data type, and number of modes are shown. Explanations of these terms are given on request in the knowledge-based component of the system. Additionallly, the objects or subjects comprising the data set can be labelled and a short comment characterizing the data can be given.

There are, of course, several ways to evaluate the information contained in such an association matrix partly depicted in Fig. 5. In the following, two approaches proposed by the knowledge-based component will be illustrated.

Suppose, the user wants to get a first impression concerning global relationships between the print ads of the cognac brands. Then, the two-mode association matrix can be transformed into a one-mode matrix reflecting (dis)similarities between the print ads themselves. To that end, some aggregation/transformation procedures are provided within the data management component which can create the desired matrix. The result of such a transformation is depicted in Fig. 6.

Obviously, the newly generated matrix is of one-mode type and symmetric.As a transformation to dissimilarities was asked for, a relabelling of the data type is automatically performed. The new matrix type is now unspecified (every matrix not explictly specified within given categories by the user is labelled that way) and named

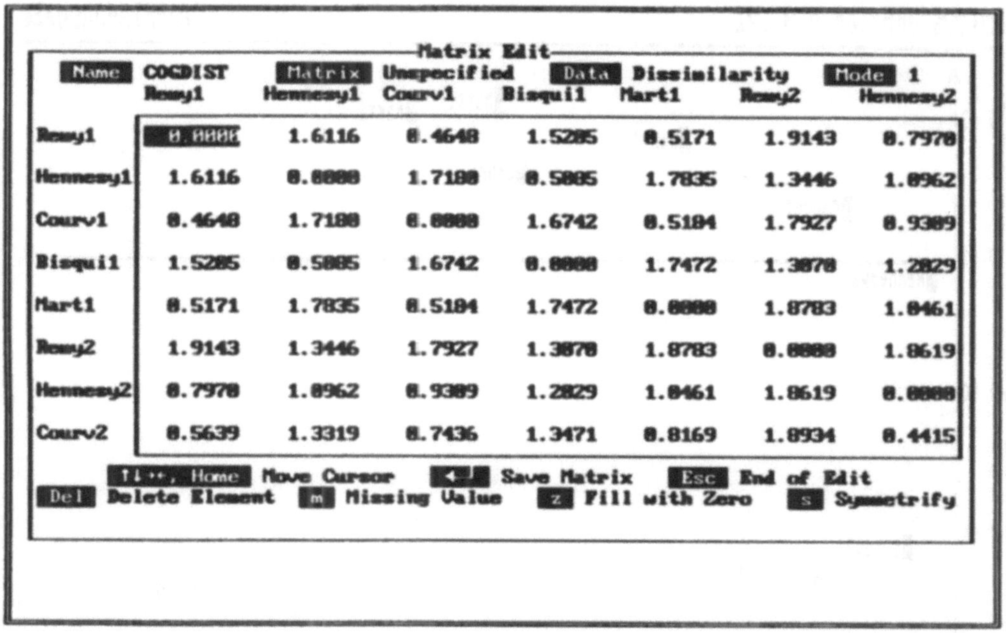

Figure 6: Part of a one-mode dissimilarity matrix obtained after transformation of the two-mode data of Fig. 5

COGDIST (DIST for DISsimilarity Transformation). The characteristics of this matrix and the new labels specifying the new column objects are adjusted automatically by the aggregation procedure.

When the user consults the knowledge-based component in the manner described in the preceding section, e.g. the following data analysis techniques would be proposed:[2] one-mode multidimensional scaling (MDS), one-mode hierarchical cluster analysis, the DEDICOM-model, and, as far as data transformations are concerned, transformation into similarities. If the user decides on getting a representation of the relationships between the print ads under study within a perceptual space, an MDS-procedure can be utilized. At this point, the knowledge-based system is being quitted, and the user communicates directly with the used MDS data analysis procedure. The way how this special program is operated will not be discussed here (the implementation was written in TURBO PASCAL, most parts of the dialogue are still in German), instead, the graphical display of a two-dimensional configuration resulting from the computations is shown in Fig. 7.

When the software part in which the individual data analysis techniques are performed is left, control is, again, transferred to the knowledge-based component, and

[2]The magnitude of the set of proposed data analysis techniques depends on several criteria which will not be discussed here in detail. One criterion is that, at least, one technique is mentioned (and marked specially) which is available either in the method management component or in our institute's subroutine library.

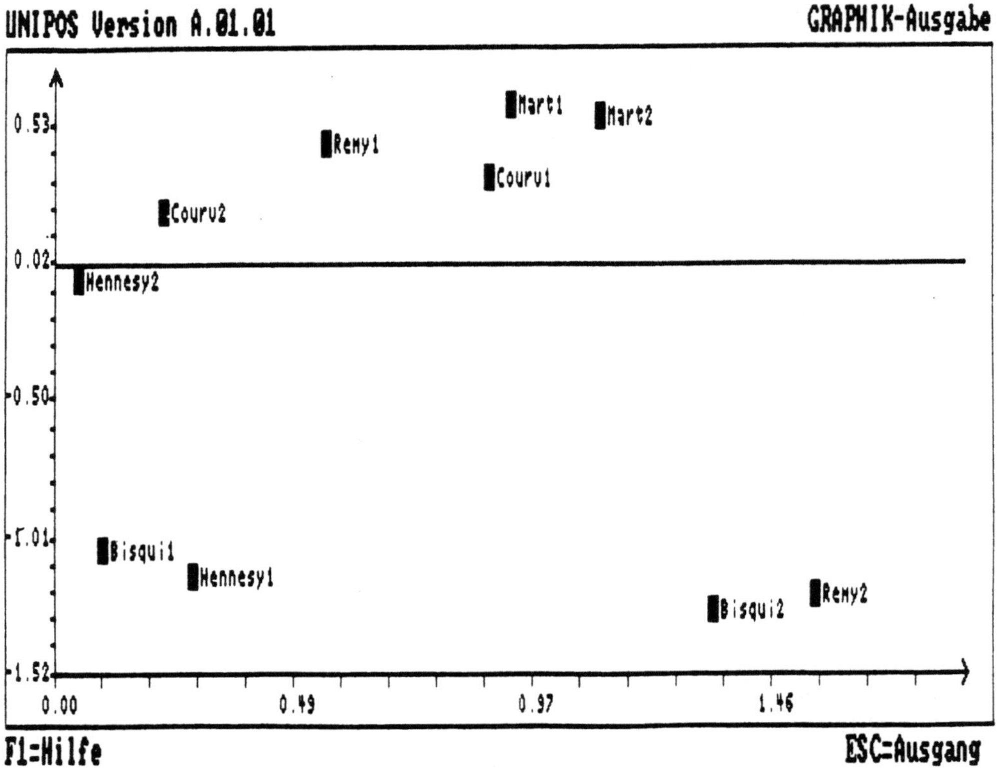

Figure 7: Graphical representation obtained by a multidimensional scaling procedure on the basis of the data of Fig. 6

the user can continue within the consultation session.

Suppose, the user also wants to evaluate the original data, depicted in Fig. 5, in such a way that the relationships between the print ads (row elements) and their associated features (column elements) are explictly taken into consideration.

Then, a two-mode data analysis would be appropriate, and the following steps are proposed by the knowledge-based component. First, the two-mode matrix of Fig. 5 should be transformed into a two-mode dissimilarity matrix. The result of such a transformation is shown in Fig. 8.

The characteristics of this new matrix are automatically adjusted by the transformation procedure. Since the resulting dissimilarities should not be interpreted as association data any longer, the type of the new matrix is, again, labelled as unspecified. Second, a consultation of the knowledge-based component concerning the evaluation of this transformed data set would e.g. result in the following proposals (see footnote 2): two-mode hierarchical cluster analysis, the unfolding model and the vector model. If the user is interested in grouping the row and column objects in clusters revealing the underlying (dis)similarities, a two-mode hierarchical cluster analysis technique should

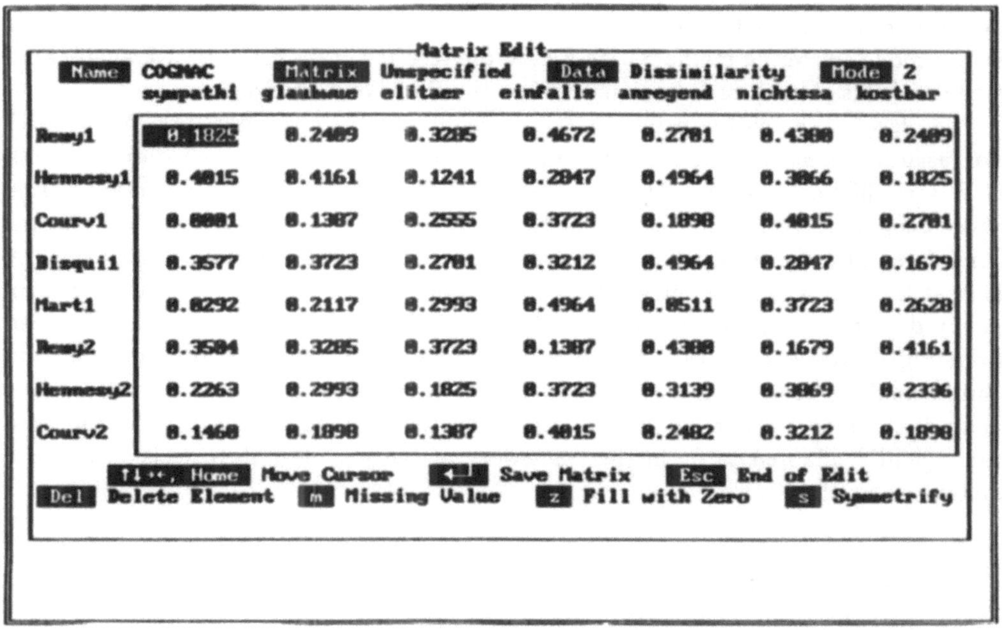

Figure 8: Part of a two-mode matrix generated from the data of Fig. 5

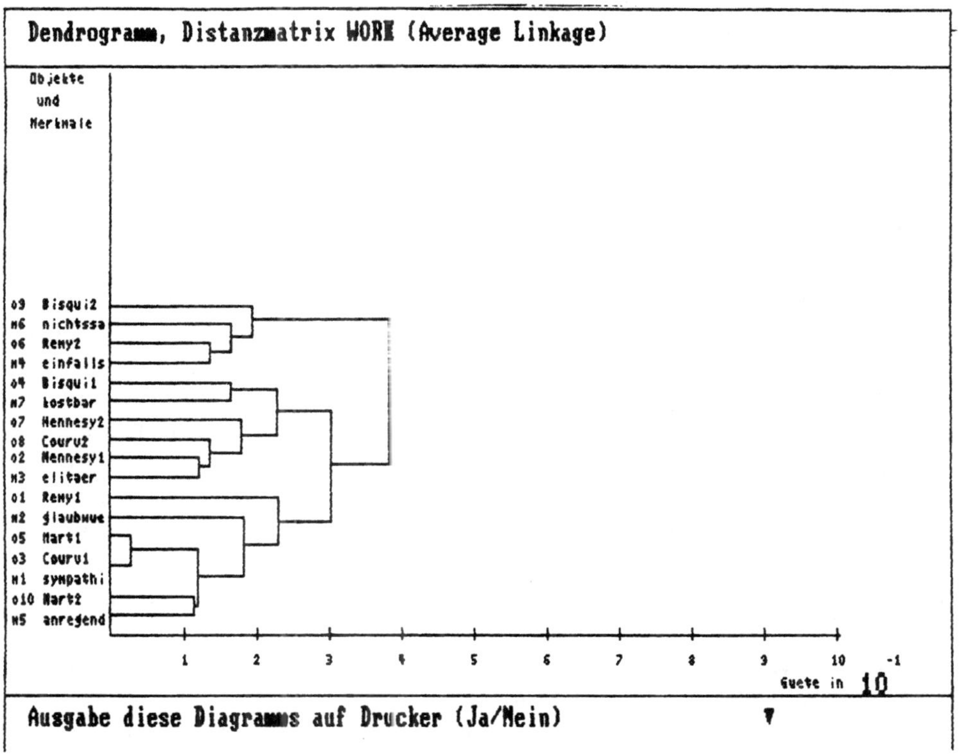

Figure 9: Dendrogram obtained by MVAL (Missing Value Average Linkage algorithm) on the basis of the data of Fig. 8

be selected (see e.g. Both and Gaul (1987) and Espejo and Gaul (1986) for a description of two-mode clustering methods). In Fig. 9, the results obtained by the average linkage version of this procedure are summarized in the shape of a dendrogram.

The level at which the print ads (O1 to O10) and the characteristics (M1 to M7) are fused into joint clusters indicates some kind of relationship between these elements of sets of different modes. At the lowest level O3 and M1 are fused, however, this effect cannot be visualized because of the limited resolution of the graphical output. Therefore, only the horizontal line between these two items indicates this cluster. A look at the corresponding entry (O3 ≅ Courvoisier, M1 ≅ sympathetic) in the matrix partly depicted in Fig. 8 confirms this finding. It has to be restated and can be seen from Fig. 7 and Fig. 9, that the user interface of both the MDS-program and the cluster analysis program is written in German. This is due to the fact that these data analysis techniques originally had been implemented as stand alone programs and were subsequently adapted to fit in the framework of the just described decision support system.

5 Outlook and Further Research

The features of the prototype presented in this paper indicate that already some of the requirements regarded as necessary for supporting decisions with respect to the analysis of marketing data have been realized. At the present implementation stage, mainly decisions about appropriate techniques for analyzing certain data structures important within marketing research are supported.

The architecture of the prototype with its three separate components allows the utilization of different implementation approaches—a more qualitative one for building the knowledge-based component and a more quantitative one for implementing the data management component and the method management component. This architecture seems to be well suited for meeting the specific requirements of the respective tasks.

Future extensions of the prototype will be aimed at supporting further stages in the analysis process, e.g. by making proposals for proper data collection or deriving clues for a substantial interpretation of the results obtained. Such extensions will, of course, entail the incorporation of subject-matter knowledge to a higher degree.

Additionally, the method management component will be extended with further data analysis procedures which have been developed on mainframes at our institute (see e.g. a variety of further one-mode cluster analysis procedures (Späth (1984)), two-mode clustering algorithms (Both and Gaul (1987)), a two-mode multidimensional scaling algorithm for contingency-tables (Böckenholt (1986)), a generalized Thurstonian scaling program, which allows for one- and multidimensional as well as internal and external analyses of paired comparisons preference data (see e.g. Böckenholt and Gaul (1986)) and algorithms which perform correspondence analysis or dual scaling (see e.g. Lebart, Morineau and Warwick (1984), and Nishisato (1980) with respect to the analysis of several kinds of qualitative data structures).

In order to adapt them to the microcomputer, data transfer interfaces as well as the user interfaces will have to be standardized and the current knowledge base will have to be extended. In view of the performance of the present version of the prototype and with respect to the potential that might arise through the enhancements just mentioned, it can be expected that the intended system will become a decision support tool for guiding an inexperienced user during the process of marketing data analysis.

References

Böckenholt I (1986) Graphical Representation of Categorical Proximities: A Maximum Likelihood Method, in: Gaul W, Schader M (eds.) Classification as a Tool of Research. North-Holland, Amsterdam, 27–34

Böckenholt I, Gaul W (1986) Analysis of Choice Behavior via Probabilistic Ideal Point and Vector Models. Applied Stochastic Models and Data Analysis 2: 209–226

Both M, Gaul W, (1987) Ein Vergleich zweimodaler Clusteranalyseverfahren. Methods of Operations Research 57, 594–605

Chambers JM (1984) Some Thoughts on Expert Software, Proceedings of the 13th Symposium on the Interface of Computer Science and Statistics. Springer, Berlin, Heidelberg, New York, pp 36–40

Espejo E, Gaul W (1986) Two-Mode Hierarchical Clustering as an Instrument for Marketing Research, in: Gaul W, Schader M (eds.) Classification as a Tool of Research. North Holland, Amsterdam, New York, Oxford, Tokyo, pp 121–128

Ferber R (ed.) (1974) Handbook of Marketing Research. McGraw-Hill, New York

Gale WA, Pregibon D (1982) An Expert System for Regression Analysis, in: Proceedings of Computer Science and Statistics, Annual Symposium on the Interface. North Hollywood, Cal., pp 110–117

Gaul W (1987) Zum Einsatz von Datenanalysetechniken in der Marktforschung, in: Opitz D, Rauhut B (eds.) Ökonomie und Mathematik. Springer, Berlin, Heidelberg

Gaul W, Böckenholt I, (1987) Generalized Thurstonian Scaling of Advertising Messages. Working Paper No. 106, Institute of Decision Theory and Operations Research, University of Karlsruhe (TH).

Gaul W, Förster F, Schiller K (1986a) Empirische Ergebnisse zur Verbreitung und Nutzung von Statistik-Software in der Marktforschung, in: Lehmacher W, Hörmann A (eds.) Statistik-Software, 3. Konferenz über die wissenschaftliche Anwendung von Statistiksoftware. Gustav Fischer, Stuttgart, New York, pp 323–332

Gaul W, Förster F, Schiller K (1986b) Typologisierung deutscher Marktforschungsinstitute: Ergebnisse einer empirischen Studie. Marketing ZFP 8: 163–172

Gaul W, Homburg C (1987) The Use of Data Analysis Techniques by German Market Research Agencies: A Causal Analysis, to appear in Journal of Business Research

Green PE, Tull DS (1982) Methoden und Techniken der Marketingforschung. 4. Auflage, deutsche Übersetzung, Poeschel, Stuttgart

Greenberg BA, Goldstucker JL Bellenger JN (1977) What Techniques are Used by Marketing Researchers in Business? Journal of Marketing 41: 62–68

Hahn GJ (1985) More Intelligent Statistical Software and Statistical Expert Systems: Future Directions. The American Statistician 39, 1: 1–16

Hand DJ (1984) Statistical Expert Systems: Design. The Statistician 37: 351–369

Hand DJ (1985) Statistical Expert Sytems: Necessary Attributes. Journal of Applied Statistics 12, 1: 19–27

Hand DJ (1986) Patterns in Statistical Strategy, in: Gale WA (ed.) Artificial Intelligence and Statistics. Addison-Wesley, Reading, Mass., pp 355–387

Harmon P, King D (1985) Expert Systems. Wiley, New York

Hayes-Roth F, Waterman D, Lenat D (eds.) (1982) Building Expert Systems. Addison-Wesley, Reading, Mass.

Lebart L, Morineau A, Warwick K (1984) Multivariate Descriptive Statistical Analysis: Correspondence Analysis and Related Techniques for Large Matrices. Wiley, New York

Lilien GL, Kotler P (1983) Marketing Decision Making: A Model-Building Approach. Harper and Row, New York

Little JDC (1970) Models and Managers: The Concept of a Decision Calculus. Management Science 16: 466–485

Little JDC (1979) Decision Support Systems for Marketing Managers. Journal of Marketing 43, 3: 9–26

Nelder JA (1977) Intelligent Programs, the Next Stage in Statistical Computing, in: Barra JR, Brodeau F, Ronner G, Van Cutsem B (eds.) Recent Developments in Statistics. North Holland, Amsterdam, pp 79–86

Nishisato S (1980) Analysis of Categorical Data: Dual Scaling and its Applications. University of Toronto Press, Toronto

Oldford RW, Peters SC (1986) Implementation and Study of Statistical Strategy, in: Gale W (ed.) Artificial Intelligence and Statistics. Addison–Wesley, Reading, Mass., pp 335–353

Pearl, J (1984) Heuristics. Addison-Wesley, Reading, Mass.

Smith AMR, Lee LS, Hand DJ (1983) Interactive User-Friendly Interfaces to Statistical Packages. The Computer Journal 26: 199–204

Späth H (1984) Cluster-Formation und -Analyse. Oldenbourg, München

Thisted, RA (1986) Representing Statistical Knowledge for Expert Data Analysis Systems, in: Gale WA (ed.) Artificial Intelligence and Statistics. Addison-Wesley, Reading, Mass., pp 267–284

Waterman D (1985) A Guide to Expert Systems. Addison-Wesley, Reading, Mass.

Wolstenholme DE, Nelder JA (1986) A Front End for GLIM, in: Haux R (ed.) Expert Systems in Statistics. Gustav Fischer, Stuttgart, New York, pp 155–177

Market-Share Analysis: Communicating Results Through Spreadsheet-Based Simulators

L. G. Cooper
Anderson Graduate School of Management, University of California
Los Angeles CA 90024-1481

Summary

This article describes the information-systems theory and the pedagogy behind the development of C.A.S.P.E.R.—Competitive Analysis System for Product Performance and Promotional Effectiveness Research. Managers must be able to learn from historical data (and graphical summaries can be very effective in this role), simulate the market response to proposals, and evaluate plans in a dynamic, competitive environment. The CASPER software performs these three basic functions using an asymmetric market-share model as the market simulator.

1 Introduction

In any information system there are three basic ingredients: data, models and the software or other vehicles which organize data and models so that they facilitate decision making. One extreme position in the design of information systems, which could be called *datum ipso loquitor*, emphasizes the data at the expense of the models, while the facilitation of decision making amounts to little more than data-base management software. Another extreme position emphasizes the facilitation of decision making by the codification of expert knowledge and/or expert decision processes—placing *content knowledge* at the disposal of brand managers. The software described by Burke and Rangaswamy (1987) is one of numerous recent illustrations of such an approach. After prompting a manager to describe the promotional and competitive conditions in a market, software helped to plan the style of marketing support which would be effective.

We advocate a third position. We believe that the comprehensiveness of the data now becoming available to brand managers could fundamentally change the conventional wisdom. We must develop and implement models rich enough to capture the diversity of these data, and develop decision-support software which, while summarizing and organizing the information in data and models, will also entice brand managers to expend more effort to understand the implications of their actions.

There are four basic questions which market information systems must address:

1. How does a firm's marketing efforts affect its brand's performance?

2. How is a brand affected by competitors' actions and reactions?

3. How does a brand's actions affect others?

4. What are the revenue and cost implications of market actions and reactions?

The marketplace is providing abundant data on sales for all brands in a category, along with the promotional environment in which those sales occur. Firms can augment these data with cost estimates of their own operations, their competitors cost and costs in the channels of distribution. Then regardless of whether a firm's objectives are cast in terms of sales, market shares or profits, sales-response models provide the relationships which tie the market conditions to the firm's objectives.

Much more information can be added to the mix. Panel-based measures of consumer loyalty (Guadagni and Little (1983)) and consumer perceptions or attribute ratings (Cooper and Finkbeiner (1984)) are just two of many potential enriching sources. While it is important that modeling frameworks are compatible with these additional sources of data, we will be using sales, prices and promotional conditions as the core. We divide the process of modeling sales response into two components—models of market share and models of total category volume. An asymmetric market-share model (Carpenter, Cooper, Hanssens and Midgley (1987)) reflects a brand's actions in a competitive context. It focuses on relative efforts, how a brand's actions stand out from the competitive context, and how the distinctiveness of a brand's efforts and the relative effectiveness of those efforts translate into shares (Cooper and Nakanishi (1983a)). The category-volume component shows how the raw levels of marketing actions by each brand relate to the total sales in that category.

Market share times total category volume will equal sales. Beyond the mathematical identity, the synthesis of these two components must be diagnostically rich to fulfill the planning role. The richness is conveyed by parameters, elasticities and simulations. In simple *constant-elasticity models* the parameters give a quick summary of the effectiveness of marketing efforts. But effectiveness of efforts is not independent of the competitive context in which those efforts occur. Constant-elasticity models provide an impoverished picture of how the effectiveness varies with different competitive responses. The move to diagnostically richer models of competitive interaction brings with it a need to look at elasticities for insight, not just parameters.

There are three vehicles for conveying to brand managers the implications of changes in elasticities. First, competitive maps (Cooper (1987)) are diagnostic tools to find out what events signal change in the competitive structure, and to visualize the patterns of competitive pressures corresponding to any set of conditions. Second, the logit ideal-point model (Cooper and Nakanishi (1983b)) provide diagnostic tools to help visualize how patterns of competitive pressures translate into sales. And third, the elasticities also provide the needed ingredients to perform equilibrium analyses (Carpenter, Cooper, Hanssens and Midgley (1987)), assessing optimal marketing-mix levels based on various assumptions about competitive reactions. The system of models is depicted in Figure 1.

While calibration of market-share models, category-volume models, the asymmetric three-mode factor analysis involved in developing competitive maps, and the equilibrium analyses are still main-frame based analyses, the use of market simulators brings us squarely into a micro-computing environment.

Simulators have two main uses in summarizing market response. The first could be called *static* simulations which report how a particular set of market conditions on a

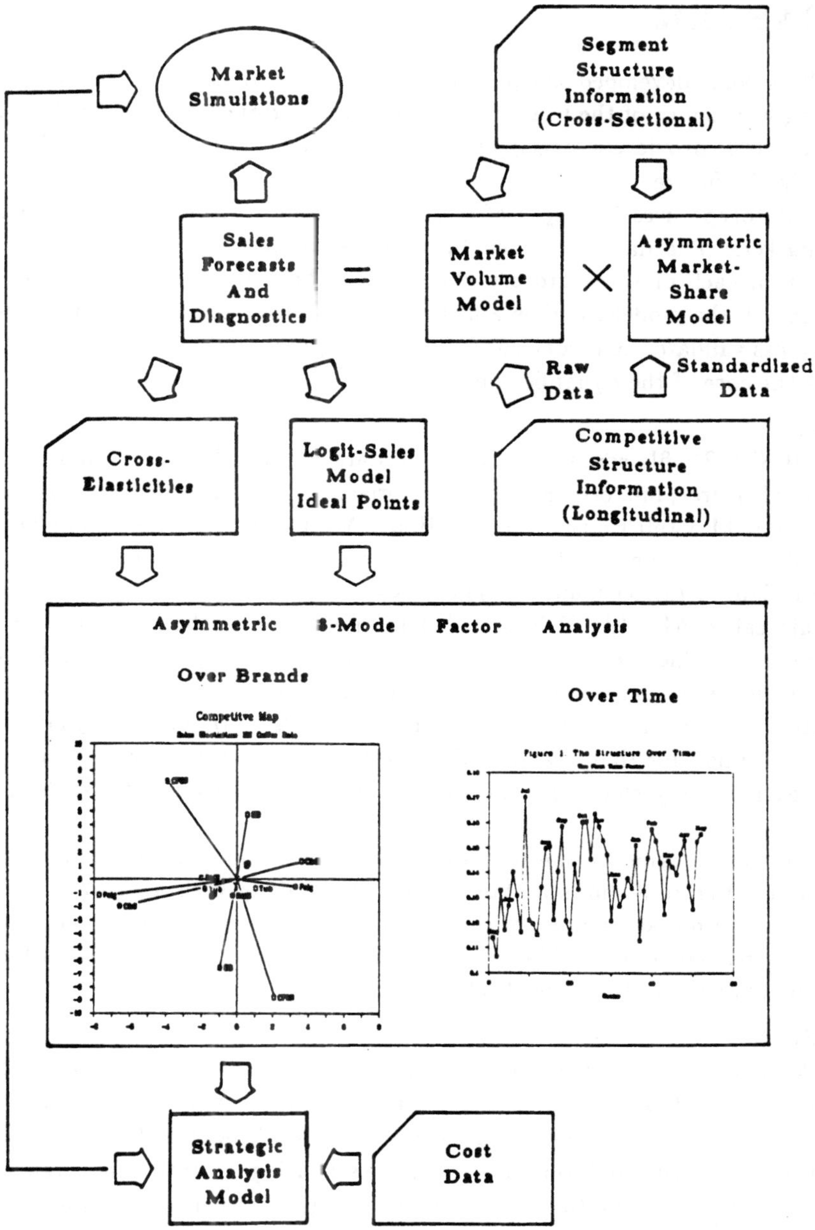

Figure 1: A System of Models for Competitive Analysis

particular occasion translates into sales (and possibly into profits). The second could be called *dynamic* simulations which show how a stream of actions over a set of time periods translates into sales (and possibly into profits). In the dynamic component the effects of advertising pulsing or wearout can be specifically modeled.

The next section reports how these ingredients are combined into software called CASPER (Competitive Analysis System for Product Performance and Promotional Effectiveness Research).

2 CASPER

CASPER is being developed as a prototype of the tools which should be available on the marketing workbench of the near-term future. Its programming in FRAMEWORK II's language FRED provides a largely open architecture for tailoring CASPER to different markets in the future.

The prototype uses 78 weeks of data on nine brands from the ground-caffeinated coffee market. The data, provided by Information Resources Inc., are weekly sales records from each of three grocery chains. The first 52 weeks of data are used for calibrating all the models, and as a historical data base. The subsequent 26 weeks are used to cross validate the models, and as the background data for the competitive game which is the core of the dynamic simulations.

HISTORY

The HISTORY file contains 52 weeks of data for each brand. Pounds sold, prices, newspaper features, in-store displays and store-coupon redemptions are tracked for Folgers, Regular Maxwell House, Maxwell House Master Blend, Hills Brs., Chock Full O Nuts, Yuban, Chase and Sanborne, an aggregate of the premium private brands called AOB (All Other Branded), and an aggregate of all the private-label economy brands for each chain called APL (All Private Labels). In addition to the raw data in HISTORY there are graphic file cabinets for each brand which contain plots such as Figure 2.

In this figure we can track market share versus price over 52 weeks with the promotional support for a brand being indicated by an "F" "D" or "C" signalling feature, display or coupon for that brand in that week. We currently track market share and sales in each grocery chain and the average over grocery chains, for each of the nine brands.

Rather than looking at one brand over time, we could summarize one time period over brands. Figure 3 shows a standard pie chart along with a digital display which summarizes the market shares, prices and promotional conditions. A complete set of such charts resides on disk. There are also menu-driven utility programs for forming custom plots or tables from the HISTORY file.

OCCASIONS

Market response is summarized by a high-parameter asymmetric market-share model (Carpenter et al. (1987), Cooper (1987)) and a category-volume model which relates internal market conditions to total category sales. With over 2000 degrees of freedom, calibration and cross validation of such models is a highly automated, relatively routine matter. But lecturing to managers on such high-parameter models is anything but routine. Simulators allow managers to experience how the market responds without dealing extensively with the methodological details of complex models. CASPER contains a menu-driven market simulator which allows the user to specify a background set of market assumptions (on prices, promotions and profits for the firms and the retailers) or accept a default set. Users can simulate market response to very flexibly specified ranges of market conditions. As a result users can assess if a promotional plan will pay out for the firm as well as for the retailers.

The results of simulations are accumulated in OCCASION files. Menu-driven utilities exist for forming plots or tables for these simulation results.

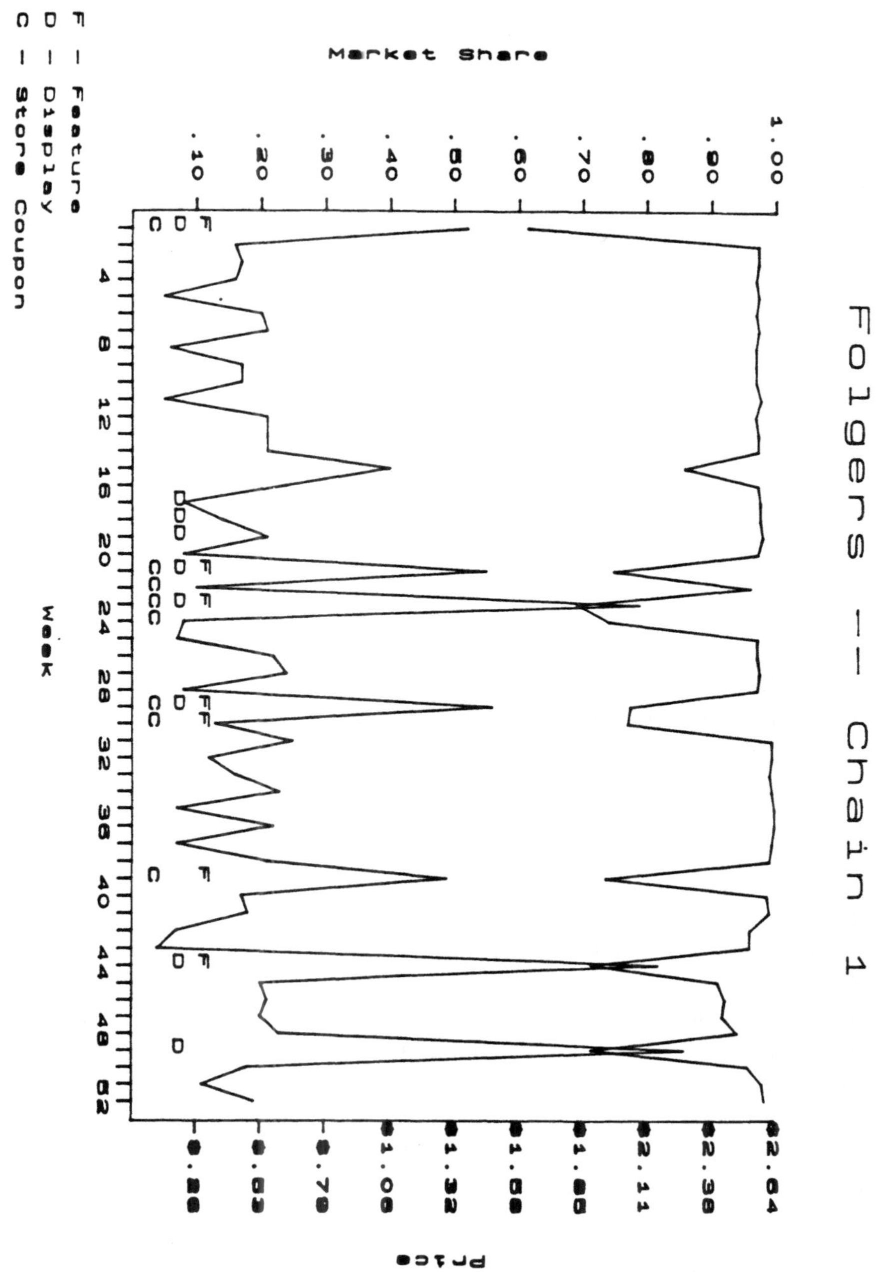

Figure 2: Market Share versus Price

COMPETITIVE GAMES

The dynamic effects of marketing plans are conveyed through competitive games. The 26 weeks of data not summarized in the HISTORY file are used as the background data. There are three promotional periods of 8 or 9 weeks each. The teams representing each brand submit a promotional plan which specifies the price to the retailer without support and the per-unit incentives for the retailer to support newspaper features, in-store displays and/or store coupons. These plans are offered to each of the three retail

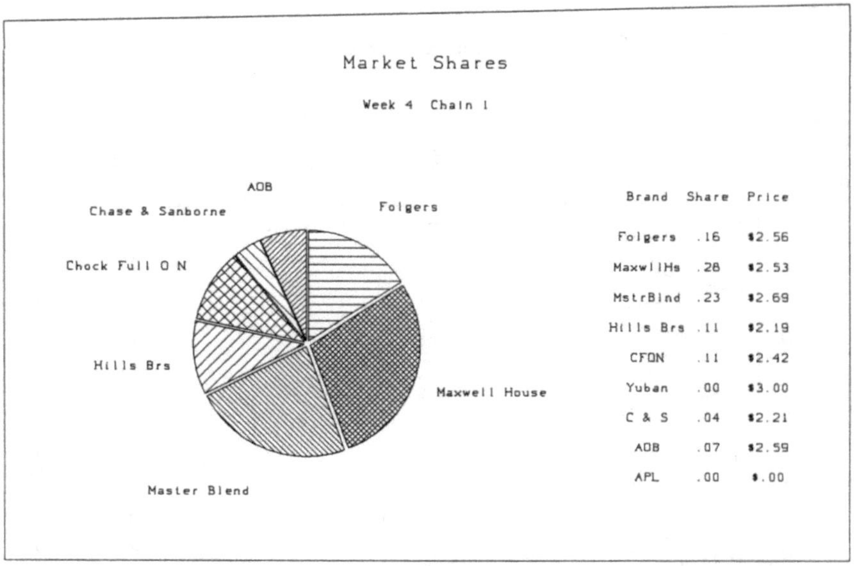

Figure 3

grocery chains in the market and can be acted upon independently by each chain. An important feature of the simulations and games is that costs and profits are broken out for the retailers as well as for the firms. The brand teams are strongly encouraged to support their plans with simulation results which show the benefits to the retailer of the firm's proposals. The game is designed so that the roles of the retailers can be played by the computer (under control of the instructor) or by other teams. In academic settings, a brand-management class could plan the brands' strategies, while a class in channels or retailing could play the roles of the stores.

After each promotional period each brand team receives three spreadsheets summarizing the results. First they see what shares, sales and profits are estimated for the actions of the real brands during this period (under the profit-margin assumptions used). Second, each team sees the results for all brands if this team's plan had competed against the decisions of the real brands in this market. And third, the teams receive the results of their plans competing head-to-head with the other brands in the game. Again, CASPER utilities and FRAMEWORK II capabilities combine to enable a wide variety of analyses of the game results.

3 Management Decision Making

Those of us involved with management research and education face the dual problems of developing relevant management tools and preparing current and future managers to use them. There are obvious tensions involved. If brand managers were captivated by the complexities of choice models or market-share models, they might well have chosen to pursue academic careers. Those of us involved in model development are rarely intrigued by the pragmatics of brand management. So where do we meet?

The design of market information systems may be as close as we can get to a common ground. This is the arena in which management science can help provide a systematic basis for utilizing data and market-response models, while management practice can use these efforts in decision making.

The emphasis on real data and real brands makes CASPER a prototype market information system which is portable to any of the hundreds of categories for which such data are available. While the development effort needed to implement CASPER in another product area is far from minor, the end result has some obvious benefits. First, brand managers spend their time learning about market response in their own product area. Second, they must make explicit the assumptions about the competition which are too often hidden or implicit in forecasts or simulations. Third, they are forced to consider the revenue and cost implications of their plans, for the firm and for the channels of distribution.

The most obvious benefit for the academicians is that their talents at research and model development can be used to advance management theory and practice without being judged for how much they know (or don't know) about selling coffee.

References

Burke R, Rangaswamy A (1987) Knowledge Representation in Marketing Expert Systems. Paper presented at the International Workshop on Data Analysis, Decision Support and Expert Knowledge Representation in Marketing and Related Areas of Research. University of Karlsruhe, West Germany

Carpenter GA, Cooper LG, Hanssens DM, Midgley DF (1987) Asymmetric Market-Share Models. Center for Marketing Studies, Anderson Graduate School of Management, UCLA, Working Paper No. 137

Cooper LG (1987) Competitive Maps: The Structure Underlying Asymmetric Cross Elasticities. Center for Marketing Studies, Anderson Graduate School of Management, UCLA, Working Paper No. 147

Cooper LG, Finkbeiner CT (1984) A Composite MCI Model for Integrating Attribute and Importance Information, in: Kinnear TC (ed.) Advances in Consumer Research, Volume XI. Association for Consumer Research, Provo, UT, pp 109–113

Cooper LG, Nakanishi M (1983a) Standardizing Variables in Multiplicative Choice Models. Journal of Consumer Research 10: 96–108

Cooper LG, Nakanishi M (1983b) Two Logit Models for External Analysis of Preferences. Psychometrika 48, 4: 607–620

Guadagni PM, Little JDC (1983) A Logit Model of Brand Choice Calibrated on Scanner Data . Marketing Science 2, 3: 203–238

A PROLOG-Based PC-Implementation for New Product Introduction*

W. Gaul and A. Schaer
Institute of Decision Theory and Operations Research, Faculty of Economics
University of Karlsruhe (TH), FRG

Summary

Activities which improve knowledge about and/or support decisions concerning NPI (New Product Introduction) are known to belong to an important area within marketing research as well as within applications of marketing research to reality. Additionally, the NPI-area seems to be well-suited for illustrating basic principles of a prototype implementation of a knowledge-based decision support system.

Thus, attempts have been made to design such a prototype to aid NPI-efforts. In this paper, a first version of an NPI-prototype is described; it allows parameter specifications adapted to the different levels of knowledge of possible users, supplies help functions, supports a GO/ON/NO classification with respect to a first attempt of NPI-decision-making, and results in a final GO/NO solution.

The prototype is implemented by means of ARITY-PROLOG on PC under MS-DOS. By a marketing example it will be demonstrated how managers applying the prototype are assisted in finally deciding upon certain NPI-situations.

1 Motivation

Lately, a new generation of information systems, promising new facilities for problem modelling and problem solving in which knowledge handling instead of data handling is a key concept, has been receiving a great deal of attention. So-called "artificial intelligence tools" and "knowledge engineering concepts" are said to be able to simplify the implementation of both more sophisticated and more user-friendly systems—labeled as "DSS (Decision Support Systems)" or "ES (Expert Systems)"—and to help to overcome some of the limitations of software based on conventional procedural programming.

"Knowledge bases", which contain e.g. facts, rules and object descriptions as knowledge elements and relationships between knowledge elements as well as inference rules by which knowledge elements can be combined to establish new knowledge elements, and which are represented by declarative (non-procedural) programming languages, are more suitable than conventional programming tools to handle incomplete, implicit and fuzzy knowledge and to represent the structure and logic of models not exclusively of algorithmic nature.

*Research has been supported by the Deutsche Forschungsgemeinschaft

Most types of knowledge engineering applications to date fall into such categories as "interpretation", "diagnosis", "prediction", "planning" and "design" (see e.g. Hayes-Roth, Waterman and Lenat (1983), Lehmann (1983) and Stefik, Aikins, Balzar, Benoit, Birnbaum, Hayes-Roth, Sacerdoti (1983)). Short definitions of the corresponding systems can be given as follows:

Interpretation systems explain information contained in given data and perform descriptions of situations on the basis of given data (e.g. observations or signals) without changing the information base.

Diagnosis systems give interpretations and indicate malfunctions on the basis of given data. Utilizing knowledge elements and interactions between them, such systems relate shortcomings to possible causes.

Prediction systems infer future consequences from given or planned situations. Here, some kind of dynamic modelling is needed in order to be able to draw conclusions about future situations.

Planning systems incorporate the (goal oriented) search for and the description of a possible action program of (optimal) decisions. Solutions should also be based on a prediction subsystem integrated into the underlying planning system.

Finally, design (construction or configuration are synonyms) systems are rather concerned with the specification of real objects where requirements and constraints have to be taken into consideration.

With respect to a concrete problem solving task different steps of the DSS building process may roughly be characterized by "problem identification", "conceptualization", "formalization", "implementation" and "testing" (see e.g. Buchanan, Barstow, Bechtel, Bennett, Clancey, Kulikowski, Mitchell, Waterman (1983)) where repeated passing of certain (sequences of) steps may be necessary.

In marketing, activities which improve knowledge about and/or support decisions concerning NPI (New Product Introduction) are known to belong to an important area within research as well as within application. Thus, it would be of interest to have knowledge-based decision support systems to aid NPI-efforts (Knowledge engineering aspects for other marketing problems are taken into consideration in e.g. Abraham and Lodish (1987), Böckenholt, Both and Gaul (1987) and Rangaswamy, Burke, Wind and and Eliashberg (1986).). In recent years, quite a number of efforts to design models and methods which allow to decide upon strategies for the market entry of own new products or defensive strategies with respect to the market entry of competing products and which forecast the success of (new) products in (new) markets have been undertaken.

In this paper, no attempt will be made to survey the relevant NPI-literature (see e.g. Böckenholt and Gaul (1987) and the references cited there). Instead, in the next section we will try to relate the just mentioned types of knowledge engineering applications and the different steps within the DSS building process with a possible NPI-situation and describe parts of the implemented NPI-prototype. This first version of the prototype described here already allows parameter specifications adapted to the different levels of knowledge of possible users, supplies help functions, supports a GO/ON/NO classification with respect to a first attempt of NPI-decision-making, and results in a final GO/NO solution. In section 3, a demonstration of a possible NPI-prototype consultation session is outlined. Finally, concluding remarks and some outlooks for further research are given.

2 A PROLOG-Based DSS-Prototype for NPI

In this section, a first version of a NPI-DSS-prototype will be explained.

2.1 General Remarks

During the development of the prototype, the different steps already mentioned within the DSS building process were passed through. Although boundaries between different steps are vague and activities of different steps may overlap, the following can be stated:

A well-defined problem out of the set of possible NPI-problems had to be selected (→ problem identification). In this first version, we confined decision support to the time period within the whole NPI-planning process when the design phase of the product itself as well as of the initial marketing plan has already been finished. This is a starting situation also used in some other NPI-approaches the findings of which were intended to be considered for comparison purposes.

Next, a characterization of important aspects of the chosen problem was needed. Besides the knowledge of the participants in the DSS building process, available resources, relevant data and variables to be used, important subproblems which could be separated, goals and the types of solutions the first prototype would be able to determine, had to be taken into consideration (→ conceptualization). From the hardware perspective, we had to get along with a PC while from the software perspective we chose ARITY-PROLOG. As one of the main tasks, the prototype should end up with an assessment of whether to launch the product under consideration and an evaluation on how to modify (parts of) the initial marketing plan.

In the following step, the problem how key concepts and different subproblems—e.g. the handling of algorithms to be incorporated and/or of non-numerical parts of knowledge processing—could be transformed to more formal representations within the knowledge engineering environment, had to be tackled (→ formalization). Here the problem of coupling symbolic and numerical knowledge elements had to be considered. Additionally, characteristics concerning data and variables, e.g. contents of data structures, inference rules, control strategies, etc., the models to be used and the set of hypotheses to be checked had to be fixed.

A mapping of the formalized concepts of the underlying problem by means of the chosen language or ES-shell into corresponding software has to follow (→ implementation). Parts of these efforts are presented in the section which describes a demonstration of a prototype consultation session.

Finally, in an iterative process of revising, a detection of parts of the current prototype which have to be altered or which can be improved (weaknesses of the knowledge base, refinements of the implementation, redesigns within formalization aspects, reformulations of concepts, etc.) is necessary (→ testing). This phase is still being performed.

In doing so, characteristics of the above mentioned types of knowledge engineering applications are met again in the concrete realization of the prototype.

First, the NPI-recommendations of the prototype depend on predicted developments of key characteristics and goal criteria (→ prediction).

Secondly, explanations of given and predicted time pattern of some of the mentioned key characteristics and goal criteria are provided (→ interpretation).

Thirdly, in order to support the managers, different input-output combinations are assessed and a description of the optimal action program, i.e. the final marketing plan (among those checked) is given (→ planning).

The incorporation of facilities, which enable to detect differences between predicted and real data and to determine possible shortcomings, becomes more important for later phases of the NPI-process when those real data are available (→ diagnosis). This part of NPI-decision support will not be emphasized in the following description of the prototype.

As has been mentioned before, the design phase of the product (→ design) has already been finished when the prototype comes into action. Thus, this type of the mentioned knowledge engineering applications is not considered within the underlying NPI-prototype.

2.2 Special Features of the Prototype

A knowledge-based DSS-prototype should be able to process concrete data and subjective judgements, to reason symbolically and to compute numerically. "Intelligent interfaces" which support possibilities of incorporation of nondeterministic solution strategies and capabilities for knowledge representation, explanation and processing would enhance the significance of numerical programming approaches, while—on the other hand—symbolic computing approaches would be improved by the acquisition of procedural knowledge in form of numerical algorithms.

Unfortunately, the development and implementation of such coupled (or hybrid) systems is still hindered by actually available knowledge engineering tools.

The first version of the NPI-DSS-prototype described here already tries to combine numerical and symbolic knowledge processing. The flow diagram of Figure 1 gives a rough first impression about how the prototype works on a given problem.

Different parts can be distinguished.

Input has to be provided in a part in which parameters and initial state specifications are needed to fix—for the first time—the model, the goal criteria and the (initial) marketing plan. Here, the user is e.g. asked to specify the product category, the company's objectives and further parts of the problem situation including reasonable combinations of different marketing activities where some pieces of information have to be provided in form of time series pattern.

Prototype evaluations follow in a next part. Here, some kind of internal sensitivity analysis may be performed to be able to come up with suggestions how feasible marketing plans would have to look like. Repeated analyses on the basis of user modifications of (parts of) the underlying marketing plans are possible which—within a GO/ON/NO-classification of possible plan success—will, finally, end up with either a satisfactory GO-solution or the answer that within the set of checked alternatives NO solution which meets the desired objectives and restrictions could be found.

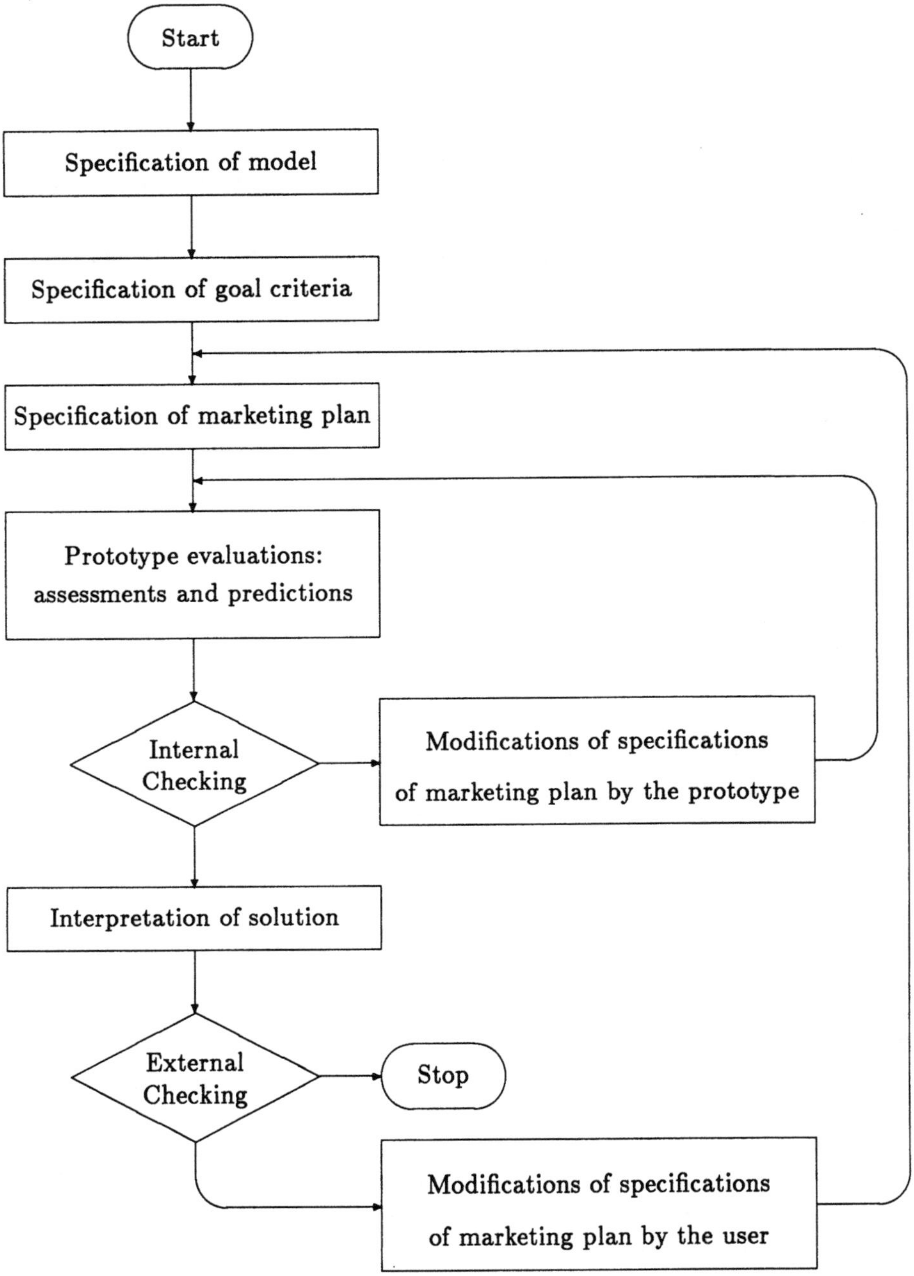

Figure 1: Flow diagram of prototype

While part of such a prototype consultation will be illustrated in the next section, here, a short description of the essentials of the numerical programming part will follow. Of course, some kind of prediction approach will be needed which transforms input data to

NPI-success characteristics. Modelling was done at an aggregate level with deterministic state changes. The principal decision variables comprise period by period advertising expenditures, prices charged and a distribution characteristic concerning availability of the product. A (low-involvement) prediction approach in which e.g. awareness, trial and (repeat) purchase stages are modeled, and in which the German NPI-situation is considered, establishes the main component. Table 1 shows how the awareness submodel of the prediction approach of the prototype fits reference data which were used in the well-known comparison of awareness forecasting models by Mahajan, Muller and Sharma (1984). On the basis of cumulative GRP (Gross Rating Points) and an initial awareness parameter A_0 awareness predictions of different models (see e.g. Blackburn and Clancy (1982), Blattberg and Golanty (1978), Dodson and Muller (1978) and Pringle, Wilson and Brody (1982)) were compared with actually observed awareness.

Cumulative GRP	Actual Awareness %	Tracker		News		Litmus		Dodson/ Muller		Prototype	
		$A_0=0$	$A_0=48$	$A_0=0$	$A_0=45$	$A_0=0$	$A_0=49$	$A_0=0$	$A_0=45$	$A_0=0$	$A_0=45$
968	54	24	54	28	53	20	54	28	53	30	54
2154	59	43	59	50	60	39	60	49	60	51	62
2879	61	57	64	56	62	47	63	55	61	58	63
3329	67	67	68	57	63	52	64	56	60	59	62
5152	72	75	72	71	70	66	70	71	69	73	71
Fit Statistics: MAE (mean absolute error)		.103	.008	.103	.019	.177	.014	.107	.026	.088	.022
TIC (Theil's inequality coefficient)		.413	.029	.355	.044	.534	.039	.363	.072	.313	.057

Table 1: Comparison of fits of awareness data from an example by Mahajan, Muller and Sharma (1984).

Using MAE (mean absolute error) and TIC (Theil's inequality coefficient) as fit measures, it can be argued that the NPI-DSS-prototype described here is able to achieve a goodness-of-fit comparable to the other approaches listed.

3 Demonstration of Prototype Consultation Session

Just at the beginning, it has to be mentioned (and will be recognized from the following figures and tables) that the user interface of this version of the prototype is in German. We assume, however, that the following description is detailed enough to avoid misunderstandings.

As underlying example, a modification of an example from Pringle, Wilson and Brody (1982) will be used for parts of the demonstration of the prototype consultation session.

When starting the session, the input part of the system collects information about the company, the product, the market and the planned NPI-strategy for first adjustments of the prototype. As an example, if a product category known to the prototype is chosen, some parameter specifications can automatically be provided, otherwise—within the limits of the methodology to be applied—questions the answers of which allow such parameter specifications have to be answered (At the moment, e.g. the examples from Pringle, Wilson and Brody (1982) and Blackburn and Clancy (1982) and own data on alcoholic beverages—more specially on the product categories "brandy" and "rye whisky"—are known to the prototype and can be used for demonstration purposes.). This proceeding of automatically specifying parameters, needed for a description of the underlying NPI-situation, is due to the (non undisputed) idea that learning from prior NPI-efforts is restricted to known product categories. Additionally, the prototype asks whether a pre- or an early-case modelling of the NPI-situation is wanted. The early-case can be applied when test-market data are available while the pre-case is designed to support the assessment of marketing plans in the pre-test-market situation.

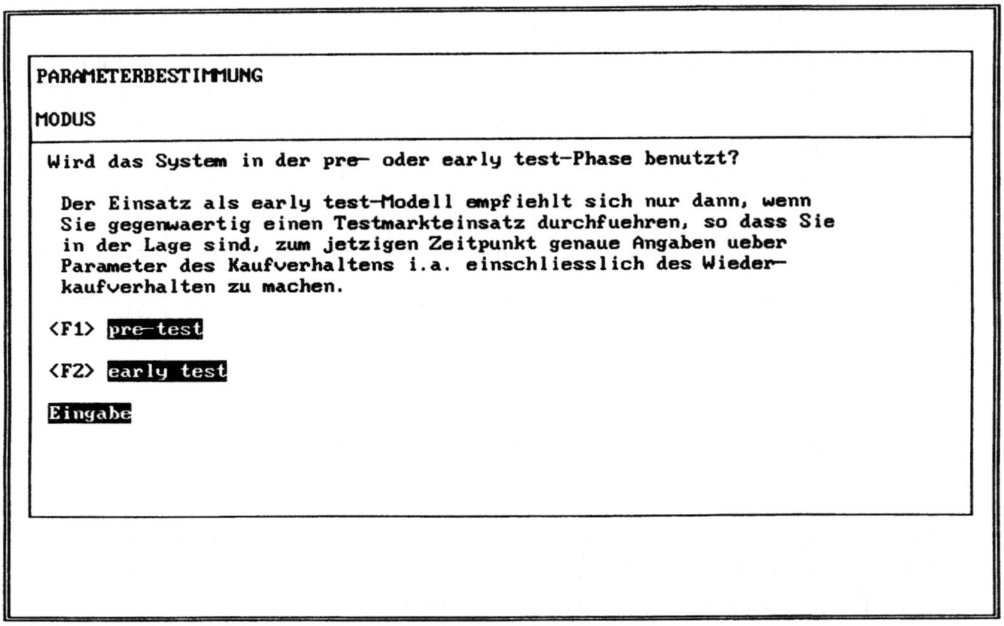

Figure 2: Example screen for pre- or early-case decision within the parameter specification part

Figure 2 shows the corresponding screen when the decision has to be made whether a pre-case or an early-case modelling should be performed. Based on this decision, different sequences of questions for further input will be asked.

Of course, within the whole input part, explanations of (technical) terms are given on request.

Table 2 shows the modified input based on the Pringle, Wilson and Brody (1982) example which will be used in the beginning of the prototype demonstration session.

Pre-case situation	
planning span of time:	48 weeks.
advertising (1000 GRP/period):	1.25 in period 1 and 2, 1.0 in period 3 (A period is assumed to contain 16 weeks.).
price:	6.5 (average price in the underlying market).
distribution:	Linear increase from 48.5% to 89% within 48 weeks.
initial awareness:	8%.
average usage volume in market:	1.6.
usage volume:	1.7.
value of target market share (at the end of planning span of time):	7.5% volume market share.

Table 2: Part of prototype input

As can be seen from Table 2, one wants to examine a pre-case situation. The planning span of time comprises 48 weeks and is divided into three periods of 16 weeks each. The GRP of 1.25, 1.25, 1.0 for the different periods of the media plan are lower than those in the Pringle, Wilson and Brody (1982) example. To exclude effects from price differences, the price is set equal to the average market price of 6.5 during the whole planning span of time while distribution rate is assumed to increase linearly within the planning span of time from 48.5% to 89%. Furthermore, an initial awareness rate of 8%, an expected usage volume of 1.7 for the new product in contrast to a slightly lower average usage volume of 1.6 within the market under study and a target volume market share of 7.5% at the end of the planning span of time are prompted to the system.

After the input part has been completed, output as shown in Figure 3 and Figure 4 is immediately available.

Figure 3 shows a first output screen containing results like awareness rate (Produktkenntnis), cumulative trial rate (Penetration Erstkaeufer), repeat purchase rate (Wiederkaeufer) and volume (Marktanteil, Menge) as well as revenue (Marktanteil, Wert) market shares which—because of the chosen price strategy (see Table 2)—are equal for the underlying situation. Additionally, a —in case of an ON-recommendation preliminary—GO/ON/NO classification with respect to the suggested NPI-strategy is given.

Such a classification is based on the comparison of target and predicted market shares and on a "checking" whether in the so-called "neighbourhood" of the current marketing plan better marketing plans would be available.

A GO-decision means that the prototype recommends the introduction of the product on the basis of the specified current marketing plan.

An ON-recommendation is always preliminary, it indicates that on the basis of the current marketing plan it is not possible to meet the target specifications, but that deviations are not too serious not to encourage the user to try to find a better marketing plan. The prototype will always proceed with a succeeding sensitivity analysis and, finally, will end up with either a GO- or a NO-decision.

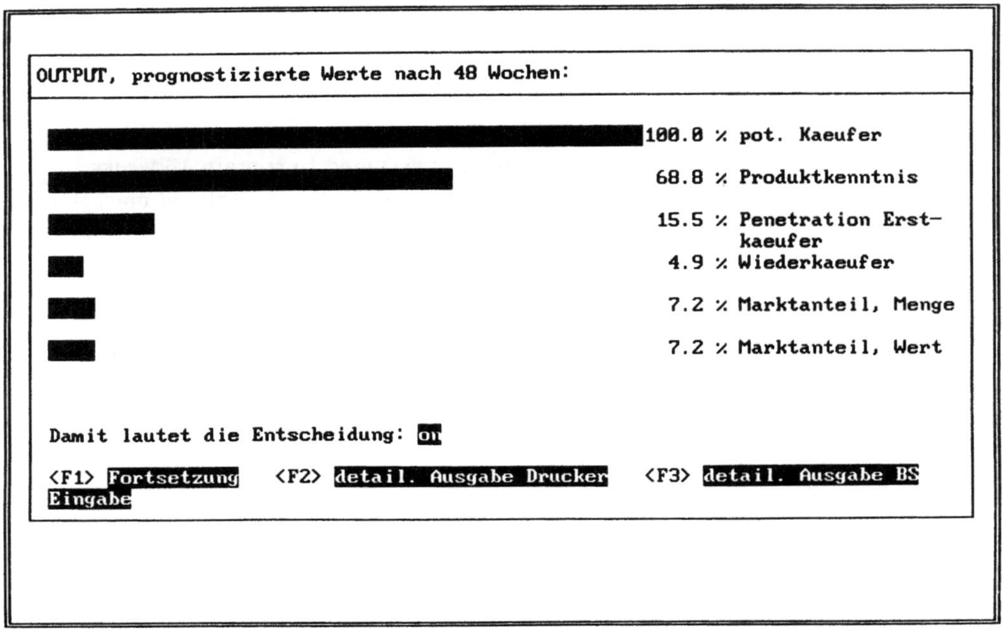

Figure 3: Example screen of prototype output

A NO-decision indicates that the target specifications cannot be reached on the basis of all checked marketing plans.

In Figure 3 it is indicated that pressing F3 (or F2 if a printed output is needed) will result in a more detailed output of the underlying NPI-situation. Figure 4 is an example of such a more detailed output.

To sum up the contents of Figure 3 and Figure 4 one recognizes that—besides the fact that Figure 4 provides additional information concerning part of the input data and period by period developments of some interesting characteristics—at the end of the planning span of time the following situation is predicted:

The product will achieve 68.8% awareness, 15.5% will have tried the product while 4.9% will have repurchased it. This will result in a market share of 7.2% (both revenue and volume because of the chosen price strategy) . As a target market share of 7.5% (see Table 2) was wanted, an ON-classification is the consequence.

In such a situation, a sensitivity analysis is started in the next step. The sensitivity analysis is intended to demonstrate the significance of changes within the current marketing plan. It takes into consideration the conclusions drawn so far (which influences selection and direction of changes proposed), and tries to reduce new input demand to the very necessary (which means that alterations are restricted to a selected part (e.g. to advertising or to distribution or to price, etc.) of the current marketing plan while others are kept fixed).

Assume, that in the underlying example the prototype suggests to examine the effects of increased advertising, first. Assume further, that the user accepts and, now,

O U T P U T

===============

Prognosezeitraum: 48 Wochen
Periodenlaenge: 16 Wochen

Werbung: wechselnder Werbedruck
Bruttoreichweiten je Periode:
1.25 1.25 1.0

Preisstrategie: konstant
Preis: 6.5
Marktpreis: 6.5

Distribution:
anfaenglich: 48.5 %
endgueltig: 89.0 %
Uebergangszeit: 48 Wochen

Prognosewerte [%]				
gewonnene P.-Kenntnis		45.6	20.7	10.0
erneuerte P.-Kenntnis:		5.1	33.6	37.5
bewahrte P.-Kenntnis:		2.0	13.1	20.5
gesamte P.-Kenntnis:	0.0	52.7	67.5	68.0
neue Erstkaeufer:		6.3	6.0	3.2
kum. Erstkaeufer:		6.3	12.3	15.5
neue Wiederkaeufer:			2.5	3.0
gesamte Wiederkaeufer:			2.5	4.9
saemtliche Kaeufer:		6.3	8.5	8.1
Mengen-Marktanteil:		3.9	6.4	7.2
Wert_Marktanteil:		3.9	6.4	7.2

Figure 4: Example screen of more detailed prototype output

prompts GRP of 2.138, 1.358, 1.25 for the different periods of the planning span of time (which are the GRP of the Pringle, Wilson and Brody (1982) example). Then, an output screen as shown in Figure 5 will be provided by the prototype.

Figure 5 indicates that the alteration of the advertising situation within the underlying marketing plan results in a GO-decison (Alternatively, an alteration of the distribution situation (e.g. a distribution which—starting from 48.5%—reaches its maximum of 89% already within 10 months) or an alteration of the price situation (e.g. a price decrease to a fixed price of 5.95) would also have resulted in a GO-decision.).

If single selected alterations are not successful in finding a GO-solution, a heuristic

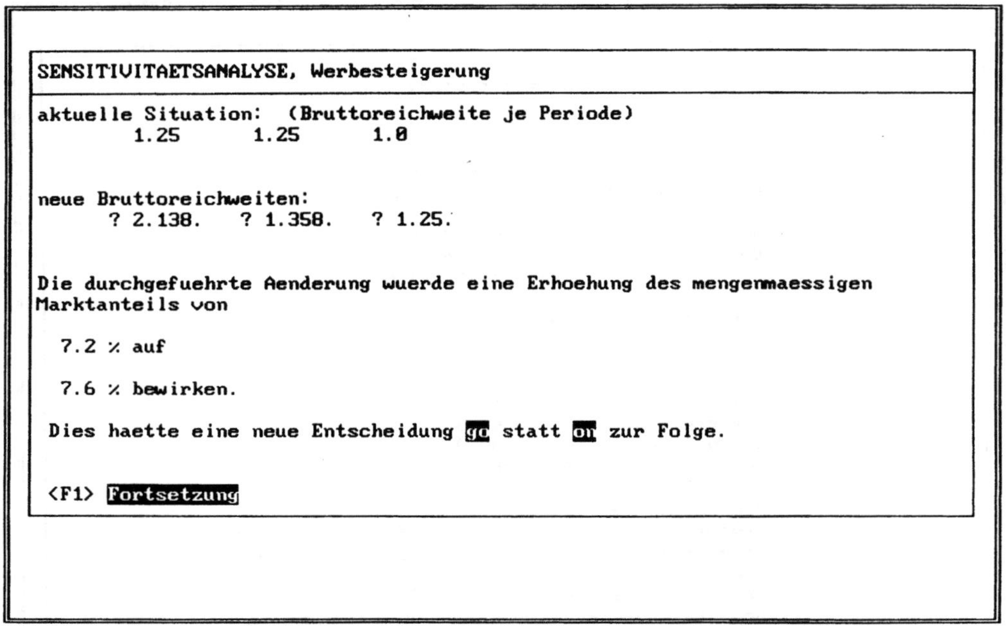

Figure 5: Example screen within the sensitivity analysis part

is automatically applied which checks the effect of the whole combination of alterations.

Again, more detailed outputs can be given on request.

Additionally, the prototype is able to answer some free format questions concerning the underlying model and the meaning (and the consequences of alterations) of certain input data (e.g.: How is a certain part of the NPI-process predicted? How far are certain input data effecting the (prediction of) results?). Further information about the NPI-process can be yielded by analyzing the predicted pattern of some interesting characteristics but will not be explained in detail.

After the actual prototype run has been finished, a restart for testing alternative scenarios can follow immediately, although—at the moment—the inability of the used PROLOG version to perform a perfect garbage collection restricts the number of restarts.

4 Conclusions

The current version of a NPI-DSS-prototype has been presented. It allows a forward chained assessment of marketing plans due to input data alterations and a goal oriented improvement of an underlying marketing plan to accomplish specified objectives.

More concretely, by coupling symbolic and numerical knowledge processing the prototype is able—besides prediction—to support parameter and (initial) state specifications of the methodology used in a way which is adapted to the different levels of knowledge of possible users, to supply help functions to explain e.g. technical terms, relations within the underlying model and decisions made, and to support a GO/ON/NO-classification with respect to the marketing plan at hand where an ON-recommendation automatically leads to further DSS-activities of the prototype, e.g. to the performance of some kind of sensitivity analysis to come up with a final GO- or NO-decision.

It should, however, be mentioned that one weakness of the prototype presented lies in the still limited knowledge base. Much more rules will have to be integrated to better support the user than it is possible at the moment.

Further developments—besides a permanent general improvement—may be devoted to an automatic generation of initial state specifications and a more stringent validation of such (initial) state specifications for completeness, consistency, conformity and plausibility.

References

Abraham MM, Lodish LM (1987) PROMOTER: An Automated Promotion Evaluation System. The Wharton School of the University of Pennsylvania, Working Paper No. 86–033 R, Draft 4

Blackburn JD, Clancy KJ (1982) LITMUS: A New Product Planning Model, in: Zoltners AA (ed.) Marketing Planning Models. North Holland, Amsterdam, New York, Oxford, pp 43–61

Blattberg R, Golanty J (1978) TRACKER: An Early Test Market Forecasting and Diagnostic Model for New Product Planning. Journal of Marketing Research 15: 192–202

Böckenholt I, Both M, Gaul W (1987) PROLOG-Based Decision Support for Data Analysis in Marketing, this volume.

Böckenholt I, Gaul W (1987) New Product Introduction Based on Pre-Test Market Data, in: Proceedings of EMAC/ESOMAR Symposium on Micro and Macro Modelling: Research on Prices, Consumer Behaviour and Forecasting, pp 77–96

Buchanan BG, Barstow D, Bechtel R, Bennett J, Clancey W, Kulikowski C, Mitchell T, Waterman DA (1983) Constructing an Expert System, in Hayes-Roth F, Waterman DA, Lenat DB (eds.) Building Expert Systems. Addison-Wesley, Reading, MA, pp 127–167

Dodson JA, Muller E (1978) Models of New Product Diffusion through Advertising and Word-of-Mouth. Management Science 24: 1568–1578

Hayes-Roth F, Waterman DA, Lenat DB (1983): An Overview of Expert Systems, in: op. cit. sub Buchanan et al. (1983), pp 3–29

Lehmann E (1984): Expertensysteme, Überblick über den aktuellen Wissensstand (1983) Siemens AG, München

Mahajan V, Muller E, Sharma S (1984) An Emprical Comparison of Awareness Forecasting Models of New Product Introduction. Marketing Science 3: 179–197

Pringle LG, Wilson RD, Brody EI (1982) NEWS: A Decision-Oriented Model for New Product Analysis and Forecasting. Marketing Science 1: 1–29

Rangaswamy A, Burke R, Wind J, Eliashberg J (1986) Expert Systems for Marketing. The Wharton School of the University of Pennsylvania, Working Paper No. 86–036

Stefik M, Aikins J, Balzar R, Benoit J, Birnbaum L, Hayes-Roth F, Sacerdoti E (1983) Basic Concepts for Building Expert Systems, in: op. cit. sub Buchanan et al. (1983), pp 59–86

Exploring the Possibilities of an Improvement of Stochastic Market Models by Rule-Based Systems

A. Geyer-Schulz [+], A. Taudes [+] and U. Wagner [++]
[+] Institut für Informationsverarbeitung und Informationswirtschaft
[++] Institut für Unternehmensführung, Quantitative Betriebswirtschaftslehre und Operations Research
Wirtschaftsuniversität Wien

Summary

In this paper we develop a method to improve the performance of stochastic models of consumer behavior and adress two problems encountered in practical market research: a way to deal with low data-quality and small sample-sizes and a way to improve strategic marketing decision making. The approach allows the integration of verbally formulated market knowledge and stochastic models of consumer behavior. Formally we construct a random level set using the estimated parameters of the market model and combine it with the Fuzzy Set derived from the experts' knowledge using the Theory of Natural Language Computations. An entropy-based measure of the difference between sources of information is given. Besides presenting the method we also discuss two empirical examples concerning buying behavior in the Austrian coffee market.

1 Introduction

Stochastic models of consumer behavior have been designed to serve as a tool for the brand manager to analyze the present market situation. Thus they support the formulation of a marketing policy in a first step and provide a benchmark for the effectiveness of marketing activities in the long run. Based on a consumer panel or scanner data they aim at providing insights into the structure of brand choice and purchase timing behavior and its determinants.

The strength of this approach, its algorithmic, empirically validatable nature, is also one of its potential weaknesses: by the very nature of construction stochastic models fail in cases where no data, only very few observations, rather vague information or incomplete data is available. According to the authors' experience such situations are encountered in empirical market research. To deal with these problems we develop a method to integrate the knowledge of marketing managers and stochastic market models in order to improve their performance in the presence of non-perfect data and extend their applicability to strategic market decision making.

In the next section we discuss the limitations mentioned in greater detail, describing an example using empirical market data. Then we give an introduction to the Theory of Fuzzy Sets and Natural Language Computations and describe a method to combine verbally formulated market knowledge and sample information. In the fourth part we present empirical applications of this approach for the Austrian coffee market.

2 Stochastic Market Models—Achievements and Limitations

The idea underlying stochastic models of consumer behavior is to regard the "purchase history", the time-ordered sequence of the consumer's buying decisions as the trajectory of a stochastic process. In the beginning of the development these approaches were limited both in scope and descriptive power, but recently they are quite general in the sense that all available statistical information is used in a unified framework: they permit the inclusion of the influence of marketing mix variables and other exogeneous factors and behavioral differences among individuals (for a survey of stochastic models of consumer behavior see Wagner and Taudes (1987)). With regard to the appropriate type of random process, a number of empirical studies concerning the buying pattern for relatively inexpensive, frequently bought consumer goods indicate (see e.g. Ehrenberg (1972)), that a proper basic model for individual purchasing is the Poisson Process. Additionally one has to account for heterogeneity, i.e, for buying habits varying over consumers, and, if the market is observed for a longer period of time, also for nonstationarity, i.e., for purchase frequencies and preferences changing due to variations in exogeneous variables like marketing mix, seasonality, etc. A purchase incidence model with substantial empirical support (Ehrenberg (1972)) is the Negative Binomial Model, which assumes that the number of purchases of a household in a number of equally long, consecutive time intervals is stationary, independent and Poisson distributed with mean purchase rate μ_k

$$P(\tilde{n}_k) = \mu_k^{n_k}.e^{-\mu_k}/n_k! \quad \forall k \tag{1}$$

with:

n_k - number of purchases of household k,

μ_k - mean purchase rate of household k,

where μ_k is Gamma distributed over the population

$$P(\tilde{\mu}) = \alpha^\beta.\mu^{\beta-1}.e^{-\alpha\mu}/\Gamma(\beta) \tag{2}$$

with:

$\alpha > 0$ - scale parameter,

$\beta > 0$ - shape parameter.

One applies the theorem of total probability and compounds (1) with (2)

$$\begin{aligned} P(\tilde{n}) = & \int_0^\infty [\mu^n.e^{-\mu}/n!].[\alpha^\beta.\mu^{\beta-1}.e^{-\alpha\mu}/\Gamma(\beta)]d\mu \\ = & \binom{n+\beta-1}{n} \cdot \left(\tfrac{\alpha}{\alpha+1}\right)^\beta \cdot \left(\tfrac{1}{\alpha+1}\right)^n . \end{aligned} \tag{3}$$

(3) represents the probability of the Negative Binomial Distribution.

We apply this model in a study of consumer behavior concerning the Austrian coffee market. A particular result for one brand, labelled A in the sequel, is depicted in

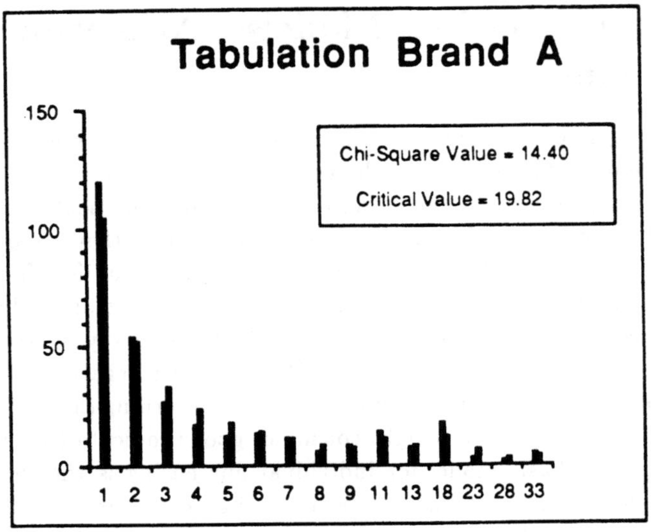

Figure 1: Tabulation Brand A

Figure 1: the model describes observed consumer behavior quite well, with the Chi-Square Statistics well below its critical value—a result in accordance with the literature. However, when confronting the managers with the findings it turns out, that the sales predicted by the model are consistently lower than those predicted by store audits. The reason for this discrepancy is found in the data-collecting procedure: A is preferred by foreign workers, who are not included in the sampling process. Thus when evaluating the forecasts of stochastic market models, one has to keep in mind the impact of imperfect sampling procedures: Using different panel data pretending to describe the same market (for example consumer panel, store audit, scanner data ...) may result in different descriptions of the market, i.e., market data does not necessarily represent market reality exactly (for a similar conclusion for econometric models in marketing see Nenning, Topritzhofer and Wagner (1981)).

The situation outlined above is described in Figure 2. The problem in such a case is that one does neither have perfect data nor the chance to clarify the issue by performing additional experiments due to the non-experimental nature of the observations. Therefore it is the task of the brand manager to subjectively balance the results provided by different sources of data against verbal informations.

For strategic marketing decision making verbal propositions about consumer behavior are even more important. Stochastic models of consumer behavior are based on the assumption of a stable, stationary market environment during the period under consideration: the number of brands stays constant and product attributes like shape, packaging, ...remain unchanged. Strategic issues, however, usually aim at changing this very attributes. (Consider e.g. launch/relaunch decisions.)

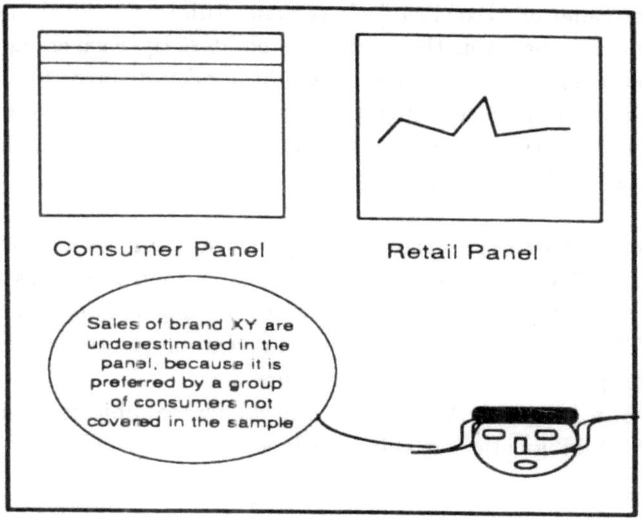

Figure 2: The Decision-Maker's Dilemma

3 Fuzzy Sets and Natural Language Computations

Fuzzy Set Theory is a generalization of traditional Set Theory in the sense that the domain of the characteristic function is extended from the discrete set $\{0,1\}$ to the closed real interval [0, 1]. More precisely, let E be a set, countable or not, and x be an element of E. A fuzzy sub-set A of E, the base-set, is a set of ordered pairs (see for example Kandel (1986)):

$$(x, m_A(x)) \forall x \in E \tag{4}$$

with $m_A(x)$ representing the degree of membership of x to A. $m_A(x)$ is restricted to the closed real interval [0,1] (Zadeh (1965)).

Generalizing the basic set operation, negation is defined as (see Zadeh (1965)):

$$m_{\bar{A}}(x) = 1 - m_A(x) \tag{5}$$

$m_{\bar{A}}$ meaning "not A".

Union and intersection of two fuzzy subsets A and B are defined as (Zadeh (1965)):

$$m_{A \cup B}(x) = MAX(m_A(x), m_B(x)) \tag{6}$$

and

$$m_{A \cap B}(x) = MIN(m_A(x), m_B(x)). \tag{7}$$

For the purpose of building models of human decision making these operations are not sufficient. (Bellmann and Giertz (see Werners (1984)) have developed a set of necessary conditions for the justification of these connectives.)

Consider the example of teaching: a student has solved an exercise using two different methods, one solution correct, the other one false. How would you grade the student?

"Fail" (Minimum Rule) or "Excellent" (Maximum Rule)? Obviously human decision-rules lie somewhere in between these extreme points. By weakening the Bellmann-Giertz conditions several classes of connectives have been defined (for an overview see Geyer-Schulz (1986)). In empirical investigations it turned out that besides generalized *and/or* connectives additional constructs to model notions like "on the average" are necessary. Thus a number of compensatory operators for aggregating sub-models has been proposed.

Mappings from verbal expressions to fuzzy sets are the subject of the Theory of Approximate Reasoning. It describes, how verbal propositions consisting of nouns, adjectives, adverbs, called "modifiers" in the sequel, and connectives, are translated into fuzzy sets. The theory consists of the concept of a Linguistic Variable, rules for the composition of propositions and rules of inference.

The concept of a Linguistic Variable describes how real objects, variables and their values are linked. A Linguistic Variable is defined as a quintupel (Kickert (1978)):

$$\{A, T(A), U, G, M\}. \tag{8}$$

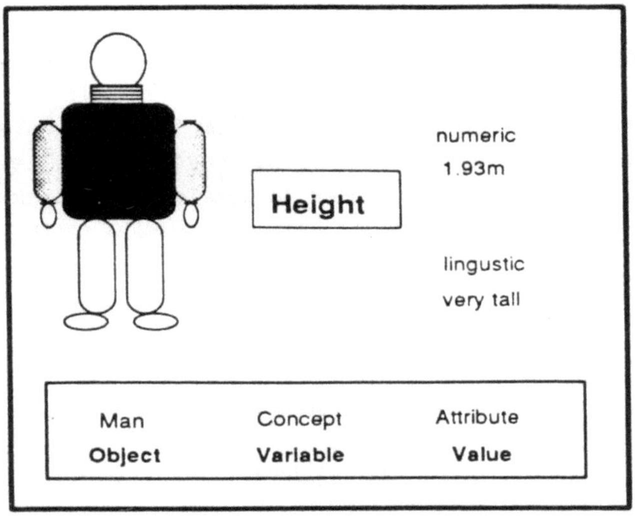

Figure 3: Linguistic Variable

A is the name of the Linguistic Variable, like "height" in Figure 3, and $T(A)$ is the domain of verbal values of A. $\{tall, medium, small, \ldots\}$ is an example for the definition of the domain of a linguistic variable by enumeration. Every single value of A, named X, represents a fuzzy set over the base-set. "tall" in Figure 3 is therefore internally represented as a fuzzy set. G is the definition of the grammar that produces the names of the values of A. U is a semantic rule, that maps every verbal value of A to a meaning $M(X)$, i.e., to a fuzzy subset of the base set. Composite expressions are defined by the grammar G. Connectives, a syntactic category of this grammar, are modelled by the set operations on fuzzy sets introduced above. Modifiers like "several, most, very, ...", another syntactic category are transformed by using the standard image-processing operations dilation, concentration and intensification (see Schmucker (1984)). Compositions of propositions are implemented by fuzzy-set operators introduced above.

Inference rules are employed to extract hypotheses about the behavior of a model. The general structure of fuzzy inference rules has the following pattern:

$$B'' = A'' \circ R : generalizedmodusponens. \tag{9}$$

$$A'' = R \circ B'' : generalizedmodustollens. \tag{10}$$

R is a fuzzy relation that represents the *IF-THEN* clause of the figure. In some applications R corresponds to the implication rule of the underlying multivalued logic. "$\circ$" is the composition rule for two relations.

An example for generalized modus ponens is:

(R) If the apple is red, the apple is ripe

(A'') The apple is very red

(B'') The apple is very ripe

An example for generalized modus tollens is:

(R) If the apple is red, the apple is ripe

(A'') The apple is very ripe

(B'') The apple is very red

For a sample of definitions for the composition rule $\circ$ and the fuzzy relation R see Geyer-Schulz (1986). We now turn to the task of mapping fuzzy sets back into verbal expressions.

The techniques proposed for this mapping are Best Fit, Successive Approximation, and Piecewise Decomposition (see Schmucker (1984)). The Best Fit Method uses a distance measure to determine the least deviation between the given fuzzy set and the fuzzy sets representing the quasi-natural language expressions in the dictionary. The dictionary contains the most useful phrases, which can be formed from $T(A)$, whereby all entries should form an equispaced grid in the scale/fuzziness plane. The Method of Successive Approximation brackets the given fuzzy set by the two closest primary terms. Modifiers are then applied to these bracket endpoints. If the resulting expression is closer to the given fuzzy sets, the bracket is replaced by the modified expressions and the range phrase constructed from them. The quasi-natural language expression corresponding to the closest fuzzy set is then chosen. The method of Piecewise Decomposition divides the base-set into intervals in such a way, that the fuzzy subsets corresponding to each partition are described by one of the verbal expressions in the dictionary. Then the resulting language expressions are combined with one of the standard connectives "and" or "or". The result is simplified to yield the most simplified linguistic term. The approach taken here is in essence a combination of the Best Fit and the Piecewise Decomposition method (see Wenstop (1980)).

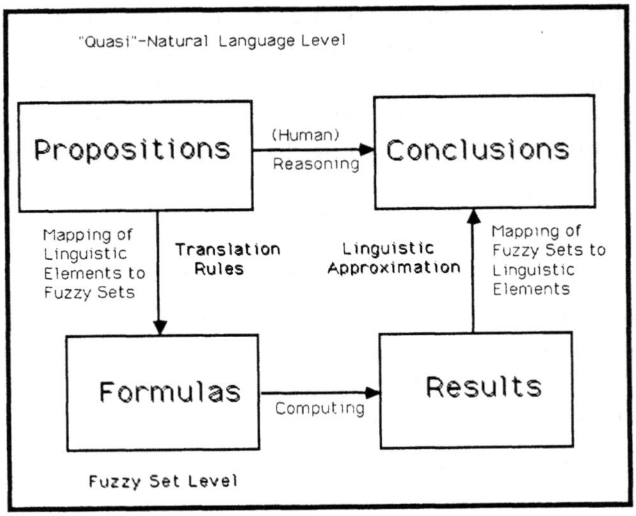

Figure 4: Natural Language Computations

Having gathered all parts necessary to transform verbal expressions into fuzzy sets and back again we are ready to summarize the method of Natural Language Computations (see Figure 4). The Theory of Approximate Reasoning and Linguistic Approximation connects the Theory of Fuzzy Sets with quasi-natural language propositions. It asserts, that conclusions are drawn in the following way: propositions are mapped into formulas on the fuzzy set level. Informally stated the mapping of linguistic elements to fuzzy sets defines the semantics of propositions, i.e., the semantic of verbal expressions is represented by fuzzy sets. This mapping is often called the "Approximate Reasoning Part" of the theory. By evaluating these formulas according to the rules of Fuzzy Set Theory a result is computed. Schmucker (1984) labelled this as "Natural Language Computations". To finally obtain a verbal conclusion, the result is mapped back to the "natural" language level of the theory. This is the "Linguistic Approximation Part" of the theory. Obviously, Natural Language Computations can be seen as a tool to model human reasoning if and only if a structural isomorphism between the model and reality holds. Furthermore there must be a "similarity" between the calculations and the conclusions drawn by humans. This notion of "similarity" is an expression of our inability to exactly formalize the meaning of natural-language expressions.

4 Integrating Different Sources of Knowledge

Having shown how to 'compute' with verbal statements, we turn to the aspect of integrating statistical and verbal information. In order to combine the parameter estimates of the stochastic model with verbal estimates a mapping from the distribution of these statistics to the fuzzy set which represents the verbal estimate is required. As Goodman (1981) has shown, such a basic canonical mapping exists: Suppose X is an arbitrary fixed space, F the collection of all fuzzy subsets A of X, each A with its membership function $m_A(x) : X \rightarrow [0,1]$ and R is the collection of all random subsets S of X. For any subset A of X, define the multi-valued mapping:

$$f_A : [0,1] \rightarrow P(X) \tag{11}$$

$$f_A(y) \stackrel{\text{def}}{=} m_A^{-1}([y,1]), \forall y \in [0,1] \tag{12}$$

If U is a random variable uniformly distributed over the interval $[0,1]$ then define the mapping:

$$S_U : F \rightarrow R \tag{13}$$

$$S_U(A) \stackrel{\text{def}}{=} f_A(U) = m_A^{-1}([U,1]), \forall A \in F, \tag{14}$$

where m_A^{-1} denotes the ordinary functional inverse of m_A. $m_A^{-1}([U,1])$ may be considered as a uniformly randomized level set of m_A. For our application we define U as level of the parameter's confidence interval. Since the number of observations in a consumer panel is usually very large, one can use a standard normal distribution in order to calculate the confidence levels associated with U instead of the computationally more elaborate t-distribution. The fuzzy set which results from this procedure is thus interpreted as a family of confidence intervals.

After representing all types of information as fuzzy sets, we combine these informations by applying one of the fuzzy set operators introduced in section 1. This is a subjective task and is directly comparable to selecting a decision-rule.

To determine the precision of the different sources of information and the combined result, we use an entropy-based measure of the index of fuzziness of a fuzzy subset (see Kaufmann (1975)):

$$H(m_A(x_1), m_A(x_2), \ldots, m_A(x_n)) = -\frac{1}{lnN} \sum_{i=1} N m_A(x_i).ln m_A(x_i) \tag{15}$$

As can be seen from (15), all ordinary subsets having a single nonzero element have entropy 0. A point-estimate thus has entropy 0, whereas blurred, fuzzy propostions have high entropy. A fuzzy subset with entropy 1 contains no information at all: all outcomes are equally possible.

Finally we summarize the method as depicted in Figure 5. The left half of Figure 5 describes the stochastic part of the method: at first the parameters are estimated, subsequently they are transformed into random level sets, which are combined with qualitiative evidence; finally a stochastic market model for each support point of the possibility distribution of models is calculated. The qualitative part of the method consists of: gathering verbal expert estimates of the parameters of the structural model, deriving the verbal model parameter estimates using the rule-base, combining of evidence, and if desired, using the model's possibility distribution in a rule-based system. Then the decision maker can use a decision-rule in order to reach a conclusion. This set of possible scenarios is immediately generated and gives hints on unintended, but highly possibly outcomes of a decision.

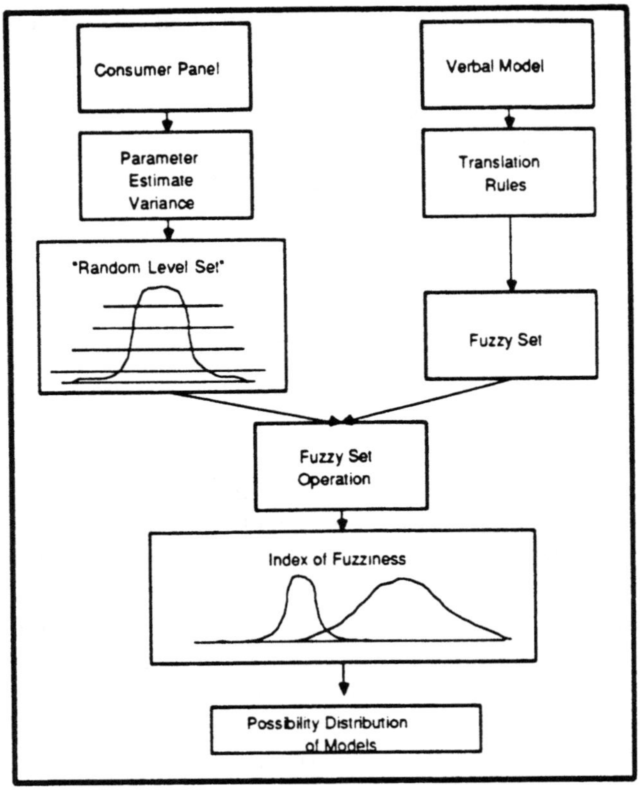

Figure 5: Combining Rule-Based and Stochastic Market Models

5 Applications

Now we demonstrate the method proposed and return to the issue of modelling buying behavior concerning the Austrian coffee market. We combine the information on the mean purchase rate of brand A provided by the data (see Section 2) with the verbal proposition that the "mean purchase rate is around upper medium" in Figure 6. This proposition reflects the managers knowledge, that foreign workers prefer brand A and are not included in the panel (see Section 2). More specifically we calculate a random level set using the observed mean purchase rate of 1.04 and its observed standard deviation of 0.1. Because of this small value the fuzziness of the random level set is small (0.0001) as well. However, combining it with the fuzzy set derived from the verbal statement results in a fuzziness measure of 0.76, and corresponding mean purchase rates which vary between 1.04 and 1.13.

Based on this fuzzy set of possible mean-purchase rates we estimate a number of different Negativ Binomial Models their possibility being identical to the possibility of the underlying mean purchase rates. Thus we end up with a broader spectrum of potential models; their validities in turn have to be evaluated by the brand manager.

The second example demonstrates the application of our approach in strategic marketing decision-making. We are interested in the consequences of possible product

Mean Purchase Rate: 1.04

Variance: 0.010

Percentage Non-Buyers: 0.790

Mean Purchase Rate is "AROUND UPPER MEDIUM"

		Index of Fuzziness
Mean Purchase Rate(Data):	"MEDIUM"	0.0001
Mean Purchase Rate(Expert):	"AROUND UPPER MEDIUM"	0.59
Combination:	"AROUND UPPER MEDIUM"	0.76

Possibility	Mean Purchase Rate	Percentage Non-Buyers
0.02	0.99	0.79
0.08	1.01	0.79
0.32	1.03	0.79
1.00	1.04	0.79
0.66	1.05	0.79
0.84	1.07	0.79
1.00	1.09	0.79
0.76	1.11	0.79
0.66	1.13	0.79
0.17	1.16	0.79

Figure 6: Empirical Results Brand A

relaunches on market-share. Once again we are dealing with the Austrian coffee market,this time we analyze the market-leader brand B. The relaunch activity under consideration is motivated by the fact of increasing world-market coffee prices and the assumed existence of a price-treshold. Thus a reduction in package size is proposed by the brand manager. The only available information on the consequences of such a marketing activity is the experience of the manager with the market. Therefore we try to merge the outcomes of the "verbal" models of the managers (i.e., "...the product relaunch will not affect market share ...", "...the mean-purchase rate will drop ...", ...) with our stochastic models. In this situation we choose the Lavington model of individual consumer-buying decisions (see Meffert and Steffenhagen (1977)) as a means to introduce the manager's experience into a quantitative approach.

Since the Lavington Model is basically of structural form, we transform it into a rule-based style. Figure 7 depicts the part relevant for the problem outlined above, Figure 8 the corresponding rule-base (due to limitations of space we restrict the presentation of the rule-base to Figure 8).

We proceed in a similar manner as in the previous example and transform the observed mean-purchase rate of brand B and its observed standard deviation into a Random-Level Set. The results are summarized in Figure 9.

Due to presentational convenience we restrict the analysis to:

- package size is 200 gramms (relaunch)
- conditioning is very high (market leader)

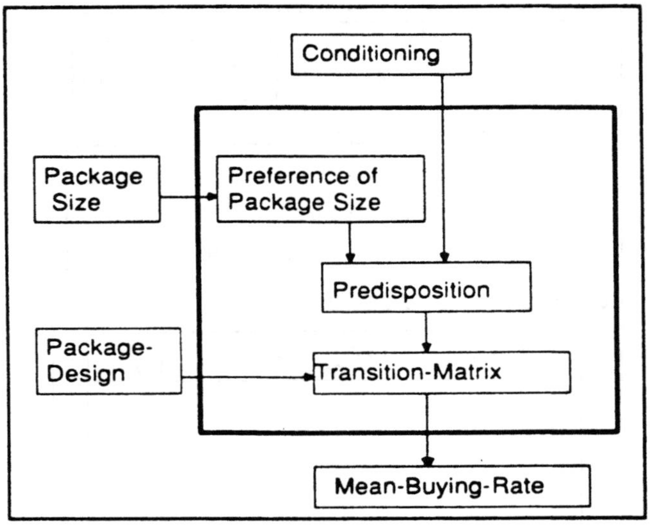

Figure 7: A Part of the Lavington Model

- package design is medium.

The Lavington Model thus infers a mean purchase rate of lower medium and the corresponding fuzzy set. It is interesting to note that in this case we arrive at two opposing propositions represented by "upper upper medium" and "lower medium", each having quite a small index of fuzziness. Their combination is characterized by a distinctly bimodal fuzzy set. The bimodality is also made evident by the *EXCEPT*-phrase of the label of the fuzzy set.

Finally we arrive at the market shares predicted by the different models and their corresponding possibilities. The two most likely models differ by 3 percent in market-share, a fact, which can be used to judge the risk of the relaunch activity under consideration.

References

Ehrenberg ASC (1972) The Pattern of Consumer Purchases. North-Holland, New York

Geyer-Schulz A (1986) Unscharfe Mengen im Operations Research, in: Dissertationen der Wirtschaftsuniversität Wien 41. Verlag der wissenschaftlichen Gesellschaften Österreichs, Wien

Goodman IR (1981) Fuzzy Sets as Random Level Sets: Implications and Extensions of the Basic Result. Applied Systems and Cybernetics 6: 2757–2766

Goodman IR, Nguyen MT (1985) Uncertainty Models for Knowledge Based Systems. Elsevier Science Publishers, Amsterdam

Kandel A (1986) Fuzzy Mathematical Techniques with Applications. Addison-Wesley, Reading, Massachusetts

Kaufmann A (1975) Introduction to the Theory of Fuzzy Subsets, 1. Academic Press, New York

Z is Preference of Package Size
R1 is (Very Low) If Package Size≤100
R2 is (Lower Lower Medium) If Package Size=150
R3 is (Lower Medium) If Package Size=200
R4 is (Upper Medium) If Package Size=250
R5 is (Rather Medium) If Package Size=300
R6 is (High) If Package Size=350
R7 is (Very High) If Package Size>350
Z is R1 OR R2 OR R3 OR R4 OR R5 OR R6 OR R7

Z is Predisposition
R1 is Low If((Preference of Package Size is(Very Low)to Lower Medium)or(Conditioning is(Very Low)to Medium))
R2 is (Rather Low) If((Preference of Package Size is(Very Low) to Lower Medium)or(Conditioning is above Medium))
R3 is (Lower Lower Medium) If((Preference of Package Size is (above Medium)to Upper UpperMedium)and(Conditioning is not below Medium))
R4 is High If((Preference of Package Size is above Upper Medium) and(Conditioning is not below Medium))
Z is R1 OR R2 OR R3 OR R4

Z is Transition Matrix
R1 is Low If((Package Design is(Very Low))or(Predisposition is below Upper Medium))
R2 is (Rather Low) If((Package Design is(above Lower Medium)) or(Predisposition is below Upper Medium))
R3 is Medium If((Package Design is(below Upper Medium)to Upper Upper Medium)and(Predisposition is above Upper Medium))
R4 is High If((Package Design is Very High)and(Predisposition is High))
Z is R1 OR R2 OR R3 OR R4

Figure 8: A Part of the Lavington Model Rule Base

Mean Purchase Rate: 4.629
Variance: 0.042
Percentage Non-Buyers: 0.372

Mean Purchase Rate is
"LOWER MEDIUM"
because
Package size is 200 gramms
Conditioning is very high
Package design is medium

		Index of Fuzziness
Mean Purchase Rate(Data):	"UPPER UPPER MEDIUM"	0.00001
Mean Purchase Rate(Expert):	"LOWER MEDIUM"	0.34
Combination:	"(NEITHERMOREORLESS HIGH)NOR MOREORLESS LOW)EXECPT(MEDIUM TO UPPER MEDIUM)"	0.51

Possibility	Market Share	Mean-Buying Rate
0.03	0.20	3.71
0.19	0.21	3.88
0.42	0.21	3.93
1.00	0.22	4.06
0.64	0.22	4.14
0.16	0.23	4.25
0.07	0.23	4.36
0.00	0.23	4.44
0.00	0.24	4.57
0.92	0.24	4.63
1.00	0.24	4.63
0.00	0.25	4.79

Figure 9: Empirical Results Brand B

Kickert WJM (1978) Fuzzy Theories on Decision Making, in: Frontiers in System Research, 3. Martinus Nijhoff Social Sciences Division, Leiden

Meffert H, Steffenhagen H (1977) Marketing Prognosemodelle—Quantitative Grundlagen des Marketing. C.E. Poeschl, Stuttgart

Nenning M, Topritzhofer E, Wagner U (1981) Empirische Marktmodellierung. Würzburg, Wien

Schmucker KJ (1984) Fuzzy Sets, Natural Language Computations, and Risk Analysis. Computer Science Press, Rockville, Maryland

Wagner U, Taudes A (1987) Stochastic Models of Consumer Behavior. European Journal of Operations Research 29, 1: 1–23

Wenstop F (1980) Quantitative Analysis with Linguistic Variables. Fuzzy Sets and Systems 4: 99–115

Werners B (1984) Interaktive Entscheidungsunterstützung durch ein flexibles mathematisches Programmierungssystem, in: Wirtschaftsinformatik und quantitative Betriebswirtschaftslehre 16. Minerva Publikation, München

Zadeh LA (1965) "Fuzzy Sets". Information and Control 8: 338–353

Zimmermann HJ, Zysno P (1980) Latent Connectives in Human Decision Making. Fuzzy Sets and Systems 4: 37–51

Zimmermann HJ, Zysno P (1982) Ein hierarchisches Bewertungssystem für die Kreditwürdigkeitsprüfung im Konsumentenkreditgeschäft. Die Betriebswirtschaft 42, 3: 403–418

Zimmermann HJ, Zysno P (1983) Decisions and Evaluations by Hierarchical Aggregation of Information. Fuzzy Sets and Systems 10: 243–260

The Development of a Knowledge Based Media Planning System

A. A. Mitchell
Faculty of Management, University of Toronto
Toronto, Ontario M5S 1V4

Summary

This paper discusses a knowledge based media planning system that we are developing. The system is designed to operate at a number of levels. At one level it operates as a decision support system while at another level it operates as a a pure expert system. The operation of the system at the decision support level is presented along with a discussion of how knowledge will be added to the system so it will operate as an expert system.

1 Introduction

The purpose of this paper is to discuss the knowledge based media planning system we are developing. A previous paper (Mitchell (1987)) discusses the media planning problem, how media planners solve the problem and the characteristics of the system we are developing. This paper will provide only a brief overview of these topics in the introduction and will, instead, focus on the structure of the system and how knowledge will be utilized in the system.

The media planning problem involves the allocation of an advertising budget to different media options over a planning horizon. For television, the media options are a commercial of a specific length (e.g., 30 seconds) in a specific daypart (e.g., prime time) during a specific week, while for magazines media options are a particular size (e.g., half page) and type (e.g., color) in a specific issue of a magazine (e.g., Newsweek). The system we are developing will generate a media plan at this level of specifity.

Characteristics of the Problem: Developing a knowledge based system for media planning is interesting for a number of reasons. First, the problem is a semi-structured or ill-structured problem (see Keene and Scott-Morton (1978); Simon (1973)) and currently few systems have been developed for these types of problems. Second, most knowledge based planning systems have been developed for domains where the relationships between the critical variables are well defined, such as job scheduling (e.g., Smith, Fox and Ow (1986)). In contrast, the effect of different elements of the media plan on sales are not well understood. This makes it difficult to evaluate a particular media plan. Third, the problem has almost an infinite number of possible solutions. This means that the system must reduce the size of the solution space quickly to solve the problem. Fourth, large amounts of data must be synthesized in developing a media plan. Since humans are poor at handling large amounts of data, a system that would aid the media planner in this task would seem to be very beneficial. Finally, a number of normative models have been developed to solve the problem (e.g., Little and Lodish (1965); Aaker (1978)), however, the evidence suggests that they are generally not used by media planners (e.g., Simon and Thiel (1980)). The primary reason they are not used seems to be that most media planners (and most academics) don't understand how these models develop a media plan. Consequently, media planners are very hesitant to turn over the control of the planning process to these models. In addition, it is difficult for media planners to evaluate a media plan developed by these models because they do not provide the information that media planners generally use to evaluate media plans. For instance, in developing media plans for television, media planners use reach and frequency measures to evaluate a plan, however, this information is not provided directly by most of the models.

When developing a media plan, media planners generally decompose the problem into subproblems and also set goals and add constraints to reduce the size of the solution space. For instance, a media planner ususally first allocates the budget across the different media and then develops a plan for each of the media separately. Examples of goals and constraints that are typically set are reach and frequency goals and scheduling constraints (e.g., no television advertising during the summer).

Characteristics of the System: The system we are developing will generate a media plan for a particular brand. In order to accomplish this task and to make the system useful to media planners it had to have a number of unique characteristics. First, it used both symbolic and numeric computation (see Kitzmiller and Kowlik (1987)). Numeric computation is used, for instance, to apply a number of different heuristics for budget allocation and to calculate a frequency distribution for a particular media schedule. Symbolic computation uses the knowledge of the media planner for reasoning. This knowledge may take many different forms. It may be cutoff values (e.g., don't buy more than 55 GRP's a week in late night television), constraints (e.g., don't advertise on television during the summer), goals (e.g., you need at least three exposures during a purchase cycle to have an effect on purchase behavior), trends (e.g., network television viewing will continue to decline) or a synthesis of data (e.g., the audience for professional basketball is skewed upward).

Second, the system is being designed to operate at a number of different levels. The first level, which we call a decision frame, is basically a decision support system. With the decision frame, the system provides the information that the media planner requires at different stages of the planning process and makes all the necessary calculations. In order to facilitate the decision making process, much of the information that is required to make a particular decision is displayed in graphical form. At this level, then, most of the expertise resides in the media planner.

At the highest level, the system acts as a pure expert system. The system develops a media plan based on the data and knowledge contained in the system. Examples of systems at intermediate levels are systems that critique a media plan developed with the decision frame system or systems that suggest improvements and indicate poor decisions at different stages of the planning process while the media planner is using the decision frame system.

Third, the system is designed to be modular. The modules are designed to conform to the different subproblems that the media planner solves in developing a media plan. This modular structure has a number of advantages. At the decision frame level, it allows the media planner to focus on a single aspect of the problem at a time. Since the modules conform to the different subproblems that are solved by media planners in developing a media plan, the decision frame system conforms to problem solving process. At the expert system level, separate production systems are written for each module instead of having a single production system for the entire planning process. This makes it easier to debug and to make changes in the system.

Finally, the system is designed to be used by different media planners. This means that differences in knowledge between media planners needs to be identified and the system has to be flexible enough to accommodate these differences (see Mittal and Dym (1985)). Currently, it appears that these differences can be accommodated by having a separate frame for each media planner that will contain his or her idiosyncratic knowledge.

In the next section, the different modules in the system and their operation at the decision frame level are discussed. Then there will be a brief discussion of how knowledge will be added to the system.

2 System Overview

The modules for network television, spot television and magazines are shown in Figure 1. These modules represent a first cut in the development of the system. It is expected there will be a number of additional changes in the modules as the development of the system proceeds.

When developing a media plan, the media planner first enters module P1, the media selection module (Figure 2). In this module, the length of the planning horizon (usually one year), the target and secondary markets, and the size of the media budget are specified. In addition, the advertising budget is allocated between network television, spot television, and magazines. A number of different methods can be used to allocate the advertising budget to the different media, such as last years dollars (adjusted for inflation) or last years percentage allocation, the dollar (adjusted for inflation) or percentage allocation of a specific competitor, or the dollar (adjusted for inflation) or percentage allocation of groups of competitors. Any four of the different allocation procedures can be displayed graphically.

The media planner can select one of the methods and then make adjustments to it in order to arrive at an allocation or she may directly input an allocation. This allocation will be used to start the media planning process, however, it may be adjusted later as the media process proceeds.

At this point, the media planner selects one of the media that has received a budget allocation and develops a plan for this media. Usually this will be the medium that has received the largest proportion of the budget and generally this medium will form the base of the plan. If other media are also used in the plan, they generally will be used to reach other target audiences, to achieve goals that may be too expensive with the base

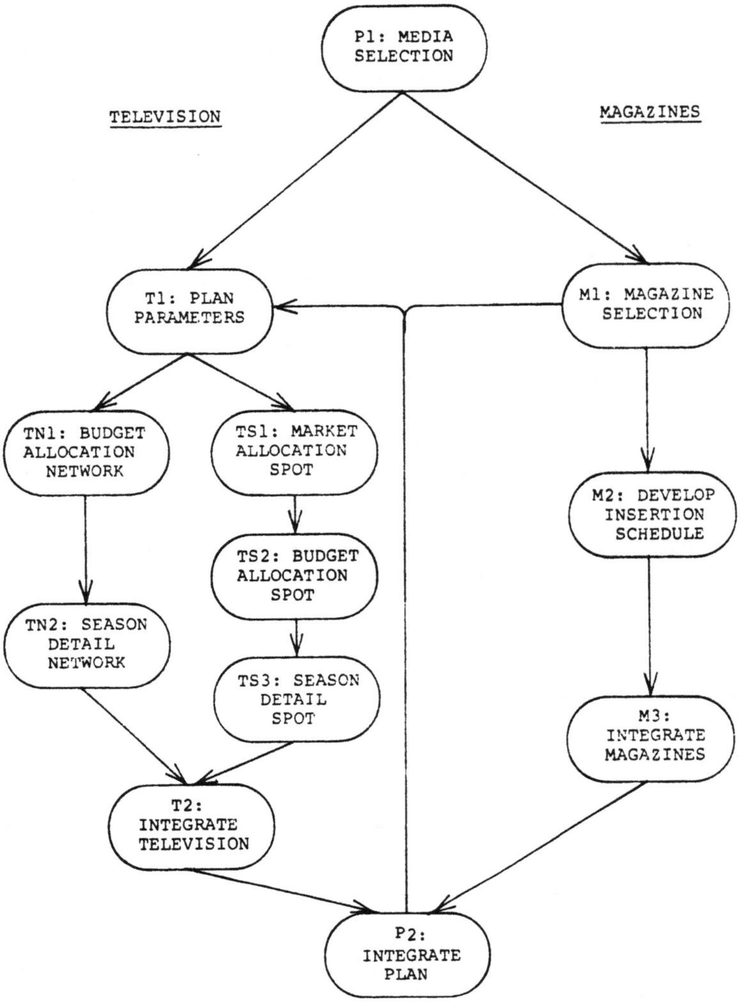

Figure 1: System Modules

media or to provide additional media weight to specific markets or audiences. For instance, network television might be used as the base media for a detergent product, however, if Spanish speaking consumers represent an important submarket, Spanish spot television may also be used to supplement the network television media plan.

Network Television: Since network television is used for most frequently purchased consumer products that have a large advertising budget, we will continue our description of the system using this medium. The media planner now enters module T1, which is the initial module for both network and spot television. In this module, the user sets scheduling constraints by indicating weeks when no television advertising is desired.

These constraints may also be used to preset "pulse" or "wave" advertising schedules by either setting off weeks or by setting the parameters for these different types of schedules. For instance, the media planner may decide that there should be no television

```
COMPANY  P & G                  PLAN  T1

CATEGORY  POWDER DETERGENT      TIME HORIZON  1 YEAR

BRAND  TIDE                          STARTING  JANUARY 1, 1987

TARGET  WOMEN 18-49

SECONDARY  NONE                 MEDIA BUDGET  50.0   ( $000,000 )

ALLOCATION GRAPH  $   ( $000,000 )


    50-  x x   x                         10-  x
     -   x x   x                          -   x x
    40-  x x x x                          8-  x x   x
     -   x x x x     x x   x              -   x x   x            x
    30-  x x x x     x x x x              6-  x x x x          x x
     -   x x x x     x x x x              -   x x x x     x    x x
    20-  x x x x     x x x x              4-  x x x x     x x x x
     -   x x x x     x x x x              -   x x x x     x x x x
    10-  x x x x     x x x x              2-  x x x x     x x x x
     -   x x x x     x x x x              -   x x x x     x x x x
     0-  x x x x     x x x x              0-  x x x x     x x x x
         -------     -------                  -------     -------
```

MEDIA:	TOTAL	NETWORK		SPOT		MAGAZINE	
PLOTS:	$	$	%	$	%	$	%
1.INPUT	50.0	35.0	70	10.0	20	5.0	10
2.LASTYR%	50.0	37.0	74	9.0	18	4.0	8
3.ALL $	42.0	29.4	70	6.2	15	6.4	15
4.ALL %	50.0	35.0	70	7.5	15	7.5	15

ALLOCATION USING METHOD 3

Figure 2: Module P1: Media Selection

advertising from the last week of November to the middle of January because of the Christmas holidays. Alternatively, the media planner may decide to preset a "wave" advertising schedule beginning the second week in January and continuing throughout the year with four weeks of advertising followed by two weeks with no advertising.

In this module, the media planner also divides the planning horizon into time periods (usually quarters) and may preset reach and frequency goals for these time periods. Finally, this module ranks dayparts on the cost efficieny of reaching the target audience and displayes both the cost per rating point and cost per thousand for the target audience for each daypart. The media planner, at this point, may delete dayparts from further consideration and change the ranking of dayparts, if desired. The display for this module is shown in Figure 3.

Next, the media planner accesses module TN1, which allocates the network television budget between the different time periods. A number of different methods are available to assist in this allocation, such as equalizing the number of GRP's that can be purchased in each time period, last years dollar (adjusted for inflation) or percentage allocation, competitor dollars (adjusted for inflation) or percentage allocation, share of voice, same percentage allocation as sales, or an allocation based on reach and frequency goals. The media planner can display any four of these methods graphically and can then adjust one of the methods to reach an allocation or may input an allocation directly. This

TELEVISION SCHEDULE CONSTRAINTS:

```
xxxxxxxxxx xxxxxxxxxxxxxx  xx xxxxxxxxxxxxxxxxxxx
xxxxxxxxxx xxxxxxxxxxxxxx  xx xxxxxxxxxxxxxxxxxxx
xxxxxxxxxx xxxxxxxxxxxxxx  xx xxxxxxxxxxxxxxxxxxx
JAN  FEB MAR  APR MAY JUN  JUL AUG  SEP OCT NOV DEC
```

SCHEDULE TYPE NONE   SEASON LENGTH 13 WEEKS

OFFWEEKS: 1,13,27,28,31,52

REACH/FREQUENCY GOALS BY SEASON:

TYPE REACH & AVG. FREQ.

SEASON	REACH	FREQ.
1	80	2.5
2	85	3.0
3	75	2.5
4	80	2.5

DAYPART EFFICIENCY RANKING:

		CPR	CPM
1	DAYTIME	900	3.22
2	LATE EVENING	1900	7.58
3	EARLY EVENING	1700	7.70

RANKING BY CPM   THRESHOLD: CPR 2100

Figure 3: Module T1: Plan Parameters

allocation is used at the next stage of the media planning process, however, it can also be adjusted later.

The next module, TN2 is used to develop the media plan within each time period given the budget allocation to that time period. Consequently, this module must be used once for each time period. In order to develop a media plan for each time period, the media planner must provide the schedule type, if this has not been set earlier, message length and priority type.

The schedule type can be "constant", "pulse" or "wave". For a "constant" schedule, the budget for this time period is allocated equally to each week in the time period that is to receive television advertising. For "pulse" or "wave" schedules, the parameters of each type of schedules are given by the user.

The message length (e.g., 30 second commercial) may vary by daypart or be fixed across dayparts. There are two priority types: budget ($) or reach. For the budget priority, the system allocates the budget to all weeks that are to receive television advertising based on the schedule type and then the media planner allocates this weekly 'budget' by dayparts. For the reach priority, the media planner first uses the ranking of the dayparts to purchase time until the reach and frequency goals are met for a typical week. This determines the amount of money that must be spent weekly to obtain these goals. This amount and the amount of money allocated to the time period determines the number of weeks of advertising in the time period. The media planner, then decides which weeks will receive advertising. Either one of these priority types can be used to develop a schedule for a particular time period. After using one of these priority types, the media planner can then make additional changes in the schedule.

After the plan for the time period has been set, the resulting GRP's and spending levels are displayed. The frequency distribution is estimated (see Rust (1986)) and either critical aspects of this distribution (e.g., effective frequency, etc.) or the entire distribution can be displayed. The media planner can now alter the plan for any week or group of weeks by either providing new reach and frequency goals or a new budget level. After any changes have been made, the summary statistics discussed above are again displayed.

As mentioned previously, this is repeated for each time period. After the media planner is satisfied with the plan for each time period, he or she moves to module T2 which displays the television media plan by dayparts across planning horizon. The media plan can be displayed for network television only, spot television only in a particular market or group of markets or network and spot television aggregated in a particular market or group of markets. The average GRP's, spending level, reach and frequency per advertising week are also displayed.

The resulting media plan can then be compared to any other media plan that is stored in the system. This may be another plan that has been generated for the same problem, last years media plan or the media plan of a competitor. The media planner may now make additional changes in the plan and the effect of these changes are displayed in the summary statistics for the plan.

Spot Television: There are a number of reasons why the media planner may want to include spot television in a media plan. First, the product or service may be available in only a limited number of markets, so network television advertising is not warrented. Second, even though the product or service has national distribution, the media planner may decide that some markets need additional advertising weight. Finally, spot television is sometimes used to compensate for weeknesses in a national schedule in some markets. For example, a national schedule of 75 GRP's in daytime television may not achieve this level in all markets. Since the latter reason can only be assessed after a particular schedule has been purchased, we will focus only on the first two reasons.

If the plan parameters for television have not been set previously, the media planner begins with module T1. Once these parameters are set, the media planner accesses module TS1 which is used to allocate the spot television budget between markets. Generally, this is a two step process. First, the markets that are to receive spot television schedules are determined and then, the spot television budget is allocated between these markets.

To assist this allocation process, the system contains data on the largest and most frequently used television markets. This data includes population, population in different demographic categories, market share and sales, BDI, CDI, competitors spending on spot television and cost per rating point for different dayparts. The media planner may use any one of these variables to rank the different markets or may use different cutoff values for sets of these variables to determine the number of markets that will receive spot television advertising.

After deciding which markets are to receive spot television advertising, the media planner must now allocate the spot television advertising budget between the different markets. If all markets are to receive the same media plan, then the markets are aggregated together and the media planner simply develops a media plan using the same procedures that were used for network television. If different media plans are to be developed for different markets, then the media planner must first make a prior allocation. To do this, the media planner can use the previously discussed data from each market to make the allocation. For instance, the media planner might consider population, target market population and cost per rating point as different ways of allocating the spot television budget. The system will display the different allocations based on these data and the media planner can either use one of these methods for making the allocation and make adjustments to it or input a specific allocation. After making this allocation, the media planner proceeds to develop a media plan for each market or for the different sets of markets.

Once the spot television budget has been allocated between markets, the media planner uses modules TS2, TS3 and T2 to develop the media plan. Modules TS2 and TS3 are identical to TN1 and TN2, so there is no need to discuss these modules further. If the media planner is using both network television and spot television, then, as discussed previously, module T2 can be used to assess the combined impact of network and spot television in the different spot television markets.

Magazines: Magazines may also be used as the base media in a media plan or may be used to supplement other media. Media planning for magazines contains three modules. The first module, M1, is used to set goals and for magazine selection. First, coverage and frequency goals can be set. Then, for magazine selection, four different effectiveness and efficiency measures are available for each magazine. These are coverage of the target market, percentage of magazine readership represented by the target market, cost per thousand circulation and cost per thousand target market readership. The media planner may analyze specific magazines or all magazines within a classification (e.g., women's shelter magazines) with these different measures. Alternatively the media planner may ask for a ranking of all magazines on one of the measures or may provide cutoff values for one or more of the measures and examine only those magazines that pass all the cutoff values.

After narrowing the set of magazines under consideration, the media planner may ask for audience duplication figures between pairs of magazines to determine which magazine should be given further consideration. The media planner may also compare the magazines graphically along one or more of the different measures.

At this point, the media planner may want to consider sets of magazines for the media plan. These different sets of magazines can be evaluated along a number of dimensions such as the coverage of the target market, the cost per thousand of this target market coverage and the amount of duplication. A comparison of the different sets of magazines along these variables can again be made graphically to facilitate the selection process.

After deciding the set of magazines that will be used, the media planner now enters module M2 where the number of insertions in each magazine is determined. In this module, he or she must give the size of the advertisement to be run in each magazine (e.g., 1/2 page), number of colors (e.g., 4 colors), bleed or nonbleed and the number of insertions to be run in each magazine. With this information, the system calculates the coverage, duplication and cost of the proposed schedule and compares it to the goals and the amount budgeted for magazine. If the proposed schedule is over or under budget, the size of the discrepancy along with the cost of one less or one more insertion in each magazine is displayed, so the media planner can select the appropriate number of insertions in each magazine to meet the budget constraint.

Now the media planner uses module M3 to schedule the insertions for each magazine. To assist the media planner in this task, the system will display a blocking chart containing fifty two weeks along with an indication of when the monthly magazines appear on the newsstands. If the media plan also contains a network or spot television schedule, this schedule may be accessed to help the media planner schedule the magazine insertions. After indicating when each insertion will appear, the system will calculate summary statistics for each quarter that include spending levels, percentage of target market reached and duplication.

Output of System: The final module P2, presents the media plan that has been developed in the previous modules. An example of the presentation format for the network television portion of a media plan is shown in Figure 4. The blocking chart indicates how many GRP's are to be purchased in each daypart for each week of the planning horizon. It also indicates the reach obtained in each daypart. Summary statistics are also provided which indicate the budget allocation by daypart and time period, and the reach and frequeny for each time period.

If spot television and magazines had also been used in the media plan, the schedules for these media would also appear in the blocking chart. For instance, the insertion schedule for magazines would indicate the size and type of advertisement to appear in a specific issue of a magazine.

3 Adding Knowledge to the System

In the previous section, an overview of the different modules was presented along with a brief description of how the system operates at the decision frame level. Modules P1, T1, TN1 and TN2 are operating and we are currently programming module T2. As we program the remaining modules, we are also adding knowledge to the system.

As mentioned previously, the system is being designed to operate at a number of of different levels. This means that different types of knowledge must be added to the system so it can operate at these different levels. This section contains a brief discussion of how knowledge is being added to the system to allow it to operate at these different levels.

First we will discuss how the decision frame system that was described earlier is being turned into an expert system. This system will contain a number of different systems operating at two levels. At one level is a control system that guides the flow of processing between the modules. At the second level are the inference systems that

COMPANY: P&G BRAND: TIDE

PLAN: T1 STARTING: JANUARY 1, 1987

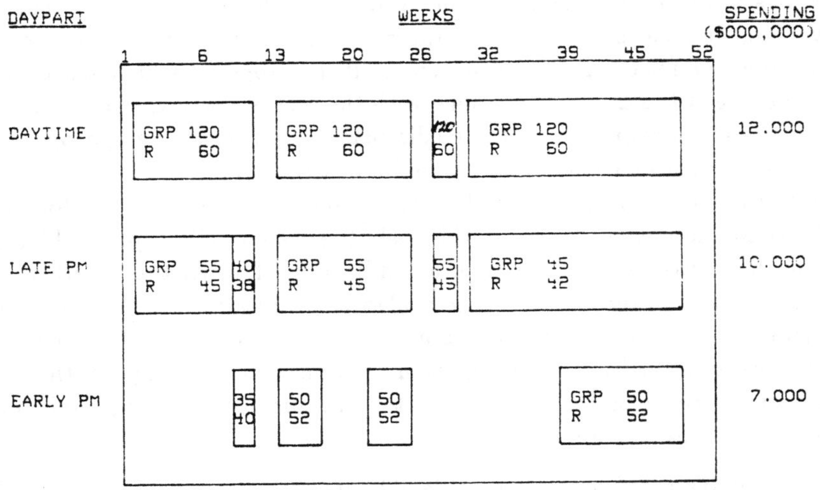

SEASON:	1	2	3	4	
TOTAL GRP (WTD AVG)	178	208	167	215	
REACH (WTD AVG ONWEEKS)	79	85	77	89	
FREQUENCY (4 WEEK AVG)	9.0	9.8	8.7	9.7	
SPENDING ($000,000)	5.821	9.673	5.468	8.438	29.400
DISTRIBUTION	19.8	32.9	18.6	28.7	

Figure 4: Output of the System

solve the local problems within each module. The subproblems solved by the modules are largely independent and if each subproblem is solved correctly, then the control system is quite simple. It simply moves the system from module to module in the appropriate sequence. If, however, a poor decision is generated in one of the modules, then the expertise within that module must decide whether to backtrack to the module that generated the poor decision. This takes place in the context of a relational database, from which each module can easily access information generated up to that point. For instance, one of the modules may make a poor allocation decision and this may only be determined after another module tries to develop a media plan based on this allocation. Currently, we hope to get around this problem by building procedures that check the viability of each decision in the modules. At this point, however, it's not clear if this alone will allow us to use a simple control structure.

In order to provide an indication of how the inference systems will operate for the different modules, we will briefly discuss how these are being developed for the network television modules. As in the <u>decision frame</u>, the basic parameters of the particular problem would need to be provided. These parameters include the brand, target audience, budget, length of planning horizon, length of time period, reach and frequency goals by time period and any scheduling constraints.

Once these parameters have been set, a number of problems remain to be solved. One problem is the allocation of the budget between time periods. In the <u>decision frame</u> system, there are a number of different methods available for allocating the budget between time periods. One of these methods or a weighted combination of methods could be pre-set for a particular media planner and/or brand. Alternatively, a number of conditions could be set for each method (e.g., if sales are highly seasonal, use the percentage of sales method) so the particular method that is selected would be based on the characterictics of a particular problem.

Another problem is the allocation of the budget between dayparts within a time period. To accomplish this, the system selects the most efficient daypart for reaching the target audience and purchases GRP's in that daypart until the reach and frequency goals are achieved or until a cutoff GRP level is reached. If the cutoff GRP level is reached without achieving the reach and frequency goals, then the system purchases in the next most efficient daypart. This procedure continues until the reach and frequency goals are achieved. This, in turn, determines the amount of money that must be spent weekly to achieve these goals.

The next problem is to develop an actual schedule for the time period. To solve this problem the system uses the budget for that time period and the number of weeks that are to receive television advertising to determine the amount of money available each week. This value is then compared to the amount of money that must be spent to achieve the reach and goals. If the former value is larger, then the difference is allocated equally to each week that receives television advertising.

If the budget allocation for that time period is not large enough to achieve the reach and frequency goals in all weeks that can receive television advertising, the system must decide which weeks should not receive television advertising. If the budget for the time period is such that a large number of weeks will not receive television advertising in order to achieve the reach and frequency goals, then these goals may be reduced or the systems will seek a larger budget allocation for that time period. If there are only a small number of weeks that will not receive television advertising, then priorities will be used to determine which weeks will receive advertising.

The second way knowledge can be used is to assist the media planner in developing a media plan with the <u>decision frame</u> system. This assistance could be provided in a number of ways. For instance, the system could check the feasibility of the goals that are set or the various allocation decisions that are made given the characteristics of the problem. For instance, setting a reach goal of 80 on network television for each quarter with a budget of $5 million is clearly not feasible unless the media planner wants to advertise only a couple of weeks per quarter. An alternative way in which the system could assist the media planner is by checking whether or not the allocation between dayparts is efficient.

Incorporating the knowledge required to provide this assistance can be done in a number of ways. It could, for instance, be provided with rules where a series of specific conditions trigger a warning (e.g., IF the network television budget is less than $3 million, THEN issue a warning). Alternatively, rough calculations could be made to provide a quick assessment of a particular decision.

Third, knowledge can also be added to the system for evaluating a particular media plan. For instance, previous experience with a particular client may indicate that he does not want to be off television for more than four weeks at a time. This information can then be used to evaluate a media plan for this client.

Finally, knowledge could also be added so the system would develop a media plan based only on the marketing strategy for the brand. Currently, the system needs to be given the goals and contraints of the media problem, however, with this expanded knowledge, the system would generate the goals and constraints based on the marketing strategy (see Mitchell (1987) for a further discussion of this).

4 Conclusions

In this paper, we have briefly discussed different characteristics of the knowledge based media planning system we are developing. The system has a number of unique aspects. One of the most important of these is that it is designed to operate at a number of different levels. At one level it is a decision support system that simply assists the media planner in developing a media plan. At another level it acts as a pure expert system by using its knowledge to develop a media plan. A second important aspect is that it is a modular system where the modules represent the subproblems that the media planner solves in developing a media plan.

In the second section, the different modules in the system and how these modules operate at the decision frame level were discussed. Then we discussed how knowledge would be built into the system so it would operate at the different levels to assist the media planner, evaluate previously generated media plans and as a pure expert system. Finally, reference was made as to how goal and constraint generation might be added to the system.

Acknowledgements

This research is partially funded by the Marketing Science Institute. The author would like to thank Ian Willson and Christopher August for the substantial contributions they have made in the development and programming of the current system.

References

Aaker DA (1975) ADMOD: An Advertising Decision Model. Journal of Marketing Research 12: 37–45

Keene PWG, Scott-Morton MS (1978) Decision Support Systems. Addison Wesley, Reading, MA

Kitzmiller CT, Kowalik JS (1987) Coupling Symbolic and Numeric Computing in Knowledge-Based Systems. AI Magazine 8: 85–90

Little JDC, Lodish CM (1969) A Media Planning Calculus. Operation Research 17: 1–35

Mitchell AA (1987) The Use of Alternative Knowledge Acquisition Procedures in the Development of a Knowledge Based Media Planning System. International Journal of Man-Machine Studies 26: 399–411

Mittal S, Dym CL (1985) Knowledge Acquisition From Multiple Experts. AI Magazine 6: 32–36

Rust RT (1986) Advertising Media Models. Lexington Books, Lexington, MA

Simon HA (1973) The Structure of Ill Structured Problems. Artificial Intelligence 4: 181–201

Simon H, Thiel M (1980) Hits and Flops Among German Media Models. Journal of Advertising Research 20: 25–29

Smith SF, Fox MS, Ow P (1986) Constructing and Maintaining Detailed Production Plans: Investigation into the Development of Knowledge Based Factory Scheduling Systems. AI Magazine 7: 45–61

Part 3

Decision Support Systems, Knowledge Representation, Applications other than Marketing

KREDIT: KEE-Based Support for Credit Decisions in a Mail-Order Firm

O. Büring and M. Schader
Institut für Informatik, Universität der Bundeswehr Hamburg
Holstenhofweg 85, D-2000 Hamburg 70

Summary

We explore ways in which a rule-based system can be applied in the decision process of a mail-order firm concerning consumer credit line limits. The first section explains the usual proceedings that are carried out when incoming orders are processed. The second section shows how the system is implemented for use in outside advisory service.

1 Problem Definition

The rule-based system KREDIT was built in cooperation with a large-scale enterprise in the merchandising business. Most of the products that are sold belong to the lower price range (DM 100.– up to DM 1000.–). The customers almost exclusively are private households, and many orders are omnibus orders.

The most preferred mode of payment is installment—with very few orders being paid immediately. Payments can be made in 3, 6 or 8 monthly installments. Thus, indirectly, credit is established without obtaining detailed information on the solvency of the customers.

For the company therefore increasing sales imply increased risk of uncollectable debts. To keep these risks small a credit department is established which analyzes all incoming orders and decides on booking or rejecting. The department distinguishes two classes of customers: *new* customers (which are known to the firm for less than 3 periods) and *regular* customers. Accordingly, two different procedures for analyzing order forms are available on the firm's mainframe computers.

In addition to the specification of the current orders only six types of data are supplied by customers: name, street, city, telephone number, date of birth, nationality (and validity of residence permit of foreigners). These data are the basis for **processing the orders of new customers.** First, a *matchcode program* is started which scores the database of the company and tries to find negative matches with parts of the data entered (e.g. payments of a member of the customer's family might be overdue, etc.). Any negative match implies that the order is rejected. In case of a foreign customer the program now compares the proposed duration of installments and the validity of the residence permit. Again, negative results lead to rejecting orders. In the last step a *scoring program* is applied in order to evaluate the risk connected with booking. The resulting number of points, say x, is compared to two critical values a and b where $a < b$.

The order is rejected if $x < a$ and booked if $x > b$. In the case $a \leq x \leq b$ additional information is obtained from a credit checking firm SCHUFA (SCHUtzgemeinschaft Für Allgemeine Kreditsicherung). If no negative information is conveyed then the order is booked and rejected otherwise. Obviously, the decision on orders of new customers results from a sequence of numerical computations or simple comparisons carried out by existing test programs.

Quite different is the **processing the orders of regular customers** which is sketched in figure 1.

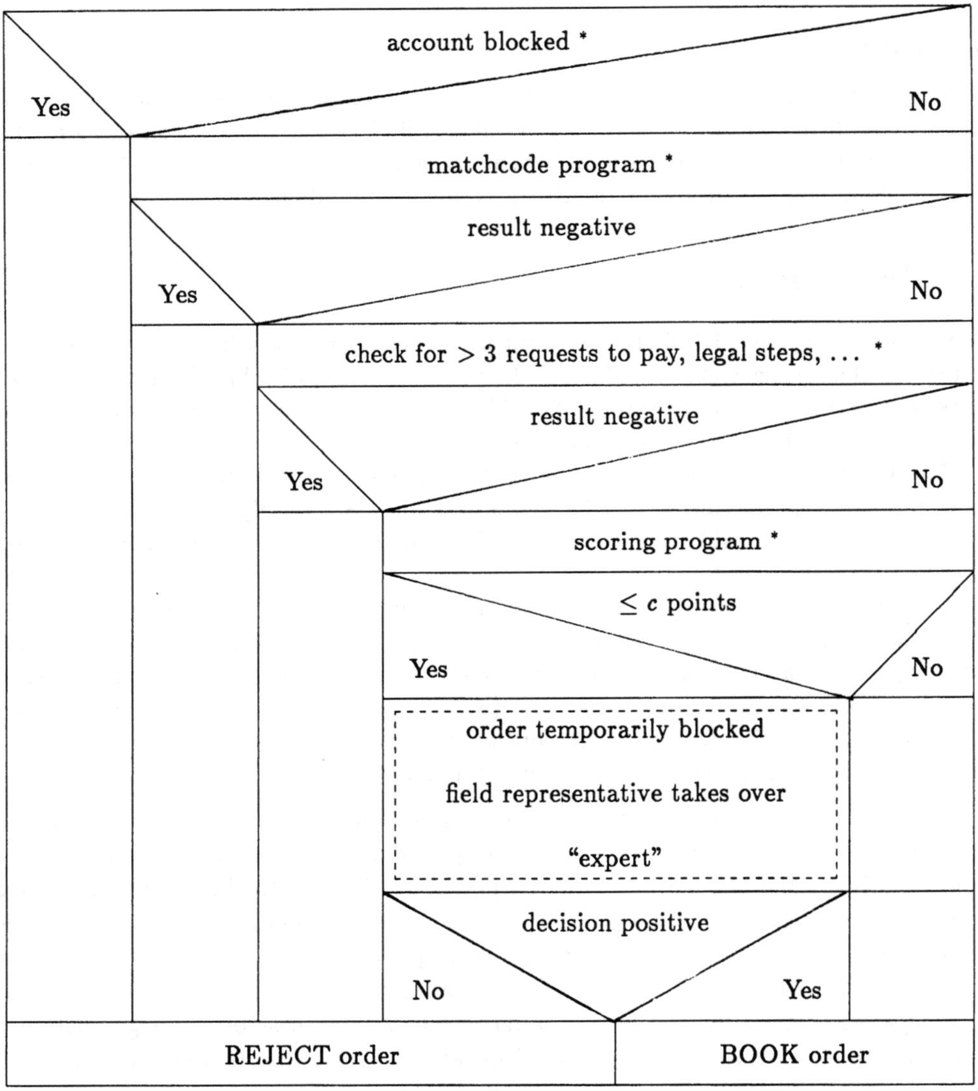

Figure 1: Processing of orders of regular customers
The tests marked * are computerized.

During the continuance of the business relation of the firm and the customer up to thirty different types of data are gathered such as customer status, current credit limit, remainders, arrears, no. of requests to pay, respites in payment, sales (5 periods), payments, ... All these data are available to the programs analyzing the orders of regular customers.

The first routine is to check if the customer's account is blocked at the moment (e.g. due to overchecking the credit limit or because installments were not paid properly). Now, again, a *matchcode program* checks if other accounts related to the customer are blocked. Subsequently, the program tests if any law-suits will be necessary or are already in progress. In case of a negative result in any of these first procedures the order will be rejected. If the order has passed the above tests then in a last step, again, a *scoring program* evaluates the payment performance of the customer in the past. The order is booked if the number of points calculated is greater than a value c. Otherwise the order is blocked temporarily and forwarded to the local field representative who finally has to decide on the acceptance.

As we have seen, the field representatives deal with those cases where the existing computer programs cannot definitely reject or accept an order. The scope of activities of a field representative can be summarized as follows: At first the account of the client is analyzed in order to find out the reasons for the blocking of the order. In many cases just five types of data are sufficient for this purpose (approximately 30 different types of information are available). Now the representative decides if the order is to be booked or to be rejected immediately. It may be necessary to call on the customer personally or by phone in order to gather more information, e.g. on reasons for arrears, customer's willingness to pay, responsibility of co-orderers for unbalanced account, possibility to respite payment, etc. Each personal call involves costs of DM 60.– to DM 120.–. A further possibility—due to lack of time or in case it is impossible to get the customer on the phone—is to send a standard letter which explains why the order cannot be processed at the moment and to suggest steps the customer should take. In addition, the representative can hand over the problem to the district manager. Any decision has to be reached in accordance with the company's guidelines.

If it is required to contact the customer the representative at some later date has to resume handling of this order and investigate additional information or take into consideration the reactions of the client. Supplied with this broader knowledge the representative finally decides on booking or rejection, and his work at the specific order is terminated.

In the past, however, this process has not produced satisfactory results. Since outdoor service receives a commission for each order booked, field representatives are interested in booking even dubious orders. Furthermore, the representatives are often overworked due to the quantity of orders that are blocked so that premature decisions often occur. And, obviously, the company's management attempts to keep the number of calls on customers to a minimum because of the costs each call involves. Due to these differing and partly conflicting objectives:

maximizing sales	minimizing risk
reducing fieldwork	receiving sufficient and reliable information on customers
flexibility given to obviously qualified customers	keeping within the guidelines concerning acceptance of orders

it would be advantageous to apply a decision support system. Analyzing the different steps of the order processing procedure (of regular customers), the decision process of the field representatives was chosen to be the first suitable subject for support by a rule-based system.
The following characteristics of the problem domain were essential in this consideration:

- Field representatives are assigned to those cases where arithmetical evaluation methods cannot arrive at definite acceptance or rejection of an order.
- Not all of the relevant variables determining whether an order will cause uncollectable claims are known.
- A direct interface to customer's data in the computer system was considered useful.

2 Development of the Rule-Based System KREDIT

One of the aims during the development of KREDIT was to incorporate the practitioners' way to evaluate the customer data and the reasoning underlying their decisions of booking or rejecting orders. Therefore—in accordance with the work of the field representatives—KREDIT is divided in two main parts (Start-1 and Start-2).

In the **first part** the customer number and the specific value of the goods ordered are entered. Now the program loads the customer data required (customer status, credit solvency class, etc.). Parts of these data are coded and have to be converted into sensible information. During tests with the company's *experts* it turned out that—compared to the forward chaining rule system of KREDIT—this kind of data processing is handled considerably faster by conventional computer programs. An improved system KREDIT II will therefore contain a program which performs the conversion in a procedural way.

Clearly, the system could operate with the coded data as well. Decoding, however, serves the following goals.

1. During the reasoning process the user is continuously informed on what the system has perceived and how it will proceed with these results.
2. In order to simplify the system, development rules were formulated in a rather verbal way e.g. instead of

```
IF (= (THE LIMIT OF ORDER) 30) AND
   (= (THE CUSTOMERSTATUS OF ORDER) 78) ...
THEN ...
```

   we used

```
IF (= (THE LIMIT OF ORDER) CONSERVATIVE.LIMIT) AND
   (= (THE CUSTOMERSTATUS OF ORDER) BIG.CUSTOMER) ...
THEN ...
```

After decoding of customer data, reasons for blocking the order are analyzed. By a forward chaining process at first rules concerning the customer status are considered. Additionally, rules concerning the development of the customer's account (sales results, reminders, respites for payment, etc.) are used.

Now backward chaining and considering rules imaging the company's guidelines, KREDIT traces recommendations for further activities of the field representative (booking, rejecting, letter, call, etc.). During backward chaining the system will possibly ask the user for missing information. In correspondance to their application by practitioners the rules are supplied with different weights. The system now saves the results obtained so far and the first part of a KREDIT session is completed.

It should be pointed out that special combinations of customer data may induce the system to a combined forward and backward chaining procedure which examines possibilities to increase the credit line. The corresponding rule is:

```
IF (THE REASON OF ORDER IS RUN.OVER.CREDIT.LINE)
DO (QUERY '(THE WARNING.SIGN OF ACCOUNT IS ?WHAT)
          'ALL
          'RULES.WARNING.SIGN
          T)
```

In case the order has not been freed for processing, the field representative now has to call on the customer or wait for reactions upon his letter. After gathering further information the second part of KREDIT may be started.

Again the customer data and the results of the first session are loaded. During backward chaining the system questions the user about the results of the call—which are required to reach a final decision. KREDIT is now able to arrange for the booking or the definite rejection of the order. One entire run through the two parts of the system is now completed.

KREDIT was developed using the KEE shell running on an Explorer system. KEE is a frame-oriented knowledge-engineering tool. Data as well as rules are stored in frames. For the representation of rules this may seem unusual since generally only static knowledge is handled in frames whereas rules are formulated in the underlying language (LISP, PROLOG, OPS5). During the development of a knowledge-based system, however, this approach is very suitable. A rule-frame consists of different slots so that the different parts of a rule (in KEE: premise, assertion and action) are easy to identify and to modify. We will give an example of such a rule-frame:

```
(RULE.WS.01
 NIL
 (RULES.WARNING.SIGN)
 NIL
```

```
()
((ACTION
  ((PUT.VALUE 'RESULT 'TEXT
    "Demand class, credit limit, date of last payment, blocking
     notes, respites and co-orderers share of current remainders
     were considered.
     It is impossible to increase the credit line.")))
 (ASSERTION (#Wff (THE WARNING.SIGN OF ACCOUNT IS ON)))
 (EXTERNAL.FORM
  (IF
   ((> (THE DEMAND.NOTES OF ORDER) 2)
    OR (THE LIMIT OF ORDER IS CONSERVATIVE.LIMIT)
    OR (> (THE LAST.WEEK OF PAYMENT) 4)
    OR (THE BLOCKING OF ORDER IS ON))
    OR (> (THE RESPITES OF ORDER) 0)
    OR (> (THE PERSONAL.SHARE OF REMAINDERS) 5000)
   THEN
   (THE WARNING.SIGN OF ACCOUNT IS ON)
   DO
   (PUT.VALUE 'RESULT 'TEXT
    "Demand class, credit limit, date of last payment, blocking
     notes, respites and co-orderers share of current remainders
     were considered.
     It is impossible to increase the credit line.")))
 (PREMISE
  (#Wff (THE PERSONAL.SHARE OF REMAINDERS IS ?VAR197)
   #Wff (THE RESPITES OF ORDER IS ?VAR196)
   #Wff (THE LAST.WEEK OF PAYMENT IS ?VAR195)
   #Wff (THE DEMAND.NOTES OF ORDER IS ?VAR194)
   #Wff ((> ?VAR194 2) OR (THE LIMIT OF ORDER IS CONSERVATIVE.LIMIT)
         OR (> ?VAR195 4) OR (THE BLOCKING OF ORDER IS ON)
         OR (> ?VAR196 0) OR (> ?VAR197 5000)))))
```

Frames may be used efficiently if various interrelations between different objects and object-classes have to be represented (e.g. different products being assembled from a stock of partly identical components). In KREDIT this capability is seldom used since the only objects are the specific customers and classification and storage of customer data is handled by conventional software. It is not intended to change this assignment of tasks.

3 A Sample Session with KREDIT

We will now give an example of the dialogue of a field representative and KREDIT concerning one of the company's customers. Let's call her Rosa Kleiber. Here are the relevant parts of her file:

name: Rosa Kleiber	street: Heilbronner Str. 51	city: 6900 Heidelberg
district: 013114100	tel.no.: 0621/685007	date of birth: 17.7.44
customer no.: 2927230	customer since: 4 72	credit limit: 3600
remainder: 3522.51	arrears: 1064.00	demand class: 3
respites: 0	sales this period: 1910.00	sales -1 period: 4200
sales -2 periods: 0	sales -3 periods: 1500	sales -4 periods: 4700
paid this month: 500.00	paid -1 month: 400	paid -2 months: 400

Table 1: Parts of a customer's data file.

Ms. Kleiber was born in 1944 and lives in Heidelberg. She has been a customer of the company since April 1972. Her credit limit is DM 3600.-. Although sales to Ms. Kleiber in this period amount to only DM 1910.- and the remainder is less than the limit she is in arrears with DM 1064.- and therefore she received already 3 requests for payment. We assume now that Ms. Kleiber has sent in an order for goods with a value of DM 800.-. After entering the customer number and the value the system displays the screen shown in figure 2.

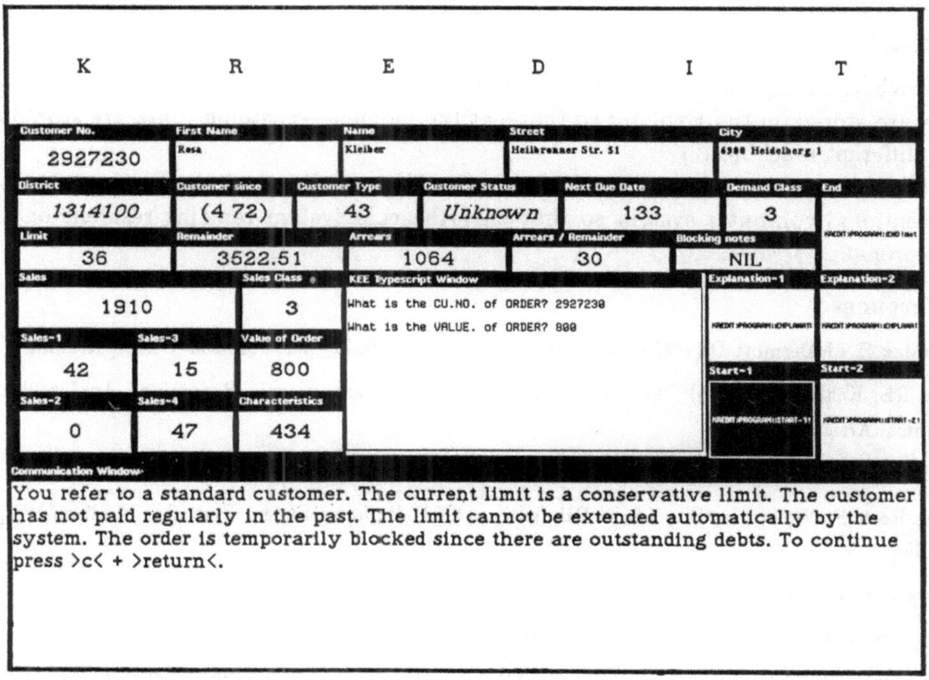

Figure 2.

In the center of the screen we see KEE's "typescript window"—this is the window KREDIT uses for displaying questions to the field representative. Also, the user's answers or questions are entered here. In the first two rows we find customer number, address, etc. The most important data are displayed in the third row: here we have credit limit, remainder, arrears and blocking notes. To the left of the typescript window we see the last sales (numbers are to be multiplied by 100) and on the right side follow some system control-buttons. In the communication window at the bottom of the screen KREDIT displays results and recommendations.

After we entered Ms. Kleiber's customer number and the value of the new order KREDIT analyzes customer data and presents the first results in the communication window: due to outstanding payments the new order is blocked temporarily and at the moment it is not possible to extend Ms. Kleiber's credit limit.

On the next two screens displayed in figure 3 KREDIT informs the field representative that the order may only be booked after the customer has balanced his account. In this specific data situation the company distinguishes according to nationality of customers and the user is asked to give this detail (typescript window). As a preliminary result of this Start-1 session the field representative is instructed to call the customer by phone.

Assuming that Ms. Kleiber has settled her account in the meantime—and the field representative has checked this information with the firm's accounting system—the Start-2 part of KREDIT will accept and book the order (see figure 4) and the system's handling of this order is completed.

Remark

A drawback of the existing version of KREDIT is that the rule system as well as customer data are stored on the Explorer so that—at the moment—customer data are stored on two different machines.

Work is now in progress (see Tüshaus (1987)) intending to link the Explorer to a conventional computer system so that only the rule system remains resident on the Explorer.

References

Charniak E, McDermott D (1985) Introduction to Artificial Intelligence. Addison-Wesley, Reading

Fikes RE, Kehler TP (1985) The Role of Frame-Based Representation in Reasoning. An IntelliCorp Technical Article

Harmon P, King D (1986) Expertensysteme in der Praxis. Oldenbourg, München

Hayes-Roth F, Waterman DA, Lenat DB (eds.) (1983) Building Expert Systems. Addison-Wesley, Reading

Sperry Corporation (1985) KEE RULESYSTEM2 Reference Manual, USA

Sperry Corporation (1985) KEE User's Manual, KEE Software Level 2.0, USA

Tüshaus, U (1987) Decision Support for Qualitative Data Analysis—KEE Shell linked to FORTRAN Programs. Paper in this volume.

Winston, PH (1984) Artificial Intelligence, 2nd ed. Addison-Wesley, Reading

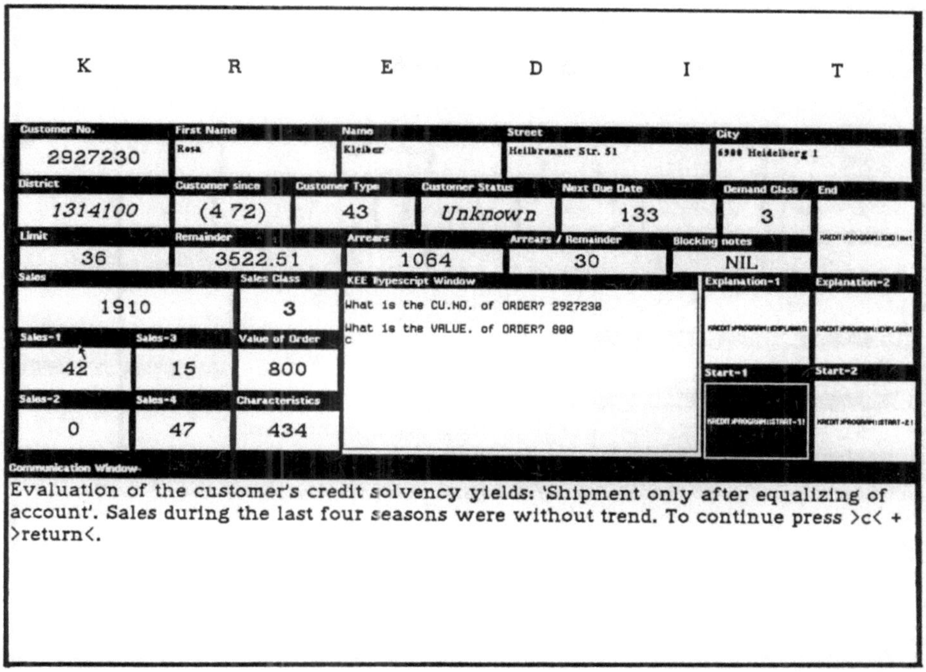
K R E D I T
Customer No.
2927230
First Name
Rosa
Name
Kleiber
Street
Heilbronner Str. 51
City
6900 Heidelberg 1
District
1314100
Customer since
(4 72)
Customer Type
43
Customer Status
Unknown
Next Due Date
133
Demand Class
3
End
Limit
36
Remainder
3522.51
Arrears
1064
Arrears / Remainder
30
Blocking notes
NIL
Sales
1910
Sales Class
3
KEE Typescript Window
What is the CU.NO. of ORDER? 2927230
What is the VALUE. of ORDER? 800
c
Explanation-1
Explanation-2
Sales-1
42
Sales-3
15
Value of Order
800
Start-1
Start-2
Sales-2
0
Sales-4
47
Characteristics
434
Communication Window
Evaluation of the customer's credit solvency yields: 'Shipment only after equalizing of account'. Sales during the last four seasons were without trend. To continue press >c< + >return<.

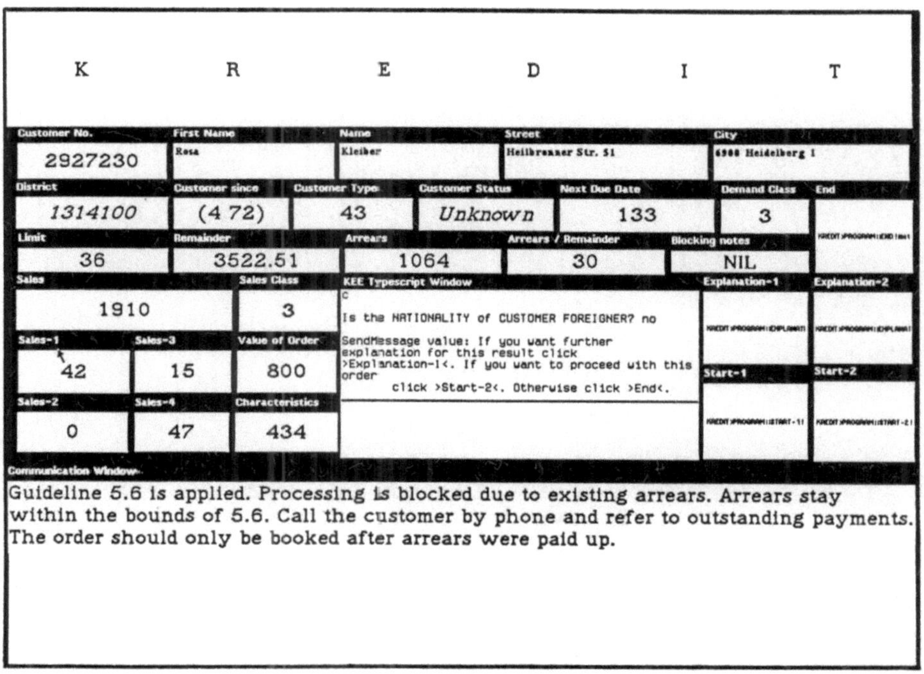
K R E D I T
Customer No.
2927230
First Name
Rosa
Name
Kleiber
Street
Heilbronner Str. 51
City
6900 Heidelberg 1
District
1314100
Customer since
(4 72)
Customer Type
43
Customer Status
Unknown
Next Due Date
133
Demand Class
3
End
Limit
36
Remainder
3522.51
Arrears
1064
Arrears / Remainder
30
Blocking notes
NIL
Sales
1910
Sales Class
3
KEE Typescript Window
c
Is the NATIONALITY of CUSTOMER FOREIGNER? no
SendMessage value: If you want further explanation for this result click >Explanation-1<. If you want to proceed with this order click >Start-2<. Otherwise click >End<.
Explanation-1
Explanation-2
Sales-1
42
Sales-3
15
Value of Order
800
Start-1
Start-2
Sales-2
0
Sales-4
47
Characteristics
434
Communication Window
Guideline 5.6 is applied. Processing is blocked due to existing arrears. Arrears stay within the bounds of 5.6. Call the customer by phone and refer to outstanding payments. The order should only be booked after arrears were paid up.

Figure 3.

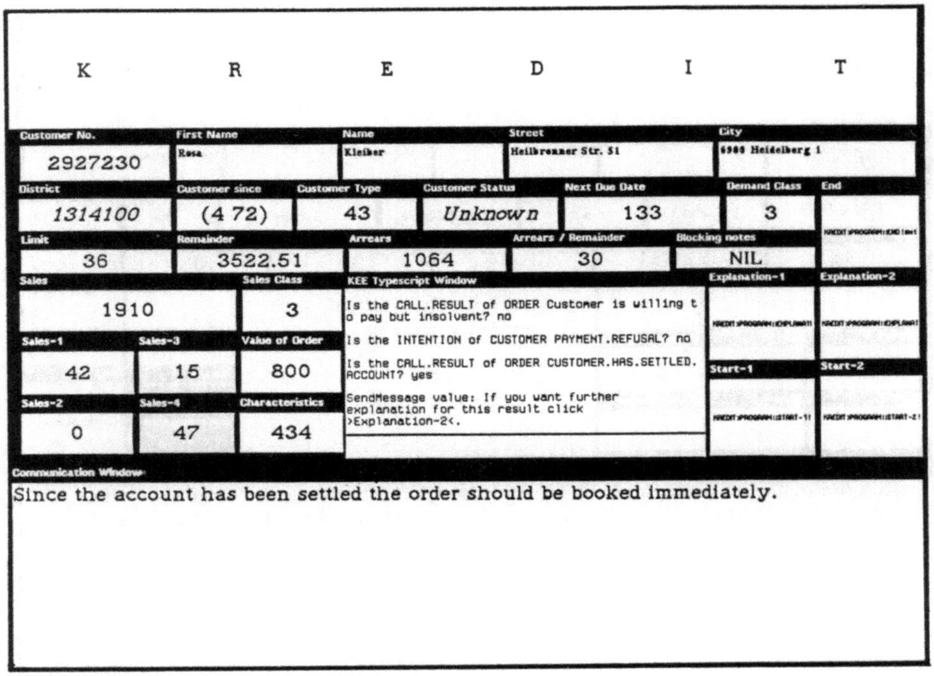
K R E D I T
Customer No.
2927230
First Name
Rosa
Name
Kleiber
Street
Heilbronner Str. 51
City
6900 Heidelberg 1
District
1314100
Customer since
(4 72)
Customer Type
43
Customer Status
Unknown
Next Due Date
133
Demand Class
3
End
Limit
36
Remainder
3522.51
Arrears
1064
Arrears / Remainder
30
Blocking notes
NIL
Sales
1910
Sales Class
3
KEE Typescript Window
Is the CALL.RESULT of ORDER Customer is willing to pay but insolvent? no
Is the INTENTION of CUSTOMER PAYMENT.REFUSAL? no
Is the CALL.RESULT of ORDER CUSTOMER.HAS.SETTLED.ACCOUNT? yes
SendMessage value: If you want further explanation for this result click >Explanation-2<.
Explanation-1
Explanation-2
Sales-1
42
Sales-3
15
Value of Order
800
Start-1
Start-2
Sales-2
0
Sales-4
47
Characteristics
434
Communication Window
Since the account has been settled the order should be booked immediately.

Figure 4.

A Decision Support System for Vehicle Scheduling in Public Transport

J.R. Daduna
Hamburger Hochbahn Aktiengesellschaft
Hamburg, Germany

Summary

In urban mass transit the timetable is determined by various political, social, economic and other factors. Making use of a module which is part of the HOT (*H*amburg *O*ptimization *T*echniques) decision support system, it is possible to alter input data in order to decrease the number of required vehicle schedules. The range of available transportation services has not to be reduced. By using this system as well, more trips may be offered for a fixed fleet size, especially in peak hours.

This special technique for vehicle scheduling is based on an assignment algorithm with an additional constraint. In an interactive procedure a sensitivity analysis will be executed during which only the departure time of a trip or special delay buffers are at users' disposal. Applications in practice show favourable results for different mass transit companies.

1 Introduction

Effective planning activities in public mass transit companies essentially depend on vehicle scheduling. In this phase of the planning process all trips on service are linked to sequences (blocks), which are assigned to buses for a day's work.The maximal number of blocks in peak hours determines the fleet size while the sum of vehicle hours produces a lower bound for staff requirement.

Manual working in solving such combinatorial problems is bounded by the size of the data set and the complexity which arises out of it. The results of recent research in this field of operations research show significant breakthroughs in model building and implementation of efficient algorithms. In conjunction with developments in computer technology it will be possible to solve these problems using computer-aided planning systems. An overview for this field of activities is given by Magnanti (1981), Wren (1981), Bodin, Golden, Assad and Ball (1983) and Rousseau (1985).

Application of these planning systems is, of course, connected with further objectives. Staff can expect to be relieved of routine work involved in manual methods. Using such instruments, it will be possible to gain a higher quality of work and to handle additional timetables. At the same time the subjective influence on planning processes may be reduced to a minimum by fixing rules.

The Hamburger Hochbahn Aktiengesellschaft has developed the HOT programme system which will be used for computer-aided planning of vehicle and staff operations in urban mass transit companies. This software package includes data management using a relational data base as well as vehicle scheduling, duty scheduling, and duty rostering.

A special component of vehicle scheduling is realized by sensitivity analysis which will be used to examine the results of strategic planning (determining the service level) from the view of operational planning. Making use of this module, the schedules which we obtain in the vehicle scheduling procedure, are analyzed, as to whether it will be possible to reduce the number of blocks in a peak hour by changing input data only in a small given range.

The proposed solution procedure is independent of the number of depots, because a schedule first - cluster second strategy is used. Assigning the trips to depots or to a set of depots, the multi-depot problem will be solved by including special constraints in the model.

2 Description of the Problem

Especially during the peak hours the gap between the distribution curves of the trips on service and the blocks yields theoretical savings (see Fig. 1). Making use of an interactive optimization procedure, possible alterations of input data are determined. To what extent potential savings will be realized depends on the decision of the user and is based on his knowledge of traffic structure, line network and timetable data.

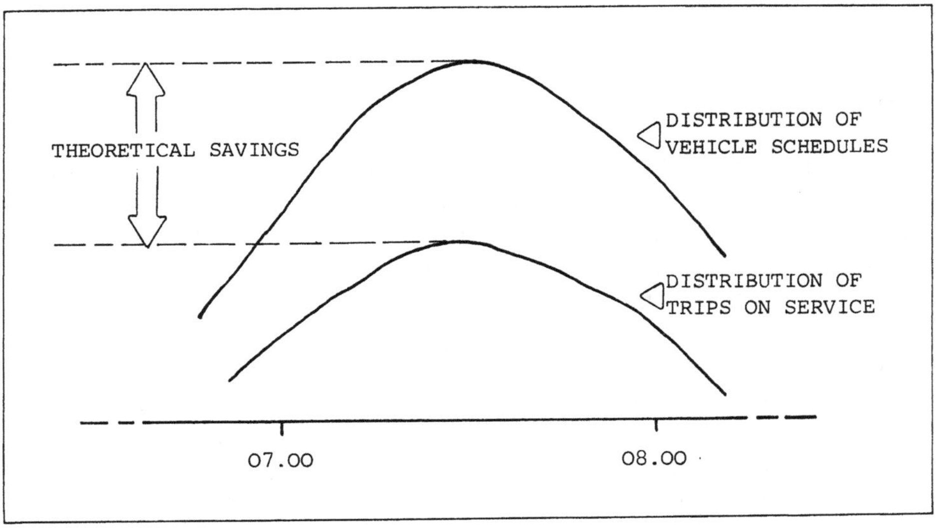

Figure 1: Distribution curves during the morning peak hour

The existing difficulties and the possibility of putting such a module into operation may be demonstrated using the example shown in Fig. 2. Carrying out eight trips on service we need five vehicles, because only three links can be realized. This result is a consequence of the data structure which does not allow to link the trip of line 140, ending in NGR at 7.03 p.m. with the trip of line 240, starting in WUB at 7.16 p.m..

One minute is missing since the necessary deadhead trip takes eight minutes while a post-layover of five and a pre-layover of one minute is required.

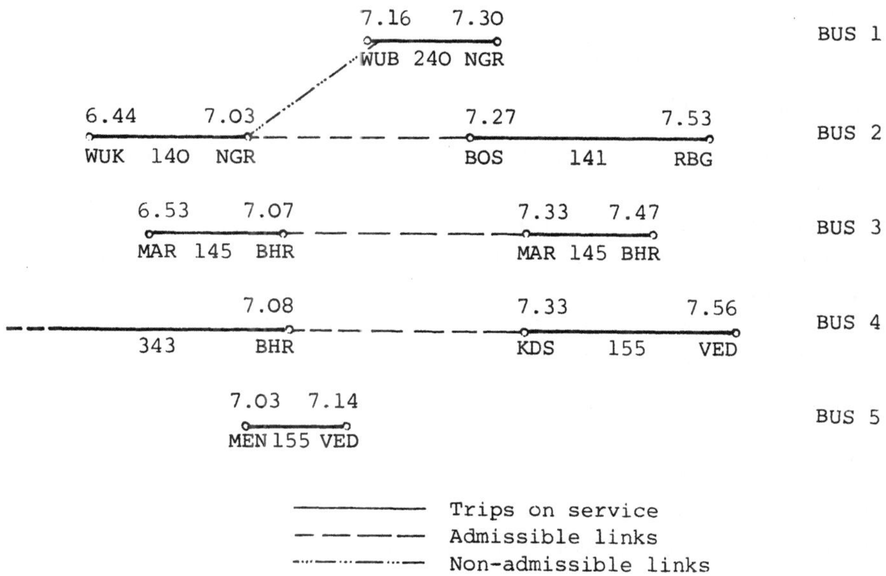

LAYOVER:

Trip on service to deadhead trip	1 min
Trips on service on the same line	2 min
Trips on service on different lines	5 min

DURATION OF DEADHEAD TRIPS:

	BOS	KDS	MAR	WUB
BHR	11	11	8	28
NGR	11	28	25	8
VED	21	11	20	38

Figure 2: Solution without deviation (example)

This result will certainly be unsatisfactory for the planning staff. Therefore we must look for alterations of special input data. But, of course, there exist essential limitations:

- It is not permitted to reduce the offered service level, which is given by the timetable. The total number of trips on service as well as routes and running times have to remain unchanged.

- In-company and contractual agreements are not allowed to be violated, e.g. layover-times and the duration of deadhead trips.

Nevertheless, it will be possible to alter departure times in a small given range according to circumstances, because this will be not a reduction but only a marginal alteration without consequences to the service level. The possible range is determined by the following aspects:

- The fixed cyclic time service has to remain essentially unchanged.

- Additional trips during peak hours are not allowed to run behind a trip on service. The difference between the departure times of these trips also may not exceed a given range, because otherwise the objective to relieve the corresponding trip on service cannot be attained.

- Connections at interchange points to other lines or different means of transport must be considered.

School trips and trips on contract hire, which are not published in the timetable, yield a greater margin to the decision maker than regular trips on service. In these cases, it only must be guaranteed that the vehicle arrives in time before start of lesson or work.In addition, special delay buffers may be reduced, since they are fixed independently by the planning staff and not by in-company or contractual agreements. Therefore, it is possible to vary these special input data within a given range.

The possible alterations offered by sensitivity analysis are:

- Altering the departure time of the first or the second trip on service.

- Reducing the delay buffer.

For the given example we can shift the departure time for the trip on line 140 as well as on line 240. The necessary alteration amounts to only one minute. The adaption of input data produces a solution which yields a saving of one vehicle (see Fig. 3).

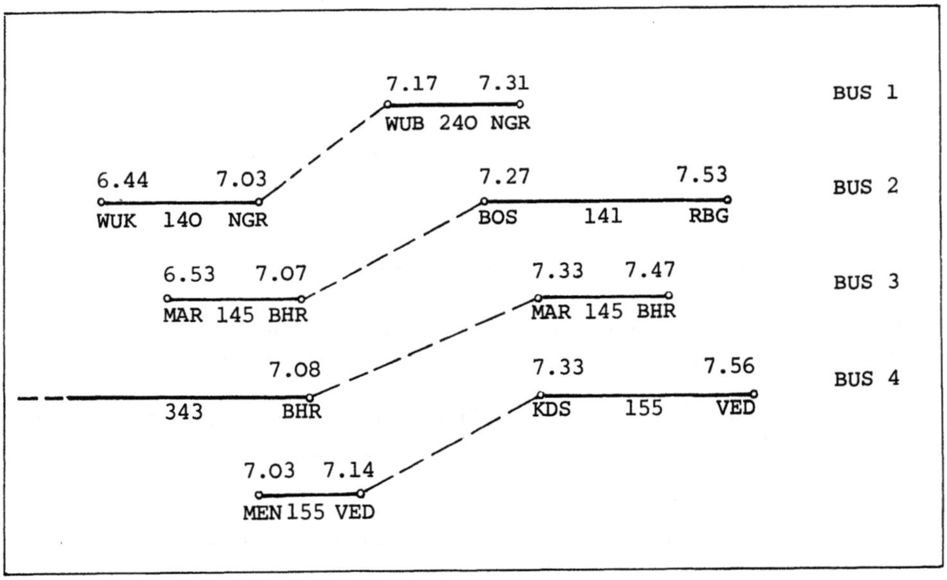

Figure 3: Solution with a deviation on departure times (example)

The given example shows a simple structure. Therefore, we can not assess whether the planning staff will be unable to find out such savings in more complex examples.

Indeed, different reasons may lead to situations in which such possibilities are not recognized.

This problem results from the following facts:

- In the process of planning the service level, the vehicle scheduling problem as a step of operational planning is not taken into consideration.
- Solving such problems in practice, the planning staff must find out possibilities for improvements from a great number of blocks.
- The complex structure results in a situation, where even well-trained and practised staff will usually be unable to identify potential savings.
- Making use of manual methods, it is impossible to spend enough time on such complex problems.

3 Mathematical Formulation

Vehicle scheduling problems show at least two objectives. The main objective is to minimize the number of blocks in peak hours (see Mojsilovic (1983), Luedtke (1985)). Besides this, the sum of deadhead times between two linked trips may be reduced in adherence to given standard working conditions.

To solve such problems using optimization algorithms, the complex structure of real world data must be reflected in a model. This process of aggregating different data is the most important step in the development of computer-aided systems, because the practical use of the results gained mainly depends on the quality of forming models.

The basic data for vehicle scheduling are the trips which will be fixed by a timetable. Since one bus may do more than one trip in the course of a day, we get the combinatorial problem of assigning trips to vehicles in such a way that (see Carraresi, Gallo (1984)):

- Each trip has to be carried out by exactly one vehicle.
- A given set of constraints has to be satisfied.
- An objective function has to be minimized.

At first, for linking two trips i and j we must take into account the following data:

$$\begin{aligned} \delta(ij) &:= \text{duration of a deadhead trip,} \\ \Delta^a(i(j)) &:= \text{pre-layover and delay buffer,} \\ \Delta^d(j(i)) &:= \text{post-layover.} \end{aligned}$$

These Δ-values which result from operations constraints are dependent on the linked trips.

A link between two trips i and j with i preceeding j will be admissible if the following conditions are satisfied:

$$s(i) + d(i) + \Delta^a(i(j)) + \delta(ij) + \Delta^d(j(i)) \leq s(j) \tag{1}$$

and

$$s(j) - \{s(i) + d(i)\} \leq T(\max) \tag{2}$$

with $s(i)$ as the departure time and $d(i)$ as the running time for trip i while $T(\max)$ defines a range to link two trips. Furthermore, the trips must be served by vehicles of the same type and must be assigned to the same depot or group of depots.

Constraints (1) and (2) only yield admissible links without a qualified rating. This part of forming models for vehicle scheduling is related to the first objective of minimizing the number of blocks. With respect to the second objective to reduce the sum of deadhead times, we also need, in addition to the quantitative conditions, qualitative weights for each link.

Defining such a value for each pair of trips, the result will be a matrix C of coefficients $c(ij)$ with:

$$c(ij) \begin{cases} \in [0; c^* \ll \infty] & \text{if it is possible to link trip } i \text{ and } j \\ = \infty & \text{otherwise} \end{cases} \tag{3}$$

The given problem may be solved as an assignment problem (see Daduna (1986) p. 313).

For the sensitivity analysis a modified coefficient matrix $\hat{C}^R$ (where R is a given number of cycles) is used with:

$$\hat{c}^R(ij) \begin{cases} = 0 & \text{if it is possible to link trip } i \text{ and } j \text{ without} \\ & \text{any deviation} \\ \in]0; \hat{c}^* \ll \infty] & \text{if it is possible to link trip } i \text{ and } j \text{ in the} \\ & \text{range of a given deviation} \\ = \infty & \text{otherwise} \end{cases} \tag{4}$$

The matrix $\hat{C}^R$ has to be updated in each iteration in accordance to users' decision (see step III in the next chapter). This extended combinatorial problem is solved by making use of an assignment algorithm with an additional constraint which can be formulated as follows:

$$\text{minimize} \quad Z_r = \sum_{i=1}^{n} \sum_{j=1}^{n} \hat{c}^R(ij)\, x(ij) \tag{5}$$

with the restrictions

$$\sum_{i=1}^{n} x(ij) = 1 \qquad \forall j = 1, 2, \ldots, n \tag{6}$$

$$\sum_{j=1}^{n} x(ij) = 1 \qquad \forall i = 1, 2, \ldots, n \tag{7}$$

$$x(ij) \in \{0; 1\} \qquad \forall i, j = 1, 2, \ldots, n \tag{8}$$

$$r \leq R \tag{9}$$

where r is the realized number of cycles for the given R.

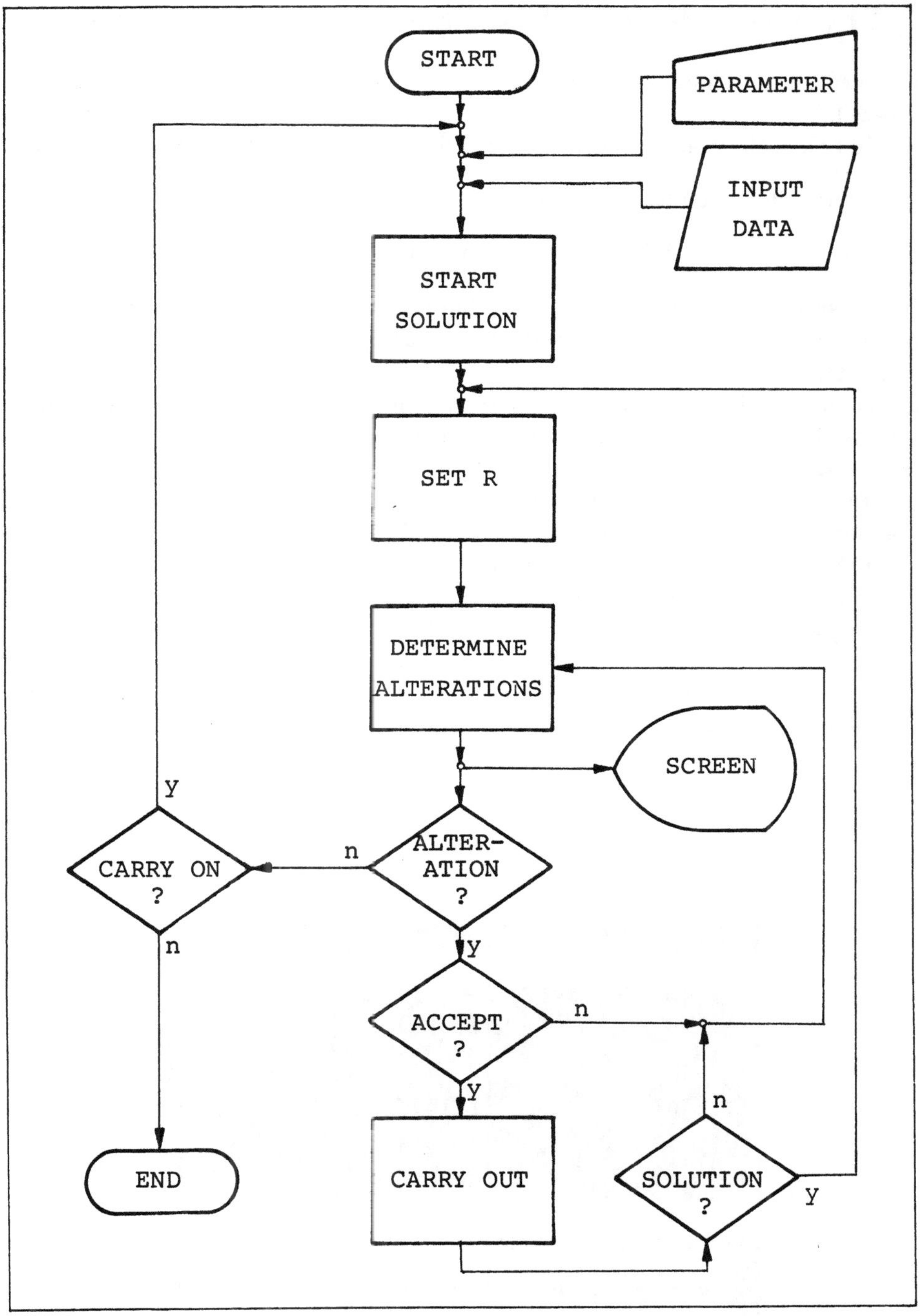

Figure 4: Flow chart for the sensitivity analysis

4 The Completion of the Sensitivity Analysis

The procedure is divided into four main steps.

Step I:

In the first step, the user must define the special parameters for the sensitivity analysis:

- maximal deviation for the departure time,
- duration of the peak hour under examination.

On the basis of these parameters and the input data for vehicle scheduling, which are stored in a relational data base, the coefficients $\hat{c}^R(ij)$ are computed.

Step II:

In a second step, for $R = \infty$ a first optimal solution is determined. The value of r represents the number of blocks in the peak hour without any deviation.

Step III:

In the third step the interactive part of this process takes place (see Fig. 4). The number of cycles R is set to $r - 1$. To get a feasible solution, input data must be changed. Starting with an actual optimal basic solution in a re-optimization procedure possibilities to attain savings are determined. These modifications are shown on screen (see Fig. 5) successively.

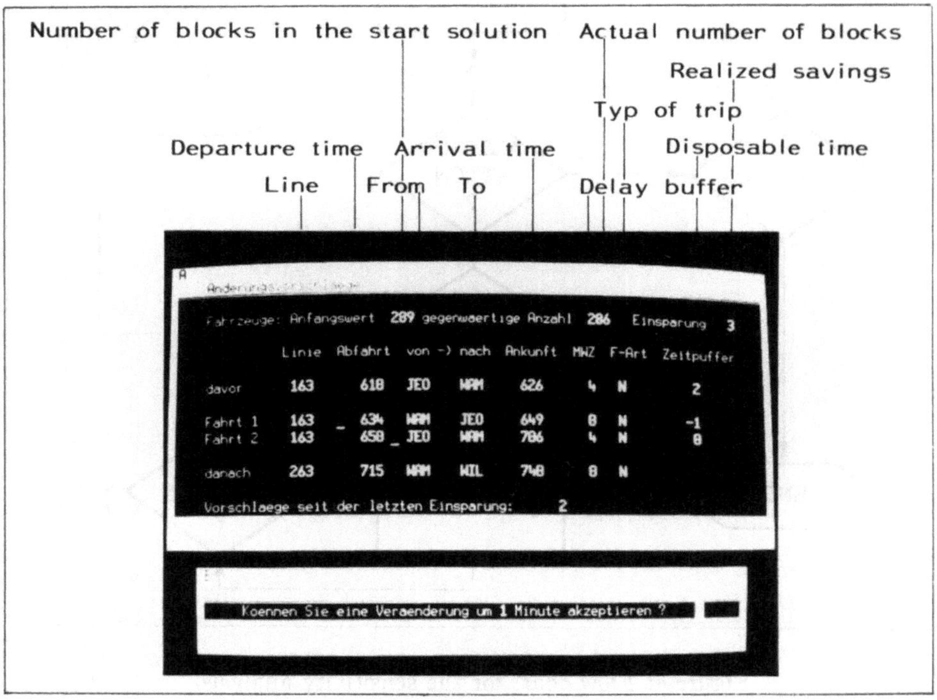

Figure 5: Example for a screen during the interactive procedure

The user must decide whether he will accept a suggested alteration or not. If he does not accept, the next suggestion will be shown. After a finite number of possible alterations a saving of one vehicle will be attained or the procedure is finished, since no feasible solution can be realized. If the procedure is carried on, R will be reduced and the re-optimization starts again. The sensitivity analysis may be repeated with different parameters or different decisions made by the user. The completion will be finished if there is no possibility for repetition or if satisfactory results are gained.

Step IV:
In the last step, the user must choose from the set of solutions what is best in his opinion. The neccessary alterations of the input data have to be carried out in the data base.

5 Conclusions

Making use of the sensitivity analysis in practice we see different aspects of the results:

- The fleet size may be reduced by decreasing the number of blocks during the peak hours. For a fixed fleet size additional capacities are made available to increase the offered service level.

- The structure of the duties (see Bodin, Golden, Assad, Ball (1983) pp. 123; Daduna (1987) pp. 78) may be improved, because the number of split duties and extra duty pieces are reduced. This may effect savings on staff costs in two ways. For split duties, which are compounded of two duty pieces with an interruption of more than two or three hours, normally, additional payments are arranged by contractual or in-company agreements. Extra duty pieces must be treated (and paid) as straight duties of a given length, if it will not be possible to serve these short pieces by workshop or temporary personel.

Carrying out the sensitivity analysis, we must analyse all peak hours separately. If the number of blocks in all peak hours is nearly the same, we only get savings in the fleet size by examining all intervals. In the case that one dominant peak exists, effects on the fleet size may be gained solely for one interval. The reduction of the number of blocks for the non-dominant peak hours yields no reduction in fleet size but a better structure of duties.

The savings on operational and staff cost gained by using this module cannot be quantified exactly, because it is impossible to isolate the influences of other system components. Comparative studies between manually compiled schedules and computer-aided schedules prepared by different companies revealed that savings on operational and staff costs in a range of 2 to 6% are achievable. But one of the most important results is a reduction of the number of vehicles used during peak hours, as has been proved by comparisons. Depending on the size of the company involved, these savings may amount to 8% of the vehicles used so far.

References

Bodin L, Golden B, Assad A, Ball M (1983) Routing and Scheduling of Vehicles and Crews: The State of the Art. Computer and Operations Research 10: 63–211

Carraresi P, Gallo G (1984) Network Models for Vehicle and Crew Scheduling. European Journal of Operations Research 16: 139–151

Daduna JR (1986) Die Anwendung einer dialog-gesteuerten Sensitivitätsanalyse bei der Fahrzeugumlaufbildung in Verkehrsbetrieben, in: Operations Research Proceedings 1985. Springer, Berlin, Heidelberg, pp 310–317

Daduna JR (1987) DV-gestützte Dienstplanbildung für das Fahrpersonal in Verkehrsbetrieben — Problematik und Lösungsansätze, in: Operations Research Proceedings 1986. Springer, Berlin, Heidelberg, pp 76–85

Luedtke LK (1985) RUCUS II: A Review of System Capabilities, in: Rousseau J-M (ed.) Computer Scheduling of Public Transport 2. North Holland, Amsterdam, New York, Oxford, pp 61–115

Magnanti TL (1981) Combinatorial Optimization and Vehicle Fleet Planning: Perspectives and Prospects. Networks 11: 179–213

Mojsilovic M (1983) Verfahren für die Bildung von Fahrzeugumläufen, Dienstplänen und Dienstreihenfolgenplänen in Verkehr und Transport, in: HEUREKA '83 — Optimierung in Transport und Verkehr, Karlsruhe, pp 178–191

Rousseau J-M (ed.)(1985) Computer Scheduling of Public Transport 2. North Holland, Amsterdam, New York, Oxford

Wren A (ed.) (1981) Computer Scheduling of Public Transport 1. North Holland, Amsterdam, New York, Oxford

Developing a Decision Support System for Personnel Disposition in a Garage —Experiences Using the KEE Shell

M. Demann, M. Schader and U. Tüshaus
Institut für Informatik, Universität der Bundeswehr Hamburg
Holstenhofweg 85, D–2000 Hamburg 70

Summary

Expert system shells offer a number of advantageous features for programmers and knowledge engineers. Typical areas of application are fault diagnosis, data analysis, system configuration, product planning, etc.

A prototype of a decision support system (DSS) covering the area of personnel disposition has been developed at the Institut für Informatik. This task was selected as an example of an area where, typically, more traditional programming techniques are in use today.

A variety of sub-problems come up managing personnel disposition; some of them were tackled successfully with expert system tools, and we feel that knowledge representation techniques may also prove valuable for modeling tasks apart from the "typical" expert system applications.

1 Introduction

During the last year we developed a prototype of a DSS designed to cover the area of personnel disposition at the operational level. We selected a specific garage of the Hamburg Urban Mass Transit Company HHA (Hamburger Hochbahn Aktiengesellschaft) where everyday personnel disposition—allocating duties of a pre-defined timetable to drivers available for disposition—is still performed manually. The need for computerized assistance in that area has been recognized and some systems for general use in practice are currently being developed. It should be pointed out that we do not deal with the problems of defining routes and level of service or vehicle and crew scheduling. Here, typically, heuristics and/or optimization procedures to "solve" the underlying organizational problems are used. For detailed information on these topics see e.g. Rousseau (1985).

We chose one of the largest garages and monitored complete "real life data" in numerous sessions. Our intention was to represent the knowledge extracted from the experts at work.

In this paper we shall describe our experiences mainly from the programmer's point of view, discussing various knowledge representation techniques and their value for our purposes. In section 2 the personnel disposition context will be briefly outlined.

In sections 3 and 4 we discuss the different types of knowledge identified and some problems of program design. A description of the prototyping process is then followed by an overview of the current DSS.

2 Personnel Disposition

Bus service at the HHA is divided into several mainly independent organizational units, called *garages*. Each driver, duty and bus is uniquely assigned to one garage. Mutual independence of these garages allowed us to select one special garage (about 200 drivers) for prototype development without simplifying reality in that regard.

A *duty* is a driver's daily work consisting of several trips. On each type of day (working day, saturday, sunday) there are different duties, but duties of a specific daytype remain fixed during one timetable period (approx. half a year). At each garage 2 or 3 operators are concerned with personnel disposition. Personnel disposition can in this context be defined as "assuring an assignment of duties to drivers (or vice versa) for every day under certain restrictions".

The duties and the number of drivers are (almost) fixed over each timetable period. For this reason it is possible to construct *duty rosters* with a computerized planning process, such providing a default pattern for assignment. The task of the operators then is to adapt these rosters to the existing situation. The assignment procedure can be divided into three parts.

1. Long-term assignment
   One fortnight in advance the duty rosters are manually adapted by the operators considering drivers absent because of vacancies, education etc. Over- and understaffing is detected.

2. Medium-term assignment
   Assignment is done for the drivers and duties not covered by the rosters. The operators constantly adapt the assignment to the changing situation (illnesses etc.). Restrictions of different kinds (to be discussed later) have to be taken into account.

3. Short-term assignment
   At the actual day it is of course more difficult to change the assignment. Therefore, responsibility for personnel disposition is then taken over from the operators by a special "task group". Additional understaffing is usually dealt with by phoning free drivers that are willing to do extra work.

In prototype development we were mainly interested in modelling the second step of the assignment procedure. There we expected most need of "expertise". Step 1 supplies the input necessary for step 2 and thus also has to be included. Information for step 3 is then—as a side effect—also available to the "task group" user.

3 Expert Knowledge

Knowledge concerning the assignment procedure consists of

- general restrictions
- knowledge about legal and union provisions as well as in-company agreements
- knowledge about the company's preferences, i.e., knowledge concerning economic aspects.
- knowledge about the driver's preferences
- knowledge about solution strategies
- knowledge about quality criteria concerning evaluation of a given solution.

General restrictions refer to the fact that some duties require special education (e.g. school bus trips) or include trips not known to all drivers.

Legal and contract provisions form necessary conditions for an assignment. In Germany, for example, a minimum spare time of 10 hours is required between two consecutive duties.

The company's main interest is to keep the monthly amount of work done by each driver as close as possible to the plan to avoid extra payment. The duty rosters take this into account, but whenever manual changes are performed, additional fine tuning is necessary.

The drivers prefer a certain pattern of duty sequences. Either they have the same kind of duty all week (first group of drivers) or they start the working period with late duties and end up with early duties (second group of drivers). Some drivers have additional individual preferences independent of the group they belong to.

The highest level of expertise is required for judging the quality of a given assignment, weighting restrictions and preferences against each other and possibly improving a given solution.

Drivers as well as duties are divided into different partly overlapping groups. Many of the restrictions in the assignment procedure refer to this object classification.

4 Problem Analysis

Before and during prototype development we identified a number of subproblems to be solved.

Data Management Our primary intention was to detect rules used by the operators, build them into a system and experiment with them. Of course, for using rules it was necessary to include a certain amount of data. For example, for every duty at least information about the begin and the end must be available. The group structure of drivers and duties must be modelled, so that the rules can handle them in a straightforward way. Most importantly, the actual state of the assignment for each of the next 14 days must be accessable simultaneously. This requires a lot of bookkeeping.

Numerous checking procedures may help maintaining consistency among the data. The duty rosters must be included to serve as a default assignment.

Knowledge Representation If knowledge about restrictions, regulations and preferences is encoded in rules it is necessary to "make these rules work", i.e., to make the system behave according to the rules. Solution strategies currently used by the operators may be dictated by their manual style of work. Instead of trying to imitate their strategies computer usage allows to include more experimenting and various search procedures.

User Interface It was intended to design a user interface satisfying the practical needs of a potential non-programmer user.

The terminology had to conform to the technical language used in the garage. A communication window may propose actions, give explanations etc. With extensive use of a mouse- and menu-technique the keybord input can be restricted to a minimum. Lots of information must be available to the user simultaneously; this requires an intelligent screen layout.

Complete control over the assignment procedure should be left to the user by making the use of the rules optional. A variety of syntactic and semantic error checking procedures can help to increase safety of program use.

The requirements described above cause numerous problems as far as program design and development is concerned. Instead of solving all of them simultaneously and from scratch, the technique of *rapid prototyping* was used.

5 Prototyping the DSS

Rapid prototyping is a programming technique commonly used by expert system designers. The expert system idea is to have the expert taking part in the program development process by discussing different prototypes with him. This is mainly done to improve system performance and to verify the rules and the terminology. Our intention was slightly different. We wanted to test a variety of solution techniques and programming tools. Instead of completely designing the system and then encoding it, small examples were generated, tested, and then discarded if necessary. Of course, rapid prototyping is only possible if high level programming languages and tools allow the system designer to concentrate on the model building task relieving him from implementation details.

It soon became evident that, before writing and testing rules, the data management task had to be solved. As soon as the "database" and the corresponding database $\leftrightarrow$ rule interface is defined, implementing the rules becomes straightforward.

The great number of objects to be managed simultaneously leads to certain problems as far as graphical interface and search procedures are concerned. Also, program performance is mainly dependent on appropriate selection of instruments and data representation.

In the following, our experiences with different knowledge representation techniques supplied by the EXPLORER hardware in addition with the KEE expert system shell are described.

5.1 LISP

LISP is the traditional programming language for developing AI applications. LISP programs typically consist of small independent functions thus permitting high modularity. The EXPLORER like other Lisp machines supplies the user with an extremely powerful and interactive LISP environment including graphics, menus, a mouse-sensitive syntax oriented editor and advanced debugging facilities. Certain LISP extensions like the flavor system for object oriented programming and a window system are also provided. The *LIS*t *P*rocessing abilities of LISP make it easy to write the functions necessary for bookkeeping.

```
(DEFMETHOD (fahrer :setze-verhinderung)       ;function called if driver
           (verhinderung fahrername)          ;is to be marked absent.

  (LET ((dienst (SEND self :dienst)))         ;compute current duty of driver.

    (COND ((MEMBER dienst **alle-dienste**)   ;if duty is a regular one, add it
           (SETQ *freie-dienste*              ;to the list of free duties.
                 (CONS dienst *freie-dienste*)))

           ((OR (EQ dienst 'unbesetzt)        ;if driver is marked
                (NOT dienst))                 ;"no assignment" or
                                              ;driver has no duty
           (SETQ *freie-fahrer*
                 (REMQ fahrername             ;remove driver from the list of
                       *freie-fahrer*))))     ;free drivers.

   (SEND self :setze-wochentag verhinderung));in any case, mark driver with
   ))                                         ;reason of absence.
```

Example of LISP function for bookkeeping

5.2 KEE

KEE (Knowledge Engineering Environment) is a powerful hybrid expert system shell. The term hybrid refers to the fact that the abilities of a production rule system are combined with a frame based system for knowledge representation. In the following, some elements of the KEE system are briefly introduced.

Frames The frame concept, first proposed by Minsky (1975), provides a means to describe real world objects or abstract concepts by hierarchically classifying them into groups and subgroups. Information about these objects (frames, in KEE terms *units*) is stored in the so-called *slots*. Slot values can be inherited, i.e., passed down the object hierarchy. Restrictions on slots provide automatic consistency checking. KEE allows creation and modification of units in an interactive mouse- and menu-style thus supporting rapid prototyping. Group structure of units is displayed graphically.

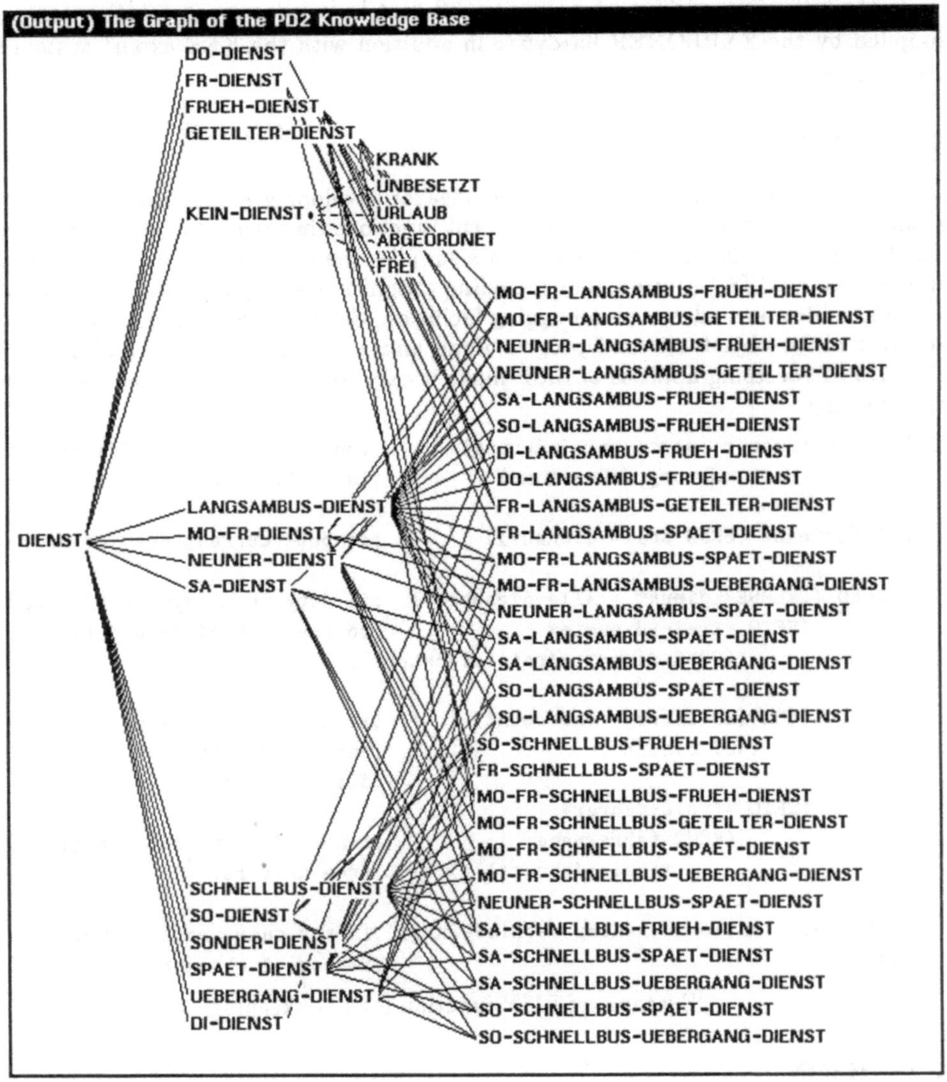

Figure 1: Group structure of duties (Classes only, individual duties are not shown. These would follow on the right side of the graph, see Figure 3)

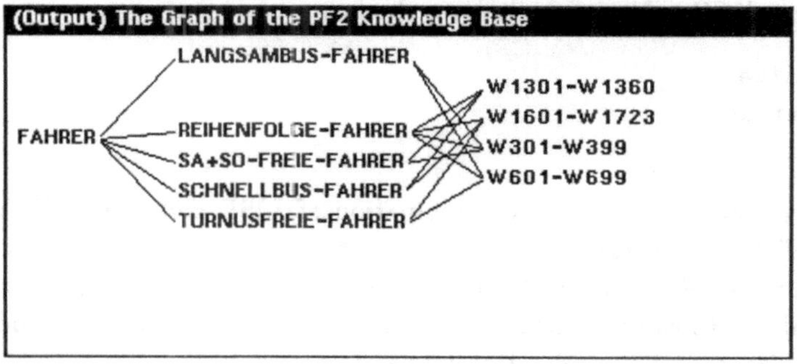

Figure 2: Group structure of drivers

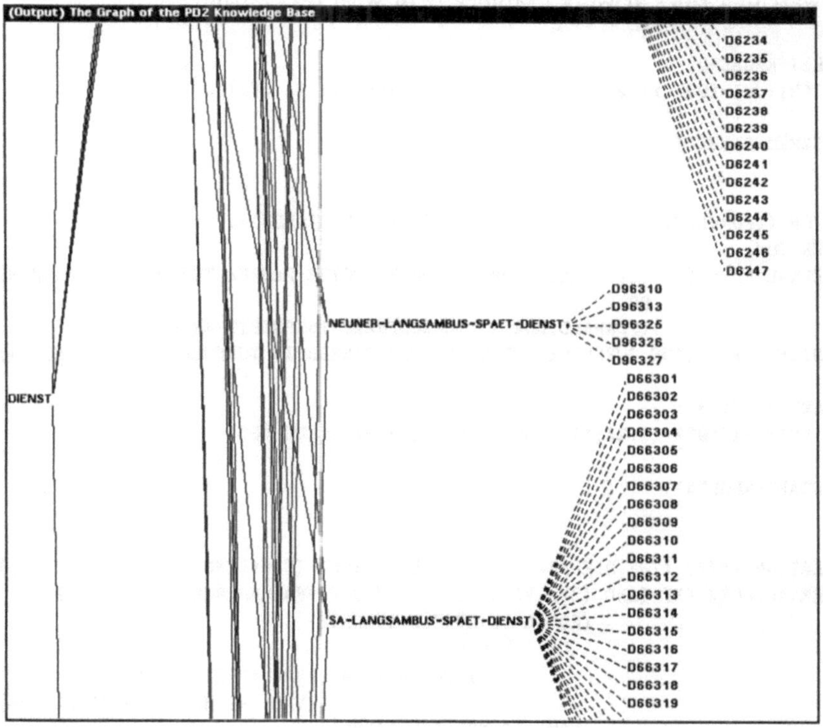

Figure 3: Part of group structure including individual duties

Rulesystem KEE rules generally have the form

```
IF   premise
THEN assertion
DO   action
```

where **premise** is an arbitrary combination of LISP code and WFFs, **assertion** consists of WFFs and **action** is a LISP form. A WFF (well formed formula) is a statement related to the KEE knowledge base (also including LISP conditions) evaluating to a boolean value. Rules are entered by the user in an "external form" and then parsed into the premise, assertion and action (see examples below).

Rules are organized in different rule classes and represented as KEE units. The user has different means to control the reasoning process by

— invoking each rule class separately;
— choosing between backward and forward chaining;
— allowing assertion of new facts with or without user prompt;
— weighting rules in their importance;
— watching rules at work graphically or with text output.

```
(TAGESZEIT-REGEL-2
  ("DE" "21-Jul-1987 11:25:29" "DE" "21-Jul-1987 11:34:47")
  NIL
  (TAGESZEIT-REGELN)
  NIL
  ()
  ((ACTION ((FORWARD.CHAIN 'TURNUSFREIE-TAGESZEIT-REGELN)))
   (ASSERTION)
   (EXTERNAL.FORM (IF (OWN.VALUE TURNUSGRUPPE MUSTER-FAHRER TURNUSFREIE-FAHRER)
                      DO
                      (FORWARD.CHAIN 'TURNUSFREIE-TAGESZEIT-REGELN)))
   (PREMISE (#Wff (THE TURNUSGRUPPE OF MUSTER-FAHRER IS TURNUSFREIE-FAHRER)))))

(DIENSTART-REGEL-3
  ("DE" "21-Jul-1987 11:24:11" "DE" "26-Jul-1987 20:05:45")
  NIL
  (DIENSTART-REGELN)
  NIL
  ()
  ((ASSERTION (#Wff (THE DIENSTART OF MUSTER-DIENST IS **LANGSAMBUS-DIENSTE**)))
   (EXTERNAL.FORM (IF (AND (OWN.VALUE GRUPPE MUSTER-FAHRER SCHNELLBUS-FAHRER)
                           (EQUAL ?WIEVIELE-DIENSTE
                                  (LENGTH
                                    (INTERSECTION (EVAL *FREIE-DIENSTE*)
                                                  (EVAL **SCHNELLBUS-DIENSTE**))))
                           (EQUAL ?WIEVIELE-FAHRER
                                  (LENGTH
                                    (INTERSECTION (EVAL *FREIE-FAHRER*)
                                                  (EVAL **SCHNELLBUS-FAHRER**))))
                           (> (* 1.5 ?WIEVIELE-FAHRER) ?WIEVIELE-DIENSTE))
                      THEN
                      (OWN.VALUE DIENSTART MUSTER-DIENST **LANGSAMBUS-DIENSTE**)))
   (PREMISE
    (#Wff (THE GRUPPE OF MUSTER-FAHRER IS SCHNELLBUS-FAHRER)
```

```
#Wff (?VAR8 = (EVAL **SCHNELLBUS-DIENSTE**))
#Wff (?VAR7 = (EVAL *FREIE-DIENSTE*))
#Wff (?VAR6 = (INTERSECTION ?VAR7 ?VAR8))
#Wff (?WIEVIELE-DIENSTE = (LENGTH ?VAR6))
#Wff (?VAR11 = (EVAL **SCHNELLBUS-FAHRER**))
#Wff (?VAR10 = (EVAL *FREIE-FAHRER*))
#Wff (?VAR9 = (INTERSECTION ?VAR10 ?VAR11))
#Wff (?WIEVIELE-FAHRER = (LENGTH ?VAR9))
#Wff (?VAR12 = (* 1.5 ?WIEVIELE-FAHRER))
#Wff (> ?VAR12 ?WIEVIELE-DIENSTE)))))
```

Examples of KEE-rules

KEE Windows KEE windows are used to display and/or alter slot values of KEE units or to invoke user functions. They are created interactively and can be modified to fit the user's purposes. Both program development speed and control over the knowledge base are increased by the use of KEE windows.

KEE Access to LISP KEE itself is written in LISP and such offers easy access to LISP functions and files. Predefined LISP functions can be used to retrieve or alter information stored in the knowledge base, and create or delete KEE units.

Large amounts of data can be stored in (compiled) LISP files independent from the knowledge base.

5.3 The Flavor System

The flavor system is a LISP extension designed for object oriented programming. Information about objects is stored in value cells and can be inherited like in a frame system. A flavor represents a class of objects. Group structures are defined by combining different flavors. Flavor objects can serve as sink or source of data and therefore provide an easy instrument for data management. Moreover, small LISP functions, called methods can be attached to flavor objects defining their behavior or relationship to other objects. Methods—like explicit values—can be inherited and combined in multiple ways. It is often useful to refer to object properties with similar underlying concepts with equally named methods, although the underlying algorithm may be different.

```
(DEFMETHOD (dienst :dauer) ()              ;duration of a regular duty is
  (- (SEND self :ende)                     ;computed by "end" minus
     (SEND self :beginn)))                 ;"begin"


(DEFMETHOD (geteilter-dienst :dauer) ()    ;for a split duty, duration is
  (- (- (SEND self :ende)                  ;("end" minus
        (SEND self :beginn))               ;"begin") minus
     (SEND self :pausen-dauer)))           ;"duration of break"
```

Example of simple use of flavors: The general method for computing the length of a duty is "overwritten" by a different method for split duties.

The LISP windows and menus are also based upon the flavor system. A variety of flavors can be combined to adapt their behavior to the user's needs. Communication with the rest of the program is easily organized by use of predefined methods. Scrollable menus store a large number of choice items in a small screen area.

6 Overview of the DSS

A typical display offered to the user is shown in Figures 4 and 5.

On the left half of the display a number of mouse sensitive *method actuators* with attached Lisp functions can be invoked by the user. These include:

— selection of any of the 14 days considered

— display of general information or information about drivers and duties

— changing the current asssignment and marking drivers with reason of absence (consistency checks included)

— saving and/or printing the current state of assignment

— selection of drivers and duties accounting for various criteria

The results of search procedures are shown in the big lower right window. Everything displayed on the screen is consistent with the terminology currently used at the garage.

A typical use of the DSS is as follows:
At first, one of the unassigned drivers—preferably with a small workload—is selected. Detailed information on this driver is made available in the five lower right windows.

A feasible solution for a driver is characterized by its duration, begin, end, etc. Using the menus of the upper right window, each of the search criteria (i.e., the duty properties desirable for the driver in question) is now either fixed by the user or is derived by a corresponding class of rules. The duties resulting from the search based on these requirements are then immediately shown. This step can be repeated if the criteria used were too weak or too strong (as indicated by the number of feasible duties found).

For the actual assignment following, more detailed information to base the decision upon is given.

In the same way, for each remaining driver his feasible duties are determined and an assignment is made.

Generally, complete control is left to the user while rule-based help is available upon request.

7 Conclusions

All the tools mentioned in the above section have proven valuable for either prototyping or encoding the current version of the DSS.

In the beginning, interactive programming with the KEE system requiring minor LISP experience helped us in structuring the problem and experimenting with different data representations and object taxonomies. It seems to be a natural choice to handle drivers and duties as KEE units using the frame representation, but soon it became

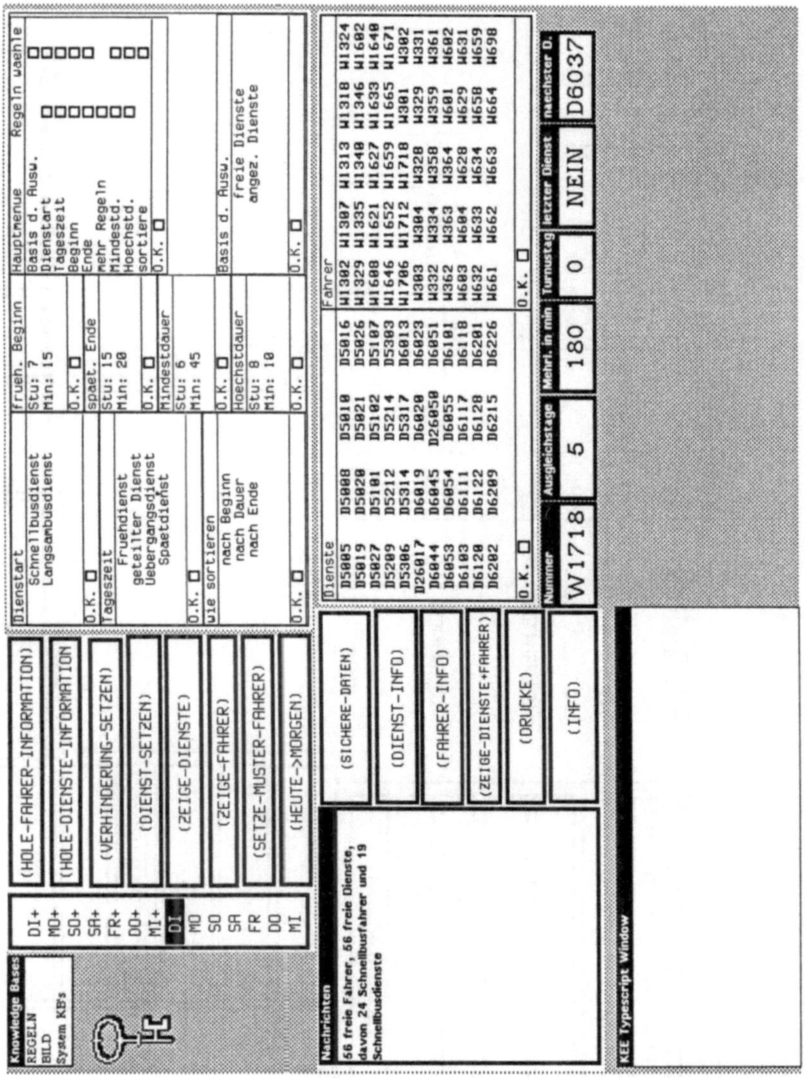

Figure 4: Typical screen of the DSS

evident that performance problems would occur with increasing amount of data. Therefore we mapped the units onto equivalent LISP objects using the flavor system. Our experiences in designing the user interface were quite similar; switching from KEE to LISP offered additional flexibility.

The rules implemented are mainly used to model the assignment restrictions mentioned above. They operate on a menu defining attributes of a prototype duty to be selected; search is then done more efficiently by LISP functions. We found that most of the current rules could have been easily substituted by simple code. The reason is that:

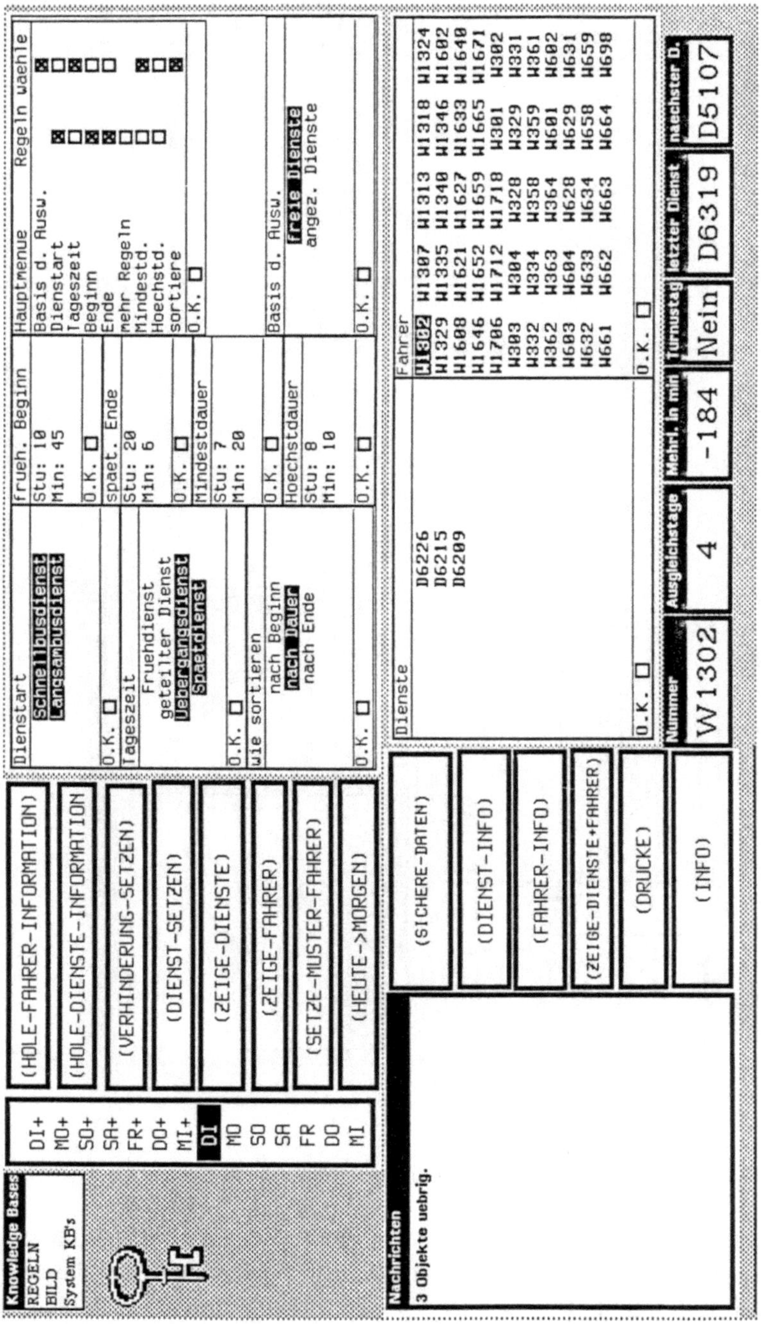

Figure 5: The DSS "at work"

— rule classes contain only few rules with mostly excluding conditions;
— forward chaining is used as reasoning strategy;
— rules do not depend on intermediate results of the reasoning process;
— additional information supplied by the user is not required for invoking the rules.

In order to improve our DSS, heading for "expert system" performance, more knowledge still needs to be added. Especially, for evaluation of a given solution and for leading the user through the whole assignment procedure some "diagnostic" rules are necessary. Here, usage of a rulesystem is clearly preferable to simple LISP coding.

To summarize, we gradually proceeded from the system-provided prototyping environment to a library of problem-specific tools. This was necessary for ensuring the efficiency and flexibility required.

As far as the problem of modelling object taxonomies is concerned we propose to separate the "knowledge" component from the data management task. Therefore, an integrated and easy-to-use connection between a frame based system and a standard database is required.

References

Fikes R, Kehler T (1985) The Role of Frame-Based Representation in Reasoning. Communications of the ACM 28: 904–920

Minsky M (1975) A Framework for Representing Knowledge, in: Winston PH (ed.) The Psychology of Computer Vision, McGraw-Hill, New York, pp 211–277

Rousseau J-M (ed.) (1985) Computer Scheduling of Public Transport 2. North Holland, Amsterdam, New York, Oxford

Sperry Corporation (1985) EXPLORER System, LISP Reference

Sperry Corporation (1985) EXPLORER System, WINDOW SYSTEM Reference

Sperry Corporation (1985) KEE Software Development System, User's Manual for EXPLORER Systems

Sperry Corporation (1985) KEE Software Development System, RULESYSTEM2 Reference Manual for EXPLORER Systems

Sperry Corporation (1985) KEE Software Development System, ActiveImages User Manual

MIDAS: An Expert Debt Management Advisory System*

M. A. H. Dempster† and A. M. Ireland
Department of Mathematics, Statistics and Computing Science
and School of Business Administration
Dalhousie University, Halifax, Nova Scotia, Canada B3H 3J5
†and Balliol College, Oxford, England OX1 3BJ

Summary

This paper describes an ongoing university/industry cooperative project within the context of the Courseware Development Project at Dalhousie University. The project integrates artificial intelligence and management science approaches within an expert decision support system to assist the treasurer of a public electric power utility in his debt management role. The prototype system under development provides optimization, simulation and object-oriented database components at the command of a menu-driven user interface and an interactive rule base. The rule base manages model runs and interprets model results to the user through text, numeric and graphic outputs. Scenario-oriented stochastic programming suggests optimal flotation and refunding decisions; the resulting suggestions can be refined heuristically through the rule base and explored in more detail with stochastic simulations consistent with the postulated scenarios. The system is being written in KEE, LISP and FORTRAN and runs in a distributed hardware and software environment on an Ethernetted Unisys Explorer and DEC MicroVAX II. It represents the use of expert system methodology for advanced mathematical model management, explanation and user interfacing in a rich—but specific—application domain.

Introduction

This paper describes an ongoing cooperative project between the Dalhousie University School of Business Administration (SBA) and a public electric utility to develop an expert decision support and advisory system for debt management. The project, called MIDAS, is being carried out within the Courseware Development Project (CDP) at the SBA. MIDAS is motivated by CDP goals, research interests and practical considerations in decision support systems and expert systems. Section 1 of the paper briefly describes the Courseware Development Project. Section 2 outlines the MIDAS project goals and conceptual design, including an example of the implementation techniques used in the

*This research and the Dalhousie Courseware Development Project are supported by the Bank of Nova Scotia, Digital Equipment Corporation, Unisys Corporation, the Nova Scotia Power Corporation, the Natural Sciences and Engineering Research Council of Canada and the Social Sciences and Humanities Research Council of Canada

prototype system. Section 3 concludes with some observations based on our experiences thus far with the project.

1 The Courseware Development Project

The Dalhousie SBA Courseware Development Project (CDP) was begun in 1985 as a large-scale restructuring of our business education and research efforts to take advantage of the current information technology environment. The project has four main goals: Level 0 provides an integrated electronic office-of-the-future environment for student labs and all faculty, with networked IBM PCs, PC-compatible microcomputers and MicroVAX IIs; electronic mail; and Ethernet and asynchronous commmunication links to DEC mainframes at Dalhousie and other universities. Figure 1 shows the current SBA and University hardware and communications environment.

Level 1 of the CDP promotes development and use of business courseware and computer-managed learning; this is changing the student learning experience from a lecture-oriented to an interactive one and freeing faculty and class time for developing communication and "people" skills. Through Level 2, realistic corporate databases are being developed to support integrated case analysis across disciplines, teaching a real-world corporate viewpoint on business problems.

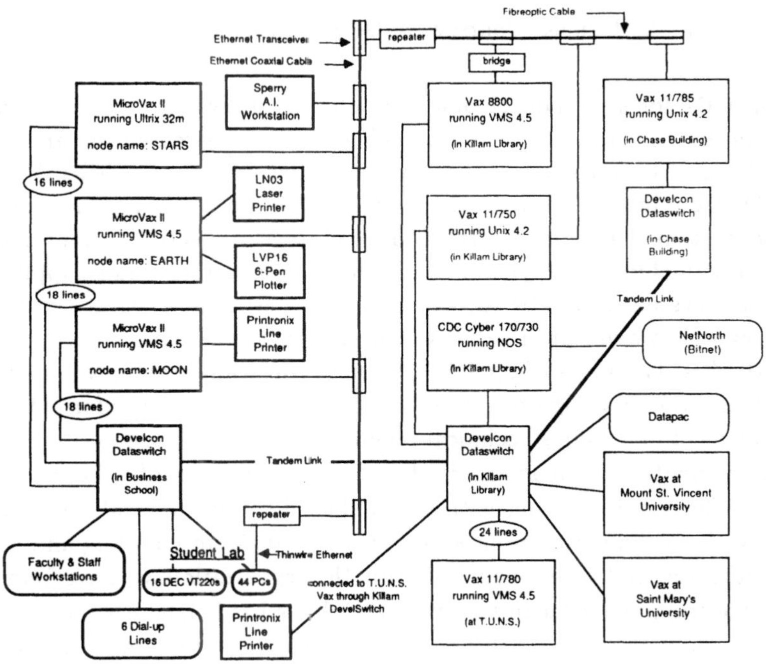

Figure 1: Dalhousie School of Business Administration/
University Computer Systems

Finally, Level 3 supports research and development in artificial intelligence (AI) and business decision support systems (DSS), fostering joint industry-university cooperation, faculty and student involvement and research accomplishments on significant AI/DSS topics. Figure 2 summarizes these project goals and our timetable for their achievement.

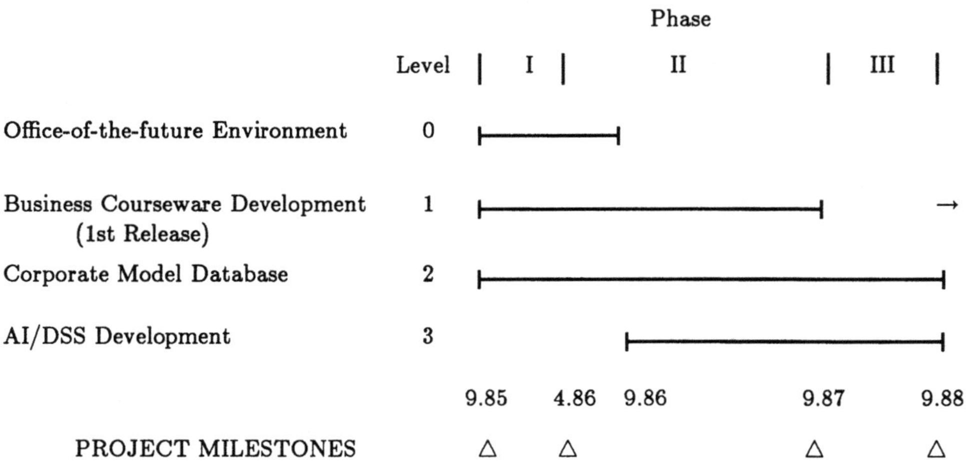

Figure 2: Business Courseware Development Project Diagram

Level 3 of the CDP focuses on developing decision support systems which take advantage of and expand on currently available technology. Our research efforts are carried out primarily with a Unisys Explorer workstation Ethernetted to our MicroVAX IIs and running KEE (from Intellicorp) and Common LISP; we are also experimenting with PC-based expert system shells for research and for student projects. Current and planned research projects include an expert system for R&D management, audit applications, an expert tutoring system and MIDAS, which explores issues in integrating management science and expert systems approaches within a DSS framework.

During the first two years of the CDP, we have learned a great deal about the technical and organizational design of education and research-oriented information systems projects. Our most demanding technical requirement has been the need for equipment and software compatability, made more of a challenge by the conflicting needs of many individuals. After experimenting with stand-alone PCs, we have also opted for a local area network to eliminate the need for extensive diskette handling and monitoring against unauthorized software copying. Within the organization, we have found that extensive, flexible training for faculty, staff and students has helped ease the transition to new work and communication facilities. Course release and research funding, although in short supply, have where available allowed development of new, exciting and useful courseware. Finally, the project has generated extremely favourable student and faculty responses and has provided a vehicle for industry-university cooperation with benefits to both sides.

2 MIDAS

Background and System Goals

The MIDAS system is intended to provide the treasurer of a Canadian Crown-owned electric utility ("the Corporation") with integrated data retrieval, financial modelling and advisory expertise in debt management. From a research perspective, debt management offers a circumscribed yet rich domain in which to study new types of decision support systems. Many debt management tasks are semi-structured in the sense defined by Keen and Scott Morton (1978); complex computation and judgment are both required for sound decisions.

Several modelling techniques have been established for application to debt management. Crane (1971), Bradley and Crane (1972, 1975, 1980), Crane, Knoop and Pettigrew (1977), Lane and Hutchinson (1980) and, more recently, Shapiro (1987) have applied scenario-based stochastic programming to optimizing the debt maturity mix and to managing fixed-income investment portfolios; the latter application transfers directly to debt management with only minor modifications once borrowing is recognized as fixed-income investing (lending) with cash flow directions reversed. These models optimize for major strategic decisions but do not incorporate the detailed risk characteristics of debt portfolios. They also tend to abstract from some detailed decisions faced by debt managers such as the specific features or covenants to include in particular debt issues. Howard (1986) uses simulation to project costs and investigate risk arising from debt management decisions; these techniques allow more detailed calculation of the expected consequences of alternative decisions. Other types of models have also been used; for example, dynamic programming techniques have been applied to bond refunding by Elton and Gruber (1971) and Kalymon (1971).

Although debt management offers a variety of well-established analytical techniques, managers also rely on heuristics to make actual borrowing decisions. Moreover, management science techniques will usually be avoided by managers when they oversimplify decision situations or present "black box" recommendations from problem representations not shared by managers (see Lane and Hutchinson (1980), McInnes and Carleton (1982), Liang (1986)). Expert systems, on the other hand, allow modelling of human non-algorithmic reasoning more likely to be trusted by managers (Buchanan and Shortliffe (1984)). It therefore appears likely that they could be used to model the reasoning of consultants who act as experts to run management science models and interpret their results so that they can be used and trusted by managers. The potential of such expert systems applications has been recognized (Turban and Watkins (1986)) and examples of decision support systems integrating heuristics and algorithmic models are now described in the literature (see, for example, Rauch-Hinden (1985) and Ganascia (1986)). However, we are not aware of a system that uses expert systems techniques to integrate the use of a variety of models as needed to support specific decisions within a selected management domain.

The project's practical motivation arises from the need to control the Corporation's debt expense, its second highest expense after fuel costs. While extensive historical data is now available to the Corporation's Treasurer, only rudimentary spreadsheet programs currently help him and his staff identify or analyze the implications of possible future borrowing decisions. An integrated, specific DSS should (a) improve the quality and quantity of current and future-oriented information available and (b) assist in effectively analyzing and interpreting this information. We have identified strategic planning as the key activity in need of support at the Corporation; our initial goal is to build a prototype system integrating models and heuristics for strategic planning assistance. The system as now under development will be able to be extended in a straightforward way to encompass additional debt management activities and decisions.

The Domain

A debt manager is typically faced with the task of obtaining financing in specified amounts, at specified times, at minimum cost. Costs include issue costs (underwriting commissions, legal and administrative costs), interest costs over the term of the debt and discounts or premiums that arise on issue or early redemption of debt. If borrowing is done in foreign markets, exchange rate fluctuations also result in gains or losses. Because future interest and exchange rates are uncertain, future debt costs are uncertain to the extent that they are not "locked in" at current rates; in general, lower costs are associated with greater risk (cost variability) over time. The debt manager must therefore make a cost-risk tradeoff consistent with the policies of the firm; in practice, this may be done implicitly and intuitively rather than with explicit projections of the variability of future debt costs. Debt management is therefore a portfolio management problem in which a mix of debt types and maturities produces a cost/risk profile consistent with borrower goals.

Major borrowing decisions include selection of borrowing sources used, timing of borrowings, term mix, particular features of bond issues (call features, sinking funds, etc.) as well as the use of foreign debt, interest rate or currency hedges and swap contracts. We can view strategic planning for debt management as development of a plan for a period of time which makes these decisions based on expected rates in the future; a scenario-based plan details decisions which are contingent on future rate movements. The plan may also include targets for debt portfolio composition, hedging, or other characteristics. Typically, a strategic plan is used as a guideline when operational decisions are made, but the individual decisions take into consideration actual rates and economic conditions at decision time.

MIDAS Conceptual Design

The MIDAS system is being developed to demonstrate the integrated use of multiple models within the debt management domain. It concentrates on strategic planning assistance using (a) optimization through stochastic programming, (b) heuristic refinement of optimization results and (c) simulation to analyze in detail the implications of possible decision alternatives. These three components are linked within a knowledge-based interface which acts as a consultant to carry out manager requests without requiring detailed technical knowledge by the manager. Query, simulation and advisory functions may be easily accessed outside the strategic planning framework through a menu system. MIDAS thus mimics an expert consultant who is able to rely on management science models or heuristics as tools and who assists the debt manager in defining, analyzing and recommending possible courses of action. In so doing, it illustrates an integrated decision support system which, while still under user control, functions at a higher level than that of simply an automated data and model manager.

Strategic debt planning consists of creating one or more borrowing plans which are viable alternatives and recommending the most favorable candidate plans to the debt manager. The task is carried out by MIDAS using a generate-evaluate-and-test approach (Figure 3).

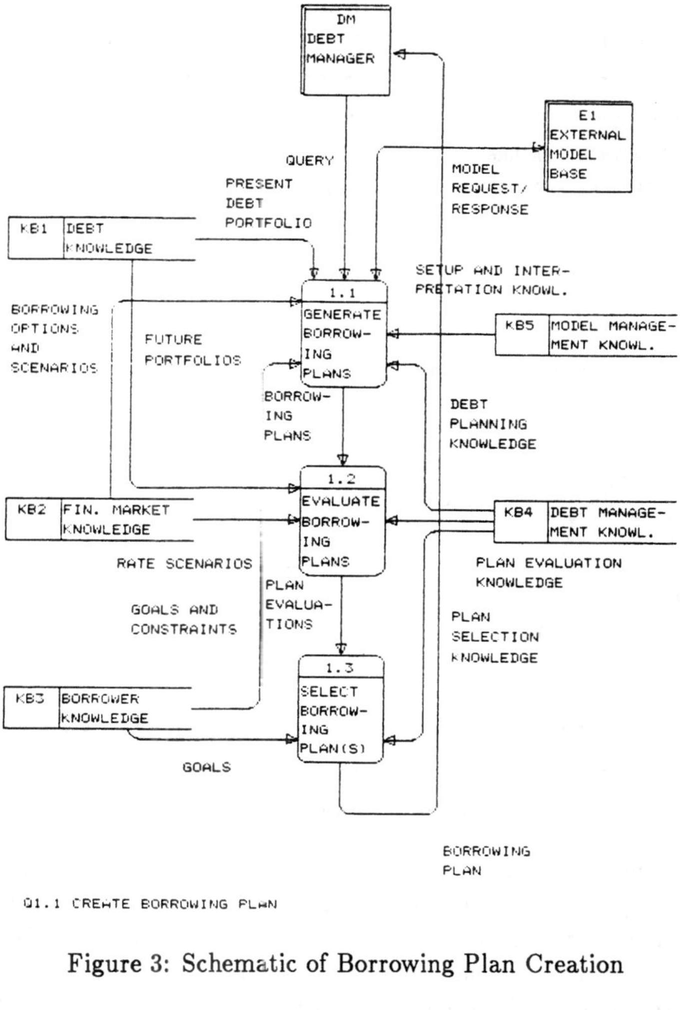

Figure 3: Schematic of Borrowing Plan Creation

The overall process is controlled by backchaining with a KEE rule set, i.e. backwards reasoning by recursively searching the rule base to find a chain of if-then statements which imply a goal consequence. This process uses knowledge from the knowledge base as far as possible, but sets up and runs available models as necessary to carry out desired analyses.

A borrowing plan can be viewed as a collection of recommended actions over a specific time period which accomplish the required financing objectives. Initially, MIDAS views these actions as specifying the debt term, timing and legal features for domestic debt issued over the time period. (Later extensions may include hedging and foreign debts.) The process of generating borrowing plans begins with optimization using a scenario-based stochastic model similar to that of Bradley and Crane. This model specifies debt source, maturity and call decisions over the planning period, given the debt manager's assessment of probable future interest rate movements. The model's suggestions are refined heuristically and completed with debt features that are required or optional in the markets where borrowing is being done. Other heuristics are applied as needed. This process results in one or more alternative borrowing plans to be evaluated and from which recommendations are selected. This process is summarized in Figure 4.

1. PICK TERM MIX (Stochastic model)
2. ASSIGN REQUIRED FEATURES (Deterministic)
3. ASSIGN OPTIONAL FEATURES (Heuristic)

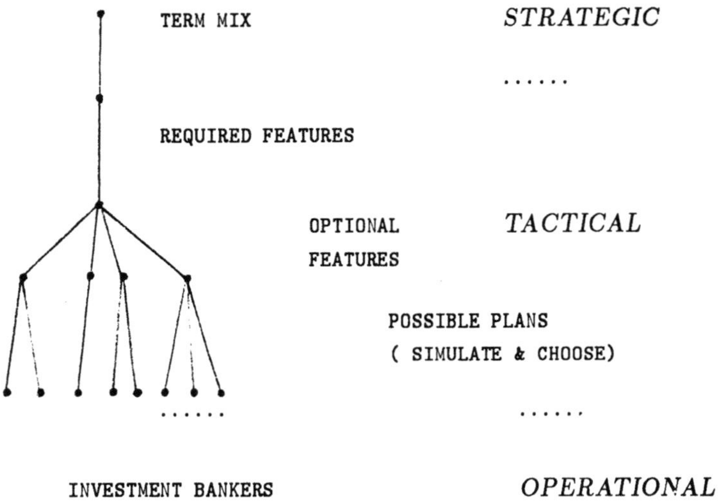

Figure 4: Borrowing Plan Generation Process

Evaluation of each plan is done using stochastic simulation, which produces a cost/risk profile for the plan. The results of the simulation are then considered together with other plan characteristics to screen undesirable plans and recommend likely alternatives to the debt manager. Recommendations are explained in report and graph format.

Actual market flotation of specific debt issues is effected by investment banking advisors in conjunction with management. Thus the MIDAS system is concerned principally with the top two levels of the traditional strategic/tactical/operational hierarchy.

The MIDAS System Knowledge Base

To make effective borrowing decisions, the debt manager relies on several types of knowledge. First, he or she must be clear about the objectives, financing needs and borrowing constraints of the firm. Second, the manager must be familiar with the requirements and behaviours of the financial markets in which borrowing might be done, as well as expectations (from external sources or subjectively determined) about future economic and rate conditions in those markets. Third, he or she must know the types of debt available in each market and their costs, restrictions and operating characteristics for the firm. Fourth, the manager must know how to choose among these debt sources and types to achieve the firm goals, based on analytical results and/or rules of thumb. And finally, certain financial analysis techniques will enhance the quality of borrowing decisions if they are understood and appropriately used.

MIDAS is designed to use a distributed frame-, rule- and model-based representation of these five types of knowledge and the corporation's debt situation (present and projected) as a resource base to handle a variety of user requests. A simplified graph of the KEE portion of the knowledge base is given in Figure 5.

KEE's object-oriented programming facility allows a concise, modular representation of facts and calculations. Each "unit" (frame) represents a class of objects or an individual object such as a financial market, debt instrument or borrowing plan. Each unit has "slots" containing descriptive data or procedural code specifying how it is to behave under certain conditions. A listing of slots for a typical bond issue is shown in Figure 6; this unit's declarative slots describe its legal features, while its "method" slots (those with names beginning with "mth.") tell how to calculate its cash flows based on its declarative slots and other facts in the knowledge base. In addition, "active value" demons maintain consistency among dependent slot values within the unit and the entire knowledge base.

Inheritance within the knowledge base allows an economical representation of related objects which applies naturally to our financial domain. For example, a callable bond issue (Figure 7) inherits most of its slots from the class of generic bonds and adds a few specialized items related to its call feature. A bond issue with a sinking fund but no call option inherits slots from generic bonds and adds slots with knowledge pertaining to its sinking fund. Likewise, the callable bond and sinking fund issues' cash flows are calculated using methods inherited from generic bonds, with applicable modifications in each case. Finally, the cash flows for an entire group of debt issues (a debt portfolio) can be easily generated by combining those of the individual group members. Rules can then refer to the cash flows or other debt portfolio features.

The KEE knowledge base also provides interfaces to both user and external models. At this time we use an extensive series of pop-up menus for user input with screen displays or hardcopy output in predefined report modules. These can be entirely generated using LISP code and KEE methods. FORTRAN models on other machines are run by calls and input from KEE via Ethernet; their output is interpreted and translated into facts in the KEE knowledge base, which again can be accessed by other methods and by rules.

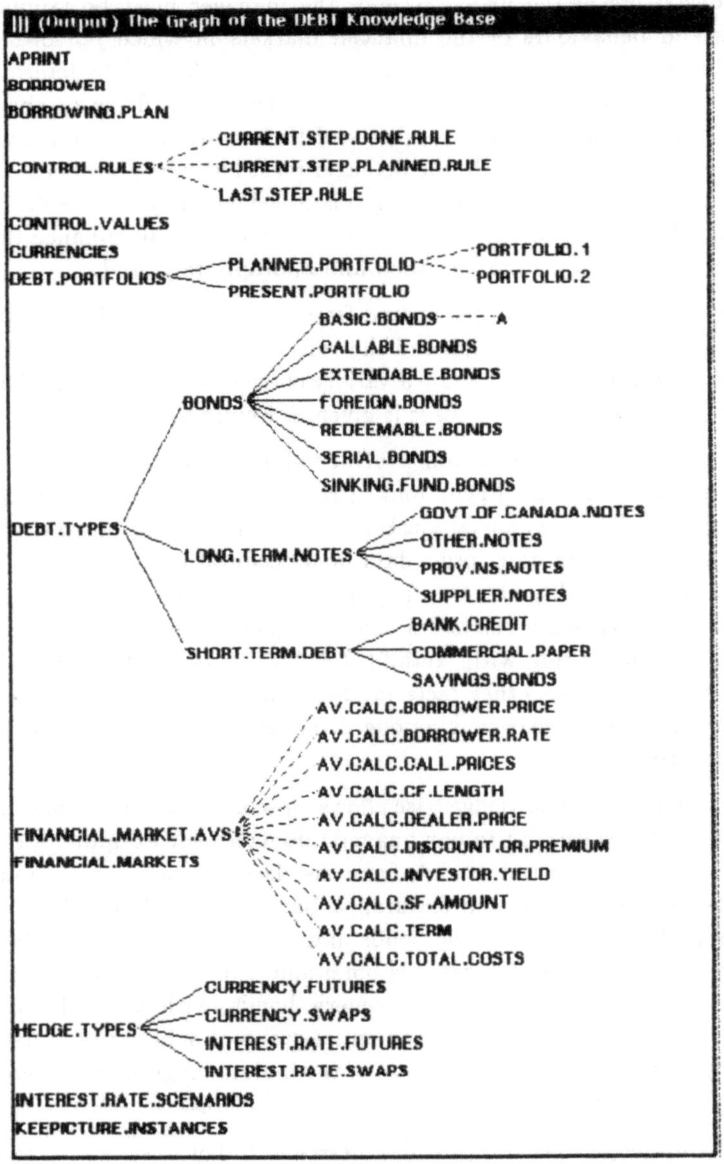

Figure 5: Schematic of KEE Knowledge Base for MIDAS

3 Conclusions and Observations

At the time of writing, the overall conceptual design for the system is completed, detailed design is in progress and the knowledge base coding is proceeding quickly. We do not yet have performance evaluations for the system, but it appears that our approach to the problem, integrating management science and expert systems, is natural and feasible for a problem domain with the semi-structured nature of debt management. Standard

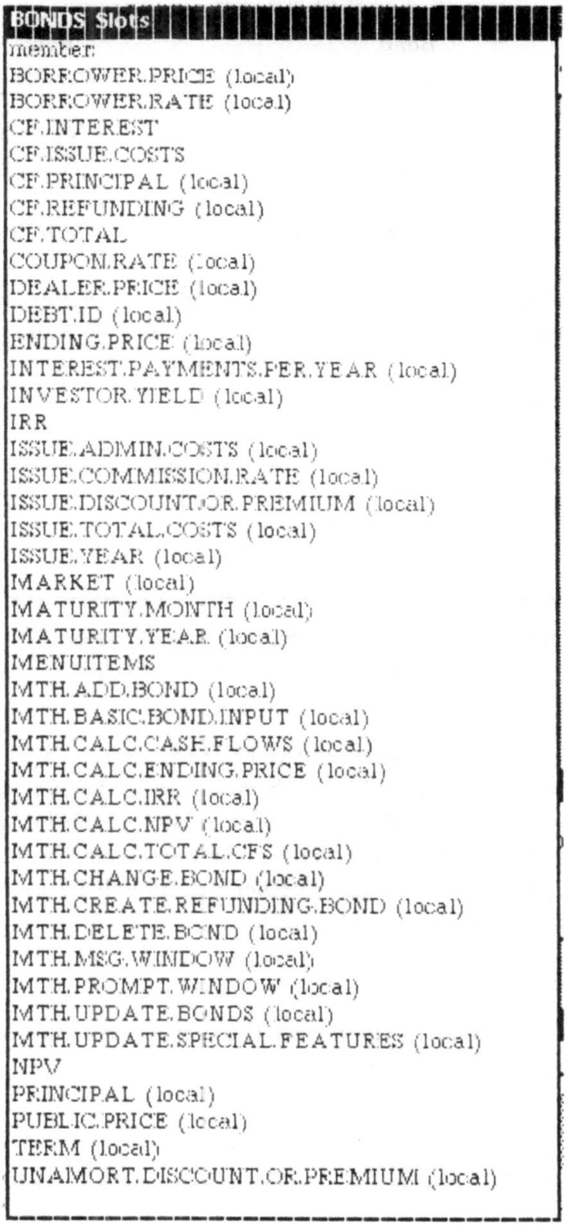

Figure 6: Representative Unit in KEE Knowledge Base for MIDAS

software engineering techniques for developing decision support systems apply. Within the chosen domain the technical problems of model management and interfacing can be solved in a straightforward manner through the KEE knowledge base and distributed processing. However, the software tools that make this possible are highly complex, requiring extensive learning time and support.

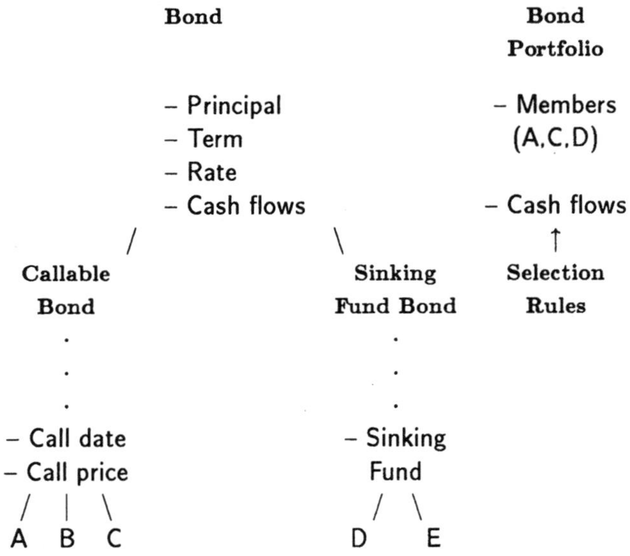

Figure 7: Representative Dependencies Between Units in KEE Knowledge Base for MIDAS

This paper has given an overview of the MIDAS project, integrating expert systems within a debt management DSS. We have outlined the system's conceptual design, briefly discussed the knowledge base which serves as the integrating component for models and heuristics used in debt management strategic planning, and noted our observations as the project progresses. Further results will be made available as the MIDAS prototype nears full implementation.

Acknowledgements

We wish to acknowledge the contributions to the material reported in this paper of our coworkers on the MIDAS project, E.G. Achorn, P.T. Cox, S.H. Hinds and S. Topiwala.

References

Bradley SP, Crane DB (1972) A Dynamic Model for Bond Portfolio Management. Management Science 19.2: 139–151

Bradley SP (1975) Management of Bank Portfolios. John Wiley, New York

Bradley SP (1980) Managing a Bank Bond Portfolio Over Time, in: Dempster MAH (ed.) Stochastic Programming. Academic Press, London

Buchanan BG, Shortliffe EH (1984) Rule-Based Expert Systems. Addison-Wesley, Reading, Mass.

Crane DB (1971) A Stochastic Programming Model for Commercial Bank Bond Portfolio Management. Journal of Financial and Quantitative Analysis 6.3: 955–976

Crane DB, Knoop F, Pettigrew W (1977) An Application of Management Science to Bank Borrowing Strategies. Interfaces 8.1.2: 70–81

Elton EJ, Gruber MJ (1971) Dynamic Programming Applications in Finance. Journal of Finance 26.2: 473–506

Ganascia J-G (1986) Using an Expert System in Merging Qualitative and Quantitative Data Analysis, in: Kowalik JS (ed.) Knowledge Based Problem Solving. Prentice-Hall, Englewood Cliffs, New Jersey

Howard CD (1986) Applications of Monte Carlo Simulation to Corporate Financial Liability Management. Paper presented at the Financial Management Association Conference, New York

Kalymon BA (1971) Bond Refunding with Stochastic Interest Rates. Management Science 18.3: 563–575

Keen PGW, Morton MSS (1978) Decision Support Systems: An Organizational Perspective. Addison-Wesley, Reading, Mass.

Lane M, Hutchinson P (1980) A Model for Managing a Certificate of Deposit Portfolio under Uncertainty, in: Dempster MAH (ed.) Stochastic Programming. Academic Press, London, pp 473–495

Liang TP (1986) Critical Success Factors of Decision Support Systems: An Experimental Study. DATA BASE 17.2: 3–15

McInnes JM, Carleton WJ (1982) Theory, Models and Implementation in Financial Management. Management Science 28.9: 957–978

Rauch-Hinden WB (1985) Artificial Intelligence in Business, Science and Industry. Prentice-Hall, Englewood Cliffs, New Jersey

Shapiro JF (1987) Stochastic Programming Models for Dedicated Portfolio Management, in: Proceedings of the NATO Advanced Study Institute on Mathematical Models for Decision Support, Val D'Isere, France. To appear

Turban E, Watkins PR (1986) Integrating Expert Systems and Decision Support Systems. MIS Quarterly 10.2: 121–136

Incorporating Knowledge in Decision Support Systems

F. Esposito
Istituto di Scienze dell'Informazione,
Università degli Studi, v.Amendola 173
(70126) Bari, Italy

Summary

The paper emphasizes the opportunity of integrating methods and techniques of AI in Decision Support Systems.

To make decisions in uncertainty conditions involves a process of hypotheses generation and verification and often needs techniques of statistical data analysis to control the phenomenon complexity. Intelligent tools to incorporate knowledge in order to reduce the search space in problem solving, to guide the selection of suitable mathematical models and to realize user friendly interfaces, enabling a more efficient decision oriented interaction, are particularly useful.

As an example of such a philosophy, an expert system aiding the user in designing and realizing experiments is presented: it, acting as a statistician consultant, assists the user in formulating the problem, gives advices about which analyses to perform, how to collect data and how to interpret the results in order to better understand the observed phenomenon.

1 Introduction

The applicability of Artificial Intelligence techniques in the development of more efficient and efficacious DSS is now being explored. Defining a DSS as a computer based system that can be used directly by decision makers to solve complex problems characterized by uncertainty conditions, by the difficulty in individuating models or prescribed algorithms for their solution or by the lack of quantitative descriptions, (Carlson and Sprague (1982)), it is straightforward how its functionality may be enhanced disposing of more "intelligent" tools. Particularly, methods to incorporate knowledge, in order to reduce the search space in problem solving or to guide the selection of appliable quantitative models, and techniques to implement friendly user interfaces, enabling an efficient decision oriented interaction, are useful.

The classical situation is that in which the decision maker starts with a certain degree of uncertainty with regard to the true situation, then he looks for additional information to reduce uncertainty and to state the actual situation, finally, he tries to foresee the phenomenon evolution and takes decisions in order to influence it or to change something. The process, in the first stage is a classical situation assessment cyclic procedure of the form

$$\text{data collection} + \text{knowledge} \longrightarrow \text{decision}$$

that ends when the decision maker knows enough about the problem; in the second stage a certain model is selected, decisions are proposed and, finally, those are chosen which seem to pursue the objectives (Ben-Bassat and Freedy (1982)).

The problems are always solved through a process of hypothesis generation and verification, a method that seems to be a universal characteristic of human thinking in complex or poorly defined environments (Anderson (1983)). So, while in the model application that may be seen as a rational way of attaching problems, the problem is already been recognized and represented, the function of the early hypotheses is that of limiting the size of the space that must be explored for solutions to the problem and methods must be applied to transform ill-structured problems into well structured problems.

Data analysis, as well as other statistical techniques, may be useful in such a structuration process, but sometimes the decision maker needs a statistician consultant who, firstly, aids him in formulating the problem, then, gives advices about which analyses to perform, how to collect data, how to interpret the results in order to "understand" something about the observed phenomenon and to make decisions with the aim of controlling it. Designing a decision aiding system implies the integration of different analytical methodologies and disciplines, including cognitive problem solving, information processing, human perception, man-machine interface in order to optimize the effect of cognitive/situational/substantive levels interaction (Andriole (1982)).

According to a proposed model of DSS (Dutta and Basu (1985)), consisting of three components, namely DIALOG, MODELS and DATA, the evolution towards a decision support expert system is evident: the DIALOG component is incorporated in the user interface and in the operational space, while the task of MODELS component is accomplished by the inference engine that dynamically activates and controls a lot of models needed by the user. This automatic instantiation of the models is performed applying series of rules of the kind

" IF condition THEN action "

according to the data collected about the situation and the knowledge stored about the particular problem. The DATA component is substituted by this "knowledge base".

An example of such a kind of expert systems in decision making may be represented by EXPER, a computer based system aiding the user in designing and realizing experiments, by means of a friendly interface, guiding him in defining the experimental units, selecting the randomization method and suggesting and performing the suitable statistical analysis. Basing upon the analysis outputs, a feedback is possible allowing to reinitialize the process from the sample definition, that, the first time, is performed on approximate evaluation of the population characteristics.

In the following, after a brief description of the characteristics of the experimental design, the functional requisites and the architecture of EXPER are presented.

2 The Design of Experiments: From the Problem Definition to the Choice of Statistical Tools

Many individuals in their professional work face the problem of experimenting (Montgomery (1976)), although they may often ignore the methods and the techniques of the experimental design or are not able to choose and to use the statistical software packages or, overcome by the hurry of reaching practical results, may neglect some aspects related to the data collection, the way of reducing the effects of undesired extraneous variables, the problem of reliability or the interrelations among different factors affecting the experimental situations.

The difficulty, therefore, is not exclusively related to the application of statistical analyses, the complexity of which, however, must not be underestimated, but is mainly inherent to the necessity of planning the experiment basing upon a defined methodology.

The basic problem of experimentation is due to the typical variability of the experimental data. Thus, drawing conclusions from results is a problem of induction from the sample to the population. The statistical theories of estimation and testing hypotheses provide solutions to this problem in the form of definite statements that have a known and controllable probability of being correct. A carefull design and analysis are necessary, these two items being clearly related since the method of analysis directly depends on the employed design. Accuracy and precision of results are of main concern in any statistical sampling experiment; thus the aim of experimental design is, within resources constraints, to attain maximal accuracy by minimizing or avoiding systematic errors, to be able to compute a confidence interval estimate of statistical errors and to increase precision by reducing random errors. It is possible to individuate three phases in performing an experiment: the experiment definition, the design and the analysis (evaluation). It is required that the questions to be answered by the experiments are correctly formulated, that a preliminary choice of the experimental method is made in light of accuracy and that the general pattern of the experiment, i.e., the number, the type and spacing of the involved variables, is stated. Such considerations fall in the experiment definition and are attached during three steps summarized in Table 1.

During such a phase the choice of the response variable is fundamental but is related to the problem definition: as in problem solving, the experimenter must be certain that the output which must be measured really provides information about the problem. As to the factor selection, the term factor is used in a general sense to denote any feature of the experimental conditions which may be assigned. A factor is a variable affecting the response and may represent environmental, apparatus and methodological conditions. It may be quantitative or qualitative where the difference is in the possibility of arranging the values in order of magnitude or not. The choice of factors is strictly related to the way of organizing the experiment: taking care of the effects of a factor on the phenomenon implies arranging the experiment so that the effects of changing each factor can be measured and separated from the effects of changing other conditions. Once the choice of factors has been performed a decision must be made about their handling.

In order to find the effect of a factor it must be varied e.g. considered at several levels. The activity of choosing the factor levels, which are referred as treatments, may

Table 1

1. RECOGNITION AND DEFINITION OF THE PROBLEM	It means to define the objective and the scope of the experiment underlying the experiment.
2. CHOICE OF THE RESPONSE OR DEPENDENT VARIABLE	The selection of the dependent variable must be done so that it supplies information about the investigated phenomenon.
3. CHOICE OF THE FACTORS	The selection of the independent variables affecting the response must be realized. These factors may be both of qualitative and quantitative nature.

Table 2

4. CHOICE OF THE FACTOR LEVELS	The choice about which factors to hold constant, about the values they may assume and the way by which the different factor levels have to be combined, must be made.
5. CHOICE OF OBSERVATIONS	It is the definition of the experimental units and of the number of observations in each unit.
6. SELECTION OF THE EXPERIMENT ORDER	It concerns the method of randomization, with the aim of averaging the effects of variables which cannot be controlled.
7. FORMULATION OF A MATHEMATICAL MODEL	A model of the experiment is required.

Table 3

8. DATA COLLECTION AND ANALYSIS	The data collection process, monitored by the experimenter, is followed by data analysis procedures.
9. INTERPRETATION OF RESULTS	Once the data have been analyzed the experimenter draws conclusions about results.

be considered the first step of the second phase, namely the design, concerning the way by which the factors must be controlled and measured, the choice of the values to use in the experiment and the selection of specific methods of design. The steps of the design phase are outlined in Table 2.

If we want to investigate k factors, factor i having L_i levels, then the number of combinations of factor levels is $L_1 * L_2 .. * L_i * .. * L_k$ and the problem is that even for few factors this number of combinations is high; therefore we try to limit the number of combinations that will be actually investigated. The design phase is based on the choice of the experimental design, that is, the definition of the different treatment combinations each of which is applied to every experimental unit, on the choice of observations concerning the definition of the smallest subdivision of the experimental material (experimental unit), on the order of experimentation, that is, stating the method of assigning treatments to the experimental units and the number of replications. It is also necessary to maintain a balance between statistical precision and costs. Once such decisions have been made, a mathematical model must be set up to describe the experiment in order to formulate the laws giving the response variable as a function of the selected factor effects, under the defined restrictions.

The final phase, namely the analysis, consists in the course of effective actions necessary to gather, to reduce and to statistically analyze the data. It consists of two steps (Table 3). This phase involves the use of statistical techniques, but the interpretation of the results remains a fundamental task for the experimenter who may use these as a feedback to design a better experiment, once certain hypotheses seem to hold. In such a sense this phase is of evaluation of the experiment and of the adopted model and preludes a new statement of the problem in a cyclic approach.

A schema, proposed by Hicks (1973), that outlines the experiments, the design techniques and some analysis tools, is in the following:

EXPERIMENT	DESIGN	ANALYSIS
1. Single factor	1. Completely randomized	1. One-way Anova
	2. Randomized blocks	2. Special Anova Regression
	3. Latin square	3. Special Anova
	4. Greco-Latin square	4. Four way Anova
2. Two or more factors		
a. Factorial	1. Completely randomized	1. General Anova
	2. Randomized blocks	2. Factorial Anova
	3. Latin square	3. Factorial Anova with replications
b. Nested experiments	1. Completely randomized	1. Nested Anova
	2. Randomized blocks	2. Nested Anova with blocks
	3. Latin square	3. Nested Anova with blocks and positions
c. Nested factorial		1. Nested Fact. Anova

The characteristics of the knowledge domain concerning the experimental design are such to allow an easy engineering of the expert system and may be summarized in:

- exhaustive search:
  the search space is small and the search methods don't imply too much time to consider the solutions;

- monotonic reasoning:
  due to the knowledge reliability, the acquisition of new data doesn't cause the invalidation of data or the retraction of facts;

- single line of reasoning:
  once the problem has been stated, the model describing the experiment is unique and alternative hypotheses are not taken into consideration.

These considerations suggest to adopt as computational mechanism and knowledge representation schema the production system approach (Davis, Buchanan and Shortliffe (1977)), widely used in the implementation of expert systems. A production system consists of a set of production rules, a data base to which the rules are applied and a mechanism for applying the rules to the data.

The choice is justified by the fact that, being the knowledge exactly codified, the problem concerns with tutoring the problem definition phase, suggesting the experiment design, choosing the suitable statistical analyses and then using them, where the first functions may be easily implemented in the production system schema, while the last one may be assured if, in the right side of the production rules, calls to statistical routines are allowed.

A particular attention must be dedicated to the user interface due to the fact that the user is a non specialized experimenter and may ignore the terms, the language and the methods of the experimental design although it depends on him the problem definition and, consequently, the successive choices influencing the statistical method selection.

3 Functional Requirements of an Expert System for the Experimental Design

Considering that experimenting is to draw inferences or to make decisions about some hypotheses, that is, to take actions in uncertainty conditions, where uncertainty does not mean the total ignorance of the phenomenon but only that the exact output is not completely predictable, the system functional requisites derive from the necessity of overcoming problems concerning the experimental design as to the data collection, the way of taking into account the effects of indesired variables, the reliability and the factor interrelations, and are also related to implementation problems, mainly concerning the exigency of putting together two programming environments, namely, one of declarative kind (the production rules in which the knowledge is codified) and the other of procedural kind (the numerical algorithms to apply).

As to the first problems, the need of activating an efficacious man-machine interaction means to design a system which discusses with the user in order to state the problem, recommends an appropriate randomization plan, having set up the experiment characteristics, suggests suitable statistical tools, carries out the analysis and, finally, aids the user to interpret the results, always supplying a guidance to explain "what" is being done and "why", or checking the assumptions and the restrictions about the data.

The difficulties mainly concern the user interface design where certain advantages may be reached analysing a concise natural language description of the problem using simple pattern matching language processing methods to detect key words or phrases (Hand (1984)), as already proposed in the design of statistical expert systems. But such a solution seems hard to realize, due to the exigency of building a sophisticated mechanism for the recognition of the natural language and, being the application field very large, to the definition of a great number of rules containing the key words used by the different users. So, an intermediate solution has been selected: first, a certain number of interviews has been conducted aiming at understanding if users belonging to different application environments have any idea, formalized or not, about the meaning of the experimental design, then, this philosophy has been reproduced in realizing the question driven interface. Once the information characterizing the experimental situation have been acquired, the factors have been defined and the experiment has been planned, the system must guide the user in organizing the experimental material and in selecting the suitable sample size. Such an operation may be objectively performed if a series of measurements, concerning the treatments, are available. In this case the randomization device, that has the task of averaging the effects of uncontrolled variables, may better operate. Further information concerning the experimental situation must be acquired also if, at this moment, the experimental data are not actually collected. Nevertheless, it's possible to suppose that the experimenter has a vague idea of the behavior of the population he is going to investigate, as well as, a rough estimate of the precision that must result. Such information are used firstly, while the exact measurements concerning the treatments will be available when the statistical analyses will be performed on the experimental data and will be useful as a feedback to design a better experiment, after the experiment evaluation.

Therefore the data collection is controlled by the system and the appropriate statistical analysis is not only suggested but performed, and the results are explained. Moreover the system must supply guidance to the user with various levels of help and must be able to justify the actions and to show the adopted lines of reasoning.

Such requirements emphasize the exigency of putting in relation the algorithmic environment and an AI programming environment in which to define the set of production rules and the inference mechanism to draw inferences and to reach conclusions. In order to satisfy these requisites a prototype version of EXPER has been realized in the POP integrated environment, where a language similar to PROLOG and a Pascal-like procedural language are available.

Being the data management completely realized within the expert system, the experimental data are handled as data files in the POP environment. All the languages available in POP are incrementally compiled in the same intermediate language, then compiled in machine code; so, it is also possible to link routines written in other languages, as Fortran, Pascal or C. Such an opportunity is interesting because there is the possibility of designing procedures for automatically generating data or for extracting the experimental data from a conventional data base system, as Oracle. This possibility is now being explored.

The possibility of developing the system in the OPS83 environment, which also allows to overcome the problem of interfacing, during the execution, two different programming environments, and which is available on a personal computer, is now being studied.

4 The Architecture of EXPER

EXPER has the classical architecture of an expert system which works as a consultant assistant. It consists of a certain number of components, as the User Interface, the Justifier, the Knowledge Base, the Inference Engine and the Case Specific Data Base which always appear in the knowledge based systems and of another component, including all the statistical routines, the significancy tests, the methods necessary to conduct the experiment, which will be referred as Statistical Module,(Figure 1).

Figure 1

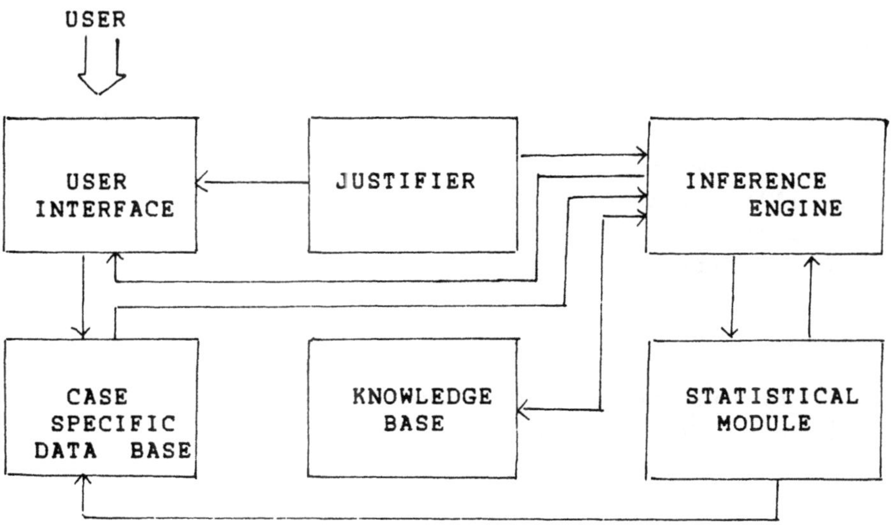

4.1 The User Interface

This module in the early version of the system (Esposito, Capozza and Altini (1986)), simply reproduced the questionnaire that was used for gathering information about the experimental situation while, in the last release acts as an interviewer for the entry of factual data to the consultation session; it, first, leaves the user free of expressing his idea of the problem, using his language, then, playing the role of a trainer, guides him in clearly formulating the problem and the experimental situation, with proper terms. The rules of interview are selected by the Inference Engine, which, having recognized, by means of a question driven menu, the user and the application field, tries to propose questions with a suitable language in order to realize a friendly interaction and to aid the experimenter to completely define the experiment characteristics. Functions of help are available, in form of possibility of consulting a dictionary of technical terms, in form of examples and solved problems, in the user application field, in form of exercises to solve in order to better explain the meaning of terms and operations, (this is explicitely referred as Didactics). This module operates emulating the iteraction between a novice experimenter and an expert statistician, aiming at suggesting the experiment design.

4.2 The Knowledge Base

It contains the statistical knowledge and expertise as a set of production rules of the general form

IF (antecedent) THEN (consequent)

where the antecedent may be a logical expression concerning the presence or not of defined conditions, a configuration of parameters characterizing the experiment, the application field, the user typology, the evaluation of the solution to a proposed problem, a set of values or computed statistics, as results coming from the statistical module routines, etc. and the consequent may be assertions or actions, that may be decisions about which rule to fire, after the left size of the rule has been satisfied, or calls to statistical analyses. So, the knowledge base has rules of different form, for example:

```
IF   ( the experiment is single factor )
     AND ( a unique block exists )
     AND ( the block is complete )
THEN ( The appropriate analysis is ANOVA two-way )
```

or

```
IF   ( the user is a novice )
     AND ( he defines the experiment as a hypothesis that must be verified )
     AND ( the application field is labeled FARMA )
THEN ( use the terms by FARMADICTIONNAIRE )
     AND ( select the question q.n )
```

or

```
IF   ( the dependent variable has an interval scale )
     AND ( its mean is hypothesized to be a value )
     AND ( the required significance is a defined value )
THEN ( call the randomization routine )
```

or

```
IF   ( three sources of variability have been individuated )
     AND ( it's possible to organize the experimental material into three groups )
     AND ( the number of treatments is admissible )
THEN ( the Greco-Latin square design must be chosen )
```

4.3 The Inference Engine

The system works as a problem solver which, provided with a set of data, entered by the user or incrementally created, suggests possible courses of actions. The lines of reasoning are selected by the Inference Engine, stringing together a number of rules deductions.

The module acts as an hypotheses generator because it has the task of evaluating the input data, namely that describing the experimental situation, and it uses these descriptions to trigger potential goal states, that is, the suitable design and the appropriate statistical methods. Moreover, the module takes care of guiding the interview, upon the exigency of new facts or data, invoked during each phase of the problem solving process and then during the analysis.

The control strategy is based upon the backward chaining mechanism of reasoning used through the production system to determine which design must be applied, which analyses are appropriate or which kind of interaction with the user must be selected.

4.4 The Case Specific Data Base

It may be defined as that part of working memory containing all the data related to an experimental situation, gathered during a session, and includes all the intermediate results, conjectures and calculated data, useful to "fire" the suitable rules in the knowledge base. During a problem solving session the case specific information are acquired in a sequential fashion, generally in response to questions generated by the expert system or are a collection of assertions coming from the application of specific rules, as intermediate hypotheses and decisions, or from the application of statistical tools, as partial or final results. It is often defined as the operative space. It differs from the conventional data base in the exigency of the incremental development: a case, namely an experimental situation, is represented by a collection of data, the order and the composition of which is suggested and guided by the system, during the consultation session.

4.5 The Justifier

It has the task of explaining, on user request, the actions of the system; generally, it answers questions about why some conclusions were reached or alternative courses of actions were rejected. It may be considered another level of help, besides the possibility of consulting a dictionary of terms, the availability of specific examples, explaining the fundations of the experiment design, or of didactic sections aiming at the acquisition, by the user, of the right terms and procedures in planning the experiment.

4.6 The Statistical Module

It contains all the statistical analyses useful in the experiment design, a certain number of tests and the randomization programs. The module is connected to the Inference Engine because the statistical routines are invoked basing upon certain verified conditions in the rules and the results are returned to the Inference Engine for soliciting rules of explanation or interpretation or, used as a feedback, for reinitializing the experiment design.

5 Example of a Session

The user is hypothesized to be a novice and the system completely guides him in defining the experiment, supplying also didactic modules and examples and giving helps on request. The user can decide to terminate the session or to go back to the precedent step, or he can ask the reasons of certain choices. The user response follows the double asterisk.

```
--------------------------------------------------------------------------------
     F-->end of session
--------------------------------------------------------------------------------
Basing upon your knowledge, which is the most appropriate definition of
"experiment" among the following?
1----> a hypothesis that must be verified by tests
2----> a perception about the behavior of defined entities that needs a
       confirmation
3----> a practical proof necessary to validate some hypotheses about the
       behavior of entities described by measurable variables
Make a choice:
** 3
--------------------------------------------------------------------------------
     P-->why       I-->back       F-->end of session
--------------------------------------------------------------------------------
The hypotheses you want to validate by means of this experiment concern:
1----> how an entity depends on one or more entities
2----> how the variation of a defined factor influences the response
3----> the comparison of the effects of different treatments on the observed
       entity.
Make a choice:
** 3
--------------------------------------------------------------------------------
     D-->didactic      P-->why      H-->help      I-->back      F-->end of session
--------------------------------------------------------------------------------
Which is the name of your observed entity?
** GROWTH IN THE WEIGHT OF THE CHICKS
--------------------------------------------------------------------------------
                    DIDACTIC MODULE
--------------------------------------------------------------------------------
In the experimental design the entity which is hypothesized to depend on other
entities and which is measured in order to understand if and how it is
influenced by variations of the others is called DEPENDENT VARIABLE or RESPONSE
while the other entities are defined INDEPENDENT VARIABLES or FACTORS.
Press RETURN to continue
                                                                      RETURN<---
```

```
---------------------------------------------------------------------------
     P-->why     I-->back     F-->end of session
---------------------------------------------------------------------------
How many factors influencing the GROWTH OF THE WEIGHT OF THE CHICKS do you want
to consider? Type the number
** 1
---------------------------------------------------------------------------
     P-->why     I-->back     F-->end of session
---------------------------------------------------------------------------
Which is the name of your factor?
** TYPE OF FEED
---------------------------------------------------------------------------
     D-->didactic     P-->why     H-->help     I-->back     F-->end of session
---------------------------------------------------------------------------
Due to the fact that you have declared to be interested in comparing the
effects of different treatments on the GROWTH OF THE WEIGHT OF THE CHICKS how
many alternatives of TYPE OF FEED do you want to consider?
Type the number
** 4
Give a name to treatment 1: ** Feed A
Give a name to treatment 2: ** Feed B
Give a name to treatment 3: ** Feed C
Give a name to treatment 4: ** Feed D
Do you confirm?(Y/N)
** Y
---------------------------------------------------------------------------
     P-->why     I-->back     F-->end of session
---------------------------------------------------------------------------
The treatments of the factor TYPE OF FEED are randomly selected from a
population of treatments?(Y/N)
** N
---------------------------------------------------------------------------
     I-->back     F-->end of session
---------------------------------------------------------------------------
If I have understood, measuring the behavior of the GROWTH OF THE WEIGHT OF THE
CHICKS and making a suitable number of tests, you want to discover if it
depends on the TYPE OF FEED and if a significant difference exists among 4
treatments, namely     FEED A     FEED B     FEED C     FEED D
Is this right?(Y/N)
** Y
---------------------------------------------------------------------------
     D-->didactic     P-->why     H-->help     I-->back     F-->end of session
---------------------------------------------------------------------------
I need to know if other factors exist which may influence the behavior of the
dependent variable GROWTH IN THE WEIGHT OF THE CHICKS. Such secondary factors
must anyhow be taken into account.
There exist secondary factors?(Y/N)
** Y
```

```
--------------------------------------------------------------------------
      D-->didactic      I-->back      F-->end of session
--------------------------------------------------------------------------
How many secondary factors do you want to consider in your experiment?
Type the number
** 1

Which is the name of the secondary factor?
** INITIAL WEIGHT OF THE CHICKS

Do you confirm?(Y/N)
** Y
--------------------------------------------------------------------------
                    DIDACTIC MODULE
--------------------------------------------------------------------------
Due to the existence of secondary factors the experiment must be made taking
into account the possibility that such factors may alter the response. The
usual exigeny of disposing of experimental material considered approximately
homogenous must be satisfied. A good way of controlling the secondary factor
incidence and the sources of variability consists in putting together the
experimental units into groups homogenous as to the secondary factors.
Generally, these groupings for homogeneity are called blocks. For example, if I
want to test different brands of tires measuring the amount of tread loss after
a certain number of miles, certainly an obvious way of setting up the
experiment, in order to assure the homogeneity of experimental material, is
that of testing the tires repeating the experiment on the same car; anyway, if
the conditions and the level of use of the car may affect the response, I can
perform the experiment using as many cars, of the same model and age, as many
brands of tires, distributing the brands on the different cars, so assuring
that the different tires are all tested in the same conditions and driven over
approximately the same terrain. In such a way, each car represents a block.
Press RETURN to continue
                                                                  RETURN<---
--------------------------------------------------------------------------
     D-->didactic      P-->why      H-->help      I-->back      F-->end of session
--------------------------------------------------------------------------
As to your secondary factor  INITIAL WEIGHT OF THE CHICKS  how many blocks do
you intend to consider? Type the number
** 4
Which is the name of block 1?** WEIGHT 12-14.5 gr.
Which is the name of block 2?** WEIGHT 14.6-18 gr.
Which is the name of block 3?** WEIGHT 19-22.5 gr.
Which is the name of block 4?** WEIGHT 22.6-26 gr.

Do you confirm?(Y/N)
** Y
--------------------------------------------------------------------------
     D-->didactic      P-->why      H-->help      I-->back      F-->end of session
--------------------------------------------------------------------------
Is it possible to apply all 4 treatments of the factor TYPE OF FEED in every
```

```
block concerning the INITIAL WEIGHT OF THE CHICKS ?(Y/N)
** N
-----------------------------------------------------------------------------
                    DIDACTIC MODULE
-----------------------------------------------------------------------------
When there are more treatments that can be put in a single block, I argue that
it is an imcomplete block design so I suggest to try to balance, if possible,
the sources of variablility, assuring that every pair of treatments occurs the
same number of times in the experiment. For example, if you dispose of three
treatments, A, B, C and of three blocks, b1, b2, b3 you can set up the
experiment in the following way:
            b1       b2       b3
A           x                 x
B           x        x
C                    x        x
The pairs of treatments AB, BC and AC appear the same number of times(1).
Press RETURN to continue
                                                                    RETURN<---
Are the external sources of variability balanced?(Y/N)
** Y
-----------------------------------------------------------------------------
      P-->why     H-->help     F-->end of session
-----------------------------------------------------------------------------
Basing upon the information you gave me I argue that the design you need is a
BALANCED INCOMPLETE BLOCK DESIGN.
Press RETURN to continue
                                                                         P<---
--------------------WHY BALANCED INCOMPLETE BLOCK DESIGN----------------------
IF the experiment is a SINGLE FACTOR experiment
AND a UNIQUE SECONDARY FACTOR is present, that is a SINGLE GROUPING is possible
AND such a GROUPING is INCOMPLETE AND BALANCED
THEN the EXPERIMENTAL DESIGN is a: BALANCED INCOMPLETE BLOCK DESIGN
AND the kind of analysis of variance to perform is: SPECIAL ANOVA.
Press RETURN to continue
                                                                    RETURN<---
Do you want I assist you in realizing the experiment?(Y/N)
** Y
-----------------------------------------------------------------------------
     D-->didactic     H-->help     I-->back     F-->end of session
-----------------------------------------------------------------------------
Now I need the experimental observations, following a randomization plan,
similar to that already suggested. Remember to supply a number (1) of
observations for each combination treatment-block. Input the data so that each
row contains the observations concerning the same treatment. For missing
for missing observations put a "x".
Press RETURN to continue
                                                                    RETURN<---
--------------------TABLE OF THE EXPERIMENTAL OBSERVATIONS--------------------
Grouping as to INITIAL WEIGHT OF THE CHICKS
```

```
                     BLOCK1  BLOCK2  BLOCK3 BLOCK4
FEED A **              13      14       x     11
FEED B **               x      15       7     12
FEED C **              13      15       8      x
FEED D **              15       x      12     15

Do you confirm?(Y/N)
** Y
--------------------------------------------------------------------------------
     H-->help     F-->end of session
--------------------------------------------------------------------------------
                              ANOVA TABLE
              SS          DF          MS          FO
Treatments    22.75        3          7.58        11.6667
Blocks        55.00        3
Error          3.25        5          0.65
TOTALS        81.00       11

Press RETURN to continue
                                                                           H<---
--------------------------------------------------------------------------------
     E-->exit help
--------------------------------------------------------------------------------
                        INFORMATION ABOUT THE TABLE
              SS          DF          MS          FO
Treatments    sst[1]       a-1[2]     mst[3]      f0[4]
Blocks        ssb[5]       b-1[6]
Error         sse[7]  (a-1)*(b-1)[8] mse[9]
TOTALS        ST[10]       N-1[11]

where  a = number of treatments in your experiment
       b = number of blocks in grouping
       c = number of observations
You may ask information about each field in the table indicating the number in
the square brackets
** 5
--------------------------------------------------------------------------------
     I-->back     E-->exit help
--------------------------------------------------------------------------------
ssb represents the sum of squares between blocks and is a measure of the
differences existing among the blocks built up grouping the experimental
material as to: INITIAL WEIGHT OF THE CHICKS. You may ask information about
each field in the table indicating the number in the square brackets
                                                                           E<---
--------------------------------------------------------------------------------
     P-->why     I-->back     F-->end of session
--------------------------------------------------------------------------------
                        CONCLUSIONS --> SPECIAL ANOVA
The conclusions about your experiment, basing upon the results of the analysis
are that:  A SIGNIFICANT DIFFERENCE EXISTS BETWEEN THE TREATMENTS OF THE FACTOR
```

```
TYPE OF FEED  THAT IS, THE TREATMENTS ARE NOT STATISTICALLY EQUIVALENT.
Press RETURN to continue
                                                               RETURN<---
-------------------------------------------------------------------------------
    P-->why    I-->back    F-->end of session
-------------------------------------------------------------------------------
It is possible to make a test on the means of the treatments concerning the
factor  TYPE OF FEED. Do you want I execute the DUNCAN MULTIPLE RANK TEST?(Y/N)
                                                                    P<---
-------------------WHY DUCAN TEST------------------------------------------
The analysis that has been applied on the data is: SPECIAL ANOVA. Such an
analysis revealed a significant difference between the treatments of the factor
TYPE OF FEED. Since the treatments have been chosen FIXED it is possible to
calculate on the means of the treatments the DUNCAN MULTIPLE RANK TEST with the
aim of determining which are the treatments that differ and which is(are) the
treatment(s) mainly influencing the observed variable GROWTH IN THE WEIGHT OF
THE CHICKS.
Press RETURN to continue
                                                               RETURN<---
Do you want I execute the DUNCAN MULTIPLE RANK TEST?(Y/N)
** Y
-------------------------------------------------------------------------------
    H-->help    I-->back    F-->end of session
-------------------------------------------------------------------------------
                   CONCLUSIONS  -->  DUNCAN TEST
TREATMENTS:        1          2          3         4
MEANS:             -1.12      -0.87      -0.50     2.50
                   <------------------->
There isn't a significant difference between the treatments: 1 and 3
Press RETURN to continue
                                                               RETURN<---
-------------------------------------------------------------------------------
    I-->back    F-->end of session
-------------------------------------------------------------------------------
Do you want to have a general synthesized view of your experiment and the
intermediate results?(Y/N)
** N
THANK YOU, THIS IS THE END OF YOUR SESSION, BYE.
```

6 Conclusions

EXPER is an expert system aiding the user to set up the experiment by means of a friendly interface, guiding him in defining the experimental units, selecting the randomization method and suggesting and performing the appropriate statistical analysis. Basing upon the analysis outputs, a feedback is possible allowing to reinitialize the process from the sample definition that, the first time, is performed on an approximate evaluation of the population characteristics.

The problem of connecting two programming environments, one of a declarative kind and the other of a procedural kind, has been solved, in the first implementation of EXPER, putting in relation the PROLOG with Pascal procedures, under CMS of an IBM 4341. Then, EXPER has been implemented in the POP integrated environment, using POP11 and POPLOG, on a VAX 730, while the implementation on a IBM PC, in OPS83 environment, is now in progress.

References

Anderson JRA (1983) The Architecture of Cognition. Harvard University Press

Andriole SJ (1982) The Design of Microcomputer-based Personal Decision Aiding Systems. IEEE Trans. Syst., Man, Cyber., SMC–12, 4: 463–469

Ben-Bassat M, Freedy A (1982) Knowledge Requirements and Management in Expert Decision Support Systems for Situation Assessment. IEEE Trans. Syst., Man, Cyber., SMC–12, 4: 479–490

Carlson ED, Sprague RH (1982) Building Effective Decision Support Systems. Addison Wesley

Davis RB, Buchanan B, Shortliffe EH (1977) Production Rules as a Representation for a Knowledge-Based Consultation Program. Artificial Intelligence 8: 15–45

Dutta A, Basu A (1985) Representation and Manipulation of Modelling Knowledge in Decision Support Systems, in: Methlie LB, Sprague RH (eds.) Knowledge Representation for Decision Support Systems, North Holland

Esposito F, Capozza F, Altini F (1986) EXPER: An Expert System in the Experimental Design. COMPSTAT '86, Roma

Hand DJ (1984) Statistical Expert Systems: Design. The Statistician 33: 351–369

Hicks CR (1973) Fundamental Concepts in the Design of Experiments. Holt, Rinehart and Winston Inc.

Montgomery DC (1976) Design and Analysis of Experiments. John Wiley & Sons

Statistical Structures for Analyzing Time-Dependent Observations

K.A. Froeschl and W. Grossmann
Dept. of Statistics and Computer Science, University of Vienna
A–1010 Wien, Universitätsstraße 5, Austria

Summary

In order to utilize statistical knowledge in a more or less automated way an appropriate symbolic data structure for capturing this knowledge is necessary. We describe such a data structure for the analysis of time dependent observations. Main emphasis is laid on the analysis of the trend component of observed processes (i.e. regression analysis). This data dependent knowledge is used later on in the phases of determination and execution of actual analyses. Furthermore, the procedural mechanism necessary for the specification of analyses is outlined.

1 Introduction

The development of program systems for supporting statistical data analysis requires the design of formal symbol structures in order to represent (operationally) statistical methodology and statistical data structures, as well as for a formalized treatment of the specific "ground domain" context of particular analyses. In addition to the customary numerical (and graphical) components such systems also shall dispose of knowledge about how and when to apply statistical methods. The tools for constructing such program systems taken into account are primarily techniques of Artificial Intelligence (AI), especially expert systems.

The following presentation deals with several considerations concerning the design of a statistical software system for the analysis of longitudinal data ("LDA" for short). Based on the characteristic data structures of such kinds of data sets (i.e. samples) this system is arranged to support the data analyst interactively by means of a collection of situation-dependent statistical analysis strategies. By longitudinal data (or trend curves) here we mean individual observations recorded at successive time points of time-dependent observables which can be interpreted as observations of a stochastic process with unknown mean value function. In contrast to time series analysis our primary interest is **not** analysis of stochastic dependencies of consecutive observations but analysis of the trend function. Hence, the elementary statistical methods used are regression analysis, and several nonparametric smoothing procedures, either.

Since there are obviously diverging views of purpose and design of (more) "intelligent" statistical software (in particular, statistical expert systems, "SES" for short), we find it both necessary and useful to outline briefly our principal view of this issue (section 2). These introductory remarks form the background of our design decisions for statistical structures dedicated to LDA. Essentially, specific structures are needed for

(N1) a semantically oriented representation of comparably complex (input) data structures (section 3);

(N2) a logical representation of actual analysis strategies (to which numerical procedures have to be linked; section 4).

In section 5 we try to illustrate some of the developed concepts by presenting an excerpt of data description structures and a dialogue fragment for the determination of a computational strategy. Finally (section 6), we briefly discuss the state of system development as well as some features of system implementation. However, we mention before that the conception of the LDA system as presented show a very tentative nature. After all, one should keep in mind both that the formal transcription of statistical methodology into software code causes considerable problems, and that, in several cases, this methodology has to be developed synchronously.

2 Some General Remarks on Statistical Expert Systems

Summarizing the trend in AI supported statistical software up to now, SES are commonly intended, or expected, to serve two (mutually compatible) purposes: help the unexperienced and possibly statistically "naive" user either to avoid misuse of statistics (e.g. by choosing inappropriate methods), or to proceed safely in a well-organized statistical data analysis.

SES of such a kind typically consist of more or less complex networks of (heuristic) decision rules for the selection of some appropriate statistical method (and sometimes also computing procedures; e.g. see Portier and Lai (1983), Hajek and Ivanek (1984), Wittkowski (1986) and, as an extreme example, Blum's (1982) attempt to create a "robot statistician"). As a rule, such a SES takes a data set, asks some questions concerning data and analysis goal, and returns some numerical and/or graphical output eventually. As a logical consequence these systems take over the conducting part of analytical sessions, thus forcing the analyst into a somewhat subordinate role. Though aiding the statistically less experienced data analyst is a creditable goal undeniably we think it is doubtful just to carry over the burden of **analytical responsibility** to a mechanized (decision) procedure (also see Velleman (1985)). Obviously, SES of this type demonstrate what is technically feasible today; on the other hand, probably the greatest potential offered to applied statistics by current AI technology is still poorly recognized: intelligent support in running interactive data analyses which relieves the human actor from the bulk of "low-level" bookkeeping and machine-serving activities. More powerful and well-tailored tools managing the lots of rather tedious organizational problems will enable the analyst to spend less time and efforts in considering **how** to get things going but, instead, enable him favorably to invest these resources in considering **what** to do (next) on a strategic level rather than a technical one. After all, recently there have been issued a few stimulating proposals pointing in this direction (see Huber

(1986), Oldford and Peters (1986a), Thisted (1986) and, to some degree also, Jöckel (1986)). Thus looking ahead a bit we can see that statistical computing can benefit from AI in rather different and even more comprehensive ways. The following figure 1 is intended to demonstrate our view of the proper position of SES among several other "intelligent" statistical software applications.

<table>
<tr><td>performance in statistics
ground domain</td><td>experienced</td><td>moderately experienced</td><td>less experienced to even naive</td></tr>
<tr><td>experienced</td><td>responsive statistical environment</td><td>SES</td><td rowspan="2">should consult a "flesh and blood" statistician at all to get reasonable results</td></tr>
<tr><td>less experienced</td><td>domain oriented expert system</td><td>should not do any sophisticated analysis on his own</td></tr>
</table>

Fig. 1: "Taxonomy" of AI-supported statistical software

Though SES at their current stage of maturity offer little to experienced statisticans (perhaps they may even hamper work by rigid and clumsy behavior), unobtrusive assistance by "attentive statistical apprentices" certainly would be welcomed. This could comprise keeping track of fruitful as well as dead ends of analyses, pointing at probably offended model assumptions, drawing attention to alternative paths of continuation, collecting material for subsequent report generation etc.. In the long run, of course, statistical software should offer qualified help with **genuinely statistical problems**. Loosely speaking, such a kind of system would have to know lots about mathematics (like algebra and optimization), statistical concepts (like asymptotic relative efficiency and multiple testing) and, last but not least, statistical literature (e.g. to provide answers to "What has been proposed already to do in comparable situations?"). If we can manage to assemble such an actively involved, responsive statistical workbench some day, we will have achieved a new stage of statistical computing. Meanwhile, the best we can do is to search for ways and means to improve today's poorly intelligent statistical software packages. After all, even conventional SES will provide valuable help to the ground domain researcher who is lacking firm statistical knowledge (though we must stipulate that, at least, he has a clear understanding of the data analytic potential of statistical methods!) by giving accurate answers and well-directed recommendations.

3 Longitudinal Data Structures

The most customary statistical data structure is the rectangular "cases by variates" data matrix whose data analytic versatility is based on its structural simplicity. Incidently, data matrices are also elementary data structures of programming languages and, hence, are dealt with easily in software. In the field of LDA, unfortunately, rectangular data matrices are of minor importance because the variates of primary interest are observed along time, and, moreover, there may be several such series of observations recorded on each case of a sample. Taking into account the additional time dimension of observations, the resulting data structure has in the main a three-dimensional shape. However, in order to make the system "intelligent" to some extent we have to add also some kind of semantic information to the data set as it is described below.

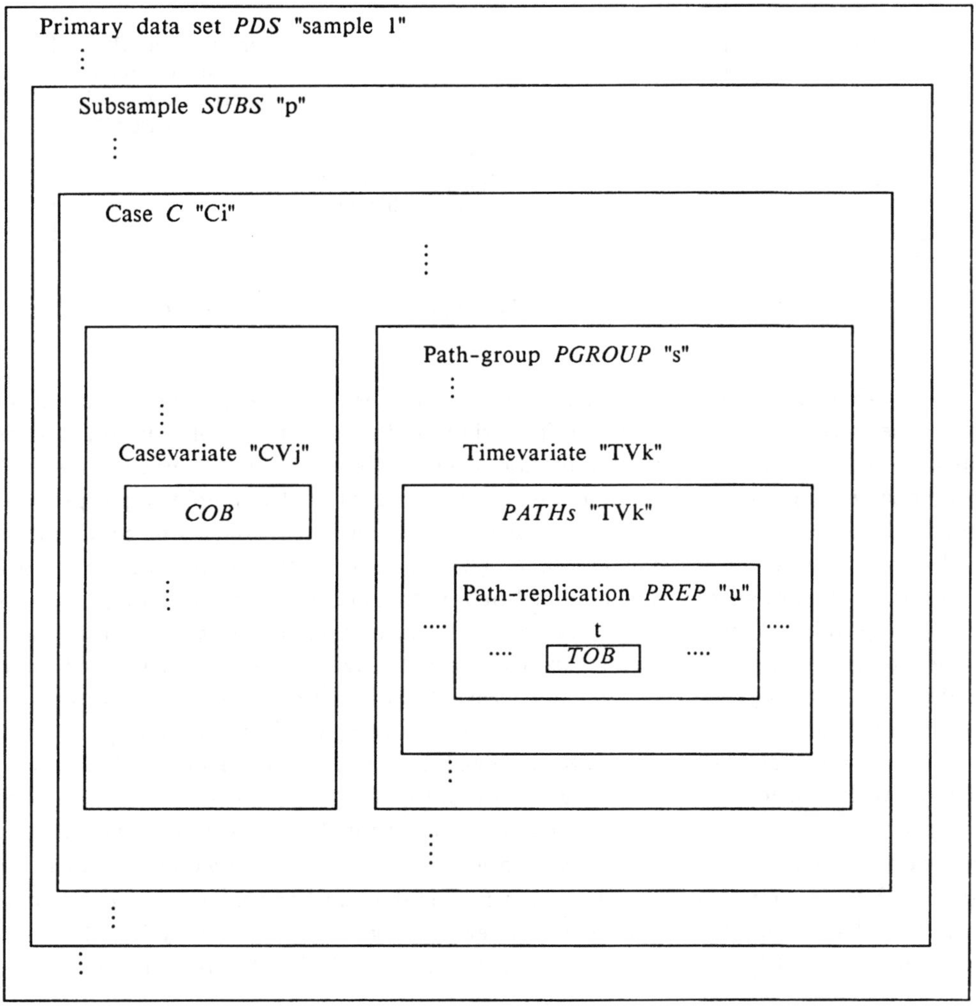

Fig. 2: Data Structure of LDA samples

A sample or <u>*primary data set*</u> *(PDS)* is a collection of <u>*cases*</u> *(Cs)* which may be grouped into <u>*subsamples*</u> *(SUBSs)*. Each case C_i comprises a set of time independent *case-observations (COBs)* as well as a set of time dependent *time-observations (TOBs)*. Each *COB* is the realization of a *casevariate* CV_k out of a set of casevariates $\{CV_1, \ldots, CV_K\}$ whereas a *TOB* is an element of the realization of a *timevariate* TV_l out of a set of timevariates $\{TV_1, \ldots, TV_L\}$. In statistical terms a timevariate TV_l is nothing else than a stochastic process $Y(t)$. For each case we observe one or more *paths (PATHs)* i.e. timeseries of that process at a case specific number of timepoints. Thus the elements of one pathobservation $y = (y_i(t_1), \ldots, y_i(t_n))$ are the *TOBs*, ordered by increasing time. In case of more than one observed path from the same timevariate for a specific case we call these paths together *path-replications (PREPs)* (e.g. monthly sales data observed for several years). Moreover, the observed paths may be grouped into *path-groups (PGROUPs)* according to some data specific semantic information about the timevariates (e.g. timevariates observed before treatment and after treatment). Fig. 2 gives a picture of the data structure. Note especially that in practise this data structure may be highly irregular w.r.t. time dimension (i.e. number, length and observation structure of paths).

The complexitiy of this data structure introduces a considerable diversity of possible semantic substructures as well as lots of data modifying, and transforming, operations which cannot enter the picture treating simple data matrices. For instance, in case of building groups now there are three basic possibilities:

- grouping of cases into subsamples *(SUBSs)*
- interpreting the paths of one case as replication of one timevariate *(PREPs)*
- grouping paths within each case into path-groups *(PGROUPs)*

As simple data transformations consider the computation of first order differences of a path with equidistant observation times or the operation of averaging over a set of path-replications with equal observation times. These examples show that the time structure of recorded *TOBs* plays an important role for transformations.

As a consequence, the structural complexity of LDA samples calls for adequate means of description. Since, for obvious reasons, a formalized representation of the semantic structure of a data set is of crucial relevance for a mechanized application of statistical methods in knowledge-based statistical software systems, a suitable descriptive language is of pre-eminent interest. It is the primary goal of this symbolic data representation to support—in response to particular situations—appropriate data transformations and applications in a "natural" way and, vice versa, to cut off doubtful or inapt operations. As a promising tool for realizing logical data set descriptions an object oriented approach has been proposed by Oldford and Peters (1986b). By detaching the logical description of observed data from matters of physical data management this approach offers an enormous flexibility and, at the same time, the advantage of easy software implementation (provided that suitable programming languages or "environments" are used). The correspondence between physical data storage and associated symbolic data description has to be maintained by an appropriate technical access organization anyhow. However, in what follows we confine ourselves to a discussion of means for symbolic data description, and even this will be exemplified merely (to save space) by structures concerning the primary data set *PDS*.

From the object-oriented view a data set and its constituent parts (e.g. *SUBSs*, *Cs*, *PGROUPs*, etc. in case of *PDS*) are represented as different individual objects which contain information about themselves as well as about their mutual relationships locally. Since the "objects" of a data set usually show a natural hierarchical dependence, they are not treated alike entirely. Typically the objects of a data set may be seperated into labeled objects (i.e. objects furnished with unique identifiers) which can be referred to directly, and unlabeled objects which can be referred to only by means of superior labeled objects. For example, the various objects of a *PDS* representing *CVs*, *TVs*, *SUBSs*, *Cs*, *COBs*, *PGROUPs*, *PATHs*, *PREPs*, *TOBs* are defined locally, w.r.t. this *PDS*. Hence, they are "visible" only within the particular *PDS* object they belong to. The hierarchical dependencies among these objects of a *PDS* are depicted in figure 3; labeled objects are printed boldfaced.

CV (-description)

PDS *TV* (-description)

SUBS *C* *PGROUP* *PATH* *PREP* *TOB*

COB

Fig. 3: PDS object hierarchy

Though each *CV*, or *TV*, in fact appears within each case or path-group resp., its individual features (e.g. level of scale, valid range etc.) are collected in an own (labeled) object. In order to support the most relevant "high level" modes of access to data descriptions (and data, too!) there is made provision for three different kinds of direct access. In addition to the "natural" hierarchical access to lower level objects according to figure 3 it is also possible to access a single case immediately even in presence of subsamples. Furthermore, if there is any grouping of paths at all, a single *PGROUP* may be addressed in its entirety (without effecting existing subsamples and case associations). On the contrary, individual *COBs*, *PATHs*, or *TOBs*, may be addressed via the case objects they are attached to. These objects' "names", then, refer to logical access paths. For instance, the observation value of the *TOB* recorded at $t = 204$ of *TV* "TV2" (out of an ungrouped set of *PATHs* with no replications) of case labeled with "C14" in *PDS* "sample1" is contained (possibly along with other features of this *TOB*) in an object identified by:

DS "sample1" *SUBS* "" *C* "C14" *PGROUP* "" *PATH* "TV2" *PREP* "" *TOB* "204".

Note that unlabeled objects may be referred to by means of positional numbers or by names if available. Usually, *COBs* are entered via *CV*-names, *TOBs* are entered via *TV*-names and time-marks.

As a principle, access to an object does neither change its contents nor its hierarchical substructure (if there is any at all). This holds also in case of a (conditional) selection of subsets of objects. For example, selecting a particular *PGROUP* from a

PDS would create another data set of which the internal structure as to *SUBS* and *Cs* would equal its *PDS* counterpart but would omit the *PATHs* not in this *PGROUP*. Naturally, conditional selection and (even) elementary data transformation (like introducing or cancelling a group structure, or merging several *PATHs* or *Cs*) cause graver modifications of symbolic data set representations. As an example, consider the selection of those *PATHs* of a *PDS* w.r.t. a particular *TV* whose values are above a critical threshold for at least a certain duration. This operation may cut off single cases, a specific path, a subsample, or a group of timevariates as well. Moreover, sometimes it will be desirable to save the information gained for selected *TVs*, e.g. the length of duration, or starting and ending points of these time intervals computed by interpolation. This, of course, necessitates additional representation structures.

To be effective, transforming symbolic data representations from some data set into another one has to be done mechanically. The main difficulty of automating this transformation process is caused by the need of managing synchronous changes of several hierarchical object levels and their interrelations. In order to better achieve both semantic integrity among various data sets derived from another and an efficient information management altogether, the derivation of new data sets is organized in the spirit of a parsimonious "principle of structural replication", i.e. substructures devolve on the new data sets by mere reference as far as they remain unchanged, and are replaced by updated substructures otherwise. For instance, eliminating just one particular *TOB* thus would generate a new data set describing only the affected case and *TVs* resp., anew but will refer to its predecessor in any other respect.

Eventually, the set of all data sets derived from a *PDS* are pooled in a further superior object called ***batch***. In particular a *BATCH* initially contains a *PDS* and its substructure only. In connection with the "principle" this pooling of data sets opens the opportunity to reconstruct the evolution of particular objects (like *SUBS*) during the course of an analysis by means of appropriate selection operations (now applied to data sets). For instance, selecting all data sets containing information about a particular case would retrieve a complete description of what is known about this case.

Stated concisely, the integration of further data set objects containing (interim or final) results of applying statistical methods into a batch is possible in a straightforward way. In principle, this holds for objects used to record protocols of selecting, transforming, and analyzing operations, as well, though these types of objects are characterized by rather different internal structures and different mutual relationships, of course. Nevertheless, we believe that the integration of all the various kinds of objects into a single uniform representation framework is an essential precondition of any manageable software system development.

4 A Formal Approach to LDA

At the outset of any particular statistical data analysis there has to be performed a mapping of an "informal" model (as we like to call it) which is mainly expressed in terms of the actual ground domain onto a "formal" statistical model (see Grossmann (1986)). The informal model is formulated in terms of the practical problem whereas the formal model is a theoretically justified statistical tool (e.g. ANOVA, or regression). Strictly speaking, the transition from informal models to formal ones may be decomposed into two (consecutive) stages (see also Hand (1986)).

(S1) Transformation of a domain problem into formal terms, i.e. replacement of (informal) phrasing of a research problem by a corresponding statistical statement of the problem.

(S2) Connection of the (perhaps somewhat idealized) statistical problem formulation of (S1) to some well suited computational strategy.

There is no doubt that mechanizing (S1) is the challenging part of any project attempting to automate statistical data analysis but depends, besides statistical knowledge, on conversational competence, on the ability to cope with the cognitive behavior of clients, and on some amount of knowledge about the subject. As far as we know up to now there are very few attempts reported aiming at this goal (Hand's (1986) proposal being the most notable exception). For pragmatic reasons the predominant research interest in mechanizing statistics is devoted to stage (S2). Evidently there are quite a few approaches imaginable e.g. checking the theoretical requirements for applying a special statistical procedure (see Smith et al. (1983) for a concrete example for ANOVA), or modelling sequences of basic analytical steps in imitation of (frequently informal) statistical practice. For example, a regression analysis may consist of the following basic steps: transformation of data, estimation of regression parameters, analysis of residuals, testing hypothesis about the regression coefficients. The analytical structures described below are in the spirit of this second approach.

Considering the particular nature of longitudinal data formal models can be characterized by four main dimensions:

- structure of input data (D-dimension)
- type of statistical task contemplated (T-dimension)
- structural form of the regression equation (F-dimension)
- error structure (E-dimension)

According to the data structure discussed in the previous section the D-dimension is specified by several functions defined on the primary data set. Two simple examples are the following functions D1 and D2. D1 is is defined on $\mathbf{C} \times \mathbf{T}$ where $\mathbf{C}$ denotes the set of all cases and $\mathbf{T}$ is the set of all timevariates. The values of this function D1 are given by

$$\mathrm{D1}(C_i, TV_k) = \begin{cases} \mathrm{D11} & \text{no replication of the path of } TV_k \text{ in case } C_i \\ \mathrm{D12} & \text{replication of the path of } TV_k \text{ in case } C_i \\ 0 & \text{path of } TV_k \text{ is missing in case } C_i \end{cases}$$

The function D2 is defined only on the set of timevariates:

$$\mathrm{D2}(TV_k) = \begin{cases} \mathrm{D21} & \text{if } \mathrm{D1}(C_i, TV_k) = \mathrm{D11} \text{ for all } C_i \text{ with } \mathrm{D1}(C_i, TV_k) \neq 0 \\ \mathrm{D22} & \text{if } \mathrm{D1}(C_i, TV_k) = \mathrm{D12} \text{ for all } C_i \text{ with } \mathrm{D1}(C_i, TV_k) \neq 0 \\ 0 & \text{otherwise} \end{cases}$$

Which of these functions has to be applied depends on the T-dimension of the problem, i.e. the task which has to be performed. Basically, we distinguish five task categories:

T1 Descriptive condensing of data (including exploratory tools)

T2 Estimation of regression functions resp. parameters

T3 Comparing groups of timevariates (testing)

T4 Classification and (taxonomic) identification

T5 Modelling of relationships

These points have to be refined and parametrized in order to arrive at a well defined statistical task. For example T2 is split into the following categories:

T21 Estimation of regression function for each case

T22 Estimation of regression function for each subsample

T23 Estimation of regression function for the whole (sub-)sample

Additional parameters are in case T21 a specific timevariate, in case of T22 and T23 we need both a particular timevariate and subsample for parametrization.

The structural form of the regression equation (F-dimension) can be either of:

F1 Parametric regression equation

F2 Nonparametric regression equation

Again, this structural model has to be refined and parametrized by the specific timevariate. For example, the specific points for F1 may be the following ones:

F11	$y = f(t, \Theta)$	(explicit time dependence)
F12	$y = f(t, CV_1, \ldots, CV_l, \Theta)$	(additional case-dependent parametrization)
F13	$y = f(t, TV_1(t), \ldots, TV_k(t), \Theta)$	(implicit time dependence)

The error dimension considers mainly the variance-covariance structure in each timevariate both within each case and between different cases. Hence it depends on the D-dimension. For example, in case of data structure D11 (no path replications for a timevariate within the case) the following types of error structures relative to a timevariate are possible:

E11 Independent errors within the timevariate, independent cases

E12 Autocorrelated error structure within the timevariate, independent cases

Quadruples of specific values in these four dimensions together with the appropriate parameters will be called a basic model (BM) (see also Froeschl and Grossmann (1986)). For example, the basic model BM = (D21, T23, F12, E12) would correspond to the following statistical problem:

- data are a sample of a timevariate and for each case we have one path observed.

- we assume a regression model of the following type:

$$y(t) = \frac{e^{\Theta(t-CV_1)/CV_2}}{1 + e^{\Theta(t-CV_1)/CV_2}} + \epsilon(t)$$

- errors are autocorrelated
- we are interested in estimating the structural parameter Θ for representing the regression function

Note that not all combinatorially possible quadruples make sense. For example, a basic model of the form (D12, T23, F11, E11) is ruled out because D12 contains only information about the data structure of cases, but not about the whole data set. Moreover, D12 would require information about the error structure within cases not contained in E11. Altogether, the proper choice of data models is determined by T-dimension and F-dimension whereas the choice of an appropriate error model depends on the D-dimension. As this example accentuates, basic models contain also semantic information implicitly.

In order to perform the analysis basic models are linked with appropriate computational models (CMs) containing computational strategies, viz. skeletons of numerical algorithms. In our example of the basic model (D21, T23, F12, E12) the algorithm could be a kind of three stage least squares procedure for multivariate regression problems and consist of the following basic steps:

- transformation of time values
- estimation of Θ with the pooled sample of all observations
- estimation of autocorrelation within each case
- estimation of Θ using the estimated covariance-matrix within each case

Note that these basic steps of the CM will need additional information about the data structure to become an executable algorithm. For example estimation of the autocorrelation is easy in case of equidistant observations within each case using the classical moment estimate of autocorrelation. In case of arbitrary distances of the time observations one has to use a numerical optimization procedure. Again the decision what method applies is based on an appropriate function defined on the data structure.

Since it is not reasonable to make results (e.g. plots of paths) visible on some output medium as soon as they become available and—more important—the requirements of exposing computed output and organizing interaction between data analyst and gathered output are rather different compared to CMs, the output management is transferred to a so-called "result model" (RM). A RM takes care of preparing obtained CM-output for closer scrutiny by supporting a wide range of modes of output investigation and, to some degree, by providing explanations and (statistical, i.e. rather formal) interpretations as well. This comprises facilities for extracting particular subsets of collected results (e.g. all cases with maximum of fitted curve greater than a critical value), drawing attention to possibly irregular cases (e.g. pointing at outliers w.r.t. shape or amplitude), minor additional calculations (e.g. computing interpolated values for some or all cases at specified time points of fitted curves), and the like.

5 Some Illustrating Examples

Though the proposed data analysis system is far from being implemented completely, we are capable to exemplify our formal concepts to a considerable degree. The following demonstration is based on a real-life clinical study concerning diabetes research. Since the recorded data set of this clinical study requires an extensive symbolic description (due to its rather complex structure), we confine our presentation to the description of a single path which is also used subsequently in the sketch of a dialogue determining a particular statistical analysis.

The sample comprises 126 cases (patients) with type I diabetes (insulin dependence) under ambulant control. Patient data are recorded 6–8 times a year at a particular hospital diabetes center. At each visit there are recorded diabetes specific measurement data (glucose, HbA-values) as well as data on the patients' physical condition. The main purpose of this study is an evaluation of new diabetes training programs compared to conventional diabetes patient training. Hence, it seemed reasonable to to split the sample into two groups of patients: treatment by new program vs. treatment by other program. Furthermore, individual measurement series can be "sliced" into consecutive intervals naturally by remarkable events concerning diabetes status (e.g. change of diet, change over to new training program, etc.). The following schedule summarizes the most important features of the diabetes data sample:

primary data set	*diabetes_data*	$(N = 126)$
subsample #1	diabetes before (new) training programs	$(n_1 = 85)$
subsample #2	no diabetes before (new) training programs	$(n_2 = 41)$

casevariates (recorded on each case, in both subsamples):

age of patient
sex of patient
age of patient at diabetes manifestation
number of relatives suffering from diabetes too

pathgroup #1 *diabetes_ control*

timevariates: *glucose, hba*

pathgroup #2 *physical_condition*

timevariates: *weight, blood_pressure*

Since we refer to timevariate *glucose* in the sequel, we specify only the replication structure of *glucose* paths:

replication #1	start of patient training	—	first training program
replication #2	first training program	—	second training program

The transformation of this quite informal (and incomplete) data set description into a formal representation stating full particulars (which also involves asking lots of queries!) finally yields—among other object descriptions—the following description of TV *glucose*:

[var_label:	*"glucose",*
scale:	*metric/0.1,*
unit:	*mg,*
range:	*0 ... 1000,*
status:	*primary - diabetes_data,*
dataset_ref:	*[pds(diabetes_data)],*
tdata:	*complete,*
tcode:	*measured - year/0.01,*
tevent:	*point,*
tstructure:	*irregular,*
tscale:	*asynchro,*
replication_type:	*sliced,*
replication_id:	*indexed,*
replication_card:	*1 ... 2,*
tob_card:	*1 ... 20,*
path_occurence:	*sectional/pgroup - [diabetes_control],*
d_functions:	*[d2: d22, d3: d32, d4: d43, d5: 20, ...]*
]	

Fig. 4: Path description

Now imagine that the process of building a formal data set representation is already finished and, hence, we are in the position to start a (first) statistical investigation. We decide, for instance, to compile some descriptive measures concerning timevariate *glucose*. The following series of "screens" is intended to give a rough idea of a dialogue as conducted by the program (note: actual screen layout is more elaborate but we try to keep the presentation concise!).

Which kind of task should be performed?

1 Descriptive condensing of data
2 Estimation of regression function
3 Comparing groups
4 Classification and identification
5 Modelling of relationships

Response = 1

Screen 1

You want to analyze
1 Timevariates
2 Casevariates
3 Both time- and casevariates
Response = 1

Screen 2

Do you want to analyze a single timevariate?
Response = yes

Screen 3

Which timevariate shall be analyzed?
*1 *glucose**
*2 *hba**
*3 *weight**
*4 *blood_pressure**
Response = 1

Screen 4

Which kind of descriptive condensing of data?
1 Descriptive analysis of time values
2 Descriptive analysis of function values
3 Combined analysis of both time and function values
Response = 3

Screen 5

Which kind of combined analysis?
1 Interpolate time/function values
2 Complete duration of path above threshold
3 Compute duration of path below threshold
Response = 2

Screen 6

Please, specify threshold value
Response = 200

Screen 7

Since now the task type (T-dimension) of the current analysis is determined exhaustively, the D-dimension of the basic model is investigated. Evaluating the functions D1 and D2 as defined above, we find immediately (cf. fig. 4):

$$\mathrm{D1}(Ci, \mathit{glucose}) = \mathrm{D12} \qquad i = 1, \ldots, N$$

hence

$$\mathrm{D2}(\mathit{glucose}) = \mathrm{D22}.$$

Moreover, if we define additionally

$$\mathrm{D3}(TVk) = \begin{cases} \mathrm{D31} & \text{number} \geq 1 \text{ of replications of } TVk \text{ is constant over cases} \\ \mathrm{D32} & \text{number} \geq 1 \text{ of replications of } TVk \text{ is not constant over cases} \\ \mathrm{D33} & \text{number} \geq 1 \text{ of replications of } TVk \text{ is not constant over cases} \\ & \text{due to missing replications} \\ 0 & \text{otherwise} \end{cases}$$

$$\mathrm{D4}(TVk) = \begin{cases} \mathrm{D41} & \text{replications of } TVk \text{ are statistically independent} \\ \mathrm{D42} & \text{replications of } TVk \text{ are dependent} \\ \mathrm{D43} & \text{replications of } TVk \text{ stem from slicing an observation series} \end{cases}$$

$$\mathrm{D5}(TVk) = \max_{Ci} \left[\max_{u} \left[\text{card} \left(\; TOBs \text{ in } PREP\; u \text{ of path } TVk \text{ in case } Ci \; \right) \right] \right]$$

then we have

$$\begin{aligned} \mathrm{D3}(\mathit{glucose}) &= \mathrm{D32}, \\ \mathrm{D4}(\mathit{glucose}) &= \mathrm{D43}, \\ \mathrm{D5}(\mathit{glucose}) &= 20. \end{aligned}$$

Now it can be inferred mechanically that the only reasonable way to perform the analysis task as specified before is to repeat the computation of durations for each case and each description of path-group *diabetes_control*. As final step the F-dimension of the basic model must be determined (since we have chosen a descriptive task E-dimension does not matter).

Which is the (assumed) kind of functional relationship between time and timevariate?
1 Linear
2 Other parametric
3 Nonparametric
Response = 3

Screen 8

The program system now has enough information to infer the proper type of estimation (i.e. relationship approximating) procedure by means of a decision rule like:

if F(*glucose*) = F2 **and** D5(*glucose*) $\leq$ 20
then METHOD = *smoothing_spline*

Provided that the program user accepts the derived computational strategy, the selected computational model will contain the following computation steps eventually:

for each case of pds*(diabetes_data)* **do :**
  for each replication of tv*(glucose)* **do :**

(1) compute a smoothing spline
(2) compute the duration of estimated spline function for path *glucose* above critical value 200

  end_do
end_do

6 Concluding Remarks

In the preceding paragraphs we discussed some concepts for representing LDA data sets and a mechanism for determining applicable statistical analysis methods depending on particular analytical constellations (i.e. type of data, model structure, investigated problem). However, we did not take care of matters of realization (this endeavor is fraught with lots of difficulties!) and illustrated our ideas by means of a few small examples instead. In order to meet the diverging requirements of numerical, graphical, and data managing components as well as of symbol processing components, we try to develop a unifying representation framework. This framework must account for object oriented storage of chunks of knowledge (about either statistical "objects" or ways of proceeding) as well as procedural execution of methodological knowledge. Moreover, the various action plans of CMs and the output preparing functions of RMs need to be coupled with their corresponding numerical and (physical) data managing counterparts. At present, we have implemented merely a prototype program based on PROLOG (Froeschl (1987)) which is aimed at supporting the formation of conditional "job step" sequences. For instance, a job step may ask a query or call a (numerical) procedure but it may also contain another lower level job step sequence to be executed. By means of combining the advantageous features of PROLOG (search, pattern matching, inference) with an embedded mechanism similar to production rule interpreters and a frame-like (see Minski (1975)) storage organization we have created already a rather powerful software tool. Currently our main efforts are dedicated to find ways and means for interlocking the execution of action plans with correspondingly self-reorganizing symbolic data descriptions.

References

Blum RL (1982) Discovery and Representation of Causal Relationships From a Large Time-Oriented Clinical Database: The RX Project. Springer, Berlin

Froeschl KA (1987) A Special-Purpose PROLOG-Based Knowledge Execution Scheme for a Statistical Expert System. TR-ISI/STACOM-46, Dept. of Statistcs and Computer Science, Univ. Wien

Froeschl KA, Grossman W (1986) Knowledge Base Supported Analysis of Longitudinal Data. Proc COMPSTAT: 289–294

Grossmann W (1986) Statistische Software—ein Ersatz für den Statistiker? ZSI 16, 3: 131–142

Hajek P, Ivanek J (1984) Artificial Intelligence and Data Analysis. Proc. COMPSTAT: 54–60

Hand DJ (1986) Patterns in Statistical Strategy, in: Gale WA (ed.) AI & Statistics. Addison Wesley, Reading, pp 355–387

Huber PJ (1986) Environments for Supporting Statistical Strategy, in: Gale WA (ed.) AI & Statistics. Addison Wesley, Reading, pp 285–294

Jöckel K-H (1986) Statistical Expert Systems and the Statistical Consultant—Considerations about the Planning Stage of Clinical Studies, in: Haux R (ed.) Expert Systems in Statistics. Fischer, Stuttgart, pp 27–44

Minski M (1975) A Framework for Representing Knowledge, in: Winston P (ed.) The Psychology of Computer Vision. McGraw-Hill, New York, pp 211–227

Oldford RW, Peters SC (1986a) Statistically Sophisticated Software and DINDE, in: Boardman TJ (ed.) Computer Science and Statistics: 18th Symposium on the Interface, ASA, Washington, pp 160–167

Oldford RW, Peters SC (1986b) Object-Oriented Data Representations for Statistical Data Analysis. Proc. COMPSTAT: 301–306

Portier KM, Lai P-Y (1983) A Statistical Expert System for Analysis Determination. Proc. ASA Stat. Comp. Section: 309–311

Smith AMR, Lee LS, Hand DJ (1983) Interactive User-friendly Interfaces of Statistical Packages. Computer Journal 26, 3: 199–204

Thisted RA (1986) Computing Environments for Data Analysis. Statistical Science 1, 2: 259–275

Velleman PF (1985) Comment on Hahn GJ More Intelligent Statistical Software and Statistical Expert System: Future Directions. Amer. Stat. 39, 1: 10–11

Wittkowski KM (1986) Generating and Testing Statistical Hypotheses: Strategies for Knowledge Engineering, in: Haux R (ed.) Expert Systems in Statistics. Fischer, Stuttgart, pp 139–154

Data Analysis and Expert Systems: Generating Rules from Data

M. Gettler-Summa, H. Ralambondrainy and E. Diday
University of Paris, IX-Dauphine
75016, France
INRIA
Le Chesnay, France

Summary

The combined viewpoints of Data Analysis and Artificial Intelligence are helpful in approaching certain problems with reviewed efficiency; for example, an easily comprehensible description of clusters may be provided by a conjunctive representation of variables in clustering; and in the techniques of learning from examples, a reduction of the order of an algorithm complexity may be obtained by hierarchical methods.

In order to work in an area dealing with "symbolic data", new tools of formalization are needed. For example, these symbolic data demand an extension of classical rectangular array of Data Analysis: case may contain an interval or several values instead of a single value as usual, and objects are not necessarily defined by the same variables.

Three algorithms are based on that knowledge representation. The first one generates clustering characterized by conjunctions of events. The second and the third generate rules that can be used in the knowledge base of an expert system: they use logical operators and counting procedures simultaneously. The purpose is to produce rules defining membership for objects belonging to a class of examples, and rules for the class of counterexamples, with discriminant and covering criteria. One of these algorithms requires the "non overlapping rules" constraint; the other does not have that constraint and its complexity may be improved by a data analysis method.

They are presented with computer programs and examples on marketing data sets.

I. Introduction

Data Analysis and Machine Learning are two fields which are both concerned with data processing.

The first one is related to statistics; therefore one can efficiently apply it to large data sets, as for example numerical taxonomy does. It uses different numerical measures of similarity to group objects of a multidimensional space into clusters; the clusters may then be represented by a center of gravity which gives a summary of their meaning.

The other one is related to Artificial Intelligence. The aim of 'Learning from Examples' methods is the search of new concepts reflecting the internal structure of a set of events supplied by an expert. One may use 'similarity detection', which differs from the previous notion of numerical similarity, so far as it accounts for a certain estimate of the effect of a 'symbolic' generalization algorithm on the processed clusters.

Now, a good Expert System requires a high quality knowledge base and one of the main problems is to obtain some selected characteristics for the 'rule base' such as: the least loss of information, coherence, clarity, absence of redundancy, concision etc. We shall propose in this paper solutions to find decision rules capable of distinguishing, from among data observations, examples and counter examples.

In order to find such rules, we shall first propose two 'learning from examples' algorithms with non structure qualitative (nominal) attributes, which are usual to Data Analysis.

But Data Analysis has also its own methods to find 'rules from data'; to extend the usual table objects $\times$ variables on which for example, clustering is applied, we shall introduce symbolic objects; such objects are not necessarily defined on the same variables and may take several numerical or logical values for each variable on which they are defined. We shall then propose an extension of the previous algorithms on that new kind of objects and present some results from the corresponding program outputs.

II. Generating Rules from Qualitative Data

1) Definitions and Notations

Let $D_1, D_2, \ldots, D_p$ be p domains where D_j is a finite domain. A data array Ω is a subset of $D = D_1 \times D_2 \times \cdots \times D_p$.
The elements of Ω are called objects and denoted:

$$\omega = (d_1, d_2, \ldots, d_p) \text{ where } d_j \in D_j \text{ for } j \in \{1, \ldots, p\} = J$$

Let us define from Ω, p variables X_j, which are the p projection functions, corresponding to the D_j domains of Ω:

$$\begin{aligned} X_j :\ & \Omega \rightarrow D_j \\ \omega = (d_1, d_2, \ldots, d_p) & \rightarrow d_j = X_j(\omega) \end{aligned}$$

Variable X_j is said to be qualitative because D_j is a finite set and its q values, $m_1, \ldots, m_q$ are the q modalities of X_j as for nominal data in Data Analysis. Assertion A is a boolean function $\Omega \rightarrow$ {true, false}. A is the identification function for the denoted set:

$$\omega_A = \{\omega \in \Omega \mid A(\omega) = \text{true}\}$$

A couple (X_j, d_j) defines an elementary assertion, $A = (X_j = d_j)$ which represents the set of Ω objects which have the value d_j for the variable X_j:

$$\begin{aligned} A = (X_j = d_j) :\ \Omega & \longrightarrow \{\text{true, false}\} \\ \omega = (d_1, d_2, \ldots d_p) & \longrightarrow A(\omega) = \text{true if } X_j(\omega) = d_j \\ & A(\omega) = \text{false if not} \end{aligned}$$

We shall consider in this paper assertion as conjunctions of elementary assertions:

$$A = \bigwedge\{X_j = d_j \mid j \in J'\} \text{ with } d_j \in D_j \text{ and } J \supseteq J'$$

where $\bigwedge$ denotes the logical conjunction.

Let us assume $J' = \{1, \dots, m\}$ with $m < p$; assertion A is the identification function for the set:

$$\omega_A = \{d_1\} \times \{d_2\} \times \cdots \times \{d_m\} \times D_{m+1} \times \cdots \times D_p \cap \Omega$$

and we have also

$$\omega_A = \bigcap \{\omega_{X_j = d_j} \mid j \in J'\}.$$

Let us associate an object $\omega = (d_1, d_2, \dots, d_p)$ with an assertion:

$$A_\omega = (X_1 = d_1) \wedge (X_2 = d_2) \wedge \cdots \wedge (X_p = d_p).$$

If A and B are two assertions, and if $A \Rightarrow B$, then assertion B is said to be more general than A and we have the inclusion $\omega_A \subset \omega_B$.

2) Recognition Problem

Data consists in a set E of examples and a set CE of counter examples, to be recognized; E and CE are both included in D. Thus, among data which describe mushrooms characteristics, one may choose as 'examples' the toxic mushrooms, and as 'counter examples' the edible ones.

From A.I. point of view, the aim is to construct a good rule base describing the concepts of edibility, that is to find 'good assertions' which will be premises for rules, capable of describing and recognizing the example set.

In Data Analysis, that would be a discriminating problem on examples and counter examples, where one looks for logical discriminant functions.

3) First Approach

a) Initial Properties

Representative rules generated for each class (examples and counter examples) should have premises which satisfy the following two conditions:

covering: for each object ω of the initial array there is a unique assertion more general than A, in the rule base.

discriminating: for any assertion A, a 'discriminating quality' $Q(A)$ is defined as

$$Q(A) = \frac{\text{card } (\omega_A \cap E)}{\text{card } \omega_A} \geq \alpha$$

where α is an arbitrary threshold.

It is usually required in learning algorithms that representative rules of a class do not recognize objects of another class ($\alpha = 1$). But according to the statistical nature of the data in Data Analysis, we shall accept approximative rules, that is a percentage of badly classified elements.

Each rule of this type defines a sufficient condition for an object to belong to a certain class and the process then comes to generate a partition on each class, according to the discrimination constraint.

Naturally, one looks for a minimum number of rules, which simultaneously maximize the covering capacity of the base and minimize the number of misrecognized objects. Consequently one looks for A_h assertions related to E and for A_l assertions related to CE such as:

$$\sum_{h=1,s} \frac{1+\text{card}\,(\omega_{A_h} \cap\ CE)}{\text{card}\,(\omega_{A_h} \cap E)} + \sum_{l=1,t} \frac{1+\text{card}\,(\omega_{A_l} \cap\ E)}{\text{card}\,(\omega_{A_l} \cap CE)} \qquad \text{(I)}$$

becomes minimum.

(s: number of sub classes for the example subset

t: number of sub classes for the counter example subset)

The knowledge is then completed by specific rules concerning common properties of all objects of a class that is with necessary conditions for an object to belong to a determinate class.

b) Sufficient Rule Algorithm

One starts from an 'empty' rule class A_{p_0} which is the most general because no value is specified for the variables.

First Step

We first determine the representative assertion corresponding to an object ω pointed out from the initial data array. Therefore we order the variables according to ω modalities occurences in the class.

One considers then the assertion:

$$A_{p_1} = A_{p_0} \wedge \{X_j = d_j\}$$

where d_j is the modality which covers the maximum number of objects in the class. The generality of the rule is thus diminished but perhaps the rule is still non discriminant. So this phase is repeated with the remaining modalities of ω, until one finds a discriminant rule such as the next attempt does not improve the covering of the rule; we have so generated a discriminant assertion which covers the maximum number of objects including ω.

Second Step

By iterating the previous algorithm for each object of E, we generate as many assertions as examples in E. We then consider $\omega_{\max}$, the object in the class, which $A_{\max}$ is related to, that is the assertion which generalizes the largest number of objects in the class. We have

$$\text{card}\,(\omega_{A_{\max}} \cap E) = \max_{i=1,\text{card}\,E} \{\text{card}\,(\omega_{A_i} \cap E)\}$$

Now, one chooses $A_{\max}$ as a premise in the rule base. One then keeps out of the class objects which are generalized by $A_{\max}$, and repeats the whole process on to the remaining objects.

The iterations go on until there is no more object to be generalized in the class; the algorithm stops after a finite number of iterations because one starts associating each object with an assertion.

c) Complexity

One notices that in order to generate the most general rules from ω, one must check all possible discriminant conjunctions of attribute-value couples. As the previous algorithm is exhaustive on E, it is not efficiently used for large data sets.

We therefore propose a quick algorithm which enables us to reduce the number of objects pointed out at the beginning of the process, according to the optimization criterium (I).

Therefore, all variable modalities are ordered according to their decreasing frequency in the class.

One then determines an ordered set O of 'fictitious objects' in the form of a tree, the root and nodes of which are defined as follows:

- each component of the root is the most frequent modality of the corresponding variable.
- let ω_F be a node in the tree. Its p sons are generated by the following way: each son is formed by changing only one value of a component of ω_F. The chosen attribute to be changed corresponds to the most frequent value among the values which have not been taken previously.

The tree is developed by 'breath first' strategy.

As the number of nodes on O is too large, one tries to find rules from the η first fictitious objects, where parameter η relates to the optimization and the complexity of the algorithm.

A fictitious object is an assertion which identifies the most frequent modalities in the class.

Therefore it may give a representative rule with the 'best chance', but in fact, such a representative rule, generated by a fictitious object, perhaps does not recognize any real object of the class.

Therefore, instead of finding rules from fictitious objects, one finds representative rules generated from their nearest neighbours in the class. The nearest neighbour of each fictitious object is defined by a distance between observations. Generally we associate each variable X_j with a weight α_j. We shall here use the Hamming ponctual distance:

$$d(\omega,\omega') = \sum \alpha_j \delta(d_j^\omega, d_j^{\omega'})$$

where

$$\delta(d_j^\omega, d_j^{\omega'}) = \begin{cases} 0 & \text{if} \quad d_j^\omega = d_j^{\omega'} \\ 1 & \text{if} \quad d_j^\omega \neq d_j^{\omega'} \end{cases} .$$

It is eventually from those η closest neighbours that the algorithm works out the rule premises.

4) Second Approach

a) Initial Properties

We now look for an assertion set which satisfies the following conditions:

1. An assertion A has to be composed of $l_{\min}$ terms at least and $l_{\max}$ terms at most:

$$l_{\min} < \text{ length } (A) < l_{\max}$$

Numbers $l_{\min}$ and $l_{\max}$ are integers in between 1 and p.

2. An assertion A has to be α-discriminating; it means that the number of counter examples which are recognized by A, must be inferior to α:

$$\text{card } (\omega_A \cap CE) < \alpha$$

3. An assertion A must recognize β examples at least:

$$\beta \leq \text{card } (\omega_A \cap E)$$

This condition makes possible the elimination of assertions reflecting too peculiar observations and provides certain robustness of the results.

The example set E is associated with an assertion A_E:

$$A_E = \bigvee \{A_\omega \mid \omega \in E\}$$

A_E will be considered as an assertion system:

$$S_E = \{A_\omega \mid \omega \in E\}.$$

S_E system recognizes the example set and no counter example.

The algorithm we shall propose is capable of generating an assertion set S according to the above requested conditions, and more general than the initial assertions A.

Therefore, let A and B be two assertions with at least one common term

$$A = \bigwedge(X_l = a_l \mid l \in L) \text{ and } B = \bigwedge(X_k = b_k \mid k \in K)$$

We define the 'generalized' of A and B, that is the assertion of maximal length which generalizes A and B. We denote it:

$$\text{Gen } (A, B) = \bigwedge\{X_m = d_m, \text{ such as } a_m = b_m\}$$

b) GENREG Algorithm

The generalized assertions are computed from assertions related to couples of examples. Assertions which do not satisfy condition (1) and condition (2) are eliminated. One repeats the whole process on to those first generated assertions, and so on, until stabilization. One then takes out of the rule base those particular assertions that do not respect condition (3).

Let S be an assertion set; the 'generalized' calculation is based on the following resemblance measure, defined on S:

$$A, B \in S \quad \begin{array}{ll} s(A,B) = 0 & \text{if } A \text{ and } B \text{ have no common term} \\ s(A,B) = m & \text{if } m \text{ is the length of GEN}(A,B) \end{array}$$

Hence $s(A, B)$ is a measure of the common term number in A and B.

The algorithm works out GEN(S) set calculation by including GEN(A, B) in GEN (S), if it had not been done yet, when s(A,B) has a 'good' length according to the previous condition.

c) Quality, Optimality and Complexity Criteria

Quality Criterium for an Assertion Set

A consequence of condition (3) may be that, for some examples of E, it might be impossible to find, in the rule base, assertions which generalize them (that cannot happen in the first approach as one starts by pointing out each element of a class).

Let E_S be the sample set recognized par S:

$$E_S = \bigcup\{(\omega_A \cap E) \mid A \in S\}$$

the percentage P_{wc} of well classified objects that is to say the percentage of the examples that S does recognize, is a criterium for measuring the quality of the recognition potential of an assertion set S:

$$P_{\text{wc}} = \text{card}\,(E_S) \times 100\,/\,\text{card}\,(E)$$

In the same way let CE_S be the counter example set recognized by S:

$$CE_S = \bigcup\{(\omega_A \cap CE) \mid A \in S\}.$$

The discrimination quality of system S is measured by the percentage of badly classified objects, P_{bc}:

$$P_{\text{bc}} = \text{card}\,(CE_S) \times 100\,/\,\text{card}\,(CE)$$

If $\alpha = 1$, assertions recognize no counter example and $P_{\text{bc}} = 0$.

Algorithm Optimality

We can prove the following result:

Proposition:

the proposed algorithm is optimal from the following point of view: it finds the most covering assertion(s), at the imposed conditions.

Algorithm Complexity

As for the first approach, the combining task is important. Let n be the number of observations. At the first step, one must calculate $n(n-1)/2$ resemblance measures to obtain the generalized assertions. Algorithm complexity is at least n^2. Nevertheless, it is possible by appropriate methods to reduce it.

If it is possible to find a Partition $P = (P_1, P_2, \ldots, P_q)$ of Ω such as $\forall\,\omega \in P_i$ and $\forall\,\omega' \in P_j$ with $i \neq j$, $s(\omega, \omega') > l_{\text{min}}$, then it is useless to calculate resemblence measures for objects which belong to distinct classes of the partition.

If n_k denotes class k cardinality, the algorithm complexity becomes

$$\sum_k n_k^2 \ll n^2$$

Now such a partition can be realized by a descending connexity algorithm (Diday (1972)):

Let m be a positive integer and let define a binary relation R_m on Ω as following:

$$\forall\, \omega, \omega' \in \Omega\,,\ \omega R \omega' \Leftrightarrow s(\omega, \omega') \geq m$$

Such a relation is reflexive, symmetrical, but not transitive. Let R_m^* be the transitive associated closing; then the m partitions related to the equivalence classes defined by R_m^* for $m > l_{\min}$, are the requested ones.

One uses the so called 'descending connexity' proposition. One calculates Γ_1 from Ω, a partition, the P_k classes of which are such as, for $\omega \neq P_k$, it exists an element $\omega' \in P_k$ which has at least one common variable with ω; then Γ_2 is calculated and so on, till $\Gamma_{l_{\min}}$. The algorithm which generates the desired assertions, is eventually applied on each class of this last partition.

III. Symbolic Approach and Related Methods of Data Analysis

1) The Symbolic Problem

The aim is to describe objects which are usual to artificial intelligence, but not to Data Analysis, and to use tools like generalization and simplification to represent clusters which can be easily interpreted by the user. As a matter of fact, Data Analysis is often considered to be efficient but to lack explanatory capabilities.

In the symbolic approach, we define objects such as:

$$\omega^* = (V_1, V_2, \ldots, V_k) \text{ where } V_j \subset D_j \text{ for } j = 1, \ldots, k \text{ with } k \leq p$$

that means that variables X_j take their values in the power set $P(D_j)$.

Example:
X_1 : mushroom foot colour
D_1 : white, yellow, pink, brown, black
X_2 : mushroom season crop
D_2 : spring, summer, autumn, winter
$\omega_1 = [X_1 = \{\text{brown, black}\}] \wedge [X_2 = \{\text{spring, summer, autumn}\}]$
$\omega_2 = [X_1 = \text{pink}] \wedge [X_2 = \{\text{summer, autumn}\}]$
$\omega_3 = [X_2 = \{\text{spring, summer}\}]$

For such objects which are easily managed by artificial intelligence languages (lisp, prolog, smalltalk, etc...), we shall propose an extension of the notion of individuals which is usually used for rows of a data analysis array. It will then be possible to adapt these new objects, points of view and methods of clustering or of any other field of Data Analysis.

2) Definition of an Event

An 'event' e, denoted $e = [X_i = V_i]$ where $V_i \subset D_i$ means that the variable X_i takes its values in V_i; more formally e is a mapping $\Omega \rightarrow \{\text{true, false}\}$ such as an 'observed event' $e(\omega)$ is true iff $X_i(\omega) \in V_i$.

If we identify each elementary object ω of Ω with the vector of observed values $(X_1(\omega), \ldots, X_p(\omega))$, Ω can be imbedded in $\Omega' = D_1 \times \cdots \times D_p$.

Let e^{-1}(true) be the subset H of Ω, composed of elementary objects such as event e is realized. We say that:

- e is an intention definition of H
- H is the extension of e in Ω

3) Assertion Objects

An assertion objects A is a conjunction of events. It is denoted

$$A\ [X_1 = V_1] \wedge \cdots \wedge [X_k = V_k] \text{ where } V_i \subset D_i,\ k \leq p$$

Variable X_i takes its value in V_i for $i = 1, \ldots, k$.

More formally A is a mapping $\Omega \rightarrow \{\text{true, false}\}$ such as:

$$A(\omega) = \text{ true iff } \forall i = 1, \ldots, k \quad X_i(\omega) \in V_i$$

Like for an event, we shall say that:

- A is an intention definition of the L subset of elementary objects from Ω which realizes A, that is of A^{-1}(true).
- L is the extension of A in Ω.

4) Extra Knowledge

The variables that we shall here consider, are, to be coherent with the exposition in the single valued case, qualitative variables, ordinal or nominal ones.

But we shall accept the following extra knowledge on a variable X:

> if the domain H verifies the properties related to a hierarchy of sets, that is if $\forall h_1, h_2 \in H$, one has $h_1 \cap h_2 = \emptyset$ or $h_1 \supset h_2$ or $h_2 \supset h_1$, we shall call X a hierarchical type variable.

Example: X_3 = mushroom crop place

one can represent the different modalities by the following encoding:

1 $\longrightarrow$ wood of Crecy
2 $\longrightarrow$ wood of Versailles
3 $\longrightarrow$ area of Paris
4 $\longrightarrow$ Ermenonville wood
5 $\longrightarrow$ North east of Paris
6 $\longrightarrow$ Yvelines
7 $\longrightarrow$ England
8 $\longrightarrow$ Europe
9 $\longrightarrow$ Roquencourt

We have the following hierarchy:

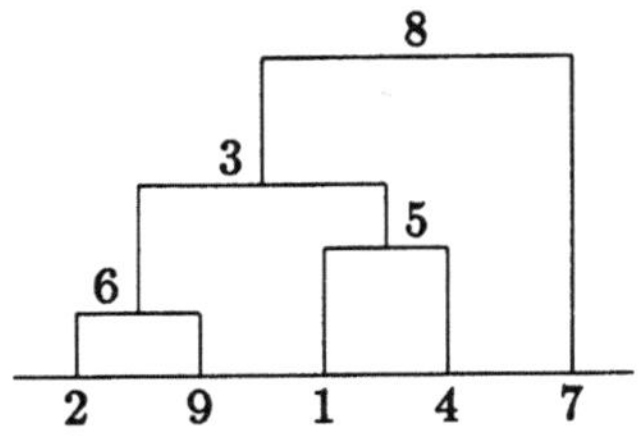

The various codes are used to simplify the representation of a class of objects.

5) Coherence Principle, Explicability Principle

a) Coherence Principle

Input and output must be expressed by the same kind of objects.

In usual Data Analysis the objects are numerical vectors, whereas in symbolic Data Analysis they are symbolic objects.

b) Explicability Principle

The results must be easily interpretable by the user even if they are less efficient.

It means, for instance, that even if a classical linear combination of variables given by a method of discrimination or regression technique is more efficient in explaining the dependent variable, we would prefer the explanations by a symbolic object because it is easier to understand by the user and may be used to build a knowledge base of an Expert System.

IV. Extension of the Rule Generating Algorithms to Assertion Objects

1) Similarity Problems

Learning methods like the ones we have just exposed, implies to evaluate an object compared with all the others in its class; one may calcalute its modality occurences in the set, or the common term number for two assertions.

In the case of generalized assertion objects, the problem amounts to calculate $d(V_i^j, V_q^j)$, a measure of the similarity between V_i^j and V_q^j where V_i^j is the variation domain of variable X_j for the object ω_i.

In fact, if one knows $d(V_i^j, V_q^j)$ for each i, j, q, one is able to calculate the generalized covering power of V_i^j in a class C by:

$$F(V_i^j, C) = \sum_{q=1}^{\text{card } C} d(V_i^j, V_q^j)$$

then one can calculate the generalized discriminating power of V_i^j:

$$D(V_i^j, C) = \frac{F(V_i^j, C)}{F(V_i^j, CE) + F(V_i^j, C)}$$

One may extend this formula to an assertion ω_a by

$$F(\omega_a, C) = \sum_{j=1}^{p} F(V^j, C)$$

and one has also:

$$D(\omega_a, C) = \frac{F(\omega_a, C)}{F(\omega_a, CE) + F(\omega_a, C)}$$

2) Some Propositions for $d(V_i^j, V_q^j)$

a) Variable Associated with a Taxonomy

One has $V_i^j \subset D_j \subset \mathbb{N}$. Each value of D_j corresponds to one of the taxonomy level. One denotes $h(V)$ the hight of the lowest level which contains the element of a domain V. One chooses:

$$\begin{aligned} d(V_i^j, V_q^j) &= \mid h(V_i^j \cup V_q^j) - h(V_i^j) \mid + \mid h(V_i^j \cup V_q^j) - h(V_q^j) \mid \\ &= 2h(V_i^j \cup V_q^j) - h(V_i^j) + h(V_q^j)) \end{aligned}$$

b) Ordered Qualitative Variable

One can define a pyramidal taxonomy (see Diday (1987)) on the set of X_j values, where a level hight is the difference of the extreme values. One chooses then for $d(V_i^j, V_q^j)$ a formula similar to the above one.

c) Non Structured Qualitative Variable

Let a be a number of common X_j modalites in V_i^j and in V_q^j.
One chooses:

$$d(V_i^j, V_q^j) = \frac{\text{card } V_i^j \times \text{card } V_q^j}{1 + a}$$

One may notice that in case of a single valued variable, that is when card $V_i = 1$ for each i, one finds that $F(V_i^j, C)$ is simply the frequence of the modality in the class.

3) Extension to the Previous Algorithms

For the first approach, we have to give a new conclusion for the occurence of V_i^j in its class, in order to give variables an order, when V_i^j is not a single value. As we consider non structured qualitative variables, we shall denote $\{v_i^j \mid j \in J\}$ the set of V_i^j elements; we shall now propose for the generalized occurence:

$$O(V_i^j, C) = \sum_{q=1}^{q=\text{card } C} \sum_{j \in J} p_q(v_i^j)$$

where

$$p_q(v_i^j) \;= 0 \text{ if } v_i^j \text{ is not in } v_q^j$$
$$p_q(v_i^j) \quad \text{is a positive number such as } \sum_{j\in J} p_q v_q^j = 1 \text{ if } v_i^j \text{ belongs to } v_q^j.$$

In the second approach, it is for the similarity between two assertions $A = \bigwedge\{(X_l = V_l \mid l \in L\}$ and $B = \bigwedge\{(X_k = W_k \mid k \in K\}$, denoted $s(A,B)$, that we have to define a new calculation.

We shall measure it by the sum of partial similarities $s_j(A,B)$ which are defined on X_j in the following way:

$$\begin{aligned} s_j(A,B) &= 1 \text{ if } V_j \cap W_k \neq \emptyset \\ s_j(A,B) &= 0 \text{ if not} \\ \text{and } s(A,B) &= \sum \{s_j(A,B) \mid j \in J\} \end{aligned}$$

Of course one has to give also a new definition to the new generalized assertions, for the multiple valued variables; it is important to choose it such as to have the same expression as for the generalized assertion for simple valued variables (when V_l and W_k are atomic values).

Eventually, the two previous algorithms may be applied with the above new definitions.

4) Computational Results

CABREXA and GENREG softwares, which correspond to the previous algorithms are implemented in FORTRAN 77. We used them on a data set which consisted in 630 mushrooms; they were examples of seven classes of edibility of mushrooms (from mortal to excellent tasting) and were characterized by 18 qualitative attributes. We looked for 'good' expert rules: the first approach proposed 37 exact rules (no badly classified objects):

Example:

```
IF          HAT COLOUR == RED
    AND     HAT FORM == BOMB
    AND     HAT SIDE == STRIA
    AND     FOOT FORM == CYLINDRICAL
    AND     RING? == NO
    AND     SPLINTER? == NO
    AND     FOOT REVETMENT == STRIA
    AND     FOOT TEXTURE == FULL
    AND     DOES THE FLESH EXCLUDE LIQUID? == NO
THEN        OBJECT BELONGS TO GROUP 4 OF GRAVE
            TOXIC MUSHROOMS
```

V. Conclusion

The algorithms we proposed in this paper, make it possible to generate rule bases from examples for Expert Systems and one may modificate them, according to the development of algorithm optimality criteria.

On the other hand, symbolic objects, which Data Analysis methods have been extended to, did already stimulate applications in clustering (see Michalsky, Stepp and Diday (1981), Quinqueton and Sallatin (1986), Ho Tu Bao, Diday and Gettler-Summa (1987)). Hence it is possible to create other developments with these objects in various other situations (see Diday (1987)) which may be concerned by both Data Analysis and Artificial Intelligence points of view.

References

Diday E (1972) Optimisation en Classification Automatique et Reconnaissance des Formes. RAIRO 6: 61–96

Diday E (1987) Orders and Overlapping Clusters by Pyramids, in: De Leeuw et al. (eds.). DSWO Press, Leiden

Diday E (1987) The Symbolic Approach in Clustering and Related Methods of Data Analysis: The Basic Choices. IFCS, Aachen

Ho Tu Bao, Diday E, Gettler-Summa M (1987) Generating Rules for Expert Systems from Observations. Rapport INRIA

Kodratoff Y (1986) Leçon d'Apprentissage Symbolique. Cepadues-editions, Toulouse

Michalsky RS, Stepp RE, Diday E (1981) A Recent Advance in Data Analysis: Clustering Objects into Classes Characterized by Conjunctive Concepts. Progress in Pattern Recognition

Quinqueton, Sallantin (1986) CALM: Contestation for Argumentative Learning Machine, in: Michalski, Carbonnel, Mitchell (eds.) Machine Learning, a Guide to Current Research. Kluwer and sons

Ralambondrainy H (1987) GENREG, Génération de règles à partir des structures, Résultats d'Analyse de Données. Rapport INRIA

Fuzzy Reasoning for Classification: An Expert System Approach

C. Granger
INRIA/ILOG, Domaine de Voluceau, Rocquencourt
BP 105, 78153 Le Chesnay, FRANCE

Summary

We present appropriate strategies and ways to represent knowledge for classification problems. These problems have noticeable characteristics, like plausible reasoning, a deep gap between data and solutions, noisy and unreliable data and they need a suitable expert system architecture. After a survey of different frameworks to represent inexact knowledge, we describe an object classification system, developed at INRIA, and based on fuzzy pattern matching techniques. We finally show how adequate control strategies may handle incomplete and contradictory data.

1 Introduction

The task of a classification problem solver is to identify an unknown object among a set of known classes. Known and finite solutions are a characteristic feature of classification, but different difficulties occur in this kind of problems:

- Classification is essentially based on heuristic reasoning. For instance, if the following rule is certain: $class_1 \longrightarrow feature_1$, the rule $feature_1 \longrightarrow class_1$ is only plausible. Classification rules are thus empirical rules often based on experience.
- Data may be noisy and unreliable. In order to handle several imprecise or contradictory solutions, conclusion parts of the rules must be applied simultaneously and the results combined.
- Data may be incomplete or too expensive to obtain. A classification system must deal with partial matching.

Different researchers have already proposed solutions through a better understanding of the classification problems.

Clancey (1984) describes heuristic classification as a two steps process. First, a phase of data abstraction is necessary because input data are rarely at the same level of abstraction than the solutions. Then, a refinement stage discriminates between the current hypothesis and refines them to a more specific classification.

Ganascia (1984) proposes a justification-based approach that must solve the problems of contradictions and ambiguities in diagnostic systems. After a consultation, the justifications of a result recall all the events that established or denied the result. With justifications, the system behavior is more clearly presented and contradictions that prevent the system to conclude, can be more easily detected.

In Protis, an expert system for medical diagnosis (Soula, Violettes and San Marco (1983)), imprecise data are represented by fuzzy events. More recently, the Diabeto system (Buisson, Farreny and Prade (1986)) offers a unified manner to represent imprecise and uncertain knowledge, using possibility distributions. The inference mechanism implemented in the Diabeto engine is based on the "generalized modus ponens" introduced by Zadeh (1979).

We propose in this paper an appropriate architecture to solve problems by classification. We designed for this purpose a system called Classic. Classic is implemented in LELISP/CEYX (Chailloux, Devin and Hullot (1984)). CEYX is an object-oriented extension of LELISP which proved to be very well adapted to the knowledge representation of the system. Besides the possibility of representing objects as structures, CEYX allows to inherit from superclasses, to describe the objects behavior by methods and to communicate with the objects via messages.

The paper begins with knowledge representation issues. The second section is a survey of the different frameworks that provide tools to manipulate inexact knowledge. Then, we propose an approach that uses fuzzy pattern matching techniques that proved very adapted to our applications and for classification problem solving in general. We finally show how adequate control strategies may handle incomplete and contradictory data.

2 Knowledge Representation

Knowledge representation is a fundamental topic in AI for the reason that a suitable knowledge representation leads to efficient control structures and natural man-machine interaction. Aikins (1980) has discussed the advantages of using an hybrid knowledge representation with a combination of production rules and frames. These frames are also called prototypes as they are stereotypical and perfect representative of their class.

2.1 The Prototypes

Prototypes contain descriptive knowledge about the class they represent. When the domain is structured in taxonomies, the prototypes are hierarchically organized from the most general class to the most specific. Prototypes can also be linked by part-of relationships to represent complex objects.
Example:

```
PROTOTYPE  E
    superclass: Early-A
    class: E
    ellipticity: [0, 0.6]
    isophotes: (smooth)
    centring: (good)
    profil: [0, 0.5]
    contour1: ContourE
    contour2: ContourE
```

Frames have usually standard facets. We have selected a subset of them that seems appropriate for the problems of classification:

- *The plausible values facet.* It contains values that can be taken by an object of the class of the prototype. In case of numerical features, this facet is an interval. In case of symbolic features it is a set of symbolic values.
- *The if-needed facet.* It contains a function that can compute a value if this value is needed.
- *The default facet.* It contains a default value which allows the system to carry on the classification, even with an important feature missing.
- *The importance facet.* It contains a weight that measures the importance of a feature in the description of the prototype.

The prototypes may have also control slots such as:

- *The threshold slot.* It contains a threshold from which it is decided that the hypothesis is confirmed or rejected.
- *The if-confirmed/if-rejected slots.* They contain a list of hypotheses that can be considered in case of confirmation (rejection), instead of following the normal order.
- *The strategy slot.* It determines the local strategy at the prototype level: forward, backward or both.

2.2 The Rules

Because most of the control knowledge is situated in the prototypes, the rules can be limited to the task of inferring new information. Nevertheless, knowledge in rules is uncertain as well as imprecise and tools must be defined to represent and manipulate it.
Example of rule:

```
RULE 3:
       if angle of contour2 far-from (5) inclination
       and ellipticity of contour2 ~> 0.3
       and inclination ~>  0.3
       then bar is present
```

3 Tools for Inexact Reasoning

Inexact reasoning characterizes classification problem solving: if we know that a given class implies a given feature, can we deduce that the observation of this feature implies the recognition of the given class? The deduction is only plausible and the weighting of this plausibility is a crucial problem.

3.1 The Limitation of Probability Theory

For a long time, probability-based models have been the only tools that could manipulate inexact information. In the probability framework, our deduction could be computed with $P(C \mid F)$ which is the conditional probability of the class C observing the feature F. From the Bayes rule:

$$P(C \mid F) = \frac{P(C) \times P(F \mid C)}{P(F)}$$

and generally, $P(C)$, $P(F)$, and $P(C \mid F)$ can be statistically estimated. Problems occur when several features are observed, when one wants to compute $P(C \mid F_1...F_n)$ and when $F_1...F_n$ are not independent.

Moreover, the relation $P(A) + P(\neg A) = 1$ does not fit with the subjectivity of the expert knowledge. If given observations lead to a probability on A, the expert does not automatically deduce that $\neg A$ has the probability $1 - P(A)$. For the same reason, the total ignorance of A does not mean $P(A) = 0.5$ and $P(\neg A) = 0.5$.

Another drawback is that the operations used to combine probabilities are multiplications and additions of numbers belonging to $[0, 1]$. After several combinations, these numbers can become unmeaningful.

The last drawback is that probabilities are not a suitable framework to represent imprecise knowledge.

3.2 An Empirical Approach

In the MYCIN project, an alternative framework has been developed, based on empirical considerations. A measure $MB(h, e)$ is defined as the belief that the hypothesis h is true knowing the evidence e. $MD(h, e)$ is the measure of disbelief that h is true knowing e. Several combination rules have been defined from these two measures (Shortliffe and Buchanan (1975)).

In this framework, the knowledge that a fact is true is clearly independent from the knowledge that this fact is false. The Bayes rule has been transformed into empirical combinations which are closer to the experts' type of reasoning.

Alternatively, the development of uncertain reasoning in computer science and especially in AI converges on important theoretical researches. The main ones are Shafer's theory and possibility theory.

3.3 Possibility Theory

Possibility theory is based on Zadeh's theory of fuzzy sets (Zadeh (1978)). In this framework, the uncertainty of an event is estimated by a possibility measure Π on a universe U that obeys to the following axioms:

$\Pi : P(U) \longrightarrow [0,1]$

$\Pi(\emptyset) = 0$

$\Pi(U) = 1$

$\forall A \in P(U), \forall B \in P(U), \Pi(A \cup B) = \max(\Pi(A), \Pi(B))$

A consequence of these axioms is the relation between $\Pi(A)$ and $\Pi(\neg A)$:

$\forall A \in P(U), max(\Pi(A), \Pi(\neg A)) = 1$

The necessity measure $N(A) = 1 - \Pi(\neg A)$ characterizes the link between A and $\neg A$.

The theory of possibility has the advantage of providing a unified way of representing imprecise and uncertain knowledge:

- An imprecise fact "X is A" (ex: "John is very tall") is described by a possibility distribution corresponding to the membership function of the fuzzy set A (ex: [1m85, 1m95]).
- An uncertain fact "X is A" (ex: "John is probably sick") is described by a pair of possibility value and necessity value.

4 Fuzzy Reasoning for Classification

Classic is a system developed at INRIA, particularly adapted for classification problem solving. Knowledge is represented by prototypes which describe the classes and rules which have the task of data abstraction from the data level to the level of description used in the prototypes. Pattern matching is a fundamental process of the system and we needed special matching mechanisms that were not all-or-nothing procedures. The possibility theory offers fuzzy pattern matching procedures (Cayrol, Farreny and Prade 1982)) that proved very well adapted to our problem.

4.1 Fuzzy Pattern Matching in the Rules

Pattern matching is the process of measuring the similarity between some data and a pattern. Usually this process returns a binary answer: true or false (1 or 0) but this answer lacks flexibility when the data and/or the pattern are imprecise or uncertain. For example, the matching of a number x with a pattern "p = 5" where 5 is an approximate threshold, is true when x = 5, untrue when x is far from 5 but the answer is uncertain around 5.

In a possibility based approach, we define a possibility distribution which is the membership function of a fuzzy interval I (here $[5 - \epsilon, 5 + \epsilon]$). The matching measures to what extend x belongs to the fuzzy interval (see figure 1) and provides a measure $\mu_I(x)$.

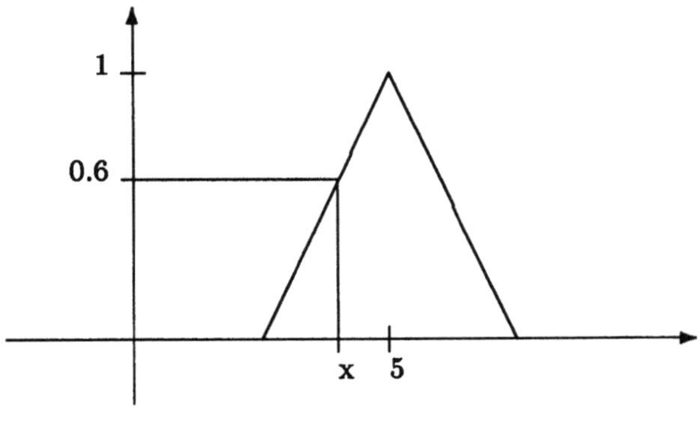

figure 1: matching of x with the pattern p ~= 5

Different predicates are thus defined in the system to manipulate imprecise numbers: `~=`, `~<`, `close-to`, `far-from` ...

Symbolic features are deduced by the rules from input data and the rules infer facts with a possibility measure $\mu_A(x)$ attached to them. Predicates that manipulate symbolic facts (`is`, `not`, `in`, `unknown` ...) have to combine these possibility measures. For instance, if we have deduced for the feature shape the values:

`shape: elliptical (0.2), average (0.7), spiral (0.3)`

if A is the fuzzy set of values taken by shape and B is the set (average, spiral), the matching with the condition "if shape in (average, spiral)" returns the possibility that shape has a value belonging to B:

$$\Pi(B|A) = \max_{val \in B} \mu_A(val) \quad (= 0.7 \ \textit{in our example})$$

4.1.1 Combination of Possibility Measures in Rules

When a rule has several conditions, the matching of each condition part returns a possibility measure. The measures are then combined together as a conjunction of patterns to provide the possibility of the rule conclusion: $\Pi(concl) = \min(\Pi(cond_i))$

Uncertainty in rules, can be measured by an estimation of the possibility of the conclusion knowing that the condition is true (Dubois and Prade (1985)). The possibility measure attached to the conclusion is then defined by:

$$\Pi(concl) = \min(\Pi(concl \mid cond), \Pi(cond))$$

4.1.2 Combination of Several Rules

A problem may occur when several rules conclude on the same value of the same descriptor and with different possibility measures.

If $cond_1$ *then conclusion*

If $cond_n$ *then conclusion*

In this case, we consider that the rules correspond to a unique rule with a disjunction of premises.

$$\Pi(conclusion) = \max_i \Pi(cond_i)$$

which corresponds to the rule:

If $cond_1$ *or, ... or* $cond_n$ *then conclusion*

4.2 Fuzzy Matching between the Prototypes and the Unknown Object

The matching process is seen here as a quantification of the similarities and the differences of both objects. Therefore, we have defined a *compatibility measure* to quantify the similarities and an *incompatibility measure* to quantify the differences. Features of the prototypes are described in fields which have one of the following types: set, interval or structured object.

4.2.1 Matching with a Field with a Set of Values

On the prototype side, the field is characterized by a set of possible values. On the object side, the field may have several values with a possibility associated to them.

1. **The measure of compatibility:** there is a compatibility between two fields if at least one value of the object field belongs to the set of values of the prototype field.

   If A_i is the fuzzy set of the possible values taken by the field i of the object,

   If B_i is the set of the possible values allowed for the field i of the prototype (in our case B_i is not fuzzy),

   the possibility that a common value exists in both fields is given by:

$$compat(field_i) = \Pi(B_i \mid A_i) = \max_{val \in B_i} \mu_{A_i}(val)$$

2. **The measure of incompatibility:** there is an incompatibility if one of the values of the object field does not belong to the set of values of the prototype field.

$$incompat(field_i) = \Pi(\neg B_i \mid A_i) = 1 - N(B_i \mid A_i) = \max_{val \in \neg B_i} \mu_{A_i}(val)$$

   where $\neg B_i$ is the complementary set of B_i

4.2.2 Matching with an Interval

When the field is an interval, the corresponding object field has a numerical value which must belong to the interval. Because of the imprecision of knowledge we consider this interval as a fuzzy interval I. The compatibility corresponds to the possibility that the value belongs to I. The incompatibility is the possibility that the value belongs to the complementary set of I.

4.2.3 Matching with a Structured Field

A structured field contains an object corresponding to a prototype in another classification tree. The object field thus contains an object that must have been sub-classified in the other classification tree. The compatibility (incompatibility) is the compatibility (incompatibility) of the class of the prototype field in the object field and it is returned by the sub-classification.

4.2.4 Global Matching

The global compatibility between the object and the prototype is given by the compatibility of *all* the fields, which corresponds to the conjunctive operation *min*.

$$compat(object, prototype) = \min_i \; compat(field_i))$$

The global incompatibility is given by the incompatibility of *at least* one field which corresponds to the disjunctive operation *max*.

$$incompat(object,\ prototype) = \max_i\ incompat(field_i)$$

compat(object, prototype) can be considered as a possibility for the object to match the prototype whereas, $1 -$ *incompat(object, prototype)* can be considered as a necessity.

Fields may have unequal importance in the description of the prototypes. In this case, it is not satisfactory that a non-important field which has a bad compatibility, causes a brutal decrease of the global compatibility. In the same way, an non-important field must not cause too high a increase of the global incompatibility.

The importance of the fields is expressed by a weight w stored in the importance facet of the field. To take these weights into account in the matching process, we use a weighted fuzzy pattern matching procedure described in Dubois, Prade and Testmale (1986):

$$compat(object,\ prototype) = \min_i\ \max(1 - w_i,\ compat(field_i))$$

$$incompat(object,\ prototype) = \max_i\ \min(w_i,\ incompat(field_i))$$

When all the weights are equal to 1, we get mere min and max operations. When a weight w_i is equal to 0, $field_i$ is not taken into account in the matching. Otherwise, the compatibility measure of $field_i$ is increased to $1 - w_i$ if the measure is below $1 - w_i$. Symmetrically, when the incompatibility measure is above w_i, it is decreased to w_i.
Example:

```
Prototype xxx : shape: (elliptical), importance (0.6)
Object yyy : shape: elliptical (0.2), average (0.7), spiral (0.3)
compat(shape) = max(0.4, 0.2) = 0.4
incompat(shape) = min(0.6, 0.7) = 0.6
```

5 Control Strategies

A suitable control strategy for classification is hypothesis directed because the solutions are known and limited. In rule based systems, this corresponds to backward chaining. On the other hand, because of incomplete and contradictory data, a maximum of knowledge is necessary to be combined. In hybrid systems, control can be assumed by prototype triggering as well as rule chaining so that different types of strategy can be chosen at the prototype level and at the rule level.

5.1 Control Strategies at the Prototype Level

At the prototype level, the strategy depends on the kind of search in the tree of prototypes. A depth-first search corresponds to a generate and refine strategy. Another type of search is to go from a solution node, up to the root. This strategy is the most focusing one but may eliminate solutions. It can be appropriate for subparts classification when trees are dense and search expensive. The default strategy is a depth-first search.

A rule structuration and compilation phase, described in Granger (1985) is performed at the knowledge base creation time, such that each node of the classification trees has small rule bases containing appropriate rules. At the beginning of the classification process, the compatibility of the unknown object with the most general class (the root of the classification tree), is checked and the rules attached to this node are activated. Then the unknown object is taken down the classification tree until no more solutions can be found. At each node, three different stages can be distinguished:

1. **The activation stage.** When a prototype is selected, the rules attached to it are activated. The rules must supply new knowledge on the discriminant features of the sons of the prototype.

2. **The matching stage.** The matching between the unknown object and the sons of the prototype returns, for each hypothesis, a measure of compatibility (how closely the hypothesis corresponds to the object) and of incompatibility (how important the incompatible values are). Low measures of compatibility and incompatibility reveal incomplete data, whereas high measures reveal contradictory data.

3. **The selection stage.** The selection depends on the thresholds of compatibility and incompatibility defined in the prototypes control slots. The set-up of their value yields different strategies that depend on the applications. When data are scarce, a low compatibility threshold and a high incompatibility threshold will support incomplete data and provide solutions that are not incompatible; when data are numerous and noisy, the reverse combination will support contradictory data and provide highly compatible solutions that may have also incompatible features.

5.2 Control Strategies at the Rule Level

At the rule level, strategies are determined by the type of chaining and the type of conflict resolution. In our system, the rule structuration process gathers rules that must be activated in the same classification context in the same rule base. Conflict resolution is thus mainly solved by the structuration stage.

Forward and backward chaining both have advantages. Forward chaining provides a maximum amount of knowledge while avoiding computational explosion (rule bases contain only useful knowledge); backward chaining allows to compute or ask or use a default value of a feature only when no rule is able to provide information on this feature.

6 Conclusion

A large number of problems can be solved by classification. We presented some fundamental common characteristics of these problems and proposed an appropriate architecture that handles the problems of uncertainty and imprecision with a possibilistic approach.

The system we described is used at INRIA for different pattern recognition applications (Thonnat (1985), Gandelin (1985)) and for an industrial application of default diagnosis.

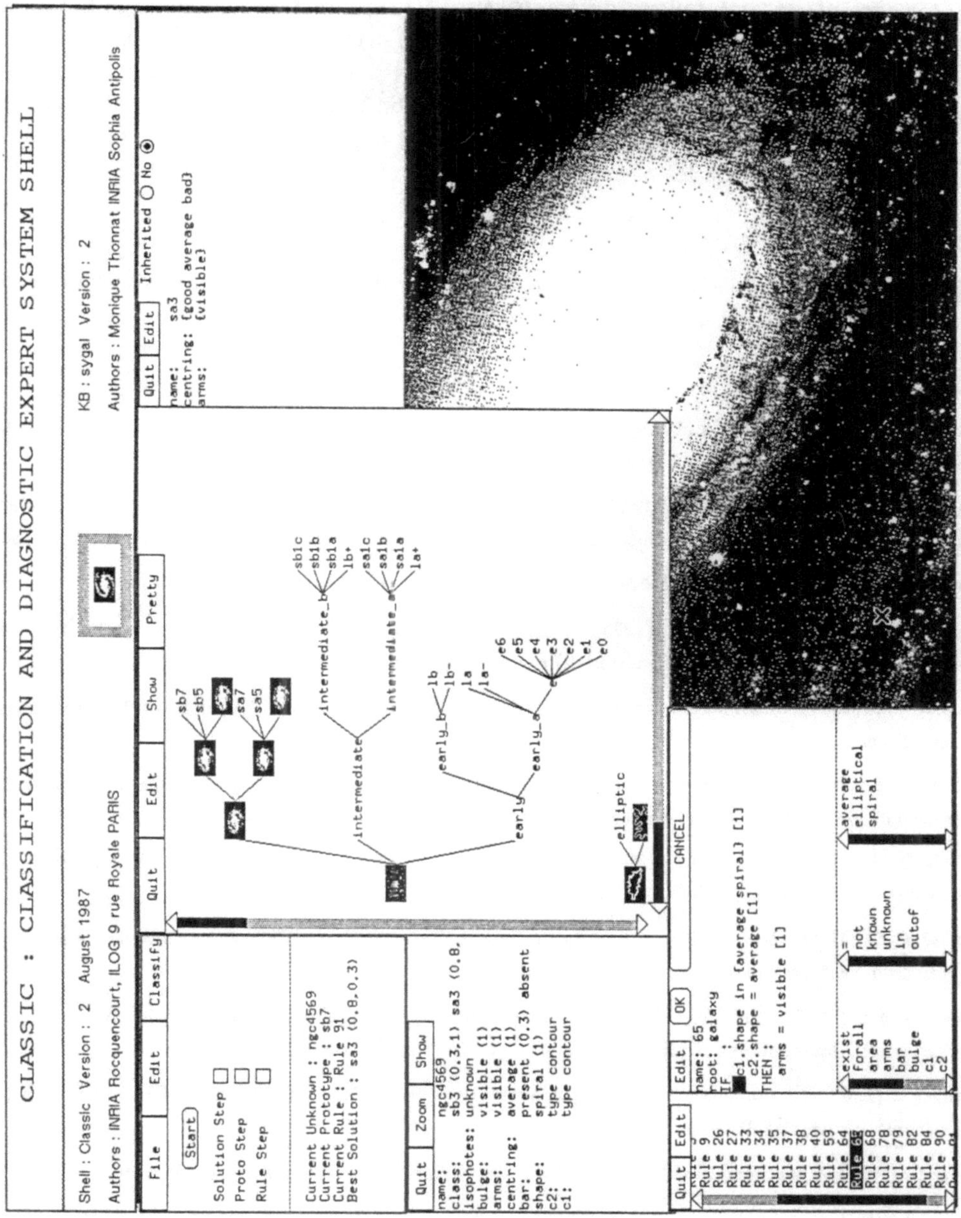
CLASSIC : CLASSIFICATION AND DIAGNOSTIC EXPERT SYSTEM SHELL
Shell : Classic Version : 2 August 1987
KB : sygal Version : 2
Authors : INRIA Rocquencourt, ILOG 9 rue Royale PARIS
Authors : Monique Thonnat INRIA Sophia Antipolis
File
Edit
Classify
Quit
Show
Pretty
Start
Solution Step
Proto Step
Rule Step
Current Unknown : ngc4569
Current Prototype : sb7
Current Rule : Rule 91
Best Solution : sa3 (0.8,0.3)
Zoom
OK
CANCEL
name: 65
root: galaxy
IF :
c1.shape in {average spiral} [1]
c2.shape = average [1]
THEN :
arms = visible [1]
intermediate
early
elliptic

Our current research follows different ways. A first direction is to enlarge the numbers of our applications to validate our approach to classification problem solving.

Another direction is to partly automate knowledge acquisition: when too many parameters have to be defined, the system adaptation to a new application can become a real burden. "Learning from examples" methods can help to define prototypes and rules in domains where a lot of examples of known class are available.

Acknowledgements

I am thankful to Didier Dubois and Henri Prade from LSI (Toulouse, France) for the fruitful discussions on possibility theory.

References

Aikins JS (1980) Prototypes and Production Rules: A Knowledge Representation for Computer Consultations. PhD thesis, Computer Science Department, Stanford University

Buisson JC, Farreny, H, Prade H (1986) Dealing with Imprecision and Uncertainty in the Expert System Diabeto-III, in: Proc. 2e Colloque International d'Intelligence Artificielle de Marseille. Marseille, France

Cayrol M, Farreny H, Prade H. (1982) Fuzzy Pattern Matching. Kybernetes 11

Chailloux J, Devin M, Hullot JM. (1984) LeLisp, a Portable and Efficient Lisp System, in: Proceedings of ACM Conference on Lisp and Functional Programming. Austin, Texas

Clancey WJ (1984) Classification Problem Solving, in: Proceeding of the National Conference on AI. Austin, Texas

Dubois D, Prade H (1985) Théorie des Possibilités. Applications à la Représentation des Connaissances en Informatique. Masson, Paris, France

Dubois D, Prade H, Testemale C (1986) Weighted Fuzzy Pattern Matching. Journée Nationale sur les Ensembles Flous, Toulouse, France

Ganascia JG (1984) Reasoning and Results in Expert Systems: Main Differences between Diagnostic Systems and Problem Solvers, in: Proceedings of ECAI84, Pisa, Italy

Gandelin M-H (1985) Etude de Faisabilité d'un Système Expert Appliqué à l'Identification Automatique d'Organismes Planctoniques. Diplôme d'Etudes Approfondies, Université de Nice

Granger C (1985) Reconnaissance d'objets par Mise en Correspondance en Vision par Ordinateur. Thèse de Doctorat, Université de Nice

Shafer G (1976) A Mathematical Theory of Evidence. Princeton University Press, Princeton

Shortliffe EH, Buchanan BG (1975) A Model of Inexact Reasoning in Medicine. Mathematical Biosciences 23

Soula G, Vialettes B, San Marco JL (1983) Protis, a Fuzzy Deduction-rule System: Application to the Treatment of Diabetes, in: Proc. MEDINFO83, Amsterdam

Thonnat M (1985) Automatic Morphological Description of Galaxies and Classification by an Expert System. Rapport de recherche INRIA

Zadeh LA (1978) Fuzzy Sets as a Basis for a Theory of Possibility. Fuzzy Sets and Systems 1

Zadeh LA (1979) A Theory of Approximate Reasoning, in: Hayes JE (ed.) Machine Intelligence. Elsevier

OPTRAD: A Decision Support System for Portfolio Management in Stock and Options Markets

S. Trautmann
Institut für Entscheidungstheorie und Unternehmensforschung, Universität Karlsruhe
Postfach 6980, 7500 Karlsruhe

Summary

OPTRAD (OPtion TRading ADvisor) is a prototype of a decision support system which helps to deal successfully in stock options and their underlying stocks. OPTRAD is especially designed for all kinds of market participants—for private investors as well as banks and other option dealers—acting at the Frankfurt Securities Exchange. At the present stage of completion OPTRAD integrates the following functions:

1. Automatic market data recording (almost in real-time) via BTX (BildschirmTeXt) communication.
2. Option valuation according to modern option valuation theory.
3. Buy/sell recommendations under consideration of institutional and financial restrictions.
4. Positionkeeping.
5. Daily and monthly portfolio revaluation.

The main program of OPTRAD is implemented in the declarative programming language PROLOG while some subroutines are written in the procedural language PASCAL. OPTRAD is running on IBM compatible Personal Computers (PCs) and needs at least 512 KB random access memory.

1 Introduction

In the last few years we have observed a phenomenal development of the options markets, mainly in the U.S. but also in other industrialized countries like Germany. An option is a contract conveying the right, but not the obligation, to buy (call option) or sell (put option) a specified financial instrument (the underlying asset) at a fixed price (exercise or strike price) before or at a certain future date (expiration or maturity date). There are two parties to an option contract: the option seller (writer or grantor) and the option purchaser (buyer or holder). The buyer purchases from the writer a commitment that the option writer will stand ready to sell or purchase a specified amount of the underlying instrument on demand. The price of this right which the option purchaser has to pay to the option seller is called option price.

Options are purchased and traded either on an organised exchange or in the over-the-counter (OTC) market. Exchange-traded options are standardized contracts on specified underlying instruments, like individual stocks, stock indices, precious metals, foreign currencies, bonds, treasury bills, futures contracts, with standardized amounts, exercise prices and expiration dates. OTC option specifications are generally negotiated as to the underlying instrument, amount, exercise price and exercise date. The rapid growth of both types of options markets indicates that many investors have found that at least one of the following reasons applies to them:

1. Options may offer a pattern of returns that could not be obtained with the underlying asset.
2. Options may provide a means of portfolio insurance.
3. Options may allow lower transactions costs than the underlying asset.
4. Options may offer tax advantages unavailable with the underlying asset.

Parallel to this rapid development of options markets there has been a corresponding progress in academic research concerned with these new securities. In two seminal papers published in 1973, Black and Scholes (1973) and Merton (1973a) provided the basic framework of modern option pricing theory. The option pricing models based on it are constructed in part to explain or predict the absolute price levels of options traded in synchronized and efficient capital markets. The observed precision of these valuation models relies primarily on preference-free, enforcable arbitrage conditions. Especially the Black/Scholes formula for valuing European-type stock options has become a widely used formula by practitioners in the options industry to guide their trading decisions: underpriced options (that is, the market price is below the corresponding model value) are considered to be good buys, and overpriced options (that is, the market price is above the corresponding model value) are considered to be good sells.

In this paper, we present a comprehensive option management tool called OPTRAD (OPtion TRading ADvisor) which helps to detect mispriced options according to modern option pricing theory. Furthermore, OPTRAD is designed to support the professional trader, broker, hedger, and portfolio manager as well as the private investor in dealing, investing, risk reducing, profit protecting and hedging strategies involving the use of options. The OPTRAD version described below has been made for users dealing in stock options and their underlying stocks at the Frankfurt Securities Exchange (Frankfurter Wertpapierbörse). The potential benefits of this OPTRAD version include the following:

1. Automatic market data recording via BTX communication. This enables the user of OPTRAD to analyse the mass of daily price data very quickly and at low cost in comparison to other real-time information services.
2. Calculation of fair values for stock options according to modern option pricing theory. Stock options which are seemingly mispriced with respect to their fair values are selected as candidates for purchase or sell recommendations.
3. OPTRAD recommends those stock options and stocks which should be bought or sold, under consideration of institutional and financial restrictions, and dependent on the user's risk preference.

4. Positionkeeping and portfolio revaluation at arbitrary instants provide solid support for trading, control, accounting and portfolio performance measurement.

The following sections describe OPTRAD's present stage of completion, outlining some of its major components and the programming environment. The main program of OPTRAD is implemented in the declarative programming language PROLOG while some subroutines are written in the procedural language PASCAL. OPTRAD is running on IBM compatible Personal Computers (PCs) and needs at least 512 KB random access memory.

2 Automatic Market Data Recording Via BTX (BildschirmTeXt) Communication

The fast detection of mispriced stock options requires the use of a real-time information service to get the actual market data. The German BTX (BildschirmTeXt) system, for instance, delivers the market data quoted at the Frankfurt Securities Exchange in almost real-time and at low costs compared with other information services like Reuters and so on.

BTX is a service offered by the German Federal postal offices (Deutsche Bundespost) since September 1983. BTX informations are transmitted through the public telephone net where the user can call information from the system and can send information to the system, too. The information and communication technology BTX is offered in many other countries under the name Videotex and is based on the British Viewdata System (see Deutsche Bundespost (1984)).

A BTX box and a BTX decoder is needed for a connection with the BTX net. These devices enable the BTX user to communicate with the central mainframe computer located at Ulm. In this machine all BTX information is organized in pages, which can be called by the user. Dependent on the type of BTX terminal the dialog occurs via a small keyboard (e.g., the remote control of a TV set) or an intelligent terminal (e.g., a homecomputer, personalcomputer or BTX terminal). Furthermore, it is possible to connect a mini or mainframe computer with the BTX system. Such a computer is able to communicate with many BTX users via Datex-P at the same time.

In this application the BTX terminal has to be an IBM compatible PC or AT with corresponding BTX hard- and software. This PC is used to receive the current stock and stock option prices via BTX and to save them on the internal fixed disk drive of the PC. It makes no difference which BTX decoder is used in the PC. The software of this application works with all decoders. During the development of this application we used the VC 2000 decoder from IMR (1987), but the installation of a different decoder is easy. A list of all certified decoders can be found under BTX page *1043031#.

In the following we will look at the information fed into the BTX system by the "Frankfurter Wertpapierbörse". The information offered by the "Frankfurter Wertpapierbörse" includes beside many other market price data the daily stock and stock option prices quoted at the Frankfurt Securities Exchange. The available market price information is structured as shown in figure 1. The opening and closing stock prices and all transaction prices between them (Fortlaufende Notierungen) you can get under

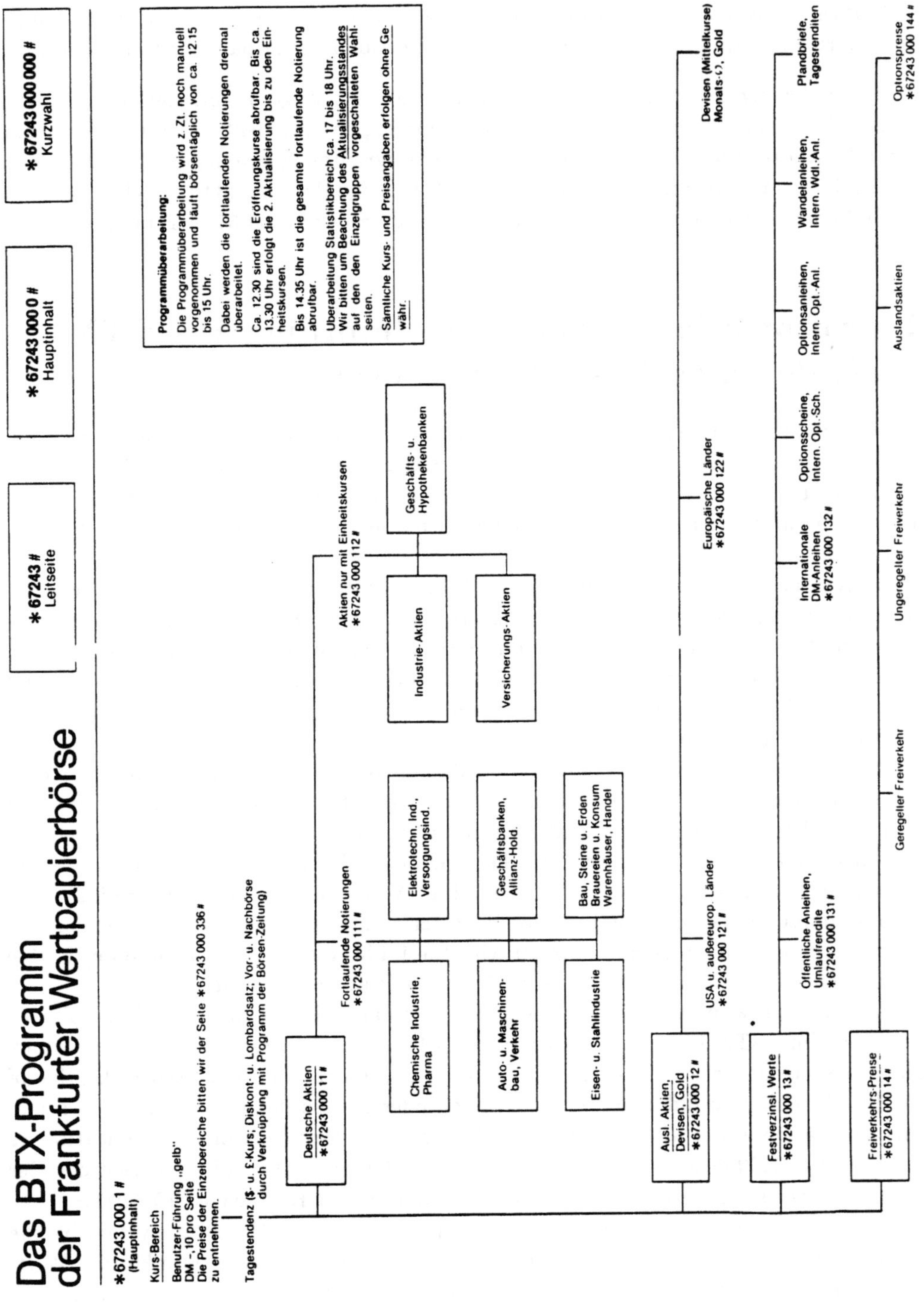

Figure 1: Structure of the market price information offered by the Frankfurter Wertpapierbörse via BTX.

page *67243000111#. These pages contain also the odd lot prices (Kassakurse). In the bottom right of figure 1 you can find the number *67243000144# representing the page with the corresponding stock option prices. Every trading day from half past eleven a.m. until four o'clock p.m. all values are updated. At the moment these data are entered manually in the BTX system, but it is already announced to be done automatically by a computer. All other market data needed by OPTRAD are available through BTX, too. This includes date and amount of dividend payments, subsidiary rights, interest rates for riskless borrowing and lending and so on. These data are available under BTX page *20027# from the "Börsen-Zeitung".

Figure 2 shows the first three BTX source data pages from June 24, 1987 for the chemistry branch stock option prices (BTX page *672430001441#). The first section, for instance, beginning with the symbol BAS comprehends all quoted prices for options written on BASF stocks. Call prices (following a "Kx:") are listed with decreasing maturities "x" while the put prices (following a "Vx:") are listed with increasing maturities "x". The first exercise price/option price entry in figure 2 ("360/4") means that at least one call option contract with exercise price K=DM 360 and expiration date January 15, 1988 was transacted at a price of DM 4. Price quotations without an additional mark denote transaction prices. Additional marks denote either bid or ask prices and are described under BTX page *672430003#.

```
Frankfurter Wertpapierboerse      0,50 DM


 Optionspreise
 Bereich: Chemie

 BAS K9:360/4 340/8TA 320/15TA 300/21TA
280/30 260/43 K6:360/3 340/5,4 320/10TA
300/16TZ 280/32TA 260/45G 240/64G K3:320
/2,7TA 300/6TZ 280/22TZ 260/41,5TZ 240/6
1,5TZ v3:320/18G 300/2TZ V6:320/20G 300/
9TZ 280/2,5G V9:320/27G 300/10TZ 280/7G


 BAY K9:400/5 380/7,5 360/10 340/20 320/
32TA 300/40G K6:400/2B 380/4 360/5,1TZ 3
40/15 320/26 300/42TZ 280/60TZ k3:360/2T
A 340/4,1 320/15TZ 300/36TZ 280/56TZ 260
/76G v3:340/7TZ V6:340/13G 320/6 V9:360/
35G 340/20 320/8,1TZ


 0 Zurueck                     weiter _
                          672430001441a

Frankfurter Wertpapierboerse      0,00 DM
```

```
 HFA K9:340/10 320/15 280/31TZ 260/50G K
6:340/5 320/10 310/15 290/19 280/25,1TZ
270/37TZ 270/35 260/45G 250/51TZ K3:320/
2,5TA 310/3,6 300/6,9TA 290/14TZ 280/25T
Z 270/33TZ 250/52 230/72 V3:300/7TZ V6:3
00/16TZ 280/8B 270/5,4B V9:300/18B 280/9
B

SCH K9:600/23 K6:550/31

 0 Zurueck     Blatt 2 von 3      Weiter _
                             672430001441b

Frankfurter Wertpapierboerse       0,00 DM

 DGS K9:650/5G 550/17B 600/13B K6:500/2
0,5 K3:490/4B

 SDF

 HEN
 RUE
 WAD3

 FDN K9:320/13TA 300/22G K6:320/10TA K3:
320/5B 30/77TA 280/28B

 0 Zurueck     Blatt 3 von 3      Weiter _
                             672430001441c
```

Figure 2: The first three BTX source data pages from June 24, 1987 for the chemistry branch stock option prices (BTX page *672430001441#).

Receiving the BTX data is done by calling the batch file HOLDATEN. This file is first calling the option data and thereafter the stock prices. If a different decoder than the IMR VC 2000 is used, this batch file must be modified. The BTX data files are not saved as normal ASCII (American Standard Code for Information Interchange) code, they are saved as ISO code (International Standardization Organisation). Therefore the first step after receiving the BTX data is the conversion from ISO to ASCII code. This conversion is done by the programm AUTOBTX. The result of this conversion is saved in the files AKTIEN.TXT and OPTIONEN.TXT. Since the main program of OPTRAD is written in PROLOG, the BTX ASCII-data files have to be converted into files of PROLOG facts. This is done by two conversion programs called WANDEL-A and WANDEL-O: WANDEL-A converts the stock data, while WANDEL-O converts the option data. Figure 3 shows the converted data, that means the PROLOG data file, which has been built through the conversion of OPTIONEN.TXT. "opxt" is a relation containing all call (x = k) or put (x = v) option data with maturity t written on a certain stock. opk9("bas",[...]), for instance, contains the exercise price and option price with corresponding price type code (e.g., price type code "0" denotes a transaction price) for all call options with maturity 9 (expiration date January 15, 1988) written on BASF stocks.

```
opk9("bas",[360,4,0,340,8,1,320,15,1,300,21,1,280,30,0,260,43,0])
opk6("bas",[360,3,0,340,5.4,0,320,10,1,300,16,2,280,32,1,260,46,
3,240,64,3])
opk3("bas",[320,2.7,1,300,6,2,280,22,2,260,41.5,2,240,61.5,2])
opv3("bas",[320,18,3,300,2,2])
opv6("bas",[320,20,3,300,9,2,280,2.5,3])
opv9("bas",[320,27,3,300,10,2,280,7,3])
opk9("bay",[400,5,0,380,7.5,0,360,10,0,340,20,0,320,32,1,300,40,3])
opk6("bay",[400,2,4,380,4,0,360,5.1,2,340,15,0,320,26,0,300,42,2
,280,60,2])
opk3("bay",[360,2,1,340,4.1,0,320,15,2,300,36,2,280,56,2,260,76,3])
opv3("bay",[340,7,2])
opv6("bay",[340,13,3,320,6,0])
opv9("bay",[360,35,3,340,20,0,320,8.1,2])
opk9("hfa",[340,10,0,320,15,0,280,31,2,260,50,3])
opk6("hfa",[340,5,0,320,10,0,310,15,0,290,19,0,280,25.1,2,270,37
,2,270,35,0,260,45,3,250,51,2])
opk3("hfa",[320,2.5,1,310,3.6,0,300,6.9,1,290,14,2,280,25,2,270,
33,2,250,52,0,230,72,0])
opv3("hfa",[300,7,2])
opv6("hfa",[300,16,2,280,8,4,270,5.4,4])
opv9("hfa",[300,18,4,280,9,4])
opk9("sch",[600,23,0])
opk6("sch",[550,31,0])
opk9("dgs",[650,5,3,550,17,4,600,13,4])
opk6("dgs",[500,20.5,0])
opk3("dgs",[490,4,4])
opk9("fdn",[320,13,1,300,22,3])
opk6("fdn",[320,10,1])
opk3("fdn",[320,5,4,30,77,1,280,28,4])
```

Figure 3: The file of PROLOG facts which corresponds to the BTX source option data presented in figure 2.

3 Option Valuation Theory

This section presents some results of modern option valuation theory which form a part of OPTRAD's knowledge base. A profound presentation of this theory can be found, for instance, in the textbook of Cox and Rubinstein (1985), while a recent survey on option valuation theory and the empirical evidence has been given by Geske and Trautmann (1986).

From a theoretical point of view, the value of an option is comprised of two components: intrinsic value and time value. Intrinsic value is the financial benefit to be derived if an option is exercised immediately, reflecting the difference between the exercise price and the market price of the underlying asset. Consequently, at the expiration date of an option its value equals always its intrinsic value. Should the stock price on the expiration date be less than the exercise price, a call option owner will not exercise his right to purchase the stock and the option will expire worthless. If, however, the stock price is greater than the exercise price, the call option will be worth the difference between the stock price and the exercise price. Thus, at the expiration date, the value of a call option can be expressed mathematically as

$$C_T = \max\,(S_T - K, 0) \tag{1}$$

where

T	denotes the expiration date,
C_T	denotes the value of the call option at the expiration date T,
S_T	denotes the price of the underlying stock at the expiration date T,
K	denotes the exercise price.

Correspondingly, a put option owner will exercise his right to sell only if it is to his advantage. If the stock price on the expiration date is greater than the exercise price, the put option owner will not exercise his right to sell the stock and the put option will expire worthless. However, should the stock price be less than the exercise price, the put option owner will exercise his right to sell the stock and the put option will be worth the difference between the exercise price and the stock price. Thus, at the expiration date the value of the put option is

$$P_T = \max\,(K - S_T, 0) \tag{2}$$

where P_T denotes the value of the call option at the expiration date T.

During the time remaining before an option expires, the price of the underlying asset can move so as to make the option profitable, or more profitable, to exercise. That is, an option whose intrinsic value is zero can get a positive intrinsic value. The chance that an option will become profitable, or more so, is always greater than zero. Therefore the selling price, or total value, of an option generally exceeds its intrinsic value which corresponds with a strict positive time value. This is especially true for an American-type call option written on a nondividend-paying stock. American-type means that the option can be exercised at any time before maturity. If an option can only be exercised at maturity, it is a European-type option. Like the stock options traded at the Frankfurt Options Exchange, most traded options are of the American type.

According to modern option pricing theory, the time value of a stock option depends on the way in which the future stock price movement is modelled. To specify such a model correctly is a crucial point, but fortunately there exist upper and lower bounds for the time value and total value of an option, respectively, which do not depend on the future stock price movement. Violations of such model-independent value bounds indicate riskless arbitrage opportunities. Riskless arbitrage opportunities in this context are situations that require no initial investment but that yield a positive amount immediately and only nonnegative amounts in the future under all possible circumstances. In the following, three examples for lower bounds will be given.

For American-type call options written on a stock that is not expected to pay dividends or issue rights during the life of the option as well as for completely payout-protected options, Merton (1973a, p. 144) derived what is called the strong European call option lower boundary condition:

$$C \geq \max\left(0, S - Ke^{-rT}\right) \tag{3}$$

where C and S denote the actual option and stock price, respectively, and r is the riskless interest rate. The term "European" stems from the fact that such an option is expected to be held until maturity. Thus, its value is effectively equivalent to an otherwise identical European call option. In well-synchronized markets the violation of (3) indicates that there is a profitable riskless arbitrage opportunity. The trading strategy to profit from a call option violating the European lower bound (3) consists of

- buying the call option,
- selling the stock and
- lending an amount equal to the present value of the exercise price,

and holding this portfolio till expiration. Since short selling is not permitted legally in Germany, this strategy can, however, only be followed by owners of the underlying stock.

Using similar arguments, Galai (1978) derived a lower bound for American-type call options written on dividend-paying stocks and unprotected against dividend payments. In Germany, exchange-traded stock options written before April 1, 1987 were partially protected against dividend payments reducing the stock price: the exercise price was reduced by the amount of the dividend on each ex-dividend date. Nowadays the stock options traded at German options exchanges are completely unprotected against dividend payments, like the options quoted at U.S. exchanges. For these "dividend-unprotected" call options which can be exercised any time until maturity, including the last moment before the stock goes ex-dividend, the early exercise dominance condition for multiple dividends over the life of the option, called pseudo-American lower bound, is

$$C \geq \max\left(0, \max_{i \in I}\left(S - Ke^{-rt_i} - \sum_{j<i} D_j e^{-rt_j}\right)\right) \tag{4}$$

where $I = (0, 1, \ldots, n+1)$, $t_0 = 0$ (the current date), $t_{n+1} = T$, and D_j denotes the amount of dividend (assumed to be non-stochastic) paid at date t_j ($j = 1, 2, \ldots, n$).

In words, (4) says that the value of an American-type call option not protected for dividends is not less than the maximum of (a) the highest of the European-type call option value for the option computed at each dividend date just before the stock goes ex-dividend, and (b) the European-type call option value assuming that the call option will be held to expiration. If premature exercise is not optimal, the trading strategy to profit from a call option violating the pseudo-American lower bound (4) consists of

- buying the call option,
- selling the stock and
- lending an amount equal to the sum of the present values of the exercise price and the expected dividends,

and holding this portfolio till expiration. If premature exercise is optimal, the trading strategy is analogous except that the position is terminated at some t instead of at T.

The third stock price drift-independent lower value bound to be presented concerns the put option. It is well known that for payout-protected European-type options the relationship between the prices of a put and a call option on the same underlying stock with the same striking price K and the same time to maturity T is given by

$$P = C - S + Ke^{-rT} \tag{5}$$

where P is the current market value of the put option. Any violation of this put-call parity relation, as originated by Stoll (1969), indicates riskless arbitrage opportunities in well synchronized, perfect capital markets. Merton (1973b) generalized this result to the case of American-type options by replacing the equality sign by the "$\geq$" sign in relation (5), which then represents a lower boundary condition (in terms of the call price) for a payout-protected put option:

$$P \geq C - S + Ke^{-rT} \tag{6}$$

Fortunately, the relation (6) remains valid even if the options under consideration are unprotected against dividend payments (see Cox and Rubinstein (1985, p. 152)). The trading strategy to profit from a put option which violates (6) consists of

- buying the put option,
- buying the stock,
- selling the corresponding call option,
- lending an amount equal to the present value of the exercise price,

and holding this portfolio either until the expiration date or the date where the call option is exercised.

In summary, it must be re-emphasized that the European and pseudo-American lower bound for call options (3) and (4), respectively, as well as the call-dependent lower bound for put options (6) are appealing because they imply hypotheses which can be tested without estimating any parameter for the stock or option return distribution.

Observations that the market price of an option did not fall within these bounds would indicate the possible existence of arbitrage opportunities, i. e., above normal profits.

In order to be more specific about the price process for options in a securities market where individuals allocate their wealth to select optimal investments, we need to be more specific about either their risk preferences, their beliefs (about the distribution of stock price changes), or both. Option valuation along the lines of Black and Scholes (1973) avoids restrictive assumptions on individual risk preferences and makes only assumptions on the price movement of the underlying stock.

In their seminal model Black and Scholes (1973) assumed that the stock price changes are continuous with a constant variance of price changes. More precisely, they assumed that the movement of the stock price can be described by a diffusion-type process

$$dS = \mu S\, dt + \sigma S\, dz \tag{7}$$

where μ is the instantaneous expected rate of return on the stock per unit time, σ is the assumed constant instantaneous standard deviation of the return on the stock per unit time, dz is the increment of a standard Gauss-Wiener process. This implies, that the logarithm of asset returns at the end of a period (with finite length) is normally distributed.

The key insight by Black and Scholes (1973) was that it is possible to construct a riskless portfolio involving positions in the stock and the underlying stock, and to avoid the possibility of arbitrage profits, the return on this riskless portfolio must be the riskless interest rate. Under the usual perfect market conditions and the assumption that the stock pays no dividends during the life of the option, the above insight and some mathematical manipulations result in a partial differential equation which must be satisfied by the value of the option. For example the call option must satisfy

$$0 = C_t + \frac{\sigma^2}{2} S^2 C_{SS} + rSC_S - rC \tag{8}$$

where subscripts denote partial derivatives. The solution of this partial differential equation, subject to the terminal condition

$$C_T = \max\,(S_T - K, 0) \tag{1}$$

is the famous Black/Scholes formula for a European-type call option on a nondividend paying stock. It reads:

$$C^{BS} = SN_1(d_1) - Ke^{-rT} N_1(d_2) \tag{9}$$

where

$$d_1 = \{\ln(S/K) + (r + 0.5\sigma^2)T\} \,/\, \sigma\sqrt{T}, \qquad d_2 = d_1 - \sigma\sqrt{T},$$

and $N_1(d)$ is the univariate cumulative normal density function with upper integral limit d.

The value of a call option given by equation (9) can be intuitively interpreted as a weighted difference between the stock price and the present value of the exercise price of the option, in which the weights can only take values between zero and one. When the option is very far "out of the money" (i.e., $S \ll K$) both weights are equal to zero and the the call option value is also equal to zero. When the option is very far "in the money" (i.e., $S \gg K$) both weights have a value of one and the call option has a value equal to the difference between the stock price and the present value of the exercise price. Loosely speaking the weights represent the probability that the option will expire in the money (where the stock price is greater than the exercise price).

Note that the Black/Scholes model value of a call option depends on five model parameters: the actual stock price S, the exercise (or striking) price K, the time to maturity T, the interest rate r and the volatility σ of the stock price. Of these parameters only the last one is not directly observable. An important feature of equation (9) is that the call option value does not directly depend on the expected rate of return of the underlying stock. The reason for this is that the current stock price S already embodies the market expectations about future stock prices.

The assumed absence of income distributions on the underlying security causes the Black/Scholes formula to overstate the value of an American-type call option on a stock with dividend payments during the option's time to expiration. A dividend paid during the option's life reduces the stock price at the ex-dividend instant, and thereby reduces the probability that the stock price will exceed the exercise price at the option's expiration.

Fortunately, there exist two different approaches which are able to consider dividend payments. Both assume that if the stock pays a certain dividend D at the ex-dividend instant t ($t < T$), then the stock price simultaneously falls by a known amount αD. This assumption causes an early exercise probability between zero and one. By means of sophisticated economic reasoning, Roll (1977) succeeded in deriving the following closed-form solution for this valuation problem:

$$\begin{aligned} C^R &= S[N_1(b_1) + N_2(a_1, -b_1; -\sqrt{t/T})] \\ &\quad -Ke^{-rT}[N_1(b_2)e^{r(T-t)} + N_2(a_2, b_2; \sqrt{t/T})] \\ &\quad +\alpha D e^{-rt} N_1(b_2), \end{aligned} \tag{10}$$

where

$$\begin{aligned} a_1 &= \{\ln(S/K) + (r + 0.5\sigma^2)T\}/\sigma\sqrt{T}, & a_2 &= a_1 - \sigma\sqrt{T}, \\ b_1 &= \{\ln(S/S_t^*) + (r + 0.5\sigma^2)t\}/\sigma\sqrt{t}, & b_2 &= b_1 - \sigma\sqrt{t}, \end{aligned}$$

and $N_2(a, b; \rho)$ is the bivariate cumulative normal density function with upper integral limits a and b, and correlation coefficient ρ. S_t^* is the ex-dividend stock price determined by

$$C^{BS}(S_t^*, T - t, K) = S_t^* + \alpha D - K \tag{11}$$

above which the option will be exercised just prior to the ex-dividend instant. The left-hand-side of relation (11) denotes the Black/Scholes value of a call option with time to maturity $T - t$, exercise price K and stock price S at time t.

Almost at the same time, Schwartz (1977) provided a numerical method by which the value of an American-type call option an a stock with known dividends can also be calculated. Moreover, this method enables the valuation of American-type call options on dividend-paying stocks as well as American-type put options on dividend-paying stocks. Since American-type options can be exercised at any instant, the boundary conditions must be checked to see if for every possible stock price at each instant, the option is worth more held than exercised (i.e. alive or dead). Thus, if t^- is the instant before exercise and t^+ the instant after, then for put options,

$$P_{t^-} = \max\left(K - S_t, P_{t^+}\right) \tag{12}$$

and for call options,

$$C_{t^-} = \max\left(S_t - K, C_{t^+}\right). \tag{13}$$

If a dividend payment D occurs during the life of the option, the stock price must fall by the previously assumed amount αD to eliminate riskless arbitrage opportunities. If t^- is the instant before the ex-dividend date t and t^+ is the instant after, then

$$S_{t^-} = S_{t^+} + \alpha D. \tag{14}$$

Merton (1973a) was able to demonstrate that call options may be exercised only at the ex-dividend dates, while the exercise boundary condition for put options must be checked at every instant. The latter implies that the valuation of an American-type put option requires the solution of the Black/Scholes partial differential equation (8) (with C replaced by P) subject to the terminal condition (2) and an infinite number of boundary conditions (12) for which no analytic solution have been found. Consequently, Schwartz (1977) devised a numerical method (more precisely, an implicit finite difference approximation scheme) for solving such problems. This numerical method, the valuation formulae of Black/Scholes (1973) and Roll (1977) as well as the boundary conditions described above, form a central part of OPTRAD's knowledge base at the present stage of completion.

4 Recommendation Rules to Purchase or Sell Options or their Underlying Stocks

The main purpose of OPTRAD is to make recommendations to purchase or sell options or their underlying stocks. The detection of options which are seemingly mispriced from the users view forms therefore an important part of OPTRAD. If an option is mispriced, there exists a trading strategy whose profit is abnormal. For a completely riskless trading strategy abnormal profit means profit in excess of the opportunity costs of the initial investment. The uncertain profit of a risky trading strategy is considered abnormal, if, after adjusting for risk by subtracting a risk premium, the expected profit exceeds the opportunity costs of the initial investment where the risk premium is determined by an asset pricing model (the Capital Asset Pricing Model (CAPM) or the Arbitrage Pricing Model (APM)).

Observed deviations between stock options' market prices and their corresponding model values may occur for the following reasons:

1. The valuation model is not valid.

2. The model parameter are not correctly specified.

3. The markets for the related assets are not well synchronized.

4. Observed market data are inaccurate.

5. The option market is inefficient (allowing abnormal profits for some option traders).

Consequently, the recommendation of trading strategies which guarantee abnormal profits is even in the presence of sophisticated option valuation models a nontrivial task.

```
                    OPTRAD - Option Trading Advisor

Select CALL options which are apparently mispriced with respect to the
       European lower bound
       Pseudo-American lower bound
       Black/Scholes model price
       Roll model price
Select PUT options which are apparently mispriced with respect to the
       Call-dependent lower bound
       Black/Scholes model price (for European-type options)
       Finite-difference model price (for American-type options )
Other: Load data for another date  -  current date: none
       Buy/sell recommendations
       Data Corrections
       BTX Source Data and Text File Corrections
       Fault finding (knowledge base listing)

Select function with cursor keys and <return>                F10 = Main menu
```

Figure 4: Main menu of the advisory dialogue (Screen-dump).

Observed violations of lower boundary conditions for both put and call options, however, can be attributed only to the aforementioned reasons (3)–(5). This enables clearer answers to the question whether the option market under consideration is efficient or not. The main menu of the advisory dialogue (see figure 4) offers therefore, first of all, the selection of options which are mispriced with respect to some model-independent lower value bound. For instance, when the OPTRAD user (say, e.g., a bank) first loads the market data of June 24, 1987 (by selecting the item "`Other: Load data ....`") and then selects the item "**`Call-dependent lower bound`**", he will get the screen image represented by figure 5. Scrolling in the output file which is displayed through the main window (headed with "`OPTRAD` - Option Trading Advisor") will enable him to select all put options which are apparently mispriced with respect to the call-dependent lower bound from the view of a bank on June 24, 1987.

The attribute "apparently" indicates, that some mispricing signals may be due to the nonsimultaneity of trade of related assets and/or market data inaccuracy. Given accurate data and synchronous trading of stock options and their underlying stock, it would have been possible to implement the aforementioned trading strategy which ensures the abnormal profits or returns (net of all observable opportunity and transaction costs and on a per contract basis) displayed in the column with the heading "Abnormal return". Since, however, neither market synchronization nor data accuracy can be guaranteed, it makes sense to examine whether these mispricing signals occured consistently during the past trading days. Figure 6 reveals the frequency of such mispricing signals during the period from June 5, 1987 to June 24, 1987.

```
Select PUT options which are apparently mispriced                          ┌ Working ─┐
with respect to the call-dependent lower bound                             │vhb       │
from the view of a bank on 24.06.87                                        └──────────┘

┌──────────────────────── OPTRAD - Option Trading Advisor ───────────────────────────────┐
  Line 1      Col 1      Indent   Insert
 Test = pcp     Investor type = bank        Date   = 240687    Price type = A

 Stock  Exp.    Striking  S/K-   Call        Put         Abnormal   Critical   Annual
 symb.  month   price     Ratio  price       price       return     int.rate   abn.re
 -----  -----   --------  -----  --------    --------    --------   --------   ------
  bas    Oct     320.00    OM     10.00TA     20.00G      152.28     0.083
  hwk    Oct     140.00    OM      4.00B      18.00G       94.79     0.097
  hwk    Jul     120.00    AM      5.00        1.00TZ      84.40     0.304          2
  khd    Jul     180.00    AM      4.80        9.00G      133.18     0.320          4
  veb    Jul     300.00    AM     12.00TA      1.00TZ     279.33     0.384          9
  vow    Jul     400.00    AM      9.00TZ      3.00G       72.35     0.114          2

└────────────────────────────────────────────────────────────────────────────────────────┘
F1:Help F3:Search F4:Subst F5:Copy F6:Move F7:Del F8:ExtEdit F9:ExtCopy F10:End
```

Figure 5: Apparently mispriced put options (with respect to the call-dependent lower bound) observed on June 24, 1987 (Screen-dump).

```
Select PUT options which are apparently mispriced                          ┌ Working ─┐
with respect to the call-dependent lower bound                             │vhb       │
from the view of a bank on 24.06.87                                        └──────────┘

┌──────────────────────── OPTRAD - Option Trading Advisor ───────────────────────────────┐
 Stock  Exp.    Striking  24 23 22 19 16 15 12 11 10  9  5
 symb.  month   price      6  6  6  6  6  6  6  6  6  6  6
 -----  -----   --------  -- -- -- -- -- -- -- -- -- -- --
  bas    Oct     320.00    *
  con    Oct     340.00                         *
  dai    Jul    1000.00       *  *  *  *
  drb    Jul     280.00                      *
  drb    Oct     300.00                      *
  hap    Jul     380.00                         *
  hwk    Jul     120.00    *     *
  hwk    Oct     140.00    *
  kfh    Oct     480.00                               *
  khd    Jul     180.00    *     *
  mmw    Jul     170.00                      *  *     *
  mmw    Oct     170.00                         *     *
  prs    Jul     170.00                         *     *
  sdf    Oct     190.00                               *
  sie    Oct     700.00                               *
└────────────────────────────────────────────────────────────────────────────────────────┘
F2:Goto line      F3:Search       S-F10:Resize window      F10:End
```

Figure 6: Mispricing signals for put options (with respect to the call-dependent lower bound) observed during the period from June 5, 1987 to June 24, 1987 (Screen-dump).

In OPTRAD a put option is considered as mispriced with respect to the call-dependent lower bound (or more popular: the Put Call Parity (=pcp)), if the put option was apparently mispriced at least "Minimum" times in the last "Frist" days. This flexible mispricing rule is called "`mispriced_pcp`" in the PROLOG code, and the complete PROLOG code for the selection of mispriced put options with respect to the call-dependent lower bound reads as following:

```
mispriced_pcp(_,_,_,_,X,X,_).

mispriced_pcp(Tag,Monat,Jahr,Frist,Minimum,Anzahl,[T,M,J,_,_|REST]):-
  Minimum>Anzahl,
  innerhalb_der_frist(Frist,Tag,Monat,Jahr,T,M,J),
  Anzahl2=Anzahl+1,
  mispriced_pcp(Tag,Monat,Jahr,Frist,Minimum,Anzahl2,REST).

mispriced_pcp(Tag,Monat,Jahr,Frist,Minimum,Anzahl,[_,_,_,_,_|REST]):-
  Minimum>Anzahl,
  mispriced_pcp(Tag,Monat,Jahr,Frist,Minimum,Anzahl,REST).
```

It is reasonable to specify the parameters "Minimum" and "Frist" such that from the apparently mispriced put options presented in figure 6, only the put option written on DAIMLER stocks (stock symbol: dai) with expiration date July 15, 1987 and exercise price DM 1000,– is considered as mispriced.

In a similar way stock options are considered as mispriced with respect to other model-independent lower bounds or with respect to some model value. However, although most parameters of the option valuation models previously discussed are in principle observable without error, the future volatility of the underlying stock is unknown. It must be estimated either from the historical or the implied volatility. The latter obtains by equating the option's actual market price to the model value, and solving (numerically) for the only unobservable parameter, the volatility. In general it is difficult to estimate or predict the future volatility precisely. Therefore OPTRAD considers an option as apparently mispriced with respect to some model value only if the deviation between the observed market price and the corresponding model value is sufficiently large. For example, according to the PROLOG rule "bsmod1" presented in figure 7, options are considered as mispriced with respect to the Black/Scholes model if the relative deviation $|BS - PR|/PR$ between the market price PR and the model value BS is larger than "Filter" percent.

Although all mispriced options detected by OPTRAD are candidates for a buy or sell recommendation, not all mispriced options can be bought or sold because of institutional and financial restrictions.

For instance, since short selling is not permitted legally in Germany, a call option which is overpriced (i.e., when the market price is above the model value) can be written or sold only by owners of the underlying stock or the call option, respectively. Clearly, OPTRAD considers only those mispriced options to be good buys or sells whose associated trading strategy is compatible with institutional and financial restrictions, the actual portfolio position, and last but not least: the investor's risk preference.

```
bsmodl(Name,Anl,PA,Filter,K,Art,Vol,T,AK,Laufzeit,Jahre,[BP,PR,P_ART|P]):-
   bsmodl(Name,Anl,PA,Filter,K,Art,Vol,T,AK,Laufzeit,Jahre,P),!,
   kurs_ok(PA,P_ART),
   zinssatz(Anl,Zins,_),
   BP>0,
   PR>0,
   R_hoch_mt=exp(-Jahre*ln(Zins)),
   E_hoch_mrt=exp(-Jahre*Zins),
   V=(ln(AK/BP)+(Zins*Jahre)+(Vol*Vol*Jahre/2))/(Vol*sqrt(Jahre)),
   normalvert_1(V,Delta),
   V2=V-(Vol*sqrt(Jahre)),
   normalvert_1(V2,Delta2),
   BSc=AK*Delta-(BP*E_hoch_mrt*Delta2),
   bs_fehlbewertet(Art,BSc,BS,AK,BP,PR,R_hoch_mt,Filter),
/*   Abweichung=(BS-PR)/PR,    */
   Gamma=exp(-V*V/2)/(2.5066283*AK*Vol*sqrt(Zins)),
   Theta=(AK*Vol*exp(-V*V/2)/(5.0132566*sqrt(Jahre)))+(BP*R_hoch_mt*log(Zins)*Delta2),
   SdK=AK/BP,finde_typ(SdK,Typ),kzt(P_ART,Zusatz,_),
   laufzeit_tage(Laufzeit,Tage),
   datum(Heute),
   Endtag=Heute+Tage,
   endtag_monat(Endtag,Monat),
   openappend(save_file,Name),
   writedevice(save_file),
   writef("  %4   %3   %8.2   %3   %7.2%2  %8.2  %5.2  %7.4  %9.2  %8.2  %1",
          K,Monat,BP,Typ,PR,Zusatz,BS,Delta,Gamma,Theta,AK,T),
   nl,
   writedevice(screen),
   closefile(save_file),
   !,
   fail.

bsmodl(_,_,_,_,_,_,_,_,_,_,_,_).
```

Figure 7: PROLOG code of the mispricing rule "**bsmodl**".

5 The Choice of the Development Language

At the beginning of the project we looked for an appropriate programming environment to write the prototype. PROLOG seemed to be a more powerful tool than procedural programming languages like PASCAL or FORTRAN for developing a decision support system.

Using PROLOG, the user is free to concentrate on issues of knowledge representation and acquisition rather than search strategies. One can naturally develop a top down algorithm. This allows rapid adjustment of decision rules in OPTRAD as recommended by brokers and financial researchers. Typically the expert does not know a priori how he thinks, and the system inevitably develops somewhat by trial and error.

However, during the process of system development we recognized that for some tasks of OPTRAD the procedural language PASCAL was the better choice. The BTX communication part and the conversion programs were exclusively written in PASCAL. The first intention to write these programs in PROLOG was dropped during the development. The BTX communication software works at assembler and BIOS (Basic Input Output System) level for communication with the BTX decoder. This is the reason for problems that would occur in case of a PROLOG implementation. Manufacturers of BTX decoders and BTX communication software told us the same experience.

Moreover, the implementation of a complete linear conversion algorithm, that is not based on any rules, can be done much faster in PASCAL than in PROLOG. For instance the following short program cut-out shows the PASCAL statements to eliminate superfluous blanks in BTX source files:

```
while not eof(FI) do
  begin
    readln (FI,SI2);
    if (SI1[length(SI1)] = ' ') and (SI2[1] = ' ') then
      delete (SI2,1,1);
    while pos('  ',SI2) > 0 do
      delete (SI2,pos('  ',SI2),1);
    writeln (FO,SI2);
    SI1 := SI2;
  end;
```

This could not have been implemented in PROLOG so fast and easy. Furthermore, the valuation of put options by the numerical methods mentioned above is very difficult to realize in PROLOG. Therefore a fast and powerful system has to include interfaces to programming languages like PASCAL and FORTRAN. Numerical procedures could then be implemented in these languages while the main program could be realized in an expert system shell or PROLOG.

Acknowledgement

I am indebted to Oliver Rietschel for programming the PROLOG parts of this OPTRAD prototype

References

Arbeitsgruppe Optionsgeschäft (1983) Das börsenmäßige Optionsgeschäft. Frankfurt

Bachem J (1987) EVA-Expertensystem zur Vermögensanlageberatung. Wiesbaden

Ball CA, Torous WN (1985) On Jumps in Common Stock Prices and The Impact on Call Option Pricing. Journal of Finance 40: 155–173

Black F, Scholes M (1973) The Pricing of Options and Corporate Liabilities. Journal of Political Economy 81: 637–659

Blaupunkt-Werke GmbH (1986) So wird der PC zum BTX Terminal. Btx: *30396# Btx: *30396#

Blaupunkt-Werke GmbH (1986) Profess. Hardware für das Kommunikationssystem BTX

Blaupunkt-Werke GmbH (1986) Profess. Software für das Kommunikationssystem BTX

Borland International (1985) Turbo Pascal 3.0. München

Borland International (1987) Turbo PROLOG 1.1. Scotts Valley

Clocksin F, Mellish CS (1984) Programming in PROLOG. Berlin–Heidelberg

Cox JC, Rubinstein M (1985) Options Markets. Englewood Cliffs

Cox PR (1984) How we build Micro Expert. in: Forsyth R (ed.) Expert Systems. Chapman and Hall, London

Deutsche Bundespost (1984) BTX Anbieter-Handbuch. Gießen

Deutsche Bundespost (1985) Nachtrag zum BTX Anbieter Handbuch. Gießen

Deutsche Bundespost (1987) Nachtrag zum BTX Anbieter Handbuch. Gießen

Frankfurter Wertpapierbörse (1986) Das BTX Programm der Frankfurter Wertpapierbörse

Galai D (1978) Empirical Test of Boundary Conditions for CBOE Options. Journal of Financial Economics 6: 187–211

Geske R, Trautmann S (1986) Option Valuation: Theory and Empirical Evidence. in: Bamberg, Spremann (eds.) Capital Market Equilibria. pp 79–133

Herausgebergemeinschaft Wertpapiermitteilungen (1987) BTX PROGRAMM. Börsen Zeitung, Düsseldorf

InfoTeSys (1986) Btx-InfoTool, Handbuch Btx1 and Btx3. Düsseldorf

Janko WH, Feurer R (1987) Eine Studie zur Beurteilung der sprachlichen Eignung der Programmiersprachen BASIC, PASCAL, APL, APL2, LISP und PROLOG zur Programmierung regelbasierter Systeme. in: Opitz, Rauhut (eds.) Ökonomie und Mathematik. pp 355–364

Merton RC (1973a) Theory of Rational Option Pricing. Bell Journal of Economics and Management Science 4: 141–183

Merton RC (1973b) The Relationship between Put and Call Option Prices: Comment. Journal of Finance 28: 183–184

Merton RC (1976) Option Pricing When Underlying Stock Returns are Discontinuous. Journal of Financial Economics 3: 125–144

Roll R (1977) An Analytic Valuation Formula for Unprotected American Call Options on Stocks with Known Dividends. Journal of Financial Economics 5: 251–258

Schwartz ES (1977) The Valuation of Warrants: Implementing a New Approach. Journal of Financial Economics 5: 79–93

Stoll H (1969) The Relationship Between Put and Call Option Prices. Journal of Finance 24: 801–824

Trautmann S (1986a) Warrant Pricing—Some Empirical Findings for Warrants Written on German Stocks. Methods of Operations Research 54: 293–306

Trautmann S (1986b) Finanztitelbewertung bei arbitragefreien Finanzmärkten—Theoretische Analyse sowie empirische Überprüfung für den deutschen Markt für Aktienoptionen und Optionsscheine (to be published). Springer Verlag

Trautmann S (1987) Die Bewertung von Aktienoptionen am deutschen Kapitalmarkt—Eine empirische Überprüfung der Informationseffizienzhypothese. Schriften des Vereins für Socialpolitik, Gesellschaft für Wirtschafts- und Sozialwissenschaften, 165: 311–327

Whaley R (1982) Valuation of American Call Option on Dividend-Paying Stocks—Empirical Tests. Journal of Financial Economics 10: 29–58

Yazdani M (1984) Knowledge Engineering in PROLOG. in: Forsyth R (ed.) Expert Systems. Chapman and Hall, London

Decision Support for Qualitative Data Analysis – KEE Shell Linked to FORTRAN Programs –

U. Tüshaus
Institut für Informatik, Universität der Bundeswehr Hamburg
Holstenhofweg 85, D-2000 Hamburg 70

Summary

For the development of a knowledge-based system for a well established application domain it is often necessary to integrate knowledge representation as well as algorithmic solution techniques. For the first part, it is desirable to use the possiblities of dedicated expert system shells like the Knowledge Engineering Environment (KEE) which integrate frame and production rule languages to form hybrid representation facilities. For the second part, most application programs, i.e. in our case data analysis algorithms for different problem types, have been implemented in command-oriented languages like FORTRAN etc. So, it seems natural to represent the expert knowledge (and the decision support process) in the KEE system and to access the data analysis programs (and the numerical processing capabilities) available on other computers. The experiences in interfacing two different working environments, here KEE/LISP and FORTRAN/MS-DOS, as well as the technical details of an experimental implementation are discussed.

1 Context of the Decision Situation

Suppose, a company plans to develop different versions of a product based on an analysis of its customer base (example from Schader (1978)). In a survey several sociographic (age, marital status) and demographic (professional status, average income) data as well as data on communication (media contact) and consumption (preferences on price/quality) are collected.

The aim of the study is then to find a structure on the set of customers which enables the company to develop products for major customers groups. As most of the data is qualitative it is planned to use a suitable data analysis method for this application. The raw data of the survey are sketched in Fig. 1.

Often several departments are involved in the different steps of the study, i.e. the definition of the aims, the planning of the survey and the computational analysis itself. Furthermore, as many analysis methods are based on theoretical models with certain assumptions, the conclusions drawn are only valid when these conditions are respected. This makes it desirable to combine available data analysis methods with knowledge-based systems which support the user in his specific application.

data matrix

customer classification

	marital status	*profession*	···	*price/quality*
customer 1	not married	teacher	···	h<l<a<m
customer 2	married	pub owner	···	l<h<m<a
⋮	⋮	⋮	⋱	⋮
customer n	not married	farmer	···	h<l<m<a

Figure 1: The data matrix of the customer study example.

For the group of qualitative data analysis methods to be used for the customer study the following questions have to be discussed.

— Are the methods envisaged adequate for the data type? The data analysis methods to be applied are based on the representation of the data as a family of binary relations on the set of objects, i.e. the set of customers (see Schader (1978), Barthélemy and Monjardet (1981), Barthélemy and Monjardet (1988), Leclerc (1988), or Schader and Tüshaus (1986) for more details on this approach). Possible structures on the variables are, for example, equivalence relations (nominal data), complete orders/preorders (cardinal data), hierarchies and others. For each variable the underlying structure type has to be tested for feasibility.

— Which transformations of the raw data are necessary? While several data types (e.g., nominal or cardinal data) transform directly into the corresponding binary relations, hierarchies, for example, must be represented by a family of relations. Other structures, if possible, have to be scaled when still quantitative.

— What type of result is meaningful for the problem data? When the catagory of each variable is known a suggestion for the result type of the analysis can be made: for nominal data, a classification of the objects, not a ranking, is natural.

— What is a reasonable interpretation of the results? The specific methods give no direct way to link the result (e.g. the classification) to the input data. On the other hand, it is now possible to investigate the raw data with respect to the outcome of the analysis. The rows of data matrix, for example, can be clusterwise rearranged and thus variables can be identified which characterize particular classes.

2 Knowledge and the Analysis Process

As it has been outlined in the previous section, the different phases of such a marketing study necessarily involve different forms of knowledge. The first step, i.e. the problem definition and the choice of the solution model, is usually performed well before - and therefore separate from - the actual computational analysis. So this will not be included, although an important part of the study as it is here where the aims of the investigation and the data necessary for it are decided.

The next steps, however, should be part of the decision support system as they are carried out in connection with the computational analysis.

In our case, at first the data matrix has to be investigated if the kind of data is appropriate to be used with the group of analysis methods envisaged: acquaintance with the theoretical background of the underlying model and its relevant assumptions (qualitative data, meaningful representation as binary relations) is required as well as knowledge of possible problem formulations and feasible solution methods. Subsequently, suitable scaling methods must be available when the raw data have to be transformed without bias into binary relations for input. The data analysis methods themselves are usually already implemented as computer algorithms and tested. For the interpretation of the results, heuristic strategies to explore the outcome are necessary as well as measures of fit to identify variables or variable values characteristic for classes.

The particular forms of expert knowledge (theoretical basis, heuristic strategies from experience and implemented numerical algorithms) are summarized in Fig. 2.

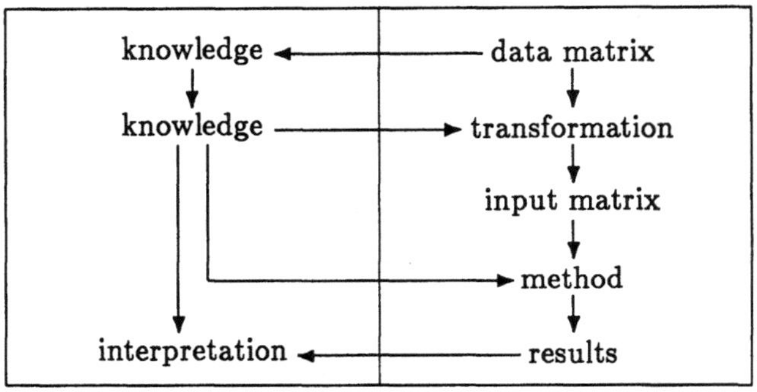

Figure 2: Knowledge in the analysis process.

Whereas knowledge on solution methods can be coded directly in algorithmic descriptions and the corresponding computer programs, an effective representation of the expert knowledge about the application is more difficult to obtain. For this purpose, it is obvious to use an expert system shell like the Knowledge Engineering Environment (KEE). Systems like this have been developed to provide the expert with facilities to express the knowledge effectively within the system, in a form which can be used easily by the system and where the (explicit and implicit) knowledge of the system is readily understood by the human expert.

The knowledge representation in KEE is based on the concept of *frames* (see Minsky (1975), Bobrow and Winograd (1977), or Brachman and Schmolze (1985) for further details). To describe the type of domain objects the expert system must model, frame languages offer the possiblity to include in the description of an object type a prototype description of individual objects (instantiations) of that type. So, when such an object becomes known to the system, the prototype can be used to create a default description of the new object. Furthermore, frames provide a structured representation of objects. Classes of frames organized in hierarchies enable the knowledge engineer to use an description-by-specialization approach: each class is described as a specialization (or subclass) of other more generic classes with controlled inheritance of properties (c.f. Fig. 3 with the definition of the variables frame (or variables unit in KEE)).

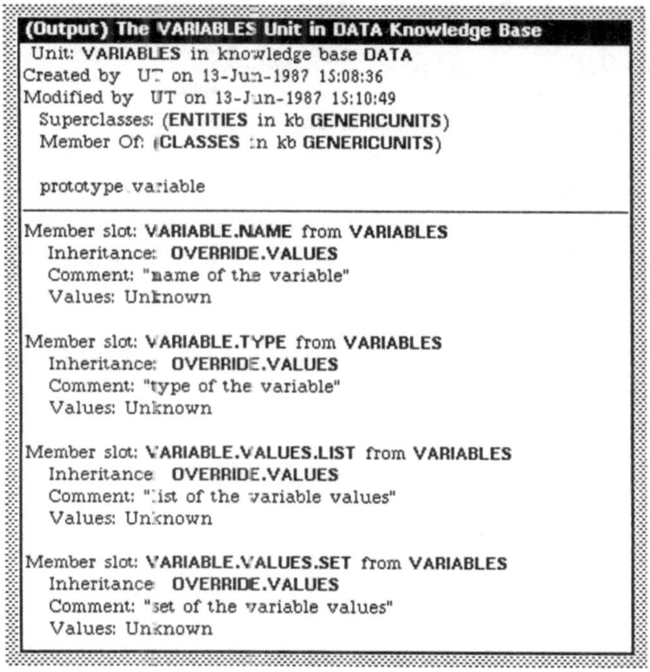

(Output) The VARIABLES Unit in DATA Knowledge Base

Unit: **VARIABLES** in knowledge base **DATA**
Created by UT on 13-Jun-1987 15:08:36
Modified by UT on 13-Jun-1987 15:10:49
Superclasses: (**ENTITIES** in kb **GENERICUNITS**)
Member Of: (**CLASSES** in kb **GENERICUNITS**)

prototype variable

Member slot: **VARIABLE.NAME** from **VARIABLES**
Inheritance: **OVERRIDE.VALUES**
Comment: "name of the variable"
Values: Unknown

Member slot: **VARIABLE.TYPE** from **VARIABLES**
Inheritance: **OVERRIDE.VALUES**
Comment: "type of the variable"
Values: Unknown

Member slot: **VARIABLE.VALUES.LIST** from **VARIABLES**
Inheritance: **OVERRIDE.VALUES**
Comment: "list of the variable values"
Values: Unknown

Member slot: **VARIABLE.VALUES.SET** from **VARIABLES**
Inheritance: **OVERRIDE.VALUES**
Comment: "set of the variable values"
Values: Unknown

Figure 3: Frames structure example for the data analysis problem.

The main advantages of frame languages are seen in the declarative form of encoding and storing beliefs about the application domain, the concise structural representation of relations between objects and the definition-by-specialization technique which together with special deduction algorithms propagates explicitly stored beliefs throughout the system.

On the other hand, frame languages have no direct way to describe how the knowledge is to be used in the reasoning process. The most popular and effective way of representing declarative descriptions of domain-dependant behavioral knowledge has been ***production rules***, i.e. pattern/action rules of the form `IF` *condition* `THEN` *assertion* `DO` *action*. Being similar to his own working strategies production rules are easily formulated and understood by the human expert. To combine the advantages of both representation techniques in hybrid systems (like KEE, LOOPS, CENTAUR, ...) has been very successful. In these environments the frame language serves as the foundation for the production rules, too. The rules themselves being stored as frames, frame taxonomies can be used to organize and to control the use of rules in a knowledge-based system.

These expert system tools usually operate in an Lisp environment which typically offers a broad range of excellent debugging and graphical services. With LISP as the common underlying language for most of the operating system and the expert system shell, within this environment the integration of system services and user written routines into the shell is very convenient.

3 Interfaces for Symbol Manipulation and Number Processing

For our customer study and for many other applications as well it is reasonable to use the facilities of an experts system shell on a Lisp machine like the UNISYS EXPLORER in our case. Features like the structured representation of knowledge and the different inference mechanisms together with tracing and debugging services are very useful.

The other part of the customer study relies on numerical algorithms which are already implemented in FORTRAN and tested. These are not easily ported to our Lisp environment as there is no FORTRAN compiler available. Some form of interface between Lisp machine and computer (with common operating system and a variety of data storage and input media) running the numerical algorithms has to be developed.

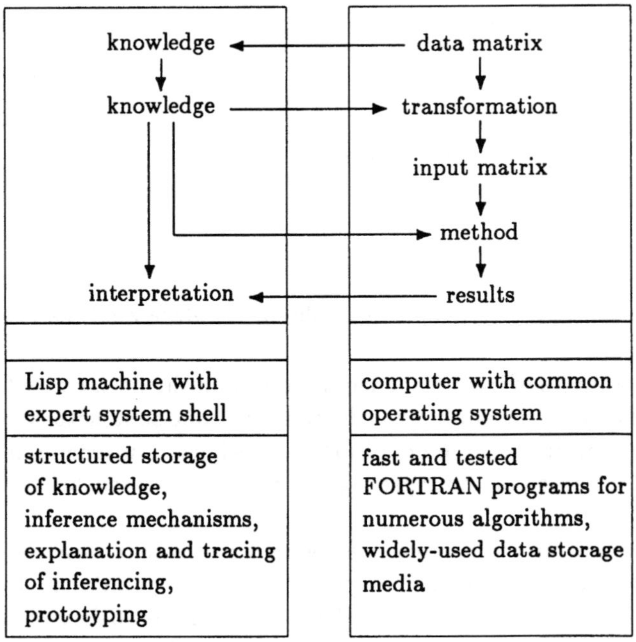

Figure 4: Symbol manipulation and number processing

Which operations are minimally required in this case shows the following example : to set the slot values in a KEE unit, i.e. altering the variable values in a frame, the KEE system offers built-in functions for nearly all purposes. Provided the data information is already stored in the file system of the Lisp machine, it is then easy to implement the necessary routines based on those KEE functions. These procedures transfer the data into the slots of the corresponding frames where the information can be accessed by the knowledge-based system. With these functions available, the task still remaining is then to transfer a data file from the remote system to the local system.

Altogether, as the diagram in Fig. 4 shows, the following minimal operations are necessary:

— get a remote data file: The data matrix can be investigated to decide on problem type and feasibility, necessary transformations of raw data and the method to be applied. Subsequently, the results can be accessed for interpretation.

— run a remote program: When the decision on the algorithm to be used has been made, the corresponding computer program on the remote machine must be started with necessary parameters like input/output files.

— send a local data file: After the required transformations of the raw data into binary relations have been made, the resulting input matrix must be made available on the remote machine for further processing. In additon, the system must be able to send a sequence of commands as a batch file to the remote machine to be executed there.

As an experimental realization, we have currently implemented a RS-232-C connection between the EXPLORER and a PC.

The main technical problem during the installation was the stability of the RS-232-C protocol, especially the XON/XOFF part on the PC side. After changing to a higher level (MS-DOS 3.1) of the PC operating system with the `ADRS232C` command as a new feature, the connection is now stable. This system command (and no longer the Basic I/O System of MS-DOS) assumes control of RS-232-C communications for the specified port. Thus additional features as buffering by interrupt and XON/XOFF line control are in effect, reducing buffer-full errors and transmission losses.

The logical connection of both systems is achieved by a batch command loop running on the remote machine, i.e. the PC is waiting for a batch file, is then processing this command sequence and going into receiver status again.

The realization of the `(get-remote-data-file)` function explains the details of this concept. With the remote machine running in server mode (via `LOOP`), on the EXPLORER as the client a file `MESSAGES.BAT` is created with all MS-DOS commands required for the file transfer from the PC. In our case, it is a call to the program `OUTFILE` to be followed by the command `LOOP` again as it is not possible from within a batch command in MS-DOS 3.1 to call another batch file and to return.

The LISP function `(file-to-rs232c)` sends `MESSAGES.BAT` to the port, finishing with 1AH as the End-Of-File character for MS-DOS. Subsequently, the function `(rs232c-to-file)` is ready to receive and store the PC file that will be sent.

Receiving the EOF, the `COPY` command finishes the transfer and stores the new file as `MESSAGES.BAT`. The following command in `LOOP` is a call to a batch file with this specific name. Thus, the transfer commands given in `MESSAGES.BAT` are executed next. As in MS-DOS the description of the length of a file is not unique (EOF-character or number of bytes), the program `OUTFILE` instead of the `COPY` command is used. `OUTFILE` is similar to `(file-to-rs232c)`. It takes an input file name as parameter and sends this file row by row to the RS-232-C port with 1AH as EOF character. This ensures functionality for all end-of-file conditions.

On the EXPLORER the function `(rs232c-to-file)` simultaneously receives this file and stores it in the local file system. After finishing the transfer, the PC is – via `LOOP` – set in server mode again.

The underlying structure of the logical interface for `(get-remote-data-file)` and (run-remote-program) is given in Fig. 5 and Fig. 6.

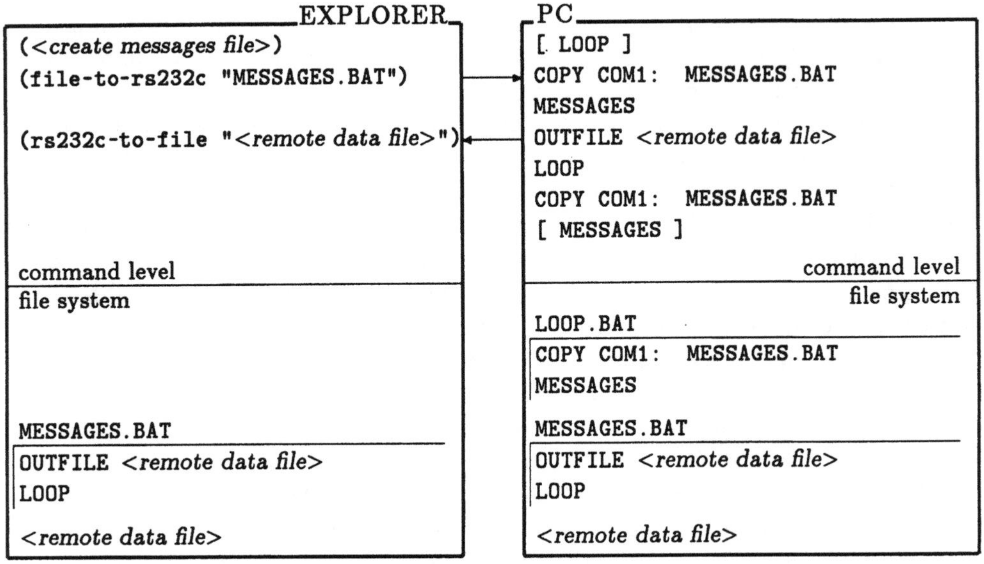

Figure 5: The structure of (get-remote-data-file).

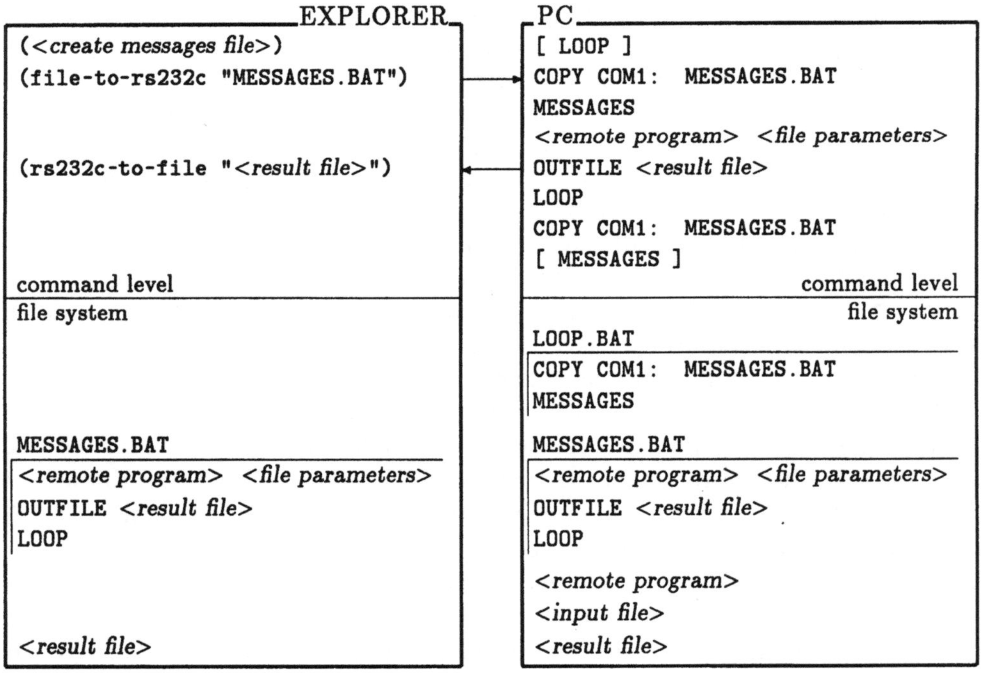

Figure 6: The structure of (run-remote-program).

Sending a local data file is more complicated as some form of timing information must be exchanged. This problem arises from the fact that the PC first has to receive the batch commands and subsequently, but separately, the local data file from the EXPLORER. The synchronization of this process can be done in a very basic manner: The PC receives MESSAGES.BAT as usual. The first of its commands, however, sends a RECEIVED.MSG message to the local machine to signal that the transfer of the batch file is complete. The PC is now ready to receive the data file. In response, the (file-to-rs232c) function on the EXPLORER sends the local data to the port. Fig. 7 summarizes the details.

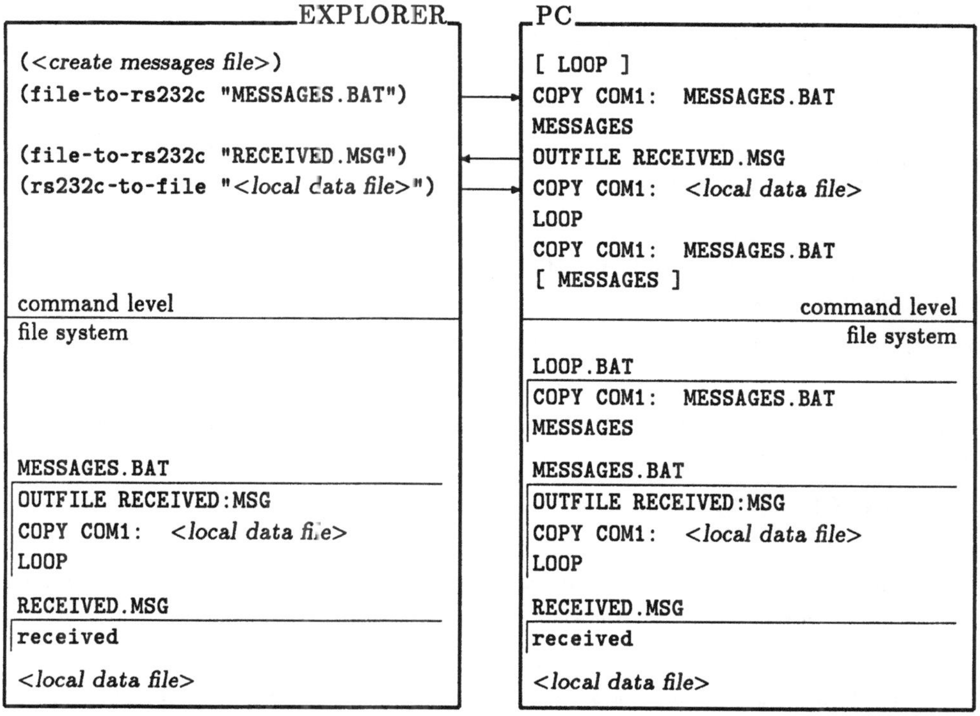

Figure 7: The structure of (send-local-data-file).

4 Future Developments

The momentary experimental design can be enhanced in different ways.

A commonly-used program for data exchange between different computer hardware is KERMIT. The interactive version running on both machines enables a stable, errror-checking transmission via RS-232-C and a more powerful local-remote communication with the server machine, giving direct access to operating system facilities.

Another significant improvement is an ETHERNET connection to the remote computer. Not only the transmission being faster and more secure, it is also possible to share resources of a host computer more directly, for example accessing files without physical transfer.

On the other hand, the need for symbol manipulation together with numerical processing capabilities arises in many application domains of knowledge-based systems. This leads to the development of hybrid computers combining the necessary hardware in one machine. The EXPLORER LX, for example, has the facilities already mentioned of a Lisp machine and in addition a complete M68020 processor system running under UNIX on a separate internal board. Now it is possible to have several LISP and UNIX windows simultaneously communicating with each other.

Hybrid systems like this enormously simplify the use of knowledge-based systems for application domains where numerical algorithms are to be controlled by LISP-based expert systems. Our case study of an data analysis problem in marketing research is just an example for areas like optimization or simulation.

References

Barthélemy JP, Monjardet B (1981) The Median Procedure in Cluster Analysis and Social Choice Theory. Mathematical Social Sciences 1:235–267

Barthélemy JP, Monjardet B (1988) The Median Procedure in Data Analysis: New Results and Open Problems, to appear in: Bock HH (ed.) Proceedings of the First Conference of the International Federation of Classification Societies. North-Holland, Amsterdam

Bobrow DG, Winograd T (1977) An Overview of KRL, a Knowledge Representation Language. Cognitive Science 1:3–46

Brachman RJ, Schmolze JG (1985) An Overview of the KL-ONE Knowledge Representation System. Cognitive Science 9:171–216

Fikes R, Kehler T (1985) The Role of Frame-Based Representation in Reasoning. Communications of the ACM 28:904–920

Leclerc B (1988) Concensus Applications in the Social Sciences, to appear in: Bock HH (ed.) Proceedings of the First Conference of the International Federation of Classification Societies. North-Holland, Amsterdam

Minsky M (1975) A Framework for Representing Knowledge, in: Winston PH (ed.) The Psychology of Computer Vision, McGraw-Hill, New York, pp 211–277

Schader M (1978) Anordnung und Klassifikation von Objekten bei qualitativen Merkmalen. Anton Hain, Meisenheim/Glan

Schader M, Tüshaus U (1986) Subgradient Methods for Analyzing Qualitative Data, in: Gaul W, Schader M (eds.) Classification as a Tool of Research. North-Holland, Amsterdam, pp 397–403

Part 4

Data Analysis and Marketing

Marketing Applications of Sequencing and Partitioning of Nonsymmetric and/or Two-Mode Matrices*

P. Arabie[†], S. Schleutermann, J. Daws and L. Hubert
Department of Psychology, University of Illinois at Champaign
603 E. Daniel St., Champaign IL 61820
[†] and Department of Computer Science, University College Dublin.

Summary

Although various authors have provided improvements to the bond energy algorithm for seriation originally proposed by McCormick, Schweitzer, and White (1972), most of these approaches have limited the types of data that can be considered (e.g., by assuming only binary input). We return to the original algorithm, free of such restrictions, and demonstrate ways of markedly improving its computational efficiency as well as the solutions it produces. These improvements enable the algorithm to sequence survey data (e.g., respondents by products' attributes) having several hundred columns and rows. Such runs require only a few hours on a personal computer. Following the successful sequencing of such matrices, it is straightforward to partition the rows and columns. We present a substantive application from marketing.

1 Introduction

As a vehicle for providing discrete representations of structure in data, clustering techniques have been used with greatly increasing frequency during the last two decades in marketing research (see Wind (1978a); Punj and Stewart (1983)). Many of these applications have occurred in market segmentation (Wind (1978b)) and in product positioning when clustering is used in conjunction with multidimensional scaling (Arabie, Carroll, DeSarbo, and Wind (1981); Arabie and Carroll (1985)).

Most clustering techniques assume as input one proximity data matrix A (or possibly several, as in Arabie and Carroll (1985)), where both the rows and columns correspond to the same set of entities. In the useful terminology of Tucker (1964), such matrices are said to be <u>one-mode</u>. A second common requirement within such matrices is <u>symmetry</u>; that is, the similarity/dissimilarity of products j and k must be the same as that between products k and j: $a_{jk} = a_{kj}$. Notable exceptions to the second requirement include work of Peay (1975) and Hubert (1973). Generalizations of techniques originally limited to one-mode data, so as to allow <u>two</u>-mode data when the rows and columns correspond to disjoint sets of entities (e.g., respondents by attributes) have been more recent: Hartigan

*This work was supported by AT & T Information Systems through the Industrial Affiliates Program of the University of Illinois and a Fulbright Award to the first author, who was based while preparing this paper at the Department of Computer Science, University College Dublin.

(1975, Ch. 14–15); Furnas (1980); DeSarbo (1982); De Soete, DeSarbo, Furnas, and Carroll (1984a, 1984b); Murtagh (1985, Ch. 1).

Clustering techniques not restricted to symmetric or one-mode data are especially needed in marketing. Concerning the former condition, we note that such commonly encountered forms of data as brand-switching matrices (Bass, Pessemier, and Lehmann (1972); Rao and Sabavala (1981); Rao, Sabavala, and Zahorick (1982); DeSarbo and De Soete (1984); McAlister and Lattin (1984); Lattin and McAlister (1985); Hutchinson (1986); Moore, Pessemier, and Lehmann (1986); Lattin (1987); Novak and Stangor (1987)) often depart markedly from symmetry. For word association (e.g., Green and Tull (1978, Ch. 8); De Soete et al., (1984b, pp. 304–305)) and other two-mode data, symmetry is meaningless. The restriction to one-mode data precludes cluster analysis of most forms of survey data unless the data are first pre-processed to convert them to one-mode data; the chance for simultaneously representing the other mode is thus lost in the process.

When the conjugate off-diagonal entries are averaged (e.g., by strategies listed in the Appendix of Arabie and Soli (1982)) to render a brand-switching proximity matrix symmetric, the data analyst loses the potential for discriminating between the (same) product as originally purchased as opposed to being the substitute for a different product (viz., in its row versus column representation; see Okada, this volume). Similarly, by obtaining separate cluster analyses of each of the modes in a two-mode matrix, the data analyst misses the opportunity to see interrelationships between the entities in the distinct modes.

We present below an approach to clustering that has neither of the restrictions just discussed and which also can accommodate data matrices with several hundred entities in each of the modes.

2 The "Bond Energy" Algorithm

McCormick, Schweitzer, and White (1972) (henceforth designated as MSW) proposed a remarkably general and straightforward approach to sequencing or seriating the rows and/or columns of proximity matrices, including those that are nonsymmetric or two-mode. This particular approach is easily generalized to the case of three-way data (e.g., sources of data by products by products, or scenarios by respondents by attributes) and lends itself as a first step prior to clustering (by partitioning) the row and column modes.

Beginning with a single M by N matrix A having nonnegative entries, MSW propose to maximize the expression

$$\{\sum\sum a_{jk}[a_{j,k-1} + a_{j,k+1} + a_{j-1,k} + a_{j+1,k}]\} \tag{1}$$

where the maximization is over all $M!N!$ possible arrays that can be obtained from permuting A. MSW presciently noted that their "bond energy" approach was equivalent to applying quadratic assignment (Koopmans and Beckmann (1957); Hubert and Schultz (1976)) to the rows and to the columns of the input matrix A.

Because this problem qualifies under the current heading of NP-complete, MSW (p. 996) proposed an easily summarized heuristic approach: Considering the columns first, place one arbitrarily in the first position. Then, each of the remaining $N - i$ ($i = 1, \ldots, N - 1$) columns is tested in each of the $i + 1$ candidate positions (viz., to the left and right of each of the i columns already placed) and placed in the one giving the largest incremental contribution by the respective column to the expression in (1). When each column has had its (one) "sub-iteration," this procedure is repeated on the rows. (Note that a subscript of i will be used to refer to the order in which a column/row is considered, as in the i-th sub-iteration. A subscript of j will refer to the position in a permuted matrix, as in the j-th column/row.)

Developments subsequent to the publication of MSW begin with Lenstra's (1974) observation that the bond energy algorithm is equivalent to two traveling salesman problems, one for the row and one for the column mode (also see Slagle, Chang, and Heller (1975)). Other authors (Bhat and Haupt (1976); Kusiak, Vannelli, and Kumar (1986); Garcia and Proth (1986)) have proposed ways of speeding up the original algorithm, sometimes at the cost of restrictions on the types of data allowed (e.g., Bhat and Haupt require that A be binary). Späth (1980, pp. 203–212) provided FORTRAN code for straightforward (and rather inefficient) implementation of MSW's bond energy algorithm. While various modifications have enabled us to improve the efficiency of the algorithm, limitations of space dictate presenting the details elsewhere. We wish instead to discuss several issues of the original philosophy of MSW.

3 Current Development of the Bond Energy Algorithm

It is important to note that MSW (p. 996) proposed only one overall iteration for the column mode and one for the row mode. While our use of additional iterations is an obvious enough development, the first iteration still merits further scrutiny. Specifically, those authors' strategy, placing each column/row in the position where it gives the largest incremental contribution to expression (1) above, implicitly assumes that all the "unoccupied" columns/rows are filled with zeroes. Thus, any replacement of such a column/row with data not all zeroes will usually increase (1), and cannot lead to a decrease. However, if a second overall iteration is conducted, or if the first iteration begins with the columns/rows already ordered (where that ordering constitutes, in effect, a first iteration), so that data values supplant the embedding matrix of zeroes assumed by MSW, there is no longer a guarantee that the value of (1) will not decrease.

Specifically, during any overall iteration after the first, when one considers repositioning a column/row to produce a maximal increase in (1), there are now two considerations not entailed in MSW's approach. First, unless the column/row considered on the i-th sub-iteration is to be placed in the first or last column/row of the matrix, it will separate the two columns/rows that soon will be its new nearest neighbors. As a result, those neighbors' current contribution to the value of (1), as computed over the entire matrix, is about to be lost. Thus, the net increase corresponding to (naive) placement according to MSW's rule for one iteration may in fact be negative. A second consideration concerns the decrement in (1) when the column/row is removed from its current j-th location to be positioned where the "net" increment in (1) is greatest.

Concretely, the j-th column/row is no longer adjacent to the neighbors most recently labeled $(j-1)$ and $(j+1)$, and is thus no longer contributing to the corresponding terms in the summation over the entire matrix, resulting in (1). On the other hand, the columns/rows previously labeled $(j-1)$ and $(j+1)$ are now adjacent and make a new contribution to (1). If both the problems in the second and the first observations are taken into account, we call the resulting computation the "net-net" increase in bond energy.

Because obtaining the net-net increase to ensure monotonicity adds such a computational burden to the algorithm, we have chosen the following "hybrid" strategy: on the i-th subiteration, compute the "net" increases for the i-th column/row at each possible position. If the net-net increase corresponding to the best net increase is positive, position the column/row accordingly. If not, consider the position corresponding to the next best net increase until one is found having a nonnegative net-net increase. The first position having such a net-net increment is assumed by the column/row being considered on the i-th sub-iteration. If no such position is found, the column/row is left in its current position. Note that there is no reason to maintain that the ordering of positions by net increase corresponds to the ordering by net-net increase, but computing the latter for all positions on each sub-iteration slows down the algorithm greatly.

In passing, we note an accidental discovery: after several iterations and when no further improvements in (1) have been found, we have occasionally allowed an additional iteration in which the requirement of monotonicity was dispensed with, just as in MSW's single iteration. This additional iteration (requiring a second run of the program) sometimes produces a better overall value of (1) than is obtained from the iterations subject to the hybrid strategy. This result, of getting a better final value of an objective function by allowing intermediate strategies leading to (temporarily) worse values, is of course the essence of simulated annealing (Kirkpatrick, Gelatt, and Vecchi (1983)).

It should be apparent from this discussion that we have no guarantees that our algorithm will produce the global optimum (i.e., best possible value of (1) for any given data set). However, the algorithm has generally produced good solutions in various simulation tests and runs very quickly.

4 Partitioning the Permuted Matrix

In the examples of applying their approach to data matrices, MSW were explicitly looking for "block checkerboard" patterns (p. 996), suggestive of submatrices having homogeneous values contrasting with those of neighboring submatrices (cf. Murtagh (1985, p. 16)). In seeking such patterns, we propose that the sequencing should be followed by partitioning the columns/rows, subject to conformity with the seriations resulting from the preceding algorithm.

A straightforward strategy is to sever the sequence between the two columns/rows contributing least to the overall bond energy in (1), to obtain a bipartition. The process can then be repeated iteratively to obtain a partition with more clusters. Such an approach is, of course, reminiscent of the well known divisive algorithm for single-link clustering (Sibson, (1973)) that exploits that method's isomorphism to the minimum spanning tree problem (Gower and Ross (1969); Hartigan (1975, Ch. 11)). Unfortunately, this approach gave disappointing results over a variety of data sets. One flaw is that for sparse matrices, the method is especially prone to splitting off columns/rows containing mostly zeroes, thus producing an uncomfortable number of singleton clusters. Other and more hypothetical reasons for the disappointing performance are suggested by Arabie and Boorman (1982, pp. 183–184).

Perhaps the best known—and certainly one of the most heavily cited—approaches to partitioning is due to MacQueen (1967). The strategy of the original paper and its many sequels is known to have severe drawbacks, in particular, dependency on the initial configuration. However, in the special case of unidimensionality (as when the order of the entities to be partitioned is known), obtaining a globally best solution is often computationally feasible. Moreover, Späth (1980, pp. 61–67) provided FORTRAN code for solving this problem. Once again, we have found various ways to improve the performance of the unidimensional k-means approach, but details will be presented elsewhere. For the present, it is sufficient to note that we use a k-means partitioning applied (separately) to the columns and to the rows according to the sequence in which each mode emerges as output from our implementation of the bond energy algorithm. Just as the rows and columns of a nonsymmetric or two-mode matrix may be represented in sequences differing between the rows and the columns, the cluster memberships and even the number of clusters may be discrepant between rows and columns.

5 Illustrative Application

Data

Bass et al. (1972) conducted an experiment in July 1969 requiring 280 subjects to select a 12-ounce can of soft drink four days a week for three weeks from the set of alternatives given in Table 1. The resulting brand-switching matrix appears in DeSarbo (1982, p. 464), with the (i,j)-th entry denoting the probability of switching from brand i in time period t to brand j during period $t+1$. Thus, the two modes are distinguished by <u>time</u> of selecting the products (even though the products are labeled identically across the two modes), and the data are not expected to be symmetric. Entries in the principal diagonal depict brand loyalty. Like DeSarbo (1982, p. 464), we treated the data as measured on a ratio scale, but did not use the normalization he described.

Table 1: Design of Products in Study by Bass, Pessemier, and Lehmann (1972)

	Cola	Non Cola
Diet	Tab Diet Pepsi	Fresca Like
Non-Diet	Coke Pepsi	7-Up Sprite

Results

Table 2 presents the results from our analysis. For various substantive reasons, we chose a solution with three row and four column clusters. Note that the entries within the partitioned matrix are probabilities, with the decimal points omitted. The values of the objective function in (1) are 2124464 for the columns and 2239530 for the rows. Considering the clusters that result from the partitioning, recall that the clusters are in a (mathematically) preferred order, up to a reflection of the rows or columns. We note that the first row cluster consists of Diet Pepsi, Tab, and Like. Although the inclusion of Like with two colas may seem surprising, DeSarbo (1982, p. 465) found a similar result. The second row cluster consists of the market leaders, Coke and Pepsi, as well as Fresca, from which subjects often switched to the former two. The final row cluster simply contains the leading non-diet non-cola soft drinks.

Table 2: Analysis of the Soft-Drink Switching Matrix from Bass et al. (1972), Using Three Row and Four Column Clusters

PARTITIONED AND PERMUTED MATRIX

	FINAL ROW PERM	1 Dt Pepsi	2 Tab	3 Like	4 7-Up	5 Coke	6 Pepsi	7 Sprite	8 Fresca
FINAL COLUMN PERMUTATION		7	3	4	2	1	5	6	8
1 Dt Pepsi	7	256	186	93	47	93	116	93	116
2 Tab	3	80	160	360	120	80	80	40	80
3 Like	4	131	87	152	152	87	239	43	109
4 Pepsi	5	26	8	30	132	177	515	75	37
5 Fresca	8	67	53	107	93	226	147	107	200
6 Coke	1	13	10	33	107	612	134	55	36
7 7-Up	2	12	5	64	448	186	140	99	46
8 Sprite	6	29	29	71	185	114	157	329	86

Note: The numbers 734 ... for the rows and columns refer to the original order or permutation of the products, as given in DeSarbo (1982, p. 464)

Turning to the column clusters, note that the first and third correspond to the diet and non-diet cola cells, respectively, of the 2×2 design in Table 1. However, 7-Up and Sprite would have to be interchanged in their cluster memberships to allow faithful correspondence to the other two cells of Table 1. Thus, results for the cola soft drinks respect Table 1 more accurately than does the organization of the non-colas. Note also that in the ordering of the products (which is independent of the partitioning), the non-cola beverages 7-Up and Fresca manifest the farthest migrations between the row and columns sequences. These discrepancies suggest that preferences for the non-cola drinks are more labile than for the counterpart colas.

What the Analysis is Doing

The goal of the bond energy algorithm is to find a preferred (unidimensional) ordering of the objects in each of the modes of the matrix. Since Table 1 indicates not one but two factors in the design of the sample of products, it is not surprising that our analysis did not perfectly recover the design of Table 1, even if the data had been perfectly consistent with such a design.

Numerically, the bond energy algorithm is trying to position the largest entries toward the center of the matrix, while relegating the smallest entries to the periphery. Thus, we should expect to find the market leaders in clusters that generally gravitate toward the centers of the modes.

Comparisons with Previous Analyses

Since DeSarbo (1982) began a tradition of using the brand-switching data of Bass et al. (1972) to illustrate new approaches to data analysis (e.g., Moore et al. (1986)), it is appropriate to compare the representation of structure in Table 2 with the results of some previous studies. DeSarbo's (1982) analysis uses his GENNCLUS model that generalizes the Shepard-Arabie (1979) ADCLUS model for nonhierarchical overlapping clustering. GENNCLUS requires the same number of clusters for both modes, and DeSarbo opted for three clusters. Somewhat surprisingly, the only difference between his two sets of clusters was that Fresca migrated from a cluster including Sprite and 7-Up for the rows to one including Tab, Like, and Diet Pepsi for the columns. (Recall that Fresca is one of the two products whose row and column positions differed most greatly in our analysis in Table 2.) We have already noted that DeSarbo's second row cluster corresponded to our first row cluster (Diet Pepsi, Like, and Tab). Presumably because GENNCLUS allows products to be found in more than one cluster (viz., clusters can overlap), it is difficult to find other simple correspondences between DeSarbo's clusters and ours.

DeSarbo and De Soete (1984, p. 607) fitted an ultrametric (hierarchical) tree to the full nonsymmetric matrix (ignoring diagonal entries but with the normalization recommended in DeSarbo (1982)), using a technique that furthered work by Furnas (1980). This method provides one hierarchical tree with all 16 entities (eight soft drinks in each of the two modes) as terminal nodes. Although there is no preferred ordering of the products/nodes, it would be possible to add an extra step of seriating the nodes. By comparing the levels in the tree at which the row and column representatives of a soft drink are joined, DeSarbo and De Soete offer a clever argument relating this aspect of the tree representation to subjects' propensity to select the same product repeatedly. Specifically, the height in the hierarchical tree at which the row and column representations of the same product are joined is inversely related to brand loyalty. A similar analysis of the (non-normalized version) of the same data in De Soete et al. (1984a) gave roughly comparable results.

DeSarbo and De Soete (1984, p. 608) note that their representation provides "an efficient way to display the structure in nonsymmetric transition matrices without having to ignore over half of the data [matrix] or having to average/smooth it." The approach presented in the present paper offers the same advantages.

McAlister and Lattin (1984), Lattin and McAlister (1985), and Lattin (1987) also used soft drink data (different from those of the present analysis), and provided an excellent review of models used for the analysis of brand-switching data. There is one point, however, with which we differ in the interpretation of clustering results. McAlister and Lattin argued that clusters resulting from such data as those of Bass et al. (1972) could only reflect structural organization based on substitutability. Like DeSarbo (1982, p. 465), we maintain that some of the clusters from this analysis can be interpreted as comprising complementary products: the presence of Fresca in the second row cluster, along with Coke and Pepsi, is much more easily explained by subjects' seeking complementary benefits than by appeals to substitutability. While the model proposed by McAlister and Lattin (1984) and Lattin and McAlister (1985) does indeed seem highly predisposed to find effects of complementarity in switching between products, clustering models do not exclude the possibility of finding evidence for reasons other than substitutability for brand-switching.

References

Arabie P, Boorman SA (1982) Blockmodeling: Developments and Prospects, in: Hudson H (ed.) Classifying Social Data: New Applications of Analytic Methods for Social Science Research. Jossey-Bass, San Francisco, pp 177–198

Arabie P, Carroll JD (1985) Product Positioning Via INDCLUS, an Individual Differences Approach to Overlapping Clustering. Paper presented at the ORSA/TIMS Marketing Science Conference, Nashville, TN

Arabie P, Carroll JD, DeSarbo W, Wind J (1981) Overlapping Clustering: A New Method for Product Positioning. Journal of Marketing Research 18: 310–317

Arabie P, Soli SD (1982) The Interface Between the Types of Regression and Methods of Collecting Proximity Data, in: Golledge RG, Rayner JN (eds.) Proximity and Preference: Problems in the Multidimensional Analysis of Large Data Sets. University of Minnesota Press, MN, pp 90–115

Bass FM, Pessemier EA, Lehmann DR (1972) An Experimental Study of Relationships Between Attitudes, Brand Preference, and Choice. Behavioral Science 17: 532–541

Bhat MV, Haupt A (1976) An Efficient Clustering Algorithm. IEEE Transactions on Systems, Man, and Cybernetics 6: 61–64

De Soete G, DeSarbo WS, Furnas GW, Carroll JD (1984a) Tree Representations of Rectangular Proximity Matrices, in: Degreef E, van Buggenhaut J (eds.) Trends in Mathematical Psychology. North-Holland, Amsterdam, pp 377–392

De Soete G, DeSarbo WS, Furnas GW, Carroll JD (1984b) The Estimation of Ultrametric Path Length Trees from Rectangular Proximity Data. Psychometrika 49: 289–310

DeSarbo WS (1982) GENNCLUS: New Models for General Nonhierarchical Clustering Analysis. Psychometrika 47: 449–475

DeSarbo WS, De Soete G (1984) On the Use of Hierarchical Clustering for the Analysis of Nonsymmetric Proximities. Journal of Consumer Research 11: 601–610

Furnas GW (1980) Objects and their Features: The Metric Analysis of Two-Class Data. Unpublished doctoral dissertation, Stanford University, Stanford, CA

Garcia H, Proth JM (1986) A New Cross-Decomposition Algorithm: The GPM. Comparison with the Bond Energy Algorithm. Control and Cybernetics 15: 155–165

Gower JC, Ross GJS (1969) Minimum Spanning Trees and Single Linkage Cluster Analysis. Applied Statistics 18: 54–64

Green PE, Tull DS (1978) Research for Marketing Decisions (4th ed). Prentice-Hall, Englewood Cliffs, NJ

Harshman RA, Green PE, Wind Y, Lundy ME (1982) A Model for the Analysis of Asymmetric Data in Marketing Research. Marketing Science 1: 205–242

Hartigan JA (1975) Clustering Algorithms. Wiley, New York

Hubert L (1973) Min and Max Hierarchical Clustering Using Asymmetric Similarity Measures. Psychometrika 38: 63–72

Hubert L, Schultz J (1976) Quadratic Assignment as a General Data Analysis Strategy. British Journal of Mathematical and Statistical Psychology 29: 190–241

Hutchinson JW (1986) Discrete Attribute Models of Brand Switching. Marketing Science 5: 350–371

Kirkpatrick S, Gelatt CD Jr., Vecchi MP (1983) Optimization by Simulated Annealing. Science 220: 671–680

Koopmans TC, Beckmann M (1957) Assignment Problems and the Location of Economic Activities. Econometrica 25: 53–76

Kusiak A, Vannelli A, Kumar KR (1986) Clustering Analysis: Models and Algorithms. Control and Cybernetics 15: 139–154

Lattin JM (1987) A Model of Balanced Choice Behavior. Marketing Science 6: 48–65

Lattin JW, McAlister L (1985) Using a Variety-Seeking Model to Identify Substitute and Complementary Relationships Among Competing Products. Journal of Marketing Research 22: 330–339

Lenstra JK (1974) Clustering a Data Array and the Traveling-Salesman Problem. Operations Research 22: 413–414

MacQueen J (1967) Some Methods for Classification and Analysis of Multivariate Observations, in: Le Cam LM, Neyman J (eds.) Proceedings of the Fifth Berkeley Symposium on Mathematical Statistics and Probability 1. University of California Press, Berkeley, pp 281–297

McAlister L, Lattin JM (1984) Identifying Competitive Brand Relationships when Consumers Seek Variety. Marketing Science Institute (Tech. Rep. No. 84–105) Cambridge, MA

McCormick WT Jr., Schweitzer PJ, White TW (1972) Problem Decomposition and Data Reorganization by a Clustering Technique. Operations Research 20: 993–1009

Moore WL, Pessemier EA, Lehmann DR (1986) Hierarchical Representations of Market Structures and Choice Processes through Preference Trees. Journal of Business Research 14: 371–386

Murtagh F (1985) Multidimensional Clustering Algorithms. Physica-Verlag, Vienna

Novak TP, Stangor C (1987) Testing Competitive Market Structures: An Application of Weighted Least Squares Methodology to Brand Switching Data. Marketing Science 6: 82–97

Peay ER (1975) Grouping by Cliques for Directed Relationships. Psychometrika 40: 573–574

Punj G, Stewart DW (1983) Cluster Analysis in Marketing Research: Review and Suggestions for Application. Journal of Marketing Research 20: 134–148

Rao VR, Sabavala DJ (1981) Inference of Hierarchical Choice Processes from Panel Data. Journal of Consumer Research 8: 85–96.

Rao VR, Sabavala DJ, Zahorick AJ (1982) Market Structure Analysis Using Brand Switching Data: A Comparison of Clustering Techniques, in: Srivastava RK, Shocker A (eds.) Analytical Approaches to Product and Marketing Planning: The Second Conference. Marketing Science Institute, Cambridge, MA., pp 17–25

Shepard RN, Arabie P (1979) Additive Clustering: Representation of Similarities as Combinations of Discrete Overlapping Properties. Psychological Review 86: 87–123

Sibson R (1973) SLINK: An Optimally Efficient Algorithm for the Single-Link Cluster Method. Computer Journal 16: 30–45

Slagle JR, Chang CL, Heller SR (1975) A Clustering and Data-Reorganizing Algorithm. IEEE Transactions on Systems, Man, and Cybernetics 5: 125–128

Späth H (1980) Cluster Analysis Algorithms (U. Bull, Trans.). Ellis Horwood, Chichester, England

Tucker LR (1964) The Extension of Factor Analysis to Three-Dimensional Matrices, in: Frederiksen N, Gulliksen H (eds.) Contributions to Mathematical Psychology. Holt, Rinehart, and Winston, New York, pp 109–127

Wind Y (1978a) Introduction to Special Section on Market Segmentation Research. Journal of Marketing Research 15: 315–316

Wind Y (1978b) Issues and Advances in Segmentation Research. Journal of Marketing Research 15: 317–337

Multidimensional Scaling in Marketing Research: An Illustrative Application to a Telecommunications Pricing Problem

J. D. Carroll, B. B. Hollister, R. T. Iosso, S. Pruzansky and J. A. Rotondo
Bell Laboratories
Murray Hill, New Jersey 07974
S. L. Weinberg*
New York University

Summary

Multidimensional scaling (MDS) has long been used extensively in marketing research, but not often in studies of telecommunications pricing. This paper illustrates a prototypical application to this domain, while pointing out general methodological aspects of application of MDS models/methods to both perceptual (similarities) and preferential choice data. Among strengths of combined use of these two data types in cases, like the present study, involving factorially designed stimuli, is providing imformation complementary to, and potentially confirmatory of, a straightforward conjoint analysis. Alternatively, if an additive conjoint analysis does not suffice, the present approach may disclose dimensions comprising "higher order" attributes, which represent complex, (possibly nonlinear) functions of basic factors, enabling a "higher order" conjoint analysis. Individual differences MDS techniques also obviate assuming a single preference order for all subjects.

1 Introduction

Multidimensional scaling (MDS) techniques have a long history of applications to marketing research. This paper will illustrate the applicability of MDS methodology to telecommunications marketing problems via an actual study of a possible family of optional calling plans which might be offered by AT&T Communications. These will be called, hereafter, simply "Optional Call Plans", or OCP's.

The motivation of this study is the increasing interest of AT&T, particularly intensified during the last several years, in tailoring telecommunication services to meet the needs of its customers. Each option in the OCP promotional pricing plan emphasizes a different service feature that is believed to be linked to a particular pattern of customer usage.

If it can be shown that these options, and combinations of them, appeal differentially to various segments of the customer populations as defined by demographics and/or calling behavior, then AT&T can be expected to improve marketing programs aimed at

*Consultant with AT&T Bell Laboratories

increasing revenues from existing customers, decreasing losses of current customers to non-AT&T companies, and attracting new customers.

The major purposes of the present study were to determine empirically the extent to which different patterns of preference do exist for the variety of plans proposed; and to determine the extent to which these different patterns of preference are linked to different segments of the customer populations as characterized by demographics and/or calling behavior (e.g., monthly billing, calling patterns).

2 Design of Study

A convenience sample of subjects, selected to be AT&T subscribers, in New Jersey (near the AT&T Bell Labs Murray Hill, NJ location) were asked to make several kinds of judgments regarding these potential OCP services. These plans were described in terms of the basic OCP service with various combinations of possible "add-on" options. These options included an Extra Discount , a class of specialized telephone credit cards to be referred to simply as "CM", and another option allowing the subscriber to purchase an additional block of time at a price commensurate with the size (in minutes) of the block (to be called the "Additional Block of Time" option). The basic OCP service, together with all possible combinations of these three "add on" options led to a total of eight possible OCP pricing packages. Basic AT&T service (without any of the OCP options) and service offered by a hypothetical competitive OCC ("Other Common Carrier"), simply called "NNN", with a tariff very much like those of AT&T's principal competitors, added two additional alternatives, for a total of 10 alternative "calling plans". These ten service plans comprised the "stimuli" involved in a series of judgments made by subjects.

Table 1: Stimuli (Calling Plans) Used in "Optional Call Plan" Study

Code	Description
att	Basic AT&T Service
bp	Basic Plan
ed	Basic Plan plus Extra Discount
ab	Basic Plan plus Additional Block of time
cm	Basic Plan plus "CM" option
ed + ab	Basic Plan plus Extra Discount and Additional Block
ed + cm	Basic Plan plus Extra Discount and "CM"
ab + cm	Basic Plan plus Additional Block and "CM"
ed + ab + cm	Basic Plan plus Extra Discount, Additional Block and "CM"
nnn	Prototypical OCC modeled after principal AT&T competitors

Table 1 provides an explicit listing of these ten stimuli, as well as indicating the coding scheme to be used in later figures. These judgments included pairwise dissimilarity ratings (on a 10 point dissimilarity scale) on all 45 pairs of the 10 stimuli, plus 4 different types of evaluative judgments:

1. Paired comparisons preferences;

2. Rank order preference;

3. A judgment of likely savings and/or losses in costs of service relative to the subject's current AT&T service; and

4. A judgment of "purchase intention" on a 10 point scale, which was included because it was felt to be the closest surrogate to actual buying behavior possible in the format of the present study.

3 Data Analysis

The subjective judgments of dissimilarity were analyzed using the SINDSCAL (Pruzansky (1975)) program for Symmetric Individual Differences multidimensional SCALing by fitting the *INDSCAL* model (Carroll and Chang (1970), Carroll (1972), Wish and Carroll (1974)). It should be noted that INDSCAL is both the name of the *model* being fitted, and of the original program for fitting it, (plus a more general class of models). SINDSCAL was derived by Pruzansky *specifically* to fit the INDSCAL model to symmetric similarity or dissimilarity data. SINDSCAL analysis of dissimilarity judgments is particularly effective in determining subjective dimensions underlying subjects' perceptions of the stimuli. It is also quite useful in characterizing individual differences in perceptions among subjects, but this was not the primary purpose of SINDSCAL in the present case. While individual differences in perception were only of secondary interest in this study, individual differences among subjects in the various preference and evaluative judgments *were* of major interest. For this reason, another MDS procedure called MDPREF (for *MultiD*imensional *PREF*erence analysis) (Chang and Carroll (1968); Carroll (1972, 1980)) was used to analyze the four different sets of evaluative judgments in terms of a model designed to account optimally for individual differences among subjects. Each of the four data sets had been analyzed separately by MDPREF, and the results indicated that a single analysis could adequately account simultaneously for all four sets.

One possible methodological problem is that, for the "purchase intention" data, no judgment was made by subjects for "AT&T"—i.e. AT&T *without* any of the OCP services added. This possible problem was handled in the present case by substituting, for each subject, the maximum value (9) on the "purchase intention" scale. This was at least partially justified by the fact that these were all already AT&T customers, while most indicated (in questions included with the demographic questions) no plans to change to another primary carrier. Most results reported here appear, based on further analyses not reported here, to be quite robust vis à vis the actual value (9) substituted for these missing data values. One other methodological point is that, in the case of the paired comparisons preference data used in the MDPREF analysis, a single preference scale was derived for each subject by standard procedures (see Chang and Carroll(1968); Carroll (1972, 1980)) that will not be described in detail here.

Both these (independent and very different) analyses, SINDSCAL applied to the dissimilarities, and MDPREF applied to the preference/evaluative data, indicated that five dimensions (which can be viewed as *subjective* features of the calling plans) were needed to account for these subjective judgments. Because of the nature of the underlying model for individual differences in dissimilarity judgments, the SINDSCAL procedure produces dimensions which are uniquely defined, (i.e., which are *not* subject to rotation of coordinate axes). On the other hand, the MDPREF procedure *does* allow rotation of the coordinate axes defining dimensions, so the dimensions in MDPREF are *not* uniquely defined until this rotational problem is solved. In two dimensions (as in a standard two-dimensional map of the United States, for example), it is easy to determine the best orientation of axes (say, to rotate the U.S. map, if it is originally in a "non-standard" orientation, to the easily "interpretable" standard orientation in terms of North-South and East-West coordinate axes, or dimensions). In five dimensions the complexity of possible rotations is enormously greater than in this simple two dimensional example, and it is generally impossible to find an optimally interpretable rotation by simple visual inspection. For this reason it is convenient in such a technique as MDPREF, in which the dimensions are not uniquely determined, to have another set of hypothesized dimensions, uniquely defined either by theory or an independent measurement process. Use of the uniquely specified dimensions from a SINDSCAL analysis provides a very useful set of such independent dimensions. Thus the MDPREF solution was rotated, using some auxiliary techniques, to optimal agreement with the (rotationally fixed) SINDSCAL solution. After this rotation, the five subjective dimensions (independently derived by these two distinct MDS procedures from the quite different types of subjective judgments) were extremely similar, as measured by standard measures of "congruence" of the two sets of dimensions (the correlations between stimulus values on the corresponding dimensions were all .97 or greater). Because these two sets of dimensions were so highly similar, we shall speak henceforth of them as though they were identical. We focus primarily now on the MDPREF results, after orthogonal rotation to SINDSCAL congruence.

4 Interpretation of MDS Dimensions and Other Analyses

The five dimensions derived related very neatly to the "formal" structure built into the definition of the stimuli (while differing in subtle, but important, ways). The dimensions were interpreted as

1. AT&T vs. the prototypical OCC ("NNN" company), simply called "service provider";
2. The service packages involving the basic OCP services (with some gradation based on number of options included) vs. either AT&T—without the basic OCP service or any of its options, or "NNN" (called "Plan vs. Non-Plan");
3. The packages involving the Extra Discount vs. those that did not (to be called "ED");
4. Those involving the "CM" option vs. those that did not; and
5. Those involving the additional block of time at a discount vs. those that did not (to be called the "Additional Block" or "AB" Dimension).

While to some degree these perceptual dimensions represented the attributes built into the definition of the service packages, their exact structure differed in important ways that could not have been predicted in the absence of these subjective data (e.g., the gradation based on number of options in the second dimension). Three planes of this five dimensional space, corresponding to dimensions 1 vs. 2, 3 vs. 4 and 3 vs. 5 are shown in Figures 1, 2 and 3.

Figure 1: 1–2 Plane of MDPREF Stimulus Space Rotated to SINDSCAL

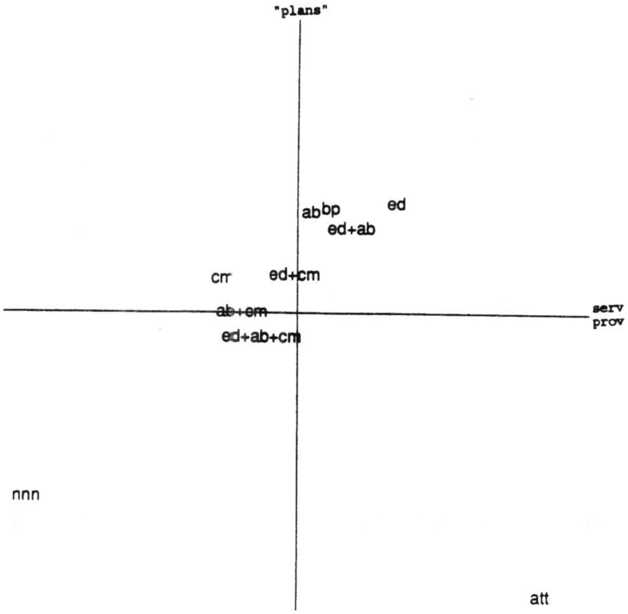

In the MDPREF representation of preferences or other evaluative data, each subject is represented by a *vector*, or directed line segment, indicating the most preferred direction (or direction of increasingly positive evaluation) for that subject. The orthogonal (perpendicular) projections of a stimulus point onto a subject's vector indicate the relative preference (evaluation) of that stimulus by that subject (e.g., the farther out a stimulus is in the subject's preferred direction, the more that subject is predicted to like the stimulus). In this case, since each subject made the four different types of preferential or evaluative judgments indicated earlier, each subject was represented by *four* such vectors (which may in some cases be fairly different from one another) so that there were represented a total of 200 vectors for 200 "pseudo-subjects" (50 "real" subjects $\times 4$ evaluative judgments). While, as indicated, the direction of the vector in the five dimensional space indicates the "most preferred" direction for that (pseudo-)subject, the length of the vector also varies, and is so defined as to represent the reliability of the evaluative judgments for that (pseudo-)subject. The projections of these vectors onto the five coordinate axes for the five dimensions defining this subjective space directly measure the "importance" of the subjective dimensions to each (pseudo-)subject in his/her preference (or other evaluative) judgments. The importance weight of a subjective dimension (coordinate axis) for a (pseudo-)subject provides a very direct measure

Figure 2: 3–4 Plane of MDPREF Stimulus Space Rotated to SINDSCAL

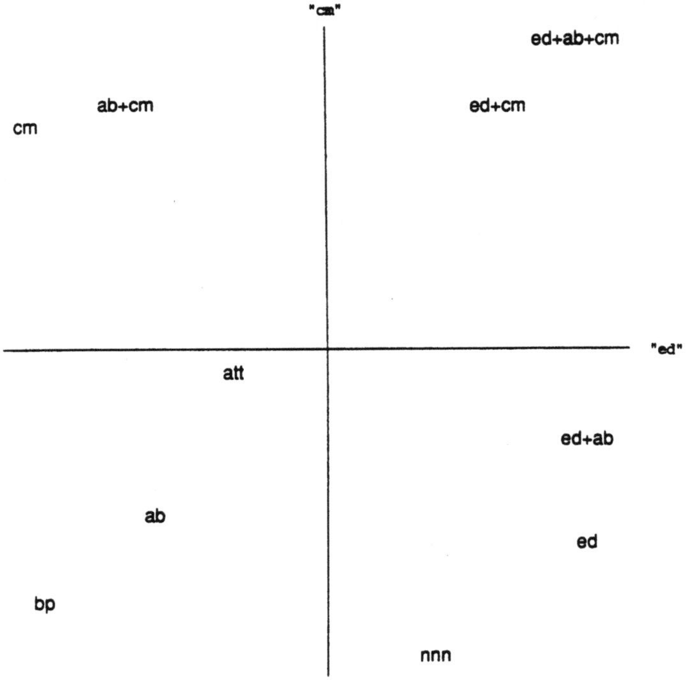

Figure 3: 3–5 Plane of MDPREF Stimulus Space Rotated to SINDSCAL

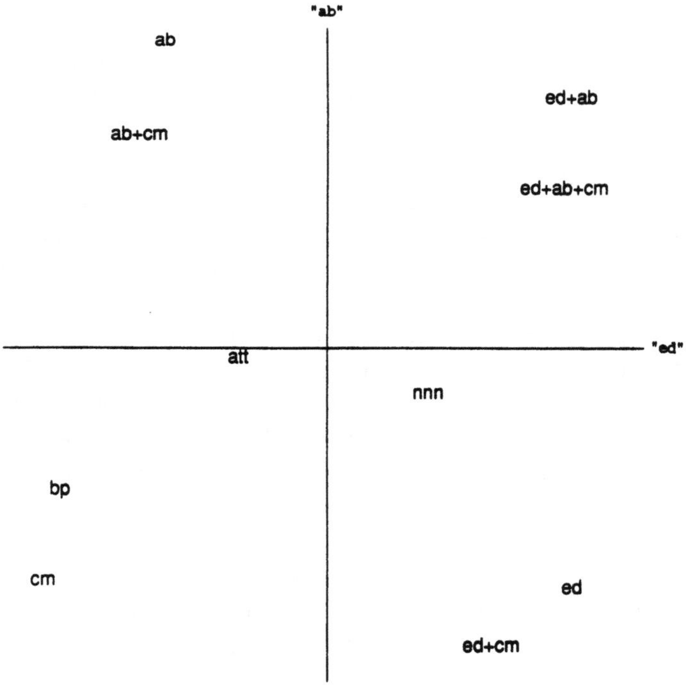

of the value of that dimension for that (pseudo-)subject. The sign of the weight indicates the valence of the dimension, (that is whether its positive pole attracts or repulses that subject), while its (absolute) magnitude indicates its overall salience (i.e., the *degree* of attraction or repulsion). (It should be kept in mind here that the "valence", defined in terms of the sign of a projection, will be reversed if the two poles of the dimension are reversed by the simple geometric operation of reflecting the dimension; e.g., the dimension contrasting AT&T to "NNN" will have an opposite pattern of signs if the poles of that dimension are interchanged in this way.)

To make the form of the MDPREF model more explicit, we may express the model, in the context of the present study, in terms of the equation

$$s_{ipj} \cong \sum_{r=1}^{R} v_{ipr} x_{jr} \tag{1}$$

where s_{ipj} is the normalized "preference scale value" for subject i on preference (or evaluative) scale p for stimulus (calling plan) j, while x_{jr} is the coordinate of stimulus j on dimension r ($r = 1, 2, \ldots, R$, with $R = 5$ in the present case), and v_{ipr} is the vector weight for subject i's preference (or evaluative) scale p on dimension r. The symbol "$\cong$" denotes approximate equality (except for error terms whose nature and distribution will not be further specified here). The form of this equation makes it clear that the preference scale values are assumed to be approximated by simple linear combinations of the coordinates of stimuli on the R (=5) dimensions. This is called the "vector" model because the linear algebraic operation defined in equation (1) is equivalent to the geometric operation of orthogonal projection of each of the n stimuli onto the vector $\mathbf{v}_{ip} = (v_{ip1}, v_{ip2}, \ldots, v_{ipR})$ so that the (normalized) preference scale values are approximated by those projections. (To be precise, the actual geometric operation is that of defining the *scalar product* between the vector defining stimulus j and that for "pseudosubject" (ip), but this scalar product operation is equivalent to projection followed by multiplication of the orthogonal projections by the length of the vector $\mathbf{v}_{ip}$; what this, plus the normalization of the scale values briefly alluded to above, means, in practice, is that the preference scale values are approximately *linear* with those projections).

Since the five subjective dimensions derived by MDS methods correspond in a very regular fashion with the components of the possible OCP calling plans, or with AT&T versus a prototypical OCC, these importance weights provide extremely critical information about (pseudo-)subjects' evaluations of these calling plans—in fact these weights can be viewed as providing a succinct summary of these judgments.

Table 2 displays these subject vector weights for the 50 subjects on the five dimensions for each of the four types of preference or evaluative judgments.

It may be instructive to compare the form of the MDPREF vector model with that of the INDSCAL model fitted to the dissimilarity data by use of the SINDSCAL procedure. In analogous notation the form of that model can be written as

$$\delta_{ijk} \cong d_{ijk} = \sqrt{\sum_{r=1}^{R} w_{ir}(x^*_{jr} - x^*_{kr})^2} \tag{2}$$

where δ_{ijk} is the (normalized) judged dissimilarity between stimuli j and k by subject i, d_{ijk} is a weighted Euclidean distance between stimuli j and k for subject i, defined

Table 2: Vector Weights for MDPREF Solution Rotated to Congruence with SINDSCAL

subj	Dimension 1 serv prov				Dimension 2 "plans"				Dimension 3 "ed"				Dimension 4 "cm"				Dimension 5 "ab"			
	pc	rank	sl	pi	pc	rank	sl	pi	pc	rank	sl	pi	pc	rank	sl	pi	pc	rank	sl	pi
1	.815	.806	.034	.681	-.028	-.053	-.698	-.723	.164	.173	.024	-.029	.025	.026	-.450	.027	-.539	-.459	-.551	-.078
2	.129	.355	-.159	.227	-.553	-.336	-.614	-.931	-.149	-.049	-.146	-.049	-.484	-.807	-.559	-.246	-.627	-.225	-.508	-.046
3	.097	.287	.000	.468	.888	.863	.000	-.228	-.213	-.246	.000	-.101	-.360	-.316	.000	-.791	-.119	-.033	.000	.128
4	-.179	-.014	-.032	.664	.357	.438	.780	.363	.125	.248	.054	-.302	.857	.716	.562	.540	.275	.470	.208	.106
5	.103	-.075	-.004	.239	.724	.670	.146	-.007	.086	.002	-.246	-.103	-.102	-.705	-.448	-.846	-.625	-.144	-.841	-.185
6	-.245	.028	.000	.343	-.536	-.585	.000	-.780	-.272	-.391	.000	-.101	-.222	-.364	.000	-.041	-.713	-.600	.000	-.449
7	-.133	.094	.018	.608	.255	.707	.734	.164	-.513	-.410	.232	-.555	.027	.159	.049	.020	-.779	-.515	.026	-.464
8	.389	.701	.300	.818	.482	.504	.348	.347	.680	.176	.545	.125	-.201	-.444	-.383	-.156	-.147	-.014	-.287	.114
9	.254	.273	.174	.682	.151	.798	.814	.181	.086	-.014	-.089	-.222	-.287	-.073	-.050	-.075	-.895	-.517	-.484	-.653
10	.057	.182	-.372	.208	-.441	-.446	-.125	-.525	-.198	-.259	.534	-.049	-.525	-.733	-.220	-.709	-.668	-.376	-.535	-.324
11	.530	.453	.613	.659	-.245	-.260	.231	-.238	.084	-.053	-.189	-.135	-.596	-.792	-.193	-.618	-.540	-.275	-.638	-.165
12	.152	.135	-.071	.219	-.435	-.446	-.331	-.572	.315	.203	-.087	.043	-.766	-.825	.128	-.748	-.295	-.032	-.607	-.195
13	.353	.762	.166	.742	-.232	.052	-.293	-.361	-.115	-.363	-.170	-.167	-.700	-.174	-.768	-.294	-.536	-.499	-.478	-.389
14	.521	.735	-.089	.772	.068	.198	-.284	-.232	-.114	-.472	.426	-.228	.262	-.386	.376	.049	-.766	-.158	.216	-.476
15	-.291	-.204	-.500	.116	-.437	-.306	.105	-.498	-.147	-.288	.163	-.248	-.230	-.505	-.228	-.262	-.760	-.645	-.726	-.760
16	-.173	-.070	-.054	.019	-.598	-.500	-.613	-.908	-.375	-.354	-.150	-.020	-.266	-.535	-.326	-.364	-.630	-.575	-.694	-.191
17	.713	.721	.058	.725	.362	-.053	.839	.232	.111	-.162	.003	-.324	-.210	.048	.335	.027	-.523	-.575	.047	-.460
18	-.046	.182	-.169	.360	.422	.140	.014	-.334	-.042	-.065	-.259	-.132	-.097	-.163	-.482	-.263	-.836	-.901	-.810	-.735
19	.238	.624	-.187	.492	-.184	-.032	-.084	-.053	-.264	-.539	-.456	-.442	.267	.086	-.119	.136	-.840	-.528	-.785	-.712
20	-.447	-.755	-.793	.721	.231	-.069	-.096	.468	.347	.386	.372	-.162	.680	.492	.464	.458	.297	.085	.078	.068
21	.283	.152	-.530	.227	-.422	-.482	-.549	-.931	-.124	-.225	-.052	-.049	-.799	-.608	-.550	-.264	-.256	-.564	-.287	-.046
22	.572	.570	.280	.525	.229	.066	-.088	-.160	.243	.401	.069	.368	-.682	-.698	-.940	-.661	.133	.087	.138	.213
23	.617	.234	.077	.110	-.199	-.419	-.174	-.801	.127	-.158	-.007	-.210	-.580	-.834	-.723	-.511	.096	-.207	.308	.023
24	.736	.844	.000	.739	.318	.183	.000	-.203	.464	.067	.000	.435	-.061	-.358	.000	-.175	-.353	.152	.000	-.274
25	.310	.702	.492	.747	.865	.439	.614	-.537	-.178	-.207	.240	-.151	-.321	-.481	-.091	-.249	-.123	-.159	.408	-.203
26	.236	.268	-.114	.713	.564	.837	.754	.126	-.165	-.170	-.253	-.380	-.370	-.189	-.142	-.359	-.477	-.155	-.571	-.182
27	-.007	.120	-.288	.585	.097	.587	.107	-.257	-.071	-.268	-.514	-.442	.491	.088	-.526	.429	-.818	-.307	-.546	-.333
28	.359	.431	-.154	.625	-.360	-.223	-.413	-.341	-.424	-.337	.050	-.343	.171	-.336	-.591	-.086	-.714	-.691	-.609	-.558
29	.691	.629	.246	.725	.363	.540	.088	.016	.054	-.226	-.002	.073	-.450	-.495	-.628	-.626	-.362	-.105	-.699	-.076
30	-.246	-.146	-.076	.082	-.319	-.388	-.327	-.599	.265	.322	.404	.368	-.221	-.245	-.440	-.259	-.843	-.791	-.711	-.516
31	.774	.860	.050	.659	.011	.060	-.286	-.155	-.227	-.077	-.141	-.323	-.218	-.264	-.566	-.468	-.500	-.206	-.745	-.353
32	.010	-.001	.466	.158	-.538	-.576	.127	-.563	.242	.169	-.020	.061	-.392	-.413	-.449	-.448	-.682	-.593	-.718	-.652
33	-.293	-.103	.143	.260	-.234	-.095	-.124	-.521	-.304	-.139	-.178	-.108	-.512	-.858	-.566	-.666	-.666	-.398	-.771	-.363
34	.424	.466	.718	.700	-.286	.351	-.040	.074	-.409	-.215	-.160	-.175	-.288	-.178	-.366	-.280	-.598	-.489	-.545	-.416
35	.463	.297	.000	.830	.340	.680	.000	.057	.786	.618	.000	.493	.114	.167	.000	.138	.113	.143	.000	.131
36	.524	.664	-.325	.591	.207	.268	.068	-.032	.123	-.337	.022	-.377	-.334	-.237	-.831	-.162	-.735	-.558	-.260	-.636
37	-.289	-.314	.000	.359	.268	.249	.000	-.486	.844	.824	.000	.732	.334	.394	.000	.275	.076	-.013	.000	.042
38	.339	.152	-.067	.429	-.320	-.482	-.495	-.306	-.263	-.225	-.002	-.204	-.582	-.608	-.543	-.540	-.611	-.564	-.656	-.615
39	.349	.014	-.101	.578	.258	.668	-.419	-.577	.528	.203	.438	-.008	.599	.316	-.426	.042	-.403	-.638	.360	-.546
40	.143	.119	-.681	.512	-.072	.744	.454	-.221	-.046	-.332	-.014	-.339	-.745	-.404	-.362	-.503	-.621	-.358	-.414	-.507
41	.665	.488	-.047	.543	-.110	-.196	-.411	-.515	.027	-.242	-.135	-.095	-.179	-.410	-.559	-.410	-.678	-.694	-.687	-.473
42	.389	.454	.112	.864	.391	.520	.341	.082	.078	.570	.547	.347	.114	.037	.169	.023	.764	.399	.705	.227
43	.532	.672	.337	.853	.483	.517	.359	.078	.553	.176	-.104	.138	-.077	-.406	-.404	-.287	.224	.068	.545	.316
44	.277	.032	.166	.854	.544	.522	-.109	-.106	.500	.236	-.036	.200	.379	-.702	-.596	-.427	.449	.167	-.700	.074
45	.013	.192	-.062	.534	.217	-.105	.720	-.479	.827	.930	.353	.613	.387	.235	-.480	.007	.324	.148	.213	.254
46	.046	.271	.022	.648	-.466	-.430	-.425	-.744	.021	.056	-.024	-.143	-.627	-.809	-.621	-.034	-.600	-.237	-.615	-.012
47	.149	.344	-.045	.580	-.329	-.301	-.069	-.427	-.413	-.483	-.326	-.476	-.359	-.169	-.456	-.058	-.687	-.719	-.621	-.350
48	.221	.210	.138	.917	.535	.691	.799	.179	.184	.186	.308	-.154	.382	.229	.296	.195	-.685	-.608	-.333	-.176
49	.350	.282	-.176	.567	-.557	-.449	-.678	-.567	.266	.088	-.056	.184	-.632	-.802	-.684	-.182	.055	-.091	.011	.291
50	.396	.396	-.004	.569	-.359	-.359	-.628	-.421	.100	.100	-.126	-.111	.042	.042	-.534	.050	-.835	-.835	.547	-.665

pc = paired comparisons preferences, rank = judged order preferences,
sl = judged savings and/or losses, pi = judged purchase intention

by the equation on the right, based on the dimension *weight* for subject i on dimension r, w_{ir}, and stimulus coordinates $x^*_{j\cdot}$ and x^*_{kr} for stimuli j and k, also on dimension r. x^*_{jr} is not precisely identical to x_{jr} in equation (1), but, as mentioned earlier, can be viewed as very nearly identical in the present case because of the orthogonal rotation of the MDREF to optimal congruence with the SINDSCAL solution, and the very high degree of congruence thus obtained (as mentioned earlier). (Of course, there is no "p" subscript here, as there was only one type of dissimilarity judgment by each subject.)

It is very important to note that the meaning of a subject's *vector* weights in the MDPREF model is quite different from that of that subject's weights in the INDSCAL model. MDPREF vector weights define the importance of dimensions in a linear compensatory model for preference (or other evaluative) judgment, while the INDSCAL subject weights indicate the relative importance of the dimensions, for the subject's *perceptions* of the stimuli, i.e., how much of a difference a change in that dimension makes to the subject's judged perceptual similarity or dissimilarity of a *pair* of stimuli. A dimension that is very important perceptually may make little or no difference to preference judgments (or vice versa). While on a theoretical basis perception may be viewed as prior to preference, in the sense that a dimension that is not perceived cannot possibly affect preference, the relationship between the effects of such dimensions on these two type of judgments is by no means a direct or simple one. This is shown in part by Figure 4 in the present case.

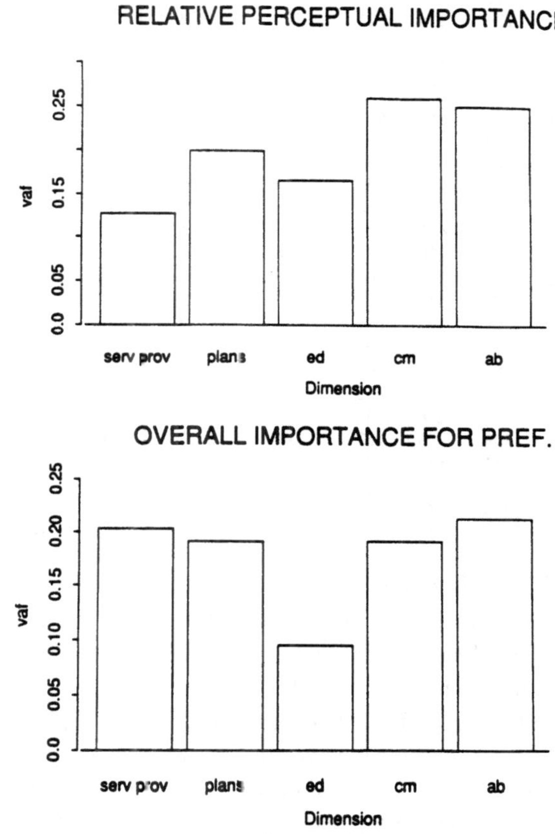

Figure 4

This figure shows the "variance accounted for" (VAF) by the five dimensions in the (estimated) scalar products derived from the dissimilarity judgments of the subjects (which can be viewed as a kind of composite measure of the relative sizes of the subject weights aggregated over all subjects for these data), together with an analogous measure for the preference and evaluative judgments, aggregated in this case over all 50 subjects and 4 judgment types. We can see from this figure that the relative sizes of these "VAF" figures are quite different for the two types of judgments. For example, dimension 1 ("service provider", contrasting AT&T with NNN) is not very important to these subjects' *perceptions* of the stimuli, but was one of the two most important dimensions for the overall *preference and evaluative* judgments. Another, perhaps more definitive, indication is given by inspection of Table 3, which gives the INDSCAL/SINDSCAL subject weights for the 50 subjects on the five dimensions. (It should be noted that, for purposes of interpretability, the INDSCAL dimensions were permuted from the order in which they were given by the SINDSCAL program, which orders them by VAF. Also, some INDSCAL dimensions were *reflected*—i.e., had all signs changed—which is also a permissible transformation.)

Table 3: Subject Weights for 5 Dimensional SINDSCAL Solution

Subj	serv prov	"plans"	"ed"	"cm"	"ab"	Subj	serv prov	"plans"	"ed"	"cm"	"ab"
1	.418	.211	.430	.426	.230	26	.205	.241	.282	.251	.454
2	.372	.431	.101	.151	.291	27	.310	.093	.376	.440	.086
3	.126	.557	.234	.314	.521	28	.389	.084	.198	.427	.287
4	.223	.585	.182	.073	.220	29	.286	.207	.365	.382	.409
5	.337	.094	.173	.425	.443	30	.367	.118	.377	.139	.543
6	.191	.715	.138	.282	.354	31	.142	.150	.060	.581	.480
7	.333	.359	.025	.447	.057	32	.320	.330	.374	.398	.134
8	.174	.066	.374	.258	.449	33	.222	.236	.093	.239	.575
9	.130	.107	.122	.035	.686	34	.514	.221	.247	.161	.226
10	.160	.287	.369	.473	.353	35	.334	.335	.242	.516	.343
11	.562	.233	.484	.224	.178	36	.050	.417	.174	.342	.461
12	−.012	.490	.344	.467	.392	37	.155	.289	.435	.220	−.169
13	.202	.185	.424	.278	.567	38	.173	.226	.222	.648	.390
14	.204	.251	.336	.353	.306	39	.263	.179	.154	.256	.376
15	.200	.447	.094	.532	.160	40	.322	.361	.128	.273	.329
16	.125	.479	.379	.490	.276	41	.139	.464	.267	.414	.358
17	.254	.096	.278	.366	.568	42	.245	.243	.399	.360	.419
18	.224	.050	.181	.611	.460	43	.125	.237	.455	.312	.154
19	.138	.133	.305	.459	.436	44	.015	.331	.407	.272	.318
20	.355	.277	.338	.276	.236	45	.187	.151	.614	.027	.230
21	.153	.522	.208	.393	.267	46	.270	.406	.223	.263	.554
22	.136	.086	.333	.531	.278	47	.178	.366	.343	.403	.448
23	.357	.141	.159	.540	.196	48	.125	.265	.135	.451	.212
24	.412	.356	.089	.363	.341	49	.110	.683	.383	.119	.314
25	.368	.159	.126	.399	.212	50	.167	.423	.449	.374	.318

Comparing these INDSCAL subject weights with the MDPREF vector weights in Table 2 shows that there is no simple or obvious relation between the sizes of these subjects' perceptual weights shown in Table 3 and the vector weights for the four types of preference/evaluative judgments in Table 2.

In addition to the INDSCAL/SINDSCAL and MDPREF analysis described, "external" analyses of the preference/evaluative data were also implemented, using the PREFMAP (Carroll (1972, 1980), Chang and Carroll (1972)) procedure for multidimensional PREFerence MAPping. In an "external" analysis, the stimulus configuration is given a priori, usually based on independent MDS analysis of similarity or dissimilarity data (in contrast to an "internal" analysis such as MDPREF, in which *both* the stimulus configuration and subject parameters, such as subject vectors, are fitted simultaneously based on the preference/evaluative data only). In the present case the "external" stimulus configuration was the one already discussed, determined by the SINDSCAL analysis of the dissimilarity data. In PREFMAP a range of models can be fitted, beginning at the simplest level with a vector model essentially the same as that fit by MDPREF (except that the SINDSCAL stimulus space was used instead of one generated by the "internal" MDPREF procedure itself). In addition, a class of "unfolding" models, in which preference/evaluation is assumed to be inversely related to distance from a subject's "ideal (stimulus) point", rather than to projections onto a vector. Three different unfolding models were fitted to these data, of increasing generality vis à vis definition of the metric, or function defining distances between stimuli and ideal points. The simpler vector model (which can be shown to be a special case of the unfolding models) was also fitted. The results of fitting the vector model to the SINDSCAL space were almost identical to the results of MDPREF after rotation to congruence with the SINDSCAL configuration. Furthermore, by some statistical significance tests built into the PREFMAP procedure it was shown that the more general "unfolding" models did not fit these data statistically significantly better than did the simpler vector model. For these reasons these results will not be discussed in further detail here. Rather we shall henceforth discuss only the MDPREF analysis, after orthogonal rotation to congruence with the SINDSCAL stimulus configuration.

A remarkable feature of the present data was the extremely high degree of variability of the subjects (despite their relative homogeneity on socioeconomic and other demographic variables). Indeed, it would not be an oversimplification to assert that, in the case of these calling plans there was essentially no consensus among subjects—i.e., no direction in the five dimensional space yielding a preference ordering of the 10 calling plans that would predict judgments of a "typical" (randomly selected) subject much better than an order corresponding to some other (arbitrary) direction. One implication of this is that it would be totally inappropriate to try to represent the preferences of these subjects by *mean* preference values, or by any analysis resulting in a single preference scale (or dimension) for all subjects. This is true despite the relative homogeneity of this particular subject sample, which varied little on major demographic variables, and so would almost certainly be much greater with a less homogeneous sample (or in the population as a whole). The need for all five dimensions of preference was reinforced by the fact that there were subjects with both positive and negative weights for each of the five dimensions, and, in fact, almost every possible pattern of signs of these five weights was exhibited by at least one of the 50 subjects (on one or more of the four evaluative scales) in this sample. This remarkable degree of individual differences is fairly atypical of preferential choice data, where, usually, there is a strong "consensus" direction representing a "typical" or "average" subject with some additional but somewhat less salient dimensions reflecting secondary individual differences. In the present case the individual differences were the *primary* phenomenon. This indicates the wisdom of making the various components of the OCP service optional, rather than building them into a single plan in an "all or none" fashion. It also indicates, from a methodological standpoint, the strong need for analyzing these data by procedures, such as MDPREF, that explicitly assume and attempt to account for individual differences in evaluation.

5 Marketing Implications

A marketing analyst, however, would obviously want to know more than the fact that there are five subjective dimensions underlying perception and evaluation of these calling plans, and that people differ widely in both the sign and magnitude of weights for these dimensions in making evaluative judgments. This analyst would undoubtedly want to relate these individual differences in evaluation to demographic variables such as family income, size of household, age of respondent and, most importantly in the present case, degree of usage of the relevant telecommunications service. For this reason an attempt was made to *predict* the importance weights of dimensions, separately for each of the four different types of evaluative judgments, from the demographic information also collected in the questionnaire. This was done by use of stepwise multiple linear regression, using the 15 demographic variables as predictors (independent variables) and each of 20 sets of evaluative weights (weights on the 5 dimensions for each of the 4 types of evaluative judgments) in turn as the criterion (dependent variable). Thus 20 separate stepwise regression analyses were done, each using the same 15 (demographic) independent variables.

While space does not permit a detailed description here, it was clear from examination of these results, as well as of the simple correlations of the twenty evaluative variables derived from the MDS analyses with the demographic variables, that the two variables that do the overall best job of predicting the evaluative variables are two variables measuring estimated dollars spent monthly on telecommunications usage of a type directly related to the type of calling involved in the OCP plans. One of these related to the telecommunications service most directly affected by the OCP calling plans, while the second was a measure of usage of a wider class of telecommunications service including this most relevant service as a subclass. Therefore, we looked closely at the simple correlations of these two variables with each of the 20 evaluative judgments. These correlations, which are shown in Table 4, together with the results from the stepwise regression procedure (not shown here), support the following general conclusions.

Table 4:

CORRELATIONS BETWEEN SUBJECT WEIGHTS ON 5 MDPREF DIMENSIONS ON FOUR DATA TYPES WITH TWO TELECOMMUNICATIONS SERVICE USAGE VARIABLES. VALUES IN PARENTHESES ARE FOR AN "OVERALL" SERVICE USAGE VARIABLE, WHILE THOSE IN SQUARE BRACKETS ARE FOR THE "MOST RELEVANT" USAGE VARIABLE.

Dimension TYPE OF DATA	DIM 1 SERVICE PROVIDER (AT&T vs. OCC)	DIM 2 PLAN vs. NON-PLAN	DIM 3 EXTRA DISCOUNT ("ED")	DIM 4 "CM"	DIM 5 ADDITIONAL BLOCK ("AB")
PAIRED COMPARISON (PR)	(−.3482**) [−.2695*]	(+.2924*) [+.3308*]	(+.3814*) [+.1914]	(+.4072**) [+.4119**]	(+.1823) [+.1297]
RANK ORDER (RK)	(−.4701A***) [−.37289A***]	(+.2100) [+.2966*]	(+.2996*) [+.19371]	(+.3736**) [+.3369*]	(+.1455) [+.1445]
PURCHASE INTENTION (PT)	(+.1051) [+.2919*]	(+.2495) [+.3828**]	(+.1481) [+.0488]	(+.3952**) [+.3967**]	(+.1282) [+.1294]
SAVINGS AND LOSS (SL)	(−.2759*) [−.2164]	(+.2295) [+.3261*]	(+.2945*) [+.2753*]	(+.3068*) [+.3608**]	(+.2259) [+.2067]

$^{*}p \leq .05$, $^{**}p \leq .01$, $^{***}p \leq .001$

Subscribers using more of the related services tend to be more favorably disposed to switching from AT&T (without the OCP plans) to an OCC (such as "NNN") than those making fewer such calls (as measured in total dollar amounts). The OCP plans appear to appeal considerably more to the high users, *particularly* the high users of one of the two classes of services (which happens to be the class of service of most value to AT&T from a revenue standpoint) suggesting that the OCP plans may tend to "save" many customers whose business is highly desirable to AT&T. The "CM" option in OCP appears to be particularly appealing to high users, of this "most relevant" service, while the Extra Discount option is less so, and in fact appears, by its pattern of correlations, to be somewhat more appealing to high users of the overall service who are not necessarily high users of the "most relevant" service. The "Additional Block of Time" option appears, somewhat paradoxically, to be more appealing to the lower users of these services than to the high users. (A precise judgment of the economic value of this option to AT&T might require detailed microeconometric modeling along the lines of a methodology called "willingness to pay" devised by members of the AT&T Bell Laboratories Business Systems Analysis Center.) A broad conclusion based on these analyses is that the basic OCP plan and at least two of its "add on" options ("CM" and "Extra Discount") appear very favorable to AT&T from a marketing point of view, while the third option ("Additional Block of Time") is somewhat questionable, appearing to require much more detailed (e.g. microeconometric) analysis to derive a solid conclusion.

The fact that the two demographic variables that relate most directly to usage patterns very closely related to the OCP services are both the best overall predictors and the most relevant from a marketing standpoint suggest that considerable effort might be worthwhile in providing more refined measures of these usage variables. This need may be met in part by obtaining, at least for AT&T users in our sample, direct measures of telecommunications usage from AT&T data banks. We have undertaken this effort, and hope to improve both the predictive and marketing efficacy of this work through use of these data. Looking to future such studies on telecommunications pricing, we may hope to produce more refined measures of various categories of telecommunications usage both through tapping such objective usage data, and through more detailed questioning of subjects regarding their *perceived* usage patterns. Multidimensional scaling and other related methods of multivariate analysis may also be quite helpful in providing better, more predictive, and more market sensitive measures of usage of the telecommunications service involved in this study (both perceived and actual), and of other telecommunications related behavior patterns.

6 General Conclusions About MDS in Marketing Research

While this paper has focussed on application of MDS to a very specific problem relating to telecommunications pricing, it is hoped that it makes clear the more general potential of this methodology for highly useful application to a broad range of marketing problems. As a whole these results, while still tentative, provide a clear illustration of the applicability and utility of multidimensional scaling to marketing problems, particularly those related to *pricing* of a service (such as the telecommunications service involved in this illustrative study), but also to a more general class of marketing problems in which it is desirable to understand the psychological dimensions underlying perception, as well as preference and evaluative judgments—and, ultimately—buying behavior of consumers. When synthesized with econometric modeling, such as "willingness to pay" modeling, this methodology should provide an even more potent tool for marketing analysis. Particularly in cases involving much more complex and less clearly defined options than this OCP domain of services, MDS enables extraction of subjective dimensions underlying customers' perceptions and evaluations of products that may be related in a very complex way to (and not simply predicted *à priori* from) physical or other variables underlying products of a more technological nature (e.g., personal computers). It might be noted, in the present case, that many of the same, or similar, conclusions could have been arrived at using the simpler and more direct approach known generically as "conjoint analysis" (see Green and Srinivasan (1978)). In many other cases, however, the subjective dimensions do not bear so simple and direct a relation to physical or other features defining the products, so that this would not be true (without, in any case, utilizing very complicated conjoint analysis models, possibly involving many higher order interaction terms). Thus the kind of MDS methodology illustrated in this paper can either confirm the applicability of a fairly straightforward conjoint analysis model when appropriate, or suggest more "relevant" subjective dimensions of products, defined as nonlinear functions of more basic features, when necessary. Even in the present case the relation between features of the calling plans and subjective dimension was not completely straightforward—and, in any case, we would not have known what this relation was without the MDS analyses discussed. In general, we view MDS and conjoint analysis as complementary approaches to the study of multiattribute consumer choice behavior.

Perhaps the single most important lesson learned as a result of this study is the need for methods, such as SINDSCAL and MDPREF, that are designed to handle individual differences among subjects (customers) in perception, and *particularly* individual differences in preferences, for products (calling plans, in this case). These individual differences MDS procedures provide particularly useful tools for market segmentation, especially when used in conjunction with demographic and other subject variables. At the same time, the *product* dimensions determined by these MDS procedures can be seen to be extremely useful for product positioning and new product development.

Multidimensional scaling provides powerful tools enabling the marketing analyst simultaneously to gain very useful insights about the perceptual structure of products, distribution of customer preferences for these products, the relationship of these customer preferences to the perceptual dimensions of the products, and the marketing implications of all of these facts.

References

Carroll JD (1972) Individual Differences and Multidimensional Scaling, in: Shepard RN, Romney AK, Nerlove S (eds.) Multidimensional Scaling: Theory and Applications in the Behavioral Sciences 1. Seminar Press, New York, London, pp 105–155

Carroll JD (1980) Models and Methods for Multidimensional Analysis of Preferential Choice (or Other Dominance) Data, in: Lantermann ED, Feger H (eds.) Similarity and Choice. Hans Huber Publishers, Bern, Stuttgart, Vienna, pp 234–289.

Carroll JD, Chang JJ (1970) Analysis of Individual Differences in Multidimensional Scaling Via an N-way Generalization of "Eckart-Young" Decomposition. Psychometrika 35: 283–319

Chang JJ, Carrol JD (1968) How to Use MDPREF: A Computer Program for Multidimensional Analysis of Preference Data. Unpublished Manuscript, Bell Laboratories, Murray Hill

Chang JJ, Carroll JD (1972) How to Use PREFMAP and PREFMAP-2: A Program which Relates Preference Data to a Multidimensional Scaling Solution. Unpublished Manuscript, Bell Laboratories, Murray Hill

Green PE, Srinivasan V (1978) Conjoint Analysis in Consumer Research: Issues and Outlook. Journal of Consumer Research 5: 103–123

Pruzansky S (1975) How to Use SINDSCAL: A Computer Program for Individual Differences in Multidimensional Scaling.

Wish M, Carroll JD (1974) Applications of Individual Differences Scaling to Studies of Human Perception and Judgment, in: Carterette EC, Friedman MP (eds.) Handbook of Perception. Academic Press, New York, pp 449–491

Inferring an Ideal-Point Product-Market Map from Consumer Panel Data

T. Elrod
Owen Graduate School of Management, Vanderbilt University
Nashville TN 37203 U.S.A.

Summary

A recent paper (see Elrod (1987)) introduced Choice Map, a model for inferring a product-market map from consumer panel data. Choice Map combines the rationale of random utility models, the parsimony of stochastic brand choice models, and the ability of multidimensional scaling procedures to simultaneously infer brand positions and consumer preferences for attributes from preference (choice) data. In its initial formulation, Choice Map represented consumers by vectors in one or two dimensions.

This paper presents an ideal-point version of Choice Map and compares it to the vector version. The ideal-point version fits a sample data set better, but brand loyalty is still underrepresented for some households.

1 Introduction

Brand managers of frequently-purchased consumer goods have access to the purchasing behavior by panels consisting of thousands of households. Scanner panel data allow the tracking of the actual purchasing behavior of households in an unobtrusive manner, and many brand managers obtain such data on a routine basis to monitor buying behavior for grocery and drug products. These data can be used to track trial and repeat rates for new brands and monitor mature product categories for changes in buyer behavior. For the latter purpose, switching matrices can be constructed periodically to determine whether or not the market is in equilibrium. Stochastic brand choice models such as the Dirichlet-multinomial (see Bass, Jeuland and Wright (1976)) are used to generate a basis for comparison by showing what switching would be expected given a stationary market, and how much of a deviation from predicted switching is within the range explainable by sampling error (see Goodhardt and Ehrenberg (1967); Morrison (1969); Morrison and Schmittlein (1981)). However, greater use of stochastic models in this way has been hampered by their neglect of brand attributes.

Choice Map in both of its versions is a brand choice model that assumes consumers perceive brands in terms of product attributes and that their evaluation of any brand is derived from their perception of the brand in terms of these attributes and the importance they attach to them; i.e., Choice Map assumes that brand choice behavior is explained by a product-market map. Furthermore, Choice Map infers the locations of brands and consumers in the map from real-world brand choice data. Rather than periodically derive switching matrices from panel data, managers can derive product-market maps. Since the maps are estimated by the method of maximum likelihood, the manager can explicitly test hypotheses about changes in the map. For example, has a new advertising campaign successfully altered buyer perceptions of the brand? Are consumers attaching less importance to a dimension than previously? Since these questions are answered by examining actual choice behavior, only changes affecting behavior will be detected.

To generate a Choice Map, the manager requires a count of the number of times each household bought each brand during the observational period. The length of time required for observation varies with the typical interpurchase time for the product category, but it appears in practice that 3–6 months of purchasing is adequate for most frequently-bought goods.

Such data are different from the type of data normally required for market structure analysis. First, there is no opportunity to effect experimental control over the choice process, such as obtaining pairwise choices from consumers. Second, the average number of purchases from the choice set is small by MDS standards—most applications of Choice Map to date have averaged 6 purchases per household for six-brand product categories, or one purchase per household per brand.

Choice Map deals with the lack of data by estimating only aggregate-level parameters. Consumer heterogeneity in purchasing is preserved by postulating a distribution of consumer preferences, and then estimating the parameters of that distribution directly. Given that the sample includes (few) purchases by a large number of households, avoiding the estimation of household-level parameters greatly increases model parsimony. However, Choice Map requires intensive numerical integration, over as many dimensions as there are dimensions in the map, which makes the estimation process slow and limits it to (at present) only one or two dimensions.

2 Model Derivation

Observed for each household is a vector of brand choice frequencies $\mathbf{y} = [y_1, \ldots, y_J]'$, where y_i is a count of the number of times brand i is bought during the observational period, and J is the number of brands. Both versions of Choice Map assume that $\mathbf{y}$ arises from a series of purchase occasions on which only a single brand is chosen. On each occasion the brand chosen (denoted X) is the one having the highest utility:

$$X = i \quad \text{if and only if} \quad U_i = \max\{U_1, \ldots, U_J\}, \tag{1}$$

where U_i denotes the utility of brand i.

Brand utilities are stochastic over time, which explains why different brands are often bought by the same household on different choice occasions. The utility for a brand is a random variable U which is the sum of a constant preference component (denoted v) and a stochastic component (denoted ϵ) of zero mean:

$$U = v + \epsilon. \tag{2}$$

Random utility models (see McFadden (1976); Manski and McFadden (1981); Currim (1982)) distinguish v as the component of utility that is explained by observed attributes of brands and/or households, and ϵ is the unobserved component of utility. In both versions of Choice Map, both v and ϵ are unobserved. Choice Map distinguishes v as being that component of utility that is unvarying over time for a given household.

McFadden (1974) has shown that if ϵ has the standard double exponential distribution and is independently distributed over brands and choice occasions, then the probability that brand i is chosen on any single choice occasion is given by:

$$\Pr[X = i] = p_i = \exp(v_i) \; / \; \sum_{j=1}^{J} \exp(v_j). \tag{3}$$

A household with purchase probabilities $\mathbf{p} = [p_1, \ldots, p_J]'$ observed for T purchase occasions will yield purchase frequencies $\mathbf{y}$ with probability given by the multinomial distribution:

$$\Pr[\mathbf{y}; \mathbf{p}, T] = (T! \; / \; \prod_{j=1}^{J} y_j!) \prod_{j=1}^{J} (p_j)^{y_j}. \tag{4}$$

Finally, Choice Map in both its ideal-point and vector versions explains a household's brand preferences ($\mathbf{v}$) as a function of the locations of the J brands in an M-dimensional map (denoted by the J-by-M matrix $\mathbf{A}$), and of the importance the household attaches to these map dimensions (denoted by the M-component column vector $\mathbf{w}$). Furthermore, both versions assume that $\mathbf{w}$ follows an M-variate normal distribution with mean μ and variance Σ. Where the versions differ is in the specification of the function specifying $\mathbf{v}$. The vector version uses the linear function:

$$\mathbf{v} = \mathbf{A}\mathbf{w}, \tag{5}$$

while the ideal-point version uses the function:

$$v_i = -\sum_{m=1}^{M} (a_{im} - w_m)^2, \quad i = 1, \ldots, J. \tag{6}$$

Lancaster (1979) has suggested that ideal-point models are similar to projections of $(M+1)$-dimensional vector maps into M dimensions. Given that Choice Map is restricted (at present) to two dimensions, an ideal-point version was expected to fit the data better, at least in the case of 4 or more brands. The intuition behind Lancaster's suggestion is seen by considering that the vector model cannot capture brand loyalty towards brands that lie interior to other brands—to be strongly preferred, a brand must lie farther in some direction than any other brand. In practice every brand has some loyal customers, so vector maps tend to locate the brands at the vertices of convex polygons. In theory, the ideal-point model suffers from no such limitation—households with ideal points very close to a brand will be loyal to it, even if it is interior to other brands.

3 Estimation Issues

The probability that a household will purchase with frequencies $\mathbf{y}$, given T purchase occasions, brand locations $\mathbf{A}$, and attribute preferences $\mathbf{w}$, is expressed as $\Pr[\mathbf{y} \mid \mathbf{w}; \mathbf{A}, T]$.

T is exogenously determined and observed, $\mathbf{A}$ is an unknown matrix of parameters to be estimated, and $\mathbf{w}$ is a vector of household-level "nuisance parameters" that is not to be estimated. Rather, we require estimates of $\boldsymbol{\mu}$ and $\boldsymbol{\Sigma}$, the parameters of the M-variate normal distribution characterizing $\mathbf{w}$. The probability that a randomly selected household will exhibit purchasing behavior $\mathbf{y}$ as a function of aggregate-level parameters (and the exogenously determined number of purchase occasions T) is given by:

$$\Pr[\mathbf{y};\mathbf{A},\boldsymbol{\mu},\boldsymbol{\Sigma},T]=\int_{-\infty}^{+\infty}\Pr[\mathbf{y}\mid\mathbf{w};\mathbf{A},T]\,n\,[\mathbf{w};\boldsymbol{\mu},\boldsymbol{\Sigma}]\,d\mathbf{w}, \tag{7}$$

where $n[.]$ represents the density of the M-variate normal distribution and the integration is over all M dimensions of $\mathbf{w}$. Assuming that all C households in the sample act independently, the maximum likelihood estimates of the parameters $\mathbf{A},\boldsymbol{\mu}$ and $\boldsymbol{\Sigma}$ are obtained by maximizing:

$$\Pr[\mathbf{y}_1,\ldots,\mathbf{y}_C;\mathbf{A},\boldsymbol{\mu},\boldsymbol{\Sigma},T_1,\ldots,T_C]=\prod_{c=1}^{C}\Pr[\mathbf{y}_c;\mathbf{A},\boldsymbol{\mu},\boldsymbol{\Sigma},T_c], \tag{8}$$

where c is an index of household.

Both versions of Choice Map accomplish the integration numerically using a 44-point rule developed by Rabinowitz and Richter (1969) that is suitable for integrating any function multiplied by a bivariate normal density. The rule exactly integrates any function so multiplied that is a polynomial of degree 15 or less.; that is, any function $f(x,y)$ of the form:

$$f(x,y)=\sum_{i=1}^{15}\sum_{j=1}^{15}b_{ij}\,x^iy^j. \tag{9}$$

Due to its reliance on this rule, Choice Map in both versions is limited to maps of one or two dimensions.

The issue of estimation includes a second matter of model identification. The parameters $\mathbf{A},\boldsymbol{\mu}$ and $\boldsymbol{\Sigma}$ are underidentified by the maximization of (8). This is the well-known indeterminacy of product-market maps—rotating, flipping, moving the origin and, in the vector version, rescaling of the axes does not affect the fit to the data. Specifically, in the vector version of Choice Map (5), $\boldsymbol{\Sigma}$ may be assumed to be the identity matrix, the map may be rotated so that $\boldsymbol{\mu}$ lies along the first principle axis, and the location of the origin is arbitrary (which means that one component of each column of $\mathbf{A}$ may be fixed) (see Elrod (1987)). This leaves $M(2J-M+1)/2$ parameters to be estimated, provided $J>M$. In the ideal-point version (6), $\boldsymbol{\mu}$ (or a component of each column of $\mathbf{A}$) may be arbitrarily fixed (to fix the origin) and the map may be rotated so that $\boldsymbol{\Sigma}$ is diagonal, leaving $M(J+1)$ parameters to be estimated. All of these restrictions are without loss of generality and merely serve to resolve notational indeterminacy. The notational indeterminacy is useful, however, because it allows managers to choose how they will standardize the map. For example, managers may wish to generate maps with their own brand at the origin.

4 Application to Panel Purchasing of Laundry Detergents

SAMI/Burke, Inc. made available purchasing data for laundry detergents. This paper examines purchasing by 676 households towards the 6 top-selling brands of liquid laundry detergent at the time the data were collected: Dynamo, Wisk, Era, Yes, Solo and Arm & Hammer. These brands had sample market shares of .12, .43, .13, .09, .13, and .09, respectively. The households purchased a total of 1714 units during the observational period. Examination of the packaging of these brands revealed that they differed in one important respect: Solo and Yes claimed to soften clothes and the other four brands claimed to remove tough stains. No brand claimed to do both.

Five models were fit to the data: the two versions of Choice Map, the Dirichlet-multinomial model, and two benchmark models (the aggregate share and the household share models). The aggregate share model computes the loglikelihood in (4) by assuming that every household has purchase probabilities equal to the market shares of the brands. The household share model computes the loglikelihood in (4) by assuming that each household has purchase probabilities proportional to their observed purchase frequencies. The fits of the five models, and the number of parameters estimated, are shown in Table 1.

MODEL	NO. OF PARAMETERS	LOGLIKELIHOOD
Household Share	3380	-280
Dirichlet-multinomial	6	-1942
Choice Map		
Ideal Point Version	14	-1962
Vector Version	11	-1983
Aggregate Share	5	-2314

Table 1: Fits of Five Models to Liquid Detergent Panel Data

The household share model fits best, which is necessarily true since all other models are a special case of it. Chi-square tests show that its better fit is statistically significant relative to only the aggregate share model. Furthermore, a previous comparison of all of these models except for the ideal-point model showed that the household share model predicted holdout purchases the worst of all (see Elrod (1987)).

The Dirichlet-multinomial model fits next best, which is surprising to those of us who believe the brands are not equisimilar. The model assumes independence from irrelevant alternatives (IIA) in aggregate as well as at the household level. Choice Map, by comparison, assumes IIA only within household over time, and not in aggregate. Reasons for the superior fit of the Dirichlet-multinomial will be examined in the next section.

The ideal-point Choice Map is shown in Figure 1. The ovals drawn in the figure represent the distribution of ideal points—the inner oval encloses half of the ideal points, the outer oval three-fourths. Unlike most multidimensional scaling algorithms that simultaneously infer ideal-points and brand locations (see Schiffman, Reynolds and Young (1981)), Choice Map did not produce a degenerate solution (such as locating all brands in the center of the map). The brands are well distributed relative to the ideal points. Furthermore, the two brands of detergent that contain fabric softener (Solo and Yes) are located close to one another. Also, the brand that founded the liquid detergent category (Wisk) is located at the center of the map. This is a reassuring result to those of us who believe that household preferences for new product categories should tend to center on the prototypical brand.

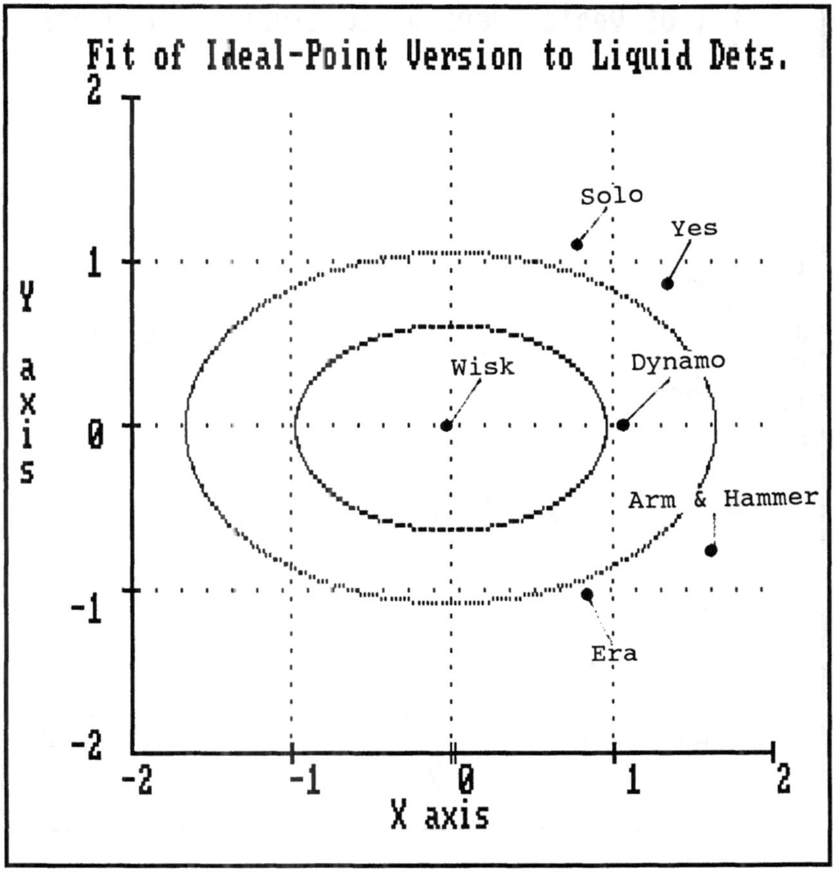

Figure 1: Fit of the Ideal-Point Version of Choice Map to the Liquid Laundry Detergent Panel Data

As expected, the vector version of Choice Map did not fit as well as the ideal-point version. The vector map is reproduced in Figure 2. The map is not very different—Solo and Yes are still located close to one another. The modal household prefers brands to the left and slightly below the horizontal axis, as is indicated by a vector from the origin pointing to the average preference μ. The variance in consumer preference for the two dimensions of the map is one in both dimensions.

Notice in the vector map shown in Figure 2 that Dynamo has moved from its interior position to be almost on top of Era, leaving no brand interior to other brands. It could be that the vector model is forced to locate Dynamo outside of its true interior position in order to capture brand loyalty observed by some households towards it. Some evidence for this is presented below, but if true, one would expect the ideal-point model to yield a greater improvement in fit than it did.

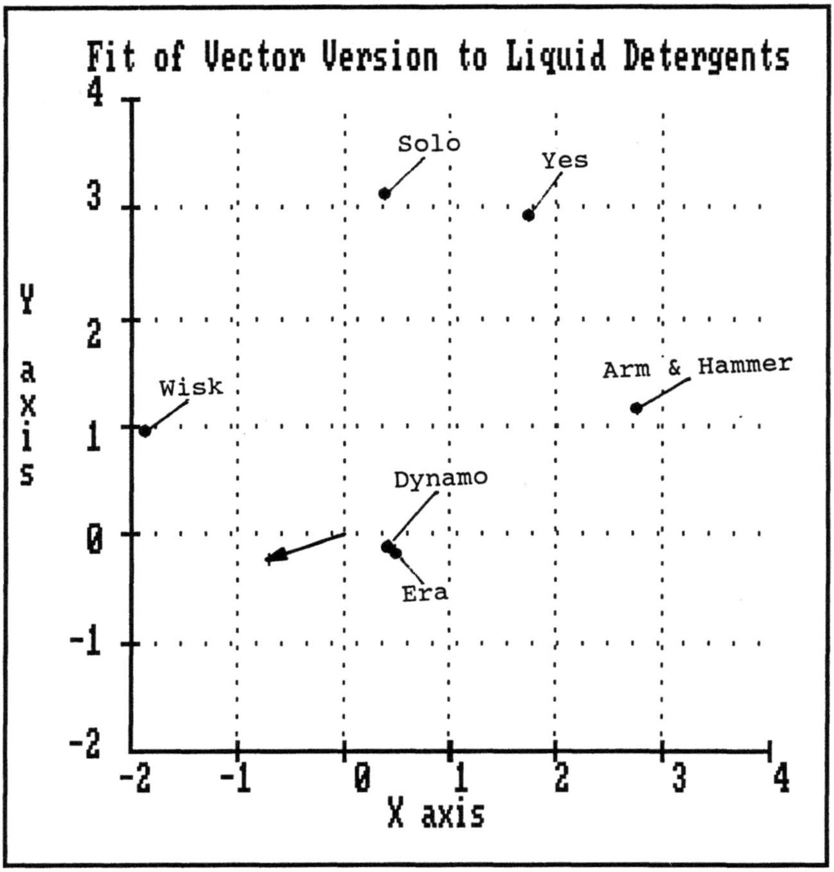

Figure 2: Fit of the Vector Version of Choice Map to the Liquid Laundry Detergent Panel Data

5 Underrepresentation of Brand Loyalty

Sources of poor fit are hard to ascertain by examining a 646-by-6 data matrix. A parsimonious method for summarizing the market structure information available is to construct a J-by-J joint purchase probability matrix (JPPM). A JPPM is an estimate, based upon the data, of what the purchasing data would look like if every purchase had been generated by households that purchased on only two occasions. Then a value of 1 would be added to cell (i, j) every time a household was observed to buy brand i on the first occasion and brand j on the second. Such a matrix is sometimes referred to as a "switching" matrix, but note that the cell values are not conditional on the choice of row, as they would be in a true (i.e. Markov) switching matrix.

Hutchinson and Zenor (1986) have proposed a method for constructing JPPMs from panel data. If a household has purchase probabilities $\mathbf{p}$, then the expected JPPM for that household is given by the J-by-J matrix $\mathbf{pp}'$. An estimate of each household's $\mathbf{p}$ vector can be taken to be the observed purchase frequency for the household divided by the number of purchase occasions $(\mathbf{f}/T)$. JPPMs were constructed in this manner for each household observed to buy liquid laundry detergent on two or more occasions. These household-level matrices were aggregated by first weighting each matrix by the number of purchases made by the household. Thus the empirical JPPM was constructed as:

$$\text{empirical JPPM } = \sum_{c=1}^{C}(\mathbf{f}_c\mathbf{f}_c' \,/\, T_c) \,/\, \sum_{c=1}^{C} T_c. \tag{10}$$

The empirical JPPM was compared to the expected JPPM constructed for all of the fitted models except for the household share model (The empirical JPPM would be the same as that fitted by the household share model if aggregation of the household-level JPPMs had not been weighted by number of units purchased.). The striking finding is that the diagonals are underrepresented in all cases. Rank-ordering the models by their degree of underrepresentation of brand loyalty exactly reproduces the ranking of the models by poorness-of-fit. Table 2 compares the diagonals of the empirical and the fitted JPPMs.

	Brand					
Model	Dynamo	Wisk	Era	Yes	Solo	A&H
(Actual)	.08	.36	.07	.06	.08	.06
Dirichlet-mult.	.06	.27	.06	.04	.06	.04
Choice Map						
Ideal Point	.03	.33	.05	.03	.05	.04
Vector	.03	.32	.03	.02	.05	.04
Aggregate share	.02	.19	.02	.01	.02	.01

Table 2: Comparison of Actual to Fitted Repeat Purchasing for Four of the Models

The Dirichlet-multinomial model fit the repeat purchasing better than all other models in all cases except for Wisk. The ideal-point version of Choice Map fit better than the remaining models in the case of all brands, and the aggregate share model underrepresented repeat purchasing in the case of all brands more so than all of the other models.

Of particular interest in comparing the two versions of Choice Map is the case of Dynamo, which is interior to the other brands in the ideal-point version but not in the vector version. Surprisingly, fitted repeat purchasing is identical in the two models. This discovery induced me to compute the probability of purchasing Dynamo for a household with an ideal point located exactly on that brand. The probability is only .37. Clearly brand loyalty is underrepresented in the map.

6 Ideas for Capturing Brand Loyalty in Product-Market Maps

At this point in time two alternatives are being considered for better capturing brand loyalty in the ideal-point version of Choice Map. The first is to recognize the existence of evoked sets. Even though the six brands studied are all major brands and presumably had 100% distribution to the scanner panel households, there is still good reason to believe that many households have zero probabilities of buying some brands (see Jacoby and Chestnut (1978)). Even with the Beta distribution's ability to represent households with purchase probabilities of zero, several studies have found that the fit of the Beta-binomial model is improved by adding a segment that has a purchase probability of zero for the brand (see Morrison (1969); Kalwani and Morrison (1976); Lehmann, Moore and Elrod (1982)). Recently, Colombo and Morrison (1987) have estimated a model that says there are J brand-loyal segments and one homogeneous segment that buys each brand with unknown purchase probabilities $\mathbf{p}$. The $2J - 1$ parameters are estimated from a JPPM, and initial fits of this model appear to be quite good. Finally, Jeuland (1979) extended the Dirichlet-multinomial model to account for varying availability of the brands in diary panel stores, but his model can be used to model evoked set as well. Each brand was assumed to be present in an unknown fraction of all stores shopped by the panel (a fraction to be estimated by the model), the probability of any brand being represented is assumed to be independent across brands, and all stores have at least one brand present. If applied to the study of evoked set, this model has the advantage of representing all possible evoked sets. But with J brands, there are $2^J - 1$ different evoked sets, or 63 for a six-brand market.

An alternative approach to better capture brand loyalty is to extend the ideal-point model in a way that generates more purchase probability vectors containing probabilities close to zero. One possibility is to allow consumers to be heterogeneous in their sensitivity to a brand's distance from their ideal point. This type of heterogeneity is common in other multidimensional scaling algorithms (see Schiffman, Reynolds and Young (1981)) that estimate individual-level parameters, but it burdens Choice Map with at least one more nuisance parameter to be integrated over numerically. The alternatives for Choice Map are then to reduce the map to one dimension (in order to integrate numerically over two parameters) or to extend the numerical procedure to integrate over a third parameter.

Both approaches to better capturing brand loyalty—incorporating evoked set and allowing consumers to differ in sensitivity to brand distances from their ideal points—are presently being pursued. At present, Choice Map in its ideal-point version already infers nondegenerate product-market maps from panel data, making it possible for brand managers to better monitor changes in buyer behavior in mature product markets.

References

Bass FM, Jeuland AP, Wright GP (1976) Equilibrium Stochastic Choice and Market Penetration Theories: Derivations and Comparisons. Management Science 22: 1051–1063

Colombo R, Morrison DG (1987) Brand Switching Model with Implications for Marketing Strategies. Colunbia University, Working paper

Currim IS (1982) Predictive Testing of Consumer Choice Models Not Subject to Independence of Irrelevant Alternatives. Journal of Marketing Research 19: 208–222

Elrod T (1987) Choice Map: Inferring a Product-Market Map from Panel Data. Vanderbilt University, Working paper

Goodhardt GJ, Ehrenberg ASC (1967) Conditional Trend Analysis: A Breakdown by Initial Purchasing Level. Journal of Marketing Research 4: 155–161

Hutchinson, Wesley J, Zenor MJ (1986) Methods for Identifying Market Partitions and Estimating Their Sizes. University of Florida, Marketing Department, working paper

Jacoby J, Chestnut RW (1978) Brand Loyalty Measurement and Management. Wiley, New York

Jeuland AP (1979) The Interaction Effect of Preference and Availability on Brand Switching and Market Share. Management Science 25: 953–965.

Kalwani MU, Morrison DG (1976) Estimating the Proportion of 'Always Buy' and 'Never Buy' Consumers: A Likelihood Ratio Test With Sample Size Implications. Journal of Marketing Research 14: 601–606

Lancaster K (1979) Variety, Equity and Efficiency. Columbia University Press, New York

Lehmann DR, Moore WL, Elrod T (1982) Development of Distinct Choice Process Segments Over Time: A Stochastic Modeling Approach. Journal of Marketing 46: 48–59

Manski CF, McFadden D (1981) Structural Analysis of Discrete Data with Econometric Applications. MIT Press, Cambridge, MA

McFadden D (1974) Conditional Logit Analysis of Qualitative Choice Behavior, in: Zarembka P (ed.) Frontiers in Econometrics. Academic Press, New York

McFadden D (1976) Quantal Choice Analysis: A Survey. Annals of Economic and Social Measurement 5: 363–390

Morrison DG (1969) Conditional Trend Analysis: A Model that Allows for Nonusers. Journal of Marketing Research 6: 342–346

Morrison DG, Schmittlein DC (1981) Predicting Future Random Events Based on Past Performance. Management Science 27: 1006–1023

Rabinowitz P, Richter N (1969) Perfectly Symmetric Two-Dimensional Integration Formulas With Minimal Numbers of Points. Mathematical Computing 23: 765–779

Schiffman SS, Reynolds ML, Young FW (1981) Introduction to Multidimensional Scaling. Academic Press, New York

An Individual Importance Weights Model for Conjoint Analysis

P. E. Green
Wharton School, University of Pennsylvania
F. J. Carmone Jr. and C. M. Schaffer
Drexel University

Summary

Increasingly, commercial applications of conjoint analysis are beset by the demand to handle larger numbers of attributes, together with the need to reduce the length of the data collection task. The proposed model is designed to estimate individual-level parameters that act as importance weights, applied to group-level part worths. Two versions of the model are described and the first version is illustratively applied to a set of field-level data.

1 Introduction

During the past several years conjoint analysis has received considerable attention (see Green and Srinivasan (1978)). In commercial applications of the methodology, two trends have been evident. On the one hand, studies are becoming more complex in terms of the number of product/service attributes that decision makers desire to include. On the other hand, it is becoming more difficult and expensive to obtain enough evaluative judgments to enable the researcher to estimate detailed, individual-level part-worth functions for input to consumer choice simuators.

One way out of this dilemma is to consider other utility models—models that still enable the researcher to estimate individual functions, while requiring less input data. This note is concerned with one such model and its application to a set of field-level data.

2 The Individual Importance Weights Model

In typical applications of conjoint analysis that utilize the full profile approach (in which all attributes can vary simultaneously), the respondent may be asked to evaluate as many as six to eight attributes, each involving four levels, or so. Even if an orthogonal main effects plan (see Green (1974)) is used, the respondent would still have to rate some 32 different card descriptions in terms of preference. If the two-factor-at-a-time approach (see Johnson (1974)) is used, some 16 different 4×4 tables may have to be evaluated in order to insure sufficient data for individual-level utility estimation.

In many empirical applications the product attributes chosen for evaluation are such that high inter-respondent agreement would be expected on the utility ordering of levels within each attribute. For example, in the context of automobiles, most people prefer more gas mileage to less, more legroom to less, greater visibility to less, and so on; high inter-respondent correlations would be expected across their rankings of levels within a specific attribute. However, inter-respondent agreement may not be high insofar as the importance weights attached to the attributes themselves, as reflected (say) in the attributes' relative ranges.

The individual importance weights model, to be described, postulates that a subset (perhaps all) of attributes exist on which high inter-respondent agreement is assumed in terms of within-attribute evaluation (in both ranking and relative spacing). However, each respondent is assumed to weight each of the (common) part-worth functions individually in order to best fit his/her particular data.

2.1 Algebraic Formulation of the Model

We let $\bar{v}_{ij}$ denote the average respondent's part worth of level i $(i = 1, 2, \ldots, I_j)$ of attribute j $(j = 1, 2, \ldots, J)$, in a simple main effects utility model. We let $a_j^{(k)}$ denote the importance that respondent k $k = (1, 2, \ldots, K)$ ascribes to the j-th attribute. Letting $V_{i_1, i_2, \ldots, i_J}^{(k)}$ denote the k-th respondent's overall preference rating of a specific profile description, the individual importance weights model is:

$$V_{i_1, i_2, \ldots, i_J}^{(k)} \cong v_0^{(k)} - a_1^{(k)} \bar{v}_{i_1} + a_2^{(k)} \bar{v}_{i_2} + \cdots + a_J^{(k)} \bar{v}_{i_J} \tag{1}$$

where $\cong$ denotes least squares approximation, and $v_0^{(k)}$ denotes an idiosyncratic constant term (intercept) for the k-th respondent.

We also assume in this model that the respondent provides some type of response (e.g., a rating or sorting of profile-description cards into numerically labeled categories) that we consider to be metric.[1] As such, ordinary dummy-variable regression can be used to estimate the a_j and $\bar{v}_{i_j}$ parameters in a two-stage manner (to be described).

Note further that the model imposes no constraints on the shape of the average respondent's part-worth function within an attribute. For example, the part-worth function need not be monotonic with increases (say) in the amount of trunk space; the respondent group might most prefer some more or less intermediate amount of trunk space. All that is required is that high inter-respondent agreement be manifested on the general shape of the part-worth function (whatever that shape is) within attribute.

2.2 A Hybrid Model

In cases where the researcher believes that respondents will differ in their within-attribute utility function shapes (e.g., their most preferred level within the attribute might vary), then those attributes can be fitted separately in a type of hybrid version of the individual importance weights model.

We first split the full set of attributes into two subsets, consisting of J and L attributes each. We let $\bar{u}_{i_j}$ denote the average respondent's part worth of level i

[1]The assumption of a metrically scaled response variable is not nearly as restrictive as might be supposed, given the general robustness of OLS regression procedures (see Carmone, Green and Jain (1978); Cattin and Wittink (1976); Green (1974))

($i = 1,2,\ldots,I_J$) of attribute j ($j = 1,2,\ldots,J$), and $b_j^{(k)}$ denote the importance that respondent k ($k = (1,2,\ldots,K)$ ascribes to the j-th attribute (as before). We let w_{m_l} denote the k-th respondent's idiosyncratic part worth of level m ($m = 1,2,\ldots,M_l$) of attribute l ($l = 1,2,\ldots,L$).

We can then write the hybrid version of the model as:

$$\begin{aligned} X^{(k)}_{i_1,i_2,\ldots,i_J,m_1,m_2,\ldots,m_L} &\cong w_0^{(k)} + b_1^{(k)}\bar{u}_{i_1} + b_2^{(k)}\bar{u}_{i_2} + \cdots + b_j^{(k)}\bar{u}_{i_J} \\ &\quad + w^{(k)}_{m_1} + w^{(k)}_{m_2} + \cdots + w^{(k)}_{m_L} \end{aligned} \quad (2)$$

where $X^{(k)}_{i_1,i_2,\ldots,i_J,m_1,m_2,\ldots,m_L}$ denotes the k-th respondent's overall preference rating of a specific profile description, $\cong$ denotes least squares approximation, and $w_0^{(k)}$ denotes the k-th respondent's constant (i.e., intercept term).

Any specific respondent's w_{m_l} parameters would be estimated from appropriately coded dummy variables (using $M-1$ levels for each such attribute, to avoid redundancy). Thus, the model of equation (2) requires more observations per respondent, since more parameters are being fitted, but not as many as would be needed in traditional conjoint parameter estimation in which all parameters are fitted individually via dummy-variable coding.

2.3 Fitting the Models

As might be surmised, fitting either version of the individual importance weights model entails a two-stage approach. In the first stage, least squares regression is applied to the J common attributes (each expressed as a set of dummy variables) and individuals are treated as replications. The group-level part worths are tested for statistical significance. Then, in case of equation (1), each individual's preference responses are regressed on the group average's utility for each attribute level exhibited by the stimulus in question. This second stage is usually carried out by a stepwise regression procedure, so as to reduce the risk of capitalization on chance. Only those importance weights that pass the user-imposed control levels (F values) are retained.

In the case of equation (2) the procedure is modified somewhat. In the first stage only the J (judged-common) attributes are entered, via dummy-variable coding, into the overall regression, where individuals are treated as replications. Having then obtained the $\bar{u}_{i_j}$ values, these are entered, along with the M idiosyncratic attributes (the latter being approximately dummy coded) in the individual regressions.

3 An Illustrative Application

For illustrative purposes we consider a small commercial study (suitably disguised to respect the sponsor's wishes) involving 186 respondents' evaluations of various attributes of imported (Japanese) luxury vans. The attributes and levels appear in Table 1.

A full factorial design of the attribute levels in Table 1 would entail $4^3 \times 3^2 \times 2 = 1152$ combinations. However, an orthogonal main effects plan can be constructed on the basis of only 32 combinations. (While this is not the minimum such plan, it provides a more satisfactory number of degrees of freedom for error estimation.)

Table 1: Group-level part worths based on first-stage regression (disguised data)

		Part-Worth			Part-Worth
A.	Cargo Height		D.	Transmission	
	1. 38"	0		1. 3-speed Manual	0
	2. 46"	0.22		2. 4-speed Manual	0.36
	3. 52"	0.96			
B.	Cargo Length		E.	Payload	
	1. 86 "	0		1. 800 pounds	0
	2. 96 "	0.20		2. 1,200 pounds	0.05
	3. 106"	0.42		3. 1,500 pounds	0.22
	4. 116"	0.55		4. 2,000 pounds	0.06
C.	Cargo Width		F.	Engine Type	
	1. 58"	0		1. 4 cylinder gasoline	0
	2. 62"	0.05		2. 6 cylinder gasoline	0.32
	3. 66"	0.11		3. 6 cylinder diesel	0.94
	4. 70"	0.48			

Still, it was thought that the data collection task would be too lengthy if each respondent had to judge all 32 combinations. Accordingly, a partially balanced incomplete block design (see Green (1974)) was set up in which each respondent had to evaluate only eight of the 32 combinations on a 1–9 sorting board, ranging from least highly liked to the most highly liked.[2] In addition, each respondent received two common or reference profiles, in order to provide a standard context for evaluating his/her test items.

All 186 respondents were "in the market" for a foreign van of the type being evaluated. Since only ten cards (out of a total of 34) had to be evaluated by any single respondent, the task was quite simple; on the average, the card sort was finished in approximately ten minutes, including instruction time.

In this application prior research had suggested that high homogenity of part worths within attribute was to be expected. Accordingly, the model of equation (1) was selected for fitting. Table 1 summarizes the group-level part worths obtained from the initial regression (across all 186 respondents) in which respondents are treated as replications.[3] All part worths were significant at the 0.05 level or better. Since one fits $t-1$ parameters for each t-level factor, a total of 14 parameters (regression coefficients) plus an intercepts term were fitted at the group level. (This, of course, exceeds the number of data points

[2]This design entails 32 blocks (respondents) in which each of the 32 test stimuli is replicated eight times (not counting the two common stimuli that each respondent gets). Six replications were made, resulting in $6 \times 32 = 192$ sets of responses. Of these, 186 were complete and usable.

[3]Incomplete block designs also permit the researcher to fit block parameters in addition to parameters based on stimuli. However, by using a common set of two reference items, the tendency for different respondents to show different average responses is reduced; hence block parameter fitting was not carried out in the illustrative case described here.

per individual respondent.)

However, for any specific stimulus, only six part worths are involved, one for each attribute level displayed by that stimulus. Hence, it is a simple matter to set up six variables (based on the part worths of Table 1) to serve as predictors for each respondent's set of ten preference ratings. This constitutes the second stage of the parameter estimation process, in which individual-respondent stepwise regressions are carried out.[4]

3.1 Second-Stage Results

As might be surmised, given the types of attributes shown in Table 1, the equation (1) fits of the group-level part worths to individual response data were quite good. Table 2 summarizes the principal results. First, we note that individual R^2's were generally high. The median R^2 was 0.84 and only 15 respondents exhibited R^2's below 0.6.

Table 2: Summary results of fitting the second stage of the individual importance weights model of equation (1)

Distribution of Individual R^2's	Frequency	Distribution of Number of Importance Weights per Respondent	Frequency
$0.9 < R^2 \leq 1.00$	43	1	7
$0.8 < R^2 \leq 0.9$	69	2	36
$0.7 < R^2 \leq 0.8$	38	3	83
$0.6 < R^2 \leq 0.7$	21	4	54
$R^2 \leq 0.6$	15	5	6
	186	6	0
			186[5]

Distribution of Attributes Entering Individual Regressions	Frequency
Attribute A[6]	144
B	92
C	80
D	75
E	62
F	121
	574

However, in no case did the stepwise regression result in all average-subject part worths being important for a single subject. As noted from Table 2, generally only

[4]A (rather stringent) F value of 3.0 was used for inclusion of predictors in the stepwise portion of the analysis.

[5]This entails a total of 574 importance weights (across the group of 186 respondents).

[6]See Table 1 for attribute descriptions

three out of the six possible part worth terms entered the stepwise regression of any individual respondent. (Of course, had the F level for inclusion been set at a less stringent level, more parameters per respondent would have entered.)

Table 2 also shows the incidence with which each of the six attributes appeared in individual regressions. Of the 574 predictors that entered the stepwise regressions, attribute A (cargo height) and F (engine type) were the most frequently occuring cases. Not surprisingly, their attribute ranges in Table 1 also show them to be the most important for the group as a whole.

In this set of data, the simple model of equation (1) appeared to provide a good representation of individual data. However, it need hardly be added that in other problems, the more elaborate model of equation (2) may be needed, albeit with fewer degrees of freedom left over for error estimation, or more observations required, as the case may be.

3.2 Consumer Choice Simulation

At this point, 186 individual utility functions had been obtained, based on the model of equation (1). Suppose the analyst is requested to evaluate four imported luxury van profiles in a consumer choice simulator. Assume that a simple selection rule, involving choosing that profile for which the respondent's computed utility is highest, is adopted. If so, what would be the share of choices garnered by each of the four options?

Table 3: Choice-option descriptions and share of first choices received in the individual importance weights model versus the average-subject-plus-error model

Choice Option	Description (see Table 1)	Individual Importance Weights Model	Average-Subject-Plus-Error Model
α	A_1; B_4; C_3; D_1; E_3; F_1	4	6
β	A_3; B_4; C_1; D_1; E_2; F_2	38	41
γ	A_2; B_1; C_2; D_2; E_1; F_2	8	13
δ	A_3; B_3; C_4; D_1; E_3; F_3	136	126
	Total Frequency	186	186

Table 3 shows a description—in terms of the attribute levels of Table 1—of the four profiles evaluated in the simulator. Also shown is the share of choices found by application of equation (1) and the highest-utility choice rule. We note that profile δ receives the major share of first choices (136 out of 186) while profile α receives only four first choices out of the total.

As a type of control case a simple alternative choice model was constructed. Here we assumed that each individual subject behaved exactly as the average subject with the addition of an error component. This was operationalized by finding the variance of individual-values of a linear combination of the model parameters of the average subject, according to the formula (see Mendenhall (1968, chap. 7))

$$\text{Var}^{[\text{error}]} = s^2[1 + \tilde{a}'(\tilde{X}'\tilde{X})^{-1}\tilde{a}] \tag{3}$$

where s^2 is the error variance around the group-average (first-stage) regression, $\tilde{a}$ is a column vector of dummy-coded variables describing each of the four choice options in Table 3, and $\tilde{X}$ is the original matrix of (dummy-coded) predictor values, augmented by a vector of unities for intercept estimation.

Since the $\tilde{a}$ vectors differ for each option, so will the error variances. To simulate the choice process random normal numbers were selected in each case and multiplied by the square root of equation (3). Each error was then added algebraically to the average subject's utility (see Table 1) for each of the four options profiled in Table 3.

Table 3 shows averaged results over several replications of this Monte Carlo procedure. While both procedures rank the options in the same way, we note sizable differences between them. In particular, the individual importance weight model accentuates the differences between the most preferred option and the less preferred ones.

4 Conclusions

The individual importance weights model represents only one of several models that fall between procedures for fitting completely idiosyncractic utility functions and a group-average function. For example, the researcher could fit a model that allows each respondent to have an idiosyncractic scale origin (intercept) or an individual scale origin <u>and</u> scale unit, as applied to a group-average set of part worths. Furthermore, the model can be combined with various kinds of clustering techniques to find individual importance weight models for subsets of respondents.[7]

In any event it seems clear that commercial applications of conjoint analysis are going to require new approaches to utility estimation—approaches that reduce the tedium of data collection while still providing enough responses to estimate some type of individual part worths that, in turn, can be utilized in consumer choice simulations.

References

Akaah IP, Korgaonkar PK (1983) An Empirical Comparison of the Predictive Validity of Compositional, Decompositional, and Hybrid Multiattribute Preference Models. Journal of Marketing Research 20: 187–197

Carmone FJ, Green PE, Jain AK (1978) The Robustness of Conjoint Analysis: Some Monte Carlo Results. Journal of Marketing Research 15: 300–303

Cattin P, Wittink DR (1976) A Monte Carlo Study of Metric and Nonmetric Estimation Methods for Multiattribute Models. Stanford University, Graduate School of Business, Research Paper 341

Cattin P, Gelfand AE, Danes J (1983) A Simple Bayesian Procedure for Estimation in a Conjoint Model. Journal of Marketing Research 20: 29–35

[7]This could be implemented by giving each respondent a small set of common (or core) stimuli and finding an initial partition of respondents on the basis of their commonality of responses to the core stimuli. This initial partitioning could then be refined via respondent assignment on the basis of the best-fitting subgroup's part worths (via a type of iterative k-means clustering procedure).

Cattin P, Hermet G, Pioche A (1982) Alternative Hybrid Models for Conjoint Analysis: Some Empirical Results, in: Analytical Approaches to Product and Market Planning: The Second Conference. Marketing Science Institute, Cambridge, MA, pp 142–152

Green PE (1974) On the Design of Choice Experiments Involving Multi-Factor Alternatives. Journal of Consumer Research 1: 61–68

Green PE, Goldberg SM (1981) A Nonmetric Version of the Hybrid Conjoint Analysis Model. Paper presented at the Third ORSA/TIMS Market Maesurement Conference, New York University

Green PE, Goldberg SM, Montemayor M (1981) A Hybrid Utility Estimation Model for Conjoint Analysis. Journal of Marketing 45: 33–41

Green PE, Goldberg SM, Wiley JB (1982) A Cross Validation Test of Hybrid Conjoint Models, in: Proceedings of 1982 Annual Meeting of the Association for Consumer Research, San Francisco.

Green PE, Srinivasan V (1978) Conjoint Analysis in Consumer Research: Issues and Outlook. Journal of Consumer Research 5: 103–123

Johnson RM (1974) Trade-Off Analysis of Consumer Values. Journal of Marketing Research 11: 121–127

Mendenhall W (1968) Introduction to Linear Models and the Design and Analysis of Experiments. Wadsworth Publishing Co., Belmont, CA

Dominated Options in Consumer Tradeoff Modeling: Is Their Occurrence Recognized?

P.E. Green, A.M. Krieger and C.M. Schaffer
Wharton School, University of Pennsylvania

Summary

Recent Monte Carlo simulations indicate that the ability of compensatory models to mimic certain non-compensatory choice rules is severely limited, particularly in Pareto optimal choice settings. This paper reports the results of an empirical analysis of choice data which suggest that consumers may not recognize dominated options in choice settings involving large numbers of attributes, even if the offered set is relatively small.

1 Introduction

Over the past 25 years, one of the most interesting developments in cognitve psychology has been the finding that linear models appear to do a surprisingly good job in modeling (seemingly) complex human judgments. An even more remarkable finding is that in many judgment situations equal (i.e., unit) weights often do as good a job as regression-derived weights (Dawes and Corrigan (1974); Einhorn and Hogarth (1975); Wilks (1938)).

As Dawes (1977) points out, the principal conditions that make linear models work are:

(a) the attributes should be oriented and scored in such a way that higher values on each variable predict higher values on the criterion, independently of values assumed by other attributes and

(b) the attributes should be positively correlated.

More recently, however, researchers have begun to question the generalization that equally weighted linear composites are good approximations to unequally weighted linear models under all circumstances (Newman (1977); McClelland (1978); Einhorn, Kleinmuntz and Kleinmuntz (1979); Stillwell, Seaver and Edwards (1981); Curry and Faulds (1986)). As these authors point out, in choice (as opposed to judgmental) contexts, the key consideration is the concept of dominance. For example, if option X is at least as good as option Y on every attribute and strictly better on at least one attribute, a rational decision maker would eliminate option Y from the set of options at the outset. The reduced set of (non-dominated) options is usually referred to as "Pareto optimal".

However, as many authors point out, the reduction of the original set of options to a Pareto optimal subset generally results in negatively correlated attributes, even though the original set of options may display either zero or positive correlations. One of the more recent papers on the topic (Johnson, Meyer and Ghose (1986)) explores this issue via computer simulation. Johnson, Meyer and Ghose (JMG) show that compensatory models (specifically, a main-effects-only multinomial logit model) fail to mimic non-compensatory choice models (e.g., lexicographic, elimination-by-aspects and a satisficing model).

More relevant to the present paper is JMG's additional finding that the inability of the logit model to mimic non-compensatory models is exacerbated if the predictions take place accross a Pareto optimal subset (which the authors call "efficient"). They further show that even a compensatory choice model is not well approximated by the (compensatory) multinomial logit in Pareto optimal subsets. All of their simulations are carried out in an illustrative context involving choice sets of four, 4-attribute options, where the attribute-level partworths are allowed to vary continuously.

On the face of it, the JMG findings are cause for concern, particularly among industry researchers, applying conjoint analysis to real world problems. In many such applications, orthogonal main effects plans (Green and Srinivasan (1978)) are used to construct full profile options, some of which may be dominated by other options. To what extent are model parameters that are calibrated in an orthogonal setting poor predictors of actual choice in (possibly) Pareto optimal choice sets?

To the best of our knowledge, no research in conjoint analysis has been reported as yet on the associated question of whether subjects actually eliminate dominated options from further consideration. It is by no means obvious that consumers even recognize dominated options, particularly if the number of attributes (and levels within attributes) are large. As Einhorn and McCoach (1977, p. 281) point out:

> "We do not believe that people use an elimination-of-dominated alternatives strategy. The cognitive work involved in scanning, searching, and holding nondominated alternatives in memory would be extreme."

To the extent that consumers recognize dominated options, we would expect that their preference orderings would be more consistent with their utility functions (since dominated options do <u>not</u> depend on errors associated with the elicitation of respondent attribute importance weights)

To address this question we examine a real-world (industry) study in which self-explicated utilities are used to predict respondent orderings of full-profile options. Specifically, we examine the question of whether respondents who receive a validation set of options containing one or more dominated items (according to their own utility functions) more accurately predict their validation-sample orderings than those who receive only Pareto optimal validation sets.

2 The Empirical Study

In 1986 a national marketing research firm conducted a conjoint survey of 501 respondents' evaluations of alternative herbicide formulations for controlling weeds/grasses in soybean crops. Respondents were owner/managers of large commercial farms distributed across the U.S..[1]

The study's sponsors were interested in respondents' reactions to alternative herbicide products that could be marketed to present (and prospecitve) soybean growers.

Table 1 shows descriptions of the attributes and levels that were used in the study. As noted, there are nine attributes, varying between three and four attribute levels, that describe actual (or potential) herbicides. A hybrid conjoint design (Green (1985)) was used in the data collection.[2] All data were collected through a combination of telephone-mail-telephone interviewing.

Table 1: Attributes and Levels Used in Commercial Study of Herbicide Formulations for Soybean Crops

A. Control of grasses
1. Some annual and perennial
2. Most annual and perennial
3. All annual
4. All perennial

B. Control of broadleaves
1. Fair control if used with crop oil
2. Good control if used with crop oil
3. Fair control if used alone
4. Good control if used alone

C. Combination effectiveness (grasses and broadleaves)
1. Very good if used alone
2. Fairly good if used alone
3. Fairly good if used with surfactant
4. Very good if used with surfactant

D. Length of effectiveness
1. May require two treatments under abnormally low temperatures
2. May require two treatments under abnormally high temperatures
3. May require two treatments under abnormally low rainfall

E. Weather risk
1. Reduced control if heavy rain
2. Reduced control if no rain
3. Reduced control under excessively high temperatures

F. Manufacturer
1. Ciba Geigy

[1] To respect the sponsor's wishes, the product class and various attribute-level descriptions have been disguised.

[2] Commercial conjoint studies often utilize nine (or more) attributes, particularly if hybrid conjoint designs are used.

2. Elanco
3. Stauffer
4. Regional supplier

G. Crop injury through overapplication
   1. Little risk
   2. Some risk of stunted growth
   3. Some risk of burned leaves

H. Packaging
   1. Metal containers
   2. Heavy plastic containers
   3. Wax-lined fiberboard pails

I. Price
   1. 20% less than leading brand
   2. 10% less than leading brand
   3. Same as leading brand
   4. 10% more than leading brand

2.1 Data Collection and Model Selection

In phase I of the data collection, each respondent evaluated the levels of each attribute in Table 1, one attribute at a time, on a 0–10 scale, ranging from completely unacceptable to highly desirable. In phase II, each respondent distributed 100 points across the nine attributes, so as to reflect their relative importance in the choice of a soybean herbicide.

In phase III each respondent received two subsets of four full-profile options each, drawn in such a way that each attribute level appeared in each set. The two subsets were drawn from a main-effects, orthogonal design of 64 combinations of the attribute levels of Table 1. For each profile the respondent was asked to state a likelihood of purchase (given that the profile was satisfactory in all other respects) if the herbicide formulations were actually marketed.

A simple hybrid model (tantamount to a linearly rescaled self-explicated model) was fitted to the total sample data.[3] We denote an illustrative profile (drawn from the master set of 64) by the vector

$$\vec{i} \equiv [i_1, i_2, \ldots, i_J]$$

in which i_j denotes level i_j ($i_j = 1, I_j$) of attribute j ($j = 1, J$). In the self-explicated tasks (phase I and II) we let

$u_{i_jk} \equiv$ respondent k's ($k = 1, K$) self-explicated desirability score for level i of attribute j (phase I),

$W_{jk} \equiv$ respondent k's self-explicated importance weight for attribute j (phase II).

[3]Hybrid models were also fitted at the subgroup level as described in Green (1984); however, only the total-sample model is used here.

In the full-profile task (phase III) we let $Y_k = Y_{i_1 i_2 \ldots i_J k}$ denote respondent k's overall response to some full-profile description. In the simple model formulation described above, we represent this by

$$Y_{i_1 i_2 \ldots i_J k} \cong A_k + bU_{i_1 i_2 \ldots i_J k} \quad (1)$$

where $\cong$ denotes least squares approximation and

$$U_{i_1 i_2 \ldots i_J k} = \sum_{j=1}^{J} W_{jk} u_{i_j k} \quad (2)$$

Equation (1) shows that a linear rescaling of equation (2) is all that is entailed, with a common slope parameter b (estimated over all respondents) and an individually estimated intercept term, A_k.

2.2 Validation

The validation procedure (phase IV) also entailed a master orthogonal design (different from that used in phase III) of 64 combinations, augmented by one additional profile. The additional profile was a sponsor supplied "base case", chosen so as to reflect the current market leader's product formulation (but not identified as such). Insofar as the respondent was concerned, the base case looked like any of the other 64 profiles.

Thirty-two validation sets, consisting of two profiles drawn from the master design plus the base case, were made up. Each respondent received one of 32 triples, assigned randomly. The respondent was asked to examine each option in the triple and rank the alternatives in order of preference. Following this, the respondent indicated his/her purchase likelihood on a 0–100 scale for each of the profiles.

3 Data Analysis

As noted above, for each triple of profiles, within individuals, three paired comparisons are possible: X versus Y, X versus Z and Y versus Z. Phase IV of the study provides data on actual option ordering behavior. Phase I (the desirability ratings) enables one to search for dominated pairs at the individual-respondent level. Phases II and III provide predictions of the paired comparisons using the full model of equations (1) and (2).

In Phase I (the desirability ratings), we can find, for each individual separately, whether any dominances exist for the three implied paired comparisons: X versus Y, X versus Z and Y versus Z (obtained from the validation-set responses in phase IV). To illustrate, Table 2 shows the case for respondent 1 in the survey. The triple X, Y, Z is the triple that respondent 1 actually evaluated in phase IV.

Comparing X to Y, we note that X is more desirable than Y on attributes C, D, E, F, G, H and I, while Y is more desirable than X on attributes A and B; there are no tied desirabilities. Comparing X to Z, we note that X is better on attributes C, E, G and I, Y is better on A, B and H, and both are tied on attributes D and F. Finally, we compare Y and Z and observe that neither dominates the other, while both are tied on attributes E and I.

Since phase II simply applies importance weights to the (scaled) desirabilities of phase I, and phase III entails a linear transformation of phase II utilities, it is clear that dominated options in phase I are not altered by the transformations in phases II and III. Thus if a respondent's desirabilities imply that any of the pairs (X versus Y, X versus Z or Y versus Z) contain a dominant member, the dominance should remain in phase IV, irrespective of the respondent's evaluations in phases II and III.

Table 2: Illustrative Examination of Dominances for Respondent 1 (Phase I)

Respondent 1's Triple	Attribute Level; (Desirabilities)								
	A	B	C	D	E	F	G	H	I
X	1 (0.4)	1 (0)	1 (1.0)	3 (0.5)	1 (0.4)	2 (0.1)	1 (0.9)	2 (0.6)	2 (0.8)
Y	4 (0.9)	4 (0.8)	4 (0.3)	2 (0.4)	3 (0.2)	4 (0)	3 (0.4)	3 (0.1)	3 (0.5)
Z	3 (0.8)	3 (0.7)	3 (0.1)	3 (0.5)	2 (0.2)	3 (0.1)	2 (0.6)	1 (0.9)	3 (0.5)

Note: Desirabilities are scaled between 0 (completely unacceptable) and 1.0 (most highly desirable) from original 0-10 point rating scale.

3.1 How Many Dominances are to be Expected?

The general problem of computing the number of pairs containing dominated options is difficult. However, one can obtain the expected number of dominances under assumptions involving sampling (without replacement) from the full Cartesian product set of conjoint profiles in which all partworths can be strictly ordered within attribute. In the present problem, assuming that all nine attributes are 4-level attributes, and assuming a presentation set of three profiles, the expected number of presentations containing a dominating-item pair is only 0.0873; hence, in a sample of 501 respondents we would expect only 44 respondents to contain a dominant pair if this simple random model were to hold. In any real data set, however, the incidence could vary considerably from this expectation.

3.2 Study Results

Table 3 shows a descriptive summary of findings for the data described earlier. First, we note that out of a total sample of 501 respondents, 134 respondents received one or more validation pairs that contained a dominant option.[4] For 116 of the respondents one such pair (out of three) was found while only 18 respondents observed a validation triple in which two of the three pairs had a dominant entry. No respondent received a triple containing three pairs with a dominating option in each pair.

In Table 3 we first consider the sample of 367 respondents, whose six pairs in the validation triple contained no dominances, as a "control" group. We note from the upper section of Table 3 that the actual proportion showing three "hits" (all correct

[4]Since some of the attributes are at three levels, attribute partworths may be tied, and sampling is not without replacement, the actual results would not be expected to agree with those of the random model.

predictions) is 0.43; this is well above the 0.167 proportion that would be observed under the null model. A statistical test indicated that the null model would be rejected; that is, the control group's self-explicated utilities (with the application of their importance weights in phase II, and the subsequent linear rescaling of phase III) predicted their ordering of the validation triples significantly better than chance.[5] Overall, we note that the control group has a prediction rate of 69.4 percent. This is also significantly higher than chance expectation.

Table 3: Descriptive Summary of Validation Triple Predictions – "Control" Versus "Treatment" Respondents

Control: No dominant-entry pairs: $N_1 = 367$

Number of "Hits"	Actual Frequency	Actual Proportion	Proportion Under Null Model
0	29	0.079	0.167
1	70	0.191	0.333
2	110	0.300	0.333
3	158	0.430	0.167
	367	1.000	1.000

Overall percentage of correct predictions:

$$[\,29(0) + 70(1) + 110(2) + 158(3)\,]/1101 = 69.4\%$$

Treatment: At least one dominant-entry pair: $N_2 = 134$

Number of Dominant-Entry Pairs	Number of "Hits" 0	1	2	Σ	Percent Correct
1	35	81	–	116	69.8%
2	3	4	11	18	72.2%
				134	

Overall percentage of correct predictions: $[\,38(0) + 85(1) + 11(2)\,]/152 = 70.4\%$

We next turn to the "treatment" group, those whose validation triple contained one or more pairs with dominant options. Of the 134 respondents receiving a validation pair with at least one dominant option, only 18 received two dominant-option pairs. As noted above, no respondent received a triple in which all three pairs contained a dominant option.

An examination of the two cases—one versus two dominant-entry pairs—showed no significantly different predictions (69.8% versus 72.2%). Moreover, in comparing the overall predictive accuracy between control and treatment groups, the results (69.4% versus 70.4%) were not significantly different.[6]

[5] This test (as well as all subsequent statistical tests) was run at an alpha level of 0.05.

[6] A statistical test was also made between the pairs containing no dominant entries in the treatment group versus the control group; again, the results were not statistically significant.

What can be concluded from these comparisons? While we have no direct evidence that the "treatment" respondents ignored dominated options, what can be said is that those respondents who did not receive any dominant-entry pairs predicted their holdout triple about as well as those who did. If some error is assumed in phase II, self-explicated importance weights, we would expect the "treatment" group to perform better than "control", since importance weights are irrelevant in cases containing dominant-entry pairs. Such evidence was not found in this study.

4 Discussion

To recapitulate, the preceding empirical analysis indicates that if dominating-option pairs appear, there is no compelling evidence that the dominances are recognized, leading to significantly better predictions than would be found in the "control" case.

How do these findings relate to other research on the question of the robustness of linear composites in Pareto optimal settings? A review of two papers in the literature leads to the following (somewhat anomalous) results.

4.1 Curry and Faulds Study

Curry and Faulds (1986) employ simulation techniques to show that a combination of negatively correlated attributes with inverted importance weights leads to poor correlations between the two linear composites computed from the synthetic data. However, if the attributes are negatively correlated but the importance weights are ranked in the same order (McClelland (1978)), the two linear composites are still highly correlated positively.

Curry and Faulds then go on to examine 385 studies envolving the German magazine, Test (which is similar to the U.S. Consumer Reports). Their empirical findings indicate that only eight out of the 385 studies showed cases where the original attributes were all negatively correlated. Their conclusions are that even with all negative correlations and reversed importance weights (eight cases), the mean correlations between composites was still positive. With zero or positive correlations, the mean correlations between composites were dramatically higher (0.90–0.99), even with reversed weights.

4.2 Johnson, Meyer and Ghose Study

The JMG simulation (1986) indicates that linear compensatory models calibrated in orthogonal environments do a poor job in mimicking non-compensatory (or even compensatory) models in Pareto optimal environments. Why is this so, given the Curry and Faulds study? Clearly, the studies are not stricly comparable, since JMG confine their attention to four-attribute profiles in choice sets of four options, a total of six pairs for evaluation by each hypothetical respondent.

As JMG show, the impact of Pareto validation sets, beyond the effect of misspecified choice model depends on the criterion—either R^2 or mean absolute error. If the former criterion is used the fits drop dramatically (e.g., from 10 to 25 percentage points, depending upon the choice model). If the latter criterion is used, the drops range from only zero to about two percentage points in the case of orthogonal compared to Pareto optimal validation sets. (Hence, poorness of fit depends markedly on the criterion used.)

4.3 Conclusions

At this stage in research involving the applicability of compensatory models to predicting consumer choice, it would appear that several issues are involved:

1. If the choice model is known to be compensatory, how well does some fitted compensatory model approximate the outcomes of the "true" model in
   a. Positively correlated attribute conditions?
   b. Orthogonal conditions?
   c. Pareto optimal conditions?
   d. Other kinds of negatively correlated attribute conditions?
2. In each of the preceding cases how sensitive are the predictions to the correct choice of attribute weights? In particular, are weights that are correctly rank ordered sufficient to produce accurate mimicking of the "true" model?
3. If the choice model is known to be non-compensatory, how well does some fitted compensatory model approximate the outcomes of the "true" model in
   a. Positively correlated attribute conditions?
   b. Orthogonal conditions?
   c. Pareto optimal conditions?
   d. Other kinds of negatively correlated attribute conditions?
4. In each of these latter cases, how much are the preconditions improved if the compensatory model is expanded to include (say) two-way interaction terms?

The preceeding questions are only illustrative of the large amount of work still needed to be done in the area of model fitting and validation. Like most research efforts, the present study has only scratched the surface. JMG's simulations demonstrate the important point that conjoint and other kind of compensatory models may <u>not</u> do an adequate job in mimicking non-compensatory choice models, particularly in Pareto optimal environments.

Associated questions concern the following issues:

1. As the number of attributes and levels within attribute increase, how frequently will non-Pareto optimal sets appear?
2. In commercial-scale conjoint problems (e.g., 8–12 attributes) how often will dominated options be recognized?
3. How does the incidence of recognition depend upon the number of options in the offered set and the form of presentation?

In the present study each full-profile option in the validation triple appeared on a separate stimulus card, organized in "bullet" fashion, where each level was listed underneath each attribute description. Other forms of presentation (e.g., one card in which all three options are listed, side by side) could make intradimensional comparisons easier across options. (Of course, this type of presentation becomes more difficult as the number of options increase.) While presentation context obviously can affect the extent to which dominance recognition occurs, relatively little is known about the impact of task on this type of information processing.

Clearly, however, the JMG simulation results should be augmented by additional kinds of research on the important question of compensatory approximations to non-compensatory choice rules in choice settings involving negatively correlated attributes. The issue of linear model robustness in choice (as opposed to judgment) modeling is still far from settled.

References

Curry DJ, Faulds DJ (1986) Indexing Product Quality: Issues, Theory and Results. Journal of Consumer Research 13: 134–145

Dawes R (1977) Predictive Models as a Guide to Preference. IEEE Tranactions on Systems, Man, and Cybernetics SMC-7: 355–357

Dawes R, Corrigan B (1974) Linear Models in Decision Making. Psychological Bulletin 81, 2: 95–106

Einhorn HJ, Hogarth R (1975) Unit Weighting Schemes for Decision Making. Organizational Behavior and Human Performance 13: 171–192

Einhorn HJ, Kleinmuntz DN, Kleinmuntz B (1979) Linear Regression and Process-Tracing Models of Judgement. Psychological Review 86, 5: 464–485

Einhorn HJ, McCoach W (1977) A Simple Multiattribute Utility Procedure for Evaluation. Behavioral Science 22: 270–282

Green PE (1984) Hybrid Models for Conjoint Analysis: An Expository Review. Journal of Marketing Research 21: 155–169

Green PE, Srinivasan (1978) Conjoint Analysis in Consumer Research: Issues and Outlook. Journal of Consumer Research 5: 103–123

Johnson EJ, Meyer RJ, Ghose S (1986) When Choice Models Fail: Compensatory Representations in Efficient Sets. Working paper, Carnegie-Mellon University

McClelland GH (1978) Equal Versus Differential Weighting for Multiattribute Decisions: There Are No Free Lunches. Report No. 207, Center for Research on Judgement and Policy, University of Colorado

Newman, JR (1977) Differential Weighting in Multiattribute Utility Measurement: Where it Should and Where it Does Make a Difference. Organizational Behavior and Human Performance 20: 312–325

Stillwell WG, Seaver D, Edwards W (198[illegible]) A Comparison of Weight Approximation Techniques in Multiattribute Utility Decision Making. Organizational Behavior and Human Performance 28: 62–77

Wilks SS (1938) Weighted Schemes for Linear Functions of Correlated Variables When There is No Dependent Variable. Psychometrica 3: 23–40

Market Segmentation by Dual Scaling Through Generalized Forced Classification

S. Nishisato
The Ontario Institute for Studies in Education (OISE) and the University of Toronto
252 Bloor Street West, Toronto, Ontario, Canada M5S 1V6

Summary

Forced classification, a technique for discriminant analysis of categorical data by dual scaling, is first presented together with its seven mathematical properties and its generalizations to dual scaling of modified data matrices. Simple and generalized forms of forced classification are then applied to hypothetical cases of market segmentation, namely, one-way classification, bipolar classification, conditional classification, classification by expert's knowledge and multi-way classification. These examples suggest also other potential applications of dual scaling to market segmentation research.

1 Introduction

Market segmentation is one of the popular concepts used in marketing research. Lilien and Kotler (1983), for example, state that "Markets ... are heterogeneous. Customers have different constraints, needs, and incentives, ... Market segmentation is the grouping of potential customers into sets that are homogeneous in response to some elements of the marketing mix" (p.289). This statement suggests that the task of market segmentation may involve a number of classification problems, hence different approaches, and that it would deal with a variety of factors associated with customers and attributes of consumer goods. Considering that many such variables as involved in market segmentation are categorical, the present study has chosen one approach, that is, dual scaling or correspondence analysis, and will explore its possible applications to the problem of market segmentation.

Dual scaling is in essence principal component analysis of categorical data, and therefore generates scores or weights of maximal discriminability. When it is used for discriminant analysis, there is a simple procedure called forced classification (Nishisato (1984)), which is an application of dual scaling to a modified data matrix with a subset of rows or columns multiplied by a large number. This procedure has been generalized (Nishisato (1986)) to dual scaling of a more general transformed matrix, where the transformation can be with respect to rows, columns, both rows and columns, or any subsection of the data matrix. In this generalized mode of forced classification, dual scaling can be used for a number of tasks of market segmentation as will be shown in this expository paper.

2 Preliminaries

Consider multiple-choice data collected from N consumers (subjects) answering n multiple-choice questions

$$F = [F_1, F_2, \ldots, F_j, \ldots, F_n], \tag{1}$$

where F_j is the $N \times m_j$ matrix of response patterns for question j, $j = 1, 2, \ldots, n$ and $F_j\mathbf{1} = \mathbf{1}$. Matrix F is $N \times m$, where $m = \sum m_j$ and $F\mathbf{1} = n\mathbf{1}$. The optimal weight vector for m options, $\mathbf{x}$, and the vector of maximally discriminative scores for the subjects, $\mathbf{y}$, are related by

$$\mathbf{y} = D_N^{-1} F\mathbf{x}/\rho \quad \text{and} \quad \mathbf{x} = D^{-1}F'\mathbf{y}/\rho \tag{2}$$

where D_N and D are diagonal matrices of row totals and column totals of F, respectively, and ρ is the product-moment correlation between responses weighted by $\mathbf{y}$ and those weighted by $\mathbf{x}$. Relation (2), used in dual scaling and correspondence analysis, is nothing but the so-called singular-value decomposition of matrix F.

Suppose that we change matrix F to

$$F(j \times k) = [F_1, F_2, \ldots, kF_j, \ldots, F_n], \tag{3}$$

where k is a scalar. It is known that the singular structure of $F(j \times k)$ is the same as that of matrix F modified in such a way that F_j is repeated k times,

$$F(j : k) = [F_1, \ldots, F_2, \ldots, F_j, F_j, \ldots, F_j, \ldots, F_n] \tag{4}$$

This relation between (3) and (4) is called the principle of equivalent partitioning (Nishisato (1984)). Thus, it is understandable that as the value of k increases, the patterns of submatrix F_j become dominant in $F(j : k)$, hence in $F(j \times k)$. As k increases to infinity, it is known that dual scaling of $F(j \times k)$ provides, among other things:

(i) The first $(m_j - 1)$ non-trivial dimensions correspond to those dimensions associated with matrix P_jF, where F is the original data matrix and P_j is the projection operator for the subspace spanned by the columns of F_j, that is, $P_j = F_j(F_j'F_j)^- F_j'$, where the symbol " $-$ " indicates a generalized inverse.

(ii) The next $(m_j - 1)$ dimensions of $F(j \times k)$ correspond to those dimensions associated with matrix $(I - P_j)F$. It is conjectured that the results (i) and (ii) may be extended to more than one criterion item. Namely, the conjecture is that dual scaling of $[F_1, F_2, kF_3, kF_4]$, for example, provide dimensions which asymptotically correspond to those of PF and $(I - P)F$, where $P = (F_3, F_4)[(F_3, F_4)'(F_3, F_4)]^-(F_3, F_4)'$.

(iii) For the first $(m_j - 1)$ dimensions of $F(j \times k)$,

$$r_{jt} = \mathbf{x}'_j F_j' F\mathbf{x} / (\mathbf{x}'_j D_j \mathbf{x}_j \mathbf{x}' F' F\mathbf{x})^{\frac{1}{2}} = 1 \tag{5}$$

where D_j is the diagonal matrix of column totals of F_j.

(iv) For the first $(m_j - 1)$ dimensions,

$$r_{jp} \geq r^*_{jp}, \tag{6}$$

where r_{jp} and r^*_{jp} are correlations between items j and p, obtained respectively from dual scaling of $F(j \times k)$ and F. In other words, forced classification with item j as the criterion offers a weighting scheme that maximizes the correlation between the criterion (i.e., the item which is multiplied by k) and a non-criterion item.

(v) The above idea of forced classification is applicable to paired comparison and rank order data, where two stimuli are typically chosen as the criteria.

Characteristics (i) through (v) hold only asymptotically, that is, in the limit $(k \to \infty)$. In practice, the word "asymptotically" becomes a key issue. Our experience indicates that the value of k need not be very large to provide a satisfactory approximation to the results obtained from dual scaling of P_jF. Figure 1, from Nishisato (1986), is an example in which twenty-four subjects answered five questions. Three variables of subjects' background information were added to the data matrix. One of the background variables was not highly correlated with any item. To see its maximal correlations with the items, this background variable was chosen as the criterion. Figure 1 clearly demonstrates that characteristic (iv) can be quickly attained as k increases from two to only five. The asymptote of each curve in Figure 1 corresponds to the value expected from P_jF. The same graph shows two other characteristics of forced classification:

(vi) Weight k does not have to be an integer. Figure 1 was generated by continuous positive values of k.

(vii) The maximal values of r_{jp} in (iv), that is, the asymptote of the curve for item p in Figure 1, remains the same even when other items are added to the data set. This invariance aspect of forced classification is very useful from the practical point of view—a large data set can be divided into subsets for analysis.

The original formulation of forced classification, as characterized by (i) through (vii), can be generalized in two respects: the mode of transformation from simple to complex forms, and the value of k from always very large (i.e., $(k \to \infty)$) to any value. Only a few such generalizations are presented here. To start with, let us generalize format (3) as follows:

$$[k_1F_1, k_2F_2, \ldots, k_jF_j, \ldots, k_nF_n], \text{ say} \tag{7}$$

Items can be differentially weighted. Let Q_j be a diagonal matrix with weights for options in the main diagonal. Then, the format

$$[F_1Q_1, F_2Q_2, \ldots, F_jQ_j, \ldots, F_nQ_n], = F(1, q_{js}) \tag{8}$$

provides a scheme to differentially weight options. This format has been applied to the case where "outlier" effects on quantification were suppressed by weights smaller than one (Nishisato (1987)). Weights for subjects can also be incorporated:

$$[PF_1Q_1, PF_2Q_2, \ldots, PF_jQ_j, \ldots, PF_nQ_n] = F(p_i, q_{js}) \tag{9}$$

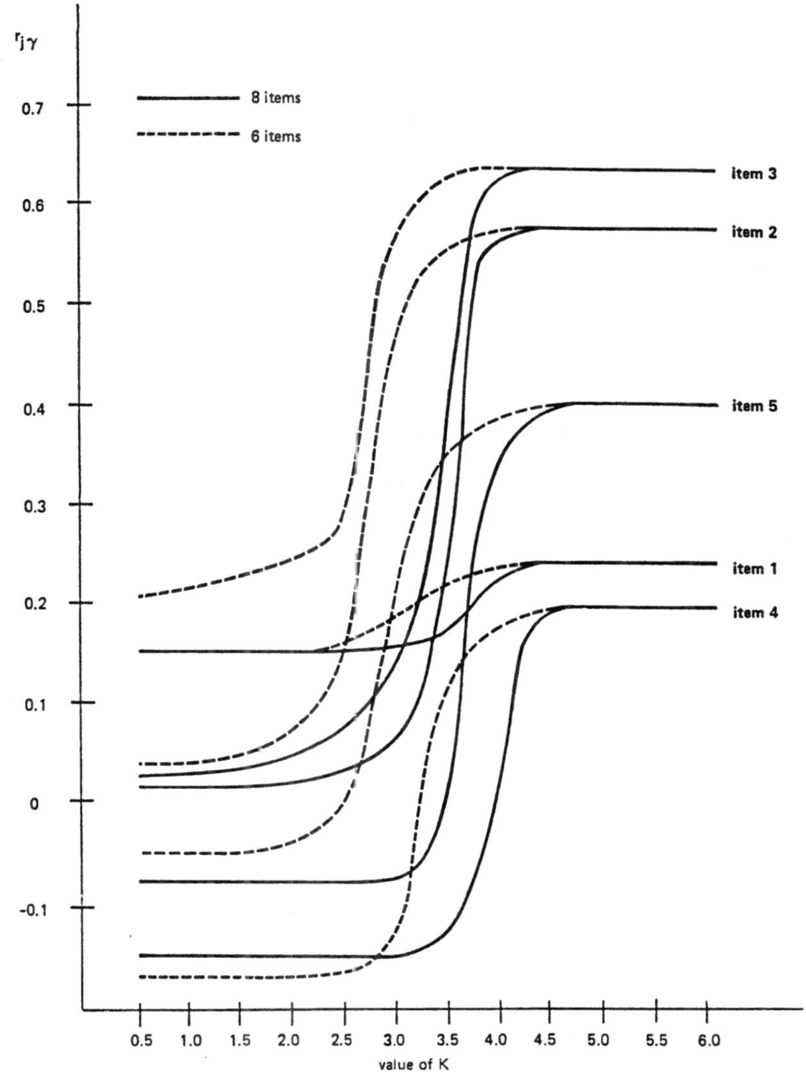

Figure 1: Continuity and Invariance of Forced Classification

If subjects are classified into subgroups, matrix F can be partitioned into row submatrices F_i^* so that we may introduce such schemes as

$$\begin{bmatrix} t_1 F_1^* \\ t_2 F_2^* \\ \vdots \\ t_i F_i^* \\ \vdots \\ t_m F_m^* \end{bmatrix} = F^*(t_i, 1) \tag{10}$$

$$\begin{bmatrix} P_1F_1^*Q \\ P_2F_2^*Q \\ \vdots \\ P_iF_i^*Q \\ \vdots \\ P_mF_m^*Q \end{bmatrix} = F^*(p_{it}, q_j) \tag{11}$$

Finally, the data matrix can be partitioned with respect to both rows and columns, resulting in the following format:

$$\begin{bmatrix} P_1F_{11}Q_1 & \dots & P_1F_{1n}Q_n \\ \vdots & & \vdots \\ P_mF_{m1}Q_1 & \dots & P_mF_{mn}Q_n \end{bmatrix} = (P_iF_{ij}Q_j) = F^*(p_{it}, q_{js}). \tag{12}$$

These different formats of forced classification can generate a large number of distinct applications. However, this paper is expository, and will present only a few examples of many possible applications.

3 Hypothetical Example

This sketchy exposition is on different applications of dual scaling to the problem of market segmentation. Let us consider a hypothetical example in which marketing of the following cosmetics was investigated:

[I] Avon, Clinique, Mary Kay, Nivea, Noxema, Oil of Olay, Revlon, Second Debut

A large number of subjects were asked to rate these products with respect to their characteristics,

[II] easing dryness; pleasant fragrance; reducing wrinkles; quickly penetrating; soft and smooth; moisturizing; making look younger; not greasy; protecting skin

and

[III] preference; overall evaluation of the products

Demographic information of subjects was also collected:

[IV] user or non-user of each product; age group; career-oriented or homemakers; modern or traditional; single or married; outgoing or homebody

Suppose that each product in [I] was rated on a seven-point scale with respect to [II] and [III]. The demographic information was collected in the multiple-choice format. The data can be arranged as in Table 1.

Table 1: Marketing Study on Cosmetic Products

	Ratings				
Product	Avon	Clinque	...	Sec. Debut	Demographic Information
Variable	1 2 ... n	1 2 ... n	...	1 2 ... n	1 2 ... t
Subj. 1	3 7 ... 1	4 5 ... 6	...	2 3 ... 7	1 2 ... 2
Subj. 2	4 5 ... 3	1 2 ... 7	...	1 4 ... 6	2 1 ... 2
⋮	⋮ ⋮ ⋱ ⋮	⋮ ⋮ ⋱ ⋮	...	⋮ ⋮ ⋱ ⋮	⋮ ⋮ ⋱ ⋮
Subj. N	2 4 ... 2	1 3 ... 5	...	3 5 ... 7	2 1 ... 1

Rating data can be treated as multiple-choice responses. If paired comparison data on the eight products are needed, one can generate pair-wise comparisons of ratings of the products on the eleven variables in [II] and [III] for each subject. Similarly, rank-order data can be obtained from the rating data, so long as many tied ranks are not too problematic for data analysis.

Given the above information, one can consider a variety of segmentation problems. In the ensuing sections, some of the interesting cases will be presented.

4 One-Way Classification With $F(j \times k)$

The basic formulation of (3) can be used with any one of the variables in [IV] as F_j, that is, the criterion. A few examples of this type are:

(a) [**Avon users vs. non-users**]: Consider the rating data on Avon and demographic information, all treated as multiple-choice data. The criterion variable is "user or non-user," which is multiplied by a large value of k. Since the criterion variable has two options, user or non-user, forced classification provides only one solution, for which (5) holds, that is, $r_{jt} = 1$. Using the property indicated by (6), this solution allows us to identify key variables which contribute to distinguishing between Avon users and non-users. These key variables may be Avon attributes in [II], to tell us which attributes are perceived differently by Avon users and non-users, or they may be demographic variables in [IV], to indicate background information which is distinct for the two groups. This type of analysis would suggest some advertising strategies for marketing Avon products.

(b) [**Clinique's appeal to different age groups**]: This example, which uses Clinique ratings and demographic information, is methodologically the same as (a), except that this criterion variable in (b) is "age." The analysis will identify patterns of responses peculiar to individual age groups . Noting that the categories of the criterion variable serve as the ideal points of respective subgroups, the analysis also suggests proximity ranking of the other variables for each subgroup.

(c) [**Preferred products by those career-oriented or homemakers**]: One can analyze data on [III] and [IV], using the variable "career-oriented or homemakers" as the criterion. This analysis will identify those products which appeal to only one of the two groups, to both groups, or to neither of the groups. In particular, it provides two distinct sets of preference ranking of the products for the two groups. It would certainly be of interest to find demographic variables which are highly correlated with such rankings.

5 Bipolar Classification

When data are paired comparisons or rank orders, forced classification typically employs two criterion stimuli. With N subjects and n stimuli, paired comparison data are arranged in the $N \times n(n-1)/2$ matrix, with elements being 1 if the first stimulus in a pair is chosen, 2 if the second is chosen, or 0 for tied preference. Rank-order data are arranged in the $N \times n$ matrix of ranks, 1 being the first choice, 2 the second choice, and so on. In both cases, the input data are transformed into the $N \times n$ (subjects-by-stimuli) dominance matrix, E, with typical element e_{ij} being the number of times subject i chose stimulus j over other stimuli minus the number of times it was not preferred to the others. Unlike the case of multiple-choice data, forced classification of these two types of data is rather complex, and is therefore described in detail using a small example.

Let us consider rank-order data from three subjects ranking five stimuli (i.e., $N = 3, n = 5$),

$$F = \begin{bmatrix} 1 & 2 & 3 & 4 & 5 \\ 2 & 3 & 5 & 1 & 4 \\ 3 & 1 & 4 & 2 & 5 \end{bmatrix}$$

Suppose that stimuli 2 and 4 are multiplied by 3 (i.e., $k = 3$), or, for the purpose of illustration, repeated three times,

$$\begin{bmatrix} 1 & 2 & 2 & 2 & 3 & 4 & 4 & 4 & 5 \\ 2 & 3 & 3 & 3 & 5 & 1 & 1 & 1 & 4 \\ 3 & 1 & 1 & 1 & 4 & 2 & 2 & 2 & 5 \end{bmatrix}$$

It is necessary to re-rank them, taking into consideration that there are now $(n-2+2k)$ stimuli,

$$\begin{bmatrix} 1 & 3 & 3 & 3 & 5 & 7 & 7 & 7 & 9 \\ 4 & 6 & 6 & 6 & 9 & 2 & 2 & 2 & 8 \\ 7 & 2 & 2 & 2 & 8 & 5 & 5 & 5 & 9 \end{bmatrix} = K = (k_{ij}), \text{ say.}$$

A typical element e_{ij} of dominance matrix E is given by $n + 1 - 2k_{ij}$, hence

$$E = \begin{bmatrix} 8 & 4 & 4 & 4 & 0 & -4 & -4 & -4 & -8 \\ 2 & -2 & -2 & -2 & 8 & 6 & 6 & 6 & -6 \\ -4 & 6 & 6 & 6 & -6 & 0 & 0 & 0 & -8 \end{bmatrix}.$$

Using the principle of equivalent partitioning, the $N \times n$ dominance matrix is finally obtained,

$$E = \begin{bmatrix} 8 & 4\times 3 & 0 & -4\times 3 & -8 \\ 2 & -2\times 3 & 8 & 6\times 3 & -6 \\ -4 & 6\times 3 & -6 & 0\times 3 & -8 \end{bmatrix} = \begin{bmatrix} 8 & 12 & 0 & -12 & -8 \\ 2 & -6 & 8 & 18 & -6 \\ -4 & 18 & -6 & 0 & -8 \end{bmatrix}$$

This transformation of F to E can be expressed by a set of formulas as follows. Let n and k be the number of stimuli and the weight for the two criterion stimuli. Suppose f_{ip} and f_{iq} are the ranks of the two criterion stimuli by subject i. Consider comparing three ranks of f_{ip}, f_{iq} and f_{ij} , where $j \neq p$, $j \neq q$. Then, the typical elements of the $N \times n$ transformed matrix, E, can be expressed as

$$\begin{cases} e_{ij} = n + 2k - 2 - 2f_{ij} & ,\text{if } f_{ij} < f_{ip} \text{ , } f_{ij} < f_{iq} \\ e_{ij} = n + 1 - 2f_{ij} & ,\text{if } f_{ij} \text{ is between } f_{ip} \text{ and } f_{iq} \\ e_{ij} = n + 3 - 2k - 2f_{ij} & ,\text{if } f_{ij} > f_{ip} \text{ , } f_{ij} > f_{iq} \\ e_{ij} = (n + 2k - 2f_{it})k & ,f_{it} \text{ is for the smaller of } f_{ip} \text{ and } f_{iq} \\ e_{ij} = (n + 2 - k - 2f_{it})k & ,f_{it} \text{ is for the larger of } f_{ip} \text{ and } f_{iq} \end{cases}$$

Although these formulas look complicated, they are easy to use, and very convenient to have especially for writing a computer program. In contrast, the paired comparison case is simpler than that of rank-order data. Suppose that three subjects compare six pairs of stimuli generated by four stimuli,

$$\begin{matrix} \text{pair} & \binom{1}{2} & \binom{1}{3} & \binom{1}{4} & \binom{2}{3} & \binom{2}{4} & \binom{3}{4} \end{matrix}$$

$$F = \begin{bmatrix} 2 & 2 & 1 & 2 & 1 & 2 \\ 2 & 2 & 2 & 2 & 1 & 2 \\ 2 & 1 & 1 & 1 & 2 & 2 \end{bmatrix}.$$

Suppose that stimuli 2 and 3 were chosen as criteria, and that k was set equal to three, in other words, the fourth column of F is repeated three times,

$$\begin{matrix} \text{pair} & \binom{1}{2} & \binom{1}{3} & \binom{1}{4} & \binom{2}{3} & \binom{2}{3} & \binom{2}{3} & \binom{2}{4} & \binom{3}{4} \end{matrix}$$

$$\begin{bmatrix} 2 & 2 & 1 & 2 & 2 & 2 & 1 & 2 \\ 2 & 2 & 2 & 2 & 2 & 2 & 1 & 2 \\ 2 & 1 & 1 & 1 & 1 & 1 & 2 & 2 \end{bmatrix}.$$

From this matrix, the dominance matrix can be calculated as

$$E = \begin{bmatrix} -1 & -1 & 3 & -1 \\ -3 & -2 & 3 & 1 \\ 1 & 3 & -5 & 1 \end{bmatrix}.$$

Notice that, in the paired comparison case, dominance numbers of non-criterion stimuli are unaffected by the value of k for the criterion stimuli. For instance, stimulus 1 in this example is free from the effects of the repeated pair (2,3). This makes it easier to calculate E from F for any value of k.

When the elements of an input matrix for dual scaling include negative numbers as in the case of matrix E, it is necessary to find "how many responses" are involved in each column and each row (Note: This is the main point of departure from correspondence analysis and analysis of quantitative data, such as principal component analysis). See Nishisato (1984) for the computation of such numbers. Let us now consider an example of analysis.

(a) [**Continuum from Noxema to Mary Kay**]: Suppose that we consider data on "overall evaluation" of [III], and that paired comparison responses to twenty-eight pairs of the eight cosmetic products are generated from ratings on their overall evaluations. Then, using the pair of Noxema and Mary Kay as the criteria, forced classification can be carried out, resulting in a bipolar continuum with Noxema at one end and Mary Kay at the other. The investigator should have a clear *a priori* knowledge as to what attribute makes the two products distinctly different from each other. With this knowledge, the derived continuum can be interpreted, and the analysis will show, for example, that Nivea and Clinique are close to Noxema and Mary Kay, respectively, on this continuum, and that some subjects placed their main emphasis for overall evaluations on this continuum.

(b) [**Continuum from Nivea to Second Debut**]: Suppose that the investigator knows that there is an attribute in data [II] which distinguishes between Nivea and Second Debut. If so, generate paired comparison data for the eight products, and carry out forced classification with the two products as its criteria.

An interesting aspect of bipolar classification lies in its non-symmetric effects on variables and subjects. While the variables are most widely distributed on the continuum with the criterion variables at the ends, the subjects are clearly divided into two groups. Therefore, it is especially appropriate for segmenting the consumers. Those interested in this aspect of bipolar classification are referred to Nishisato and Nishisato (1984) for a numerical example.

6 Conditional Classification

If data on Revlon and demographic information are subjected to fored classification with the variable "user vs. non-user" as the criterion, Dimension 1 maximizes the difference between the two groups of the criterion variable, and Dimension 2 provides dual scaling results expected when the effect of the criterion variable is partialled out. Thus, for example, when the sample happens to be unbalanced with respect to the group sizes, it may be useful to look at Dimension 2, that is, the dimension least contaminated by the group size imbalance. After the elimination of the group size effect, one may wish to find variables, for example, that contribute to popularity of Revlon. To carry out the entire analysis together, the task requires two criteria, "user vs. non-user" and "preference." Which dimension should we look at in order to find the answer to our problem? With two binary criterion variables, we expect four dimensions of interest, which correspond to the following basic structures: $P_{use}F$, $(I-P_{use})F$, $P_{pref}F$, and $(I-P_{pref})F$, where P_{use} and P_{pref} are projection operators for subspaces "users vs. non-users" and "preferred vs.

not preferred," respectively. Thus, it may be difficult to find out which of the forced classification dimensions corresponds, for example, to $(I - P_{use})F$. Furthermore, our interest lies in the basic structure of $P_{pref}(I - P_{use})\,F$, instead of that of $(I - P_{use})\,F$. In practice, therefore, it is advisable to carry out forced classification of matrix $(I - P_{use})F$ with the criterion variable being "preference".

7 Expert's Knowledge as Criterion

Forced classification with a large value of k is an asymptotic form of canonical analysis with one set of data being criterion variables and the other set the remaining variables. Thus, it is easy to incorporate expert's knowledge into the classification framework.

(a) [**Expected response patterns**]: Suppose that an expert in marketing research has theory on three distinct types of consumer behaviour, and that the researcher generates three sets of model (expected) responses to the data collection inventory. We have now introduced three model subjects and their responses to the data set as criteria for forced classification. In this instance, there will be in general three dimensions extracted, and one can classify subjects into three groups in terms of correlations between each of the three model subjects and real subjects.

(b) [**Response models**]: Similarly, the researcher may have a special behavioural theory (e.g., conjunctive, disjunctive, compensatory models), which states, for instance, that specific combinations of responses to a particular set of questions determine distinct types of behavioral category. If this is the theory to be applied to market segmentation, the data file should be scanned with respect to these variables, and the response patterns to them should be used to classify subjects into subgroups. The original data file is now augmented by introducing this new classification variable, say F_c , and dual scaling of $[F, kF_c]$, with a large value of k, should be carried out. Analysis will also identify other variables which contribute to this classification theory. In particular, if the analysis identifies a single variable which is highly correlated with the criterion, the variable can be used, in lieu of a combination of variables, to classify subjects into subgroups by forced classification with this variable as the criterion.

8 Multi-Way Classification

There are cases in which we wish to find the effects of a few classification variables simultaneously on consumer behaviour. For instance, we want to know if age and profession have significant effects on consumer's purchasing patterns, singly, jointly in an additive manner, or jointly with interactions. Another example may be the situation in which purchasing of different packages of consumer goods are examined in conjunction with a variety of demographic variables. In these examples, the use of projection operators (e.g., Lawrence (1985); Nishisato (1976, 1980, 1982); Poon (1977)) offers an immediate analysis, the only problem being that of computation—projectors for the subject's subspaces are all $N \times N$, where N is the number of subjects. In contrast, the forced classification approach would provide a computationally simple alternative. However, the exact relation between these two approaches in the multi-way classification problem is only conjectured to exist, and is yet to be proven.

9 Concluding Remarks

The present paper provided only a glimpse of what forced classification and its generalized version can do for market segmentation. When dual scaling is regarded as singular-value decomposition of a modified data matrix (e.g., $F(j \grave{\times} k), E$), one can see a large number of its potential applications to marketing research. Although a number of theoretical issues of the current approach are still open for debate, it needs to be applied to real situations. Only through constant interplay between methodological work and applications will we expect to develop an effective method for routine use.

Acknowledgements

This study was supported by the Natural Sciences and Engineering Research Council of Canada (Grant A 7942 to S. Nishisato).

References

Lawrence DR (1985) Dual Scaling of Multidimensional Data Structures: An Extended Comparison of Three Methods. Unpublished Doctoral Dissertation, University of Toronto

Lilien GL, Kotler P (1983) Marketing Decision Making: A Model-Building Approach. Harper & Row, New York

Nishisato S (1976) Optimal Scaling as Applied to Different Forms of Data. Technical Report No.4, Department of Measurement and Evaluation, The Ontario Institute for Studies in Education

Nishisato S (1980) Analysis of Categorical Data: Dual Scaling and Its Applications. University of Toronto Press, Toronto

Nishisato S (1982) Quantifying Qualitative Data: Dual Scaling and Its Applications. Asakura Shoten, Tokyo

Nishisato S (1984) Forced Classification: A Simple Application of a Quantification Method. Psychometrika 49: 25–36

Nishisato S (1986) Generalized Forced Classification for Quantifying Categorical Data, in: Diday E et al. (eds.) Data Analysis and Informatics IV. North-Holland, Amsterdam, pp 351–362

Nishisato S (1987) Robust Technique for Quantifying Categorical Data, in: McNeil IB, Umphrey GJ (eds.) Foundations of Statistical Inference. D. Reidel Publishing Co., Dortrecht, The Netherlands, pp 209–217

Nishisato S, Nishisato I (1984) An Introduction to Dual Scaling. MicroStats, Toronto

Poon W (1977) Transformations of Data Matrices in Optimal Scaling. Unpublished Master's Thesis, University of Toronto

Asymmetric Multidimensional Scaling of Car Switching Data

A. Okada
Department of Industrial Relations
School of Social Relations, Rikkyo (St. Paul's) University
3 Nishi Ikebukuro, Toshima-ku, Tokyo 171 JAPAN

Summary

Car switching data among 16 car segments was analyzed by an asymmetric multidimensional scaling. The car switching data was formed by rescaling a 16×16 car switching matrix whose (j, k) element represents the frequency with which any car in car segment j was traded-in for any car in car segment k. The asymmetric multidimensional scaling utilized in the present study represents each car segment as a point and a circle (shpere, hypershpere) centered at the point representing the car segment in a multidimensional Euclidean space. The resulting three-dimensional solution revealed size or price dimension, imports-captive imports-domestic dimension, and specialty dimension. It seems that radii of shperes might represent the relative dominance or attractiveness of car segments.

1 Introduction

The importance of asymmetries in various kinds of areas of research such as journal citation (Coombs (1964)), international trade (Chino (1978)), telephone calls (Harshman and Lundy 1984)), social mobility among occupations (Blau and Duncan (1967); Laumann and Guttman (1966); McDonald (1972); Okada (1986)), and inflow and outflow of migration (Coxon (1982)) has been growing recently (Carroll and Arabie (1980)).

But the majority of the studies has not been aware of the importance of asymmetries in the data. These studies simply ignored the asymmetries in the data and thought of the asymmetries as a noise or an error. The typical style of dealing with asymmetries in one-mode two-way data matrices was to obtain the average of the two elements which, they thought, should be equal to each other (Lorr (1983)), or to map the two asymmetric elements onto the same interpoint distance in a multidimensional space (Laumann and Guttman (1966); Shepard (1963)).

On the other hand, theoretical developments (Krumhansl (1978); Rips, Shoben and Smith (1973); Rosch (1975); Smith and Medin (1981); Tversky (1977)) have been made to explain asymmetries in similarity or dissimilarity judgment. And quite a few numbers of methods have been introduced to analyze asymmetric data (Bishop, Fienberg and Holland (1975); Chino (1978); Constantine and Gower (1978); Cunningham (1978); Gower (1977); Harshman (1978, 1981); Harshman, Green, Wind and Lundy (1982);

Holman (1979); Okada and Imaizumi (1984, 1987); Tobler (1977, 1979); Weeks and Bentler (1982); Young (1975)).

In marketing research, there also is a broad class of data which is not symmetric by nature. (Harshman et al. (1982), p. 206). For example, word association frequencies among stimulus phrases collected from female users of hair shampoo (Green, Wind and Jain (1973)) were asymmetric. The obtained word association frequency matrix is asymmetric. And the word association frequency matrix was asymmetrically analyzed by DEDICOM (Harshman et al. (1982)). The result was clearly improved compared with the result obtained by a symmetric analysis. Car switching data among 16 car segments, a 16×16 matrix whose (j, k) element represents the frequency with which any car in segment j was traded-in for any car in segment k $(j, k = 1, 2, \ldots, 16)$, is another example of asymmetric data in marketing research (The 16 car segments are shown in Table 1). The car switching data matrix was also analyzed asymmetrically by DEDICOM (Harshman et al. (1982)). The result was significantly improved compared with that obtained by a symmetric analysis. The car switching data matrix was also analyzed by the asymmetric multidimensional scaling (Okada and Imaizumi (1987)). In these two studies on the car switching data matrix, the asymmetric relationship of the car switching among 16 car segments was successfully accounted for.

In Harshman et al. (1982) the analysis was adjusted to deal with the differences in market share. The adjustment was based only on off-diagonal elements of the car switching data matrix (Table 4 of Harshman et al. (1982)) and excluded diagonal elements. In Okada and Imaizu (1987) the car switching data matrix was rescaled to deal with the differences in market share. And corresponding to the adjustment by Harshman et al. (1982), the rescaling was based only on off-diagonal elements of the car switching data matrix and excluded diagonal elements such that the results of the two studies could easily be compared. Although these studies focus their attention on the car switch among 16 car segments, that does not necessarily justify the adjustment or the rescaling based only on off-diagonal elements of the data matrix.

Each of the diagonal elements of the car switching data matrix represents the frequency with which any car in some segment was replaced by any car in the same segment. Although these diagonal elements of the car switching data matrix were excluded in the adjustment or the rescaling in previous studies, each of the diagonal elements is a constituent part of the number of cars traded-in and of the number of cars purchased in the segment. In the present study, the rescaling based on all the elements of the car switching data matrix (the rescaling procedure which did not exclude the diagonal elements) was done, and the rescaled car switching data matrix was analyzed by the asymmetric multidimensional scaling introduced by Okada and Imaizumi (1987).

2 Method

Since the details of the present asymmetric multidimensional scaling which is nonmetric in nature is fully described elsewhere (Okada and Imaizumi (1984, 1987)), the model and the algorithm of the asymmetric multidimensional scaling are recapitulated only briefly.

2.1 Model

The model of the present asymmetric multidimensional scaling was developed from the model of Weeks and Bentler (1982). The later model was generalized and improved such that

1. ordinally scaled similarities or dissimilarities can be analyzed nonmetrically (similarities or dissimilarities have to be at least interval scaled in Weeks and Bentler's model), which widens the applicability of the present multidimensional scaling to the data from various kinds of fields of research, and

2. the interpretation of the meaning of the term r_j, which was introduced to account for skew symmetries in similarities or dissimilarities and corresponds to c_j of Weeks and Bentler's model, can be uniquely determined irrespective of whether similarities or dissimilarities are analyzed. (On the contrary c_j has two opposite meanings depending on whether similarities or dissimilarities are analyzed.)

Let s_{jk} be the similarity or dissimilarity of stimulus j to k. The present definition of s_{jk} does not mean that s_{jk} equals to s_{kj}. Then it is assumed that s_{jk} is monotonically decreasingly related with m_{jk} (when s_{jk} is similarity) or is monotonically increasingly related with m_{jk} (when s_{jk} is dissimilarity) and m_{jk} is

$$m_{jk} = d_{jk} - r_j + r_k. \tag{1}$$

In Equation (1) the first term d_{jk} represents the Euclidean distance between stimuli j and k defined by

$$d_{jk} = [\sum_{t=1}^{p} (x_{jt} - x_{kt})^2]^{1/2} \tag{2}$$

where x_{jt} is the t-th coordinate of the point representing stimulus j in a p-dimensional Euclidean space. The terms r_j and r_k are introduced to represent skew symmetries in s_{jk}. They are normalized by imposing the condition

$$\min_j(r_j) = 0. \tag{3}$$

In the present model, s_{jk} is related with m_{jk}, and the definition of m_{jk} is not altered according to whether s_{jk} is assumed to be monotonically increasingly or decreasingly related with m_{jk}. And therefore the meaning of r_j is not altered irrespective of whether similarities or dissimilarities are analyzed.

In the geometric representation of the model, r_j can be represented as a radius of a circle (sphere, hypersphere) centered at the point which represents stimulus j. When r_j is too large to be represented in a stimulus configuration, r_j can be represented as a line segment embedded in the configuration (Okada (1986)). The two-dimensional model, where r_j is represented as a radius of a circle, is illustrated in Figure 1.

2.2 Algorithm

An algorithm which iteratively obtains a configuration (a stimulus configuration and a radius of a circle centered at each point) from a square asymmetric similarity or dissimilarity matrix was developed. The algorithm itself is the adaptation of that of Kruskal's nonmetric multidimensional scaling (Kruskal (1964a, 1964b), Lingoes and

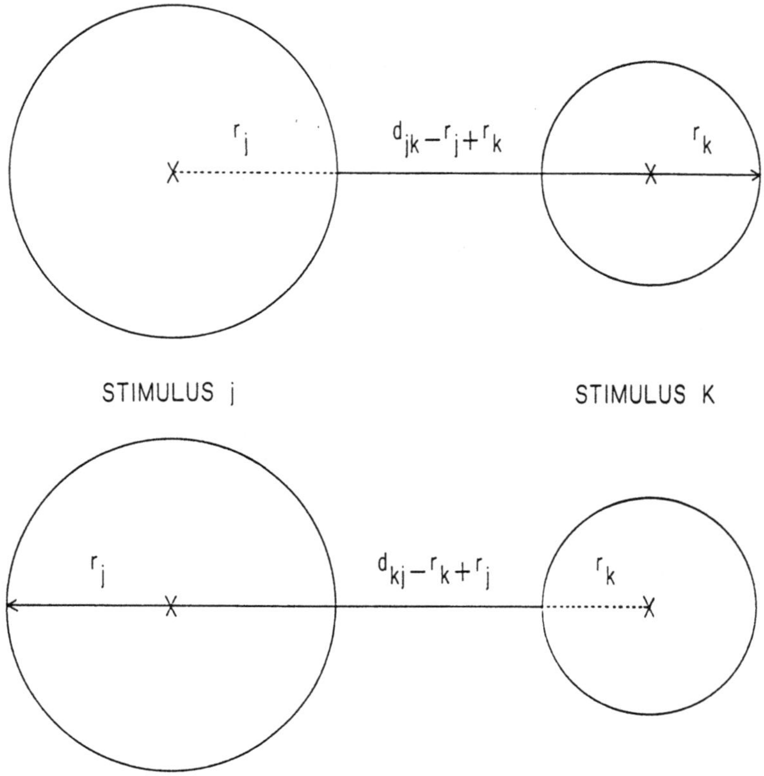

Figure 1: Geometric representation of the model in a two-dimensional space

Roskam (1973)) for the present model.

The measure of goodness of fit of m_{jk} to the monotone relationship with s_{jk} is defined as

$$S = \Big(\sum_{j\neq k}^{n}(m_{jk} - \widehat{m}_{jk})^2 \ / \ \sum_{j\neq k}^{n}(m_{jk} - \overline{m})^2\Big)^{1/2} \tag{4}$$

where $\widehat{m}_{jk}$ represents the disparity defined by Kruskal's monotonicity principle, and $\overline{m}$ is the mean of m_{jk}. Then the configuration (the stimulus configuration and the radii) which minimizes S is derived by the steepest descent method for a given dimensionality. It is very interesting that the square of the denominator of S can be divided into two terms as

$$\text{square of the denominator of } S = \sum_{j\neq k}^{n}(d_{jk} - \overline{d})^2 + 2n^2\text{var}\,(r_j) \tag{5}$$

where $\overline{d}$ is the mean of d_{jk} and is always equal to $\overline{m}$. The first term of the Equation (5) is the twice of the square of the denominator of stress formula two (Coxon (1982)) and is connected with the symmetric component of a configuration. The second term is the $2n^2$ times of the variance of radii and is connected with the skew symmetric component of a configuration. The relative weights of the two terms to the sum of them plays an important role in the performance of the algorithm (Okada and Imaizumi (1987)).

3 Rescaling the Car Switching Data

The car switching data matrix was rescaled to remove the differences in market share. The rescaling based on all elements of the car switching data matrix (diagonal elements were not excluded) was done by multiplying the rescaling coefficient to each row and column such that the row j plus column j sum in the rescaled car switching data matrix is equal to the mean row plus column sum across 16 row plus column sums in the original data matrix for any j. The rescaling coefficients are shown in Table 1. And the resultant rescaled car switching data matrix is shown in Table 2.

Table 1: Rescaling Coefficients

	Car segments	Rescaling coefficients
1	SUBCOMPACT DOMESTIC	0.777
2	SUBCOMPACT CAPTIVE IMPORTS	4.885
3	SUBCOMPACT IMPORTS	0.826
4	SMALL SPECIALTY DOMESTIC	0.721
5	SMALL SPECIALTY CAPTIVE IMPORTS	114.679
6	SMALL SPECIALTY IMPORTS	2.547
7	LOW PRICE COMPACT	0.923
8	MEDIUM PRICE COMPACT	1.728
9	IMPORT COMPACT	4.072
10	MIDSIZE DOMESTIC	0.474
11	MIDSIZE IMPORTS	3.547
12	MIDSIZE SPECIALTY	0.581
13	LOW PRICE STANDARD	0.673
14	MEDIUM PRICE STANDARD	0.640
15	LUXURY DOMESTIC	0.960
16	LUXURY IMPORT	4.716

4 Results

The car switching data matrix of Table 2 was analyzed by asymmetric multidimensional scaling by Okada and Imaizumi (1987). The analysis was done for five through uni-dimensional spaces. The resulting minimized S values are 0.312, 0.336, 0.360, 0.409, and 0.603 respectively. The elbow or scree criterion tells that the three-dimensional configuration should be chosen as a solution. And the substantive interpretation supports the decision. The three-dimensional configuration was rotated such that the interpretation given to the stimulus configuration becomes as clear as possible. The rotated stimulus configuration and radii (which are not affected by the rotation) are shown in Table 3. The configuration is illustrated geometrically in Figure 2.

Table 2: Rescaled Data

From segment	To segment 1	2	3	4	5	6	7	8
1	14049	5644	6741	10639	4367	4589	8854	5453
2	12350	26581	12163	9353	12888	6855	4323	7547
3	7282	4899	17736	5838	4454	11362	2487	1932
4	6576	4197	6640	19974	5706	8959	4023	2909
5	4189	3362	0	9675	52637	0	0	9714
6	3506	2700	7621	6340	4674	34045	2616	1378
7	13222	8411	9266	10136	6880	3821	23107	9859
8	13910	5850	8340	7934	7930	2685	9924	22308
9	8267	9568	23486	5440	4671	10609	4904	4448
10	12150	5375	8621	10116	5977	5058	9178	9951
11	3563	1975	8334	3176	2034	6974	4932	2771
12	5855	2782	3967	7913	6460	5092	1978	1754
13	14540	6211	7214	7757	2624	2267	11751	6785
14	8594	4033	5941	5283	3008	3033	4563	6829
15	2783	2016	3684	4091	661	1520	1463	1731
16	385	921	3884	2050	0	4096	326	448

From segment	To segment 9	10	11	12	13	14	15	16
1	1724	4646	1326	7365	2223	1178	708	465
2	4356	3869	3864	5706	3043	1687	1153	852
3	7593	2033	3830	4003	1283	851	849	1122
4	2733	2904	3010	10001	1570	2039	2846	1394
5	0	5977	0	666	0	0	0	0
6	7654	1968	9666	7299	579	1468	3202	5513
7	3138	9140	1853	8219	6039	2131	806	740
8	3969	7875	2666	9763	4187	6077	1267	693
9	25470	5281	14516	2340	1244	2581	2122	2439
10	4886	11893	3596	16871	8925	10275	4459	1577
11	8161	6418	38485	4853	1406	2387	2965	9953
12	2210	3177	2706	18882	4280	6939	6987	1582
13	3238	9027	2238	14600	30762	12428	4252	952
14	3355	6345	2378	11209	6591	33466	13488	1653
15	1860	1395	2822	4775	1914	5639	58489	7173
16	3380	337	9852	2075	501	2280	5585	69479

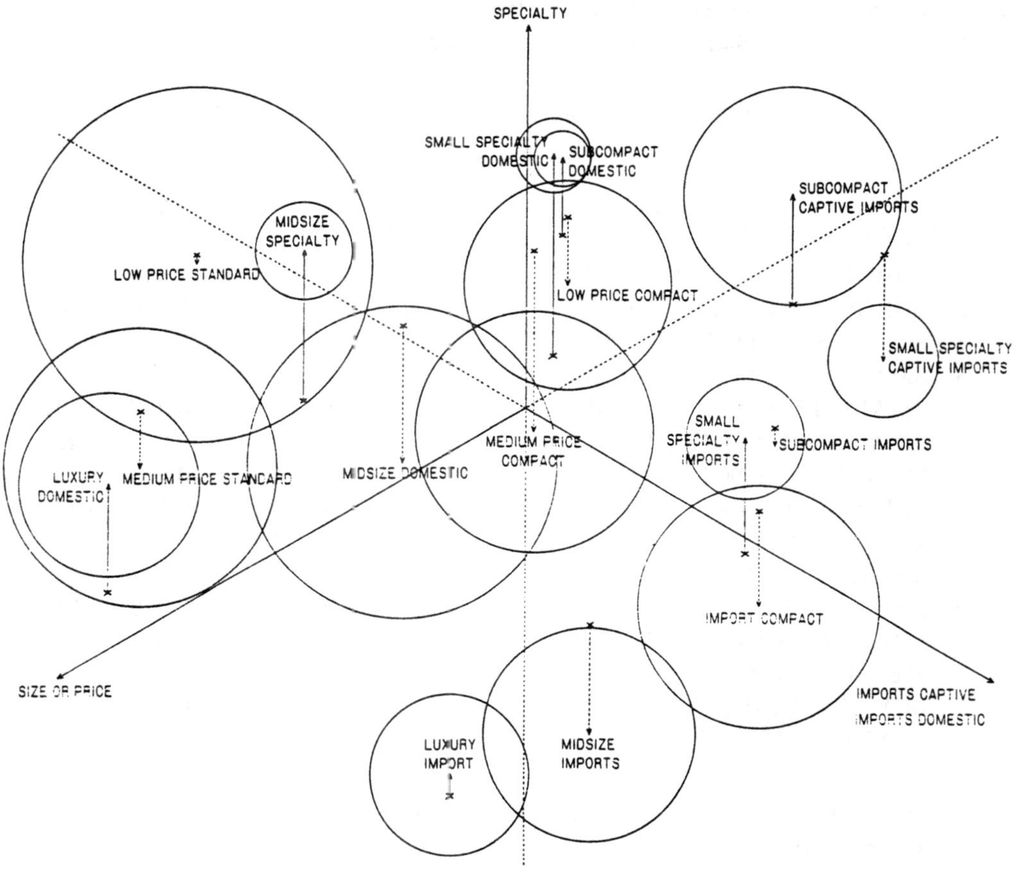

Figure 2: Three-dimensional representation of the configuration

(Each car segment is represented by an arrow head and the sphere centered at the arrow head. The arrow head represents the location of the stimuli in the three-dimensional space and the X represent the projection of the arrow head onto the two-dimensional space formed by size or price dimension and imports—captive imports—domestic dimension. The solid line shows that the specialty dimension is positive, and the dotted line shows that the specialty dimension is negative.)

The three dimensions of the solution seem to represent size or price (dimension 1), imports—captive imports—domestic (dimension 2), and specialty (dimension 3) respectively. The three dimensions unveiled in the present study are very close to those obtained in the study previously done by Okada and Imaizumi (1987) where the rescaling without diagonal elements of the car switching data matrix was done. Similarly to the three dimensions of the previous study, the dimension 1 of the present study corresponds to the first (plain large - midsize), the third (fancy large), and the fourth (small) factors of Harshman et al. (1982), and the dimension 3 of the present study corresponds to their second (specialty) factor. The dimension 2 of the present study does not correspond to any of the factors given by Harshman et al. (1982). The dimension

1 and dimension 2 also correspond to the traditional ways of dividing the auto market (Urban and Hauser (1980)).

Table 3: Stimulus Configuration and Radii

		Dimension			
	Car segments	1	2	3	Radii
1	SUBCOMPACT DOMESTIC	-0.623	-0.469	0.252	0.080
2	SUBCOMPACT CAPTIVE IMPORTS	-0.805	0.158	0.341	0.342
3	SUBCOMPACT IMPORTS	-0.396	0.611	-0.056	0.000
4	SMALL SPECIALTY DOMESTIC	-0.211	-0.106	0.625	0.114
5	SMALL SPECIALTY CAPTIVE IMPORTS	-1.130	0.173	-0.329	0.171
6	SMALL SPECIALTY IMPORTS	0.049	0.846	0.362	0.187
7	LOW PRICE COMPACT	-0.668	-0.525	-0.212	0.326
8	MEDIUM PRICE COMPACT	-0.511	-0.475	-0.569	0.369
9	IMPORT COMPACT	-0.107	0.743	-0.301	0.375
10	MIDSIZE DOMESTIC	-0.039	-0.480	-0.426	0.482
11	MIDSIZE IMPORTS	0.546	0.789	-0.347	0.327
12	MIDSIZE SPECIALTY	0.376	-0.420	0.468	0.144
13	LOW PRICE STANDARD	0.124	-1.073	-0.034	0.553
14	MEDIUM PRICE STANDARD	0.713	-0.678	-0.180	0.430
15	LUXURY DOMESTIC	1.339	-0.167	0.341	0.280
16	LUXURY IMPORT	1.344	1.076	0.065	0.244

The radii of Table 3 are slightly larger than those of the previous study, but the two sets of radii are very close ($r = 0.995$). They also highly negatively correlate with the figures obtained by subtracting row j sum from column j sum ($r = -0.966$). And this seems to mean that the radius of each car segment might represent the relative dominance or attractiveness of the car segment which governs the asymmetries in the car switching.

Identically to the previous study, SUBCOMPACT IMPORTS has the smallest radius, and LOW PRICE STANDARD has the largest radius. The mean radii for the imports, the captive imports, and the domestic are 0.227, 0.257, and 0.309 respectively. And the mean radii for the subcompact, the small specialty, the compact, the midsize, the standard, and the luxury are 0.141, 0.157, 0.357, 0.318, 0.492, and 0.262. These figures tell that the smaller cars, the imported cars, and the luxurious cars are predominating over the domestic cars, and the plain or simple cars in the auto market.

5 Discussion

The car switching data matrix which was rescaled to remove the differences in market share was analyzed by asymmetric multidimensional scaling. The resulting stimulus configuration was successfully explained by the three dimensions and the radii are compatible with the superiority or inferiority relationship in car switching. Although the rescaling was based not only on off diagonal elements but based on all elements of the matrix, the obtained stimulus configuration and the radius are very similar to those previously obtained by analyzing the car switching data rescaled without diagonal elements (Okada and Imaizumi (1987)). The previously obtained stimulus configuration was rotated to be congruent with the present stimulus configuration (Cliff (1968)). Then the mean (z-transformed) product moment correlation coefficient between the two sets of coordinates over three dimensions was calculated to be 0.973. The product moment correlation coefficient between the two sets of radii is 0.995 as described earlier. Thus the two solutions seem to be almost identical to each other. But the dimension 2 of the present solution discriminates captive imports from imports and domestic more clearly than that of the previous study. Thus the dimension 2 of the present solution seems to satisfactorily divide the car segments into three classes (imports, captive imports, and domestic), whereas the dimension 2 of the previous study divides the car segments into two classes (imports, domestic (includes captive imports)). In both solutions SMALL SPECIALTY CAPTIVE IMPORTS fails to have a large positive coordinate on dimension 3. The inclusion of diagonal elements in the rescaling of the car switching data matrix leads to reveal dimension 2 which is clearly improved than that of the previous study. The ratios of the first and second terms of Equation (6) to the sum of them of the present solution is 0.849 and 0.151 respectively. The corresponding ratios of the previous study are 0.837 and 0.163. Thus the relative weight of the asymmetric component of the present solution is much the same as that of the previous solution. And the asymmetric component of the solutions is much smaller than that of another study (Okada (1986)).

The rescaled car switching data matrix of Table 2 was analyzed by symmetric nonmetric multidimensional scaling. The minimized stress values from five- through unidimensional stimulus configurations were 0.490, 0.512, 0.528, 0.564, and 0.688 respectively. The three-dimensional stimulus configuration was rotated to be congruent with the present stimulus configuration given by the asymmetric multidimensional scaling. The mean (z-transformed) product moment correlation coefficient between the two sets of coordinates over three dimensions is 0.993. In case of the four-dimensional configuration the corresponding figure is 0.987. And the product moment correlation coefficient between the radii of Table 3 and the coordinates of the fourth dimension of the rotated configuration is -0.208. These product moment correlation coefficients tell that the stimulus configuration of the solution given by the asymmetric analysis is very close to that given by symmetric analyses, and that the radii given by the asymmetric analysis can not be provided by symmetric analyses (Okada and Imaizumi (1987)).

An external analysis procedure where radii are derived for a given stimulus configuration has been incorporated into the present asymmetric multidimensional scaling program (Okada and Imaizumi, in press). The external analysis was executed to derive radii for the three-dimensional stimulus configuration given by the symmetric analysis. The derived radii are slightly larger than the radii of Table 3, but they are almost identical (r = 0.997). Thus the external analysis seems to be practical when the stimulus configuration has been already obtained.

A lower triangular matrix of symmetric car switch data matrix was constructed by defining a (j,k) element (where $j < k$) of the matrix as the sum of (j,k) and (k,j) elements of Table 3. Then the lower triangular matrix was analyzed by HCS (Johnson

(1968)). The minimum method represented more satisfactory results than the maximum method. The tree diagram is shown in Figure 3.

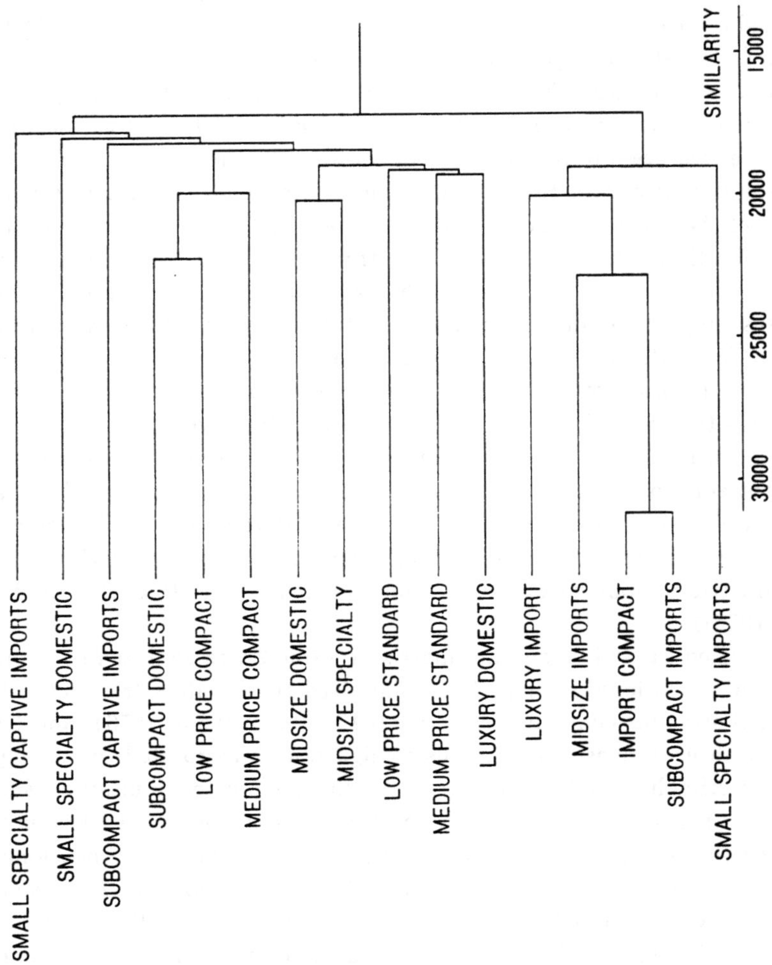

Figure 3: Tree diagram produced by the minimum method

The result given by the minimum method seems to be compatible with the stimulus configuration shown in Figure 2, and with the traditional way of dividing the auto market. This also substantiates the validity of the present configuration.

The car switching data among 16 car segments which was given by the rescaling based on all elements of the matrix was analyzed by the asymmetric multidimensional scaling algorithm. Each car segment was represented by a point and a radius of a sphere centered at the point in a three-dimensional Euclidean space. The solution was very similar to the solution given by analyzing the data rescaled without diagonal elements. The solution seems to be compatible with the traditional ways of dividing the auto market, and with the results given by the minimum method of cluster analysis. There are various kinds of asymmetric data in marketing research. And it seems to be very important to unveil the characteristics and features of the data, which the symmetric analysis might not be able to disclose, by asymmetric analyses.

Acknowledgments

The present research is supported by a grant from the Rikkyo (St. Paul's) University Research Fund

References

Bishop YMM, Fienberg SE, Holland PW (eds.) (1975). Discrete Multivariate Analysis: Theory and Practice. The MIT Press

Blau PM, Duncan OD (1967) The American Occupational Structure. Wiley, New York

Carroll JD, Arabie P (1980) Multidimensional Scaling. Annual Review of Psychology 31: 607–649

Chino N (1978) A Graphical Technique for Representing the Asymmetric Relationships between N Objects. Behaviormetrika 5: 23–40

Cliff N (1968) Orthogonal Rotation to Congruence. Psychometrika 31: 33–42

Constantine AG, Gower JC (1978) Graphical Representation of Asymmetric Matrices. Applied Statistics 27: 297–304

Coombs CH (1964) A Theory of Data. Wiley, New York

Coxon APM (1982) The User's Guide to Multidimensional Scaling. Heinemann Educational Books, Exeter

Cunningham JP (1978) Free Trees and Bidirectional Trees as Representations of Psychological Distance. Journal of Mathematical Psychology 17: 165–188

Gower JC (1977) The Analysis of Asymmetry and Orthogonality, in: Barra JR, Brodeau F, Romier G, van Cutsem B (eds.) Recent Developments in Statistics. North Holland, Amsterdam, pp 109–123

Green PE, Wind Y, Jain AK (1973) Analyzing Free-Response Data in Marketing Research. Journal of Marketing Research 10: 45–52

Harshman, RA (1978) Models for Analysis of Asymmetrical Relationships Among N Objects or Stimuli. Paper presented at the First Joint Meeting of the Psychometric Society and the Society for Mathematical Psychology at McMaster University, Hamilton, Ontario

Harshman RA (1981) DEDICOM Multidimensional Analysis of Skew-Symmetrical Data. Technical Memorandum, Bell Telephone Laboratories

Harshman RA, Green PE, Wind Y, Lundy ME (1982) A Model for the Analysis of Asymmetric Data in Marketing Research. Marketing Science 1: 205–242

Harshman RA, Lundy ME (1984) The PARAFAC Model for Three-Way Factor Analysis and Multidimensional Scaling, in: Law LG, Snyder CW, Hattie JA, McDonald RP (eds.) Research Methods for Multimode Data Analysis. Praeger, New York, pp 122–215

Holman EW (1979) Monotonic Models for Asymmetric Proximities. Journal of Mathematical Psychology 20: 1–15

Johnson SC Hierarchical Clustering Schemes. Psychometrika 32: 241– 255

Krumhansl CL (1978). Concerning the Applicability of Geometric Models to Similarity Data: The Interrelationship between Similarity and Spatial Density. Psychological Review 85: 445–463

Kruskal JB (1964a) Multidimensional Scaling by Optimizing Goodness of Fit to a Nonmetric Hypothesis. Psychometrika 29: 1–27

Kruskal JB (1964b) Nonmetric Multidimensional Scaling: A Numerical Method. Psychometrika 29: 115–129

Lingoes JC, Roskam EE (1973) A Mathematical and Empirical Analysis of Two Multidimensional Scaling Algorithms. Psychometrika Monograph Supplement 19

Lorr M (1983) Cluster Analysis for Social Scientists. Jossey-Bass., San Francisco

Laumann EO, Guttman L (1966) The Relative Associational Contigiuty of Occupations in an Urban Setting. American Sociological Review 31: 169–178

McDonald KI (1972) MDSCAL and Distances between Socio-Economic Groups, in: Hope K (ed.) The Analysis of Social Mobility. Charendon Press, Oxford, pp 211–234

Okada A (1986) Asymmetric Multidimensional Scaling of Intergenerational Occupational Mobility, in: Proceedings of the Second Japan China Symposium on Statistics. Kyushu University, Fukuoka, Japan, pp 197–200

Okada A, Imaizumi T (1984) Geometric Models for Asymmetric Similarity Data. Research Report, Rikkyo (St.Paul's) University

Okada A, Imaizumi T (1987) Nonmetric Multidimensional Scaling of Asymmetric Proximities. Behaviormetrika 21: 81–96

Okada A, Imaizumi T (in press) How to Use Nonmetric Asymmetric Multidimensional Scaling Program (NAMS Version 1. 1f). Journal of Applied Sociology

Rips LJ, Shoben EJ, Smith EE (1973) Semantic Distance and the Verification of Semantic Relations. Journal of Verbal Learning and Verbal Behavior 12: 1–20

Rosch E (1975) Cognitive Reference Points. Cognitive Psychology 7: 532–547

Shepard RN (1963) Analysis of Proximities as a Technique for the Study of Information Processing in Man. Human Factors 5: 33–48

Smith EE, Medin DL (1981). Categories and Concepts. Harvard University Press, Cambridge

Tobler W (1977) Spatial Interaction Patterns. Journal of Environmental Systems 6: 271–301

Tobler WR (1979) Estimation of Attractivities from Interactions. Environment and Planning A 11: 121–127

Tversky A (1977) Features of Similarity. Psychological Review 84: 327–352

Urban GL, Hauser JR (1980) Design and Marketing of New Products. Prentice Hall, Englewood Cliffs

Weeks DG, Bentler PM (1982) Restricted Multidimensional Scaling Models for Asymmetric Proximities. Psychometrika 47: 201–208

Young FW (1975) An Asymmetric Euclidean Model for Multi-Process Asymmetric Data, in: Proceedings of the US Japan Seminar on the Theory, Methods and Applications of Multidimensional Scaling and Related Techniques at the University of California San Diego, La Jolla, California

Evolving Principal Clusters: Theory and Application to Management Monitoring

Y. Schektman and A. Ibrahim
Aegide, Grecc-CNRS 59 Universite Toulouse Le MIRAIL
31058 Toulouse Cedex, FRANCE

Summary

Principal Clusters (PC) and Evolving Principal Clusters (EPC) constitute applications of inner products (distances) with relationship effects and the general theory of symmetrical (CARS) and dissymmetrical (CARDS) relationship association indices defined in Schektman (1978, 1987).

PC are obtained by maximizing CARS or CARDS, i.e., inertia of well design configurations of points in a well chosen euclidean space. By proving intermediate PC, EPC simulates evolution between two PC obtained on the same population. So EPC provides a "measure" of mobility for individuals which change classes.

Applications of EPC to manage a population of 41 restaurants is presented; restaurants to be monitored are pointed out with the help of a friendly program running on IBM PC.

1 Introduction

Theoretical complements to our last paper (Ibrahim and Schektman (1986)) are presented and a more important application than (Schektman and al., (1986)) is described. Now, theoretical framework of Principal Clusters are linked to more general results (Schektman (1987)) and a friendly program for users is running on IBM-PC.

In this paper, we describe how to use principal clusters for managing an homogeneous population of institutions. In the numerical example, presented in section 5, the institutions are the restaurants of the "Central Office of Social Activities (CCAS)" of E.D.F-G.D.F. staff (French Electrical and Gaz Industries).

The problem to be solved in this application needs to take into account the direction of associations which are analysed. Thus, dissymmetrical measures of associations must be used. A general theory of these indices is presented in the following section.

2 Some General Results on Association Measures

2.1 Generalities

The results described just below are based on distances with relationship effects (Schektman (1978)) and some general structural properties on distances (Schektman (1983,

1984)). In this paper, the particular case of two sets of variables is described in details. In fact, this case is sufficient for defining principal clusters. However, the results presented here should constitute a useful guideline for holding more than two sets. Consider a multivariate sample defined by n individuals and two sets of variables $[x_j]$ $(j = 1, \ldots, p)$ and $[y_k]$ $(k = 1, \ldots, q)$. We suppose, without loss of generality, that all variables have zero means. Let x_{ji} be the value of the ith individual on the jth variable, and y_{ki} the similar value on the variable y_k. For any definition referring to x, a similar definition referring to y exists. So, we shall not give the definitions referring to y subsequently. All the values x_{ji} are regarded as forming a (n,p) rectangular data matrix, denoted by X, with x_{ji} in ith row and jth column. Let $\mathcal{F} = \mathbb{R}^n$ be the variable-space and $\mathcal{E} = \mathbb{R}^{p+q} = \mathcal{E}x \oplus \mathcal{E}y$ be the individual-space, where $\mathcal{E}x$ is the p-dimensional subspace associated by duality to the columns of X. Let M and D be the inner products in $\mathcal{E}$ and $\mathcal{F}$, respectively. Generally, the matrix associated to D is a (n,n) diagonal one with the (i,i)th element equal to the weight w_i of the ith individual, but D may be more complex. In this paper, it is sufficient to suppose (H_0) that the restriction of M to $Sx \subset \mathcal{E}x$ is an inner product, where Sx is the subspace spanned by the row vectors of the $(n, p+q)$ matrix $[X \mid 0]$.

According to the variables partition in two sets and to the corresponding partition of $\mathcal{E} = \mathcal{E}x \oplus \mathcal{E}y$, the covariance matrix between all variables , denoted by V, and the matrix of M may be written:

$$V = \begin{bmatrix} Vx & Vxy \\ Vyx & Vy \end{bmatrix} \qquad M = \begin{bmatrix} Mx & Mxy \\ Myx & My \end{bmatrix}$$

where $Vx = X'D\,X$, $Vy = Y'D\,Y$, $Vxy = X'D\,Y$.

Definition 1: M is with relationship effect for $(\mathcal{E}x, \mathcal{E}y)$
if $Mxy = Mx[(Vx\,Mx)^{1/2}]^+\,Vxy\,My\,[(Vy\,My)^{1/2}]^+$
where $[(Vx\,Mx)^{1/2}]^+$ is the Moore-Penrose inverse of $(Vx\,Mx)^{1/2}$ with respect to Mx.

One can find properties of this inner product or euclidean distance in (Schektman (1978, 1983, 1984, 1987); Croquette (1980); Grau (1983); Ibrahim and al. (1986)). V^-x denotes the matrices V^+x or χ^2_x (chi-square) which define useful distances when variables are quantitative (linearly independent or dependent), or Centered Dummy Variables (C.D.V.) associated to a categorical variable. It is easy to show that $Qx = X\,V^-x\,X'\,D$ is the orthogonal projection onto $\mathcal{F}x$, where $\mathcal{F}x$ is the subspace spanned by the column vectors of X. If $\mathrm{Im}[\mathrm{In}x\;M^+x] = Sx$ (see hypothesis H_0), for example $Mx = V^+x$ or Vx, then $Px = \mathrm{In}x\;M^+x\;\mathrm{In}x'\;M$ is the orthogonal projection onto Sx, where $\mathrm{In}x$ is the canonical injection from $\mathbb{R}^p$ into $\mathcal{E}$. Besides, if $[x_j]$ are C.D.V. and if $Mx = \chi^2_x$, as $\mathrm{In}x[(\chi^2_x)^{-1}]\mathrm{In}x'\;M\;\mathrm{In}y$ is equal to $\mathrm{In}x\;Vx\;\mathrm{In}x'\;M\;\mathrm{In}y$, then the restriction to $\mathcal{E}y$ of $Px = \mathrm{In}x[(\chi^2_x)^{-1}]\;\mathrm{In}x'\;M$, is also the orthogonal projection onto Sx.

Let $y(i)'$ be the ith row of $[0 \mid Y], Ny = [y(i), (i = 1, \ldots, n)]$ the corresponding configuration of individual vectors in $\mathcal{E}y$ and $Ix[Ny] = \sum w_i \|Px[y(i)]\|^2$ the inertia of the orthogonal projection of Ny onto Sx. Note that if M is with relationship effect, $Ix[Ny]$ depends upon Vxy, i.e the statitical relationships between variables $[x_j]$ and $[y_k]$. Let us give a useful expression of $Ix[Ny]$:

Property 1:
If M is with relationship effect for $(\mathcal{E}x, \mathcal{E}y)$ and
if Mx is full rank or equal to $V^{+}x$ or to Vx
then $Ix[Ny] = \mathrm{Tr}[Vxy\, My\, Vyx\, V^{+}x]$.
Proof:
$Ix[Ny] = \mathrm{Tr}[Px\ \mathrm{Iny}\ Vy\ \mathrm{Iny}'\ M] = \mathrm{Tr}[M^{+}x\ Mxy\ Vy\ Myx]$

As we suppose $\mathrm{Im}[\mathrm{Inx}M^{+}x] = Sx$, thus $M^{+}x\ Mx$ is the orthogonal projection onto Sx, that yields $M^{+}x\ Mx\ [(Vx\ Mx)^{1/2}]^{+} = [(Vx\ Mx)^{1/2}]^{+}$.
By using definition 1, we obtain:

$$\begin{aligned} Ix[Ny] &= \mathrm{Tr}[[(Vx\ Mx)^{1/2}]^{+} Vxy\ My\ Vyx\ Mx\ [(Vx\ Mx)^{1/2}]^{+}] \\ &= \mathrm{Tr}[Vxy\ My\ Vyx\ Mx(Vx\ Mx)^{+}] \\ &= \mathrm{Tr}[Vxy\ My\ Vyx\ V^{+}x] \end{aligned}$$

because

$$\begin{aligned} Mx\ (Vx\ Mx)^{+} &= V^{+}x && \text{if } Mx \text{ is full rank} \\ &= V^{+}x\ Vx\ V^{+}x \\ &= V^{+}x && \text{if } Mx = V^{+}x \\ &= Vx\ (V^{2}x)^{+} \\ &= V^{+}x && \text{if } Mx = Vx \end{aligned}$$

Note (Schektman (1986)) that, under the same conditions as property 1, $Px\ Py$, $Py\ Px$,$Qx\ Qy$ and $Qy\ Qx$ have the same non zero latent roots.

2.2 Symmetrical Association Indices

Let $[r_{cj}]$ be the Canonical Correlation Coefficients of (Fx, Fy, D).
As $\sum(r_{cj})^2 = \mathrm{Tr}[Qx\ Qy]$, using expressions of Qx and Qy it follows:

Property 2: $\sum(r_{cj})^2 = \mathrm{Tr}[Vxy\ V^{-}y\ Vyx\ V^{-}x]$.

For C.D.V., $X\ \chi^2_x\ X'D = Qx = Q^2x = X\ V^{+}x\ X'D\ X\ \chi^2_x\ X'D = X\ V^{+}x\ X'D$, indeed $Vx\ \chi^2_x$ is a projection matrix onto $\mathrm{Im}[Vx\ \chi^2_x] = Sx$ since χ^2_x is a generalized internal inverse of Vx. Thus properties 1 and 2 imply:

Property 3: If M is with relationship effect for $(\mathcal{E}x, \mathcal{E}y)$ and
if Mx is full rank or equal to $V^{+}x$ or to Vx and $My = V^{-}y$
then $Ix[Ny] = \sum(r_{cj})^2$.

In a similar way $Iy[Nx] = \sum(r_{cj})^2$. Thus, if M is with relationship effect, $Mx = V^{-}x$ and $My = V^{-}y$ then $Iy[Nx]$ and $Ix[Ny]$ are equal to the

- "Pearson coefficient of mean square contingency" when $[x_j]$ and $[y_k]$ are the C.D.V. associated to two categorical variables,

- "generalized correlation ratio" when $[x_j]$ are quantitative and $[y_k]$ C.D.V..

In conclusion, whatever the type of variables, property 3 points out that classical symmetrical association indices can be expressed by the same formula $Ix[Ny]$ (or $Iy[Nx]$). That leads to the following general definition:

Definition 2: Given M with relationship effect for $(\mathcal{E}\,x, \mathcal{E}\,y)$, Symmetrical Relationship Association Coefficients between variables $[x_j]$ and $[y_k]$, are defined by

$$\text{CARS}[x, y/Mx = V^{-}x, My = V^{-}y] = Ix[Ny] \;/\; (Ix[Nx]\; Iy[Ny])^{1/2}.$$

Note that these formulas must be used with suitable distances, concerning $Ix[Ny]$, for example, one must choose:

- $My = \chi^2_y$ when $[y_k]$ are C.D.V.,
- $My = V^{+}y$ when $[y_k]$ are quantitative variables.

Besides, it is easy to verify that $\text{CARS}[x, y/\chi^2_x, \chi^2_y]$ is equal to the "Tschuprow coefficient" when $[x_j]$ and $[y_k]$ are C.D.V.. One can find theoretical framework of these results in (Schektman (1983, 1984); Grau (1983); Fabre (1986)). However, we can give an intuitive justification: for $My = V^{-}y$, as $Vy\; My = Vy\; V^{-}y$ is a projection matrix onto Sy, then $Iu[Ny] = 1$ for any line Δu belonging to Sy, moreover as M is with relationship effect for $(\mathcal{E}\,x, \mathcal{E}\,y)$ thus the "shape" of $Px[Ny]$ mainly depends on the relationships between variables $[x_j]$ and $[y_k]$.

2.3 Dissymmetrical Association Indices

Classical dissymmetrical association indices (Goodman and Kruskal (1954); Stewart and Love (1968)), from variables $[x_j]$ to $[y_k]$, can be defined in a geometrical way by: $\sum \|Qx(y_k)\|^2 \;/\; \sum \|y_k\|^2$.

Property 4: $\sum \|Qx(y_k)\|^2 = \text{Tr}[Vxy\; Vyx\; V^{-}x]$

Proof:

$$\begin{aligned}
\sum \|Qx(y_k)\|^2 &= \sum D\,[Qx(y_k), Qx(y_k)] \\
&= \sum D\,[Qx(y_k), y_k] \\
&= \text{Tr}[Y'\,D\,Qx\,Y] \\
&= \text{Tr}[Y'\,D\,X\,V^{-}x\;X'\,D\,Y] \\
&= \text{Tr}[Vyx\;V^{-}x\;Vxy].
\end{aligned}$$

As $\sum \|y_k\|^2 = \text{Tr}[Vy] = Iy[Ny]$ for $My = \text{Id}_q$, where Id_q is the q-dimensional identity matrix, properties 1 and 4 imply:

Property 5: If M is with relationship effect for $(\mathcal{E}\,x, \mathcal{E}\,y)$ and if Mx is of full rank or $Mx = V^{+}x$ or $Mx = Vx$ and if $My = \text{Id}_q$ then $Ix[Ny] \;/\; Iy[Ny] = \sum \|Qx(y_k)\|^2 \;/\; \sum \|y_k\|^2$.

That leads to the following general definition:

Definition 3: Given M with relationship effect for $(\mathcal{E}\,x, \mathcal{E}\,y)$, Dissymmetrical Relationship Association Coefficients from $[x_j]$ to $[y_k]$ are defined by

$$\text{CARDS}[x \rightarrow y/Mx, \text{Id}_q] = Ix[Ny] \;/\; Iy[Ny].$$

Consequently following association indices are CARDS:

- "Goodman and Kruskal's tau" (1954), for two categorical variables,

- "Steward and Love's association" (1968) for two sets of quantitative variables.

$[x_j]$ being quantitative variables and $[y_k]$ C.D.V., thus it is natural to propose the $\mathrm{CARDS}[y \to x/My, \mathrm{Id}_p]$ for measuring dissymmetrical association from the factor y to the observed variables $[x_j]$ in a MANOVA environment. Note that $Mx = \mathrm{Id}_p$ corresponds to classical dissymmetrical association indices, but other choices for Mx, more or less near to $V^{-}x$, would provide more or less dissymmetrical association indices.

3 Principal Clusters

In this section, $[y_k]$ are C.D.V. associated to an unknown partition.

Definition 4: Given Mx and My, $[y_k]$ are C.D.V. of Principal Clusters of $[x_j]$ if

$$\mathrm{CARDS}[y \to x/My, Mx] = \max_{(s)} \mathrm{CARDS}[s \to x/Ms, Mx].$$

This criterium is similar to the one used to define the first axis in Principal Component Analysis. Note that it does not depend on the choice of My, so one may decide $My = \mathrm{Id}_q$, but we suggest to take $My = \chi^2_y$ in order to get a simple expression of Mxy. The degree of dissymmetry will depend on Mx: in our application (section 5) $Mx = \mathrm{Id}_p$ (Schektman (1984)). Now, no analytical solution has been pointed out, so we propose an iterative algorithm described in section 4.

Evolving Principal Clusters (EPC) are useful when one wants to simulate, on the same population of individuals, the evolution from Principal Clusters of variables $[x_j]$ to Principal Clusters of variables $[z_l]$.

Definition 5: Given Mx, My and Mz, for a fixed $a \in [0, 1], [y_k]$ are C.D.V. of Evolving Principal Clusters from $[x_j]$ to $[z_l]$, if

$$(1-a)\ \mathrm{CARDS}[y \to x/My, Mx] + a\ \mathrm{CARDS}[y \to z/My, Mz] \text{ is MAXIMUM.}$$

According to this criterium, EPC summarizes as well as possible the data arrays X and Z with respect to the value of a. In a different way, if we wish to approach a given theoretical partition $[z]$, as well as possible with respect to the data array X, then it may be better to use the following criterium:

$$(1-a)\ \mathrm{CARDS}[x \to y/Mx, My] + a\ \mathrm{CARDS}[y \to z/My, Mz] \quad \text{is MAXIMUM.}$$

4 Algorithm

A transfer algorithm is used to maximize the preceeding criteria. The program is written in B.M.A.D. (Schektman and al (1987)). Individuals are examined sequentially. At each loop of the algorithm:

(i) for each individual i ($i = 1, \dots, n$) and for each cluster k ($k = 1, \dots, q$) the individual i is virtually tranferred into cluster k and the criterium is calculated,

(ii) at the end ($i = n, k = q$), for a given percentage of individuals, among the better according to the criterium increase, we decide to do tranfers.

The iterative process stops when no increase of criterium is observed.

The following property simplifies the program. Let $[uy_k]$ be the uncentered D.V. associated to the centered D.V. $[y_k]$ and $R\mathcal{E}uy$ be the restriction to the subspace $\mathcal{E}uy$, property 6 shows that one may handle $[uy_k]$ instead of $[y_k]$.

Property 6: If M is with relationship effect and if $My = Muy = \chi_y^2$ then $Vxuy = Vxy$, $Mxuy = Mxy$, $R\mathcal{E}uy[Px] = R\mathcal{E}y[Px]$, $R\mathcal{E}x[Puy] = R\mathcal{E}x[Py]$.

Proof:

- $Q1_n$ is the orthogonal projection onto the line spanned by $(1,\ldots,1)' \in \mathbb{R}^n$, $Vxuy = X'\,D\,UY = [(Id_n - Q1_n)\,X]'D\,UY = X'\,D(\mathrm{Id}_n - Q1_n)\,UY = X'\,D\,Y = Vxy$.
- As $My = \chi_y^2 = V^{-1}uy = Muy$ then $Vxuy\,Muy\,[(Vuy\,Muy)^{1/2}]^+ = Vxy\,My$ thus $Mxuy = Mxy$.
- $R\mathcal{E}uy[Px] = \mathrm{In}x\;M^+x\;\mathrm{In}x'\;M\;\mathrm{In}uy = \mathrm{In}x\;M^+x\;Mxuy = \mathrm{In}x\;M^+x\;Mxy = R\mathcal{E}y[Px]$.
- $R\mathcal{E}x[Puy] = \mathrm{In}uy\,Vuy\,Muyx = \mathrm{In}y\,M^+y\,Myx = R\mathcal{E}x[Py]$.

5 Management Monitoring of CCAS Restaurants

Numerical and graphical results given below concerned application of Evolving Principal Clusters to a subset of 41 CCAS restaurants. Each is characterized by the following five ratios (variables), calculated during a period of 12 months: wages (WAG), food (FOO), sundry (SUN), receipt (REC), deficit (DEF). In this application, elements of $X(41,5)$ and $Z(41,5)$ are ratios corresponding to two successive periods: [april 1984 – march 1985] and [april 1985 – march 1986].

In figure 1, restaurants are represented on the first principal plane of (X, Id_5) , the first digit of each restaurant number is equal to principal cluster number provided by the algorithm for $q = 4$ and $Mx = Id_5$.

In table 1, integers represent the cluster numbers ($k = 1,\ldots,4$) and "-->" indicates, for each value of a, the real transfer for the restaurant identifies on the first row. The only restaurants that move are in it.

These results (figure 1, table 1) and other classical statistics bring to the manager knowledges on the "health" of his institutions during a given period. In table 1, the arrows may be interpreted as a warning. Let us consider restaurant 110 for example, it is transferred ($a = .75$) from cluster 1 (1984–85) to cluster 3 (1985–86): in this case, we clearly observed a bad evolution for this restaurant on the data (table 2) .

A friendly program running on compatible IBM-PC provides:

(i) dynamic graphics to follow the evolution of institutions,

(ii) all statistics on the restaurants to monitor,

(iii) many graphical facilities (identification, location, characteristics of restaurants or clusters, moving or deleting elementary piece of a graphic, ...).

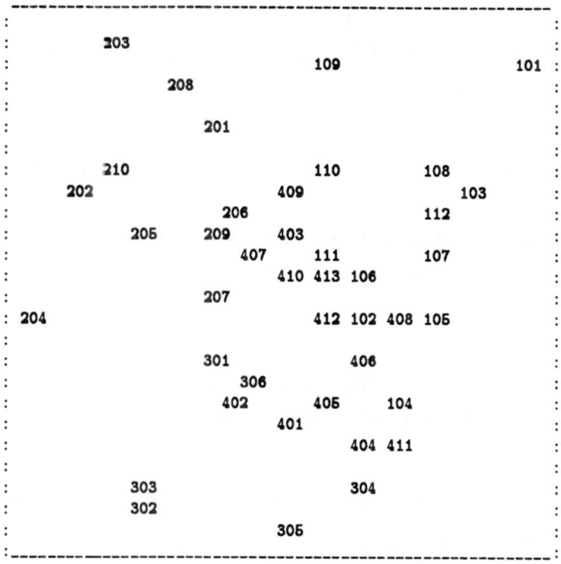

Figure 1: Principal Clusters (1984–1985)

102	1	1	1	1	1	--> 3	3	3
105	1	--> 4	4	4	4	4	4	4
106	1	--> 4	4	4	4	4	4	--> 3
107	1	1	1	1	--> 4	--> 1	1	1
109	1	1	1	1	1	1	1	--> 2
110	1	1	1	1	1	1	--> 3	3
201	2	2	--> 4	4	4	4	4	4
206	2	2	--> 4	4	4	4	4	4
207	2	2	2	--> 3	3	3	3	3
209	2	2	2	--> 3	3	3	3	3
302	3	3	3	3	3	3	--> 2	2
401	4	4	--> 3	3	3	3	3	3
402	4	4	4	--> 3	3	3	--> 2	2
403	4	--> 2	2	2	2	2	2	2
404	4	4	4	4	--> 3	3	3	3
405	4	--> 2	2	--> 3	3	3	3	3
406	4	4	4	4	4	--> 1	1	1
407	4	4	4	4	4	4	--> 2	2
408	4	4	4	4	--> 1	1	1	1
a	.0	.2	.3	.4	.6	.7	.75	1

Table 1: Evolving Principal Clusters

	WAG	FOO	SUN	REC	DEF
1984–1985	24.33	10.07	0.90	15.71	19.59
1985–1986	32.02	11.71	1.77	18.69	26.81

Table 2: Values of ratios for restaurant 110.

Note that this management monitoring may be improved by getting data on shorter periods, every three months for example instead of every year.

References

Croquette A (1980) Quelques Resultats Synthetiques en Analyse de Donnees Multidimensionnelles: Optimalite et Metriques a Effets Relationnels. These de 3eme cycle, Universite Paul SABATIER (U.P.S.), Toulouse

Fabre C (1986) Contribution a la Protection des Methodes Relationnelles. These de 3eme cycle, U.P.S.

Goodman LA, Kruskal WH (1954) Measures of Association for Cross Classifications. J.A.S.A. 49: 732–764

Grau D (1983) Mesures des Effets Relationnels, Applications. These de 3eme cycle, U.P.S.

Ibrahim A (1982) Quelques Applications des Analyses en Composantes Principales sous Contraintes et des Metriques a Effets Relationnels en Analyse des Donnees. These de 3eme cycle, U.P.S.

Ibrahim A, Schektman Y (1986) Principal Cluster Analyses, in: Gaul W, Schader M (eds.) Classification as a Tool of Research, Elsever Science Publisher B.V., North Holland, pp 217–223

Schektman Y (1978) Contribution a la Mesure en Facteurs dans les Sciences Experimentales et a la Mise en Oeuvre des Calculs Statistiques. These de doctorat d'Etat, U.P.S.

Schektman Y, Ibrahim A, Barouin L (1986) Quelques Applications des Analyses en Partitions Principales. Journees Francophones de l'A.S.U. (Lille): 4

Schektman Y, Jockin J, Vielle D, Hamad A, Sadeg B (1987) Bibliotheque Mathematique pour l'Analyse de Donnees (B.M.A.D.). Resume des Communications XIX, J.F.A.S.U., Lausanne

Schektman Y (1983) Quelques Reflexions sur les Metriques: Une Approche Originale pour la Protection des Methodes Relationnelles et l'etude de la Regression Multidimensionnelle. Note Interne, MLAD-UPS

Schektman Y (1984) Metriques et Analyse de Donnees. Quelques Contributions. Communication au 2eme colloque Franco-Sovietique "Statistique et Analyse de Donnees", Paris

Schektman Y (1986) Cours de DEA (Universites Toulouse et Paris Dauphine)

Schektman Y (1987) A General Euclidean Approach for Measuring and Describing Associations between Several Sets of Variables, in: Recent Developments in Clustering and Data Analysis. Proceedings of the 1st French-Japanese Scientific Seminar, Tokyo, pp 31–42

Stewart D, Love W (1968) A General Canonical Correlation Index. Psychol. Bull. 70

The Importance of Unidimensional Unfolding for Marketing Research

W. H. van Schuur
Faculty of Social Sciences, University of Groningen
Oude Boteringestraat 23, 9712 GC Groningen, The Netherlands

Summary

Unfolding has been neglected as a data reduction technique, especially for Likert-type rating scales. Reason for this neglect are given and the relationship between unfolding and factor analysis is briefly discussed. A new unfolding model is proposed, based on the analysis of dichotomous items. (Partial) rank orders of preference can be used as 'pick k/n' data and Likert-type rating scales as 'pick any/n' data. Criteria for unidimensional unfoldability are derived from ordered triples of stimuli. These criteria are used in exploratory or confirmatory procedures. Both procedures have been applied to Green and Rao's breakfast food items. For twelve of the fifteen items a good fitting unidimensional unfolding scale is found. Reasons for lack of representability of the remaining items are discussed.

Introduction

The unfolding model, as developed by Coombs (1950, 1964) for analyzing preference data, received considerable attention in its early stages from researchers in the area of marketing (e.g., Green and Carmone (1970); Green and Rao (1972)). And still today, new developments in unfolding analysis often have a marketing origin (e.g., DeSarbo and Rao (1984), DeSarbo and Hoffman (1986), Böckenholt and Gaul (1986)).

Whenever the unfolding model is appropriate for modeling preference data, full rank orders of preference obtained from a set of subjects for a fixed set of stimuli can be represented in a space with one or few dimensions. Scale values for stimuli and subjects are found in such a way that the order of distances between a subject-point and each of the stimulus-points from small to large reflects the order of preference for the stimuli by the subject from high to low. The dimensions of this space will be interpreted as the criteria for preference. The scale values assigned to a subject are the positions on the dimensions for which the subject has the highest preference.

Subject scale values can be regarded as measurements of subjects along new variables, which in turn can be used either as dependent or independent variables for explanatory purposes. In this respect unfolding can be regarded as a special kind of a data reduction technique analogous to, but distinct from, factor analysis or cumulative scale analysis. However, unfolding is often used only as the end stage of analyzing preferences, with the purpose of finding target groups of subjects with certain values on the latent dimensions. Most applications of unfolding do not emphasize its potential as a data reduction, for a number of reasons. Further, unfolding is rarely used to analyze preferences collected in the form of Likert-type rating scales. Many applied empirical researchers seem to believe that unfolding is not necessary as a technique for data analysis or data reduction, because factor analysis is sufficient for this purpose.

In this chapter I outline some of the reasons why unfolding has been neglected as a data reduction technique, and propose a new unfolding model that overcomes previous problems. In addition, I argue that the view that unfolding is unnecessary, given factor analysis, is mistaken. To illustrate how the model works, I apply it to a classical dataset in marketing research: Green and Rao's (1972) breakfast food items. I will show that, even though the full dataset can not be well represented as a unidimensional unfolding scale, a well-fitting unfolding scale of 12 items can be found, and there are several plausible reasons for the poor fit of the other items.

1 Problems in Some Widely Used Unfolding Models

In applying a number of widely used unfolding models (e.g., MINIRSA, Roskam (1968); KYST, Kruskal et al. (1973), ALSCAL, Takane et al. (1977)) the following problems are often encountered:

1. The number of subjects that can be processed is limited, which makes unfolding unfeasible for the analysis of large data sets.

2. Input data are required to consist of full rank orders of preference; information about metric distances between subjects and stimuli is even better. This requirement makes unfolding unfeasable for many types of data. Most datasets in marketing consist of answers to easy questions, with only a few response categories, which do not demand too much of the subjects. Such data often contain ties, which in unfolding analyses tend to lead to insufficiently specified and sometimes degenerated results.

3. Certain assumptions are overly strict. All unfolding models can be regarded as giving other answers to the question: why does a simple, perfectly deterministic unidimensional unfolding scale not apply to the data at hand? Unfolding analysis often does not give satisfactory results because the data do not fully satisfy the assumptions of the deterministic model. One way to overcome this problem is to use a probabilistic unfolding model. Even though several such models have been proposed (e.g., DeSarbo, DeSoete and Jedidi (1987)), they have not been widely applied because sometimes the data must contain a type of information that is even more difficult to obtain than full rank orders of preference: probabilities that a subject prefers one stimulus over another. Another problem is that some probabilistic models incorporate rather unrealistic assumptions (see Jansen (1983), for discussion). Nevertheless, the concept of a probabilistic unfolding model is worthwhile, and is used in the approach to be presented in this paper.

A second way to deal with problems when the data do not fully meet the assumptions of the model is to argue that some of these assumptions may be unreasonably strict. One assumption that is arguably too strict is the specification that all subjects agree in their perception of the metric positions of the stimuli along the dimensions. Social psychological literature from the sixties (see Davison (1979) for a brief overview) indicates that subjects are able to make relatively fine discriminations in the area around their own 'ideal' position, but tend to make coarser and more stereotypical discriminations among stimuli that are farther away. If subjects differ in their 'ideal' position, then they will not agree on the metric position of all stimuli along the continuum, although they may still agree about their order along that continuum. For practical applications, therefore, finding a qualitative J-scale rather than a metric one—also known as 'ordination' or 'seriation'—may, from a substantive point of view, be the best we can hope for.

A second assumption of most multidimensional unfolding models that may be too strict is that, if subjects use more than one criterion in making preference judgments about a set of stimuli, they use these criteria simultaneously and independently, rather than in an hierarchical order. The possibility that subjects use different criteria for different stimuli, or the same criteria in an hierarchical way, has been mentioned by Coombs (1964) in his 'Portfolio Model' and by Tversky (1972) in his 'Elimination By Aspects' model, respectively.

Related to the assumption about using all criteria for preference simultaneously is the assumption that subjects are able to make valid preference judgments about all stimuli, irrespective of how much the stimuli are known and liked. Subjects who do not know certain stimuli well, or who are indifferent about them, may violate the unfolding model when they are required to make judgments about them. A proposed solution to this problem is to not use full rank orders of preference, but rather dichotomous data, in which the most preferred stimuli are dichotomously distinguished from the remaining ones.

Another assumption is that the unfolding model is valid for all subjects and all stimuli in the data. But some subjects may use entirely different criteria, or may respond randomly, and some stimuli may be unknown to some subjects, or may be confused with other stimuli. A strategy for overcoming these difficulties is to find an unfolding scale for only a subset of subjects, or for only a subset of stimuli. Obviously, if all subjects and all stimuli are hypothesized to be representable along the same unfolding scale, then the researcher should try to find plausible explanations for the (unexpected) nonrepresentability of stimuli or subjects that do not form part of the final unfolding scale.

Unfolding models that aim at representing all subjects and all stimuli of a dataset, and that do not indicate which subjects or stimuli fit poorly, generally resort to representations in more than one dimension. But a representation of only a subset of stimuli or a subset of subjects in one dimension is more parsimonious and generally easier to interpret than a multidimensional solution. An additional advantage of a unidimensional solution is that there are no problems in interpreting the best rotation of the dimensions in the space, since the problem of rotational invariance does not apply in one dimension.

2 Unfolding and Factor Analysis

Apart from problems that arise in trying to carry out unfolding analyses, the possible advantages of unfolding over other data reduction techniques are not always clear to the applied researcher. In particular, the difference between unfolding and factor analysis is not always sufficiently appreciated. Several mathematical psychologists (e.g., Coombs and Kao (1960); Coombs (1964), Ross and Cliff (1964), Davison (1977)) have pointed out that a factor analysis of data that conform to an unfolding model artificially leads to one factor (or dimension) too many, but this warning does not seem to have been attended to in the more applied literature.

One major reason for this neglect is that unfolding has always been associated with the data collection technique of eliciting full rank orders of preference, whereas factor analysis has been associated with the use of Likert-type rating scales. Nevertheless, Likert-type rating scales may conform to the unfolding model as well. For example, we may ask subjects to rank order cups of tea with different amounts of sugar in terms of preference, and find an unfolding scale with an underlying 'amount of sugar' dimension. But we could just as well ask whether subjects like each of these cups of tea (1) very well (2) somewhat (3) neutral (4) not much (5) not at all. These answers could also be represented on the same unfolding dimension. The reason in practice that Likert-type rating scales are rarely subjected to an unfolding analysis is that, as mentioned above, such data usually contain many ties, and thus lead to insufficiently specified and degenerate results. This means that many different representations can be found that all have a good fit, which makes the actual representation useless.

3 A New Unfolding Model

The problems outlined above about the usefulness of the unfolding model are often not solved by making the model more complicated, for instance by inserting individual weight values for dimensions, or by rotating dimensions idiosyncratically, as in the PREFMAP-model (Carroll (1972)). Rather, we need to find ways to simplify the model and make it more accessible to the daily demands of empirical research. The unfolding model I propose is a combination of some of the strategies discussed above. It will find an unfolding representation of a maximal subset of stimuli and an unlimited number of subjects in one dimension on the basis of dichotomous or dichotomized data, using a probabilistic model. Dichotomous data are used rather than 'rank' data for two reasons. When the number of preferred stimuli compared to the total number of stimuli is small (e.g., 3 out of 10), the difference in information content between an 'pick $3/n$' analysis and a 'rank $3/n$' analysis is small, and the most reliable information is likely to be contained in the first few most preferred stimuli. Moreover, the use of dichotomous data makes this model also applicable to data that have not been collected as 'rank' data. A documented computer program called MUDFOLD, for Multiple UniDimensional unFOLDing, is available to perform the necessary calculations.

3.1 Dichotomous Data and the Concept of 'Error'

The method proposed here has been described in Van Schuur (1984, 1987a). Its basic principles are as follows. The data used are either already dichotomous or made dichotomous by changing each response pattern into (most) preferred (1) and not (or least) preferred (0) responses. In this respect the model is similar to those of Leik and Matthews (1968), Coombs and Smith (1973), Davison (1980), Andrich (1984), and DeSarbo and Hoffman (1986). However, a well-fitting representation is defined differently than these other models. If the responses can be represented in an unfolding scale, then all 'positive' (1) responses should only be for the stimuli closest to each subject's ideal point and therefore only to adjacent stimuli. An unfolding representation is falsified if two nonadjacent stimuli are both 'picked' as preferred, while one or more intermediate stimuli are not 'picked'. More concretely, if three stimuli—A, B, and C—are hypothesized to form an unfolding scale in this order, then a subject who prefers A and C should also prefer B. If he does not, his response pattern is said to contain an 'error' for the proposed unfolding scale.

If subjects must judge more than three stimuli, the number of errors in their response patterns, relative to any proposed unfolding order of the stimuli, is defined as the number of triples in that response pattern that contain an 'error'. For instance, if the following four stimuli—A, B, C, and D— are hypothesized to form an unfolding scale in this order, then the response pattern ($ABCD$, 1010)—in which stimuli A and C are 'picked' and stimuli B and D are not 'picked'—contains one error, since only the triple ABC contains an error, but the triples ABD, ACD, and BCD do not. On the other hand, the response pattern ($ABCD$,1011) contains two errors, since not only does triple ABC contain an error, but also triple ABD.

The number of errors in a dataset, relative to any candidate unfolding scale, is defined as the sum of the number of errors over all subjects' response patterns. Since the number of errors in each response pattern is defined in terms of all triples of stimuli, the number of errors in the dataset can also be defined as the number of times each triple of stimuli contains an error, summed over all triples. This makes it possible to evaluate how much any individual stimulus contributes to the overall amount of error by calculating the number of errors for each individual stimulus in terms of the number of errors in the triples that contain that stimulus. For instance, the number of errors in stimulus A in an unfolding scale $ABCD$ can be regarded as the sum of the errors in the triples ABC, ABD and ACD.

3.2 Goodness of Fit

The goodness-of-fit of a scale solution in the present model does not depend directly on the absolute number of errors observed in the scale. Rather, as in Mokken's nonparametric cumulative scale analysis, (Mokken (1971); Mokken and Lewis (1982)), goodness of fit depends on the *relative* amount of error, where the amount of error observed is compared to the amount of error we could expect if subjects' preference judgments for different stimuli were statistically independent.

The determination of the number of errors expected for a triple of stimuli under statistical independence depends on the data collection procedure. In the case of 'pick any/n' data, a subject can mention as many or as few stimuli as he likes as (most) preferred. Data can be dichotomized to conform to this pattern even when subjects have been asked to use thermometer-type scales (e.g., 9-point rating scales), or Likert-type rating scales by specifying a 'cutoff' point between preferred and not preferred alternatives (e.g., between the values 7 and 8 on a 9-point scale, or between the values 1 and 2 on a 4-point scale). For data of this type the expected number of errors for each triple of stimuli in a given permutation (e.g., for the scale ABC) is $Np(A)\{1-p(B)\}p(C)$, where N is the number of subjects in the total sample and $p(A)$ is the relative frequency with which stimulus A is 'picked' as preferred.

In the case of 'pick k/n' data, each subject mentions the same number of stimuli as preferred out of a given set of n stimuli. The researcher can transform data into this pattern even when subjects have been asked to give full or partial rank orders of preference by coding the k highest preferred stimuli as 'preferred' and the remaining stimuli as 'not preferred'. For this kind of data the preference judgments for the different stimuli are not independent, which means that it is more complicated to calculate the expected number of errors under statistical independence. The procedure is as follows:

For pick $3/n$ data the expected number of errors is calculated by first determining the frequency with which each triple of stimuli would have been chosen under the assumption of statistical independence, where the marginal popularity of each stimulus is taken into account. These frequencies are found by applying the 3-way quasi-independence model known from the loglinear literature (e.g., Bishop et al. (1975)).

The expected frequency of errors for a given triple in a given permutation can now be regarded as the sum of those triples that contain the two outer stimuli plus every stimulus other than the middle one of the triple under consideration. For instance, given five stimuli A, B, C, D, and E, the expected frequency of errors for the triple ABC consists of the sum of the expected frequencies of the triples that contain stimuli A and C, and a third stimulus which is not stimulus B: $ACD + ACE$.

An analogous procedure can be used for each value of k in 'pick k/n' between 2 and $n-2$: first the expected frequency of each k-tuple is calculated using the k-way quasi-independence model; the expected error frequency of a given triple of stimuli in a given permutation is the sum of all k-tuples that contain the two outer stimuli plus all $(k-3)$-tuples of remaining stimuli, except those that contain the middle stimulus of the triple under consideration. Discussions of this procedure can be found in Van Schuur and Molenaar (1982) and Van Schuur (1984).

3.3 Constructing an Unfolding Scale on the Basis of Information About All Triples.

In contrast to a cumulative scale, where the order of the stimuli along an underlying dimension can be determined by the marginal popularity of the stimuli, it is not *a priori* possible to determine the order of the stimuli along an unfolding scale. In principle all permutations of all subsets of stimuli might be investigated to find out whether they conform to an unfolding scale. Rather than following this time-consuming procedure, which is also vulnerable to capitalization on chance, I have adopted a search procedure analogous to Mokken's procedure for nonparametric cumulative scaling. This can be regarded as a 'bottom-up' clustering procedure: it begins with a search for the 'best' smallest unfolding scale, and then adds in new stimuli to the existing scale as long as the criteria for scalability are still satisfied.

The major criteria for scalability in the search procedure make reference to a coefficient of homogeneity, H, which is analogous to Loevinger's (1948) coefficient of homogeneity for a cumulative scale: $H = 1 - O/E$, where O is the frequency of errors observed and E is the frequency of errors expected under statistical independence. This coefficient H can be used to assess the unfoldability of a set of stimuli as one unfolding scale; additionally, if O and E are appropriately redefined, it can also be used to assess the scalability of each individual stimulus, and also of each triple of stimuli in each of its three different permutations. Perfect unfoldability is obtained when $H = 1$; conversely, the hypothesis of statistical independence of the data cannot be rejected if $H = 0$. A minimum requirement for unfoldability is that all the relevant $H(ijk)$-values are positive. Note that a reflexion of a permutation of a triple of stimuli does not change the amount of error in that permutation. This is because an unfolding scale may just as well run from 'left' to 'right' as from 'right' to 'left'. The only thing that is reversed is the order in which the stimuli in the scale are interpreted.

Since the amount of error for the scale as a whole depends on the amount of error in each triple, and since the amount of error of each stimulus depends on the amont of error in each triple containing that stimulus, the first step is to determine the amount of error observed and the amount of error expected for each triple in each of its three different permutations. This information is collected in the 'H-matrix'. On the basis of the information in the H-matrix we can distinguish four types of triples:

1. Unique triples, which have a positive $H(ijk)$-value in only one of their three different permutations. These triples are unfoldable in only one order, and are therefore important for determining the 'best' smallest unfolding scale.

2. Positive triples, which have a positive $H(ijk)$-value in all three permutations. Such triples generally consist of stimuli that are far apart on the underlying unfolding dimension.

3. Dual triples, which have two positive and one negative $H(ijk)$-value.

4. Negative triples, which have a negative $H(ijk)$-value in all three permutations. Such triples violate the assumption of an unfolding scale: it is impossible to represent all three stimuli of a negative triple in the same unfolding scale.

The first criterion formulated for a candidate unfolding scale is that all triples in the scale in their scale order must have a positive coefficient of homogeneity $H(ijk)$. The second criterion is that all the stimuli in the candidate scale must have a positive coefficient of scalability that is larger than some user-set lower boundary larger than zero. This is necessary if we want to be able to interpret our scale, once we have found one that has only positive coefficients of homogeneity, since small positive numbers in the sample need not be significantly larger than 0 in the population. As a rule of thumb, a lower boundary of 0.30 is generally maintained. Mokken also suggests this boundary for his cumulative scaling procedure. The requirement that all stimuli have a coefficient of homogeneity higher than a given lower boundary insures that the scale as a whole will also have a coefficient of homogeneity higher than this lower boundary.

The search procedure for an unfolding scale consists of two steps:

1. Either find the best elementary unfolding scale, which is a scale that consists of three stimuli, or begin with a user-selected startset of stimuli in a specified order.

2. Successively find the best additional stimuli for the scale. In both cases the two criteria for scalability described above must be satisfied. If a user-selected startset contains triples with a negative $H(ijk)$-value, these triples will be flagged by the computer program MUDFOLD.

In addition, since the order of the stimuli along the unfolding dimension has to be derived as a result of the unfolding procedure, the order in which the stimuli can be represented as an unfolding scale should ideally be unique. This latter specification constrains us to look only at the unique triples in our search for the best elementary unfolding scale. The best elementary unfolding scale is defined as that unique triple for which the sum of frequencies of the perfect patterns with two or three items 'picked' is highest. For instance, the triple ABC is the best elementary unfolding scale if $H(ABC) > 0.30$; $H(BAC)$ and $H(ACB) < 0$, and the sum of the frequencies of admissible response patterns in which two or three of the stimuli are 'picked—$ABC(110) + ABC(011) + ABC(111)$—is higher than the comparable sum of the frequencies of all other unique triples with a positive H-value > 0.30. High H-values may also occur among unique triples containing only unpopular stimuli. A scale begun with such a triple will not be useful in discriminating among subjects, since there may be too many subjects who do not select any of the stimuli of the best triple. Note that the best triple therefore does not necessarily have the highest H-value.

An additional stimulus is a candidate for addition to an existing unfolding scale if the H-values of all the triples containing the new stimulus and all pairs of stimuli in the existing unfolding scale are positive, and if the H-value of the new stimulus is larger than the user-specified lower boundary (e.g., 0.30). A new stimulus that conforms to these requirements, but that can be represented in the existing scale in two or more positions that are not adjacent, will not be added to the scale. Ideally, one would like to insist on a unique ordering of *all* stimuli in an unfolding scale. In practical applications, however, this requirement appears to be too strict and leads to rather short scales. Therefore, the computer program accepts stimuli that can be represented in adjacent positions in an existing scale (e.g., stimulus D in scale ABC forming either scale $ADBC$ or scale $ABDC$) in whichever position gives the highest H-value for the scale as a whole. If two or more candidate stimuli differ in the number of adjacent positions in which they can be added to the scale, the stimulus that can be added in the fewest positions will be selected. For instance, if scale ABC can be extended with stimulus D, making either scales $ADBC$ or $ABDC$, or with stimulus E, making either scales $EABC$, $AEBC$ or $ABEC$, stimulus D is selected rather than stimulus E, regardless of the size of the H-values of the resulting scale. The choice between scale $ADBC$ and $ABDC$ does depend on the H-value of the scale, however. If no additional stimulus can be added to an existing unfolding scale because one or more $H(ijk)$-values containing the additional stimulus is negative, or because its $H(i)$-value is lower than the user-set lower boundary, then the existing scale is the maximal subset of unfoldable stimuli.

Since the stimuli that are not representable in the initial unfolding scale may still form (part of) a second unfolding scale, the search procedure can be applied again to the remaining stimuli. Because more than one unidimensional unfolding scale can thus be found among a set of items, this procedure is called 'multiple unidimensional scaling'.

3.4 Additional Criteria for Goodness of Fit

Besides the criteria for scalability involving the homogeneity coefficients, two other criteria for the unfoldability of a set of p stimuli are implemented. These are the visual inspection of the dominance matrix and the adjacency matrix, respectively. The dominance matrix for a candidate scale is a square matrix of order $p \times p$ containing information about each pair of stimuli, in which rows and columns represent the stimuli in their unfoldable order. In this matrix each off-diagonal cell (i, j) gives the frequency with which the row stimulus i is 'picked' but the column stimulus j is not 'picked',—in other words, the frequency with which stimulus i dominates stimulus j. According to the unfolding model, the probability that for a pair of stimuli one stimulus dominates the other increases with the distance between these stimuli. The dominance matrix for perfectly unfoldable data therefore gives a pattern of characteristic monotonicity in which for each row the values decrease from the left to the diagonal, and increase from the diagonal to the right. This pattern should be (closely) approximated in the dominance matrix of the scale under evaluation.

In an adjacency matrix of order $p \times p$, each cell (i, j) indicates the frequency with which row stimulus i and column stimulus j are both 'picked'. According to the unfolding model, the probability that both members of a pair of stimuli are picked should decrease as the distance between the stimuli increases. The symmetric adjacency matrix should therefore show a simplex pattern: cell frequencies should decrease from the diagonal to the left and from the diagonal downwards.

3.5 Scale Values for Stimuli and Subjects

If we have found a maximum subset of stimuli that forms an unfolding scale, we can assign scale values to subjects. This is not part of the MUDFOLD program, but it can be done with any data management program. The scale value of a stimulus is defined as the rank number of that stimulus in the unfolding scale. The scale value of a subject is defined as the mean value of the scale values of the stimuli (s)he picks. A subject who has not picked any of the stimuli in the scale does not get a scale value, and is regarded as a missing datum. All other subjects receive a scale value, independent of the number of errors in their response pattern or the number of stimuli they picked.

4 A Marketing Application of Unidimensional Unfolding: Breakfast Food Items

Green and Rao (1972) tried to show the applicability of unfolding to the analysis of full rank orders of preferences for fifteen different breakfast food items by 42 subjects (21 student couples). The items were (in the order in which they were presented): Toast pop-up (TP) —Buttered toast (BT) — English muffin and margarine (EMM) — Jelly donut (JD) — Cinnamon toast (CT) — Blueberry muffin and margarine (BMM) — Hard rolls and butter (HRB) — Toast and marmalade (TMd) — Buttered toast and jelly (BTJ) — Toast and margarine (TMn) — Cinnamon bun (CB) — Danish pastry (DP) — Glazed donut (GD) —Coffee cake (CC) — Corn muffin and butter (CMB). The stimulus set and respondent group were chosen mainly for convenience. Although Green and Rao discuss a number of substantive questions, their primary motivation was methodological (Green and Rao (1972, p. 3)). ·

Green and Rao were not very successful in finding a well-fitting representation of their dataset: "...the stress values are so poor as to limit severely any attempt at interpretation" (p. 89). They decided on a two-dimensional representation, which they tentatively interpreted as a type of sweetness dimension and as a toast/nontoast dimension based on the extent of required preparation.

I have reanalyzed this same dataset with the proposed unfolding procedure, using the MUDFOLD program. Even though it is not possible in this procedure to find a two-dimensional representation, it will be possible to compare my results with those of Green and Rao.

4.1 Application of the Search Procedure to Pick 3/15 – Pick 6/15 Data

The full rank orders of preference of the 42 subjects can be dichotomized in different ways by the researcher, who can specify which value of k (in 'pick k/n') differentiates the most preferred from the least preferred stimuli. I have chosen four different values of k: 3, 4, 5, and 6. This allows me to show some specific possibilities and problems with this approach. I did not use $k = 2$ because the number of subjects is very small and the scaling procedure then becomes vulnerable to incidental outliers in the data. The value of n is fixed at 15.

In a perfect unfolding scale, scaling procedures for different values of k ought to lead to the same result, irrespective of the value of k. This is not the case for this dataset, unfortunately. All four analyses (for $k = 3, 4, 5$, or 6) lead to two unfolding scales of subsets of the items, but the subsets are different, and so is the order of some of the stimuli along the scales:

	scale 1	scale 2
pick 3/15:	CT-EMM-CC-DP-TP (H=1.00)	BMM-CMB-BT-HRB-TMd-GD-JD (H=0.81)
pick 4/15:	TMn-BT-EMM-CMB-CC-DP-CB-TP (H=0.82)	CT-BTJ-TMd-JD-GD-BMM (H=0.60)
pick 5/15:	HRB-EMM-BMM-CC-DP-GD-CB-JD-TP (H=0.61)	CT-BTJ-BT-TMn (H=0.42)
pick 6/15:	HRB-BT-EMM-BMM-CC-DP-GD-JD (H=0.67)	TMn-TMd-BTJ-CT-CMB-CB(H=0.51)

The major reason for this disappointing result lies in the model's insistence on positive $H(ijk)$-values for each triple of stimuli. With the given small number of subjects (42) and the large number of triples $\{(15 \times 14 \times 13)/6 = 455\}$ the expected error frequency of all triples is small, and for a large number of triples even less than 1. This effectively makes the model a deterministic model, in which one violation leads to rejection of the model, because for many triples an observed error frequency of 1 already leads to a negative $H(ijk)$-value.

4.2 Using the Unfolding Procedure in a Confirmatory Sense

The next step in the analysis therefore was to ignore the negative $H(ijk)$-values temporarily, use the eight scales that we found in the first series of search procedures as startsets, and determine where the remaining stimuli would best fit in the resulting scales. For each of the eight startsets this gives us a final scale with a qualitative ordering of all fifteen items along an unfolding dimension. For each of these scales we get:

a) a list of triples of items with a negative $H(ijk)$-value;
b) the $H(i)$-values for each of the fifteen items;
c) the H-value;
d) the dominance matrix;
e) the adjacency matrix.

On the basis of this information the unfolding procedure is now used in a more confirmatory sense: That order of stimuli along one unfolding dimension is now hypothesized that has the smallest number of negative $H(ijk)$-values, the highest $H(i)$- and H-values, and that gives a dominance matrix and an adjacency matrix that corresponds best to the expected characteristic monotony. The unfolding results for this hypothesized order are given in Table I.

It turns out that the stimuli Toast pop-up, Cinnamon Toast, and Corn muffin and butter form part of the majority of triples with a negative $H(ijk)$-value. The adjacency matrices indicates why this is the case: preference for one of these items does not co-occur with preference for only a few other items, adjacent to this item along the unfolding scale, but rather with preference for sets of items that are not themselves adjacent on the unfolding scale. For instance: Cinnamon toast is picked together with other toast items by some subjects, but together with Cinnamon bun, which is not a toast item, by other subjects. This implies that the best representation of Cinnamon Toast is somewhere between the toast items and Cinnamon bun. But there are a number of other items, especially the different muffins, that are also represented between the toast items and Cinnamon bun. This suggests that preference for Cinnamon toast should co-occur with preference for the different muffins, but this is not the case. Toast pop-up and Corn muffin and butter are relatively unpopular items. Toast pop-up is ocasionally preferred, but together with a wide variety of other items, rather than with only a few adjacent items. Although Corn muffin is preferred together with the other muffins, it often happens that English muffin or Blueberry muffin is preferred, but Corn muffin is not, which violates the unfolding hypothesis.

To a lesser extent, violations of the unidimensional unfolding model can also be

Table I: unfolding scale of 15 breakfast food items in one dimension. Items are in their unfoldable order along the J-scale from top to bottom.
$p(i)$: proportion of subjects who picked item i as preferred among 15 items.
$H(i)$: coefficient of scalability for item i in this unfolding scale.

		pick	3/15	pick	4/15	pick	5/15	pick	6/15
		$p(i)$	$H(i)$	$p(i)$	$H(i)$	$p(i)$	$H(i)$	$p(i)$	$H(i)$
TMn	Toast and margarine	.10	.82	.12	.60	.21	.68	.29	.37
TMB	Hard rolls and butter	.14	.78	.21	.50	.26	.49	.29	.46
BT	Buttered toast	.29	.66	.31	.58	.31	.58	.36	.56
TMd	Toast and marmalade	.12	.37	.19	.45	.21	.48	.24	.44
BTJ	Buttered toast and jelly	.17	.43	.26	.48	.29	.49	.36	.44
TP	Toast pop-up	.02	.40	.02	.33	.05	.38	.12	.27
CT	Cinnamon toast	.10	.48	.21	.31	.33	.33	.36	.29
CMB	Corn muffin and butter	.05	.40	.07	.43	.14	.39	.17	.34
EMM	English muffin and margarine	.21	.48	.26	.35	.31	.35	.43	.30
BMM	Blueberry muffin and margarine	.24	.62	.33	.47	.43	.51	.60	.47
CC	Coffee cake	.45	.66	.57	.54	.64	.57	.67	.49
DP	Danish pastry	.52	.41	.52	.48	.60	.43	.67	.35
CB	Cinnamon bun	.19	.39	.24	.48	.40	.66	.50	.48
GD	Glazed donut	.21	.59	.38	.52	.40	.53	.50	.55
JD	Jelly donut	.19	.72	.29	.58	.40	.50	.48	.49
			H=.55		H=.48		H=.49		H=.41
		N=42		N=42		N=42		N=42	

Table II: Unfolding scale of 12 breakfast food items in one dimension. Items are given in their unfoldable order from top to bottom.
$p(i)$: proportion of subjects who picked item i as preferred among 12 items.
$H(i)$: coefficient of scalability for item i.

		pick	3/12	pick	4/12	pick	5/12	pick	6/12
		$p(i)$	$H(i)$	$p(i)$	$H(i)$	$p(i)$	$H(i)$	$p(i)$	$H(i)$
TMn	Toast and margarine	.10	.82	.14	.71	.21	.70	.31	.45
HRB	Hard rolls and butter	.14	.77	.26	.61	.26	.60	.33	.52
BT	Buttered toast	.29	.76	.31	.65	.33	.66	.36	.61
TMd	Toast and marmalade	.14	.46	.19	.48	.24	.50	.31	.44
BTJ	Buttered toast and jelly	.21	.57	.26	.54	.36	.52	.50	.43
EMM	English muffins and margarine	.24	.65	.29	.54	.40	.58	.48	.46
BMM	Blueberry muffins, margarine	.26	.66	.40	.58	.52	.57	.67	.49
CC	Coffee cake	.45	.64	.60	.62	.64	.64	.71	.51
DP	Danish pastry	.52	.48	.52	.53	.64	.55	.71	.36
CB	Cinnamon bun	.19	.47	.31	.55	.43	.69	.60	.43
GD	Glazed donut	.26	.57	.38	.50	.50	.62	.52	.57
JD	Jelly donut	.19	.65	.33	.61	.45	.59	.50	.55
			H=.62		H=.57		H=.60		H=.48
		N=42		N=42		N=42		N=42	
number of negative $H(ijk)$'s:		39		23		12		16	

ascribed to English muffin and to Danish pastry. The problem with Danish pastry is the reverse of the problem with Toast pop-up. Danish pastry is the most popular item, but it is popular not only among subjects who also prefer items close to Danish pastry on the unfolding scale, but also among subjects whose other preferences are for items that are far away. So, whereas Toast pop-up should be represented far away from most other items, Danish pastry should be represented close to most other items.

Deleting a few items from an unfolding scale means that all those subjects who picked one or more of the deleted items have not picked exactly k items out of the remaining 12, and therefore that the expected number of errors calculated for each triple will no longer be correct. After deciding to delete three items from the scale (Toast pop-up, Cinnamon toast, and Corn muffin and butter), we therefore have to assess the scalability of the remaining twelve items again, now in pick 3/12, pick 4/12, pick 5/12, and pick 6/12 analyses, respectively. Since we have a complete rank order of preference from each subject it is possible to distinguish the most preferred stimuli from the remaining ones, even if several stimuli are not incorporated in the analysis. The results of these analyses are shown in Table II.

As an example, the dominance matrix and the adjacency matrix for the pick 5/12 analysis is given in Table III and IV below.

Table III: dominance matrix for pick 5/12 analysis of 12 breakfast foods. In cell (i,j): percentage respondents who mentioned item i, but not item j.

	TMn	HRB	BT	TMd	BTJ	EMM	BMM	CC	DP	CB	GD	JD
TMn	-	7	2	10	7	10	17	21	17	21	19	19
HRB	12	-	7	17	12	10	14	19	19	26	24	24
BT	14	14	-	19	10	12	19	26	26	33	31	29
TMd	12	14	10	-	5	17	19	17	12	21	21	19
BTJ	21	21	12	17	-	19	26	24	21	33	29	26
EMM	29	24	19	33	24	-	12	17	26	33	29	38
BMM	48	40	38	48	43	24	-	14	17	31	29	36
CC	64	57	57	57	52	40	26	-	14	26	24	31
DP	60	57	57	52	50	50	29	14	-	29	26	26
CB	43	43	43	40	40	36	21	5	7	-	10	12
GD	48	48	48	48	43	38	26	10	12	17	-	14
JD	43	43	40	40	36	43	29	12	7	14	10	-

There still are several violations of the expected characteristic monotonicity (e.g., cell EMM-TMd is too high in the dominance matrix — 33 — and too low in the adjacency matrix — 7). Nevertheless, both matrices show the expected monotonicity patterns to a large extent. The number of negative $H(ijk)$-values in the pick 3/12 case is rather high (39). Most negative $H(ijk)$-values can be attributed to triples containing English muffin and margarine or Danish pastry. Still, most of these negative $H(ijk)$-values are based on very small numbers of observed errors: in 18 cases on only 1 observed error, and in another 12 cases on only 2 or 3 observed errors. The number of negative $H(ijk)$'s for analyses with other values of k (4,5,6) is not too high, given that for 12 items a total of 220 triples (12.11.10/6) have to be considered. Reassuringly, the scalability values are rather high, at least compared with applications in the field of political attitudes (Van Schuur (1984)).

Table IV: Adjacency matrix from pick 5/12 analysis of breakfast foods. In cell (i,j): percentage of respondents who mentioned both item i and j.

	TMn	HRB	BT	TMd	BTJ	EMM	BMM	CC	DP	CB	GD	JD
TMn	-											
HRB	14	-										
BT	19	19	-									
TMd	12	10	14	-								
BTJ	14	14	24	19	-							
EMM	12	17	21	7	17	-						
BMM	5	12	14	5	10	29	-					
CC	0	7	7	7	12	24	38	-				
DP	5	7	7	12	14	14	36	50	-			
CB	0	0	0	2	2	7	21	38	36	-		
GD	2	2	2	2	7	12	24	40	38	33	-	
JD	2	2	5	5	10	2	17	33	38	31	36	-

This unfolding scale (see Table II) can be interpreted in terms of the labels used by Green and Rao: toast/non-toast, or non-sweet/sweet, where 'toast' corresponds with 'non-sweet', and 'non-toast' with 'sweet'. There is a remarkable similarity between the results found with the MUDFOLD procedure and the results found by Green and Rao (page 88, Figure 4.3): the order of unfoldable stimuli according to the MUDFOLD scale is represented along a horse shoe in the twodimensional Green and Rao representation. Toast pop-up, the least popular item, is placed far away from the remaining items in their representation. The problems found with Corn muffin and butter do not show in Green and Rao's representation: this item is represented close to English muffin and Blueberry muffin. The representation of Cinnamon toast according to Green and Rao is different from the best possible representation that is found with MUDFOLD.

The horse shoe is well known as a two-dimensional representation of what is essentially a unidimensional structure (e.g., Shepard (1974)); it is therefore less parsimonious than is desirable. It is found mainly for two reasons. First Green and Rao insisted on representing items that seem to violate the assumption of the unfolding model that if two pairs of items (say AB and AC) are both highly preferred then the pair (BC) will also be highly preferred; this assumption can be regarded as an application of the triangular inequality. This problem can be illustrated with the adjacency matrix of Table IV: 17% of the subjects 'pick' HRB and EMM together, and 12% 'pick' EMM and GD together; these are still relatively high percentages that suggests that EMM lies close to HRB and GD. But only 2% 'picks' HRB and GD together, which suggests that HRB and GD are not close together. Since the coefficients of scalability in the MUDFOLD unfolding analysis are based on the *relative* number of errors, rather than on the absolute number, this example does not violate the MUDFOLD model, whereas it does violate the unidimensional deterministic unfolding model. Secondly, Green and Rao insisted on using the full rank order of preferences as basic data. As can be seen from pick k/n analyses with subsequent increase in the value k, the scalability of the scale drops gradually. Subjects apparently violate the unfolding model to a greater extent when they are required to make preference judgments about stimuli they like decreasingly well, or are indifferent to.

5 Discussion

Unfolding analysis has often been unsuccessful in the past, as is illustrated by the difficulty Green and Rao experienced in trying to unfold their breakfast food items. Some reasons for difficulties in finding a good unfolding representation can be shown, using results from the MUDFOLD procedure.

First, the quantitative unfolding model assumes that the metric position of all stimuli along the scale is perceived identically by all subjects. This is apparently not the case for certain items (Toast pop-up, Cinnamon toast, and Corn muffin and butter) in the present dataset. In our final unfolding scale, these items were deleted. In addition, the relative positions of the remaining Toast-items along the qualitative unfolding dimension seem to be less stable than the relative positions of the cakes and the donuts, since the Toast-items could be represented in more than one adjacent position on the dimension. Perhaps the different Toast items should not be represented as points along a dimension, but simply as a cluster of items from which subjects who prefer toast items can pick any item indiscriminately. Some work is currenly being done in our department to establish a 'nonuniqueness' coefficient for each item, which will specify how many positions a stimulus can occupy in the scale without violating the scalability criteria.

Second, the decreasing H- and $H(i)$ values for pick-conditions with increasing values of k show that the degree of structure in subjects' preferences fades when choices have to be made among less and less preferred stimuli. Analysis techniques that require full rank orders of preferences for all items from all subjects are therefore prone to more error than analysis techniques that allow the user to distinguish only the most preferred from the least preferred items. Monte Carlo studies are being done in our department to establish the dependence of the scalability coefficient on factors such as the values of k and n in 'pick k/n', and the distribution of the stimuli or the subjects along the dimension. Rigorous statistical tests are being developed to assess the hypothesis that in the population H, $H(i)$, or $H(ijk)$-values are larger than 0. Such a test can then be used to try to prevent type II errors: rejecting an unfolding scale on the basis of a sample even though the scale may be valid for the population.

To conclude, the present unfolding model has the following two advantages over a number of widely used unfolding models. First, MUDFOLD operates best with a lower limit of about 100 subjects, whereas this approaches the maximum number of subjects posssible for MDS programs. The second advantage is that since MUDFOLD uses dichotomous data, almost all types of data, including Likert-type rating scales, can be subjected to an unfolding analysis. This makes the multiple unidimensional unfolding model also particularly applicable in the area of marketing research.

The MUDFOLD program plus documentation is available for 100 Dutch guilders from the Dutch Inter University Expert Center 'GAMMA', Kraneweg 8, 9718 JP Groningen, The Netherlands. Mainframe versions run on IBM, VAX, DEC, and CDC-Cyber; Floppy disk versions run on IBM-compatible PC's with 640K RAM memory. Applications of MUDFOLD to preferences for German political parties can be found in Van Schuur (in press), and to sympathy ratings for European pressure groups in Van Schuur (1987b).

References

Andrich D (1984) The Construction of a Probabilistic Model for the Psychological Scaling of Unfolding Choice Data. Unpublished paper

Bishop YMM, Fienberg SE, Holland PW (1975) Discrete Multivariate Analysis: Theory and Practice. MIT Press, Cambridge, Mass.

Böckenholt I, Gaul W (1986). Analysis of Choice Behavior Via Probabilistic Ideal Point and Vector Models. Applied Stochastic Models and Data Analysis 2: 209–226

Carroll JD (1972) Individual Differences Scaling, in: Shepard R et al. (eds.) Multidimensional Scaling, Vol. I: Theory. Seminar Press, New York, pp 105–155

Coombs CH (1950) Psychological Scaling Without a Unit of Measurement. Psychological Review 57: 148–158

Coombs CH (1964) A Theory of Data. Wiley, New York

Coombs CH, Kao RC (1960) On a Connection Between Factor Analysis and Multidimensional Unfolding. Psychometrika 25: 219–231

Coombs CH, Smith JEK (1973) On the Detection of Structure in Attitudes and Developmental Processes. Psychological Review 80: 337–351

Davison ML (1977) On a Metric, Unidimensional Unfolding Model for Attitudinal and Developmental Data. Psychometrika 42: 523–548

Davison ML (1979). Testing a Unidimensional Qualitative Unfolding Model for Attitudinal or Developmental Data. Psychometrika 44: 179–194

Davison ML (1980) A Psychological Scaling Model for Testing Order Hypotheses. British Journal of Mathematical and Statistical Psychology 33: 123–141

DeSarbo WS, Rao VR (1984) GENFOLD2: A Set of Models and Algorithms for the GENeral unFOLDing Analysis of Preference/Dominance Data. Journal of Classification 2/3: 147–186

DeSarbo WS, Hoffman DL (1986) Simple and Weighted Unfolding Threshold Models for the Spatial Representation of Binary Choice Data. Applied Psychological Measurement 10: 247–264

DeSarbo WS, DeSoete G, Jedidi K (1987) Probabilistic Multidimensional Scaling Models for Analyzing Consumer Choice Behavior. Communication and Cognition 20: 93–116

Green PE, Carmone FJ (1970) Multidimensional Scaling and Related Techniques in Marketing Analysis. Allyn and Bacon, Boston

Green PE, Green VR (1972) Applied Multidimensional Scaling; A Comparison of Approaches and Algorithms. Holt, Rinehart and Winston, New York

Jansen PGW (1983) Rasch Analysis of Attitudinal Data. Catholic University of Nijmegen—Rijks Psychologische Dienst, Den Haag, unpublished dissertation

Kruskal JB, Young FW, Seery JB (1973). How to Use KYST, a Very Flexible Program to Do Multidimensional Scaling and Unfolding. Bell Laboratories, Murray Hill

Leik RK, Mathews M (1968) A Scale for Developmental Processes. American Sociological Review 54: 62–75

Loevinger J (1948) The Technique of Homogeneous Tests Compared with Some Aspects of "Scale Analysis" and Factor Analysis. Psychological Bulletin 45: 507–530

Mokken RJ (1971) A Theory and Procedure of Scale Analysis, with Applications in Political Research. Mouton, The Hague

Mokken RJ, Lewis C (1982) A Nonparametric Approach to the Analysis of Dichotomous Item Responses. Applied Psychological Measurement 6: 417–430

Roskam EE (1968) Metric Analysis of Ordinal Data. VAM, Voorschoten

Ross J, Cliff N (1964) A Generalization of the Interpoint Distance Model. Psychometrika 29: 167–176

Shepard RN (1974) Representation of Structure in Similarity Data: Problems and Prospects. Psychometrika 39: 373–421

Takane Y, Young FW, de Leeuw J (1977) Nonmetric Individual Differences MDS: An Alternating Least Squares Method with Optimal Scaling Features. Psychometrika 42: 7–67

Tversky A (1972) Elimination by Aspects: A Theory of Choice. Psychological Review 79: 281–299

Van Schuur WH, Molenaar IW (1982) MUDFOLD, Multiple Stochastic Unidimensional Unfolding, in: Caussinus H, Ettinger P, Thomassone R (eds.) Proceedings in Computational Statistics, COMPSTAT 1982 part I. Physica-Verlag, Vienna, pp 419–424

Van Schuur WH (1984). Structure in Political Beliefs; A New Model for Stochastic Unfolding with Application to European Party Activists. CT Press, Amsterdam

Van Schuur WH (1987a) Stochastic Unfolding, in: Gallhofer I, Saris WE (eds.) Advances in Sociometric Research, Vol. I: Data Collection and Scaling. McMillan, London, pp 137–158

Van Schuur WH (1987b) Constraints in European Party Activists' Sympathy Scores for Interest Groups; the Left-Right Dimension as Dominant Structuring Principle. European Journal of Political Research 15: 347–362

Van Schuur WH (in press) Unfolding the German Political Parties: A Description and Application of Multiple Unidimensional Unfolding. Zeitschrift für Sozialpsychologie [illegible] (19[illegible]) The [illegible] Data Compared with [illegible] and Factor Analysis, [illegible]

M[illegible] (197[illegible]) A Theory [illegible] Analysis [illegible]

Wallace [illegible] (19[illegible]) [illegible]

[illegible] (19[illegible]) Metric [illegible] N.M., New York

[illegible] (19[illegible]) [illegible] for Interpoint Distances [illegible] 29, [illegible]

[illegible] (19[illegible]) [illegible] Nonlinear [illegible]

[illegible] Y., Young F.W., de Leeuw J. [illegible] ALSCAL [illegible] Squares Method with Optimal Scaling Features, Psychometrika 41, [illegible]

[illegible] A. (1972) [illegible] of [illegible] Psychological Review 79, [illegible]

[illegible] Schuur W.H. [illegible] Stochastic Unfolding [illegible] Springer-Verlag, [illegible]

Van Schuur W.H. (19[illegible]) Stochastic [illegible] A New Model [illegible] Unfolding [illegible]

Van Schuur W.H. (19[illegible]) [illegible] Research, Vol. [illegible] Methods, London, [illegible]

[illegible] Schuur W.H. (19[illegible]) [illegible] Party [illegible] Research [illegible]

Van Schuur W.H. (19[illegible]) [illegible] Applied [illegible] Models [illegible]

Part 5

Data Analysis

The Effect of Measurement Error on Determining the Number of Clusters in Cluster Analysis

M. C. Cooper and G. W. Milligan
Faculty of Marketing, Faculty of Management Sciences
The Ohio State University
1775 College Road, Columbus, Ohio 43210

Summary

Market researchers examining market segmentation and other aggregation issues can use cluster analysis to form segments of consumers or organizations. When the segments are formed using attitude information or even demographic data, the possibility of measurement error exists.

Previous research (Milligan and Cooper (1985)) had indicated two stopping rules for determining the number of clusters in a data set were superior in the error-free data sets examined. The present research reconfirmed the performance of the pseudo-t and pseudo-F statistics as the best rules in a larger number of replications of error-free data. In addition, the present research examined the performance of stopping rules in low-error and high-error conditions. Low-error would be representative of small measurement error in the data collection instrument or due to respondent error. High error is more severe and can obscure clusters due to the overlapping cluster boundaries.

As one would expect, the ability to recover the true cluster structure deteriorated as more error was introduced into the data. Some stopping rules had differing recovery at different numbers of clusters in the data sets. Two clusters were particularly difficult to recover.

The two best stopping rules for the error-free data were also clearly superior in the error pertubed conditions. Thus, these rules appear to be robust across the conditions tested here.

1 Introduction

Clustering is used by market researchers as a means of a posteriori grouping of consumers or organizations into market segments. See the review article by Punj and Stewart (1982) for numerous references and examples. The researcher who chooses clustering as a means of data analysis should examine the decisions made at each step of the research process outlined in Milligan and Cooper (1988). One of the steps in a cluster analysis involves determining the number of clusters present in the data. The existing lack of guidance for researchers faced with this decision prompted the current study.

Before proceeding, a few clarifications of terms used in the paper are in order. An hierarchical method clustering n subjects provides n different solution sets: n clusters, $n-1$ clusters, $n-2, \ldots,$ until one cluster is obtained consisting of all subjects. Each solution set is referred to as an hierarchy level in the clustering process. The researcher selects the number of clusters by deciding at which level to stop the clustering process. Clearly, the researcher needs some criterion for selecting the appropriate number of clusters. These criteria are known as stopping rules.

Numerous stopping rules have been suggested. Thirty of these were tested on four hierarchical clustering algorithms using error-free data when the true number of clusters was known (Milligan and Cooper (1985)). Some of the better known stopping rules did not perform well, including Trace W, log (SSB/SSW), and the McClain and Rao procedure. These rules did not indicate the correct number of clusters in half of the trials. In total, the fifteen least effective rules from the study of error-free data were omitted from the present study.

Few would argue that market research data are free from error. Subjects may not be accurate in their responses, the collection instrument may not measure the desired variables properly, and there is the possibility of error in recording, data entry, and processing which add noise to the measurement process. While a stopping rule cannot correct for the error in the data, one can hope to find a reasonably robust rule. Two error conditions are examined in the present study. The low error condition may be similar to small recording errors or responses that are off by, say, a point on a semantic differential scale from the respondent's true perceptions. A high error condition is representative of more severe processing errors and lack of clarity of the measurement instrument.

2 Methodology

2.1 Data Sets and Methods

Artifical data sets were constructed by varying the number of clusters, the number of dimensions, and the patterns of assigning observations in the data set to specific clusters as described in Milligan (1985). There were either $2, 3, 4$, or 5 clusters. Of course, the advantage of using constructed data is that the true number of clusters is known exactly. The number of dimensions was the number of measures used for clustering. These could represent attributes of a reduced 4-, 6-, or 8-dimensional space, such as the result of a factor analysis. Observations were assigned so that in one third of the data sets, the clusters were of equal size. In another third, one of the clusters contained only 10% of the observations to represent a small cluster in the data. In the last third, one of the clusters contained 60% of the observations. These variations increase the generalizability by considering data sets with different configurations. Six replications of the $4 \times 3 \times 3$ design were used in the present study, resulting in 216 data sets for each error level.

Individual clusters were constructed to have internal cohesion among points within clusters and external isolation between clusters for distinct cluster structure. The clusters were distinct and well seperated in the variable space. The boundaries of a cluster were 1.5 standard deviations away from the cluster mean. The separation between cluster boundaries on the first dimension varied from .25 to .75 times the sum of the standard deviations of the two clusters involved. Other dimensions were permitted to have overlapping clusters. The data sets were then error-pertubed. A random error was subtracted or added to each dimension to alter the error free distances between observations. This is more representative of real data sets where measurement error exists and cluster boundaries may be less clear. The error-pertubed distance between observation j and k was $d_{jk} = [\sum_i (A_{ij} - A_{ik} - \gamma e_{ijk})^2]^{1/2}$. A_{ij} and A_{ik} are the responses of observations j and k on dimension i. They are the coordinate values generated from multivariate normal distributions. Different multivariate normal distributions correspond to different clusters in the variable space The e_{ijk} represent the error-perturbation to the error-free distance between the A_{ij} and A_{ik}. The e_{ijk} were randomly generated from a univariate normal distribution with a mean of 0 and a standard deviation equal to the average standard deviations on dimension i of the clusters containing j and k. Low and high error were defined by γ which was either 1.0 or 2.0. Low error makes cluster boundaries slightly "fuzzy". High error reduces cluster separation and distinctness.

Four hierarchical methods were used for more generalizable results: single link, complete link, group average, and Ward's minimum variance. These methods have been compared in numerous studies and provide a range of differing results for analysis of the stopping rules.

2.2 Stopping Rules

Table 1 describes the fifteen stopping rules examined. In the remainder of the paper the different rules are referred to by the number assigned to each in Table 1. The various stopping rules which have been proposed use different approaches to determining the number of clusters. In an hierarchical method, this is equivalent to deciding when to stop the clustering. For rules 1, 5, 12, and 14, calculations are based only on the information from the two clusters being merged, ignoring the rest of the data. The other rules use most or all of the data and information about the cluster structure prior to the hierarchy level under consideration. For example, rules 1 and 2 have been referred to as the pseudo T-test and the pseudo F-test because of their formulations.

Table 1: Description of Stopping Rules

Rule	Description	Cluster level Selected
1. Pseudo T-test (Duda & Hart)	test ratio against critical value; Ratio is sum of squared errors for 2 clusters (Je(2)) vs. 1 cluster (Je(1))	first time ratio is less than critical value
2. Pseudo F-test (Calinski, Harabasz)	Trace Cov$\underline{B}$ / Trace Cov$\underline{W}$, where $\underline{B}$ and $\underline{W}$ are sums of squares and cross product matrices	maximum value
3. C-Index (Dalrymple-Alford)	$[\underline{d}_u - \min(\underline{d}_w)] / [\max(\underline{d}_w) - \min(\underline{d}_w)]$ $\underline{d}_w$ = sum of within-cluster distances	minimum value
4. Gamma (Baker & Hubert)	$[\underline{S}(+) - \underline{S}(-)] / [\underline{S}(+) + \underline{S}(-)]$ $\underline{S}(+)$ = number of consistent comparisons $\underline{S}(-)$ = number of inconsistent comparisons	maximum value

5. Beale	F-test on increase in mean square deviation from cluster centroids from 2 clusters to 1 cluster	first time hypothesis of 1 cluster rejected
6. G^+ (reviewed in Rohlf)	$[2S(-)] / \underline{n}_d(\underline{n}_d - 1)]$ $S-$ = number of inconsistent comparisons $\underline{n}_d$ = number of within-cluster distances	minimum value
7. Cubic clustering criterion (Sarle)	[natural log $(1 - E(R^2)) / (1 - R^2)]*$ $[((np / 2)^{.5}) / ((.001 + E(R^2))^{1.2})]$ R^2 = proportion of variance by clusters p = estimate of dimensionality of between cluster variation	maximum value
8. Point-biserial	correlation of matrix of distance between 2 pairs of observations and 0/1 matrix of whether both observations are in the same cluster	maximum value
9. Davies & Bouldin	measure of cluster separation: $R = 1/N(R_i)$; R_i = maximum R_{ij} for clusters i, j $R_{i,j} = \frac{\sigma_i + \sigma_j}{d_{ij}}$ N = number of clusters with more than one observation	minimum value
10. Mojena Rule 1	test against critical value $= \bar{\alpha} + KS$ α = fusion value for hierarchy level $\bar{\alpha}$ = mean of α's used in this and previous levels S_α = standard deviation of α's K = Constant	level prior to (1 more cluster) exceeding critical value
11. Stepsize (Johnson)	within-cluster distances	level prior to (one more cluster) maximum difference
12. Log (p) (Gnanadeskian, et al.)	absolute log of p-value from Hoteling's $\underline{T}^2$ test on 2 clusters to be merged	maximum difference
13. Frey & Groene-woud ratio	ratio = increase in outsider cluster distances between levels divided by increase in within-cluster distances between levels	level prior to (1 cluster more) last time the ratio falls below 1.0
14. Sneath $\underline{t}_w$	$\underline{t}_w$ = distance between 2 cluster centroids to be merged/overlap of the two clusters	$\underline{t}_w$ exceeds critical score
15. Tau (reviewed in Rohlf)	tau correlation of matrices in point-biserial calculations	maximum value

Table 2: Aggregate Results for Error-free, Low Error and High Error Conditions

		Error-free	Low Error	High Error
1.	Pseudo T-test	94%	86%	61%
2.	Pseudo F-test	94	88	65
3.	C-Index	87	71	36
4.	Gamma	87	73	40
5.	Beale	84	72	46
6.	$G+$	79	61	27
7.	Cubic Clustering Criterion	74	70	52
8.	Point Biserial	74	63	44
9.	Davies and Bouldin	69	47	24
10.	Mojena	67	57	38
11.	Stepsize	65	53	40
12.	Log(p)	56	45	34
13.	Frey & Groenewoud	53	47	37
14.	Sneath	52	32	17
15.	Tau	49	46	35

3 Results

The fifteen stopping rules were each run on the 216 error-free data sets, the 216 low-error data sets, and the 216 high-error data sets. With four hierarchical methods tested on each data set, a total of 864 results was generated for each stopping rule under each error condition. Table 2 presents the percent of the data sets where exactly the correct number of clusters was recovered for the error-free, the low error and the high error conditions. Generally those rules which tended to work well in the error free data also worked better than other rules in the two error conditions. Rules 1 and 2 consistently ranked highest across the three conditions. The other rules had similar rankings between the error-free and low error conditions. Recall that the low error condition makes the cluster boundaries fuzzy. In the high error condition, many of the rules simply did not recover the true cluster structure prior to error-perturbation because some clusters may be hidden due to limited overlap on some dimensions used in the clustering. Rule 7 is the only rule besides 1 and 2 to recover the cluster structures in more than half of the data sets. The top seven rules for the error-free data are plotted in Figure 1.

Tables 3 and 4 present detailed results of the top eight stopping rules. (See Cooper (1987) for results of all 15 rules.) The results are aggregated as percentages into three categories: correct choice of the number of clusters, type B, and type A errors. A type B error occured if the stopping rule indicated fewer clusters than were in the data set. This is viewed as a serious error for market researchers since potentially distinct clusters (segments) would be merged together, thus losing valuable information about the subjects.

Type A error occured when too many clusters were indicated. While this result is not desirable either, more information about the observations is preserved. A researcher may wish to know whether a stopping rule is prone to type B errors, as well as how often the correct number of clusters is found.

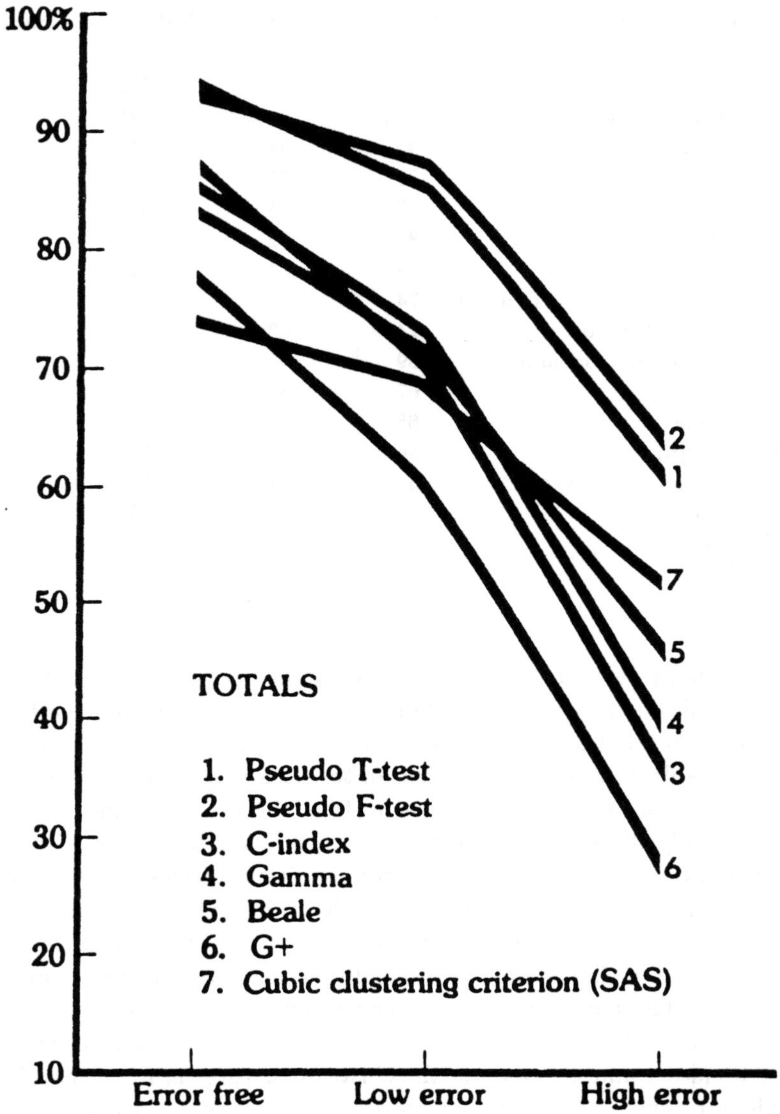

Figure 1.

In the low error condition, the first eight rules performed fairly well, although they all had lower recovery rates at two clusters than for three to five clusters in the data. The researcher will have a difficult time finding only two clusters in the data when measurement error is present. Rule 2 showed increasing recovery rates with an increase in the number of clusters in the data.

In the high error condition, recovery rates decreased substantially, so that all stopping rules performed poorly. Rules 1 and 7 again had lower recovery rates when two clusters were present in the data. Rule 1 exhibited increasing recovery rates for more clusters in the data, while rule 2 dropped at three clusters and then rose again. Rule 7 exhibited differing patterns across the number of clusters for the low and high error conditions.

Table 3: Stopping Rule Performance on Low-Error Data

	Number of Clusters 2	3	4	5	Total
1. Pseudo T-test					
Type B	18.1%	3.7%	6.5%	5.1%	8.3%
Correct	73.6	91.7	84.7	91.7	85.8
Type A	8.3	4.6	8.8	3.2	6.3
2. Pseudo F-test					
Type B	0	12.5	7.4	2.8	5.7
Correct	83.8	85.6	88.4	93.5	87.8
Type A	16.2	1.9	4.2	3.7	6.5
3. C-Index					
Type B	0	9.3	8.8	13.0	7.8
Correct	54.6	72.7	74.1	84.5	70.7
Type A	45.4	18.0	17.1	5.6	21.5
4. Gamma					
Type B	0	9.3	9.7	11.1	7.5
Correct	57.4	74.5	75.9	84.7	73.2
Type A	42.6	16.2	14.4	4.2	19.3
5. Beale					
Type B	39.3	12.5	9.7	6.5	17.0
Correct	51.4	76.4	81.0	77.8	71.7
Type A	9.3	11.1	9.3	15.7	11.3
6. $G+$					
Type B	0	6.5	5.6	11.1	5.8
Correct	36.6	59.7	65.7	81.5	60.9
Type A	63.4	33.8	28.7	7.4	33.3
7. Cubic Clustering Criterion					
Type B	19.4	2.8	1.9	1.4	6.4
Correct	64.4	81.5	67.6	65.7	69.8
Type A	16.2	15.7	30.6	32.9	23.8
8. Point Biserial					
Type B	0	15.3	48.6	55.6	29.8
Correct	74.5	82.9	50.0	44.4	63.0
Type A	25.5	1.8	1.4	0	7.2

Type B errors grew substantially from the error-free to the low error and then to the high error conditions. Even the best three rules, 1, 2, and 7, had type B errors in excess of twenty percent. This is a concern when information is lost by aggregating true clusters together.

Table 4: Stopping Rule Performance on High-Error Data

	Number of Clusters 2	3	4	5	Total
1. Pseudo T-test					
Type B	44.0%	28.7%	22.2%	14.4%	27.3%
Correct	44.9	57.9	66.7	75.9	61.4
Type A	11.1	13.4	11.1	9.7	11.3
2. Pseudo F-test					
Type B	0	35.6	32.4	14.4	20.6
Correct	67.6	52.8	62.5	75.0	64.5
Type A	32.4	11.6	5.1	10.6	14.9
3. C-Index					
Type B	0	5.1	24.1	11.1	10.1
Correct	17.6	29.2	38.9	59.3	36.2
Type A	82.4	65.7	37.0	29.6	53.7
4. Gamma					
Type B	0	5.6	23.6	11.1	10.1
Correct	24.5	28.2	44.5	63.0	40.0
Type A	75.5	66.2	31.9	25.9	49.9
5. Beale					
Type B	64.4	51.4	36.1	19.0	42.7
Correct	23.6	38.0	55.1	67.6	46.1
Type A	12.0	10.6	8.8	13.4	11.2
6. $G+$					
Type B	0	5.1	11.1	6.5	5.7
Correct	17.6	13.0	26.4	52.3	27.3
Type A	82.4	81.9	62.5	41.2	67.0
7. Cubic Clustering Criterion					
Type B	54.2	21.3	11.6	5.6	23.2
Correct	33.8	57.4	54.6	63.4	52.3
Type A	12.0	21.3	33.8	31.0	24.5
8. Point Biserial					
Type B	0	19.9	58.8	61.6	35.1
Correct	43.1	60.2	36.6	37.5	44.3
Type A	56.9	19.9	4.6	0.9	20.6

4 Discussion

The results suggest that:

1. High error substantially reduces the ability of the stopping rules studied to select the appropriate number of clusters and tends to moderate differences between stopping rules. That is, they all exhibited substantial decrements in performance.

2. With relatively low error in measurement, some stopping rules are clearly better than others under the conditions studied.

3. Certain rules are able to recover two cluster solutions better than five cluster solutions, and vice versa.

Of course, with respect to this last point, a researcher would normally want to avoid techniques whose performance is dependent on unknown characteristics of the data such as the number of clusters.

Rules 1 and 2 performed best in the three conditions tested here. The Statistical Analysis System (SAS) has incorporated these two rules into its clustering program based in part on the results of this study. Rule 7 was developed at SAS and performed rather well in these tests. Rule 1 is a pseudo T-test in that only the two clusters considered for merging are used in the calculations. Rule 2 is a pseudo F-test since all the data are used. Looking at the combination of results of these three rules can help the researcher to decide about the number of clusters present in the data. Rules 1 and 2 tend to do better as the number of clusters increases. Rule 7 works well except for the two cluster situation. Thus, depending on how many clusters the researcher may suspect are in the data, these rules may converge on the appropriate number.

Finally, the researcher is urged to look up and down the hierarchy one or two cluster levels from the selected level since the error in the data make finding the correct number of clusters difficult. Not only should the researcher seek mathematically justifiable cluster solutions, but also solutions that make sense given the purpose of the research and the data. See Milligan and Cooper (1988) for a review of the literature on interpreting clusters and cluster structure.

References

Baker FB, Hubert LJ (1972) Measuring the Power of Hierarchical Cluster Analysis. Journal of the American Statistical Association 70: 31–38

Beale EML (1969) Cluster Analysis. Scientific Control Systems, London

Calinski RB, Harabasz JA (1974) A Dendrite Method for Cluster Analysis. Communicatons in Statistics 3: 1–27

Cooper MC (1987) The Effect of Measurement Error on Determining the Number of Clusters. Working Paper Series, College of Business, The Ohio State University, Columbus, Ohio

Dalrymple-Alford EC (1970) The Measurement of Clustering in Free Recall. Psychological Bulletin 75: 32–34

Davies DL, Bouldin DWA (1979) A Cluster Seperation Measure. IEEE Transactions on Pattern Analysis and Machine Intelligence 1: 224–227

Duda RO, Hart PE (1973) Pattern Classification and Scene Analysis. Wiley, New York

Frey T, Van Groenewoud HA (1972) A Cluster Analysis of the D-Squared Matrix of White Spruce Stands in Saskatechwan Based on the Maximum-Minimum Principle. Journal of Ecology 60: 873–886

Gnanadesikan R, Kettenring JR, Landwehr JM (1977) Interpreting and Assessing the Results of Cluster Analyses. Bulletin of the International Statistical Institute 47: 451–463

Johnson SC (1967) Hierarchical Clustering Schemes. Psychometrika 32: 241–254

Milligan GW (1985) An Algorithm for Generating Artificial Test Clusters. Psychometrika 50, 1: 123–127

Milligan GW, Cooper MC (1985) An Examination of Procedures for Determining the Number of Clusters in a Data Set. Psychometrika 50, 2: 159–179

Milligan GW, Cooper MC (1988) A Review of Clustering Methodology. Applied Psychological Measurement, in press

Mojena R (1977) Hierarchical Grouping Methods and Stopping Rules: An Evaluation. The Computer Journal 20: 359–363

Punj G, Steward DW (1983) Cluster Analysis in Marketing Research: Review and Suggestions for Application. Journal of Marketing Research 20: 134–148

Rohlf FJ (1974) Methods of Comparing Classifiations. Annual Review of Ecology and Systematics 5: 101–113

Sarle WS (1983) Cubic Clustering Criterion. Technical Report A–108, Cary NC, SAS Institute

Sneath PHA (1977) A Method for Testing the Distinctness of Clusters: A Test of the Disjunction of Two Clusters in Euclidean Space as Measured by Their Overlap. Mathematical Geology 9: 123–143

On the Use of Simulated Annealing for Combinatorial Data Analysis

G. De Soete*
Department of Psychology, University of Ghent
Henri Dunantlaan 2, B–9000 Ghent, Belgium
L. Hubert and P. Arabie†
Department of Psychology, University of Illinois at Champaign
603 E. Daniel St., Champaign IL 61820

Summary

Simulated annealing was compared with a (locally optimal) pairwise interchange algorithm on two combinatorial data analysis tasks, viz., least-squares unidimensional scaling of symmetric proximity data and a particular unidimensional scaling method of dominance data. These two tasks are representative of a larger class of combinatorial data analysis problems for which globally optimal solutions are, in general, computationally intractable to obtain even when the number of objects is moderate.

It was found that, contrary to theoretical expectations, simulated annealing was not markedly superior to the more traditional pairwise interchange strategy in avoiding local optima.

1 Introduction

A variety of data analysis tasks in the social and behavioral sciences involve some type of combinatorial optimization. In these problems, a finite set of potential solutions can be specified along with an objective function that numerically evaluates the goodness or badness of each solution. The problem amounts to searching for the solution that optimizes the objective function. Many of the combinatorial optimization tasks of interest in the social and behavioral sciences fall within the class of problems for which no algorithms have been found that can guarantee an absolute best solution (i.e., a solution that globally optimizes the objective function) with reasonable computational effort (i.e., the NP-complete and NP-hard categories discussed in, say, Garey and Johnson (1979)). More specifically, the best we can do when globally optimal solutions are sought for these problems is to devise algorithms where computational effort increases exponentially with respect to problem size. Two prototypical examples of such data analysis tasks are unidimensional scaling of symmetric proximities data and unidimensional scaling of asymmetric dominance data.

*Supported as "Bevoegdverklaard Navorser" of the Belgian "Nationaal Fonds voor Wetenschappelijk Onderzoek".

†Supported in part by a grant from American Telephone and Telegraph (AT&T) to the Industrial Affiliates Program of the University of Illinois and by a Fulbright award.

2 Two Combinatorial Data Analysis Tasks

Unidimensional Scaling of Symmetric Proximities Data Let $\mathbf{A} = \{a_{ij}\}$ be an $n \times n$ symmetric (one-mode) proximity matrix, where a_{ij} numerically indexes the dissimilarity between objects i and j. Thus, the larger values in $\mathbf{A}$ are assumed to refer to the more dissimilar objects. Also, the main diagonal entries are irrelevant and are set equal to 0, i.e., $a_{ii} = 0$ for $1 \leq i \leq n$. Our task is to locate the n coordinates $x_1, x_2, \ldots, x_n$ such that the least squares criterion

$$\sum_{i<j}(a_{ij} - |x_i - x_j|)^2 \tag{1}$$

is minimized. In the explicit least-squares sense, the distances between the points along the continuum should reconstruct the corresponding values in the matrix $\mathbf{A}$ as closely as possible.

As shown by Defays (1978), the set of optimal coordinates can be defined through a particular combinatorial optimization task. Let $\Psi(\cdot) \equiv \Psi$ represent a one-to-one permutation on the first n integers and let $\{a_{\Psi(i)\Psi(j)}\}$ denote the original proximity matrix with its rows and columns permuted by Ψ, e.g., the row/column k of $\{a_{\Psi(i)\Psi(j)}\}$ is the original $\Psi(k)$ row/column of $\mathbf{A}$. Also, define

$$t_i^{(\Psi)} = (u_i^{(\Psi)} - v_i^{(\Psi)})/n \tag{2}$$

where

$$u_i^{(\Psi)} = \sum_{j=1}^{i-1} a_{\Psi(i)\Psi(j)}, \quad \text{for } i \geq 2;$$

$$v_i^{(\Psi)} = \sum_{j=i+1}^{n} a_{\Psi(i)\Psi(j)}, \quad \text{for } i < n;$$

and $u_1^{(\Psi)} = v_n^{(\Psi)} = 0$. Thus, $u_i^{(\Psi)}$ is the sum of the proximities in row $\Psi(i)$ of $\{a_{\Psi(i)\Psi(j)}\}$ from the extreme left to the main diagonal and $v_i^{(\Psi)}$ is the sum from the main diagonal to the extreme right. Defays (1978) showed that the optimal coordinates can be found from

$$x_i = t_i^{(\Psi^*)} \tag{3}$$

where Ψ^* denotes a permutation maximizing

$$\sum_{i=1}^{n}(t_i^{(\Psi)})^2. \tag{4}$$

In short, the set of possible solutions to the unidimensional scaling task is the set of $n!$ possible permutations of n integers (or, since reflections are indistinguishable, the effective number of possible solutions is $n!/2$). The objective function values corresponding to a specific permutation Ψ is given in (4) and an optimal solution, Ψ^*, maximizes (4). Once Ψ^* is found, the actual coordinates minimizing the least squares criterion can be obtained through (3).

Unidimensional Scaling of Asymmetric Dominance Data. Assume that the data are collected in an $n \times n$ asymmetric dominance matrix $\mathbf{P} = \{p_{ij}\}$, where p_{ij} numerically indexes the degree of dominance of object i over object j. Thus, if $p_{ij} > p_{ji}$, object i is assumed to dominate object j, with larger values of p_{ij} indicating larger degrees of dominance. Again, the main diagonal entries of $\mathbf{P}$ are irrelevant and are set equal to 0, i.e., $p_{ii} = 0$ for $1 \leq i \leq n$. A well-known example of this kind of data in the social and behavioral sciences is paired comparison data where p_{ij} indicates the proportion of times object i was preferred to object j. Our task is to order from left to right the n objects along a single dimension from most to least dominant, i.e., if object i is placed to the left of object j, then object i should dominate object j and p_{ij} should be greater than p_{ji}. Stated differently, if the rows and columns of $\mathbf{P}$ are reordered appropriately by the permutation Ψ to form $\{p_{\Psi(i)\Psi(j)}\}$, then an entry above the main diagonal, $p_{\Psi(i)\Psi(j)}$ for $i < j$, should be larger than the conjugate entry below the main diagonal, $p_{\Psi(i)\Psi(j)}$.

As a specific measure of how successful any particular ordering is in achieving this property of having the larger entries above the main diagonal, we will choose the obvious criterion defined through the sum of above-diagonal entries. Thus, the explicit optimization task is to find a permutation $\Psi^*(\cdot)$ such that

$$\sum_{i<j} p_{\Psi(i)\Psi(j)} \tag{5}$$

is maximized. Again, the set of possible solutions to this unidimensional scaling task is the set of $n!$ possible permutations on n integers (see Hubert (1976), for a review).

3 The LOPI and SA Algorithms

Both unidimensional scaling tasks just discussed fall within the class of combinatorial optimization problems having computational burdens that grow exponentially with the number of rows/columns of the data matrix. Existing methods that guarantee globally optimal solutions are all limited as to the size of the problems that can be handled with reasonable computational effort, usually n's less than, say, about 15. For instance, dynamic programming methods are available both for the Defays approach (see Hubert and Arabie (1986)) and for maximizing the sum of above-diagonal entries in a dominance matrix (see Hubert and Golledge (1981)). In both cases, the task of evaluating a solution space of size $n!$ is reduced to evaluating 2^n possible subsets. Even though 2^n tends to be much smaller than $n!$, the former still grows exponentially and limits the matrix sizes that can realistically be attacked. Obviously, moderate sized matrices can only be handled by heuristic methods. What are needed are heuristic procedures that find "good" solutions in an efficient way. However, such solutions are not guaranteed to be globally optimal.

Most heuristic algorithms for solving the type of combinatorial data analysis problems considered in this paper are iterative. A candidate solution is repeatedly improved by applying some local operation until no further improvement is possible. A local operation that seems natural for the two combinatorial tasks discussed here amounts to interchanging two integers in the current permutation Ψ. Hubert and Schultz (1976) have suggested a heuristic procedure that is based on this pairwise interchange operation and that can be used for solving the unidimensional scaling tasks considered here. In this procedure the effect of all possible $n(n-1)/2$ pairwise interchanges on the objective function is evaluated and the interchange that most improves the objective function is accepted. This process is continued until no further improvement is possible through pairwise interchanges. Because at each iteration, the locally best solution is found, this procedure will be referred to as the *l*ocally *o*ptimal *p*airwise *i*nterchange (LOPI) strategy.

More recently, a procedure—called *s*imulated *a*nnealing (SA)—has been suggested in the literature for solving combinatorial optimization problems (see Kirkpatrick, Gelatt and Vecchi (1983)). In this method—which is based on a simulation of the physical process of annealing—the effect of a randomly applied local operation is evaluated at each step. If the operation improves the objective function, the change is always accepted. Otherwise, when the interchange does not improve the objective function, the change is accepted with a certain probability that is gradually decreased. Because (especially in the early stages of the optimization process) changes are sometimes accepted that do not improve the objective function, SA is expected to be better at avoiding local optima than are most other heuristic combinatorial optimization methods. Schematically, a simulated annealing algorithm for minimizing some objective function $\mathcal{F}(\mathbf{x})$ can be generally outlined as follows:

```
Determine the initial value of x and T;
while (stopping criterion is not satisfied)
      {
      while (inner loop criterion is not satisfied)
            {
            Perturb x to get x*;
            If F(x*) < F(x), accept x*;
            If F(x) ≥ F(x), accept x* with probability exp[-(F(x*) - F(x))/T];
            If accept x*, x ← x*;
            }
      Decrease T;
      }
```

In order to define a SA algorithm completely, the two stopping criteria need to be specified as well as the particular methods that will be used for perturbing $\mathbf{x}$ and for decreasing T.

The SA approach can be applied to the two unidimensional scaling tasks discussed above. In the case of least-squares unidimensional scaling of symmetric proximities, the loss function $\mathcal{F}(\Psi)$ is defined as

$$-\sum_{i}(t_i^{(\Psi)})^2, \tag{6}$$

while in the case of unidimensional scaling of dominance data, $\mathcal{F}(\Psi)$ is defined as

$$-\sum_{i<j} p_{\Psi(i)\Psi(j)}. \tag{7}$$

Following Burkard and Rendl's (1984) SA algorithm for solving the Quadratic Assignment Problem, a simulated annealing algorithm can be implemented for solving the undimensional scaling tasks as follows:

```
Choose a random permutation Ψ;
T = 2.5 × F(Ψ);
stop = .FALSE.;
r = 2n;
while (not stop)
      {
      stop = .TRUE.;
      repeat r times
            {
            Apply a random pairwise interchange to Ψ yielding Ψ*;
            If F(Ψ*) < F(Ψ), accept Ψ;
            If F(Ψ*) ≥ F(Ψ), accept Ψ* with probability exp[−(F(Ψ*) − F(Ψ))/T];
            If accept Ψ*
              {
              Ψ ← Ψ*;
              stop = .FALSE.;
              }
            }
      T ← T/2;
      r ← r × 1.1;
      }
```

For a representative numerical application of how the LOPI and SA algorithms work, we use the same example as Hubert and Arabie (1986), originally reported by Robinson (1951). Hubert and Arabie (1986, p. 194, Table 2) give a proximity (dissimilarity) matrix for the Kabah collection of archaeological deposits based on 2.00 minus the Robinson measure of similarity; thus, we would hope that larger proximities would correspond to deposits relatively distant from each other in time. This table has been reordered so that the identity permutation actually gives the (globally) optimal set of coordinates obtained by using the dynamic programming method discussed in Hubert and Arabie (1986). In particular, the coordinate locations for the optimal solution are given by $t_1 = -1.13$, $t_2 = -.86$, $t_3 = -.51$, $t_4 = -.43$, $t_5 = -.23$, $t_6 = -.15$, $t_7 = -.08$, $t_8 = -.01$, $t_9 = .01$, $t_{10} = +.10$, $t_{11} = +.17$, $t_{12} = +.29$, $t_{13} = +.43$, $t_{14} = +.48$, $t_{15} = +.55$, $t_{16} = +.65$, $t_{17} = +.71$; the optimal value of $\sum_i t_i^2$ is 4.30 (all to two decimal places).

When applying the SA algorithm to these data using 25 random permutations as starting configurations, the global optimum could be identified 13 times. Figure 1 shows the behavior of the objective function $\mathcal{F}(\Psi)$ for a run that converged to the global optimum. As can be seen from the figure, in the beginning of the minimization process, ascent steps are accepted. However, as the minimization process progresses, ascent steps are less likely to occur. In comparison, 25 random starts of the LOPI algorithm resulted in an identification of the global optimum (which as mentioned above, was found with dynamic programming) all 25 times. Considering computational effort, the average number of function evaluations over the 25 runs was 1460.6 for SA and 2105.3 for the

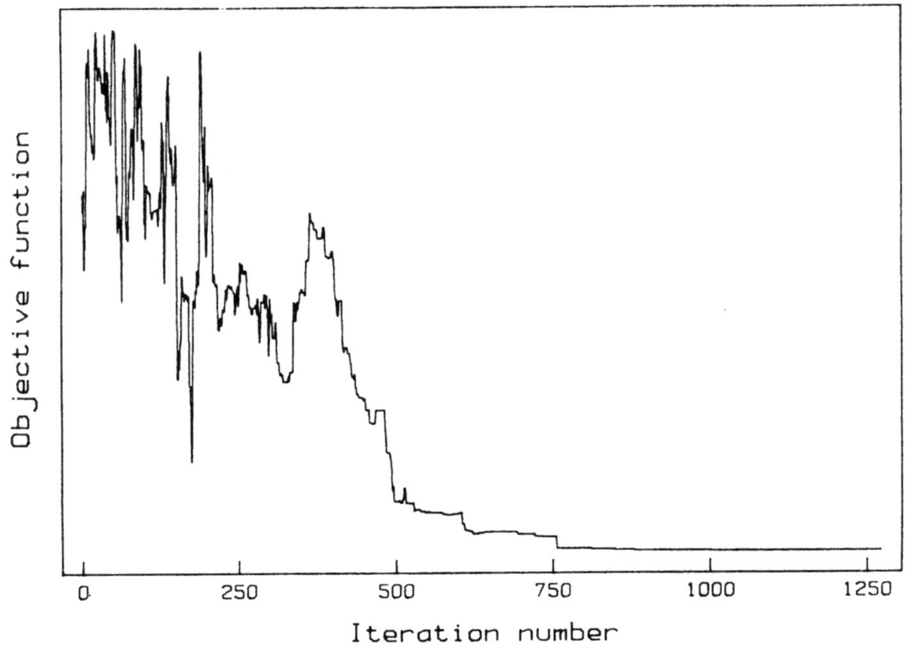

Figure 1: Behavior of the Loss Function during a Typical Run of the SA Algorithm on the Kabah Collection Data

LOPI method (a single function evaluation is defined as an evaluation of $\mathcal{F}(\Psi)$). Thus, LOPI was "more expensive" computationally, but it did perform somewhat better in locating the optimal solution. In order to compare the two approaches more thoroughly, two Monte Carlo studies were performed.

4 Monte Carlo Comparisons

The Monte Carlo comparisons we present follow the implementation of the two methods as discussed in analyzing the Kabah collection, but on artificially constructed data. We begin with the least-squares approach to unidimensional scaling of symmetric proximity matrices.

Two factors were varied: (a) the size of the proximity matrices (15×15 and 30×30), and (b) the error imposed on the proximities (no error, 16% and 33% error, and uniformly distributed proximities). For these four error levels (including the first "no error" condition), the interobject distances were computed from coordinates generated by uniformly sampling from [0,1). In the "no error" condition, these distances form the proximities directly (subject to the integer conversion mentioned below). In the 16% (33%) error variance condition, central normally distributed error was added with a variance equal to 19% (50%) of the variance of the true distances so that approximately 16% (33%) of the generated proximities could be attributed to error. In the fourth condition, the proximities were merely sampled at random from the uniform distribution on [0,1). In all cases, the data were converted to integers through a multiplication by 100 and a rounding to zero decimal places. For each of the eight conditions (two matrix sizes by four error levels), five data sets were generated and analyzed 50 times—25 with SA and 25 with LOPI. The initial permutation for each run was generated at random. (The two algorithms were programmed in the "C" language with an attempt to make the coding as efficient as possible, using register variables, etc.)

Table 1: Results of the Monte Carlo Comparison for Unidimensional Scaling of Symmetric Proximities—Number of Times the "Best" Solution Was Found

Matrix	Repli-	Error Condition			
size	cation	No Error	16%	33%	Random
		Results for SA algorithm			
	1	16	4	1	9
	2	21	6	2	3
15 × 15	3	18	2	6	9
	4	14	1	3	4
	5	19	1	1	12
	1	15	1	0	0
	2	15	0	1	1
30 × 30	3	16	0	0	1
	4	21	1	1	5
	5	19	0	0	3
		Results for LOPI algorithm			
	1	25	10	3	10
	2	25	9	7	2
15 × 15	3	25	3	9	14
	4	25	3	5	3
	5	25	4	1	18
	1	25	0	1	1
	2	25	1	0	0
30 × 30	3	25	1	1	1
	4	25	0	1	6
	5	25	1	1	5

Tables 1 and 2 summarize the major results of the Monte Carlo comparison under each of the eight conditions. Table 1 presents the number of times the "best" solution was found for each replication, where "best" is defined with respect to the smallest observed value of the objective function given in (6) located with either strategy (in some cases, distinct permutations may have given this same smallest value). Because of the enormous computational costs (even using dynamic programming) associated with finding all of the actual optimal values of the objective function when the matrices are 15 × 15 and the intractability for the 30 × 30 case, (globally) optimal solutions were not explicitly found for comparison; thus, we can offer no assurance that the

Table 2: Results of the Monte Carlo Comparison for Unidimensional Scaling of Symmetric Proximities—Average Number of Function Evaluations per Run

Matrix size	Replication	No Error	Error Condition 16%	33%	Random
		Results for SA algorithm			
15 × 15	1	1296.7	1098.3	1023.4	1286.2
	2	1506.9	1138.6	905.2	1189.6
	3	1345.8	1057.0	1110.3	1186.8
	4	1198.8	921.4	956.4	1132.3
	5	1452.8	1278.9	964.5	1056.7
30 × 30	1	4112.5	3555.4	2859.2	3601.2
	2	4108.7	3272.9	3209.6	4020.0
	3	4077.6	3356.7	3174.1	3877.9
	4	4143.0	3478.8	3193.8	3917.6
	5	4064.0	3204.4	3028.9	4309.5
		Results for LOPI algorithm			
15 × 15	1	1419.6	1323.4	1373.4	1465.8
	2	1482.6	1419.6	1293.6	1365.0
	3	1373.4	1297.8	1344.0	1445.0
	4	1352.4	1260.0	1461.6	1419.6
	5	1381.8	1314.6	1188.6	1470.0
30 × 30	1	13606.8	12145.2	11605.8	14442.0
	2	13154.4	12719.4	12528.0	14581.2
	3	12562.8	12632.4	12371.4	12772.6
	4	12458.4	13189.2	13084.8	15503.4
	5	13084.8	12423.9	12493.2	14981.4

best solutions reported are actually optimal, other than for the error-free condition—although we might speculate rather hesitantly on optimality when the same solutions were repeatedly obtained. In addition to the count of best solutions of Table 1, Table 2 summarizes the computational effort required by providing the number of function evaluations averaged over the 25 runs of a single data set with the same algorithm.

As expected for LOPI, the number of function evaluations grows rapidly as the number of objects increases.

Referring to Table 1 in the error-free condition, LOPI always obtained the same (optimal) solution and SA identified it most of the time. In the 16% and 33% error variance conditions, both methods found the same best solutions at least once when the number of objects was 15; however, when the number of objects was 30, both methods found the same best solution only for replication 4 under the 33% error condition. In the random data condition, both methods performed reasonably well with 15 objects and in 3 of the 30 object sets, both approaches located the same best solution. In short, SA does not appear markedly better or worse in this Monte Carlo comparison than a more traditional LOPI strategy in locating "best" solutions. Considering computational effort, relative to the specific way we have operationalized the methods, SA may have a marked advantage, at least in the 30×30 conditions. As noted below, however, such an advantage might be viewed as specific to the particular combinatorial optimization task under study.

The structure of the second Monte Carlo comparison for the unidimensional scaling of dominance data was based on optimizing the sum of above-diagonal entries but otherwise was conducted in much the same way except for the inclusion of one additional annealing schedule that allows a greater number of repetitions of the trial interchange process at each given value of T. Explicitly, the initial number of repetitions for the previous Monte Carlo comparison, $r = 2n$ (labeled SA1 below), is also compared with $r = n^2/2$ (labeled SA2 below), to investigate whether a slower "cooling process" might be more effective in locating "best" solutions. In the first three error conditions, the lower diagonal entries in each data matrix were generated by sampling from the uniform distribution on $[0, 1/2]$. In the 16% (33%) error variance condition, central normally distributed error was then added with a variance equal to 19% (50%) of the variance of the given dominance values so that approximately 16% (33%) of the generated proximities could be attributed to error. Each corresponding entry above the main diagonal was then defined by 1.0 minus the below-diagonal entry. In the fourth (random) condition, the lower diagonal entries were generated by sampling from the uniform distribution on $[0, 1)$ with the above diagonal entries again constructed by taking 1.0 minus the below-diagonal entries.

Tables 3 and 4 correspond respectively to Table 1 and Table 2 and present the major results of the Monte Carlo comparison. In all cases, the effect of a particular interchange was evaluated in $O(n)$ operations as suggested by Burkard and Rendl (1984) for the more general Quadratic Assignment Problem. In the error-free condition of Table 3, the LOPI strategy always obtained the same (optimal) solution and both SA1 and SA2 identified it very consistently. In the 16% error variance condition, all methods found the same best solutions at least once except for replication 1 for 30 objects where both LOPI and SA1 failed to locate the best solution identified by SA2. For 33% error, LOPI failed to identify the best solution 4 times (including once when the matrix size was 15×15); SA1 failed four times in the 30×30 condition, and SA2 failed once. For random data, SA2 always identified the best solutions except for one replication in the 15×15 case; LOPI and SA1 never identified the best solution for 30 objects; for 15 objects, LOPI was successful for a single replication and SA1 for three. In brief, since SA2 always identified the best solutions except for two replications and SA1 and LOPI failed 12 and 14 times, respectively, SA2 has the advantage. This conclusion, however, must be tempered rather severely considering the much greater computational effort required for SA2, as indicated in Table 4.

Given the availability of a fixed amount of computational effort, it is still an open question which method might be preferable. One suggestion of our results is that a slower cooling schedule entailing much more computation for SA might give markedly improved results. What is rather obvious is that SA, as implemented here, is not a panacea for avoiding local optima in the two prototypic combinatorial optimization problems we have chosen, contrary to initial theoretical expectations. There are some practical as well as theoretical problems that should be noted when comparing SA

Table 3: Results of the Monte Carlo Comparison for Unidimensional Scaling of Dominance Data—Number of Times the "Best" Solution Was Found

Matrix size	Replication	No Error	16%	33%	Random
		Results for SA1 algorithm			
	1	23	15	1	1
	2	22	7	2	1
15 × 15	3	20	9	1	0
	4	23	18	5	2
	5	20	6	2	0
	1	19	0	0	0
	2	22	4	1	0
30 × 30	3	19	3	0	0
	4	23	1	0	0
	5	20	2	0	0
		Results for SA2 algorithm			
	1	25	16	2	2
	2	25	5	4	0
15 × 15	3	24	9	5	1
	4	25	24	5	2
	5	25	9	5	1
	1	25	3	1	1
	2	25	7	3	1
30 × 30	3	25	6	0	1
	4	25	1	1	1
	5	25	7	2	1
		Results for LOPI algorithm			
	1	25	9	0	0
	2	25	10	4	0
15 × 15	3	25	8	2	0
	4	25	20	4	2
	5	25	3	6	0
	1	25	0	0	0
	2	25	3	1	0
30 × 30	3	25	6	2	0
	4	25	4	0	0
	5	25	7	0	0

Table 4: Results of the Monte Carlo Comparison for Unidimensional Scaling of Dominance Data—Average Number of Function Evaluations per Run

Matrix size	Replication	Error Condition No Error	16%	33%	Random
		Results for SA1 algorithm			
15 × 15	1	2689.8	2648.6	2499.7	1864.8
	2	2499.7	2797.8	2673.4	1353.3
	3	2444.5	2575.6	1884.0	2023.6
	4	2799.7	2198.7	2179.2	2255.7
	5	2104.4	2454.2	2636.5	1784.6
30 × 30	1	7592.8	7865.8	8048.4	7684.4
	2	8148.9	8072.8	7854.4	7668.2
	3	7852.8	8703.4	8081.1	7982.4
	4	8100.4	7949.0	8060.9	7585.2
	5	7566.9	8440.6	7987.1	7849.5
		Results for SA2 algorithm			
15 × 15	1	11088.0	11044.7	9603.3	8372.6
	2	10296.8	11971.7	11003.9	5233.3
	3	10296.3	8963.5	9006.7	9409.7
	4	11655.3	10251.8	8653.1	9343.1
	5	9332.8	10475.7	10245.9	4780.2
30 × 30	1	57264.3	59047.4	56634.2	55560.6
	2	63202.6	59796.3	54949.6	58968.3
	3	62875.4	59415.8	59038.4	57807.9
	4	59821.8	59280.5	60571.2	55133.9
	5	53805.5	58419.8	59682.2	58503.8
		Results for LOPI algorithm			
15 × 15	1	1440.6	1402.8	1209.6	1024.8
	2	1503.6	1377.6	1222.2	873.0
	3	1663.2	1491.0	1327.2	1062.6
	4	1558.2	1524.6	1251.6	1096.2
	5	1596.0	1428.0	1344.0	999.6
30 × 30	1	16303.8	14563.8	11971.2	9935.4
	2	14877.0	15138.0	13032.6	8874.0
	3	15277.2	14250.6	13328.4	8787.0
	4	15764.4	15312.0	13885.2	9831.0
	5	15625.2	14790.0	12928.2	10109.4

and any other interchange technique. First, SA is heavily dependent on the particular schedule selected for reducing T and on how the number of repetitions at any given temperature is chosen. In fact, it can be argued that SA should never be worse than the LOPI strategy, since at convergence of T to 0, only improvements in the objective function are allowed in SA, and if a sufficient number of repetitions of the random interchange process had been attempted, any result from SA should be locally optimal with respect to all pairwise interchanges as well. Theoretically, this argument may be defensible but it presents a practical difficulty in any implementation requiring the use of some type of convergence criterion for accepting a solution as "final" as we have done. In any actual use of SA, for example, we would expect that, at convergence, the researcher would at least check the solution for local optimality with respect to, say, all pairwise interchanges. What is fairly clear from our Monte Carlo comparisons is that SA might be considered a competitor to an iterative improvement strategy such as LOPI. But unfortunately, we were looking for a markedly superior performance, given the theoretical expectations that surround the method's ability to avoid local optima. This latter problem is still with us.

References

Burkard RE, Rendl F (1984). A Thermodynamically Motivated Simulation Procedure for Combinatorial Optimization Problems. European Journal of Operational Research 17: 169–174

Defays D (1978) A Short Note on a Method of Seriation. Journal of Mathematical and Statistical Psychology 3: 49–53

Garey MR, Johnson DS (1979). Computers and Intractability: A Guide to the Theory of NP-Completeness. Freeman, San Francisco

Hubert LJ (1976) Seriation Using Asymmetric Proximity Measures. British Journal of Mathematical and Statistical Psychology 29: 32–52

Hubert L, Arabie P (1986) Unidimensional Scaling and Combinatorial Optimization, in: de Leeuw J, Heiser WJ, Meulman J, Critchley F (eds.) Multidimensional Data Analysis. DSWO Press, Leiden, The Netherlands, pp 181–196

Hubert LJ, Golledge RG (1981) Matrix Reorganization and Dynamic Programming: Applications to Paired Comparisons and Unidimensional Seriation. Psychometrika 46: 429–441

Hubert L, Schultz JV (1976) Quadratic Assignment as a General Data Analysis Strategy. British Journal of Mathematical and Statistical Psychology 29: 190–241

Kirkpatrick S, Gelatt CD, Vecchi MP (1983) Optimization by Simulated Annealing. Science 220: 671–680

Robinson WS (1951) A Method for Chronologically Ordering Archaeological Deposits. American Antiquity 16: 293–301

Some Thoughts on Comparing Multivariate Data with the Map Locations at which they are Observed

K. R. Gabriel
University of Rochester

Summary

Much statistical data is multivariate and its observations are made at different geographical locations. Analysis of such data needs to examine if and how the data's variability depends on geography. Two approaches are examined in this paper, (1) to regress each variable onto longitudes and latitudes, (2) to compare (by regression and/or rotation) the first two principal components with longitudes and latitudes. Both approaches are complemented by examination of residuals with or without local smoothing. The paper compares the two approaches on the basis of Illinois rainfall data.

1 The Problem

Data are frequently observed at a set of geographical locations: one datum, possibly multivariate, being observed at each location. These data may depend on the geography in some systematic manner, such as a trend across the region, or similarities that decrease with distance, possibly more rapidly in some directions than in others. It may be of interest to model this systematic dependence as a function of the location coordinates and highlight individual locations whose data do not fit the general pattern.

We consider multivariate data observed at each of a number of locations, and attempt to relate the data's variability to the map of the locations. We try

(I) the direct approach of regressing the observations onto the location coordinates, and

(II) the indirect approach of first representing the observations as vectors in a planar ordination and then comparing that ordination with the geographical map.

Assume, then, that we are given an m-variate vector of observations at each of n locations, as well as map coordinates for each location. To ease the comparison of observations and coordinates, we center each set of vectors to zero and norm them to average length unity. We write the centered and normed observations and coordinates as rows of matrices $Y(n\text{-by-}m)$ and $X(n\text{-by-}2)$, respectively. Both X and Y then have squared Euclidean norms of n and each of their columns sums to zero.

As an illustration, we use data of monthly precipitation in Illinois: $n = 60$ stations for $m = 12$ months. These are averages for the years 1901–80, from a data base we assembled at the University of Rochester. For the purposes of this paper, both station means and month means have been subtracted out, so our 60-by-12 matrix Y consists of the "interactions", and our 60-by-2 matrix X gives the longitudes and latitudes of the stations, also centered on the Illinois mean. Both matrices were normed to have their mean squared row lengths equal to one. A "map" of the 60 stations is displayed in Figure 1. Some familiar locations are 10 and 28 for Chicago and Joliet, 35 for Moline, 55 for StLouis and 56 for Urbana.

2 The Direct Approach: Regression and the Map-Biplot

We regress each of the m variables' observations, i.e., each column of Y, onto the location coordinates, i.e., onto the 2 columns of X. We write the regression coefficients for the j-th variable as 2-element vector $\mathbf{r}_j$, and define matrix R(m-by-2) to have j-th row $\mathbf{r}_j$, $j = 1, \ldots, m$. Standard linear least squares then gives

$$R' = \text{inv}(X'X)X'Y,$$

and the regression fits to Y are XR'.

These regression fits can be displayed in the plane by plotting the centered and normed coordinates $\mathbf{x}_i$, $i = 1, \ldots, n$ (these are the rows of X), as well as the regression coefficient vectors $\mathbf{r}_j$, $j = 1, \ldots, m$ (the rows of R). This display of n location markers and m variable markers is a biplot of Y since the inner product of $\mathbf{x}_i$ with $\mathbf{r}_j$ approximates observation element y_{ij}. This follows from XR' being the regression fit for Y. Since this construction has the row markers $\mathbf{x}$ displaying the map of locations, it is referred to as a MAP-BIPLOT (this was first proposed by Kempton (1984) and differs from the better known principal component biplot (Gabriel (1971, 1981)) in which both sets of markers are chosen to optimize the joint fit).

The map-biplot gives an excellent display of the planar dependence of all the variables on the map. The regressions of the columns of Y onto those of X fit each variable's observations at the n locations by a plane defined over the map. The $\mathbf{r}_j$ marker on the map-biplot describes the regression plane for the j-th variable: its direction indicates where the plane has its maximum gradient; its length shows the slope of the plane in that direction. The m regresssion planes displayed on the map-biplot fit the data to the extent that the variables depend planarly on location.

The Illinois precipitation map-biplot—Figure 2—has a $\mathbf{x}_i$ marker for each station i (numbered by the station label i), and a $\mathbf{r}_j$ marker for each month j (highlighted by a vector from the origin and labeled by the number j of the month, with a minus sign to distinguish it from station labels). As usual with biplot display (Gabriel (1971, 1981)) a station i which is marked in the positive (negative) direction of the j-th month marker indicates more (less) than average precipitation at that station in that month. We note two main sheaves of month markers: November through March and May through October. They are differentiated along a NNW to SSE axis, with November to March having more precipitation in the SSE and less in the NNW, and vice versa for May to October.

The map-biplot does not provide any information on the deviations from planarity of dependence on location, but analysis of the residuals

$$Z = Y - XR'$$

may provide such information.

Outliers may be detected by inspecting the residuals Z, though that could be done more satisfactorily if resistant methods were used to obtain the regresssion coefficients R.

The residuals' patterns of dependence on location cannot be planar (as the planar component has been subtracted out), so the above regression and map-biplot methods cannot help in studying them. Fitting higher order terms or transformations of latitudes and longitudes might be useful, but assumes that one has a way of identifying which transformations would be helpful.

Contours of each variable's residuals plotted on the map might indicate patterns, but it would usually be difficult to consider contours for m variables' residuals simultaneously. To avoid that we may study some "typical" residuals, such as some of their principal components. Thus, we may approximate Z by n-by-m matrix

$$Z_{\{1\}} = \mathbf{j}_{\{1\}}\mathbf{k}'_{\{1\}},$$

(an outer product) of rank one, or by matrix

$$Z_{\{2\}} = \mathbf{j}_{\{1\}}\mathbf{k}'_{\{1\}} + \mathbf{j}_{\{2\}}\mathbf{k}'_{\{2\}}$$

of rank 2. If we choose the $\mathbf{k}$'s to be orthonormal, then $\mathbf{j}_{\{1\}}$ and $\mathbf{j}_{\{2\}}$ are, respectively, the first and the second principal component (PC) scores of the residuals Z.

We now wish to display the first PC score $j_{\{1\},i}$ (or the vector

$$\mathbf{j}_i = (j_{\{1\},i}, j_{\{2\},i})'$$

of the first two PC scores) at map location $\mathbf{x}_i$ and see if a "typical" pattern emerges. Such a pattern might suggest a quadratic model, or some transformation of the coordinates, or a distortion of the geography that does not follow a simple mathematical form. We would then see if we could incorporate that into modeling the geographical dependence of the data, or merely describing it.

Displaying the PC scores is not straightforward. Their relation to the geography is to be brought out, but they do not have geographical dimensions of their own. One may place glyphs representing them on the map, each score $\mathbf{j}_i$ (of one or two PCs) being shown at location $\mathbf{x}_i$. The choice of glyphs may be experimented with. Inspection of such a map of glyphs moight reveal patterns.

For the Illinois precipitation data, two alternative displays of the first PCs are given in Figures 3 and 4, using arrows and rectangles, respectively. We are concerned that the arrows in Figure 3 (whose direction was chosen arbitrarily) might be misinterpreted as having a geographical sense, and therefore prefer Figure 4. Either way it is apparent that there are positive residual PCs in the North and South, and a band of negative values through the middle of the state and toward its NE corner (below the lake). This pattern might in part be modeled by a quadratic term in latitudes, but the large negative values in the East (below the lake) are unlikely to be fitted by a longitude quadratic or any simple polynomial.

For two PCs one may use a directed arrow, and there again one has the choice of scale and of the direction of the axes of representation. If one has animated display capability, one might want to look at a variety of directions.

This is illustrated in Figure 5, but we must warn against the natural tendency to interpret the arrows' directions geographically. It would seem that these data have no "outlying" stations: None of the arrows are strinkingly different from others around them.

Interpretation of the residuals' patterns would be facilitated by smoothing the $\mathbf{j}_i$'s and possibly plotting contours. That should lead to decomposing the residuals into the smooth and the rough. The former should be described and, if possible, modeled, whereas the latter should be inspected for outliers and otherwise ascribed to noise.

3 The Indirect Approach: Principal Components and the Map

We first approximate the matrix of observations $Y(n\text{-by-}m)$ by a matrix of rank two, $Y_{\{2\}}$ say, which is equivalent to seeking two factor matrices $G(n\text{-by-}2)$ and $H(m\text{-by-}2)$ whose product is the approximation, i.e.,

$$Y_{\{2\}} = GH'.$$

The least squares solution is well known to be provided by PC analysis, and may be written

$$Y_{\{2\}} = P'LQ,$$

where diagonal L has the first (largest) two singular values of Y and the columns of P' and Q' contain the orthogonal column and rows of the corresponding singular components. Resistant solutions are also available (Gabriel and Odoroff (1984)) but require heavier computing.

The rows $\mathbf{g}$ of G reflect the statistical scatter of the n locations' observations. But the factorization $Y_{\{2\}} = GH'$ is clearly not unique: Indeed, for any non-singular 2-by-2 R, there is an equivalent factorization $Y_{\{2\}} = (GR)(H \text{ inv}(R'))'$. This multiplicity of possible factorizations may result in $\mathbf{g}$'s reflecting different aspects of the multivariate scatter. Thus, if $G = P'L$ of the above SVD (singular value decomposition), then the $\mathbf{g}$-metric is the same as the Euclidean metric of the rows of $Y_{\{2\}}$, and approximates the Euclidean metric of the rows of Y. Similarly, if $G = P'$, the $\mathbf{g}$-metric becomes that of the Mahalanobis distances of the rows of $Y_{\{2\}}$. Also, if $G = P'PX$, the $\mathbf{g}$-scatter is optimally (least squares) close to the $\mathbf{x}$-scatter, but the resulting $\mathbf{g}$-metric is not easy to interpret in terms of the data alone. In the following, we have chosen the first type of factorization, so that the $\mathbf{g}$-scatter reflects the Euclidean distances of the rows of the data matrix.

Both the data and the location coordinates had been zero centered and normed to mean row length unity. (One may or may not wish to similarly renorm the rank 2 approximation.) But the orientation of the rows of G is entirely arbitrary. Replacing factorization $Y_{\{2\}} = GH'$ by $Y_{\{2\}} = (GO)(HO)'$ for any orthogonal matrix O(2-by-2) does not change the distances or angles of the rows' configuration. For example, if the **g**-metric is that of Euclidean data distances, the **g** O-metric will be the same. Hence we facilitate the (**x** , **g**) comparison by rotating the **g**'s to the optimal orientation, which is the one that makes them closest to the corresponding **x**'s.

(NOTE: For any given factor G, the Euclidean norm $\|X - GO\|$, where O is orthogonal, is minimized by Procrustes rotation (see, for example, Gordon (1981) Section 5.5). The solution is $O = MN'$, where MTN' is the SVD of $G'X$, with $MM' = M'M = NN' = N'N = I$ and T diagonal.)

The rank 2 approximation to the Illinois precipitation data is shown in Figure 6 in a row-metric-preserving (rmp) biplot which is chosen so that the inter-station marker distances approximate Euclidean distances (as in the first factorization mentioned above). This biplot is read just like that in Figure 2, form which it differs in that its station markers are not constrained to their map locations, but only rotated to be near the station locations. Clearly, this biplot provides a closer fit to the data than the map-biplot. In Figure 7 it is reproduced after Procrustes rotation, so as to be more readily compared to the map and the map-biplot—Figure 2. We will not comment on this biplot further, except to note that since the length of the month markers correspond to the month standard deviations, the variability of rainfall across Illinois is seen to be rather small in April and May and October. Also, since the cosines of the angles between month markers indicate correlations, one notes the very high correlations between the months June–September and between the November–March months, and the strong negative correlation between these two sets of months.

The distances in the **g**'s-scatter are calculated only from the data, not the locations. To see how the data depend on the locations, we now compare the rows $\mathbf{g}_i$ with the location coordiates $\mathbf{x}_i$, $i = 1, \ldots, n$. This comparison can be made by plotting the **x**'s and the **g**'s jointly and linking each location $\mathbf{x}_i$ with the corresponding datum $\mathbf{g}_i$. (For a discussion of such linked plots see Diaconis and Friedman (1980), Tukey and Tukey (1981), and Wegman (1986).)

If the $(\mathbf{x}_i, \mathbf{g}_i)$ links are short, the data, in its rank 2 approximation, correspond closely to the map pattern. In other words, the observations differ more, or less, according to the greater, or lesser, distance between the locations. Individual outliers would be represented by long links.

The map-to-PC links for Illinois precipitation are shown in Figure 8. The pattern here is very clear, the data induced **g**'s are narrowing the geographic **x**'s and shifting the Central part of Illinois to the west and compensating from the other parts. Note also that the very Southern stations are farther away than suggested from the geography. (That agrees with what was observed on different residual PCs displayed in Figures 3 to 5, above.)

If the links form a systematic pattern of pointing towards, or away from, two axes, these axes may indicate the directions of the gradients for the PCs planar dependence on the location. If we suspect such a systematic dependence, we represent it by a regression fit. Thus, we adjust the i-th location to $\overset{\#}{\mathbf{x}}_i$, the i-th row of

$$\overset{\#}{X} = X\mathrm{inv}(X'X)X'G.$$

We then decompose the link $(\mathbf{x}_i, \mathbf{g}_i)$ into the two components $(\mathbf{x}_i, \overset{\#}{\mathbf{x}}_i)$ for planar regression fit and $(\overset{\#}{\mathbf{x}}_i, \mathbf{g}_i)$ for residuals from this fit. In examining the possibility of non-planar dependence, we examine the $(\overset{\#}{\mathbf{x}}_i, \mathbf{g}_i)$ links for patterns. Again, smoothing might help to differentiate the smooth from the rough.

For the Illinois data the two sets of links are shown in Figures 9 and 10, respectively. Figure 9 shows a very clear regression toward a NNW to SSE axis, Figure 10 shows distortions from planarity in that central stations are displaced in a WSW direction whereas Northern and Southern stations compensate by moving to the East and somewhat to the center latitude.

4 Some Comparisons of the Two Approaches

The direct approach uses four dimensions to fit the data—the first two geographical, and the last two chosen to fit the residuals optimally. The indirect approach compares two sets of two dimensions—two geographical and two chosen to fit the data optimally. Clearly, the direct approach must give a better fit to the data. But its four dimensions are not related to each other easily and make it hard to trace non-planar dependencies since these are partitioned between the first two and the last two dimensions. Such dependencies may be more easily traced by comparing the map with the rank 2 approximation to the data. We would be out of luck, however, if the planar dependence was not strong enough to dominate the first two principal components—our indirect approach would miss it.

The illustrative Illinois precipitation example showed that very similar conclusions were drawn from graphical displays of both approaches. They seem to complement and support each other. (More elaborate modeling, as suggested by these analyses, are not illustrated here as that is not the topic of this paper.)

The moral seems to be that an exploration should use both approaches in parallel and compare their findings.

5 Attemps at Smoothing

Regressing the PCs onto the coordinates explores planar dependence on the geography. Other patters may be studied by smoothing the data locally, i.e., within relatively small geographical regions. For a first attempt to do this we have defined the neighborhood of each location as a disc shaped subset of other locations within a given radius 'dis' of it. We then regressed the $\mathbf{g}$'s within that disc on the corresponding $\mathbf{x}$'s, and defined the smoothed $\hat{\mathbf{g}}_i$ as the regression fit at $\mathbf{x}_i$. We tried unweighted regression within the disc by using regression of all locations with indicator weights

$$v_{i,e} = \begin{cases} 1 & \text{if } 0 < \|\mathbf{x}_e - \mathbf{x}_i\| < \text{dis} \\ 0 & \text{otherwise,} \end{cases}$$

and we also tried regression weighted inversely to distance within the disc, using weights

$$w_{i,e} = \begin{cases} 1 - (\|\mathbf{x}_i - \mathbf{x}_e\| \,/\, \text{dis})^2 & \text{if } 0 < \|\mathbf{x}_e - \mathbf{x}_i\| < \text{dis} \\ 0 & \text{otherwise.} \end{cases}$$

The results of this smoothing are shown in Figures 11–13, for weights w with radius dis = 0.5.

Figure 11 shows a systematic pattern in which the east-central stations are displaced westward, whereas the west-central stations move to in a North-easterly direction. Also, the station farthest to the South (#6) becomes more separated, suggesting it was rather more different from the rest of Illinois than accounted for by its geographic location.

Figures 12 and 13 display the "rough" $\mathbf{g}_i - \hat{\mathbf{g}}_i$ for each station, i.e., the part of its precipitation pattern that is not part of a smooth geographical pattern. Its most obvious feature is the large rough for station #6 in the South, which makes one wonder whether smoothing had worked well for that station. The other stations with sizeable "roughs" are #4 and #55, both in the StLouis region. Could that be evidence of an urban effect?

An alternative would be to smooth the deviations $\mathbf{d}_i = \mathbf{g}_i - \overset{\#}{\mathbf{x}}_i$ from the regressions on the locations. Using the same methods as above, one would obtain display of the smooth and of the "rough". For the Illinois example the rough is virtually indistinguishable from that of the above smoothing of the PCs $\mathbf{g}$'s, so the sum of the regressed PCs $\overset{\#}{\mathbf{x}}$ and the smoothed $\hat{\mathbf{d}}$ must be much the same as the smoothed PCs $\hat{\mathbf{g}}$. That is not surprising. The advantage of the latter type of smoothing would be that the relation of PCs to locations be decomposed into three parts, as follows,

locations to regressed PCs	$\mathbf{x}_i$ to $\overset{\#}{\mathbf{x}}_i$
regressed PCs to smoothed PCs	$\overset{\#}{\mathbf{x}}_i$ to $\hat{\mathbf{d}}_i + \overset{\#}{\mathbf{x}}_i$ [apx. $\hat{\mathbf{g}}_i$]
smoothed PCs to PCs	$\hat{\mathbf{d}}_i + \overset{\#}{\mathbf{x}}_i$ to $\mathbf{g}_i$

This decomposition with weights and radiuses 'dis' suggests that smoothing is not crucially dependent on them, within a small range. However, the type of smoothing introduced here does not appear to deal well with edge effects. That needs further investigation.

Acknowledgement

It is a real pleasure to acknowledge Nick Fisher's friendly and lively critical review of my attempts to deal with problems of geostatistical variation.

This work was supported in part by the NSF Contract ATM-8610028 on Studies of Temporal and Spatial Fluctuations of and Other Severe Storm Conditions, awarded to the University of Rochester: S.A. Changnon and K.R. Gabriel, co-investigators.

References

Diaconis PI, Friedman JH (1983) M and N Plots. SLAC Report PUB-2495, Stanford

Gabriel KR (1971) The Biplot—Graphical Display of Matrices with Application to Principal Component Analysis. Biometrica 58: 3453–3467

Gabriel KR (1981) Biplot, in: Kotz S, Johnson NL, Read C (eds.) Encyclopedia of Statistical Sciences. Wiley, New York, pp 23–30

Gabriel KR, Odoroff CL (1984) Resistant Lower Rank Approximations of Matrices, in: Diday E et al. (eds.) Data Analysis and Informatics. North Holland, Amsterdam, pp 23–30

Gordon AW (1981) Classification. Chapman and Hall, London

Kempton RA (1984) The Use of Biplots in Interpreting Variety by Environment Interactions. Journal of Agricultural Science 103: 123–135

Tukey PA, Tukey JW (1981) Preparation; Prechosen Sequences of Views, in: Barnett V (ed.) Interpreting Multivariate Data. Wiley, London, pp 189–213

Wegman EJ (1986) Representing Multivariate Meterological Data Using Parallel Coordinates. Preprints of the Tenth Conference on Weather Modification. American Meteorological Society, Boston

Figure 1: Map of Illinois stations

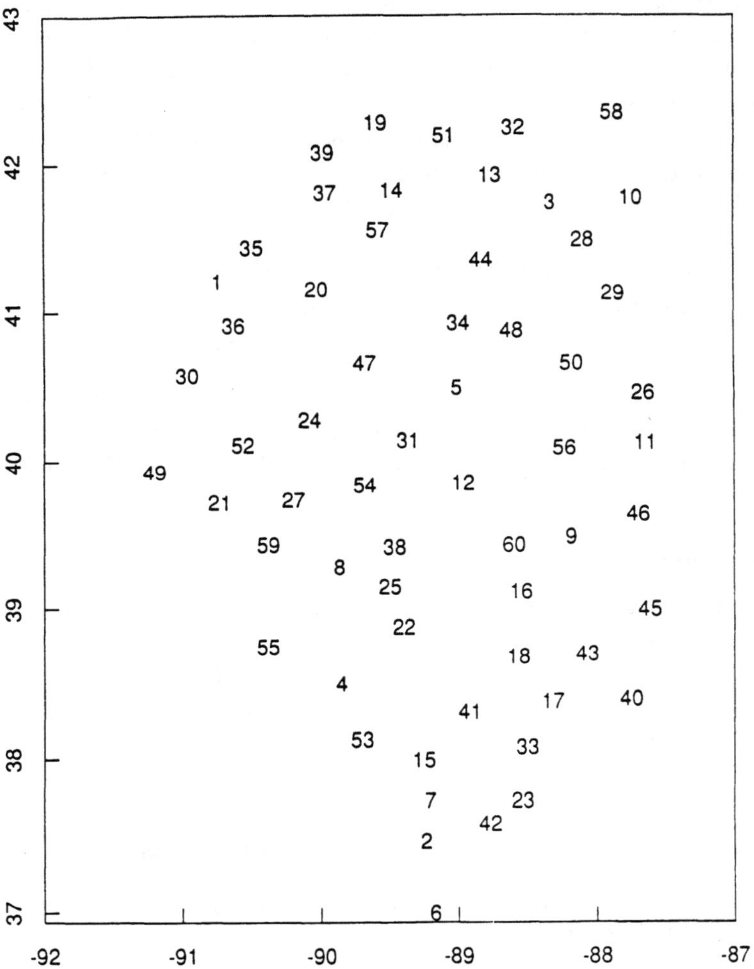

Illinois precip RMP

Figure 2: Map-biplot - stations and months

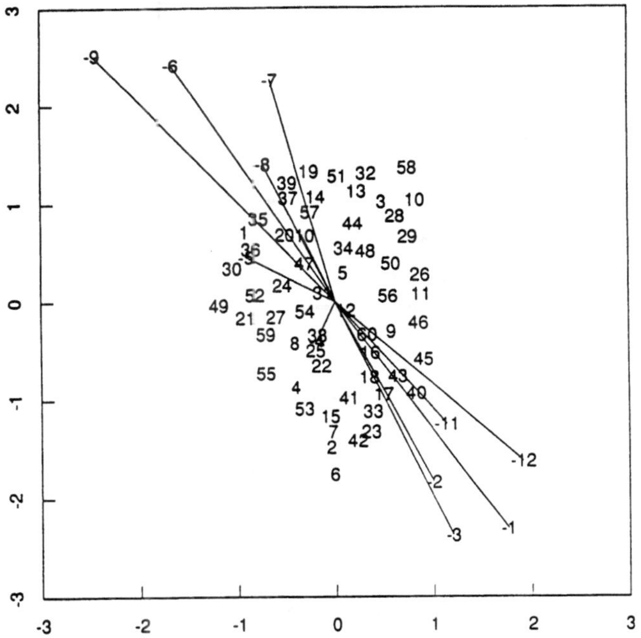

Illinois precip RMP SS from regr= 13.16282

Figure 3: Map plus first residuals PC arrows

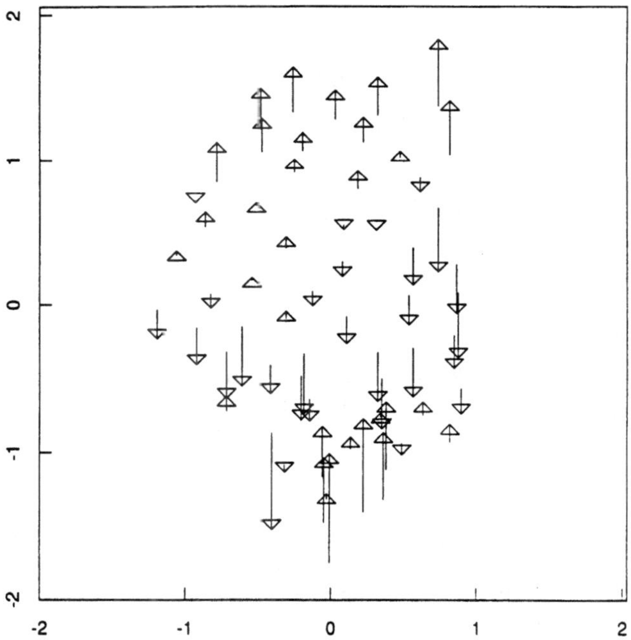

Illinois precip RMP SS one reg residual PC= 4.731636

Figure 4: First principal component of residuals
(vertical is positive, horizontal negative)

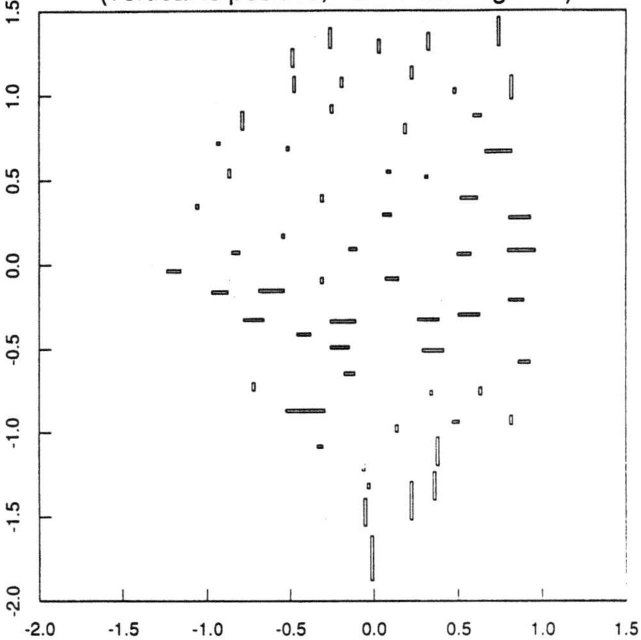

Illinois precip RMP SS one reg residual PC= 4.731636

Figure 5: Map plus two residuals PC arrows

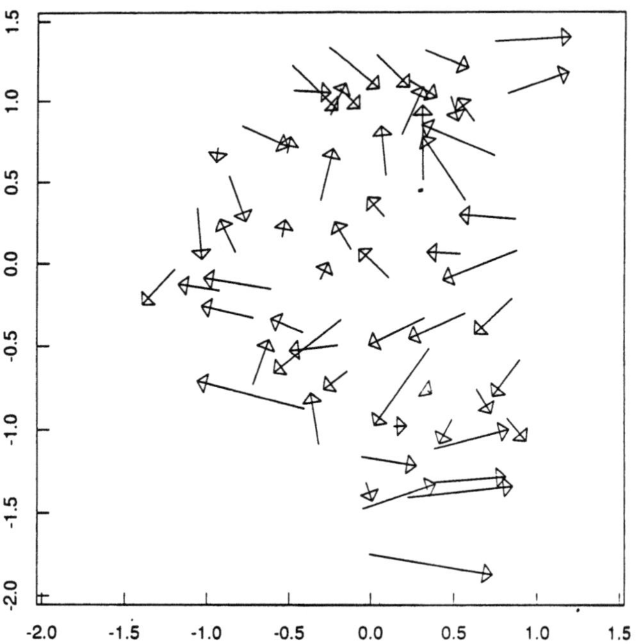

Illinois precip RMP SS two reg residual PCs= 4.731636 2.233167

Figure 6: Row-Metric-Preserving Biplot

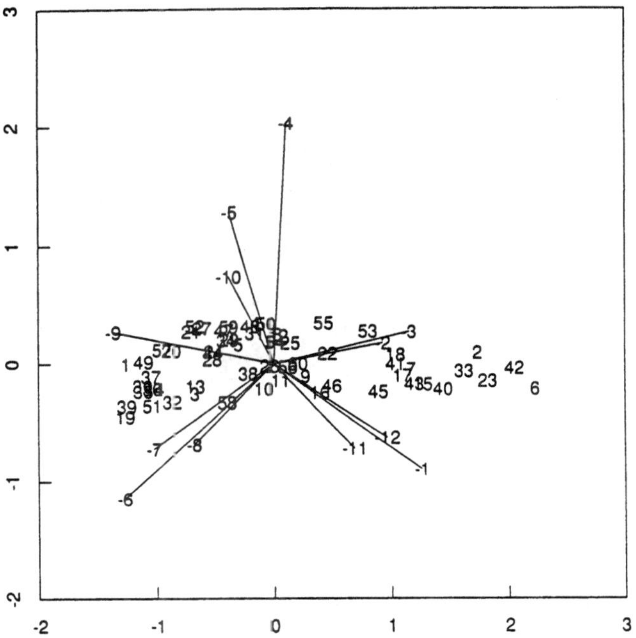

Illinois precip RMP Biplot fit= 0.874143 SS Devs= 7.55144

Figure 7: Map-rotated rmp-biplot

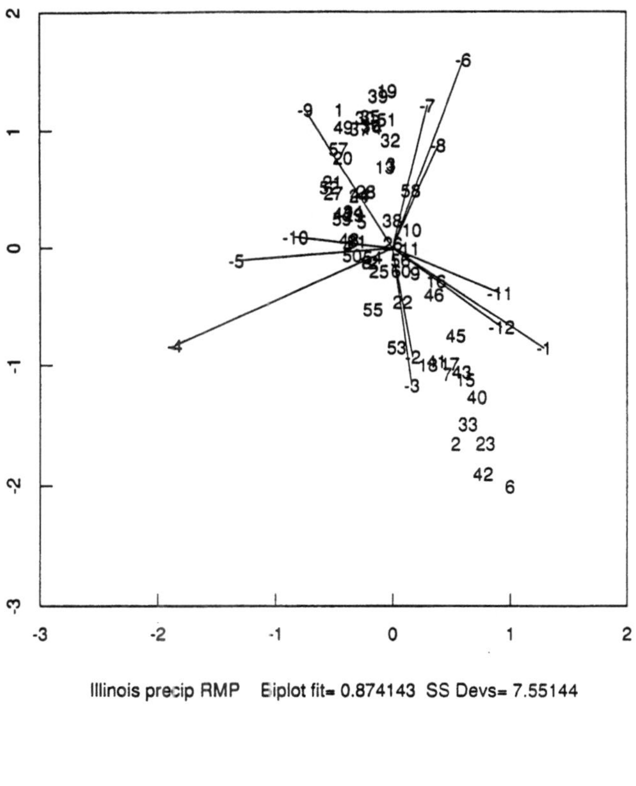

Illinois precip RMP Biplot fit= 0.874143 SS Devs= 7.55144

Figure 8: Map locations pointing to rmp PCs

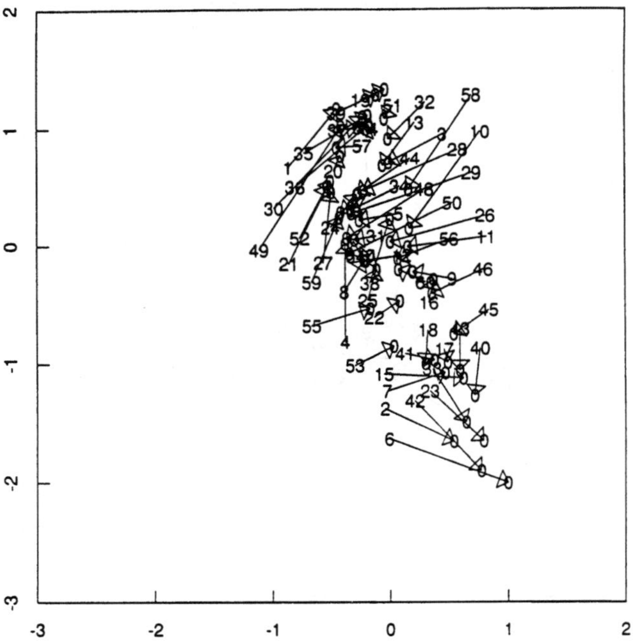

Illinois precip RMP SS= 20.96415

Figure 9: Locations pointing to affine transformation

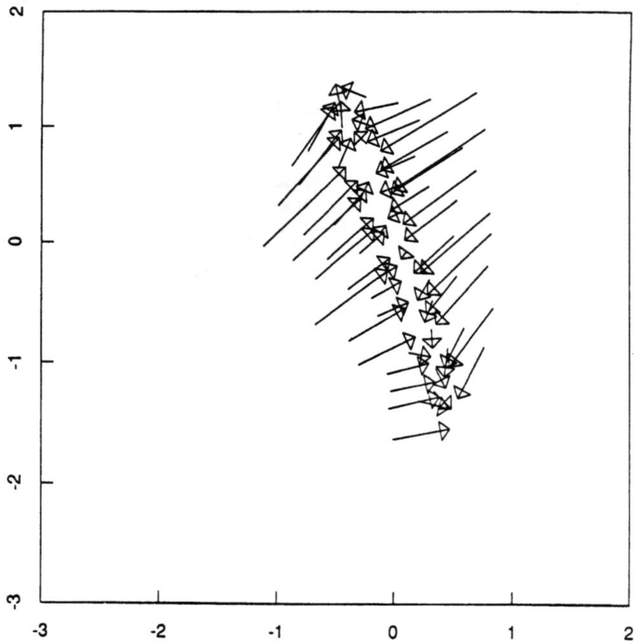

Illinois precip RMP

Figure 10: Affine transformation pointing to PCs

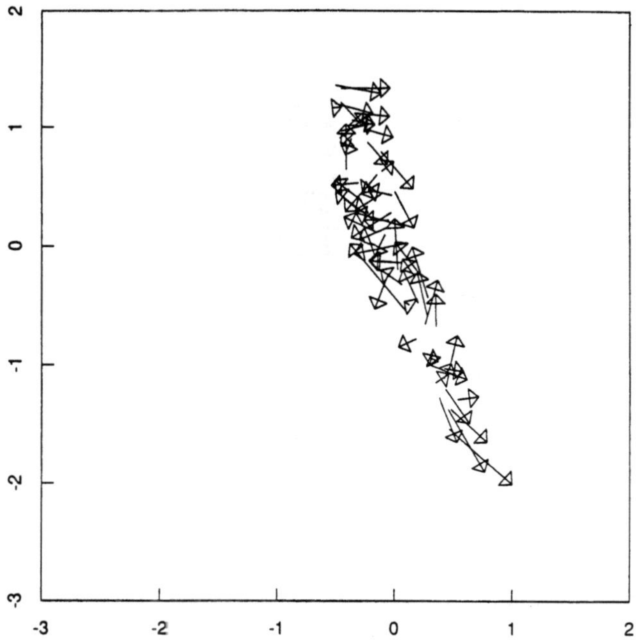

Illinois precip RMP SS= 6.20222

Figure 11: Locations pointing to smoothed PCs

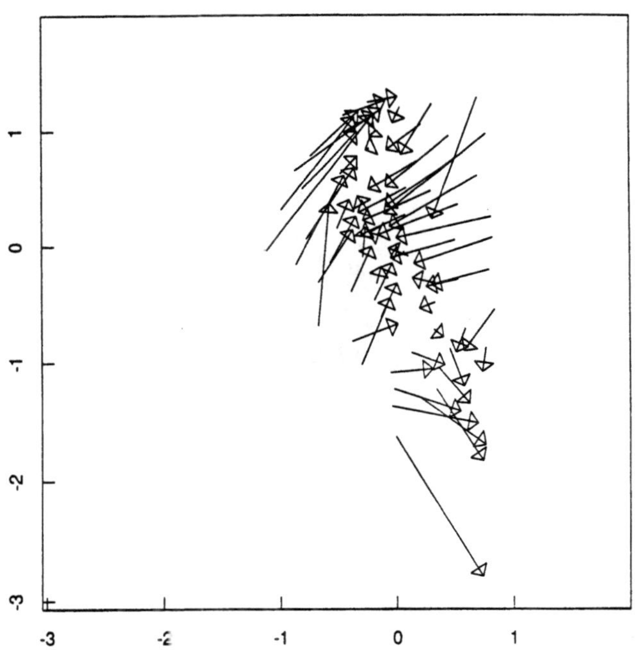

Illinois precip RMP dis= 0.5

Figure 12: Smoothed PCs pointing to PCs

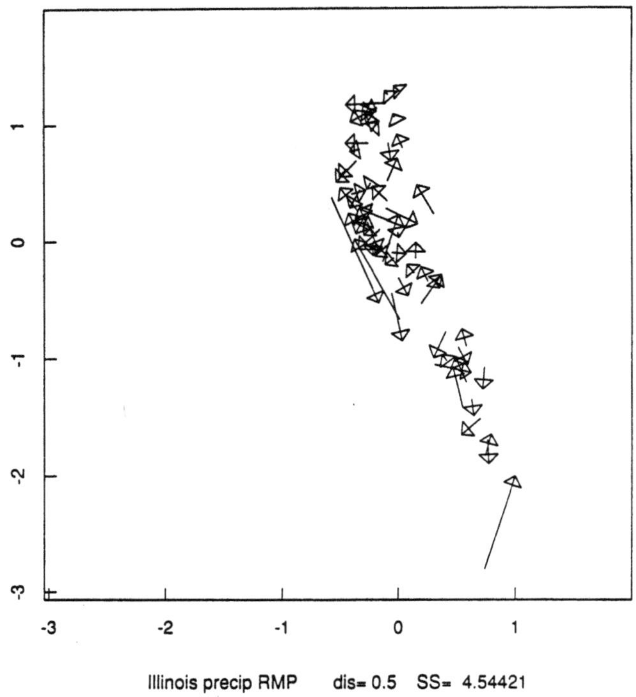

Figure 13: Deviations from smoothing resids PC

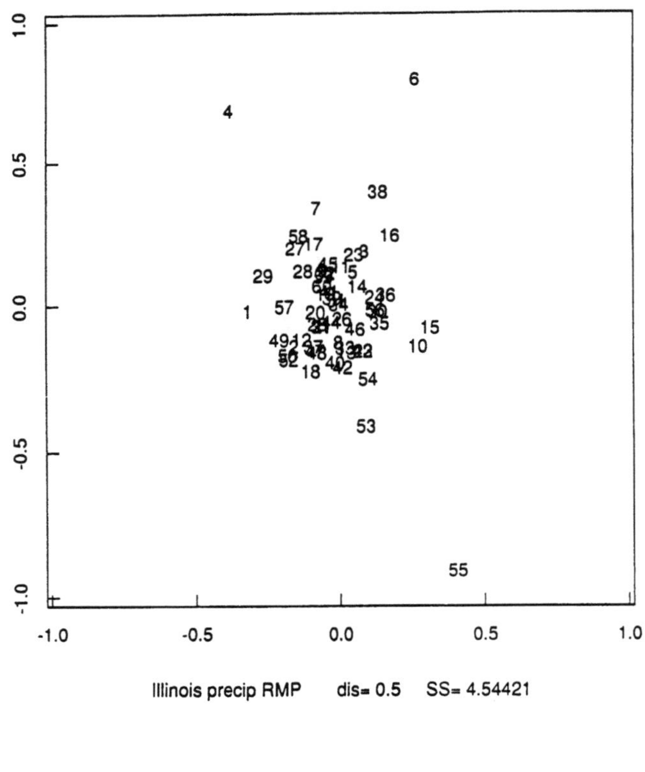

Classification of Microcomputers and Marketing Interpretation

J. Janssen and P. Van Brussel
CADEPS/ULB
Av. F. Roosevelt, 50 CP 194/7, B1050 Brussels

Summary

Forty Microcomputers representative of the market were selected in 1985. They were described with a set of heterogeneous data, including both quantitative and qualitative variables. The first problem is to draw the structure of this simplified market by classifying them with the help of classical Data Analysis methods such as Correspondence Analysis and Hierarchical Classification. The next step is to study the evolution of this structure on two consecutive years. This can be made by using the powerful "Supplementary Elements" technique. Finally, it will be shown how this technique can be at the root of a small simulation model for the choice of a microcomputer.

1 Introduction

The aim of the paper is to explain how combinations of several Data Analysis tools such as Correspondence Analysis and Hierarchical Classification can help to find solutions for some general problems in Marketing. More specifically, three applications of the so-called "Supplementary Elements" technique (Lebart, Morineau, Tabard (1977)) will be given in order to see what contribution it has in the study of the structure of a market, the evolution of this structure and finally in the problem of placing an existent or non-existent product in relation to others. Furthermore, this technique can be at the root of simulations models.

The basic idea of the "Supplementary Elements" technique is to perform a "visualized" regression. Additional information (individuals and/or variables) is projected in the structure issued of the analysis of a given data set, in order to explain it using this structure. This paper will attempt to illustruate this approach with the help of a didactic example. It will consequently be designed in a very practical way.

The origin of this example is a problem presented at the "Third International Workshop on Data Analysis" (Brussels (1985)) by S. Chah (Janssen, Marcotorchino, Proth (1987)). The problem was to classify 40 microcomputers described by a heterogeneous data set, including both qualitative and quantitative variables. Several approaches were proposed (Chah, Guttman, Van Brussel, Lewi) that all converged on the same results. The list of the individuals, of the variables and the data matrix can be found in the appendix.

2 The "Supplementary Elements" Technique

In this part, we only give a short overview of the "Supplementary Elements" technique. Let us assume that a Correspondence Analysis has been performed on the X data table. Let us also assume that we have additional information that we would like to "explain" by the structure issued from the Correspondence Analysis. The problem is to place the new "profiles" in relation with the structure, i.e. the factorial axes. This can be schematically explained as follows:

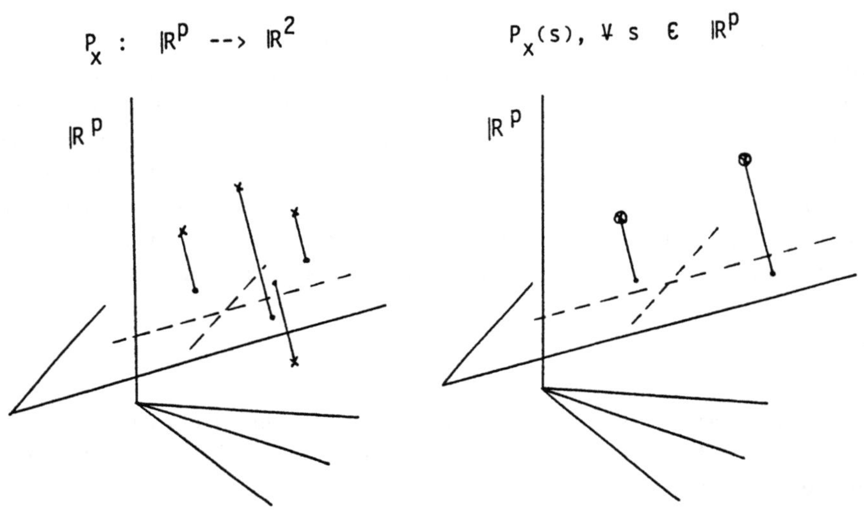

Figure 1

Rows (resp columns) of data matrix X will define a projector Px when building the structure. Each supplementary element will be projected in the structure using Px. Thus the interpretation is given by the position of the supplementary element with respect to the factorial axes, i.e. with respect to the structure of the data set. For further information, see Lebart, Morineau, Tabard (1977).

3 Structure of the PC Market

As mentioned in the introduction, several approaches of the problem were presented and all converged to the same results. More specifically, several classical Data Analysis methods were used, each of them corresponding to a different coding of the variables. That is the reason why only one will be presented here: the Multiple Correspondence Analysis approach. First at all, it is necessary to transform quantitative variables to make them qualitative. This has been done in a very classical way by dividing them in classes.

- Prize:
  1 : 20.000 - 30.000 FF
  2 : 30.001 - 40.000 FF
  3 : 40.001 - 50.000 FF
  4 : more than 50.000
- RAM configuration:
  1 : less than 64 Kb
  2 : 64 Kb
  3 : 64 - 128 Kb
  4 : 128 Kb
  5 : 128 - 256 Kb
  6 : 256 Kb
  7 : more than 256 Kb
- RAM maximum:
  1 : less than 256 Kb
  2 : 256 Kb
  3 : 256 - 512 Kb
  4 : 512 Kb
  5 : 512 - 1024 Kb
  6 : 1024 Kb
- Mass storage:
  1 : less than 320 Kb
  2 : 320 Kb
  3 : 360 Kb
  4 : 360 - 720 Kb
  5 : 720 Kb
  6 : more than 720 Kb

Multiple Correspondence Analysis will be performed with the analysis of the Burt's table (Burt (1950); Lebart, Morineau, Tabard (1977)). Since Burt's table is only crossing variables, it does not permit to visualise the individuals. Nevertheless, the "Supplementary Elements" technique will make us able to do it by adding the identity matrix as supplementary variable. The data matrix will look as follow:

"Active" Variables	"Supplementary" Variables
	1000 000
	0100 000
Qualitative	0010 000
	....
+	....
	....
Quantitative	0000 100
	0000 010
	0000 001

Figure 2 contains the results of the Multiple Correspondence Analysis. Only the first factorial plane was represented.

- Axis 1 (horizontal) opposes the PCs using a 16 bit-processor (16B) to the others (8B - 32B). Those computers are running under DOS (DSS) with a standard mass storage of 320 Kb (320) or 360 Kb (They support color monitor (MCS) and a 10 Mb hard disk (H10).).
- Axis 2 (vertical) separates two groups of microcomputers. On the upper side of the axis, we found PCs running under CP/M (CPS) operating system. They are characterised by having a 8 bit-processor (8B) and supporting no color monitor

(HDX). On the lower side, several microcomputers running under other operating systems (ASS) are to be found. Some of them are using a 32 bit-processor (32B) and support a 5 Mb hard disk (HD5).

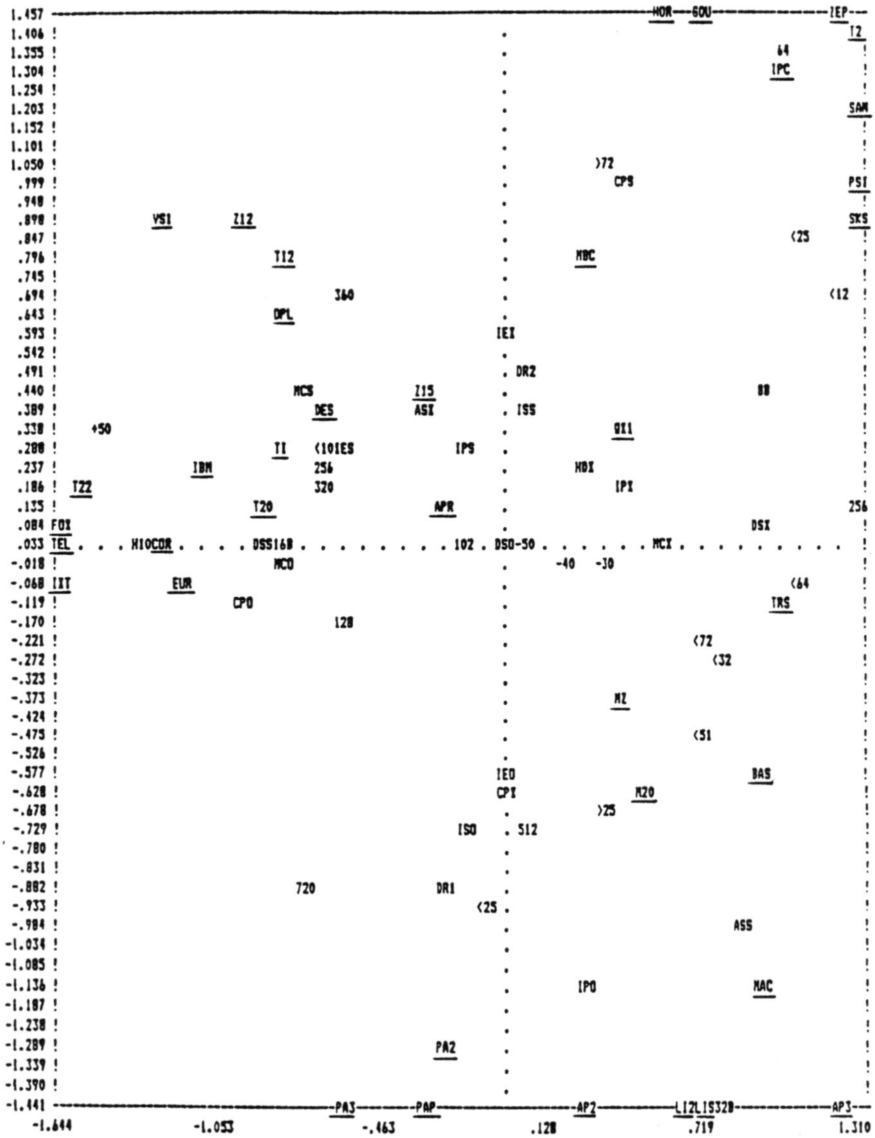

Figure 2: Multiple Correspondence Analysis (Factorial Plane (1,2))

This structure separates the microcomputers (underlined in the figure) in four groups:

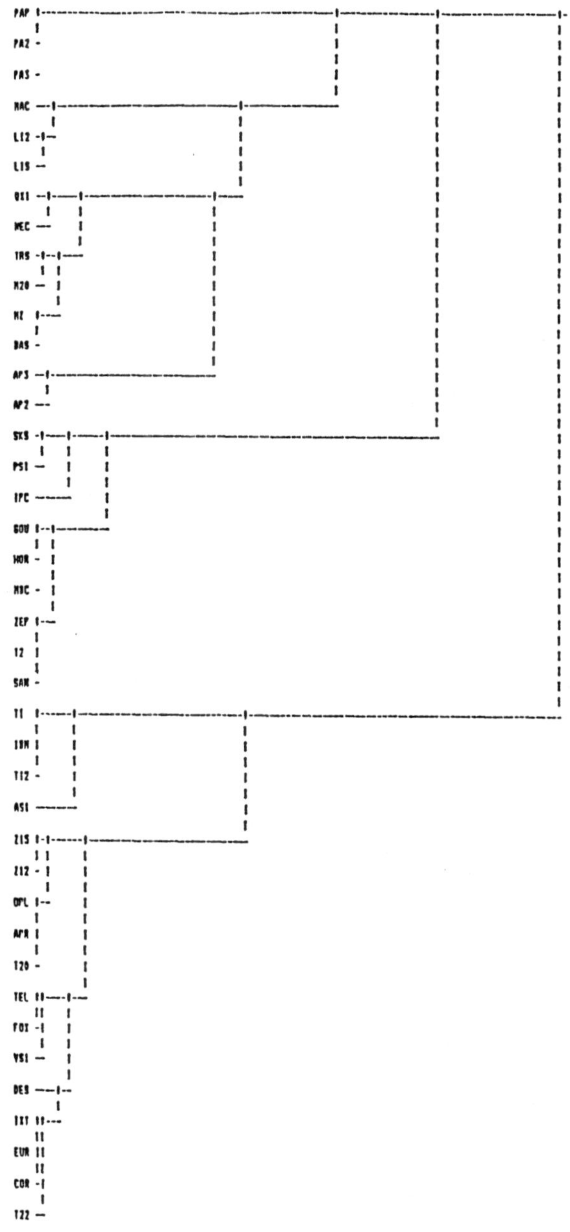

Figure 3: Hierarchical Classification on Factorial Coordinates

- All "IBM like" computers running under DOS with a 8088-8086 processor. The highest level of price are to be found in this group.
- The CP/M microcomputers that use the Z80 processor and are the less expensive but also the less powerful.

- The third group contains all APPLE machines and also those that are not standard. We shall name these "APPLE like" machines whose characteristics is the use of the 6502-6809-68000 processors.

- Finally, the last group contains the three TOSHIBA computers PAP (PAP, PA2, PA3) which are similar to the IBM standard according to the operating system and the processor and close to the APPLE because of a non-standard 720 Kb mass storage (720).

Since Correspondence Analysis only gives a plane vision of the data, the solution found above can be validated by performing a hierarchical clustering analysis (Ward algorithm) on the factorial coordinates with respect to the six first factorial axes. Figure 3 shows the classification tree. As we can see, the four clusters appear very clearly.

4 Evolution of the Market's Structure

Here, we are going to give another illustration of the use of the "Supplementary Elements" technique for studying the evolution found in the preceding paragraph. The approach is based on the so-called "Table Comparison" method (Cullus, Guttman, Janssen, Van Brussel (1987)).

Binary Correspondence Analysis has been performed on a disjunctive table just as it was a contingency table. This table contains data related to 171 PCs that represent the PC market in 1986. Those were the "active" elements. The forty PCs of previous problem were added as supplementary elements.

Figure 4 shows the position of the variables in the first factorial plane. It will allow us to identify the new structure.

- Axis 1 (horizontal) opposes 16 bit-processor (16BS) to 8 bits-processor (08BS). On the left side of the axis, we find DOS operating system (DOSS) which is opposed to both CP/M (CPMS) and "Other" (0.SS) operating systems on the right side. As we can see, those two points are very close together. In the same way, the axis also distinguishes hard disks with a total mass storage greater than 10 Mb (HD10: 10 Mb, HD20: 20 Mb, H>20: more than 20 Mb) from the others (H<10: less than 10 Mb, HDXX: no hard disk).

- Axis 2 appears like a "price" axis. On the upper side, we find the lowest level of price and on the other side, the highest levels are to be found, due to the presence of the new "PC-AT" products.

Figure 5 gives the position of the 40 microcomputers as supplementary elements. There are only two classes left: on the left side, we find all "IBM compatible" machines (classes 1 and 4 in the previous classification). As we can see, the presence of the new "PC-AT" machines has caused a simplification of the market.

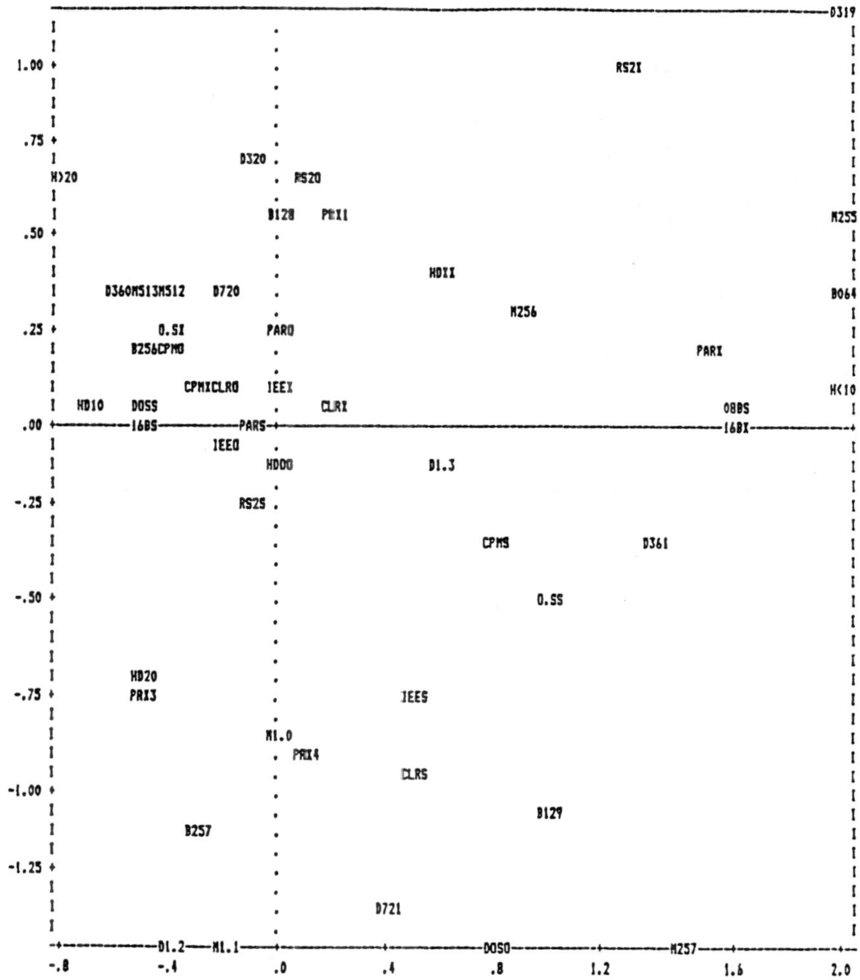

Figure 4: Binary Correspondence Analysis (Factorial Plane (1,2): Variables)

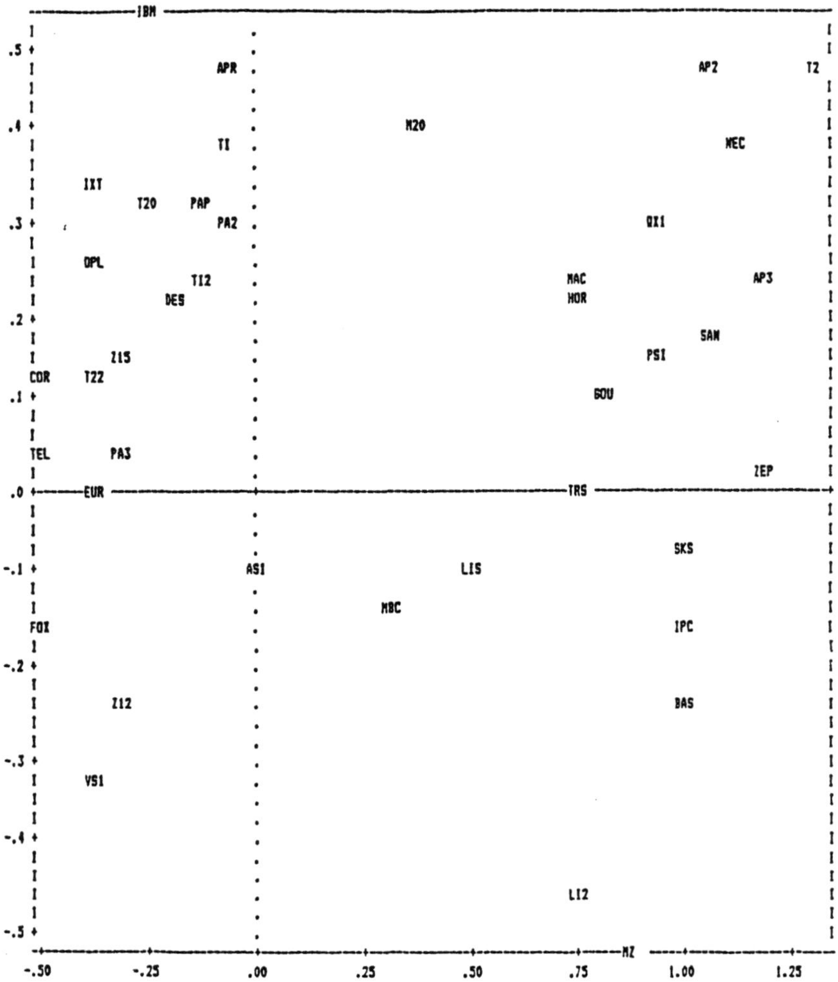

Figure 5: Binary Correspondence Analysis (Factorial Plane (1,2): Supplementary Elements)

5 A Simulation Model

The "Supplementary Elements" technique can also be at the root of simulation models. In this part, we will illustrate this possibility with the help of a small model written in LOTUS 123.

The structure of the model is the following:

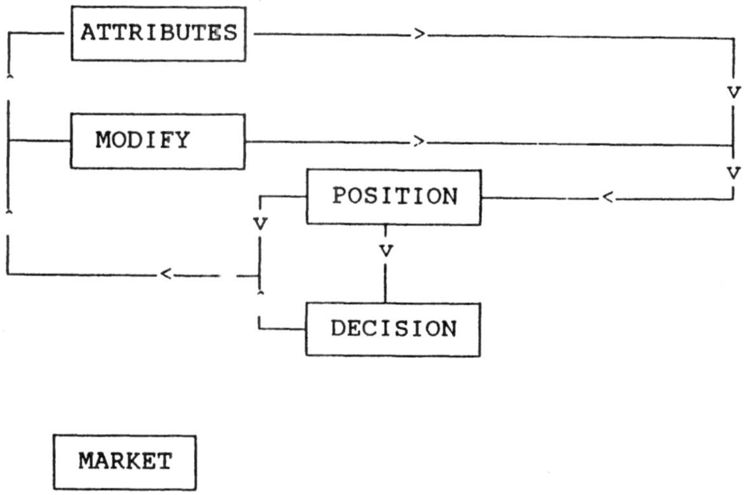

where:

- Attributes: Input of the New PC's characteristics.
- Modify: Modification of one characteristic.
- Position: Display the position of the New PC in the Structure.
- Decision: Gives the 10 closest PCs.
- Market: Display the structure of the market.

Figure 6 gives the layout of the screen when function "Market" has been invoked. As we can see, only one label is displayed for each group to make the graphic more readable. Each label is centred on the mean point of its cluster.

Let us assume we need a PC with the following characteristics:

- Color monitor
- DOS operating system
- 16 bit-processor
- Parallel interface
- Serial interface
- 10 Mb hard disk
- About FF 40,000
- 512 Kb RAM
- 360 Kb mass storage

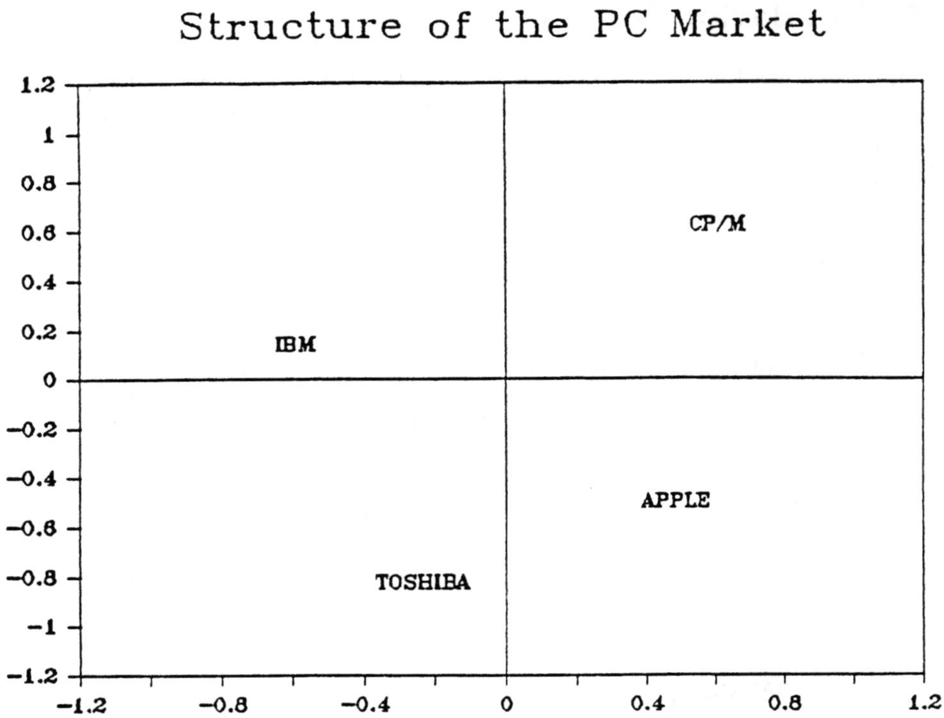

Figure 6

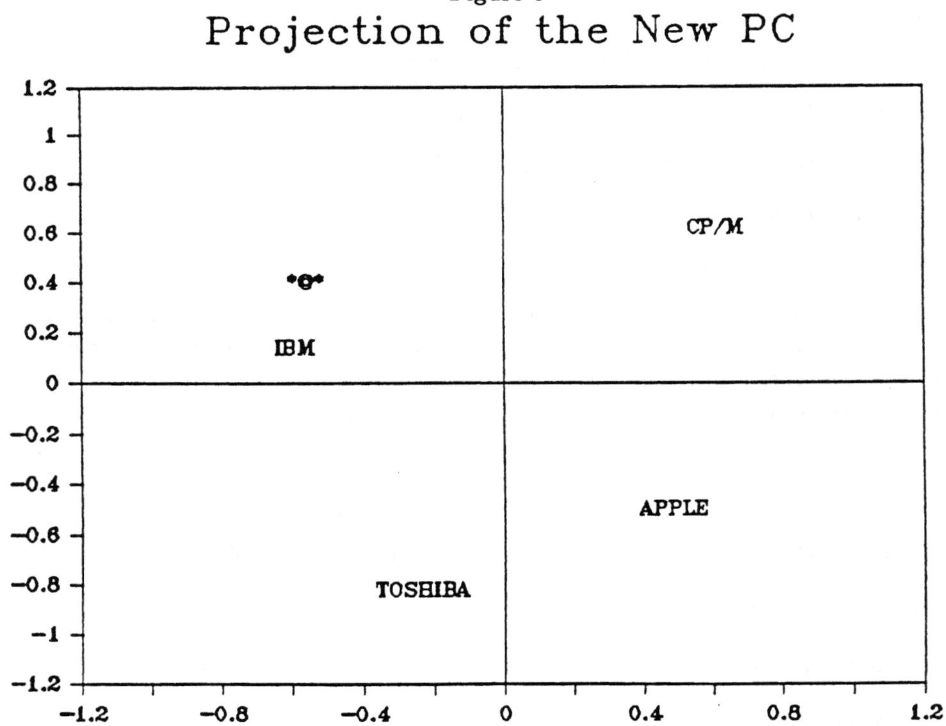

Figure 7

These characteristics are introduced in the model by invoking the "Attributes" function. The program generates a record with the same format as the data and computes its position in the figure. The "computational kernel" is the projector Px (Cf supra) which has been extracted from the Correspondence Analysis results. The model has only to perform the scalar product of the new attributes vector by the projector. The result of the simulation is displayed in Figure 7. The new PC is represented by the "* @ *" symbol. Finally, invoking function "Decision" lists the 10 closest PCs with respect to the euclidian distance computed on the six first factorial coordinates. This function has of course to be considered as a primary selection and could be completed by classical multicriteria methods or by an expert system.

6 Conclusion

Combining several Data Analysis methods such as Factorial Analysis and Hierarchical Classification appears as a quite appropriate and very powerful tool to solve classical marketing problems. Factorial Analysis allows a visualisation of a structure and therefore an easy identification of the clusters. Nevertheless, it is limited to a plane vision, so using Hierarchical Classification on factorial coordinates allows a validation of the structure.

The "Supplementary Elements" technique appears to be a quite appropriate method, that gives more flexibility to the approach. Its main advantage is that it uses the results of a Factorial Analysis, so that only one analysis is necessary.

References

Chah S, Cullus P ,Guttman L, Lewi P, Van Brussel P (1987) Classification of Heterogeneous Data Related to Microcomputers, in: Janssen J, Marcotorchino F, Proth JM (eds.) Data Analysis: The Ins and Outs of Solving Real Problems. Plenum

Cullus P, Guttman L, Janssen J, Van Brussel P (1987) A Comparison of Results of European Elections, in: Janssen J, Marcotorchino F, Proth JM (eds.) Data Analysis: The Ins and Outs of Solving Real Problems. Plenum

Greenacre MJ (1984) Theory and Applications of Correspondence Analysis. Academic Press

Janssen J, Marcotorchino F, Proth JM (1983) New Trends in Data Analysis and Applications. North Holland

Janssen J, Marcotorchino F, Proth JM (1985) Data Analysis in Real Life Environment: the Ins and Outs of Solving Problems. North Holland

Janssen J, Marcotorchino F, Proth JM (1987) Data Analysis: The Ins and Outs of Solving Real Problems. Plenum

Lebart L, Morineau A, Tabard N (1977) Techniques de la Déscription Statistique: Méthodes et Logiciels pour l'Analyse des Grands Tableaux. Dunod

Lebart L, Morineau A, Fenelon JP (1979) Traitement des Données Statistiques. Dunod

THE VARIABLES:

The Qualitative Variables:

Color Monitor {0,1,2}
Operating System CP/M {0,1,2}
Operating System DOS {0,1,2}
Operating System "Other" {0,1,2}
Processor {1(8 bits),2(16 Bits),3(32 Bits)}
Parallel Interface {0,1,2}
Serial Interface {0,1,2}
IEEE 488 Interface {0,1,2}
Hard Disk {0(does not exist),1(5 Mb),2(10 Mb)}
Number of Disk Drives {1,2}
(0: Feature does not exist
1: Feature is optional
2: Feature exists)

The Quantitative Variables:

Price (F.F.)
Random Access Memory: Basic configuration (Kb)
Random Access Memory: Maximum configurartion (Kb)
Mass Storage: Floppy disk unit (Kb)

THE INDIVIDUALS:

PAP (Toshiba)
QX 10 (Epson)
MACINTOSH (Apple)
TI PC (Texas Instruments)
PAP (2) (Toshiba)
APRICOT (ACT)
Z 150 (Zenith Data System)
GOUPIL 3 (SMT)
APPLE 3 (Apple)
TANDY 2000 (Tandy)
IBM PC-G (IBM)
TI PC (2) (Texas Instruments)
APPLE 2E (Apple)
TELE PC
PAP (3) (Toshiba)
IBM PC-XT (IBM)
Z 150 (2) (Zenith Data System)
TANDY 2000 (2) (Tandy)
VICTOR S1 (Victor Technologies)
T 200
AS 100
MZ 35 (Sharp)
BASIS 108
LISA 2 (Apple)
EUROPE PC (Brit)
PSI 80 (Kontron)
CORONA PC 2 (Corona)
OPLITE (Normerel)
HORIZON (Horizon Systems)
FOXY
SKS 2500
ZEPHYR (Horizon Systems)
MBC 4050 (Sanyo)
SANCO 8000 (Sanco)
IPC Mod. 15
DESKTOP 10 (Data General)
LISA 2-S (Apple)
NEC PC 8000 (Nec)
M 20 (Sord)
TRS 80 Mod. 12 (Tandy)

THE DATA MATRIX:

PAP	0	0	2	0	2	1	1	1	0	1	20000	192	512	720
QX1	1	2	0	0	1	2	1	1	0	2	23500	192	250	320
MAC	0	0	0	2	3	0	2	0	0	1	26000	128	512	400
TI	2	2	2	0	2	2	1	0	0	1	26300	128	768	320
PA2	0	0	2	0	2	1	1	1	0	2	27200	192	512	720
APR	0	0	2	0	2	2	2	1	0	2	28400	256	768	315
Z15	0	0	2	0	2	2	2	0	0	2	28500	320	640	360
GOU	0	2	0	0	1	2	2	0	0	2	29700	64	1024	360
AP3	0	0	0	2	1	1	2	1	1	1	35000	256	256	140
T20	1	0	2	0	2	2	2	0	0	2	30200	128	768	720
IBM	1	1	2	0	2	2	1	0	0	2	36100	128	640	320
TI2	2	2	2	0	2	2	1	0	0	2	39000	256	768	320
AP2	1	1	0	2	1	1	1	1	1	1	39400	128	832	140
TEL	1	0	2	0	2	2	2	1	2	1	59200	256	640	360
PA3	0	0	2	0	2	1	1	1	2	1	47400	192	512	720
IXT	1	1	2	0	2	2	1	0	2	1	51000	128	640	320
Z12	0	2	2	0	2	2	2	0	2	2	51500	320	640	360
T22	1	0	2	0	2	2	2	0	2	2	52200	128	768	720
VS1	1	2	2	0	2	2	2	1	2	2	66000	256	896	1228
T2	0	2	0	0	1	2	2	0	0	2	22500	64	64	256
AS1	2	1	2	0	2	2	2	2	0	2	32000	128	512	640
MZ	1	0	2	2	1	2	2	0	0	2	34000	136	372	400
BAS	1	0	0	2	1	2	2	1	0	2	28500	384	384	160
LIS	0	0	0	2	3	2	1	1	0	1	35500	512	512	400
EUR	1	0	2	0	2	2	2	0	2	1	47400	128	1024	327
PSI	0	2	0	0	1	2	2	0	0	2	47800	80	256	308
COR	1	1	2	0	2	2	2	1	2	2	45000	256	512	320
OPL	1	0	2	0	2	2	2	0	0	2	33500	256	640	360
HOR	0	2	0	0	1	2	2	0	0	2	35000	64	576	360
FOX	1	1	2	0	2	2	2	1	2	1	51000	256	1024	360
SKS	0	2	0	0	1	1	2	1	0	2	32000	64	256	800
ZEP	0	2	0	0	1	2	2	0	0	2	41400	64	64	640
MBC	0	2	0	0	2	2	2	0	0	2	35600	256	1024	640
SAN	0	2	0	0	1	2	2	0	0	2	26100	70	192	400
IPC	0	2	0	0	1	0	2	0	0	2	43000	64	512	782
DES	0	1	2	0	2	0	2	1	0	2	44800	128	768	360
LI2	0	0	0	2	3	2	1	1	1	1	47400	512	1024	400
NEC	0	0	0	2	1	2	1	1	0	2	31800	32	64	320
M20	0	0	0	2	2	2	2	1	0	2	21600	128	512	286
TRS	0	0	0	2	1	2	2	0	0	1	32000	80	768	422

Second Order Regression and Distance Analysis

J. J. Meulman and W. J. Heiser
Department of Data Theory, University of Leiden
Middelstegracht 4, 2312 TW Leiden

Summary

This paper discusses alternative strategies in a data analytical situation where one would usually apply multiple regression analysis. The target units of the analysis are a set of predictor variables on the one hand and a criterion variable on the other hand. In the first place we move away from the multiple regression approach by allowing the influence of the predictor set to be channeled through a latent variable that does not have to fit in the predictor space. This technique will be shown to have certain distance properties. These properties are emphasized by introducing a loss function that is defined explicitly on the distances. A special feature of this loss function is that the result of the analysis might be multidimensional. An example is given that investigates the predictive properties.

1 Introduction

In the data analytical situation that will be discussed is this paper the basic units of analysis are a set $\mathbf{Z}$, consisting of m predictor variables $\mathbf{z}_1, \ldots, \mathbf{z}_j, \ldots, \mathbf{z}_m$, and a criterion variable $\mathbf{y}$. Both $\mathbf{Z}$ and $\mathbf{y}$ are defined on a common set of n objects or individuals. Both the predictor variables and the criterion are assumed to have zero mean and sum of squares equal to 1. The objective of multiple regression is to predict the values of the criterion variable $\mathbf{y}$ by taking an optimal linear combination $c_1\mathbf{z}_1 + \ldots + c_j\mathbf{z}_j + \ldots + c_m\mathbf{z}_m$. The equation to be fitted is written as $\mathbf{y} = \mathbf{Zc}$, and the model can be depicted in a path diagram as is shown in Figure 1, where we have 5 predictor variables. At the left side the multiple regression model is shown in a form that will be used throughout this paper. A bold square with a capital indicates multidimensionality, and a bold arrow, pointing in the direction of the variable that is to be predicted, denotes a set of weights. For the sake of clearness, it is shown at the right hand side where this representation is the abbreviated version of.

Geometrically, the predictor data consists of a collection of points in an m-dimensional predictor space; each object corresponds to one point, and the scores on the m-variables are the coordinates of the n points in the m-dimensional space. Similarly, the criterion variable gives the coordinates for the n objects in a one-dimensional space. The multiple regression model then assumes that the criterion variable fits perfectly into the space spanned by the predictor variables.

When fitting the model to actual data, however, the latter will usually not be true. Then the lack of predictability can be measured by the least squares loss function

$$\sigma(\mathbf{c}) = (\mathbf{Zc} - \mathbf{y})'(\mathbf{Zc} - \mathbf{y}) \tag{1}$$

and fitting the multiple regression model comes to the minimization of (1) over $\mathbf{c}$. The optimal $\mathbf{c}^*$ is obtained as $\mathbf{c}^* = (\mathbf{Z}'\mathbf{Z})^{-1}\mathbf{Z}'\mathbf{y}$. The result of applying the weights in $\mathbf{c}$ to the variables in $\mathbf{Z}$ gives a so-called *latent variable*, say $\mathbf{x}$, that is exactly in the predictor space $\mathbf{Z}$, while being at the same time as close as possible to $\mathbf{y}$.

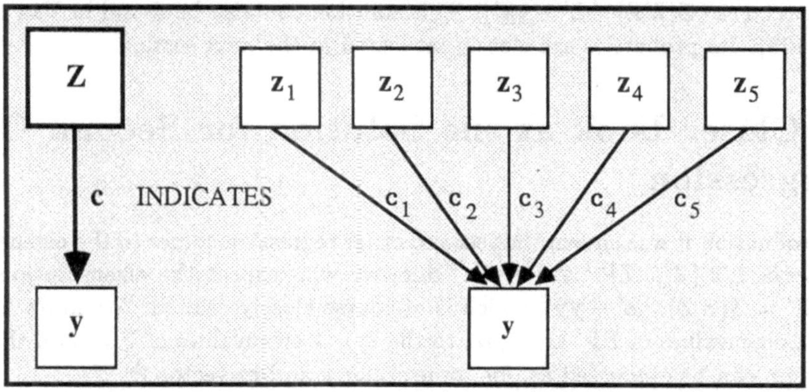

Figure 1: Path diagram for multiple regression

In case we obtain nonperfect fit, the multiple regression model can be slightly modified. This alternative model channels the influence of the predictor variables through a latent variable $\mathbf{x}$ that is *not restricted* to be a subspace of $\mathbf{Z}$. The optimality of $\mathbf{x}$ is now defined by its being at the same time as close as possible to an optimal one-dimensional subspace of $\mathbf{Z}$ and as close as possible to $\mathbf{y}$. For this model two equations have to be fitted simultaneously; these are $\mathbf{x} = \mathbf{Z}\mathbf{a}$ and $\mathbf{y} = b\mathbf{x}$. We will call this technique *second order regression*. The accompanying path diagram is given in Figure 2, where the latent variable $\mathbf{x}$ is denoted by a circle. It is important to recognize the asymmetric role of $\mathbf{Z}$ and $\mathbf{y}$ with respect to $\mathbf{x}$. The model says that $\mathbf{x}$ should be predicted from $\mathbf{Z}$, while $\mathbf{x}$ itself should predict $\mathbf{y}$.

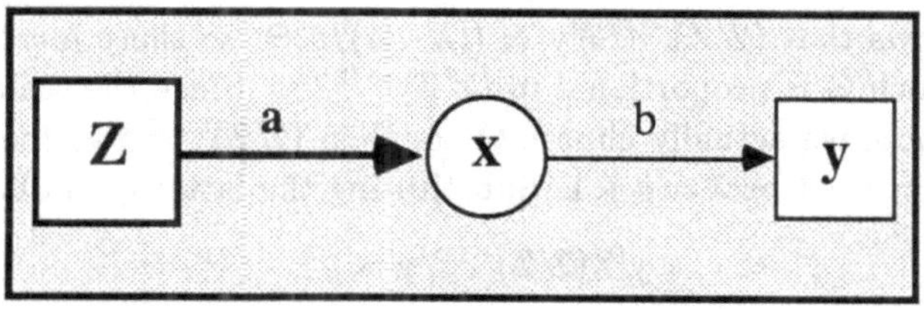

Figure 2: Path diagram for second order regression

The second order regression model is fitted by minimizing the least squares loss function

$$\sigma(\mathbf{x};\mathbf{a};b) = 1/2\,\{(\mathbf{Z}\mathbf{a}-\mathbf{x})'(\mathbf{Z}\mathbf{a}-\mathbf{x}) + (b\mathbf{x}-\mathbf{y})'(b\mathbf{x}-\mathbf{y})\}. \tag{2}$$

It will be clear that ordinary multiple regression (1) can be seen as a special case of (2), when we restrict $\mathbf{x}$ to be exactly equal to $\mathbf{Z}\mathbf{a}$. In the present, more general, case $\mathbf{x}$ is free, except for the requirement that $\mathbf{x}'\mathbf{x} = 1$.

Firstly, we solve for $\mathbf{a}$ and b by equating the partial derivatives to zero. This gives $\mathbf{a}^* = (\mathbf{Z}'\mathbf{Z})^{-1}\mathbf{Z}'\mathbf{x}$ and $b^* = \mathbf{x}'\mathbf{y}$. Substitution of these results in (2) shows that the loss can be written in terms of $\mathbf{x}$ as

$$\sigma(\mathbf{x};*;*) = 1/2\,[\mathbf{x}'\mathbf{x} - \mathbf{x}'\{\mathbf{Z}(\mathbf{Z}'\mathbf{Z})^{-1}\mathbf{Z}' + \mathbf{y}\mathbf{y}'\}\mathbf{x} + \mathbf{y}'\mathbf{y}] \tag{3}$$

(an asterisk denotes an element over which the loss function has been minimized). Next $\sigma(\mathbf{x};*;*)$ is minimized over normalized $\mathbf{x}$ by maximizing $\mathbf{x}'\{\mathbf{Z}(\mathbf{Z}'\mathbf{Z})^{-1}\mathbf{Z}'+\mathbf{y}\mathbf{y}'\}\mathbf{x}$. This maximization problem can be solved by an eigenvalue decomposition: the optimal solution for $\mathbf{x}$ consists of the eigenvector that is associated with the largest eigenvalue of the matrix $1/2\,\{\mathbf{Z}(\mathbf{Z}'\mathbf{Z})^{-1}\mathbf{Z}'+\mathbf{y}\mathbf{y}'\}$. This solution can also be found in Van de Geer (1986, p. 128). Its properties are closely inspected in the next section.

2 A Closer Look at the Solution for Second Order Regression

In the introduction it was shown that second order regression comes to the eigenanalysis of the matrix $1/2\,\{\mathbf{Z}(\mathbf{Z}'\mathbf{Z})^{-1}\mathbf{Z}'+\mathbf{y}\mathbf{y}'\}$. Here we will inspect the eigensolution of the matrix $\mathbf{F}\mathbf{F}'=\mathbf{Z}(\mathbf{Z}'\mathbf{Z})^{-1}\mathbf{Z}'+\mathbf{y}\mathbf{y}'$, which is of course closely related. We know that the first $m+1$ eigenvalues of $\mathbf{F}\mathbf{F}'$ are equal to the $m+1$ eigenvalues of $\mathbf{F}'\mathbf{F}$, and the latter eigenproblem can be expressed as, for some scalar g and m-vector Θ,

$$\begin{matrix}1\\2\\\vdots\\m+1\end{matrix}\quad\left[\begin{array}{c|c}1 & \mathbf{y}'\mathbf{Z}(\mathbf{Z}'\mathbf{Z})^{-1/2}\\\hline(\mathbf{Z}'\mathbf{Z})^{-1/2}\mathbf{Z}'\mathbf{y} & \mathbf{I}\end{array}\right]\left[\begin{array}{c}g\\\hline\Theta\end{array}\right]=\lambda\left[\begin{array}{c}g\\\hline\Theta\end{array}\right]. \tag{4}$$

Now (4) yields the following two equations:

$$g+\mathbf{y}'\mathbf{Z}(\mathbf{Z}'\mathbf{Z})^{-1/2}\Theta=\lambda g, \tag{5a}$$

$$g(\mathbf{Z}'\mathbf{Z})^{-1/2}\mathbf{Z}'\mathbf{y}+\Theta=\lambda\Theta. \tag{5b}$$

From (5b) it follows that $(\mathbf{Z}'\mathbf{Z})^{-1/2}\mathbf{Z}'\mathbf{y}=((\lambda-1)/g)\Theta$, so there must be at least one eigenvector in which Θ is proportional to $(\mathbf{Z}'\mathbf{Z})^{-1/2}\mathbf{Z}'\mathbf{y}$. Since the scale of eigenvectors is arbitrary, suppose we actually choose Θ equal to $(\mathbf{Z}'\mathbf{Z})^{-1/2}\mathbf{Z}'\mathbf{y}$; then it also follows from (5b) that $g=\lambda-1$ or $\lambda=g+1$. Substituting the latter quantity in (5a) yields

$$\mathbf{y}'\mathbf{Z}(\mathbf{Z}'\mathbf{Z})^{-1}\mathbf{Z}'\mathbf{y}=g^2. \tag{6}$$

So there must be one eigenvector that is associated with $g_a=\{\mathbf{y}'\mathbf{Z}(\mathbf{Z}'\mathbf{Z})^{-1}\mathbf{Z}'\mathbf{y}\}^{1/2}$ and with eigenvalue $\lambda_a=1+\{\mathbf{y}'\mathbf{Z}(\mathbf{Z}'\mathbf{Z})^{-1}\mathbf{Z}'\mathbf{y}\}^{1/2}$, and another one associated with $g_b=-\{\mathbf{y}'\mathbf{Z}(\mathbf{Z}'\mathbf{Z})^{-1}\mathbf{Z}'\mathbf{y}\}^{1/2}$ and eigenvalue $\lambda_b=1-\{\mathbf{y}'\mathbf{Z}(\mathbf{Z}'\mathbf{Z})^{-1}\mathbf{Z}'\mathbf{y}\}^{1/2}$, both with the same choice of $\Theta=(\mathbf{Z}'\mathbf{Z})^{-1/2}\mathbf{Z}'\mathbf{y}$.

The remaining $m-1$ eigenvectors must be orthogonal to the two found so far. So for any of those the pair (g_r,Θ_r) must satisfy

$$g_rg_a+\mathbf{y}'\mathbf{Z}(\mathbf{Z}'\mathbf{Z})^{-1/2}\Theta_r=0, \tag{7a}$$

$$g_rg_b+\mathbf{y}'\mathbf{Z}(\mathbf{Z}'\mathbf{Z})^{-1/2}\Theta_r=0. \tag{7b}$$

From (7a) and (7b) it follows that $g_r g_a - g_r g_b = g_r(g_a - g_b) = 0$. But since $g_a = -g_b$ and g_a is nonnegative, this can only be the case if $g_r = 0$. From (5a) it now follows that Θ_r must be orthogonal to $(\mathbf{Z}'\mathbf{Z})^{-1/2}\mathbf{Z}'\mathbf{y}$, and from (5b) that all those vectors are associated with $\lambda_r = 1$. So we find $m-1$ equal eigenvalues, and $\lambda_a \geq \lambda_r \geq \lambda_b$.

There is an interesting relation between the solutions for $\mathbf{Zc}$ in (1) and $\mathbf{x}$ in (3). Recall that $\mathbf{x}'\mathbf{x} = 1$, so we can write the correlation between the two solutions as

$$r(\mathbf{Zc},\mathbf{x}) = \frac{\mathbf{y}'\mathbf{Z}(\mathbf{Z}'\mathbf{Z})^{-1}\mathbf{Z}'\mathbf{x}}{\{\mathbf{y}'\mathbf{Z}(\mathbf{Z}'\mathbf{Z})^{-1}\mathbf{Z}'\mathbf{y}\}^{1/2}}. \tag{8}$$

At the moment we take $\mathbf{x}$ as the eigenvector associated with λ_a, so it is the first eigenvector. Furthermore we know that $\mathbf{x}$ satisfies

$$[\mathbf{Z}(\mathbf{Z}'\mathbf{Z})^{-1}\mathbf{Z}' + \mathbf{y}\mathbf{y}']\mathbf{x} = \lambda_a\mathbf{x}. \tag{9}$$

Therefore we find that, since $\mathbf{y}$ is normalized as $\mathbf{y}'\mathbf{y} = 1$,

$$\mathbf{y}'\mathbf{Z}(\mathbf{Z}'\mathbf{Z})^{-1}\mathbf{Z}'\mathbf{x} + \mathbf{y}'\mathbf{x} = \lambda_a\mathbf{y}'\mathbf{x}, \tag{10}$$

so that the numerator of (8) becomes

$$\mathbf{y}'\mathbf{Z}(\mathbf{Z}'\mathbf{Z})^{-1}\mathbf{Z}'\mathbf{x} = (\lambda_a - 1)\mathbf{y}'\mathbf{x}. \tag{11}$$

Now the correlation between $\mathbf{Zc}$ and $\mathbf{x}$ can be written as

$$r(\mathbf{Zc},\mathbf{x}) = \frac{(\lambda_a - 1)\mathbf{y}'\mathbf{x}}{\{\mathbf{y}'\mathbf{Z}(\mathbf{Z}'\mathbf{Z})^{-1}\mathbf{Z}'\mathbf{y}\}^{1/2}}, \tag{12}$$

and because $\lambda_a = 1 + \{\mathbf{y}'\mathbf{Z}(\mathbf{Z}'\mathbf{Z})^{-1}\mathbf{Z}'\mathbf{y}\}^{1/2}$, (12) says that

$$r(\mathbf{Zc},\mathbf{x}) = \mathbf{y}'\mathbf{x} = r(\mathbf{y},\mathbf{x}). \tag{13}$$

Thus $\mathbf{x}$ is equicorrelated with $\mathbf{Zc}$ and $\mathbf{y}$.

We will also prove the stronger result that $\mathbf{x}$ is exactly in between $\mathbf{Zc}$ and $\mathbf{y}$. This implies that it can be obtained, up to a scaling factor, as a weighted combination of $\mathbf{Zc}$ and $\mathbf{y}$; it is in the plane spanned by them.

Suppose $\underline{\mathbf{x}} = \mathbf{Z}(\mathbf{Z}'\mathbf{Z})^{-1}\mathbf{Z}'\mathbf{y} + \beta\mathbf{y}$. We know it must also satisfy $[\mathbf{Z}(\mathbf{Z}'\mathbf{Z})^{-1}\mathbf{Z}' + \mathbf{y}\mathbf{y}']\underline{\mathbf{x}} = \lambda\underline{\mathbf{x}}$. In that case we must have

$$(1+\beta)\mathbf{Z}(\mathbf{Z}'\mathbf{Z})^{-1}\mathbf{Z}'\mathbf{y} - \mathbf{y}(\mathbf{y}'\mathbf{Z}(\mathbf{Z}'\mathbf{Z})^{-1}\mathbf{Z}'\mathbf{y} + \beta) = \lambda\mathbf{Z}(\mathbf{Z}'\mathbf{Z})^{-1}\mathbf{Z}'\mathbf{y} + \lambda\beta\mathbf{y}. \tag{14}$$

Now

$$(1+\beta)\mathbf{Z}(\mathbf{Z}'\mathbf{Z})^{-1}\mathbf{Z}'\mathbf{y} = \lambda\mathbf{Z}(\mathbf{Z}'\mathbf{Z})^{-1}\mathbf{Z}'\mathbf{y} \text{ if } 1+\beta = \lambda, \tag{15}$$

which gives β as $\{\mathbf{y}'\mathbf{Z}(\mathbf{Z}'\mathbf{Z})^{-1}\mathbf{Z}'\mathbf{y}\}^{1/2}$, and

$$\mathbf{y}(\mathbf{y}'\mathbf{Z}(\mathbf{Z}'\mathbf{Z})^{-1}\mathbf{Z}'\mathbf{y} + \beta) = \lambda\beta\mathbf{y} \text{ if } \mathbf{y}'\mathbf{Z}(\mathbf{Z}'\mathbf{Z})^{-1}\mathbf{Z}'\mathbf{y} + \beta = \lambda\beta, \tag{16}$$

which gives β as $\{\mathbf{y}'\mathbf{Z}(\mathbf{Z}'\mathbf{Z})^{-1}\mathbf{Z}'\mathbf{y}\}^{1/2}$ as well. So

$$\underline{\mathbf{x}} = \mathbf{Z}(\mathbf{Z}'\mathbf{Z})^{-1}\mathbf{Z}'\mathbf{y} + \mathbf{y}\{\mathbf{y}'\mathbf{Z}(\mathbf{Z}'\mathbf{Z})^{-1}\mathbf{Z}'\mathbf{y}\}^{1/2}. \tag{17}$$

Finally we will have a look at the normalization details taking into account that we in fact work with the eigenvalues of $1/2\,\mathbf{FF}'$ instead of $\mathbf{FF}'$. The matrix $1/2\,\mathbf{FF}'$ has eigenvalues μ, where $\mu = 1/2\,\lambda$. If $\underline{\mathbf{x}}$ satiesfies (17) then

$$\begin{aligned}\underline{\mathbf{x}}'\underline{\mathbf{x}} &= 2\mathbf{y}'\mathbf{Z}(\mathbf{Z}'\mathbf{Z})^{-1}\mathbf{Z}'\mathbf{y} + 2\mathbf{y}'\mathbf{Z}(\mathbf{Z}'\mathbf{Z})^{-1}\mathbf{Z}'\mathbf{y}\{\mathbf{y}'\mathbf{Z}(\mathbf{Z}'\mathbf{Z})^{-1}\mathbf{Z}'\mathbf{y}\}^{1/2} \\ &= 2\lambda\mathbf{y}'\mathbf{Z}(\mathbf{Z}'\mathbf{Z})^{-1}\mathbf{Z}'\mathbf{y} = 4\mu\mathbf{y}'\mathbf{Z}(\mathbf{Z}'\mathbf{Z})^{-1}\mathbf{Z}'\mathbf{y}.\end{aligned} \tag{18}$$

So the normalized solution $\mathbf{x}^*$ becomes

$$\mathbf{x}^* = 1/(2\mu^{1/2})[\mathbf{Z}(\mathbf{Z}'\mathbf{Z})^{-1}\mathbf{Z}'\mathbf{y} \,/\, \{\mathbf{y}'\mathbf{Z}(\mathbf{Z}'\mathbf{Z})^{-1}\mathbf{Z}'\mathbf{y}\}^{1/2} + \mathbf{y}]. \tag{19}$$

Furthermore the correlation between $\mathbf{x}^*$ and $\mathbf{y}$ is equal to

$$\mathbf{x}^{*\prime}\mathbf{y} = [\{\mathbf{y}'\mathbf{Z}(\mathbf{Z}'\mathbf{Z})^{-1}\mathbf{Z}'\mathbf{y}\}^{1/2} + 1] \,/\, 2\mu^{1/2} = \mu^{1/2} = b. \tag{20}$$

Therefore the vector $b\mathbf{x}^*$ in the second order regression problem can be written as

$$b\mathbf{x}^* = 1/2\,[\mathbf{Z}(\mathbf{Z}'\mathbf{Z})^{-1}\mathbf{Z}'\mathbf{y} \,/\, \{\mathbf{y}'\mathbf{Z}(\mathbf{Z}'\mathbf{Z})^{-1}\mathbf{Z}'\mathbf{y}\}^{1/2} + \mathbf{y}]. \tag{21}$$

So $b\mathbf{x}^*$ is the vector that lies exactly in between $\mathbf{y}$ and the normalized projection, and it has length $\mu^{1/2}$, the square root of the largest eigenvalue of $1/2\,\mathbf{FF}'$. All vectors that have been discussed in this section are displayed in Figure 3.

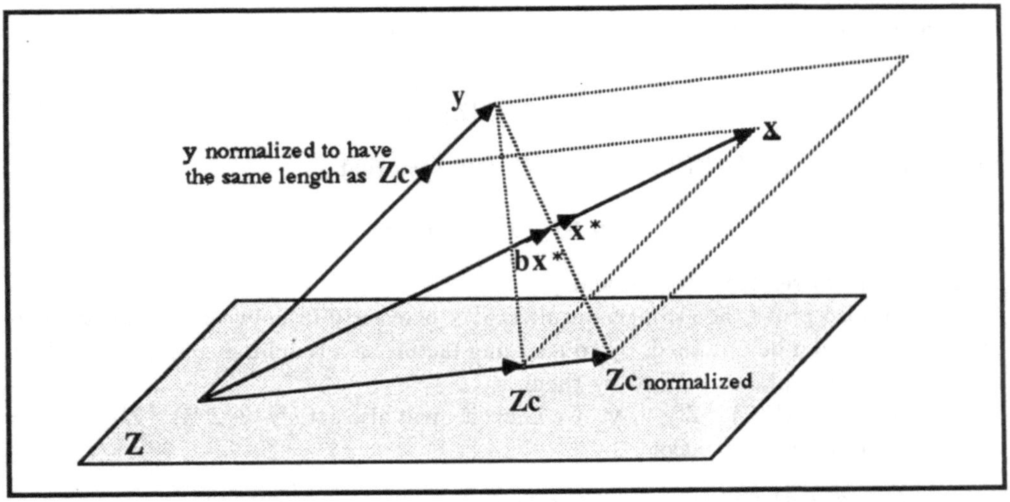

Figure 3: Relation between the solutions for multiple regression ($\mathbf{Zc}$) and second order regression ($\mathbf{x}^*$).

3 Distance Properties of Second Order Regression

When $\mathbf{x}^*$ is normalized to have sum of squares equal to the largest eigenvalue of $1/2\,\{\mathbf{Z}(\mathbf{Z}'\mathbf{Z})^{-1}\mathbf{Z}' + \mathbf{yy}'\}$, we obtain $b\mathbf{x}^*$ and this variable appears to have interesting distance properties. When we speak about distance properties we mean that the coordinates in $b\mathbf{x}^*$ are a solution to a particular multidimensional scaling problem. Multidimensional scaling methods find distances in an unknown low-dimensional space that approximate distances in a known high-dimensional space. One of the well-known MDS methods is called classical or Torgerson-Gower scaling, the latter after the independent contributions of Torgerson (1958) and Gower (1966). An important ingredient in this MDS method is the modified Young-Householder process, applied to the distance matrix $D(\mathbf{Q})$, and written as $-1/2\,\mathbf{J}D^2(\mathbf{Q})\mathbf{J}$. $\mathbf{J}$ is a centering operator that is defined by $\mathbf{J} = \mathbf{I} - \mathbf{uu}'/\mathbf{u}'\mathbf{u}$, with $\mathbf{I}$ the $n \times n$ identity matrix and $\mathbf{u}$ an n-vector with all elements equal to 1. $D^2(\mathbf{Q})$ denotes the matrix containing the *squared* distances between the rows of $\mathbf{Q}$; its elements are the squared Pythagorean distances

$$d^2(\mathbf{q}_i, \mathbf{q}_k) = (\mathbf{q}_i - \mathbf{q}_k)'(\mathbf{q}_i - \mathbf{q}_k) = (\mathbf{e}_i - \mathbf{e}_k)'\mathbf{QQ}'(\mathbf{e}_i - \mathbf{e}_k), \tag{22}$$

($\mathbf{e}_i$ is the i'th column of $\mathbf{I}$). Torgerson-Gower scaling finds a one-dimensional scaling solution $\mathbf{x}$ by computing the first eigenvector of the matrix $-1/2\,\mathbf{J}D^2(\mathbf{Q})\mathbf{J}$ and by normalizing the result on the largest eigenvalue. The loss then is measured by the STRAIN function

$$\begin{aligned} \text{STRAIN}(\mathbf{x}) &= \text{tr}\,(-1/2\,\mathbf{J}D^2(\mathbf{Q})\mathbf{J} - \mathbf{xx}')'(-1/2\,\mathbf{J}D^2(\mathbf{Q})\mathbf{J} - \mathbf{xx}') \\ &= 1/4\,\text{tr}\,\mathbf{J}(D^2(\mathbf{Q}) - D^2(\mathbf{x}))'\mathbf{J}(D^2(\mathbf{Q}) - D^2(\mathbf{x}))\mathbf{J}, \end{aligned} \tag{23}$$

(the name STRAIN has been adopted from Carroll and Chang (1972)).

The distance properties of second order regression are derived from the fact that, because the columns of $\mathbf{Z}$ and $\mathbf{y}$ are assumed to have zero mean, we can write the following equality

$$1/2\,\{\mathbf{Z}(\mathbf{Z}'\mathbf{Z})^{-1}\mathbf{Z}' + \mathbf{yy}'\} = -1/4\,\mathbf{J}\{D^2(\mathbf{Z}(\mathbf{Z}'\mathbf{Z})^{-1/2}) + D^2(\mathbf{y})\}\mathbf{J} = -1/2\,\mathbf{J}\underline{D}^2\mathbf{J}, \tag{24}$$

where $\underline{D}^2 = 1/2\,\{D^2(\mathbf{Z}(\mathbf{Z}'\mathbf{Z})^{-1/2}) + D^2(\mathbf{y})\}$. It appears that by finding $\mathbf{x}$ we have minimized (23) with $\underline{D}^2$ in the role of $D^2(\mathbf{Q})$. Minimizing this loss function, however, is equivalent to the minimization of the more complicated STRAIN function

$$\begin{aligned} \text{STRAIN}_R(\mathbf{x}) = {} & 1/2\,\text{tr}\,\mathbf{J}(D^2(\mathbf{Z}(\mathbf{Z}'\mathbf{Z})^{-1/2}) - D^2(\mathbf{x}))'\mathbf{J}(D^2(\mathbf{Z}(\mathbf{Z}'\mathbf{Z})^{-1/2}) - D^2(\mathbf{x}))\mathbf{J} \\ & + 1/2\,\text{tr}\,\mathbf{J}(D^2(\mathbf{x}) - D^2(\mathbf{y}))'\mathbf{J}(D^2(\mathbf{x}) - D^2(\mathbf{y}))\mathbf{J}. \end{aligned} \tag{25}$$

This is the case because $\text{STRAIN}_R(\mathbf{x})$ is the sum of the proper $\text{STRAIN}_P(\mathbf{x})$

$$\text{STRAIN}_P(\mathbf{x}) = \text{tr}\,\mathbf{J}(\underline{D}^2 - D^2(\mathbf{x}))'\mathbf{J}(\underline{D}^2 - D^2(\mathbf{x}))\mathbf{J} \tag{26}$$

and STRAIN_H due to heterogeneity, which is

$$\begin{aligned} \text{STRAIN}_H = {} & 1/2\,\text{tr}\,\mathbf{J}(D^2(\mathbf{Z}(\mathbf{Z}'\mathbf{Z})^{-1/2}) - \underline{D}^2)'\mathbf{J}(D^2(\mathbf{Z}(\mathbf{Z}'\mathbf{Z})^{-1/2}) - \underline{D}^2)\mathbf{J} \\ & + 1/2\,\text{tr}\,\mathbf{J}(D^2(\mathbf{y}) - \underline{D}^2)'\mathbf{J}(D^2(\mathbf{y}) - \underline{D}^2)\mathbf{J}, \end{aligned} \tag{27}$$

and since the latter is a constant term, we minimize (25) by minimization of (26).

Having identified (25) as the loss function for which the solution for the renormalized $\mathbf{x}$ from the previous section is the minimizer, we have come to the point where the distances involved need special attention. It is clear that the two sets $\mathbf{Z}$ and $\mathbf{y}$ are treated asymmetrically. With respect to $\mathbf{y}$ we note that we deal with the ordinary,

Pythagorean, distance as defined in (22). With respect to $\mathbf{Z}$, on the other hand, we are dealing with so-called Mahalanobis distances between the objects, which are defined by

$$d_M^2(\mathbf{z}_i, \mathbf{z}_k) = (\mathbf{z}_i - \mathbf{z}_k)'\mathbf{V}_Z^{-1}(\mathbf{z}_i - \mathbf{z}_k) \tag{28}$$

where $\mathbf{V}_Z^{-1}$ is the inverse of the covariance matrix between the variables in $\mathbf{Z}$. We note that the Mahalanobis distance function corrects for the intercorrelations between the variables.

We conclude that second order regression has the following distance properties: it simultaneously approximates the Mahalanobis distances in the predictor space $\mathbf{Z}$ and the Pythagorean distances in the criterion space $\mathbf{y}$ by distances in a one-dimensional space $\mathbf{x}$.

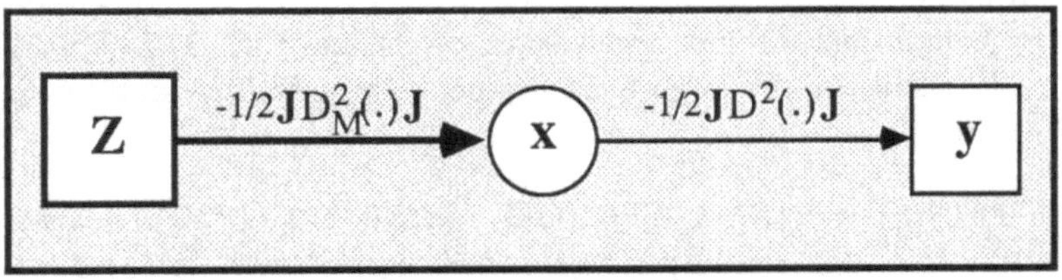

Figure 4: The path diagram for second order regression via STRAIN

The translation in terms of the path diagram is given in Figure 4. Here the arrows describe the modified Young-Householder process. The model says that $\mathbf{xx}' \cong -1/2\,\mathbf{J}D^2(\mathbf{Z}(\mathbf{Z}'\mathbf{Z})^{-1/2})\mathbf{J}$, while $\mathbf{yy}' \cong -1/2\,\mathbf{J}D^2(\mathbf{x})\mathbf{J}$. The asymmetry characteristic for the second order regression model is translated into the fact that we deal with Mahalanobis distances in $\mathbf{Z}$ and with Pythagorean distances in $\mathbf{y}$.

A final, but crucial, remark should be made about the type of approximation that is involved. In the first place, the minimization is not defined over the distances themselves, but over their squares. In the second place it is true for each pair $\{d_{ik}(\mathbf{x}), \underline{d}_{ik}\}$ that $d_{ik}(\mathbf{x}) \leq \underline{d}_{ik}$. Thus the fitted distance will *always be smaller* than the average distance that is to be approximated. This phenomenon, called approximation from below, is explained by the fact that the solution follows from a projection from high-dimensional space into low-dimensional space, and it is characteristic for Torgerson-Gower scaling.

4 From Classical Scaling to Least Squares Distance Fitting

Both Kruskal (1964) and Guttman (1968) propose an MDS method that can be considered as an alternative for classical MDS. Although they are mostly credited for their work on nonmetric MDS, where the distances to be approximated are transformed by a monotonic function, their approach also has consequences for the metric case. Here a loss function is minimized that is defined on the distances themselves, and not on the scalar products that result from the Young-Householder process. As a result, when such a loss function is minimized, the distances themselves will be approximated *from both sides,* and no longer from below: some distances in low-dimensional space may be larger than the associated distances in high-dimensional space. The loss function associated with this method has been called STRESS, and it is the dominant loss function in the majorization approach to MDS as described in, among others, De Leeuw and Heiser (1980), De Leeuw (1984), and Heiser (1985). This section translates the distance properties of second order regression into the STRESS framework. This implies that we remove the squares and the centering operator $\mathbf{J}$ from the STRAIN function (25).

This transition from STRAIN to STRESS has another interesting property. Suppose we wish to find more than one latent variable, say p of them, and we wish that $\mathbf{y}$ is to be predicted from this set of p variables $\mathbf{X}$. We have seen, however, that the eigenvalues of the matrix $1/2\,\{\mathbf{Z}(\mathbf{Z}'\mathbf{Z})^{-1}\mathbf{Z}' + \mathbf{yy}'\}$ have a very special structure: apart from the largest and the smallest eigenvalue (where the latter equals 1 minus the largest eigenvalue) all other eigenvalues are equal to 0.5. Although we usually can take more than one eigenvector for a classical scaling solution, we would not know which one to select in the present case.

In second order regression via STRESS, however, we are not dealing with an eigenanalysis. And there exists a genuine more-dimensional $\mathbf{X}$ in which the distances approximate the Mahalanobis distances and the Pythagorean distances in the two spaces. This $\mathbf{X}$ is found by minimizing the STRESS function:

$$\begin{aligned}\mathrm{STRESS}(\mathbf{X}) \;=\;& 1/2\,\mathrm{tr}\,(D(\mathbf{Z}\mathbf{V}_Z^{-1/2}) - D(\mathbf{X}))'(D(\mathbf{Z}\mathbf{V}_Z^{-1/2}) - D(\mathbf{X})) \\ & +1/2\,\mathrm{tr}\,(D(\mathbf{X}) - D(\mathbf{y}))'(D(\mathbf{X}) - D(\mathbf{y})).\end{aligned} \tag{29}$$

By analogy with equation (25), (26) and (27), this minimization can be carried out by minimizing the more simple proper STRESS

$$\mathrm{STRESS}_P(\mathbf{X}) = \mathrm{tr}\,(\underline{D} - D(\mathbf{X}))'(\underline{D} - D(\mathbf{X})), \tag{30}$$

where $\underline{D}$ is the average distance $\underline{D} = 1/2\,\{D(\mathbf{Z}(\mathbf{Z}'\mathbf{Z})^{-1/2}) + D(\mathbf{y})\}$. An important ingredient in the majorization approach to MDS mentioned before is the so-called Guttman transform $\overline{\mathbf{X}}$ of a configuration $\mathbf{X}$, which is defined as

$$\overline{\mathbf{X}} = n^{-1}B(\mathbf{X})\mathbf{X}. \tag{31}$$

It remains to describe what the $B(\mathbf{X})$ matrix looks like when we wish to minimize (30). First we define an off-diagonal matrix $B^0(\mathbf{X})$, with elements

$$b^0_{ik}(\mathbf{X}) = \underline{d}_{ik}/d_{ik}(\mathbf{X}) \quad \text{if } i \neq k; \tag{32a}$$

$$b^0_{ik}(\mathbf{X}) = 0 \quad \text{if } d_{ik}(\mathbf{X}) = 0 \tag{32b}$$

and a diagonal matrix $B^*(\mathbf{X})$, with diagonal elements

$$b^*_{ii}(\mathbf{X}) = \mathbf{u}'B^0_i(\mathbf{X})\mathbf{e}_i. \tag{33}$$

Then $B(\mathbf{X})$ itself is defined by

$$B(\mathbf{X}) = B^*(\mathbf{X}) - B^0(\mathbf{X}), \tag{34}$$

and repeatedly computing the update $\mathbf{X}^+ = n^{-1}B(\mathbf{X})\mathbf{X}$ defines an algorithm that guarantees a convergent series of configurations for problem (30).

Figure 5 gives the translation of second order regression via STRESS in the path diagram. The arrows now describe the distance function $D(.)$. The second order regression model expresses that $D(\mathbf{X}) \cong D(\mathbf{Z}(\mathbf{Z}'\mathbf{Z})^{-1/2})$, while $D(\mathbf{Y}) \cong D(\mathbf{X})$. As a special characteristic we note that the latent space $\mathbf{X}$ can now be *multidimensional.* And because we minimize a STRESS function, the average distance $\underline{d}_{ik}$ is approximated directly from both sides.

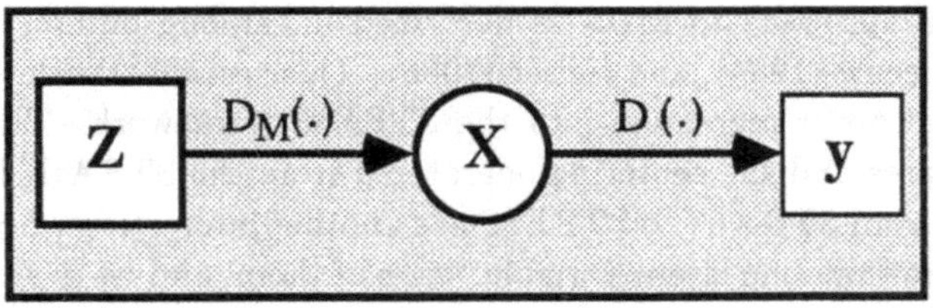

Figure 5: The path diagram for second order regression via STRESS

5 Predicting the Criterion Score for an Additional Object

In some cases it happens that we have fitted the multiple regression model and that we afterwards use the weights to predict the unknown criterion value y^* for an additional object when $\mathbf{z}^*$, a row vector with predictor scores, is given for this object. One $\mathbf{c}^*$ is regarded as a fixed estimated set of weights, $\mathbf{z}^*\mathbf{c}^*$ forms the desired prediction. In second order regression prediction is not as simple, due to the fact that the latent variable is a function of both $\mathbf{Z}$ and $\mathbf{y}$. Yet we would like to have the same possibility when we have applied second order regression. We propose the following strategy, valid for the STRAIN and STRESS approach alike, except for the fact that for STRAIN the latent variable is one-dimensional.

- In a first step we fit the criterion vector $\mathbf{y}$ into the configuration space $\mathbf{X}$. The coordinates of the criterion variable are obtained by minimizing $(\mathbf{y}-\mathbf{Xb})'(\mathbf{y}-\mathbf{Xb})$ over $\mathbf{b}$. The optimal $\mathbf{b}^*$ is found as

$$\mathbf{b}^* = (\mathbf{X}'\mathbf{X})^{-1}\mathbf{X}'\mathbf{y}. \tag{35a}$$

- In the second step we compute weights $\mathbf{A}^*$ by taking

$$\mathbf{A}^* = (\mathbf{Z}'\mathbf{Z})^{-1}\mathbf{Z}'\mathbf{X}. \tag{35b}$$

- In the third step we find the coordinates for the additional object $\mathbf{x}^*$ by

$$\mathbf{x}^* = \mathbf{z}^*\mathbf{A}^*. \tag{35c}$$

- Finally we perform the orthogonal projection of this object point onto the criterion vector by taking

$$\mathbf{y}^* = \mathbf{x}^*\mathbf{b}^*. \tag{35d}$$

The first and second step are performed only once; the third and the fourth can be repeated for any number of additional objects. The predictive properties of this procedure will be investigated in the next section.

6 An Application

In order to illustrate the technique, incorporating the prediction of criterion scores, a re-analysis has been performed of a set of data from 1977 concerning the 50 states of the

U.S.A. (see Meulman (1986) for the origin of this composite set of data). The variables chosen in the predictor set are: *per capita income in dollars, life expectancy in years, homicide rate, unemployment rate, percentage of high school graduates* and *illiteracy rate*. These variables are assumed to predict the criterion variable *rate of failure on an ability test*. In order to investigate the predictive properties of the method, 10 percent of the 50 states have been randomly omitted from the analysis. These are Wisconsin (WI), Washington (WA), Minnesota (MN), Kansas (KS) and Virginia (VA).

After the configuration $\mathbf{X}$ was obtained, the criterion variable FAIL has been fitted into the space (step 1). The correlation between the values for FAIL in $\mathbf{X}$ and the given, actual values of $\mathbf{y}$ is .92. After obtaining the predictor weights (step 2), the omitted states were fitted into the configuration space (step 3). Next the points were projected onto the FAIL vector to obtain estimates for the FAIL-values (step 4).

These values have been compared with the actual values and in addition with the results obtained by performing an ordinary multiple regression. The figures are given in Table 1, summarized by the root mean square of the residuals.

Table 1: Comparison of predicted values and actual values

	Second order regression	Actual values	Ordinary multiple regression
WI	−.099	−.113	−.107
WA	−.144	−.140	−.145
MN	−.139	−.140	−.162
KS	−.121	−.113	−.161
VA	.085	.125	.080
RMS	.043		0.70

One of the advantages of the approach described in the previous section, is the possibility to make informative graphical displays. The analysis that has been performed results in the display given in Figure 6.

This Figure gives a lot of information. The 45 states that were active in the second order regression are indicated by an asterisk; the coordinates for the 5 omitted points are indicated by a speckled circle. States that are closely together resemble each other according to the predictor variables and the criterion variable. It is clear that the Southern states are represented predominantly at the right hand side of the picture. They project highly on the FAIL vector. For the sake of interpretation, the predictor variables have also been fitted into the space. They all extend from the origin, which is indicated by a black dot. Before interpreting the projections of the states on the predictor variables, we should take into account how well they fit into the space. The length of the vectors in the Figure has been adapted to the size of the configuration; their real length is equal to their correlation with the original values; these correlations are .81 for INCOME, .71 for LIFE, .79 for HOMIC, .46 for UNEMP, .73 for SCHOOL, and .88 for ILLIT. Thus we can interpret the predictor directions quite safely, except for UNEMP.

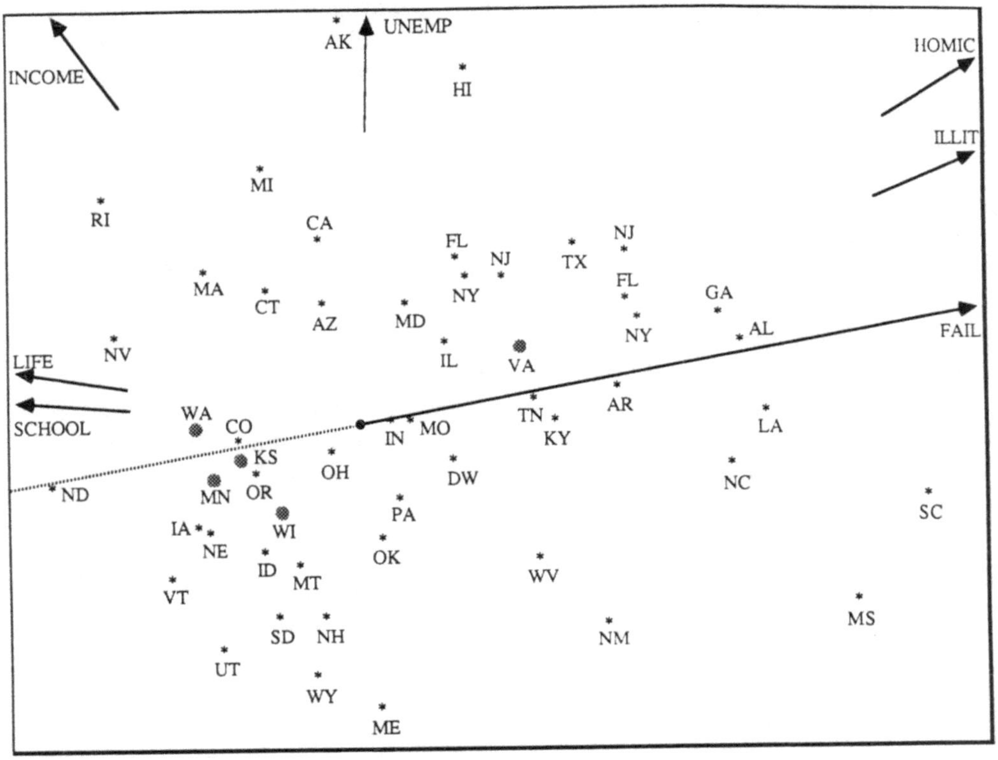

Figure 6: Two-dimensional display of second order regression.

It is also important to realize that the configuration **X** is the result of distance approximation. Therefore it will usually have a certain shape, where the configuration is usually displayed in principal axes orientation. This implies that the axes have different lengths, and therefore technically we cannot interpret the angles between the vectors as approximations of the correlations between the variables, which would have been the case when both axes have unit length in addition to being orthogonal. It happens to be the case in Figure 6, however, that the position of the vectors resembles the original correlations quite closely. This can be seen by comparing Table 2, containing the actual correlations, with Table 3, which gives the cross products of the fitted variables (the diagonal gives the squared fit values).

Table 2: Original correlations between all variables

	INC	LIFE	HOMIC	UNEMP	SCHOOL	ILLIT	FAIL
INC	1.00	.34	−.23	.10	.63	−.43	−.43
LIFE	.34	1.00	−.71	−.16	.52	−.50	−.69
HOMIC	−.23	−.71	1.00	.16	−.46	.68	.71
UNEMP	.10	−.16	.16	1.00	−.13	.15	.21
SCHOOL	.63	.52	−.46	−.13	1.00	−.64	−.71
ILLIT	−.43	−.50	.68	.15	−.64	1.00	.82
FAIL	−.43	−.69	.71	.21	−.71	.82	1.00

Table 3: Cross products between fitted variables

	INC	LIFE	HOMIC	UNEMP	SCHOOL	ILLIT	FAIL
INC	.66	.44	−.20	.27	.42	−.29	−.43
LIFE	.44	.50	−.47	.03	.51	−.55	−.62
HOMIC	−.20	−.47	.62	.16	−.51	.69	.69
UNEMP	.27	−.03	.16	.21	.01	.14	.07
SCHOOL	.42	.51	−.51	.01	.53	−.59	−.65
ILLIT	−.29	−.55	.69	.14	−.59	.77	.79
FAIL	−.43	−.62	.69	.07	−.65	.79	.84

Since Figure 6 displays the result of a distance analysis, we wish to inspect it in terms of distance approximation. The total STRESS value, as given by (29), can be decomposed as is shown in Table 4. We note that the proper STRESS is quite small, that because we are dealing with two sets each of the sets contributes the same amount to STRESS due to heterogeneity, and that the Pythagorean distances in **y** are better fitted than the Mahalanobis distances in **Z**.

Table 4: Decomposition of the total STRESS in second order regression

$\text{STRESS}_P(\mathbf{X})$	$=$	$(\underline{D} - D(\mathbf{X}))'(\underline{D} - D(\mathbf{X})) =$		.141
STRESS_H	$=$	$1/2\,(D(\mathbf{Z}(\mathbf{Z}'\mathbf{Z})^{-1/2} - \underline{D}))'(D(\mathbf{Z}(\mathbf{Z}'\mathbf{Z})^{-1/2} - \underline{D})) =$	.437	
	$+$	$1/2\,(D(\mathbf{y}) - \underline{D})'(D(\mathbf{y}) - \underline{D}) =$	.437	
				.874
$\text{STRESS}(\mathbf{X})$	$=$	$1/2\,(D(\mathbf{Z}(\mathbf{Z}'\mathbf{Z})^{-1/2} - D(\mathbf{X}))'(D(\mathbf{Z}(\mathbf{Z}'\mathbf{Z})^{-1/2} - D(\mathbf{X})) =$	.640	
	$+$	$1/2\,(D(\mathbf{X}) - D(\mathbf{y}))'(D(\mathbf{X}) - D(\mathbf{y})) =$	.375	
				1.015

7 Discussion

In the previous sections the multiple regression model has been modified by allowing for one or more latent variables that are intermediaries between the predictor variables and the criterion variable. The resulting technique, called second order regression, could be interpreted in a distance framework. A rationale for the least squares distance fitting performed in section 4 is the conjecture that distances are much more stable than weights. This might have positive consequences for the case where we are dealing with high multicollinearity between the predictor variables. Moreover, the formulation of the technique in terms of the minimization of a least squares loss function gave way to multidimensional solutions for the second order regression problem. Choosing for multidimensionality can be justified in several ways. In the first place, the more-dimensional solution will always fit the criterion variable better than a one-dimensional solution. In the second place, it gives the possibility for informative graphical displays. And finally, the multidimensional model can be taken as the starting point for the formulation of more complicated path models.

Second order regression is a specimen in a variety of well-known multivariate analysis techniques that all can be placed in a distance framework. This has been done in Meulman (1986). In order to identify an MVA technique with a particular distance model, it is crucial to specify the number of high-dimensional spaces, and the type of distances that operate in them. Table 5 gives an overview.

Table 5: Multivariate analysis techniques in a distance framework

MVA technique	Number of spaces	Distance function
Multiple correspondence analysis	number of variables	Chi-squared
Principal components analysis	1	Pythagorean
Generalized canonical analysis	number of sets	Mahalanobis
Redundancy analysis	2	Mahalanobis in first and Pythagorean in second space

Finally we wish to remark that all these methods can be generalized to a nonlinear variety. Here the qualification nonlinear signifies that the models incorporate nonlinear transformations of the variables (see Gifi (1981); Young (1981)). These nonlinear transformations are optimal in the sence that they minimize the approximation error resulting from fitting the distance model to actual data. It has been shown in Meulman (1986) how the majorization algorithm that was described in section 4 can be adapted for the various MVA techniques in order to obtain transformations of the high-dimensional spaces in which the coordinates are monotonic functions of the original coordinates.

References

Carroll JD, Chang JJ (1972) IDIOSCAL: A Generalization of INSCAL Allowing for IDIOsyncratic Reference Systems as Well as an Analytic Approximation to INDSCAL. Paper presented at the Psychometric Society Meeting, Princeton

De Leeuw J (1984) Convergence of the Majorization Algorithm for Multidimensional Scaling. Research Report RR-84-07, Dept. of Data Theory, Leiden

De Leeuw J, Heiser WJ (1980) Multidimensional Scaling with Restrictions on the Configuration, in: Krisnaiah PR (ed.) Multivariate Analysis V. North-Holland, Amsterdam, pp 501–522

Gifi A (1981) Nonlinear Multivariate Analysis. Department of Data Theory, Leiden

Gower JC (1966) Some Distance Properties of Latent Roots and Vector Methods Used in Multivariate Analysis. Biometrica 53: 325–338

Guttman L (1968) A General Nonmetric Technique for Finding the Smallest Coordinate Space for a Configuration of Points. Psychometrika 33: 469–506

Heiser WJ (1985) A General MDS Initialization Procedure Using the SMACOF Majorization Algorithm with Constraints. Research Report RR-85-23, Dept. of Data Theory, Leiden

Kruskal JB (1964) Multidimensional Scaling by Optimizing Goodness of Fit to a Nonmetric Hypothesis. Psychometrika 29: 1–28

Meulman JJ (1986) A Distance Approach to Nonlinear Multivariate Analysis. DSWO Press, Leiden

Torgerson WS (1958) Theory and Methods of Scaling. Wiley, New York

Van de Geer (1986) Introduction to Linear Multivariate Analysis. DSWO Press, Leiden

Young FW (1981) Quantitative Analysis of Qualitative Data. Psychometrika 46: 357–387

MIX
Papier aus verantwortungsvollen Quellen
Paper from responsible sources
FSC® C105338

If you have any concerns about our products,
you can contact us on
ProductSafety@springernature.com

In case Publisher is established outside the EU,
the EU authorized representative is:
Springer Nature Customer Service Center GmbH
Europaplatz 3, 69115 Heidelberg, Germany

Printed by Libri Plureos GmbH
in Hamburg, Germany